IISS

Strategic Survey 2013
The Annual Review of World Affairs

published by

Routledge
Taylor & Francis Group

for

The International Institute for Strategic Studies

The International Institute for Strategic Studies
Arundel House | 13–15 Arundel Street | Temple Place | London | WC2R 3DX | UK

Strategic Survey 2013
The Annual Review of World Affairs

First published September 2013 by **Routledge**
4 Park Square, Milton Park, Abingdon, Oxon, OX14 4RN

for **The International Institute for Strategic Studies**
Arundel House, 13–15 Arundel Street, Temple Place, London, WC2R 3DX, UK

Simultaneously published in the USA and Canada by **Routledge**
270 Madison Ave., New York, NY 10016

Routledge is an imprint of Taylor & Francis, an Informa business

DIRECTOR-GENERAL AND CHIEF EXECUTIVE Dr John Chipman

EDITOR Alexander Nicoll

EDITORIAL Sarah Johnstone, Mona Moussavi, Nicholas Payne, Chris Raggett, Alexa van Sickle, Jens Wardenaer
MAP EDITOR Jessica Delaney
DESIGN/PRODUCTION John Buck
COVER Kelly Verity
ADDITIONAL MAP RESEARCH Wafa Alsayed, Islam Altayeb, Nathan Beauchamp-Mustafaga, Henry Boyd, Elly Jupp, Antonio Sampaio
CARTOGRAPHY Martin J. Lubikowski

COVER IMAGES Getty Images
PRINTED BY Bell & Bain Ltd, Glasgow, UK

British Library Cataloguing in Publication Data
A catalogue record for this book is available from the British Library

Library of Congress Cataloguing in Publication Data

ISBN 978-1-85743-693-8
ISSN 0459-7230

Contents

	Events at a Glance July 2012–June 2013	**5**
Chapter 1	**Perspectives**	**17**
Chapter 2	**Strategic Policy Issues**	**31**
	South Asia's Nuclear Arms Race: Lessons of the Cold War	31
	European Defence Cooperation: Ways Forward	44
Chapter 3	**The Americas**	**59**
	The United States: Raw Data	59
	Latin America's New Leadership Challenges	77
Chapter 4	**Europe**	**111**
	France: Hollande's Fraught First Year	114
	Germany: Merkel's Strong Position	124
	United Kingdom: Anti-Europe Sentiment Grows	129
	European Defence: Budget Cuts	137
	Turkey: Contentious Transition	143
Chapter 5	**Russia and Eurasia**	**153**
	Russia's Rising Conservatism	153
	Georgia's New Pluralism	170
Chapter 6	**Middle East/Gulf**	**175**
	Spreading Conflict in the Levant	179
	North Africa's Difficult Transitions	188
	Gulf States: Containing Change	204
	Israel and Palestine: Status Quo Amidst Regional Upheaval	216
	Iran: Persistent Confrontation	221
	Iraq: Political Deadlock	236
Chapter 7	**Africa**	**247**
	West Africa's Troubled Year	248
	The Horn, Central and East Africa: Qualified Progress	258
	Southern Africa: Quest for Integration	270
Chapter 8	**South Asia and Afghanistan**	**281**
	India: Slow Economy Prompts Contentious Reforms	282
	Pakistan: Sharif Returns	290
	Sri Lanka: UN Censure	294
	Afghanistan: Elections Loom as Foreign Troops Depart	295
Chapter 9	**Asia-Pacific**	**309**
	China: New Leadership	309
	Japan: Abe's Radicalism	325
	The Koreas: New Leaders Face Old Challenges	333
	Australia: Policy Initiatives Precede Leadership Change	348
	New Zealand: US Relations Deepen	353
	Southwest Pacific: Steps to Democracy	354
	Southeast Asia: Back to the 1960s?	355
Chapter 10	**Prospectives**	**375**
	Index	**385**

Strategic Geography (after p. 174)

Reasons for hope in the fight against global disease II
The shifting dynamics of world oil markets IV
Maritime disputes in focus VI
The United States' gun debate rumbles on VIII
Antarctica: the quiet race for national influence X
Colombia: FARC rebels' changing tactics XII
Could Scotland go it alone? XIII
Islamic extremism in West Africa XIV
Syria's increasingly internationalised civil war XVI
Afghanistan: the long drawdown XVIII
North Korea does it again XX

Index of Regional Maps

The Americas 58
Europe 110
Russia and Eurasia 152
Middle East 176
Africa 246
South and Central Asia 280
Asia-Pacific 308

Events at a Glance

July 2012–June 2013

July 2012

1 **Mexico:** Institutional Revolutionary Party (PRI), which held power from 1929 until it was ousted in 2000, returns as its candidate Enrique Peña Nieto wins presidential election with 38% of the vote. The candidate of the incumbent National Action Party (PAN) is knocked into third place.

11 **Myanmar:** US President Barack Obama eases sanctions on Myanmar, allowing American companies to do business there.

16 **North Korea:** Army chief Vice-Marshal Ri Yong-ho is removed. The decision is seen as an assertion of control over the military by Kim Jong-un, the country's leader, seven months after taking office.

18 **Bulgaria:** Suicide bomber kills five Israelis and the Bulgarian driver of a bus carrying Israeli tourists from the airport at the Black Sea city of Burgas. In February 2013, Bulgarian investigators conclude that Hizbullah, the Lebanese militia, was behind the attack.

18 **Syria:** Bomb explosion at national security headquarters kills Dawoud Rajiha, defence minister, and Assef Shawkat, deputy defence minister and brother-in-law of President Bashar al-Assad.

20 **United States:** Heavily armed gunman kills 12 people after opening fire on the audience in a cinema in Aurora, a suburb of Denver, Colorado.

20 **China:** Beijing establishes prefecture-level 'city' of Sansha (upgrading it from a county-level administrative division) to administer disputed islands in the South China Sea, with its centre on Woody Island, largest of the Paracel Islands. The Central Military Commission authorises deployment of a military garrison there.

23 **Iraq:** More than 100 people are killed in bombings in 13 cities, including more than 40 in an attack at Taji, north of Baghdad. The attacks are believed to be orchestrated by al-Qaeda in Iraq.

24 **Ghana:** President John Atta Mills dies suddenly. He is replaced by John Dramani Mahama, vice-president, who is then elected president in December 2012.

26 **China:** Gu Kailai, wife of disgraced politician Bo Xilai, is charged with murder of British businessman Neil Heywood. On 9 August, her trial takes place. On 20 August, she is found guilty and is given a suspended death sentence.

26 **Rwanda:** The Netherlands suspends aid after UN experts group accuses Rwanda of supplying weapons and fighters to M23 rebel group in the Democratic Republic of Congo.

26 Mario Draghi, president of the European Central Bank, says the ECB is ready to resume purchases of eurozone members' government bonds. He says there has been extraordinary progress to reduce budget deficits and introduce economic reforms, and the ECB 'is ready to do whatever it takes to preserve the euro. And believe me, it will be enough.' On 7 September, his plans crystallise as the ECB announces a programme of 'outright monetary transactions': purchases of short-term bonds of governments that obtain a bailout from EU rescue funds and agree to economic reforms supervised by the EU and IMF. German Chancellor Angela Merkel supports the programme but Bundesbank president Jens Weidmann opposes it. Markets see it as reducing uncertainties and push up bond prices of Italy and Spain.

August 2012

2 **Syria:** Kofi Annan, former UN secretary-general, resigns as special envoy for Syria, citing political impasse, militarisation of the conflict and inadequate international action. He is later replaced by veteran Algerian diplomat Lakhdar Brahimi. The northern city of Aleppo is gripped by heavy fighting. On 6 August, Prime Minister Riad Hijab resigns and defects to the rebels, two months after he was appointed.

5 **Egypt:** Sixteen Egyptian soldiers are killed in an attack by Islamic militants in Sinai, near the border with Israel. A week later, President Muhammad Morsi sacks top military figures including long-time defence minister Field Marshal Mohamed Hussein Tantawi, who was the country's interim leader from the 2011 revolution until Morsi's election on 30 June 2012. The president also takes back some powers appropriated by the army.

16 **South Africa:** Police open fire on striking platinum miners at Marikana mine, killing 34 people and sparking further strikes and violence. Two hundred and seventy miners are arrested and charged with the murder of their colleagues. The charges are later set aside pending an inquiry into the incident. On 18 September, the platinum miners accept an 18% pay increase and return to work. However, unrest in the mining industry continues.

17 **Russia:** Three members of female punk band Pussy Riot are sentenced to two years in jail for singing a protest song about President Vladimir Putin in a Moscow cathedral. They are found gulity of 'hooliganism motivated by religious hatred' for singing 'Mother of God, Drive Putin Out'. The sentence of one woman is later suspended.

20 **Syria:** A mass killing occurs over several days in Daraya, a suburb of Damascus. Later estimates indicate that some 500 people were killed. Mass graves are found. While there are divergent claims about who was responsible, official media speak of cleansing the area of 'terrorist groups'. Killings are said to have been carried out by regime forces and pro-regime militia. In one basement, 120 bodies are reported to have been found.

21 **Ethiopia:** Prime Minister Meles Zenawi, Ethiopia's leader since 1991, dies at 57 of an illness. He is succeeded by Hailemariam Desalegn, who was foreign minister.

24 **Norway:** Anders Breivik, who killed 77 people in 2011 with a car bomb in Oslo and in a shooting spree at a political summer camp for young people, is sentenced to the maximum term of 21 years in prison, although this could be extended indefinitely. Judges reject prosecutors' request that he be found insane and put into psychiatric care.

September 2012

4 **Colombia:** Government and FARC guerrillas agree a road map towards an end to their long-running conflict. On 20 November, FARC declares a unilateral two-month ceasefire as talks continue.

10 **Somalia:** Legislators in Somalia's newly elected parliament choose Hassan Sheikh Mohamud as president of the new republic, the formation of which ends the eight-year tenure of the Transitional Federal Government. Abdi Farah Shirdon is appointed prime minister.

10 **Japan:** Government agrees deal to buy from a private owner three of the disputed Senkaku islands (called Diaoyu by China), prompting objections from Beijing, which sends maritime surveillance vessels to carry out patrols near the islands. Anti-Japanese demonstrations occur across China. On 25 September, about 40 Taiwanese fishing vessels, escorted by coastguard ships, make an incursion into waters close to the islands and are met by Japanese patrol ships using water cannon.

11 **Egypt:** Protesters attack the US Embassy in Cairo over a film, made in the United States, which denigrates the Prophet Mohammed. Protests also occur over four days in many other countries, including Libya. The US government denounces the film.

11 **Pakistan:** Fire in a textile factory in Karachi kills nearly 300 people.

11 **Libya:** US Ambassador Christopher Stevens and three other Americans are killed in an attack on the consulate in the eastern city of Benghazi, apparently by an extreme Islamist militant group.

12 **Germany:** German constitutional court rejects bid to block the creation of the European Stability Mechanism, the eurozone's $500 billion rescue fund.

12 **Netherlands:** People's Party for Freedom and Democracy, led by Mark Rutte whose coalition government had resigned because of opposition to austerity measures and eurozone rescues, wins largest share of vote in general election and, after eight weeks of negotiations, forms new coalition with second-placed Labour Party. Rutte remains prime minister.

13 **United States:** Federal Reserve, the US central bank, launches a third round of 'quantitative easing', undertaking to buy large amounts of mortgage-backed securities in an aggressive effort to lower real-estate lending rates and unemployment.

18 **Russia:** Moscow expels USAID development agency, accusing it of using grants to influence Russian politics and elections.

21 **Turkey:** Court sentences 331 serving and former military officers to prison for alleged involvement in plans for a military coup.

October 2012

1 **Georgia:** Georgian Dream alliance easily wins parliamentary elections, defeating the party of President Mikheil Saakashvili, who is due to remain in office for a further year. Bidzina Ivanishvili, a wealthy businessman turned politician, becomes prime minister.

3 **Syria/Turkey:** Mortar fire from Syria kills five Turkish civilians, and Turkish forces respond with artillery attacks on targets in Syria. On 4 October, Turkish parliament authorises military to deploy troops into Syria. On 9 October, NATO Secretary-General Anders Fogh Rasmussen says the alliance has 'all necessary plans in place to protect and defend Turkey if necessary'. On 10 October, Turkish fighters force a Syrian Air passenger aircraft, en route from Moscow, to land at Ankara airport on suspicion of carrying weapons for the Assad regime. In November, Turkey requests NATO to deploy *Patriot* anti-missile batteries near the Syrian border, and in January 2013 the deployment of Dutch, German and US systems begins.

5 **United Kingdom:** Abu Hamza, Egyptian-born Islamist preacher convicted of terrorism offences and imprisoned in the United Kingdom for eight years, is extradited to the United States to face terrorism charges.

7 **Venezuela:** President Hugo Chávez wins fourth presidential term with 55% of vote. However, he remains ill with cancer and in December he designates Nicolas Maduro, vice-president, as his successor.

7 **Mexico:** Heriberto Lazcano, head of the Zetas drug cartel, is killed in a shoot-out with Mexican marines.

11 **France:** French police say they have foiled a bomb plot and dismantled the most dangerous terrorist group found in France since 1996. Seven people are detained, and bomb-making materials found. One suspect is shot dead after firing at police.

15 **United Kingdom:** UK and Scottish governments sign agreement allowing Scotland to hold a referendum on independence in 2014.

15 **Philippines:** Government signs framework peace agreement with Moro Islamic Liberation Front, intended to end 40-year conflict with the Muslim secessionist group. The accord provides for an autonomous region to be administered by Muslims on the southern island of Mindanao.

19 **Lebanon:** Car bomb in Beirut kills eight people including Wissam al-Hassan, intelligence official who played a key role in an investigation that implicated Syria in car bomb assassination of former prime minister Rafik Hariri in 2005. The killing provokes street clashes in Beirut and elsewhere.

29 **United States:** Hurricane Sandy sweeps across northeastern United States, killing more than 130 people and causing widespread damage and power outages. It previously killed more than 100 people in Haiti.

November 2012

6 **Russia:** Anatoly Serdyukov, reformist defence minister, is sacked by President Vladimir Putin following allegations of corruption. Three days later, the chief of the general staff, General Nikolai Makarov, is also sacked.

6 **United States:** Barack Obama wins second presidential term, defeating Republican candidate Mitt Romney. Obama retains all states won in 2008 election except Indiana and North Carolina. Senate elections result in a net gain of two seats for the Democrats, bringing their total to 53 out of 100. Republicans lose a net eight seats in the House of Representatives to hold 234 out of 435.

9 **United States:** David Petraeus, CIA head and former military commander in Afghanistan and Iraq, resigns because of an extramarital affair.

11 **Syria:** Opposition factions, meeting in Qatar, agree to form a national coalition. It is recognised as the sole representative of the Syrian people by Gulf Co-operation Council members, and then by France, and later by the United States and many other countries.

14 **Israel/Palestine:** Israeli air-strike in Gaza kills Ahmed al-Jabari, commander of military wing of Hamas. The strike is part of a bombardment intended to weaken the military capability of Hamas, which responds by firing hundreds of rockets at Israel, including Tel Aviv and Jerusalem. On 21 November, a truce is

brokered by Egypt. More than 160 Palestinians and five Israelis are killed in the exchanges.

15 **China:** Xi Jinping is appointed head of the Chinese Communist Party and of the military, and in March 2013 succeeds Hu Jintao as president.

21 **India:** Mohammed Ajmal Kasab, the only surviving participant in the 2008 terrorist attack on Mumbai, is executed by hanging.

22 **Egypt:** President Muhammad Morsi grants himself additional powers and declares his decisions immune from legal challenge, pending the election of a new parliament. The move provokes widespread protests and is later rescinded, although a referendum on a controversial draft constitution is to proceed.

29 **Palestine:** UN General Assembly votes by 138 to 9 (with 41 abstentions) to grant Palestine the status of 'non-member observer state'.

December 2012

12 **North Korea:** A long-range rocket is successfully launched, and the government claims a satellite has been put into orbit. UN Security Council condemns the launch.

14 **United States:** Gunman kills 26 people, including 20 children aged 6 and 7, at elementary school in Newtown, Connecticut. He also kills his mother and himself. The shooting prompts renewed debate on gun control.

16 **Japan:** The Democratic Party of Japan, which has governed for three years, is ousted in a general election. The Liberal Democratic Party, which has ruled since 1955 with two interruptions, sweeps back to power. Shinzo Abe, prime minister for 12 months until September 2007, takes up the office again. There were five prime ministers in the intervening period.

19 **South Korea:** Park Geun-hye, a conservative, is elected president, succeeding Lee Myung-bak. She is the daughter of Park Chung-hee, an authoritarian president who was assassinated in 1979.

26 **Egypt:** A new constitution takes effect after being formally approved in a referendum by 63.8% of voters, though turnout was only 32.9%. The upper house of parliament is given legislative powers pending the election of a new lower house. However, unrest continues over the constitution and economic problems.

January 2013

1 **Turkey:** Government begins talks with Abdullah Ocalan, jailed head of PKK militant group. On 10 January, three female PKK members, including Sakine Cansiz, a co-founder and Ocalan associate, are found murdered in Paris.

1 **United States:** Congress votes to increase taxes on high earners, averting 'fiscal cliff' combination of automatic tax rises and spending cuts.

2 **Syria:** UN says 60,000 people have been killed so far in Syria's civil war.

6 **Central African Republic:** South Africa sends 400 troops to help the army to counter an advance of the Seleka alliance of rebel groups. Cameroon, Chad, Gabon and Republic of Congo have also sent troops. On 11 January a ceasefire is signed in Gabon. Under its terms, President François Bozizé appoints Nicolas Tiangaye, an opposition politican nominated by the rebels, as prime minister. A national unity government is to be formed.

8 **Egypt/Qatar:** Qatar provides $2.5bn of emergency finance to Egypt to stem the weakening of the Egyptian pound. However, the currency continues to fall.

10 **Pakistan:** Three bombs kill 96 people in Quetta, capital of Baluchistan, prompting widespread protests by Pakistan's Shia community. The attacks are blamed on a Sunni group linked to the Taliban. The province's chief minister is sacked.

11 **Mali:** France launches military operation to help Mali's armed forces to counter advances into southern Mali by Islamist rebels. French and Malian forces stop rebel advance towards Mopti, but rebels take Diabaly. French aircraft hit rebel positions in northern towns. Later, French and Malian forces recapture Diabaly, Gao, Douentza, Léré and Timbuktu.

15 **Syria:** Two explosions at Aleppo University kill more than 80 people.

16 **Algeria:** Islamist militants led by Mokhtar Belmokhtar attack and overrun the In Amenas gas plant in eastern Algeria, close to the border with Libya, taking some 800 workers hostage, including about 130 foreigners. The plant is operated by Sonatrach of Algeria with BP of the UK and Statoil of Norway. Next day, Algerian special forces launch an attack in which about 30 hostages are killed. By 18 January, most of the hostages have escaped or been freed. On 19 January, the plant is retaken in a final assault. The final death toll is 37 foreigners and one Algerian, as well as 29 of about 40 militants. Among the dead hostages are 10 Japanese, eight Filipinos, five Norwegians and five Britons.

22 **Israel:** In elections, the right-wing Likud party headed by Prime Minister Benjamin Netanyahu remains the largest party with 31 Knesset seats, but loses 11, while new centre-left party Yesh Atid, headed by television personality Yair Lapid, wins 19 seats to become second-largest party. They form a coalition with two other parties, with Netanyahu remaining prime minister.

23 **United Kingdom:** Prime Minister David Cameron says UK will hold a referendum on whether to remain in the European Union by end-2017.

27 **Egypt:** President Muhammad Morsi declares state of emergency in Port Said, Ismailia and Suez amid protests and clashes that left 40 dead.

30 **Japan/China:** A Japanese naval vessel in the East China Sea is 'painted' by the fire control radar of a Chinese frigate, according to the Japanese government, though China denies the allegation. The incident increases tensions between the two countries over disputed islands.

30 **Syria:** Israeli jets are reported to have struck a convoy of trucks inside Syria, apparently carrying SA-17 anti-aircraft missiles bound for Hizbullah in Lebanon. A Syrian research centre believed to be involved in chemical weapons is also damaged.

February 2013

6 **Tunisia:** Chokri Belaid, a leftist and secular opposition politician and critic of the Islamist government, is shot dead outside his home. Hamadi Jebali, prime minister of the Islamist-led government, immediately proposes to dissolve his cabinet and form a technocrat government as a means of uniting the country pending elections. However, this is rejected by Jebali's An-Nahda party, and on 19 February he resigns.

11 **Vatican City:** Pope Benedict XVI announces his resignation on grounds of poor health, at the age of 85. The German-born pope is the first to leave the office voluntarily since 1294. Jorge Mario Bergoglio of Argentina is elected the next head of the Catholic Church, and takes office as Pope Francis on 13 March.

12 **North Korea:** North Korea carries out a third undergound nuclear test, following those in 2006 and 2009. UN Security Council passes a resolution condemning the test.

15 **Russia:** A meteor breaks up and crashes into the Ural Mountains, creating a huge fireball and injuring about 1,000 people.

24 **Italy:** General election produces no clear result, and deadlock ensues in negotiations involving centre-left coalition led by Pier Luigi Bersani, centre-right grouping headed by Silvio Berlusconi, and anti-establishment Five Star Movement led by comedian Beppe Grillo. Mario Monti remains caretaker prime minister of technocrat government.

March 2013

4 **Kenya:** Uhuru Kenyatta, deputy prime minister, is elected president, winning 50.5% of vote and defeating Raila Odinga, prime minister, with 43.7%.

5 **Venezuela:** President Hugo Chávez dies of cancer at 58. Nicolas Maduro, vice president, succeeds him and on 14 April is elected president, narrowly defeating Henrique Capriles.

6 **Syria:** UN says the number of people who have left Syria as refugees in the civil war has reached one million.

16 **Cyprus:** Government agrees bailout deal with European authorities under which all bank depositors would be subject to a levy, contrary to EU plans to insure all deposits under €100,000. However, Cyprus scrambles to renegotiate the deal following an outcry and rejection by parliament. Banks remain closed to prevent runs. The Russian banking system is thrown into uncertainty because of the large amount of Russian deposits in Cypriot banks. On 25 March, a new €10bn bailout agreement is reached with the EU and IMF that drops the plan for a levy on depositors with accounts less than €100,000. However, larger deposits will be subject to a 'haircut', and one of the two biggest banks, Laiki Bank, is to be wound down with 'good' parts merged into the other, Bank of Cyprus. Capital controls are introduced to prevent flight of money.

18 **Democratic Republic of Congo:** Bosco Ntaganda, former general and a leader of the M23 rebel group, gives himself up at the US Embassy in Rwanda and is transferred to The Hague to face war-crimes charges.

20 **Myanmar:** Sectarian violence breaks out between Buddhists and Muslims, with 43 people killed in the town of Meiktila. It spreads to other towns, including Yangon, with Buddhist mobs reported to be attacking Muslims. Thousands of Muslims flee their homes.

21 **Turkey:** Abdullah Ocalan, imprisoned PKK leader, declares an immediate ceasefire in 30-year conflict between Kurdish separatists and Turkish government.

22 **Lebanon:** Najib Mikati resigns as prime minister as a result of divisions over the Syrian civil war. Tammam Salam, a Sunni politician, is asked to form a government.

24 **Central African Republic:** Seleka rebel coalition seizes control in Bangui, the capital, ousting President François Bozizé. Thirteen South African soldiers are killed. On 13 April, Michel Djotodia is elected president by a transitional parliament.

30 **North Korea:** Pyongyang says it is entering a 'state of war' with Seoul. On 3 April, United States says it will deploy a missile defence battery to Guam as a precaution against the threat of North Korean ballistic missiles. On 9 April, North Korea warns foreigners to leave South Korea because of the danger of conflict. US Secretary of State John Kerry says Pyongyang's threats are 'unacceptable by any standard'.

April 2013

4 **Japan:** Bank of Japan, the central bank, seeks to end two decades of economic malaise by a substantial easing of monetary policy that could double the amount of money in circulation within two years.

15 **United States:** Two bombs explode near the finish line of the Boston marathon, killing three people and injuring more than 250. Following a manhunt, two brothers of Chechen origin are identified as suspects. Tamerlan Tsarnaev, 26, is

killed in a shoot-out with police on 19 April. Dzokhar Tsarnaev, 19, is arrested and charged with using a weapon of mass destruction. It emerges that Russia had warned the United States of the elder brother's activities.

19 **Serbia/Kosovo:** Prime ministers of Serbia and Kosovo sign an agreement to normalise relations, following mediation by Catherine Ashton, EU foreign-policy chief. The accord paves the way for Serbia to begin talks on EU membership.

24 **Bangladesh:** A garment factory building collapses in Dhaka, killing 1,130 people.

25 **Syria:** Obama administration says Syrian government has probably used chemical weapons on a small scale, though it does not have definitive proof.

28 **Italy:** Two months after general elections, Enrico Letta of the centre-left Democratic Party becomes prime minister of a grand coalition including the centre-right People of Freedom Party. This follows the resignation of Democratic Party leader Pier Luigi Bersani who was unable to form a government.

May 2013

3 **Syria:** Israel again launches air-strikes against targets in Syria, reported to include missiles in transit from Iran to Hizbullah in Lebanon, and a military research centre.

11 **Turkey:** Bomb explosions kill about 50 people in the town of Reyhanli, close to the Syrian border.

11 **Pakistan:** Pakistan Muslim League (N) ousts the Pakistan People's Party from power in general elections, and Nawaz Sharif becomes prime minister for the third time. Pakistan Tehreek-e-Insaf, led by former cricketer Imran Khan, takes second-largest vote share.

14 **Nigeria:** President Goodluck Jonathan declares state of emergency in three northeastern states amid growing violence blamed on the Boko Haram militant group.

19 **Sweden:** Riots and arson attacks break out in a suburb of Stockholm, following the killing by police of an immigrant reportedly brandishing a knife in his apartment. Disturbances continue nightly for a week in the area, which has a predominantly immigrant population and very high youth unemployment.

22 **United Kingdom:** A British soldier is hacked to death on a London street. Two attackers, both Britons of Nigerian descent with Islamist views, are shot after waiting for police to arrive, and are later charged with murder.

27 **Syria:** EU foreign ministers agree to lift the embargo on supply of arms to Syrian rebel groups. In response, Russia says it will proceed with supplies of

S-300 anti-aircraft missiles to the Assad regime. On 14 June, United States says it will provide military support to Syrian rebels.

29 **Pakistan:** Drone attack kills Wali-ur-Rehman, a senior commander in the Pakistani Taliban.

31 **Turkey:** Anti-government protests break out in Istanbul and spread to other Turkish cities, met by police with tear gas and water cannon. The protests spring from plans to redevelop the Taksim Square area of Istanbul, including nearby Gezi Park, where police used violence in breaking up an environmentalist camp, sparking the wider protests and occupation of the square. Prime Minister Recep Tayyip Erdogan calls the protesters 'looters' under the influence of foreign powers. On 11 June, police attempt to storm Taksim Square, and on 15 June they try to clear Gezi Park. However, battles between protesters and riot police continue in Istanbul and other cities.

June 2013

5 **Syria:** Government forces recapture the town of Qusair, an important point on rebels' supply route from Lebanon.

6 **United States:** *Guardian* newspaper of the UK reveals the existence of US surveillance programmes that routinely gather data on the telephone and Internet communications of private citizens. The UK is alleged to share information. The US administration says it is necessary to gather data to guard against terrorist attacks. Edward Snowden, a former CIA and defence-contractor employee, later reveals that he leaked the information. He goes on the run from Hawaii to Hong Kong, and later to the transit area of Moscow's Sheremetyevo airport.

14 **Iran:** Hassan Rouhani, a moderate candidate, easily wins presidential election with 51% of the vote, with Tehran mayor Mohammad Baqer Qalibaf coming second with 17%.

17 **Brazil:** Mass protests break out in many Brazilian cities after police fire rubber bullets at a small demonstration against a rise in São Paulo's bus fare. Hundreds of thousands take part in peaceful marches, expressing dissatisfaction with government failings and the high cost of staging the 2014 football World Cup.

25 **Qatar:** Sheikh Hamad bin Khalifa al-Thani abdicates as emir and is succeeded by his 33-year-old son, Sheikh Tamim bin Hamad al-Thani. Sheikh Hamad bin Jassim al-Thani is immediately replaced as prime minister by Sheikh Abdullah bin-Nasser al-Thani.

26 **Australia:** Julia Gillard is ousted as Labor Party leader by Kevin Rudd, who returns as prime minister three years after she removed him in a similar manner.

30 **Egypt:** Protesters gather in Cairo's Tahrir Square and elsewhere to demand the resignation of President Muhammad Morsi, one year after he took office. The army announces it will remove Morsi from office unless he complies with the protesters' demands. On 3 July, it does so.

Chapter 1

Perspectives

The power struggles set in train by the Arab uprisings of 2011 held centre stage over the past year, as Syria's bloody civil war showed no sign of resolution and the Egyptian army intervened for a second time to unseat a government in response to massive popular protests.

These confrontations, though closely watched by the world's major powers, were taking place without their direct intervention. US President Barack Obama, re-elected for a second term, showed no more inclination towards interventionism than he had in his first. His more detached approach to international affairs – focusing instead on economic and social wellbeing at home – was not seriously contested in Washington. But it meant that America had become an astonishingly different global actor when compared with the one that provoked millions of protesters on to the streets around the world with its invasion of Iraq just a decade ago.

Obama understood early on that Washington had a limited ability not only to delineate the outcomes it desired in the Middle East, but also to make them happen. Events in Iraq and Afghanistan had underlined this. In Syria, for example, it would be almost impossible to achieve an international consensus on any possible concrete action. Moreover, if any such agreed action were to be military, it would be similarly challenging to win domestic political backing, and to pay for it. Obama did keep on the table the possibility of strikes against Iran's nuclear facilities, but this clearly remained his last option.

As the global power balance continued to shift, newer powers encountered challenges associated with the rising prosperity and expectations of their citizens. The Chinese Communist Party ushered in new leaders, with Xi Jinping ascending as expected to the summit and inaugurating the 'Chinese dream', intended to revitalise the country's economic drive and to counter official corruption. He did so after the authorities tried hard over an extended period to restrain expressions of dissent. The transition, though smooth on the surface, was marked by frantic factional manoeuvring as former top party officials protected their interests. Moreover, the leadership suffered extreme embarrassment from the downfall of party high-flier Bo Xilai, whose wife was given a suspended death sentence for the murder of a British businessman. In addition, investigative reporting by foreign media highlighted the wealth of families of senior government figures, including Xi. There remained questions about Xi's ability to exert authority over the party structure, and about how much he could achieve with his populist approach.

Meanwhile, China's diversion of criticism into nationalist feelings saw large protests against Japanese manoeuvres regarding a group of tiny, uninhabited islands and rocks in the East China Sea, over which there seemed – extraordinarily – to be a risk of conflict.

If China is well practised at suppressing domestic dissent, other rising powers are not. Spontaneous expressions of popular discontent have become much more common, fuelled by the instant ability to communicate offered by social media. The Arab uprisings of 2011 were the biggest example of this, as ordinary people expressed the frustrations built up over decades of dictatorship. The past year has seen mounting mass protests again in Egypt, and large demonstrations in Brazil and Turkey. The means of expression were similar, but the issues that sparked them were very different. Brazil, like China and India, has seen the fruits of rapid growth spread very unevenly amongst its population, so that a bus-fare hike in São Paulo was enough to trigger mass protests about how money was being spent by the government. In Turkey, a protest about plans to build over a park in Istanbul similarly broadened into the expression of multiple grievances, as a rising young middle class collided with an Islamist government that had grandiloquent goals. In both cases, a clumsy, aggressive response by police to a local protest triggered nationwide public outrage. In India, the rape and murder of a medical student on a Delhi bus prompted protests that highlighted the cultural challenges arising from economic liberalisation. While the protests in Brazil, Turkey and India did not seem to threaten the established order, the lesson of the Arab uprisings was that the outcome of modern protests was unpredictable.

No such upheavals were taking place in the industrialised world, which still struggled to break free of the economic stagnation that began with the financial crisis of 2008. The United States had begun to display reasonable growth as well as progress in reducing the fiscal deficit, but Europe's economic performance remained flat. The most positive development was the easing of the three-year crisis that stemmed from the financing difficulties of some of the 17 countries that use the euro as a common currency. This was achieved through decisive action by Mario Draghi, head of the European Central Bank, who undertook to make unlimited purchases of government bonds issued by problem debtors that agreed to reform programmes. This provided sufficient confidence to encourage investors to bid up the prices of Spanish and Italian debt, paradoxically removing the need for those governments to negotiate bailouts and agree with creditors on reform programmes. Draghi thus won the battle for the euro's survival – at least for the time being – without having to fire a shot. Meanwhile, however, a bitter debate continued among economists about the correct medicine for the industrialised world's economic ills, with some arguing that governments were correct to pursue 'austerity' programmes of public-sector cuts, while others said that Keynesian stimulus was essential to shake off the malaise. In practice, European governments began to compromise on this issue as Germany, which had insisted on austerity in debtor countries such as Greece in return for financial support, acquiesced in the granting of longer periods for countries to lower their budget deficits to the agreed level of 3% of GDP.

Other long-standing issues continued to overshadow international affairs. Iran's nuclear programme remained a pressing issue that could cause an outbreak of conflict in the near future, unless serious talks can begin that would require both the regime in Tehran and Western governments to make concessions that they have so far rejected. It was unclear whether the election of a somewhat more moderate president, Hassan Rouhani, would change the nature of the confrontation. North Korea, which carried out its third nuclear test in February 2013, took an extremely belligerent tone under its young leader Kim Jong-un, but both South Korea and the United States shrugged their shoulders in a determined show of indifference.

Meanwhile, terrorist attacks in the United States, the United Kingdom, Algeria and elsewhere demonstrated that al-Qaeda, though now a set of diffused entities pursuing mainly regional issues, continued to inspire young men to embrace violent jihadism. Radical Islamist groups were also a growing presence among Syrian rebels.

These elements of world affairs were no less threatening for being familiar. But new themes were also evident, principally those that arose from the ubiquity of the Internet and of web-based communications and systems. The United States and China traded accusations about cyber intrusions into government bodies and commercial companies, and no one seriously doubted that each side was daily attempting to disrupt the other. Meanwhile, disclosures by a young American, who had worked for government agencies and defence contractors in a short career, brought home the degree to which the ordinary citizen's daily life could be tracked by the government, and by Internet and communications companies.

Egyptian tumult, Syrian morass

Whatever Egypt's 2011 revolution was, it was not Islamist. It was only after Hosni Mubarak's regime had been swept away by the country's young middle classes, whom the army declined to oppose, that the Muslim Brotherhood emerged from its former suppression and became an overt political actor. But by the June 2012 elections, voters were faced with a choice between Muhammad Morsi, the Brotherhood candidate, and Ahmed Shafiq, a senior military figure from the old regime. It was not surprising that Morsi won. But this was not a strong democratic foundation from which to go forward. Indeed, even before he was elected, the military had dissolved the Islamist-dominated lower house of parliament after the country's highest court ruled that the electoral process was unfair – a decision that Morsi tried and failed to reverse.

Morsi, a hard-working, middle-class professor of engineering, religious but pragmatic, seemed likely to be more in tune with the average Egyptian than the elite that had flourished under Mubarak. The challenges that he faced should not be underestimated: a dominant army anxious not to lose its role and privileges, closely allied with a judiciary also wary of losing its powers; the disorganised factions produced by the revolution; an economy in a poor state; and a strong bureaucracy. He replaced the military chiefs. But as he was dealing with so many vested interests, it was not long before he began to suffer further setbacks, to which his response was to resort to authoritarian rule. He rushed through what was seen as a politicised constitution that leant towards Islamic law and did not reflect a post-revolutionary consensus. He issued and was then forced to withdraw an edict making his own decisions immune from judicial review. These moves sparked protests from demonstrators who began to equate Morsi's regime with that of Mubarak. From that point on, there was a steady deterioration into mass demonstrations and violence, with Morsi's government accused of incompetence and worse. As the one-year anniversary of his rule approached, opponents claimed to have gathered 22 million signatures for a petition asking him to step down. Within days, the army had removed him.

This was, in one sense, democracy at work, since opponents had no democratic processes left through which they could seek to exercise their will. Hence, it was argued by some that this was not a military coup, especially as it was supported by a broad plurality of Egypt's religious and political factions. Others, however, took the view that the removal of an elected government by the military could not be called anything but a coup. Regardless of this distinction, the future of democracy in Egypt was hard to predict as the Muslim Brotherhood's supporters would be disillusioned by the experience, and there was no unity between other groups. The world looked to Washington, which provides more than $1 billion in military aid annually, to offer an opinion, but the Obama administration studiously sought to avoid giving succour or criticism to any side. The Gulf's monarchies, who had viewed Mubarak's removal with alarm and (with the exception of Qatar) the Muslim Brotherhood with distaste, perhaps obtained some comfort from the Islamists' removal. However, the biggest and most successful of the Arab uprisings had been cast back into rank uncertainty. This was very uncomfortable for Egyptians and their neighbours as they looked at the sequence of events that had been triggered by the uprising in Syria.

By mid-2013, the death toll in the Syrian conflict was estimated at 100,000. A rebellion that had started, as in other Arab countries, as a popular expression of protest against an entrenched regime, had become suffused with radicalism. In spite of efforts to create a unified opposition and a command organisation, there was very limited central authority over the multiple rebel units and factions. While rebels made advances and took control of cities in the second half of 2012, the regime of President Bashar al-Assad concentrated on what it needed to control in order to survive. This effort was effective, and in the first half of 2013 it was taking back territory from the rebels, and had added to its military capabilities with help and training from its Shia allies, Iran and the Lebanon-based Hizbullah. Gulf states, seeking to contain Iranian influence, funnelled weapons and money to the rebels: Syria was the latest cockpit for the long proxy battle between the region's traditional rivals. As refugees flooded over Syria's borders, the conflict was destabilising for Lebanon and Jordan, and created difficulties for Turkey, which obtained the deployment by NATO of *Patriot* missiles on its borders. Thus, the Syrian conflict had drawn in many outside actors, and seemed set to continue to do so, at the cost of many Syrian lives, the destruction of its cities and any hope of stability in Syria's vicinity.

Selective intervention

International intervention in Syria – at least, any action with UN backing – was blocked for the foreseeable future by Russia and China. But this was in fact convenient for the governments of the United States and European countries, since they had no real appetite for action. While France and the United Kingdom took the most activist approach and succeeded in overturning an EU ban on supplying weapons to the rebels – soon followed cautiously by the United States – there was no move at all to take a significant hand in the conflict. Few in the West could determine whom exactly they might support, or to what end. It was hard to define a desired outcome beyond an end to the fighting or to predict where any possible intervention might lead. Though the imposition of no-fly zones on government forces had been mentioned as a possibility from the start, military counsel tended towards pointing out the practical difficulties and the unknown consequences of such action. Following the trials of Iraq and Afghanistan – and given the fragile state of Libya, where US Ambassador Christopher Stevens was murdered – it was not surprising that there was no wish to get involved anywhere else in the Middle East. Here again, the world had turned.

Financial Times columnist Gideon Rachman captured the change neatly. 'Those who are urging the US to get more deeply involved in the Syrian conflict now are living in the past,' he wrote. 'They assume that America can and should continue to dominate the politics of the Middle East.' Four fundamental changes, he said, made it 'no longer realistic, or even desirable, for the US to dominate the region in the old way'. These were the failures in Afghanistan and Iraq, the recession, the Arab uprisings and the prospect that the United States would attain energy independence.

Nevertheless, the United States would continue to have an important interest in shaping outcomes in the Middle East and elsewhere. While Obama's evident reluctance to send troops on new adventures was understandable and in tune with the American populace, over time Washington – and other Western powers – would want to find new ways to influence events. Military might was not the only instrument available. Plenty of outside actors, including Russia, were at work in different ways in the Syrian conflict. Washington could hardly stand back from such confrontations forever. In a sense, the pursuit of American interests might necessitate a reversion to more traditional diplomatic arts.

As if to underline the shifts that were under way, defence-spending cuts continued across the Western world, with 'sequestration' triggering significant automatic cuts at the Pentagon after the absence of any serious Congressional effort to bridge the political divide and agree on an alternative. During 2012, Asian defence spending overtook that of Europe, and the trend in both regions seemed set to continue. France and the United Kingdom, Europe's two defence powers, retained important all-round capabilities, but both have lowered their ambitions for the size and sustainability of interventions in recent years: in 2013, a French defence review froze planned spending in nominal terms, but this meant that it would decline after adjustment for inflation. As an essay in this book indicates (pp. 44–57), European countries' efforts at cooperation that could improve both military capabilities and value for taxpayer had promising elements but were making limited headway.

France, however, remained an important actor in Africa, and in January 2013 it commenced a surprise military operation in Mali, helping the armed forces of the coup-ridden country to beat back an advance by separatist Islamist militants, who had taken over the long-standing Tuareg rebellion in the north. The French action – a rare single-country intervention, although military assets of other nations were also used in support – was praised as well-planned and executed. It showed the advantage of rapid decision-making by French President François Hollande, after international efforts to support Mali had been slow in gestation. However, Europe's ability to sustain longer-term interventions would become more limited as budget cuts took effect.

Economic hopes revive

The good news on the economic front was that budget cuts and other measures taken since the 2008 financial crisis appeared to be having an effect in reducing the risks that had been hanging over the global economy. This did not mean that the situation had suddenly become rosy: growth in the industrialised world was slow or non-existent, and in the large emerging nations it had decelerated considerably. Europe's economies, constrained by fiscal austerity measures intended to reduce budget deficits, failed to move out of the doldrums. The banking system, so close to collapse in 2008, was not yet in robust health.

In the United States, the needed reduction in the budget deficit was being achieved by sequestration: overall, the deadlock between Republicans and Democrats showed no sign of easing, though an agreement was reached that averted the triggering of the so-called 'fiscal cliff', a combination of tax increases and spending cuts that threatened to halt economic recovery. In spite of the politicians, the American economy was showing moderate growth and the Federal Reserve, the central bank, indicated that it would continue to maintain an accommodative monetary policy – even after a bout of worries about this had caused a period of global volatility and had pushed up money-market interest rates in May and June 2013.

The strong hand taken by the Federal Reserve since 2008 – and similarly by the Bank of England in the United Kingdom – was matched over the past year by their counterparts in the eurozone and Japan. In Europe, through a combination of measures taken by governments and central banks' actions, enough appeared to have been done to avert financial disaster. This calmer atmosphere allowed for the prospect that economic growth might resume, albeit at a slow pace.

In Japan, the new government of Shinzo Abe attempted to break the deflationary malaise that had for so long afflicted the economy. He introduced a large fiscal stimulus, and the Bank of Japan substantially eased monetary policy. It was not yet clear whether this would end the chronic decline of consumer prices, which stifled demand as shoppers were put off purchases.

Power shifts

The 2008 crisis had altered the world in several ways: it caused a wrenching change to economic growth and prospects, forcing many governments, including that of the United States, to focus on domestic economic and social issues; it underlined important issues for Europe's future, causing tensions within and between countries, and raising questions about the EU's original goal of ever-closer union; and it accentuated shifts in the global balance, towards rising nations such as China, India and Brazil – and, in Europe, towards Germany. But these countries were not inclined to assume the role of hegemonic powers to which the twentieth-century world had been accustomed.

Moreover, they were not immune from domestic political and economic realities, as was shown over the past year by the slowing of Chinese growth, by the political difficulties involved in introducing new economic reforms in India, and by the protests in Brazil. Meanwhile, the United States and Europe had become either less willing or less able to achieve their aims through the flexing of diplomatic and military muscle. The effect of this was to create a more uncertain world, in which unexpected developments could have large and unpredictable effects.

. urther altering the global strategic picture was radical change in the energy market, where new oil and gas extraction techniques were behind the United States' shift towards energy independence. Over time, this seemed bound to alter the priorities and interests that went into the making of foreign policy in many countries, especially those that had depended heavily on energy imports or exports. The United States would become far less beholden to small states in the Middle East, even though it would still consider it to be against its interests for unrest in that region to spread far beyond the countries that had already been destabilised.

These shifts in the global balance of power were being accompanied by important shifts of power within societies. From some developments in the year to mid-2013, it was hard to escape the conclusion that governments, whether democratically elected or not, generally had less power to control the activities of their citizens than they used to have. In Turkey, a democratic government with no serious political opposition was reduced to flailing against supposed Western conspiracies as it failed to address properly the grievances raised by mass popular protests. In China, a non-democratic government sought daily to keep the lid on domestic protests expressed in social media and in so-called 'mass incidents'. The example of public protest that was set by Arab populations was being copied elsewhere as web-based media and smart-phone communications were used for rapid, spontaneous mobilisation. Savvy leaders such as Obama had used such platforms to good campaigning effect, but to other politicians these methods represented a threat rather than an opportunity.

Disclosures about the methods of the National Security Agency (NSA), the signals-intelligence branch of the US government, highlighted both sides of the equation. Edward Snowden, a 29-year-old who had worked as a technician for the Central Intelligence Agency and for private-sector contractors, leaked documents to newspapers that revealed NSA surveillance programmes of the communications of citizens. These did not cause political outrage, except in some European countries that were revealed as being treated for intelligence purposes as not the most closely trusted of US allies. But in the United States and in the United Kingdom, which was shown as sharing in the surveillance activities, there was a high level of acceptance that the gathering of 'metadata' – details of whom you are in contact with rather than what you say – was a useful means to detect and track potential terrorists. In addition, political and judicial safeguards, intended to deter surveillance deemed too intrusive, were said to be in place.

However, the Snowden disclosures highlighted the extent to which the world had drifted into new territory. It was through access to the data of private-sector companies that governments were obtaining the metadata. This served as a reminder that businesses such as Google and Apple, as well as other providers of Internet services and mobile communications, were gathering an enormous amount of knowledge about users' activities. Customers had acquiesced in companies having such knowledge in return for the convenience and pleasures of the services they offered. But the effect was to change fundamentally people's relationship with information and their expectations of privacy. In past times, information about people had been much more scarce, guarded and valuable; in the twenty-first century, it is ubiquitous and cheap. Countries in which there remain high expectations of privacy will struggle to adjust to this, and to regulate it. Moreover, even if the safeguards on NSA-type activity are deemed to be sufficient at present, the longer-term possibilities for official abuse of the private sector's data-gathering capabilities, especially in authoritarian states, seem significant.

Persistent threats

Amidst such discussions of new power balances, it was important to remember that the world was still at risk from long-standing dangers. Nuclear proliferation remained a serious threat, and the jihadist message of al-Qaeda was still inspiring terrorist attacks. As an essay in this book demonstrates (pp. 31–43), Pakistan and India were developing new nuclear doctrines that were doing nothing to reduce the risk that, if conflict were to break out again in their long-standing rivalry and territorial argument, it could turn nuclear.

Iran's nuclear programme was continuing to approach the point of development at which Israel – and perhaps the United States – might feel that military action was needed to prevent the production of nuclear weapons. Rouhani, the president-elect, was well versed in nuclear issues the programme continued to have wide popular support in Iran, and Supreme Leader Ayatollah Ali Khamenei had so far scotched any tentative progress made in international negotiations.

As North Korea's Kim Jong-un took a bellicose approach, China appeared inclined not to offer him support, but had not decisively veered away from the regime, no doubt worried about the disruptive effects of its eventual collapse. Kim made other efforts to assert control, sacking key members of his father's ruling clique, but it was hard to draw any definitive conclusions as to the course of the new regime. What was clear was that Pyongyang's drive towards nuclear weapons was unchecked and that it remained a threat.

While al-Qaeda's central organisation appeared to have been neutralised by the death and capture of many of its leaders, the message of violent extremism that it propagated was still powerful. Partly through online magazines, it attracted young people, especially men, to espouse grievances about wrongs they perceived to have been perpetrated against Islam. This was the case with two brothers of Chechen origin, but American education, who exploded bombs at the finish line of the Boston marathon, and two Britons of Nigerian origin who killed a British soldier in London. In both cases, at least one of the attackers had previously come to the attention of intelligence agencies. But security services faced a difficult task in detecting which of the thousands of alienated people on their watch lists might turn to violence. Meanwhile, Islamist groups in other countries, involved in local and regional conflicts, were also pursuing an extremist agenda that involved violence: Boko Haram in Nigeria, as well as militants in Pakistan, Mali, Libya, Yemen and Somalia. A foreign-owned gas plant was attacked in Algeria, and extremist groups were a factor in the uprising in Syria.

America's use of drone strikes to eliminate suspected extremists, seen especially in Pakistan and Afghanistan but also in Yemen and Somalia, was increasingly questioned on legal and ethical grounds. The number of strikes was falling, and the administration indicated that this method would be used in future in more tightly defined circumstances. Obama, seeking to bring American military interventions to a close, also sought to draw a line under the 'war on terror' declared by his predecessor,

George W. Bush. 'Our systematic effort to dismantle terrorist organisations must continue,' he said. 'But this war, like all wars, must end.'

However, even if the United States had entered a less interventionist era, the legacies of past actions remained. Iraq, free of foreign troops, had an authoritarian government and a high level of political violence. Afghanistan, plagued by corruption, was facing presidential elections in 2014 with no clarity about candidates who might succeed Hamid Karzai, leader since the West's military action in 2001. Though the withdrawal of foreign combat troops, due to be completed in 2014, was fully under way, stability in Afghanistan and its surrounding region was far from assured. The West may be less willing to participate in the world's trouble spots, but that will not prevent them from causing trouble.

Chapter 2

Strategic Policy Issues

South Asia's Nuclear Arms Race: Lessons of the Cold War

The continuing expansion of Pakistan's and India's nuclear capabilities, and major differences between the countries' force structures and defence policies, create ever greater concern about an intensifying nuclear arms race in South Asia. Pakistan's prospective introduction of tactical nuclear weapons increases the chance that a nuclear exchange will occur if a conflict breaks out, perhaps sparked by an act of terrorism. In addressing this strategic instability, India and Pakistan could learn from a comparison of their rivalry with NATO–Soviet competition during the Cold War. The analogy is somewhat problematic – particularly because India's nuclear posture is cast as primarily shaped by competition with China – but there are important similarities between the contests that shed light on the development of India's and Pakistan's nuclear policies.

South Asia's nuclear age began long before India and Pakistan tested nuclear weapons in 1998. In 1974, 12 years after its defeat by China in a border war, India carried out its first detonation of a nuclear device, referring to the event as a 'peaceful nuclear explosion'. Pakistan, whose eastern territories seceded to form Bangladesh in 1971, had by the late 1970s begun secretly working to acquire its own bomb to deter India.

By the mid-1980s, both India and Pakistan had a notional capability to deploy fission bombs. The subsequent period of 'recessed' deterrence lasted until the countries' 1998 tests established them as overtly nuclear-armed states.

Fifteen years later, South Asia is in the second phase of this nuclear stand-off. India and Pakistan have roughly equivalent nuclear inventories of about 100 warheads, double the number they had a decade ago. Both states have the capability to further expand their arsenals, and Pakistan is doing so explicitly, including by introducing rockets for use with tactical nuclear weapons. India and Pakistan are also developing naval nuclear weapons to add to their current ballistic-missile and aircraft-delivery platforms. Lately, the countries' declared nuclear doctrines of 'minimum credible deterrence' have seemed less and less concerned with minimisation. Concern about the dangers of nuclear war finds little expression in South Asia.

Both sides reject comparisons with the Cold War, arguing that – unlike NATO and the Soviet Union – they are reluctant nuclear powers. But in recent years the two governments have lacked the political will to use diplomacy to alleviate an arms race. India and Pakistan have not engaged in significant nuclear risk-reduction talks since 2007. This considerably strengthens reasons to consider Cold War lessons, especially with regard to the need to enhance strategic stability by moving away from reliance on tactical nuclear weapons and towards agreements to reduce arsenals and increase transparency.

Increasing competition

Nuclear competition between India and Pakistan was exacerbated by two developments in 2005. That year, New Delhi reached a landmark agreement with Washington to overturn more than three decades of US non-proliferation policy, which had prevented trade in nuclear materials for non-military purposes with countries not party to the Treaty on the Non-Proliferation of Nuclear Weapons. (Neither India nor Pakistan have signed the treaty.) Under the 2005 agreement, which became the basis for an arrangement with the International Atomic Energy Agency and the Nuclear Suppliers Group, India could import uranium and even dual-use nuclear technology. Eight existing Indian reactors for electricity generation, as well as planned fast-breeder reactors, were exempt from international inspection and were therefore presumably available for weapons-grade plutonium production as well as for civilian purposes. By 2008, all other nuclear exporters had agreed to the same exemptions for India. In theory, the ability to import uranium for civilian nuclear reactors would free up India's domestic uranium resources for use in nuclear weapons. However, India would be able to do this without international cooperation because of the small amount of uranium required for military applications.

Pakistan also began to expand its plutonium-production capabilities in 2005. The country was not offered the same agreement with the United States but cited the Indian deal as justification for this expansion. Other reasons, however, included a perceived need to catch up with India's larger plutonium stockpile and to produce more plutonium for tactical nuclear weapons. Pakistan had begun to assess the usefulness of such weapons as a response to India's consideration of plans to fight a limited conventional war. Growing economic disparity with India also increased Pakistan's reliance on nuclear weapons as a means of compensating for conventional-weapons inferiority.

Two additional plutonium-producing reactors being built at Khushab, in Punjab province, as well as a new plutonium-reprocessing facility, will allow Pakistan to double the number of weapons it produces each year: very roughly, from about 10 to 20. Although both New Delhi and Islamabad insist that they are not engaged in an arms race, Pakistan looks set to overtake the United Kingdom as the owner of the world's fifth-largest nuclear weapons stockpile. India will probably remain in seventh or eighth place, depending on the size of Israel's undeclared arsenal. Since 2009, Pakistan has blocked any discussion of a treaty to ban further production of fissile material for weapons use at the UN Conference on Disarmament. It argues that a treaty addressing only new production and not existing stocks would cement India's advantage of having more plutonium on hand for military use.

Beyond fissile material, India and Pakistan have focused on enhancing the range, composition and sophistication of their nuclear weapons. In 2005 Pakistan began testing nuclear-capable cruise missiles that would require smaller (plutonium-based) warheads. The *Hatf-7* (*Babur*) and *Hatf*-8 (*Ra'ad*) cruise missiles have a fuselage diameter of 52 centimetres and ranges of 700 kilometres and 'over 350km' respectively, limiting them to in-theatre use. Since April 2011, Pakistan has carried out three tests of the *Hatf*-9 (*Nasr*), a solid-fuelled artillery rocket with a range of 60km that is said to be designed for use as a tactical nuclear weapon. Pakistan indicated that the missile tests were only a technological demonstration and that no decision had been made to produce the system. A decision to move to production could worsen the crisis. Pakistan has also said that the nuclear-capable *Hatf*-2 (*Abdali*) missile – which has a range of 180km, and testing of which resumed in 2011, following a five-year hiatus – provides an 'operational-level capability', meaning for in-theatre use.

In 2010 India unveiled the first of at least three *Arihant*-class nuclear-propulsion submarines, the fruit of three decades of cooperation with Russia. The vessel was expected to start sea trials with its own reactor by mid-2013. In 2012 Indian defence scientists claimed to have developed a two-layer defence capability against missiles with ranges of up to 2,000km. They also claimed to have mastered the technology behind multiple independent re-entry vehicles. Although the claims were seen by many as premature, they encouraged worst-case threat perceptions in Pakistan.

Indian scientists also suggested that additional advances were on the horizon. After India completed its twelfth test of a sea-launched ballistic missile in January 2013, Vijay Kumar Saraswat, outgoing director of India's Defence Research and Development Organisation (DRDO), said the system would soon be ready for deployment on the country's submarines. The development of the nuclear-capable *Nirbhay* – a subsonic cruise missile that was first flight-tested in March 2013 and can be launched from multiple platforms – will also add to India's capabilities. Further ahead, Pakistan is working to develop naval tactical nuclear weapons for use against Indian carrier groups.

Cycle of escalation

Neither India nor Pakistan has explained how their emerging capabilities fit with their expressed posture of minimum deterrence. On the contrary, both countries continue to develop doctrines on the possible use of nuclear weapons, with the intention of making their deterrence postures more credible.

Pakistan's concern that India has formulated a policy for a limited conventional war – which would not cross what New Delhi perceives to be Islamabad's 'red line' for nuclear retaliation – was exacerbated in 2004. That year, Indian military officials called for a 'Cold Start' doctrine that would enable them to respond more quickly to Pakistan-linked terrorist attacks, such as the 2001 assault on the New Delhi parliament building. Although the initiative failed to win support from Indian political leaders, Pakistan is nonetheless seeking to deter a conventional attack by lowering the threshold for the use of nuclear weapons and developing short-range rockets that could carry nuclear warheads.

Such thinking contributes to a cycle of escalatory policies. By threatening to respond to Pakistani-sponsored terrorism with conventional military forces, India seeks to compensate for what it perceives as a shortfall in its ability to deter Pakistan. Denying any links with terrorism, Pakistan seeks to deter India's conventional military attacks by threatening retaliation with nuclear weapons on the battlefield. For Islamabad, a higher threshold for nuclear retaliation leaves it vulnerable to a conventional assault by India. India's conventional-military retaliation for a Pakistan-linked terrorist attack could therefore precipitate the use of tactical nuclear weapons by Islamabad – to which New Delhi, according to its doctrine, would respond with massive nuclear retaliation. Former Foreign Secretary Shyam Saran, who sits on India's National Security Advisory Board, emphasised this doctrine in a forceful speech on 24 April 2013.

Risk of nuclear conflict

This doctrinal mismatch is clearly a recipe for instability, especially in a climate of volatile nationalism. On the one hand, it is possible that nuclear deterrence has helped to maintain the fitful peace that has prevailed since 1999, when India and Pakistan engaged in a limited conflict in the Kargil area of Kashmir. The countries had previously fought three wars since becoming independent in 1947. On the other hand, nuclear weapons may have encouraged risk-taking and increased tension in South Asia.

There is a high risk of a renewed crisis: anti-Indian terrorist groups maintain a strong presence in Pakistan, and could strike India again. New Delhi finds it difficult to accept that Pakistani authorities are not associated with such attacks. Given the ties that Pakistan's Directorate for Inter-Services Intelligence has had with such groups, New Delhi would probably trace a future terrorist attack back to Islamabad. Although India rejected the 'Cold Start' doctrine, it does have a stance of 'proactive defence', a loose policy formulation under which it aims to deter Pakistan, and to punish it if necessary.

India's response to a future terrorist attack is difficult to predict. Some influential Indian strategists note that the country would face difficult questions about whom to target, what forces to use and how to keep control of events amid public outcry for revenge. Anticipating the worst, Pakistan believes that within days of a political decision, India would deploy eight division-sized integrated battle groups, accompanied by heavy support, to advance 40–60km into Pakistani territory. This is precisely the kind of operation that a nuclear-armed *Hatf*-9 would be intended to deter. Pakistan calculates that because such a weapon would have a relatively low nuclear yield, India would have neither the justification nor the political will to respond with overwhelming nuclear force, as Indian doctrine prescribes.

However, it is unclear whether Pakistan has developed a warhead small enough to fit into the *Hatf*-9 or other short-range systems. Such weapons have not been tested and there are no reports of Pakistan obtaining a miniaturised warhead design from China. Moreover, there are questions about doctrine and intent. It is hard to determine whether the purpose of using tactical nuclear weapons would be to slow or halt Indian forces, and whether Pakistan would fire them across the border into India rather than using them within its own territory. Nor has Islamabad indicated whether it would use *Hatf*-9 if India carried out precision conventional strikes against terrorist camps in Pakistan rather than Pakistani military forces or population centres.

India also has the potential to develop tactical nuclear weapons. In 2011, three months after the *Hatf*-9 was first tested, India tested the *Prahaar*, a ballistic missile that has a range of 150km and is seen by some

Pakistani analysts as potentially giving New Delhi a tactical nuclear capability of its own. India's DRDO has long had an interest in such a capability, and some Indian defence analysts have argued that a tactical nuclear option is needed. However, the *Prahaar*'s 200 kilogramme warhead capacity means it is unable to carry India's smallest nuclear weapon, which weighs 500kg, and tactical nuclear weapons are not compatible with the country's defence policy.

Accordingly, there is increasing cause for concern about a nuclear conflict resulting from miscalculation. On the bright side, both India and Pakistan are seen as having recessed postures for their nuclear forces, which involve separating warheads and delivery systems, refraining from the deployment of missiles and avoiding a launch-ready status. However, this could change. Pakistani analysts have warned that India's use of conventional military force at short notice and plans for ballistic-missile defence necessitate a more launch-ready posture. The deployment of naval systems, which require warheads to be deployed, would inherently raise the country's alert status. The dangers posed by misunderstanding and a lack of communication are exacerbated by the ambiguity of Pakistan's and India's dual-use systems, which make it very difficult to discriminate between incoming nuclear and conventional attacks.

Cold War attitudes

One aspect of the Cold War that is particularly relevant to South Asia is NATO's shift away from reliance on tactical nuclear weapons and towards arms control and transparency. In the 1950s, NATO placed these weapons, referred to as 'non-strategic nuclear weapons', at the centre of its defence plans. Designed to offset the weaknesses of its conventional forces in Europe against a Warsaw Pact attack, the weapons were seen as a more credible deterrent than the threat of massive retaliation against Soviet cities. The United States' strategy of forward defence in Europe was seen as delegating the authority to use tactical nuclear weapons to the US commander in Europe, with the aim of guaranteeing success in operations such as the defence of Berlin. The early stages of the Cold War therefore saw nuclear weapons being targeted at soldiers and tanks rather than cities and infrastructure. But doubts about the strategy began to emerge among the US Army and its European allies, as war games indicated that the escalation and spread of radiation caused by the use of tactical nuclear weapons would result in the large-scale destruction of European countries.

This realisation led to a more nuanced approach, with differentiated responses to various scenarios. There was progressively less delegation to theatre commanders and, ultimately, a change of doctrine from a massive, immediate response to the use of nuclear weapons only as a last resort. Targeting policies evolved considerably as NATO tended towards minimal use of nuclear force. By 1967 NATO envisaged that nuclear weapons would only be used in extreme circumstances: to end a war and restore deterrence. The more caveats that were added to the use of nuclear arms, the less relevant tactical nuclear weapons became. Having had approximately 7,500 tactical nuclear weapons stationed in Europe in the 1970s, by 1992 the US Army no longer had any such weapons there. The US Air Force kept about 200 of the weapons in Europe, mainly to reassure new NATO members and act as future bargaining chips with Russia. By this stage, NATO had recognised that the use of small-yield short-range nuclear weapons would always have strategic implications.

In response to its rival, the Soviet Union initially developed its own multilayered tactical-nuclear-weapons capability, and subsequently mirrored NATO reductions in reliance on these weapons. In 1991, when the United States withdrew its nuclear artillery shells and short-range ballistic-missile warheads, and removed tactical nuclear weapons from surface ships, Soviet President Mikhail Gorbachev announced that the Soviet Union would do the same. Gorbachev ordered that the remaining tactical nuclear weapons be moved to central Russia, away from Western Europe. In December 1991, following the dissolution of the Soviet Union and Gorbachev's resignation, Russian President Boris Yeltsin confirmed these commitments. Although Russia is estimated to still possess 2,000 tactical nuclear weapons, they remain in central storage.

NATO's abandonment of tactical nuclear weapons was closely linked to the wider evolution of thinking about nuclear arms. Defence planners had realised that crossing the nuclear threshold would be disastrous.

The idea of nuclear first use lost credibility because it was likely to lead to uncontrollable escalation.

Lessons for South Asia

From an outsider's perspective, the lessons that Cold War defence planners and policymakers took many years to learn are eminently applicable to South Asia, where tactical nuclear weapons are only beginning to become important. India does not have any such weapons and there is reason to question whether Pakistan, which has only been talking about the weapons for two years, has them either. Pakistan is yet to develop command-and-control, support, operational-security, situational-awareness and force-protection infrastructure for tactical nuclear weapons. Doing so requires different procedures from those used for conventional weapons systems. One encouraging sign is that the Pakistani military has apparently decided against deploying tactical nuclear weapons in forward positions and delegating their use to field commanders. However, the country could go further in this regard by learning from the Cold War. NATO concluded that precision-guided missiles, multiple-launch rocket systems and attack helicopters were a more effective defence against a limited conventional attack than tactical nuclear weapons, and had the additional benefit of being usable in other contexts. Western analysts argue that tactical nuclear weapons are expensive; add little to deterrence; invite pre-emption; are ineffective against mobile and armoured forces; complicate command, control and communications; require time-consuming launch-approval procedures; are difficult to secure when deployed and are not decisive on the battlefield.

Islamabad rejects NATO analogies regarding the development of tactical nuclear weapons, but Pakistan's reliance on such weapons is even more problematic than it was for NATO during the Cold War. NATO's development of such weapons in the 1950s was partly driven by concern about a massive Soviet ground invasion coming through a bottleneck such as the Fulda Gap, an area between Frankfurt am Main and what was the East German border. Pakistani experts recognise that there is no such bottleneck at which invading Indian forces would be massed in either Punjab or Rajasthan. This fact weakens the case for using tactical nuclear weapons because striking dispersed armoured forces entering Pakistan through many routes could require hundreds of tactical nuclear weapons, depleting the country's nuclear stockpile. Their use would also lead to significant fallout on non-military targets. In such a scenario, parts of Pakistan's densely populated agricultural heartland could become a nuclear wasteland. Pakistan's north–south communications lifelines, which lie only 50–60km from the border, could also be damaged by blowback from the explosions.

Islamabad regards any nuclear policy suggestions that single it out as discriminatory, especially if they come from Western nuclear-armed states. But the lessons NATO learned about tactical nuclear weapons during the Cold War also apply to India, and may reinforce New Delhi's disinclination to develop such capabilities. Given India's and Pakistan's differing nuclear postures and defence perceptions, it is inevitable that one side will feel unfairly singled out by cautionary comparisons with NATO. And although the discussion surrounding tactical nuclear weapons is currently more applicable to Pakistan, other lessons from the Cold War, such as those on arms-control talks and strategic stability, may be more relevant to India.

Arms control and confidence-building measures

Tactical nuclear weapons and dual-use delivery systems create the need for better ways of exchanging information and signalling intent to maintain crisis stability. India and Pakistan are not new to arms control. The first phase of South Asia's nuclear age stabilised thanks to several face-to-face bilateral negotiations and agreements between India and Pakistan between 1988 and 2007. Since 2002, both sides have kept to the agreements. Although tensions were raised in January 2013, a ceasefire on the Line of Control in Kashmir has largely held since 2003. The two sides have also worked together to promote a UN resolution calling for a reduction of nuclear threats by de-alerting nuclear weapons. In addition, India and Pakistan have maintained voluntary weapons-testing moratoria, agreed to in 1999. Since 2011, bilateral talks between the countries have resumed at the highest level. But there has been no real discussion of the factors that contribute to growing nuclear risks. This worries Western policymakers, who recall the dangerous nuclear experiences of the Cold War and the arms-control measures that were undertaken to reduce such risks.

Early in the Cold War, events such as the Suez stand-off, the Hungarian uprising, the Berlin crisis and the Cuban missile crisis made leaders on both sides realise that they needed mechanisms for engagement to escape the grave consequences of a failure of deterrence. Starting with US President Dwight Eisenhower and Soviet Premier Nikita Khrushchev, leaders cultivated a strong risk perception of nuclear weapons, made particularly acute by consideration of the potential for misperception and formidable other challenges of mounting surprise attacks with such weapons. Despite conflicts in Asia and elsewhere during the Cold War, NATO and the Soviet Union saw it as in their interests to negotiate processes and agreements that reduced the threat posed by their nuclear armouries and related defence doctrines.

This did not happen overnight. East and West made significant, if gradual, progress in two complementary ways. At the bilateral level, the United States and the Soviet Union engaged in arms-control talks that led to constraints and reductions in their offensive and defensive nuclear weapons. At the multilateral level, NATO and the Warsaw Pact engaged in conventional confidence- and security-building measures, which from 1975 involved information exchange, notification of activity, mutual observation and, by 1990, limitations on forces and challenge inspections. Following the Cold War, US–Russia transparency was enhanced by the 1992 Treaty on Open Skies.

Building this institutional machinery and reaching negotiated commitments helped bring about an end to the NATO–Soviet stand-off. To devise new means of building trust, government leaders, diplomats, military strategists and scientific experts used a new lexicon and a full range of negotiating tools, from high-level summits down to regular working-level meetings. They also created binding verification frameworks for their agreements and institutionalised gains with reciprocal, limited-duration commitments that were usually renewed. Such agreements also reduced the danger of mistaken signalling, such as occurred in NATO's *Able Archer* exercise in 1983, which the Soviets wrongly interpreted as a surprise attack.

Such developments are relevant to South Asia. Strategic stability requires that concerns about surprise attacks be addressed. India and Pakistan would benefit from taking up Islamabad's long-standing proposal to discuss elements of a 'strategic restraint regime'. The lesson of the 1973 Conference on Security and Co-operation in Europe – which fully acknowledged the differences between the conventional forces of NATO and the Soviet Union – is that strategic talks between rivals with militaries of varied strengths can succeed. It is worth noting that India and Pakistan have already made progress on one large issue that the Cold War blocs were unable to agree upon before the 1975 Helsinki Accords. In 1972 India and Pakistan signed the Simla Agreement, which refers to respect for each other's territorial integrity, albeit with the status of Kashmir left unresolved.

In recent years, meetings between non-governmental Indian and Pakistani experts have produced some useful suggestions to improve both strategic and crisis stability. These include setting up a regular face-to-face meeting between Pakistan's director general for military operations and his Indian counterpart, who are already connected by a hotline and hold a weekly conversation. They also include adding a declaration not to attack each other's nuclear command-and-control organisations, including via cyber warfare. Other proposals focus on preventing incidents at sea; creating a nuclear risk-reduction centre; establishing a binding framework to keep communication channels open during a crisis; designating organisations as official crisis messengers; admitting defence attachés to each other's military exercises to enhance fact-based threat assessments; creating military liaison missions; promoting service-specific military links between the two sides; establishing a hotline for the countries' national security advisers; assigning roles to weapon systems to eliminate dual-use ambiguities and concluding an agreement on the de-alerted status of nuclear weapons.

In India and Pakistan, arguments against comparisons with the Cold War often refer to the much lower alert status of nuclear forces in South Asia. India rejects bipolarity arguments altogether, given its need also to defend against China. Pakistan, for its part, emphasises that it is a sovereign state capable of ensuring internal cohesion without the kind of declaratory doctrines used by NATO.

In addition to these objections, there are institutional challenges to strategic talks. Firstly, no serving head of the Indian army has met his Pakistani counterpart since 1949, and there are no regular, prolonged military-to-military interactions for two-star generals and above. In comparison, by December 1987 Sergei Akhromeyev, chief of the general staff of the Soviet armed forces, was reportedly able, in the words of the *New York Times*, to 'march into the Pentagon and barely cause a ripple'. The meeting between Pakistan's director general of military operations and his Indian counterpart does not allow for discussions off the agenda. Although the crisis hotline between these officials has been used to reduce tensions, including in 2008, there is a stigma attached to being the first to pick up the phone, and the line has even been disconnected during certain crises.

Secondly, there are major differences between the countries' command-and-control structures. Lieutenant-General (retd.) Khalid Kidwai, who is head of Pakistan's Strategic Plans Division and controls the country's nuclear forces, has no counterpart in India's civilian-led Nuclear Command Authority (although Kidwai technically became a civilian upon retirement from the military). The Pakistani military's influence over nuclear policy, both in long-term strategic decision-making and operations planning, is at odds with India's institutions and strategic culture. Notwithstanding these institutional differences, however, the similarities between India and Pakistan – which include a shared culture and history – are greater than those between NATO countries and the Soviet Union.

South Asian strategists are familiar with the history of the Cold War and its nuclear doctrines. However, the means by which the West and the Soviet bloc developed processes to reduce nuclear risks are less well known. These include the methods used to devalue and recess tactical nuclear weapons and the ways in which NATO and Warsaw Pact political leaders made painstaking efforts at all levels to prepare for negotiations. With a new Pakistani government in place and India's general elections planned for spring 2014, there may soon be a chance for further political efforts to address the strategic environment. New leaders resuming talks on the mitigation of nuclear risk could benefit from the lessons of the Cold War.

European Defence Cooperation: Ways Forward

The amount of money that European nations spend on defence remains substantial: Europe's armed forces retain extensive capabilities that collectively should enable them both to defend their countries and to play significant roles in the world's trouble spots. However, defence budgets are falling quite rapidly, and well-known shortfalls in capabilities persist.

The decline in available resources is giving rise to concerns in defence establishments that European countries individually, and Europe as a whole, will in future be less able to control their own destinies and to influence global affairs. This is sometimes referred to as a loss of sovereignty, though what is in question is not each state's (or Europe's) political independence but rather the freedom of action to ensure that independence is preserved over the longer term.

Such concerns can be overstated. It is worth recalling that the fall in European defence spending was already occurring well before the financial crisis of 2008. It reflects a fundamental belief that threats to European security are at a lower level than they were during the Cold War. Admittedly, fiscal troubles have accelerated the decline, forcing difficult decisions to be made, including the elimination of important military capabilities. However, Europe's problem in the area of defence is not that the resources it devotes to armed forces are hopelessly inadequate: rather, it is one of balance and coordination – and of value for taxpayers' money, since it is unbalanced and uncoordinated spending that makes for wasteful use of resources and the failure to obtain the collective capabilities that should come from the substantial amount of money spent. Improved cooperation between countries seems a very important part of the solution.

There are paths forward. Useful models are already in existence, such as a cooperation agreement between Scandinavian countries and treaties agreed in 2010 between the United Kingdom and France. They could be copied and expanded. Greater awareness of the practical benefits to be gained from collaboration could help to overcome understandable fears that national sovereignty and jobs will be undermined. Bilateral and small-group initiatives offer particular promise, since it is easier to bring together an effective combination of political and budgetary support, as well as military buy-in, if only a small number of countries are involved. Through such efforts, not only can budgetary savings be made, but participating countries can devote resources to the capabilities and technologies that they are likely to need in coming decades, while dispensing with those that seem less likely to be of use.

Cooperation: bottom-up and top-down

Cooperation can originate at many levels: for example, from individual governments, armed services, and defence-industrial companies. There is also a role for top-down encouragement; since the Cold War, there have been several grand plans, especially those hatched by NATO, to improve Europe's capabilities, with the United States acting as cheerleader. The more ambitious and all-encompassing the plan, the more likely it was to be hobbled by bureaucratic, political and military inertia.

Several current efforts seem more promising precisely because they rely on individual countries or small groups to drive advances in specific areas. NATO has undertaken a 'Smart Defence' initiative, while the EU has a parallel 'pooling and sharing' programme. Meanwhile, the 2010 defence cooperation treaty between the UK and France, Europe's two biggest defence powers, has the potential to foster technological advances in specific areas and to influence the structure of Europe's defence industries.

The Chicago summit, bringing together NATO heads of government in May 2012, established Smart Defence – brainchild of Secretary-General Anders Fogh Rasmussen – as a central element in the Alliance's provision and use of capabilities. Leaders agreed that member states would set priorities with guidance from NATO, cooperate more among themselves on developing and maintaining military capacities, and give new consideration to specialisation of roles and tasks. By better allocating budgets, Allies would retain the ability to meet NATO's defence-planning goals. A list of 29 projects was compiled, some of which address shortfalls that had been repeatedly exposed, most recently in the 2011 Libya conflict, such as availability of munitions and of maritime patrol aircraft.

Smart Defence has the potential to change markedly the way in which many NATO members think about their armed forces. It could lead them away from traditional, deeply rooted notions of autonomy and national security. However, this would inevitably take time. It is not yet clear whether Smart Defence will generate the game-changing momentum for which Rasmussen hoped. Nevertheless, the principles behind it – prioritisation, cooperation and specialisation – seem essential whatever collaborative framework is applied.

Separately, Herman Van Rompuy, President of the European Council, triggered a flurry of discussion in the committee rooms of Brussels, as well as in European capitals, by placing defence firmly on the agenda of the Council summit in December 2013, when new proposals on reshaping the Common Security and Defence Policy, as well as on EU defence strategy and military structures, are likely to be put forward. The Council's decisions could provide improved strategic rationale and political backing for capability improvements, as well as a stronger impetus for cooperative efforts. (See European Defence, pp. 137–142).

Numbers and experience

It is important to set the background for discussions about cooperative efforts. Europe as a whole, and some individual European countries on their own, remain important military powers. The United Kingdom, France and Germany are in the top eight global defence spenders, and Europe accounts for 17.6% of global spending. In 2012 it was overtaken by Asia and Australasia, which together accounted for 19.9% (compared with North America's 42%). The most striking feature of the global defence picture is China's development as a military power, with a large army and rapid modernisation of technical capabilities under way. But it is notable that Europe's combined defence expenditure is 1.8–2.8 times that of China in absolute terms, four to six times that of China per head of population, and 1.9–2.8 times that of China per person in uniform. (All figures are derived from the IISS publication *The Military Balance 2013*, and some make use of purchasing-power-parity calculations.)

In terms of equipment, Europe has considerable capabilities in high-technology equipment, as well as some recognised gaps. It has, for example, over 2,300 fast-jet combat aircraft, well behind the United States but ahead of the 1,800 mostly less capable Chinese equivalent aircraft and just over 1,200 possessed by Russia. In its navies, Europe has

151 cruisers, destroyers and frigates, compared with 109 in the United States, 77 in China and 32 in Russia.

Of course, these figures only give an overall impression of Europe's military might, and one that undoubtedly suffers under closer scrutiny. The first point is that defence budgets are being reduced in all the major economies. The $260 billion spent by NATO's European members in 2012 was 11% lower in real (inflation-adjusted) terms than their defence expenditure in 2006, and the total will undoubtedly drop still further. In April 2013, France announced that it would freeze annual defence expenditure in nominal terms for the next six years, meaning that in real terms there will be a significant reduction, with personnel numbers cut quite sharply. The UK's defence review of 2010 similarly forced personnel cuts, as it reduced spending in real terms by 8% over four years. It eliminated unfunded equipment programmes from future procurement plans; lowered expeditionary ambitions; eliminated carrier strike capability for at least a decade; cancelled a maritime patrol aircraft programme and forced a restructuring of the army. In southern European countries, heavily affected by the eurozone crisis, defence spending fell in real terms by 11.9% between 2010 and 2012.

Secondly, Europe's deficiencies in terms of modern capabilities have been frequently exposed. Many nations have not invested enough in intelligence and surveillance, and so find themselves reliant on American assets. The same applies to other enabling assets such as air transport and refuelling, and in some countries to precision-guided munitions. These gaps have been noted repeatedly, and therefore seem likely to be felt again in future operations. Some of them will be filled by procurements and projects now under way, but budget austerity means that the resources available to address them are limited.

The third and most important disadvantage from which European nations are suffering is that, even though they are almost always taking part in multinational operations, their forces mostly deploy, operate and are supplied separately. They also, in most cases, purchase and support their equipment separately. Moreover, the fact that budget cuts are almost entirely uncoordinated creates risks of dangerous weaknesses emerging in some capability areas while duplications remain in other, perhaps less vital, fields. Countries therefore do not make the most of the advantages that their collective investments in defence should offer. This is the area in which there is most scope for improvements that could provide real tactical, strategic and economic benefits.

On the other side of the equation, European armed forces have one significant advantage: the large amount of operational and combat experience that they have amassed over the past 20 years. Since the end of the Cold War, NATO as an alliance has been involved in long missions in Bosnia, Kosovo and Afghanistan, and its members have been involved in cooperative deployments to Iraq and numerous other places in the Middle East and Africa. These have provided participating countries with invaluable experience of both high- and low-intensity operations, and have improved their ability to operate alongside each other. Important new skills have been developed, many of them involving the use of technologies that have emerged within the past two decades. While the planned withdrawal of combat forces from Afghanistan by the end of 2014 will provide a welcome respite, experience suggests that there will be more missions to undertake in Europe's vicinity, for example in Africa and the Middle East, and the hard-won improvement in multinational combat effectiveness will need to be preserved. Closer cooperation will therefore be vital.

Sovereignty and models of cooperation

Whatever type of cooperation is attempted, the principles of the Smart Defence initiative are important. Firstly, it is vital to set clear priorities that are based on a country's desired future role in the world and in European security, as well on the threats to national security that it perceives. Only on the basis of these can good decisions be made about what capabilities to keep and develop, and what to do without. Secondly, these decisions are far more likely to be implemented effectively if dwindling resources are pooled – not only money, but also military, industrial and technological skills. Thirdly, since not even the largest countries can afford to keep all the capabilities and assets that they would like, specialisation is inevitable. It is far safer and more effective for European countries to make choices about specialisation in a coordinated fashion, establishing some degree of mutual dependence. However, all of these steps require difficult debates about two sets of issues: national identity and sovereignty on the one hand, and defence-industrial cooperation and consolidation on the other. Within these lie the largest obstacles to closer defence cooperation in Europe, but it is possible at least to begin to untangle them.

Admittedly, setting priorities is hard. Virtually every national defence review by European governments stresses deep uncertainty as perhaps the one key characteristic of the strategic environment. This makes it challenging to predict future contingencies and, thus, future requirements. Governments worry about giving up capabilities that they might need urgently in the future. They know how difficult it would be to regenerate what has been lost. But in the end, budget imperatives demand that choices about priorities are made. This means favouring one capability over another, and in doing this a government is, in effect, making a choice to specialise. The largest countries, and especially the UK and France, seek to keep as full a spectrum of capabilities as they can even while cutting defence budgets. But for others, this is simply not feasible.

'Specialisation by default' is under way as NATO members engage in uncoordinated defence cuts that often involve the complete elimination of some capabilities. As a result, NATO's collective capacity suffers. Those nations that still possess the capabilities in question are left with specialised roles purely as the result of other nations' actions. But the other side of the coin is that the Alliance is also left with capabilities that are duplicated to an unnecessary degree. NATO's goal through Smart Defence, therefore, is to achieve 'specialisation by design' to the greatest extent possible. For this to happen, NATO Allies would need to reduce to an acceptable level the risks that nations perceive. Among these is the danger of placing reliance on another country which might then fail to deliver a particular capability when the operational need arises.

This is the crux of any decision to specialise. How and to what degree can access to a capability be assured? It has been suggested that one method would be for countries to enter into legally binding agreements to deliver a predetermined capability after receiving notice that it was required. However, there are disadvantages to such an approach. It ignores political realities. If a country saw no reason to put its military assets (and lives) at risk in a particular operation, it could well refuse to take part, binding agreement or not.

Less formal models are therefore needed. Some already exist. For example, sharing arrangements have provided numerous nations with access to tactical and strategic transport aircraft. The five-nation European Air Transport Command (EATC) was established in 2010, with Belgium, France, Germany and the Netherlands as the launch nations, joined by Luxembourg in 2012. EATC provides a pool of nearly 150 transport aircraft across a variety of classes from medium and light military airlifters to business jets. Assets are declared to the command by each nation, and each nation retains the ability to withdraw aircraft. During 2011, 7,000 missions were flown. The command provides cost savings while making better use of available capacity. Missions in which an aircraft flies one leg of a journey empty have been reduced by an average of 8%, with a similar percentage reduction in the requirement to outsource medical evacuation flights.

Crucially, partners retain a 'red card' giving them national veto with regard to participating in particular operations. A 'black cell', under which national elements can be temporarily removed from EATC, addresses national sensitivities to specific air movements, giving nations the ability, for example, to run special-forces operations through separate command chains. By the end of 2012, the red card had been exercised once in two years, and the black cell had yet to be used. This suggests that while it is important to accommodate concerns about lost sovereignty, actual instances in which the common arrangements are affected by national issues may be rare – an encouraging sign.

While the EATC goes some way towards improving participating nations' tactical and medium airlift resources, requirements for strategic airlift and outsize cargo have been addressed through other arrangements. Participating NATO nations and partner states have obtained access to two types of large aircraft: the Antonov An-124 and the Boeing C-17, the former through the Strategic Airlift Interim Solution (SALIS), and the latter through a separate Heavy Airlift Wing based at Papa Air Base in Hungary. SALIS, set up in 2006, involves 14 NATO nations and provides charter access to six An-124s. Meanwhile, ten NATO and two partner nations have signed up to the C-17 project, established in 2008, with access to three aircraft. The entry of the delayed Airbus A400M airlifter into service will go a considerable way towards filling this gap.

There are other models of collaboration. For example, the German/Netherlands Corps is a collaboration in the arena of high-intensity operations. The corps has acted as a kind of 'think tank' for best practices. It has conceptualised Smart Defence as a trade-off between cost and dependency – the greater the degree of sovereignty lost, the lower the cost of defence provision. For example, if states were to cooperate in training alone, this would create a relatively low degree of dependency, and hence only a small loss of sovereignty. However, the total cost would remain relatively high, due to the limited scope for efficiencies and the expense associated with constructing shared training facilities. At the other end of the spectrum, more extensive role specialisation would enable more efficient allocation of resources, and thus greater cost savings, but would create a higher level of dependency and thus a relatively large loss of sovereignty. The German/Netherlands Corps sees itself as falling in the middle range of the cost-dependency trade-off, and could serve as a test case for other states as they seek to define how far they are willing to go in accepting mutual dependency.

One development of this approach would be for nations to establish mentoring agreements among themselves. The aim would be to provide a nation that agreed to disinvest from some capabilities with a partner who ensured that a minimum level of skills, training and doctrine were maintained. Such residual capability would speed up the process of regeneration should the need arise. It is likely that larger member states would provide the anchor for several smaller ones. However, while there may be some benefit for the larger state, such as more efficient use of training and education facilities, the benefit to the smaller state would probably be greater.

The Anglo-French Lancaster House treaties of 2010 provide one of the most important examples of collaborative approaches. These significantly expanded cooperation between Europe's two biggest defence powers, which have similar strategic cultures and armed forces, and a shared appetite for expeditionary operations. Both are frequently involved in foreign deployments, and in leadership roles. Both have similarly capable armed forces and defence-industrial bases. One treaty envisages a series of cooperative ventures including the creation of a

Combined Joint Expeditionary Force (CJEF) and industrial collaboration in several types of technology, including A400M aircraft maintenance and training, submarine systems and satellite communications. The other outlines specific areas of nuclear collaboration, including maintenance of warhead stockpiles.

Since the treaties were signed, much time has been spent setting up governance structures for the relationship. However, the CJEF has already undertaken exercises and is planned to be at full operational capability by 2016. Following the announcement of the French *Livre Blanc* in April 2013, a joint project to develop an anti-ship missile was added to the list of projects. Although the agreement is not specifically exclusive, the manner in which other countries might engage with the bilateral relationship remains open to debate.

These examples – and there are plenty of others, such as the Nordic Defence Cooperation (NORDEFCO) arrangement between Denmark, Finland, Iceland, Norway and Sweden – offer several pointers about successful cooperation. Firstly, they give participating nations confidence that could help them to specialise in particular areas and leave other areas to their partners. Secondly, they afford nations sufficient flexibility: they do not assure access to capabilities beyond doubt, because this is impossible – a decision can always be taken by a national government not to take part in a specific mission. Creative mechanisms such as 'red cards' can mitigate this. Thirdly and as a consequence, some redundancy should be allowed to remain across Europe in each type of capability, though this should not be taken too far as otherwise there is wasteful duplication. Fourthly, successful collaborations can act as laboratories, creating a strong bottom-up dynamic, as well as an understanding of the potential trade-offs between benefits and costs.

Effective industrial collaboration

About a quarter of NATO nations' defence budgets are spent on the acquisition of military equipment. Add the cost of lifetime maintenance, which can amount to three or four times the purchase price, and the proportion of defence spending taken up by equipment is considerable. As governments seek to obtain better value from shrinking budgets, this is therefore an important area on which to focus.

This was recognised by NATO leaders at the Chicago summit: 'Maintaining a strong defence industry in Europe and making the fullest possible use of the potential of defence-industrial cooperation across the Alliance remain an essential condition for delivering the capabilities needed for 2020 and beyond.' Similarly, EU leaders decided in December 2012 to advance their 'pooling and sharing' initiative, and develop 'a more integrated, innovative and competitive European defence technological and industrial base'.

As budgets fall, the question for European governments is how to ensure that industry continues to be able to meet their needs on a profitable basis and maintains the capacity to develop new technologies. Again, the principles of Smart Defence seem central. As budgets fall, it is only through cooperation that countries can marshal the resources – both financial and technological – to acquire and support the equipment needed by their armed forces. Prioritisation is essential: it means concentrating resources on what will be needed for the military of the future, and dispensing with legacy programmes that are often kept going for reasons beyond the requirements of defence. Specialisation is closely related to the setting of these priorities: it involves identifying centres of excellence within industry and ensuring that they receive the investment necessary to develop new technologies.

There is already enormous experience of collaboration between countries on acquisition of equipment. This has delivered weapons systems that constitute key elements of national inventories, including *Tornado* and *Typhoon* aircraft, and the NH90 helicopter. Current programmes will add to this list: the F-35 *Lightning* combat aircraft, the A400M airlifter and *Meteor* missiles.

It is also undeniable, however, that much more could have been achieved. Collaborative programmes are typically subject to long delays and cost escalation. Requirements inevitably change, resulting in wasted resources. 'Juste retour' principles have meant that industrial arrangements for the development and production of weapons systems have been far from optimal: jobs may be maintained, but at considerable cost to taxpayers. Moreover, though produced jointly, equipment is maintained separately by nations.

The scope for more cooperation is indicated by IISS research: in 2008, European countries were engaged in a total of 41 procurement programmes with a value of €1bn or more. Of these, 30 (73%) were single-country acquisitions. By 2012, the list of programmes worth €1bn or more had shrunk to 31, but there had been no progress towards greater collaboration. Of the total, 22 were single-country acquisitions, and only nine collaborative. No collaborative programme had been initiated since 2002 (see *Survival: Global Politics and Strategy*, vol. 54 no. 1, February–March 2012, 'The Struggle for Value in European Defence', pp. 53–81). In short, there has been no visible move at all in recent years among governments to pool equipment requirements, as domestic priorities such as jobs and protection of intellectual property have predominated. One reason for the absence of new large-scale collaborative projects, apart from lack of money, could be a tendency towards buying 'off-the-shelf' products developed by other countries instead of developing new ones. But even this activity – though sensible – appears limited in scope.

Nor has Europe's defence-industrial base become significantly more consolidated across borders. After a burst of mergers and acquisitions in the late 1990s and early 2000s, rationalisation has largely stalled. The biggest moves by European companies have been to build their presence in the United States. Increasingly, companies are looking to the growing defence market in Asia as a future source of business, rather than to their home governments. This means that, to ensure that they will retain a measure of control over what capabilities they can purchase, European governments will need to ensure that their own supplier base is correctly sized, resourced and skilled. This will demand far more effective consultation and coordination than there has been in decades past.

This need is urgent. Europe's defence industry faces the prospect of a sudden fall-off in demand from its main customers. Currently, it remains busy with programmes that have been under way for many years, and which still occupy a large chunk of nations' defence expenditure. These include the F-35, *Typhoon* and *Rafale* combat aircraft, Airbus transport and air-to-air refuelling aircraft, as well as various destroyers, frigates and submarines and, in Britain's case, two aircraft carriers. Helicopters, armoured vehicles and intelligence, surveillance and reconnaissance systems are also on order. Europe's defence industry thus has plenty to do for the next few years. But as production of existing orders comes to an end, manufacturers will find themselves facing a much less secure future. Difficult questions will arise for governments about the continued funding of manufacturing capacity, know-how and technologies. Failure to provide satisfactory answers could lead companies to prioritise other customers with more money to spend – for example, in Asia – or else to quit the defence business altogether. This would contribute to an erosion of European countries' ability to determine their own destinies.

How then should governments cooperate on acquisition and support in ways that offer better value than methods attempted in the past? Again, promising models exist.

An oft-cited example is the purchase by the UK and France of the same cruise missile (called SCALP EG by France and *Storm Shadow* in the UK), from the same manufacturer (MBDA, a cross-border joint venture), in separate programmes. This avoided the necessity for joint agreements and joint contracts, and for the creation of additional legal entities, but did require a considerable amount of trust, especially by the contractor. It represented, if informally, a harmonisation of two sets of national requirements, and it produced timely delivery of capability for both nations, which proceeded swiftly to use them in operations. However, it left the missile industry still a long way from true cross-border consolidation and integration. Moreover, SCALP/*Storm Shadow* has been in service for more than a decade, during which time this procurement method has not been replicated. The two governments do now plan to upgrade the system.

A useful starting point is the list of nearly 30 projects created under the Smart Defence initiative itself, some of which contain significant potential for industrial cooperation. For example, Project 1 is to enable jets to use munitions from different sources and nations, increasing operational flexibility. The scope for industry to play a key role seems obvious. Project 2 is to identify robots to clear bombs – central to the increasing focus of industry on developing unmanned systems – and promote collaborative acquisition of such systems. Project 3 seeks to create a pool of maritime patrol aircraft – again, something in which industry could play a role. Meanwhile, 'pooling and sharing' projects overseen by the

European Defence Agency include air-to-air refuelling, modular field hospitals and maritime surveillance.

It is also important that industrial companies show initiative in promoting cooperative projects. However, they will need some encouragement from their customers that any investment they make in this direction is likely to generate profitable business over the long term. Governments will also need to afford industry more flexibility over how best to structure itself so as to meet their equipment needs most cost-effectively – especially given the coming decline in new orders. Some companies are already anticipating that time: for example, the two largest European defence manufacturers, BAE Systems and EADS, proposed a merger in 2012. But this was blocked by the German government for domestic political reasons.

If the two biggest suppliers saw the need to combine to ensure a healthy future, what chances are there for the smallest? The supply chain could be significantly impaired if small and medium-sized enterprises, seeing their defence-related work drying up, were to opt en masse to quit the business. It is in governments' interest, therefore, to persuade companies of the benefits of staying in the defence business. The days are long gone in which a country's arsenal was, in effect, a subsidised arm of the state, and thus could be counted upon to be there to meet its needs. Industry executives need to be confident that contracts will be profitable over the long term. It is therefore in the interests of customers to ensure that there is a measure of stability and predictability for their suppliers. The British government has, for example, produced a future equipment plan covering about £159bn of spending over ten years. Such a plan could be created at a wider European level, with a particular focus on technologies meeting new military needs, such as unmanned systems and cyber. Industry could be given a say in shaping procurement and support models, including alternative funding sources. The SCALP/*Storm Shadow* model, as well as uses of public/private partnerships in acquisition and support, has shown the scope for innovation, and suppliers can offer innovative solutions. Companies could also be invited to offer innovative packages to customers in the support of equipment – an obvious case would be the A400M transport aircraft due to come into service in several countries, which could benefit from shared support arrangements.

If uncoordinated budget cuts continue along the pattern of the past few years, and are not mitigated by cooperation, prioritisation and specialisation, governments will undoubtedly see the erosion of key elements of their national defence-industrial bases. For each country – and for Europe as a whole – the defence industry is a strategic asset, an essential component of military capability. Decisions by companies to close factories, dispense with skilled staff, or even exit from defence will make it impossible for European nations to maintain full-spectrum capabilities without relying much more significantly than at present on external suppliers. Such reliance would entail a loss of bargaining power: for example, European countries could face constraints on the use of technologies, and thus on how their militaries could be used. The supplier countries that might benefit would not just be the United States, but could include emerging powers such as India and Brazil, as well as Russia. The loss of European sovereignty – whether viewed collectively or nationally – would be accelerated.

Solutions

European governments face key issues over the future of their armed forces and over the industries that supply them. These will not be resolved overnight, nor is there any magic bullet for them. Indeed, the issues have remained remarkably static for many years, with the picture worsening, but in slow motion. Europe has for decades lacked key capabilities, and during this time it has had problems in collaborating to fill the gaps. Nevertheless, it has engaged in multiple military operations and has acquired vital new technologies and equipment. The picture is far from being all black. There is time to devise more effective long-term solutions and, as outlined above, there are good ideas that offer hope for more cost-effective European defence in the future. The need is for mutual efforts and the political, military and industrial will to cooperate to assure Europe's future place in the world.

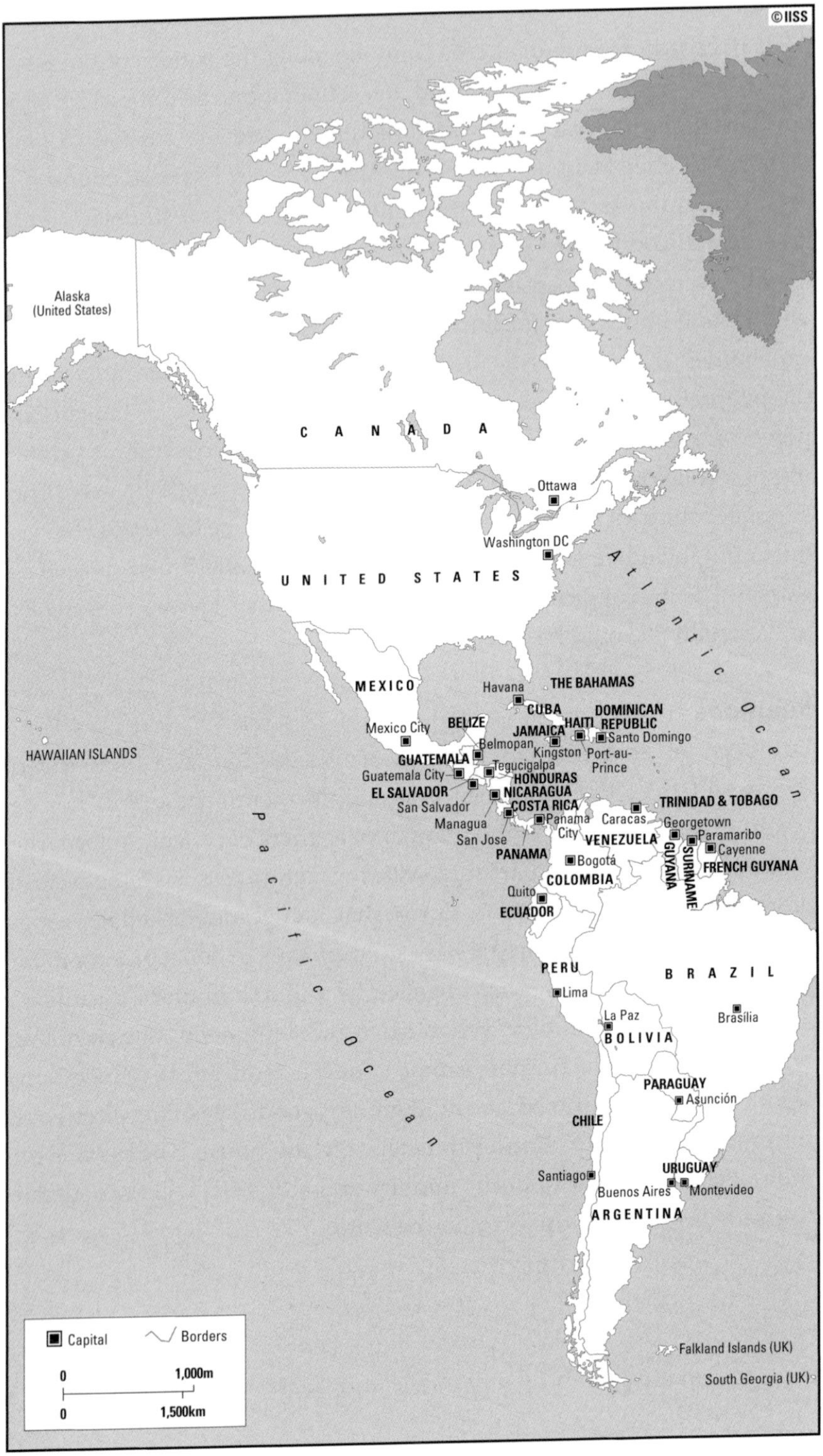
©IISS
Alaska
(United States)
CANADA
Ottawa
Washington DC
UNITED STATES
Atlantic Ocean
MEXICO
Havana
THE BAHAMAS
CUBA
DOMINICAN
REPUBLIC
HAITI
JAMAICA
Santo Domingo
Mexico City
BELIZE
Belmopan
Kingston
Port-au-
Prince
HAWAIIAN ISLANDS
GUATEMALA
Tegucigalpa
Guatemala City
HONDURAS
EL SALVADOR
NICARAGUA
San Salvador
COSTA RICA
TRINIDAD & TOBAGO
Managua
Panama
City
Caracas
Georgetown
Paramaribo
San Jose
VENEZUELA
GUYANA
SURINAME
Cayenne
PANAMA
Bogotá
FRENCH GUYANA
COLOMBIA
Pacific Ocean
Quito
ECUADOR
PERU
BRAZIL
Lima
La Paz
Brasília
BOLIVIA
PARAGUAY
Asunción
CHILE
URUGUAY
Santiago
Buenos Aires
Montevideo
ARGENTINA
Capital
Borders
0
1,000m
0
1,500km
Falkland Islands (UK)
South Georgia (UK)

Chapter 3

The Americas

The United States: Raw Data

The iconography expressed the zeitgeist, which involved data. A video clip, spread virally with some help from gloating Democrats, showed Republican strategist Karl Rove in evident consternation, objecting to the decision by Fox News statisticians to call Ohio, and with it the 2012 presidential election, for President Barack Obama. Rove, the man who had charted George W. Bush's political rise and now a regular commentator on Fox, felt there were too many outstanding precincts with enough potential Republican votes to tip the state the other way. So Fox anchor Megan Kelly walked, under camera's gaze, down a succession of white corridors to the Fox 'decisions desk', where she interviewed two of the statisticians who had made the call. They told her that Cuyahoga County, containing overwhelmingly Democratic Cleveland, had significant precincts still to report. '99.95%' sure of Obama's victory, said one of them. 'There just aren't enough Republican votes left for Romney to get there,' said another. Fox News at this point was showing a split screen with giddy celebrations at the Obama campaign's Chicago headquarters on one half, and Rove still protesting on the other. At another point in the evening, Kelly asked Rove: 'Is this just math you do as a Republican to make yourself feel better, or is this real?'

The contest, in the end, was not very close: Obama's re-election margin, though smaller than his first victory in 2008, was still a healthy five million votes, while his electoral-college margin – 332 to 206 – constituted a modest landslide. That so many pundits considered the race to be a toss-up showed the sway of a rather inexact attitude towards hard numbers. Those gloating Democrats, on the other hand, might have remembered their own levels of confidence from eight years earlier: the failure of the George W. Bush presidency, they had felt, was manifest; a tide of righteous anger was moving against Bush and would install John Kerry in the White House. Eight years later, conservatives experienced similar anguish as their unfounded confidence burst. Mitt Romney was, according to aides, 'shell-shocked' when the election results came in and every swing state except North Carolina fell to President Obama. *Wall Street Journal* columnist Peggy Noonan had seen Romney 'quietly rising' because 'the Republicans have the passion now, the enthusiasm. The Democrats do not. Independents are breaking for Romney.' *Washington Post* columnist George Will predicted a Republican landslide. Special derision was reserved for the *New York Times'* statistician and forecaster Nate Silver, who kept repeating the same simple arithmetic: Obama was consistently ahead in well-polled swing states, giving him 303 electoral votes. But it was impossible, conservatives argued, that African-Americans, Hispanics and the young – all of them obviously disillusioned by Obama's failed presidency – would turn out in numbers comparable to 2008. Yet turn out they did. (Silver's forecast accurately called every state, including, by election eve, Florida, which Obama won by approximately 74,000 votes and a margin of less than one percentage point.)

Political realignment?

Obama's re-election meant that the Democratic candidate had won the popular vote in five of the past six national elections, spanning almost one-quarter of a century. It raised the possibility that the conservative realignment that took hold from Richard Nixon's narrow victory in 1968, through the two terms of Ronald Reagan and the single term of George H.W. Bush, had been superseded by a new, more liberal era in American politics.

Political realignments can only be identified, with any degree of certainty, in historical hindsight. It is clear in retrospect that a centre-left consensus underpinned the Democratic ascendancy from Franklin D. Roosevelt's election in 1932 through the tumultuous end of Lyndon Johnson's presidency in 1968. That 36-year span saw the triumph of an American New Deal version of the communitarian creeds that emerged in Europe amidst the economic and political disasters of the first half of the century: Catholic Christian Democracy and secular Social Democracy on the continent; Labour Party socialism in Britain. In the American circumstance, where the disasters were not so complete, the New Deal welfare state was somewhat weaker, while strong conservative currents included very religious and messianic anti-communists, as well as white supremacists. Many of the latter, however, were New Deal Democrats, a reflection of America's complex political landscape. The old Confederacy, relatively impoverished, was known as the 'Solid South' – solid, that is, for the Democrats and, as such, an important component of the Roosevelt coalition. Three decades later, however, the Democratic Party's (notably President Johnson's) embrace of civil rights left an opening for Richard Nixon and other Republicans to target disaffected Southern whites. Thus civil rights and race were the specifically American factors in the breakdown of the centre-left consensus that was also under pressure elsewhere in the world. (With the end of cheap oil, the neo-Keynesian welfare states in Europe and the United States had run into some common difficulties, including a tendency towards inflation.)

And those specifically American racial factors endure: a glance at the election-night map for the most recent contest shows that Romney's victories were mainly confined to the old Confederate states of the South. (He also won some western prairie and mountain states that look large on the map but contain few voters.)

To be sure, the civil-rights confrontation was not the only trauma of the 1960s and 1970s. Drugs, the counter-culture, a sexual revolution, and anti-Vietnam War protests that included, on the margins, small-scale terrorism, tended to delegitimise the more left-wing party in the eyes of the more inherently 'small-c' conservative voters, who had worked hard and achieved much from the New Deal and post-war economy, and were angry to see it repudiated by long-haired, seemingly privileged students. Moreover, a series of urban crime waves crested through the 1960s, 1970s and 1980s; and perceived liberal leniency towards criminals was another source of middle-class disaffection.

The subsequent Nixon–Reagan realignment drew strength from these particular traumas. It was also, however, part of a broader shift to the right among most Western democracies. The symbolic spearhead of this shift was Margaret Thatcher's British government, with its determined assault on the power of trade unions. Even in France, under the socialist government of François Mitterrand, a dose of neo-liberal austerity was deemed necessary to maintain export competitiveness and the value of the French franc against the German mark. In the United States, for the entire period between 1968 and 1992, Democrats still controlled at least one House of Congress. And Republican control of the White House was interrupted, of course, by the one-term presidency of Jimmy Carter, a consequence of Nixon's self-destruction in the Watergate scandal. There was little question, however, that during this period the centre of American political debate had moved significantly to the right. The 'Reagan Revolution', though manifestly failing its stated goal of reducing the size of government, did have this real intellectual and political impact.

In the late 1960s, Nixon strategist Kevin Phillips wrote a seminal book, *The Emerging Republican Majority*, which in effect predicted the revolution. In 2002, John B. Judis and Ruy Teixeira – a liberal journalist and historian, and a liberal political scientist, respectively – published their own mirror analysis, *The Emerging Democratic Majority*. In the book's introduction, they stated: 'A longer trend … is leading American politics from the conservative Republican majority of the 1980s to a new Democratic majority. Democrats aren't there yet, but barring the unforeseen, they should arrive by the decade's end.'

Like Phillips 33 years earlier, Judis and Teixeira were writing in the face of considerable intuition and street-level evidence to the contrary. George W. Bush's election in 2000 may have been disputed, but 2002 was the year that Republicans took control of the Senate, thereby placing the White House and both Houses of Congress in conservative hands for the first time since the 1930s. Following the terrorist attacks of 11 September

2001, Republicans were well placed to exploit the advantages that they had traditionally enjoyed in voters' minds regarding national security, and Bush indeed took advantage, winning re-election in 2004 on his strengths as a 'war president', even though the main war in question – in Iraq – was going badly. Moreover, there was a case to be made that Bill Clinton's two terms in office had manifested rather than repudiated the thesis of a conservative ascendancy. Clinton used decidedly centrist language – for example, declaring the 'era of big government' to be over. In any event, he had been helped into office in both of his victories (in 1992 and 1996) by the third-party candidacy of Ross Perot, who arguably siphoned more votes from Republicans than Democrats.

And yet – like Phillips in 1969 – the theorists of an emerging Democratic majority in 2002 pointed to what they regarded as inexorable socio-political trends favouring their argument. The black vote was going to remain a certainty for the Democrats. The growing Hispanic population, on which Karl Rove had set his sights, believing in their Catholic affinity with conservatism, was in fact trending the other way. (Even without the problem of harsh anti-immigrant attitudes that animated the Tea Party wing of the Republican Party, polling indicated that Hispanics were disposed to favour an active state with a remit for at least modest redistribution of wealth.) A significant stratum of well-educated whites – a traditional source of moderate Republicanism – were becoming more liberal: this would easily compensate for some Democratic losses among the white working class. Women were voting in greater numbers for Democrats. And it was deemed highly significant that the youth vote was turning more liberal – not because the young would stay young, but because voting habits, once established, tend to stay more or less fixed.

Obama's triumph in 2008 could be interpreted as a singular event: a consequence of voters' deep disaffection with the George W. Bush administration; of the effects of a traumatic financial crisis; and of the excitement of transcending America's long-standing racial divide. His win in 2012, however, may have indicated something more lasting: its ingredients were precisely those that Judis and Teixeira had predicted would lead to a realignment by the end of the last decade. One should be cautious about sweeping predictions: Romney won just under half the votes cast, and there are no permanent realignments in American politics. But Republicans now have a problem based on a pattern. Every four years, the electorate is likely to be even younger and ethnically more diverse than the last time. Demography is not destiny; the Republican Party can and, most likely, will adapt. But it probably will not suffice to simply change the mode of discourse on social issues, including abortion, contraception and gay marriage, and to offer more liberal policies on immigration reform. Over half the voters – including a large majority of Hispanics – have more or less explicitly endorsed a moderately redistributionist welfare state based on progressive taxation. This was a model of state and society that an earlier generation of Republicans – including Dwight Eisenhower, Nelson Rockefeller, Nixon, Romney's father George, and even in certain respects Reagan – embraced or came to terms with.

Against the welfare state

Modern Republicans have repudiated this model, and one thing that must be said about the 2012 election campaign is that it offered voters a sharp and genuine philosophical choice. Romney, having shown moderation as governor of Massachusetts from 2003–07 – the years during which he in fact enacted the state-wide model for 'Obamacare' – might have seemed a weak avatar for this radical right-wing challenge. But he did his best.

One line of attack was to ignore the technical aspects of providing universal health care using market mechanisms and instead criticise the very idea of guaranteed access as inimical to freedom because insidiously 'European'. This association became the Republican standard-bearer's frequent refrain. 'I want you to remember', said Romney in a campaign speech after winning the New Hampshire primary in early 2012, 'when our White House reflected the best of who we are, not the worst of what Europe has become'. Obama's intended dystopia was a 'European-style entitlement society … this president takes his inspiration from the capitals of Europe; we look to the cities and small towns of America.' Romney carried the theme from speech to speech. 'He's taking us down a path towards Europe. He wants us to see a bigger and bigger government, with a health-care system run by the government. He wants to see people paying more and more in taxes.' In another speech, Romney claimed that Obama 'wants to fundamentally transform America', and added, 'I kind of like America. I'm not looking for it to be fundamentally transformed. I don't want it to become like Europe.'

Romney was hardly the only Republican candidate or politician to repeat this refrain, which seemed politically odd since most Americans, according to opinion polls, held favourable and even warm views of European allies. The explanation had to be that Romney and other conservatives believed sincerely in what they saw as a contrast between the American way of economic freedom and Europeans' more communitarian ethos. Conservatives condemned the American version of this ethos as expressed in a popular YouTube clip of a talk that Harvard professor and Massachusetts Senate candidate Elizabeth Warren gave to a group of supporters early in her campaign: 'There is nobody in this country who got rich on his own', Warren had said. 'Nobody. You built a factory out there – good for you. But I want to be clear: you moved your goods to market on the roads the rest of us paid for; you hired workers the rest of us paid to educate; you were safe in your factory because of police forces and fire forces that the rest of us paid for. You didn't have to worry that marauding bands would come and seize everything at your factory ... Now look. You built a factory and it turned into something terrific or a great idea – God bless! Keep a big hunk of it. But part of the underlying social contract is you take a hunk of that and pay forward for the next kid who comes along.'

Republicans latched on to an Obama stump speech in which he argued, echoing Warren, that individuals' economic success rests on a broader community effort. Businesses are possible because of the infrastructure, the education, the regulation and the social safety net that only government can provide. Such an argument only restated the consensus philosophy that had emerged as part of Franklin Roosevelt's New Deal liberalism, but Obama in this particular speech had slightly garbled the message – so he could be represented, tendentiously and out of context, as denying all credit to businessmen and women for their own success. Leaving this misrepresentation aside, conservatives seemed genuinely offended by the (in historical terms, rather mild) communitarian instincts of the president and his party. Unfortunately for Romney, he got caught in a rather crude expression of the underlying belief that real freedom is a matter of economic freedom and economic success. A secretly recorded video, obtained by David Corn of *Mother Jones* magazine, showed Romney in front of wealthy donors expressing disdain for those many Americans – half the country, in his telling – supposedly dependent on government largesse: 'There are 47% of the people who will vote for the president no matter what … who are dependent on government, who believe they are victims, who believe the government has a responsibility to care for them, who believe that they are entitled to health-care, to food, to housing, to you-name-it … my job is not to worry about those people. I'll never convince them they should take personal responsibility and care for their lives.'

August and September had already been unkind to the Romney campaign. Among other problems, the Republicans had a lacklustre nominating convention, while the Democrats staged a boisterously successful one. In the weeks that followed, Romney stumbled through a knee-jerk attack on the White House in the very hours that US diplomats were under attack, and dying, in a US compound in Benghazi, Libya. Then the video surfaced. Portraying almost half of Americans as indolent moochers was unlikely to win him new supporters, and polls suggested that it didn't.

Romney's supporters did take heart from his performance in the first presidential debate, in Denver, Colorado, at the beginning of October. The Republican was sharp, engaged and composed, while President Obama looked like he would have preferred to be somewhere else. The president was back on form, however, in the next two debates, and although margins remained close, Romney never pulled ahead in polling averages. In key swing states such as Ohio, moreover, Obama had built what turned out to be insurmountable leads.

Obama's second term

If the Republicans saw the threat of America's leftward tilt to be dire, they did have at least one formidable defence: the division of powers embedded in the nation's eighteenth-century constitution. Even during his first two years in office, when the Democrats held majorities in both Houses of Congress, Republicans had exploited arcane Senate rules to impose the innovative requirement of a supermajority – 60 out of 100 votes – to pass any legislation. (The filibuster and its associated parliamentary manoeuvres, such as individual senators placing 'holds' on presidential nominees, were not new as such, but had never before been used on such a routine basis.) Thus, it was only in the narrow window of 134 days – between a contested Minnesota recount that put Democrat Al Franken into the Senate, and Republican Scott Brown's swearing-in to replace deceased Massachusetts Senator Edward Kennedy – that Obama enjoyed that bare supermajority needed to pass his landmark healthcare reforms.

After Republicans retook the House of Representatives in the midterm elections of 2010, the exploitation of Senate rules had less importance in blocking Democratic legislation, but remained crucially important in stopping the president from filling executive and judicial vacancies. Thus, for example, the US Court of Appeals for the District of Columbia Circuit, the second-highest judicial authority in the land, maintained its very conservative majority as a result of Senate Republicans' refusal to confirm a single Obama nominee. Obama decided in June 2013 to attack the problem with a salvo of nominations to fill all three vacancies at once – a challenge to Republicans that had not yet played out when this book went to press.

The difficult reality for Obama, often glossed over by domestic and foreign commentators alike, is that not only his legal authority but also his power of persuasion are strictly limited. The president may have received a narrow popular mandate for more liberal policies, and even in the House elections, more votes were cast for Democrats than Republicans. But because of the way voters are distributed and concentrated in Congressional districts, Republicans comfortably kept control. Many Republican Congressmen have little to fear from a Democratic challenger, but everything to fear from a Tea Party challenge from the right. This situation could cause considerable further damage to the Republican Party as a whole, but in many individual cases, seats will be best safeguarded by continuing to refuse to compromise.

This basic dynamic was evident in the early showdown after Obama's re-election, involving the same fiscal matters that had brought the United States to the edge of default on its national debt in the summer of 2011. At that time, Congress and the administration had been unable to reach agreement on long-term debt reduction, but had created a kind of doomsday mechanism of automatic sequestration cutting deeply into both civil and defence spending. The logic was that the automatic cuts would be unpalatable to both sides, thereby forcing them into a deal. On 31 December 2012, the sequestration would coincide with the end-of-year expiration of the George W. Bush-administration tax cuts, resulting in a so-called 'fiscal cliff'. Economists considered that this combination of tax rises and spending cuts was likely to stall the recovery and could return the economy to recession.

To avert the plunge, Obama and House Speaker John Boehner seemed to be coming close to an agreement after Boehner put forward a proposal implicitly conceding that the election result required softening Republican opposition to any increase in marginal tax rates. Boehner's offer included tax increases on incomes of greater than $1m; Obama countered with a proposal that would set the threshold at $400,000 of family income, in a package that included spending cuts and a mechanism for restraining cost-of-living increases for Social Security (the state-provided pension system). It also extended unemployment benefits and provided for new stimulus spending for infrastructure projects. The use of the requirement for Congressional approval of each rise in the federal debt ceiling as a form of hostage-taking, which Republicans had employed to such scary effect in 2011, would be taken off the table for two years.

Obama appeared to be in a slightly stronger position because going over the cliff might not have proved as devastating as some predicted. The counter-stimulus would not have been delivered all at once. Moreover, without a deal, the president would have found himself confronting a policy landscape much more to his liking and much less to that of Republicans. Plenty of revenue would suddenly have been available for the medium term, and he could have expected that the opposition party would be ready to negotiate about restoring some of the tax cuts and some of the sequestered spending. Obama's leverage was presumably increased in such a scenario by the knowledge on both sides that he had campaigned explicitly for higher taxes on the wealthy and polling showed that most voters agreed with him.

But Boehner could not persuade his Republican caucus to accept any compromise. Instead, the Obama administration and Senate leaders, including Republicans, negotiated a compromise bill that passed the Senate at around 2:00am on New Year's Day. To get it through the House, Boehner had to abandon the so-called 'Hastert rule': an informal, two-decade-old principle against introducing a bill without the support of a majority of the Republican majority. Votes from the majority of Democrats and a third of Republicans in the House put it through.

The measure signed by Obama raised taxes for families earning more than $450,000 and individuals earning more than $400,000 a year. Hence the Bush tax cuts of 2001 – arguably the most important medium-term driver of federal budget deficits – became permanent for all but the richest 2% of Americans. There was a one-year extension of unemployment benefits, affecting two million people and costing $30 billion, but Obama lost a key stimulus measure: the 2% cut to payroll taxes enacted in 2010. Employee payroll taxes rose back to 6.2%.

Crucially, Obama's demand that the question of raising the debt ceiling be kept off the table was not part of the package. Soon enough, Boehner, under extreme pressure from within his party, returned to the Republicans' 2011 position: no raising of the debt ceiling unless spending programmes were cut by an equal amount. Obama was equally adamant that Congress was obligated to authorise the servicing of debt that it had already incurred on behalf of the United States, and said he would refuse to let this question enter into any of his negotiations with Republicans. A new crisis was possible in autumn 2013.

Sequestration did go into effect on 1 March 2013, mainly because there was not enough basic trust between the parties to prevent it. But there was another dynamic at play. In the original stop-gap deal, Democrats had succeeded in exempting from the knife Social-Security benefits and mandatory programmes for the poor, including Medicaid and food stamps. What was left was a 7.9% reduction in defence spending for 2013, a 5.3% reduction in discretionary domestic spending and a 2% reduction in Medicare costs. The unexpected dynamic was the Republicans' relative equanimity about the defence cuts. In the new, tea-flavoured House of Representatives, fiscal hawks turned out to be much stronger than traditional Republican defence hawks.

To be clear, the Tea Party version of a fiscal hawk is a distinctive bird. Not concerned so much about the deficit in terms of a balance between spending and revenue, he or she is focused above all on lowering taxes and cutting the size of government. It is an Ayn Randian ethos that is too often confused with the preoccupations of many Beltway and financial insiders, who had spent most of Obama's presidency warning that fiscal deficits and the growing debt were approaching catastrophic dimensions. Yet their preoccupations also seemed to have been misguided, for the stunning reality of Obama's second term was that the US fiscal deficit was melting away – indeed, it was perhaps falling too quickly, given the still anaemic US recovery. After reaching $1.4 trillion in 2009 following the 2008 financial crisis, it had fallen to a projected $845bn in fiscal year 2013. The Congressional Budget Office estimated that the 'cyclically adjusted deficit' – if the economy was near full employment – would be just $423bn, well below the sustainable level at which the US economy grows faster than the federal debt.

This progress on the deficit was not really surprising: its ballooning in Obama's first year had been the consequence of increased costs and decreased revenues in the Great Recession, and even modest economic growth was taking care of much of that problem. A longer-term problem was posed by rising health-care costs for an increasingly elderly population; yet even here there was some promising, albeit tentative, news. According to the Kaiser Family Foundation, a think tank, health spending had grown 3.9% each year from 2009 to 2011, the lowest rate of growth since records began in 1960. The reasons were unclear – the weak economy probably caused some, but not all, of the slowdown. But this was evidence that the cost curve could be made flatter.

American exceptionalism

On the morning of 14 December 2012, 20-year-old Adam Lanza shot his mother dead in their Connecticut home, then carried a Bushmaster rifle, a Glock handgun and a Sig Sauer handgun to nearby Sandy Hook Elementary School, where he went on a killing spree that ended the lives of 20 terrified children and eight adults, including himself. As teachers and staff tried to barricade doors and hide the children in their care, Lanza entered a first-grade classroom where he found and killed the teacher and children hiding in the adjacent bathroom. The only survivor was a six-year-old girl who played dead. In the second classroom, Lanza walked to the back of the room and shot the children hiding under their desks, as well as the teacher who attempted to shield them. One first grader was killed as he shouted for his classmates to run. Six of them made it to safety. Five others survived by hiding in the closet. Lanza managed to kill three more: a special-needs student and two teacher's aides, before finding that all remaining doors had been barricaded. When the police came, he shot himself to death.

Such mass killings were familiar events in the United States: in July of the same year, another disturbed gunman had killed 12 and injured 70 at a midnight showing of *The Dark Knight Rises* at a cinema in Aurora, Colorado; in January 2011, another had critically injured Arizona Congresswoman Gabrielle Giffords and shot 18 others, killing six of them, outside a Safeway in Tucson, Arizona, where she was meeting constituents. In fact, over the four years since January 2009 there had been an average of more than one mass shooting (defined by the FBI as murdering at least four people with a gun) per month in the United States. Indeed, between the December 2012 Sandy Hook shooting and 31 May 2013, the total number of people killed by guns in the United States exceeded the number of US troops killed during the Iraq War, according to figures compiled by the *National Journal.*

The Sandy Hook massacre of children, however, galvanised popular feeling, and Obama rolled out a plan for the most sweeping changes to gun laws in nearly two decades. These included banning the sale of certain semi-automatic rifles and high-capacity ammunition magazines, and requiring background checks for all gun buyers. A scaled-back version was put together by Senators Joe Manchin, Democrat of West Virginia, and Pat Toomey, Republican of Pennsylvania. But their bipartisan and strong gun-state credentials were not enough to overcome the opposition of the National Rifle Association (NRA), which drove five Democrats to join 41 Republicans in blocking consideration of the bill – another example of Republicans using Senate procedure to stop legislation even though it was backed by a majority of Senators.

Non-Americans mystified by this result should probably understand that the NRA derives much of its lobbying power from the way that gun culture infuses the fiercely held identity of so many rural Americans. To block the bill, which would hardly have challenged that identity, the NRA exaggerated its possible consequences and exploited lurid conspiracy manias about federal government – read, Obama socialist – plans to impose totalitarian rule and rob free citizens of their guns. Urban Democrats had seemingly lost the heart for this battle after convincing themselves, rightly or wrongly, that their association with gun control had cost candidate Al Gore his native Tennessee in 2000, and with it the presidency. But after the gun bill's defeat, there were some signs that this could change. 'Mayors Against Illegal Guns', an organisation spearheaded by New York Mayor Michael Bloomberg and largely funded out of his deep pockets, promised to target Democrats who had voted against the measure, no matter what their views on other issues.

Another issue of long-standing divisiveness was deemed, after the election, to be a rare opportunity for compromise. Republican leaders had decided that their perceived hostility to Hispanics had proven a significant electoral liability, at least for presidential elections, and so they decided to support reform legislation that would offer a path to citizenship for the estimated 11 million immigrants who were in the United States illegally. Thus in late June, a significant number of Republican senators joined the Democratic majority to pass legislation that coupled the mechanisms for such normalisation with greatly increased spending on border security, as well as heightened requirements for employers to scrutinise their employees' citizenship.

But at mid-2013, the bill's prospects in the House were murky. Conservatives saw the citizenship mechanisms as rewards for illegal behaviour; their constituents remained hostile to the whole idea; and the main political dynamic was a familiar one – in right-leaning districts, successful challenges to their re-election were more likely to come from the right than the left. Thus, Speaker Boehner faced a dilemma reminiscent of the fiscal fights: he could allow the bill to pass with mainly

Democrats' votes, but at the risk of his speakership if angry conservatives staged a revolt.

Foreign policy

In the face of such limits at home, there is a natural temptation for presidents to build their legacy in foreign affairs, where they have more power. Yet, although Obama has a fairly ambitious foreign-policy agenda, he has always maintained that the prerequisite for avoiding a decline of American global power is to restore the basis of economic strength at home. And he has been clear in his view that such strength requires not only investment in infrastructure and education, but also a reversal – or at least a deceleration – of the 30-year trend of increasing American income inequality. If his view is correct, then the absolute paralysis between the parties regarding the role of government in domestic affairs seems bound to affect America's international position. Republican efforts to stymie the implementation of Obama's health reforms – which constituted a major initiative of income redistribution – looked set to continue for the foreseeable future.

There was, however, one area of overriding foreign-policy importance where the president decided to test the limits of his domestic authority: the challenge of climate change. In a June 2013 speech at Georgetown University, the president announced a package of measures including, most importantly, regulations to limit carbon emissions by power plants. These were simple executive orders, not requiring congressional legislation, because the Supreme Court had previously found that carbon emissions are 'pollutants' that the Environmental Protection Agency can regulate. But the plans will require the administration to formulate and implement some complex regulations over the next few years, with the goal of meeting the US diplomatic commitments to reduce the country's greenhouse-gas emissions by at least 17% between 2005 and 2020. If successful, the United States might regain a modicum of leadership on the issue, for later efforts to craft a truly global regime that can limit the increase in mean temperatures. The sudden plenitude of natural gas extracted by hydraulic fracturing, considerably cleaner than coal, might help America and other countries in the transition to a low-carbon economy. But it seems clear that a sustainable path to this future will not be possible so long as one of the major parties is united with coal-state and other energy interests in rejecting the very idea that climate change is a serious problem requiring a government-led solution.

It is hard to say whether the partisan divisions that have made domestic policymaking so intractable will continue to spill over into foreign policy. There was certainly an effort during the campaign to accuse the president of appeasement, including what looked like the extraordinary intervention by Israeli Prime Minister Benjamin Netanyahu on the side of Romney. (Some Israelis countered that Netanyahu's election-eve agitation for action to halt Iran's nuclear programme was simply a coincidence of timing, because the Iranian threat was reaching what he viewed as the crisis point.) After Obama's victory, his nomination of former Republican Senator Chuck Hagel as defence secretary set the stage for a dispiriting spectacle: allegations of anti-Israeli and even anti-Semitic bias were thrown at him on the basis of his previous criticism of Israeli policies and his aversion to military action against Iran. Hagel won Senate confirmation with only four Republican votes, which indicated that whatever else the president may have achieved by nominating a conservative Republican to his cabinet, it did not include any credit from across the aisle.

Early in his second term, the president travelled to Israel, correcting what was possibly the diplomatic error of not going there in his first term. If there were expectations that Obama might try to punish Netanyahu for the latter's tilt towards Romney and rejection of the administration's démarche for a permanent freeze on Jewish settlements in occupied territories, there was no evidence of it on this trip. Obama did give a moving speech before an assembly of mainly young Israelis, in which he articulated the visceral emotional ties between Americans and Israel, but also asked them to think a little harder about the plight of the Palestinians: 'Put yourself in their shoes – look at the world through their eyes. It is not fair that a Palestinian child cannot grow up in a state of her own, and lives with the presence of a foreign army that controls the movements of her parents every single day. It is not just when settler violence against Palestinians goes unpunished. It is not right to prevent Palestinians from farming their lands; to restrict a student's ability to move around the West Bank; or to displace Palestinian families from their home.'

It looked as though the administration was going to try persuasion rather than pressure. Obama's new secretary of state, John Kerry, was said to be fixated on the issue of an Israel–Palestine peace, and he spent his early months in shuttle diplomacy to re-establish peace talks. Few outside observers gave him much chance of success, and there was some criticism that he was focusing on this problem to the exclusion of other tumultuous changes in the Middle East.

But it was hard to say which policy options he was neglecting. The United States was naturally ambivalent about the coup that toppled President Muhammad Morsi in Egypt, but it was not about to cut off aid to the Egyptian military for heeding the liberal demands of thronged demonstrators. On Syria, Obama himself was deeply reluctant to see the United States dragged into a civil war, but having set a 'red line' at the Assad regime's use of chemical weapons, the administration decided on US weapons deliveries to rebels. The strategic imperative of 'rebalancing' US attention towards the Asia-Pacific was still an Obama doctrinal principle, but commitments to stop Iran from developing nuclear weapons prolonged the danger of another military conflict involving the United States. The election in Iran of moderate cleric Hassan Rouhani as president offered some hope of a diplomatic solution, yet both sides were locked in the logic of antagonism. It was not clear that the Obama administration could offer major concessions, even if it were inclined to do so.

Big data

The notion of a hobbled second-term president became popular when a narrative of scandal hit Obama's remarkably scandal-free administration. The first incidence was born of conservatives' obsession with the killing of Ambassador Christopher Stevens and four others by Islamists at a diplomatic and CIA compound in Benghazi, Libya, on 11 September 2012. This scrutiny was reasonable insofar as diplomats died and there were real questions about security. However, the line of criticism concerned the question of when the administration had started calling the attacks 'terrorism', as opposed to the spontaneous reaction to an anti-

Islamic film produced in the United States. The theory seemed to be that the Obama administration, running for re-election on having killed Osama bin Laden, did not want to admit that there were terrorists any more. This was a bizarre theory, in any event, and might have been considered null when Obama bested Romney in one of their election debates with the simple reminder that he had called it terrorism from the earliest days of the crisis.

The second chapter of the narrative arose from the attempt by Internal Revenue Service (IRS) employees in Ohio to expedite the evaluation of certain organisations' applications for tax-free status by looking for such keywords as 'Tea Party'. The accusation arose that the Obama administration was seeking to punish its political enemies through the tax system – an accusation redolent of the Nixon administration's targeting of its 'enemies'. However, there was no evidence that any elected official or any of their appointees had anything to do with the activities of this IRS field office, which in any event also searched for putative left-wing code words, such as 'progressive'.

Both supposed scandals were swallowed up by the revelations of Edward Snowden, a former employee of the federal contractor Booz Allen Hamilton working for the National Security Agency. Snowden fled to Hong Kong – and later to Moscow airport – and admitted to being the source for a series of *Washington Post* and *Guardian* articles about the US intelligence community's capabilities and practices for mining 'metadata' from phone calls and Internet communications. The collection of this data, though admittedly vast, was apparently conducted in accordance with the law that enabled it. For Americans a major issue was that the legislation and the way it had been interpreted had not been made explicit. But monitoring of other nations' communications was also exposed, and after the WikiLeaks dump of diplomatic cables from two years earlier, this was another diplomatic embarrassment. Allies of the United States presumably knew they were being spied on but were loath to admit it to their citizens. The disclosures added to the impression that, especially since the 9/11 terrorist attacks in 2001, the United States had grown into a Leviathan national-security state. Barack Obama came into office in 2009 promising to end some of that state's excesses. But he never promised to dismantle it, and nor does he have the intention of doing so.

Latin America's New Leadership Challenges

If Latin America had been 'lost' in the 1980s, it found itself during the early years of the twenty-first century. The region has become stronger economically and increasingly independent and self-assured on the political front. In contrast, Washington, which for decades attempted to play a part in the region's domestic affairs, is routinely criticised for its mounting deficits and political polarisation. Events in 2003 especially marked this sea change. That year, under President George W. Bush, the United States invaded Iraq. The ensuing occupation would come at a huge cost to Washington's fiscal health and international standing. In Brazil, meanwhile, Luiz Inácio 'Lula' da Silva of the Workers' Party was inaugurated on 1 January 2003. Despite having virtually no formal education, Lula would preside over the country's most significant period of growth since the 1970s. In contrast to previous eras, the poor's income would rise faster than that of the rich, reducing Brazil's chronic inequality. Lula was the poster child of a new Latin America with inclusive growth, vibrant democracies and increasing clout in global affairs.

In the past decade, the region has been transformed in important ways. Global demand for Latin America's commodities has fuelled fairly robust growth that, coupled with a reinvigorated government commitment to the social agenda, has resulted in all-time lows for poverty and inequality. Furthermore, its middle class has ballooned from 103m in 2003 to 152m in 2009, according to the World Bank. Brazil and Mexico, Latin America's two largest countries, are now considered by many to be middle-class societies. And while the United States' international influence was constrained by its wars in Iraq and Afghanistan, its southern neighbours became increasingly assertive in international organisations such as the International Monetary Fund (IMF) and the World Trade Organisation (WTO) – the latter of which is now headed by Roberto Carvalho de Azevêdo, a Brazilian. The region also witnessed the birth of new organisations, such as the Bolivarian Alliance for the Peoples of Our America (ALBA) in 2004, the Union of South American Nations (Unasur) in 2008, the Community of Latin American and Caribbean States (CELAC) in 2010 and the Pacific Alliance in 2012. In short, Latin

America is now wealthier and more confident in its leadership than at any other time in recent memory.

Yet a decade after Lula assumed office, it seems increasingly difficult for the region to sustain its momentum. The years of easy money from commodity sales, which were boosted by China's breakneck development, may be waning. A slowdown in the country's growth to 7.5% of GDP, high by any other standard, would correspond to an estimated 10% decrease in the region's commodity prices. This could spell trouble not only for the private sector. Countries such as Ecuador, Venezuela, Bolivia and Argentina are exceedingly reliant on natural-resource rents to finance their governments.

In the social realm, the region's policies require meaningful renewal. Pioneered by Mexico and made famous by Brazil, the conditional cash transfer has become a hallmark of Latin America and has been adopted across the region (even New York implemented a pilot). These programmes offer poor families a modest monthly stipend, with the stipulation that their children are vaccinated and attend school. The schemes have been a crucial element of Latin America's success in combating indigence, but they alone are not enough to help individuals escape poverty outright. Around 40% of Latin Americans are now classified as 'vulnerable': neither very poor nor solidly middle class. To serve this stratum, governments must go about the complicated business of improving their countries' education, fiscal, pension and health care systems. A growing middle class is a positive development, but one that raises expectations for elected officials; whether they are up to the task remains an open question.

Latin America is at a crossroads. Continued progress requires tough reforms and sound management to diversify the region's economies and accommodate the heightened demands of its citizens. But while the last ten years have produced some highly capable leaders, governance in Latin America remains decidedly mixed. Democratic norms are routinely threatened or disregarded by elected officials in a number of countries across the Americas. Moreover, the proliferation of regional forums has not been matched by increased cooperation or the strengthening of the inter-American system. Latin America's leaders face crucial decisions that will determine whether the region can continue its recent success. Although few things are certain, they can rest assured that the solutions will not come from Washington.

Mexico: ambitious reforms

Mexico's July 2012 presidential election was the most crucial in Latin America that year, yet produced no clear mandate for the country. The Institutional Revolutionary Party (PRI) secured victory after 12 years in opposition, although Enrique Peña Nieto, its candidate, obtained only 38% of the vote. The left did surprisingly well but remains in flux in the election's aftermath. Andrés Manuel López Obrador of the Party of the Democratic Revolution (PRD), the country's most prominent leftist party, came in second with 32%, but resigned shortly afterward to start his own political project. Perhaps the clearest message was the electorate's dissatisfaction with the status quo. Finishing third, Josefina Vázquez Mota of the conservative National Action Party (PAN) had the difficult task of taking up the mantle of unpopular incumbent Felipe Calderón without the support of her own party, whose leadership threw their weight behind Peña Nieto during the campaign.

Before he took office, many in Mexico had low expectations for Peña Nieto. Not only had nearly two-thirds of the electorate voted for another candidate, but concerns surrounded his party's return to power. For over 70 years, the PRI had monopolised politics in Mexico. Elections, while routine, were neither free nor fair as incumbents effectively hand-picked their successors in a process dubbed the *dedazo* (literally, 'big finger'). The PRI also developed a dubious reputation for working with business monopolies and criminal syndicates. As a candidate, Peña Nieto did little to assuage these worries. During the final weeks of the campaign, reports surfaced that he had paid for favourable media coverage as governor of Mexico State, angering many young, educated Mexicans. His good looks, marriage to a soap-opera actress and close ties to the PRI establishment all solidified his image as the young face of the old guard.

However, the first few months of his presidency were surprisingly productive. Specifically, the legislative gridlock of the previous six years was largely replaced with partisan cooperation and an ambitious reform agenda. As president-elect, Peña Nieto coordinated the Pact for Mexico, a commitment to 95 wide-ranging policy goals signed by all three major parties. This was an impressive feat because it not only came on the heels of a bitter presidential campaign but was also carefully managed and produced no major media leaks. Also before his inauguration, Peña Nieto facilitated the passage of a significant labour reform. The measure seeks to modernise the country's labour force and incorporate the 34% of Mexicans who work outside the formal economy by making it easier to hire and fire workers. Although more remains to be done, analysts heralded the legislation as an important first step in making the country more competitive.

As president, Peña Nieto continued to push for change. In February 2013, the legislature amended Mexico's constitution to pass the most sweeping education reform in 70 years. Under the old system, the country's powerful teachers' union – which has 1.5m members – had total control over the hiring and firing of educators. The reform seeks to weaken unions, institute a more meritocratic system for promotions and hiring, implement a census to ascertain the number of students currently enrolled in the country and increase the number of learning hours. Immediately after the president signed the reform, Elba Esther Gordillo, the union's leader, was arrested on charges of embezzlement. Gordillo's lavish lifestyle and taste for designer clothing is well known, making her one of the country's most reviled establishment figures. Her arrest was well received by the public and sent a clear message not to stand in the president's way.

Another notable reform sought to overhaul the country's telecommunications industry. Monopolies dominate the sector: Televisa controls around 60% of the broadcast market, while Carlos Slim's América Móvil owns about 70% of the country's mobile networks and 80% of landlines. These measures seek to introduce competition and foreign investment, as well as create a new, more effective regulatory agency. The most eagerly awaited reform, however, is a combined energy–fiscal package that will open up Mexico's nationalised resource endowments and decrease the state's reliance on oil revenues. The government signalled that this legislation would be introduced in the second half of 2013; if passed, it would be a huge accomplishment.

Peña Nieto proved a capable negotiator with the PAN and the PRD, which, to their credit, have been more cooperative in opposition than the PRI. The president was also willing to take on vested interests and long-time PRI allies, such as conglomerates and unions. These trends indicate that the party has become more democratic – on the national level, at least – and are an encouraging sign for Mexico. Nevertheless, three looming long-term challenges may significantly complicate Peña Nieto's remaining years in office.

Firstly, while the president and his party are adept at turning legislation into law, implementation is a separate battle. This is especially true in Mexico, whose markedly federalist system ensures that states wield considerable influence. Fortunately for Peña Nieto, roughly two-thirds of Mexico's governorships are controlled by the PRI. It is critical that federal and state regulators are not unduly influenced by those they seek to control.

Secondly, while an impressive political feat, the Pact for Mexico has shown signs of fragility. Accusations that public resources were being used to influence state elections led to the temporary suspension of the agreement in April 2013. The episode is indicative of the complicated position in which the opposition now finds itself. Although all parties have heeded Mexicans' call for change, the PAN and the PRD are wary of letting Peña Nieto call all the shots and ceding their party banners to the PRI. To portray themselves as viable alternatives in the near future, opposition parties may find it more beneficial to obstruct the president rather than follow him.

Finally, the administration's Achilles' heel remains Mexico's tenuous security situation. In light of the unpopularity of Calderón's 'war on drugs', Peña Nieto has promised lower levels of violence, despite having proposed few concrete changes to his predecessor's approach. Since assuming office, the most appreciable shift has been rhetorical. Peña Nieto prefers to avoid the subject of drugs-related violence, and most of his solutions hinge on prevention programmes, anti-poverty initiatives and job creation. These are all worthy causes, but are inherently long-term solutions. The president has also promised a new, 40,000-strong gendarmerie, but this too will take time, and it is unclear how it will be financed or what its exact duties will be.

It is likely that much of Peña Nieto's strategy will be a continuation of Calderón's, which is well established within the country's large security apparatus. The new president has made certain modifications, such as consolidating security policy under the interior ministry, but any large-scale changes will be difficult. Early indicators suggest the new administration may adopt a strategy of 'harm reduction', which seeks to mitigate the damage caused by narcotics themselves and reduce prohibition's negative effects on society. For example, analysts point to a recent decrease in prosecutions of petty drug traffickers, which under Calderón swelled the prison population. It is much too soon, however, to draw any definitive conclusions regarding the administration's security policy. Violence, although down from its peak in 2011, is still unacceptably high. The infighting between criminal groups that accounts for much of the bloodshed continues. Even tourist 'havens', such as Acapulco and Cancún, have succumbed to territorial disputes between the cartels. If the death toll stays high, Peña Nieto will struggle to retain his focus on an ambitious economic agenda.

The United States, for its part, has followed Mexico's lead in adjusting the framework of security cooperation. The centralisation of Mexico's security policy has required adjustments in its coordination with Washington, which previously maintained independent relations with several Mexican agencies at once. And while security will continue to be an important element of the bilateral agenda, the United States has shown a willingness to shift the tone of the relationship away from the issue. Moreover, two reforms that were sticking points during the negotiations over the North American Free Trade Agreement in the 1990s – immigration in the United States and energy in Mexico – made great progress in the first half of 2013. Should this legislation pass, there is tremendous potential for deepening the relationship outside the security agenda.

Central America's 'northern triangle': mitigating violence

Comprising El Salvador, Honduras and Guatemala, Latin America's 'northern triangle' is its most troubled territory by far. Flanked by the world's leading consumer of drugs and its largest producers of cocaine, Central America is a principal corridor for the trafficking of people, arms and illegal narcotics. Weak institutional capacity has allowed criminal gangs to thrive as contracted transportistas (carriers) of illicit goods. Smugglers have long used the isthmus' coastline but, since 2006,

Mexico's military offensive against drug traffickers has fuelled competition between armed groups for more Central American territory. This, coupled with the violent legacy of civil wars and rampant impunity, has led to the world's highest homicide rates. Guatemala and El Salvador both demonstrate the difficulty of restoring state capacity, while the situation in Honduras continues to deteriorate.

For many, Otto Pérez Molina's 2011 election as the president of Guatemala, Central America's largest country, was a worrying development. A general in the country's brutal civil war, Pérez Molina alarmed human-rights advocates with his tough-on-crime rhetoric as a candidate. Iron-fisted (or *mano dura*) responses to crime are common in Central America, but have proven to be counterproductive in improving citizen security. Observers braced themselves for more violence as the president expanded the military's role to combat drug trafficking. The early warnings may have proven true. After a steady decline from 2009 to 2012, the first half of 2013 saw a marked increase in homicides. Since so few cases are investigated, it is difficult to determine the precise cause or extent of the change; some attribute it to abuses by the military, while others point to spillover from Honduras and El Salvador.

Pérez Molina has been a reformer in some respects. He boldly called for the legalisation of narcotics ahead of the 2012 Summit of the Americas, putting the issue on the regional agenda and prompting other heads of state to openly question US drug policy. He also increased funding of the attorney general's office, which has made impressive strides in the struggle against impunity. A massacre of six protesters in October 2012 led to the arrest of several soldiers which, alongside several cases against military officers for crimes committed during the civil war, is a sign that the armed forces are no longer getting a free pass. Tax increases have bolstered the government's notoriously underfunded operations, and the president has expanded the social agenda to target poverty.

Yet the challenges are daunting. Large swathes of territory remain out of the government's control and drug smuggling continues to imperil communities. The trial of former dictator Efraín Ríos Montt exemplified the difficulties of ushering in a new era in Guatemala. Initiated in January 2012, the proceedings were the first against a Latin American head of state on charges of crimes against humanity and genocide. Testimony was given both in Spanish and Ixil, the language of the indigenous community the army systematically targeted during the 1980s. But there have been major hurdles. In April 2013, a dozen members of the Guatemalan establishment, some with strong human-rights backgrounds, published an advertisement lambasting the charges as a betrayal of the peace. In May, the Constitutional Court annulled Ríos Montt's conviction on the grounds that he had been temporarily left without a defence counsel, setting the trial back by months. Securing justice after decades of violence is an ongoing challenge that threatens the country's elite – even Pérez Molina is rumoured to have participated in the genocide – and will be exceedingly difficult.

With the world's second-highest homicide rate in 2011 (71 per 100,000 people), El Salvador has suffered from breathtaking levels of violence due to a long-standing conflict between the country's two largest gangs: Mara Salvatrucha and M-18. But in March 2012, authorities helped broker a truce that, more than a year later, has seen murders decrease by over-40%. Significant doubts about the sustainability of the process remain, but this dramatic fall in killings has been a welcome respite. The federal government downplays its involvement in the ceasefire, but has begun to take a more proactive role maintaining the truce. Although prevention programmes have traditionally been underfunded, the administration of President Mauricio Funes has promised $72m for 18 'peace zones': municipalities intended to reintegrate at-risk youth through employment and education programmes. It is too early to tell what the lasting effects of this initiative will be. The first zone, a district of San Salvador named Ilopango, had a rough start as several murders took place in February 2013, but efforts continue. Complementing the government's efforts, convict employment initiatives by private companies have also received increased attention of late.

Programmes targeting poor young people, run by both the government and the private sector, are critical to ending criminality in El Salvador. Although still a factor, trafficking plays less of a role in the country than it does in nearby states. Instead, the bulk of the violence is carried out by street gangs known as *maras*, which are more involved in extortion and territorial disputes at the local level than transnationally. These groups are composed of young people with few employment prospects, many of whom have been deported from the United States. The recent push to provide opportunities for young Salvadoreans is heartening and fundamental to realising long-term reductions in violence. Upcoming presidential elections in 2014, however, may cut this undertaking short. Gangs have little public sympathy, and candidates are likely to adopt a hard line against them to win popular support.

El Salvador experienced an institutional crisis in the summer of 2012, when the constitutional chamber of the Supreme Court voided several of congress' judicial appointments on a technicality. The five-member chamber has not held back from taking on the political establishment since four new officials were appointed in 2009. This independence has stoked animosity in congress, which cried foul when the chamber declared its appointments unconstitutional. The dispute led to the simultaneous operation of two Supreme Courts for over a month, and many feared a prolonged and destabilising impasse. Fortunately, the resolution of the crisis was anti-climactic, as Funes mediated dozens of meetings with party leaders, who agreed to appoint judges in accordance with the court's mandate. The episode was seen as a victory for democracy and the separation of powers.

In contrast, there have been few such encouraging signs in Honduras. When the country's constitutional chamber declared a police-reform bill unconstitutional in December 2012, congress promptly removed four justices from office. Unlike their counterparts in El Salvador, the Honduran political class was not able to negotiate a solution in favour of democracy. This bodes ill as the country prepares for an unpredictable presidential election in November 2013. As of mid-year, the race was a three-way tie between Juan Orlando Hernández, the conservative president of congress; Xiomara Castro de Zelaya, whose husband, Manuel Zelaya, was deposed from the presidency in a 2009 coup; and Salvador Nasralla, a TV personality and anti-corruption advocate. As Zelaya had done while in office, President Porfirio Lobo Sosa proposed a popular vote on constitutional and legislative questions that would operate in tandem with the presidential election. Worryingly, such referenda could muddle the results and serve as a basis for the election's losers to contest the outcome. With no clear front-runner and weak democratic institutions, Honduras is prone to further instability.

Are Gang Truces Good Policy?

If cutting homicide rates by over 40% overnight seems too good to be true, it probably is. Of course, the dramatic fall in violent deaths since the announcement of a truce between El Salvador's two largest gangs is a positive development, but it has left much of the public worried about what comes next. According to an April 2013 poll by Consulta Mitofsky–TCS, over 60% of Salvadoreans do not think the pact is working. These doubts are important to the debate over the merits of government mediation between criminal groups.

Victimisation in El Salvador continues much as it always has: gangs still extort communities and some non-lethal violent crimes, such as rape, have reportedly increased. Some also contend that disappearances have risen, suggesting that killers may simply have become more discreet. The peace zones announced by the leaders of the pact may succeed, but it is far too early to gauge the feasibility of the initiative.

The durability of these agreements is also in doubt. The Salvadorean truce surprised many by lasting for over a year, but similar accords in Los Angeles, Medellín and Belize demonstrated that violence can quickly rise to previous levels once an agreement falls apart. In Trinidad and Tobago, gangs exploited a Church-brokered ceasefire to regroup and rearm, which led to even worse long-term violence. To its credit, the Salvadorean government has taken advantage of this moment to increase spending on reintegration programmes and solidify these gains.

El Salvador's criminal landscape is distinct in that it is dominated by two large gangs, whose leaders have remarkable control over their members and which are less involved in the drug trade than the Mexican cartels or the Central American transportistas. The pact is therefore difficult to replicate elsewhere. A similar truce was recently announced in Guadalajara, for instance, but reportedly many gang members were unaware of it. Various criminal groups operate in the city, as is the case in many areas in the region, rendering any agreement nearly impossible to negotiate or enforce.

Gang truces also raise serious questions about rule of law. The Funes administration, for example, has been evasive about its role in negotiating with gangs. Despite clear government involvement in the transfer of incarcerated gang leaders to lower security facilities, officials continue to deny having negotiated with criminals. Without knowing what the gangs were promised, it becomes impossible to accurately assess the value of the policy. Furthermore, NGOs have complained of being sidelined during the negotiation and implementation of the pact, while the majority of Salvadoreans disapprove of the truce. Such important processes suffer from this lack of transparency.

The pact may also boost organised crime. Salvadorean street gangs had not previously sought to become political actors but the government concessions they received as part of the deal could set a dangerous precedent. Gaining privileges in exchange for not committing murder is little more than extortion and, perversely, grants the greatest bargaining power to the most violent groups. Policymakers outside El Salvador may have shown interest in the country's pact, but in creating similar initiatives they must establish strict, transparent parameters that ensure short-term reductions in homicides do not come at the expense of the long-term rule of law.

This political drama is unfolding against a backdrop of extreme violence. 2012 was another record year for homicides: the country was estimated to have had 85–92 murders per 100,000 inhabitants. Much of this violence occurs in contested smuggling territories, in addition to contract killings targeting journalists, human-rights advocates, lawyers and political opponents. Although a strike in April 2013 drew attention to abysmal police salaries, efforts to reform law enforcement institutions have been hamstrung by a dysfunctional political system and the difficulty of restoring faith in an institution with known criminal links. Efforts are being made to ramp up cooperation with the United States in this regard, but have been complicated by corruption and botched joint operations. In the face of such a severe crisis in governance, even small successes have been hard to find in Honduras.

Colombia: finding a role for the FARC

On 4 September 2012, Colombian President Juan Manuel Santos announced that his government would begin formal peace negotiations with the Revolutionary Armed Forces of Colombia (FARC) in Oslo and Havana, sparking hope that Latin America's longest internal armed conflict was finally coming to an end. Since the struggle began, violence in the Colombian countryside has displaced millions of people and claimed hundreds of thousands of lives. Negotiating a peace would be a monumental step towards addressing Colombia's many social ills.

Disarming the nation's largest insurgency is an irresistible legacy for a Colombian head of state and, sensing an opportune moment for peace, Santos began laying the groundwork for negotiations as soon as he took office in 2010. In foreign policy, he quickly patched relations with Venezuelan President Hugo Chávez, who went on to play an important role in bringing FARC to the table. For two years, the Santos administration secretly engaged the insurgency in preliminary negotiations while pushing through an ambitious legislative agenda at home.

Santos has also worked closely with congress to set the stage for a peace process, beginning with the Law of Public Order in February 2011. Dubbed the 'spinal cord' of the dialogues, the measure suspends arrest warrants for representatives of the insurgency and authorises negotiations to take place outside the country. In June 2011, historic legislation was adopted to provide restitution to the victims of armed conflict. Returning lands and supporting those displaced or harmed by violence will facilitate the reintegration process in a post-conflict environment. Also importantly, in June 2012 legislators approved a constitutional framework for bringing justice to demobilised guerrillas. Once the planned laws are in effect, the reform will institute alternative sentencing procedures for FARC combatants, should an agreement in Havana materialise.

Santos' effort marks the fourth instance in which the Colombian government has been seated opposite FARC at the negotiating table, the last round having taken place under the 1998–2002 presidency of Andrés Pastrana Arango. Despite this legacy of frustrated attempts, many are at least moderately optimistic. Colombia has changed in important ways over the last decade, and the architects of the process have made an effort to avoid the mistakes of the past. Overall, the situation has never seemed more favourable for a successful outcome.

The most important development is the weakening of FARC. During the last peace process, the insurgency had 18,000 members and half of the country lacked a state-security presence. Largely on the defensive, the government was unable to push for an agreement and the talks ultimately failed. A turnaround, however, was ushered in by Pastrana's successor, Álvaro Uribe, who served as president from 2002–10. Bolstered by $7bn of US assistance, an aggressive military response vastly diminished the rebels' capabilities. Between 2002 and 2009, FARC forces were reduced to roughly 9,000 fighters, while many of its leaders were captured or killed. In contrast to 11 years ago, FARC knows it cannot win this fight through strength of arms, even if its leaders claim otherwise in public. This new awareness may increase the chances of an agreement more than any other factor.

Improvements have also been made to the peace negotiations themselves. Whereas the agenda of the Pastrana talks consisted of ten articles covering over 100 issues, this time the two sides have agreed to discuss only six items: rural development, FARC's political participation, ending the conflict, drug trafficking, victims' rights and the implementation of the agreement. Holding the talks abroad is intended to reduce leaks and 'lower the temperature' in Colombia, with Venezuela and Chile accompanying the process and Cuba and Norway acting as guarantors. During the last round of talks, the government ceded a zone the size of Switzerland, which the FARC used to hide victims of kidnap and regroup its forces. With no demilitarised areas or ceasefires offered by the Santos administration, this time there is greater pressure on the guerrillas to reach an accord in a timely manner.

The FARC's lack of popularity is the biggest hurdle to an agreement. The insurgents view themselves as legitimate actors fighting against a repressive government, and are therefore working to obtain an agreement that grants them the right to participate in the political process and immunity from prosecution for the scores of massacres, displacements and kidnappings for which they are responsible. It is safe to say that any agreement signed in Havana will include some degree of amnesty and a path for FARC to enter politics. Colombians, however, starkly disapprove of such concessions. In April 2013, a poll from Colombia Opina found that 67% of citizens oppose political participation for the rebels and 69% believe they must serve jail time. Paradoxically, while 63% of Colombians support peace negotiations over a military solution, the majority of them are unwilling to grant the concessions necessary for the FARC to lay down arms. This contradiction in public opinion puts the president in a tough position. Any agreement will need to be ratified, potentially by popular referendum, but allowing FARC members to become senators instead of prisoners may be too bitter a pill for Colombians to swallow. Legislation will also need to be passed for any agreement to take effect, including the specific judicial procedures through which the rebels will be processed. These measures would be among the most unpopular elements of a peace accord, and are sure to meet resistance in congress.

Santos has set November 2013 as the deadline for an agreement. Colombians, however, will vote in congressional and presidential elections in March and May of 2014. If negotiations continue right up to the deadline, congress could find itself passing a highly contentious piece of legislation while in full re-election mode. Uribe, meanwhile, has become the most vocal critic of the current president and the peace process, censuring Santos for going soft on security and for negotiating with terrorists. His criticisms have gained traction. According to Colombia

Opina, as of April 2013 only 31% of Colombians support Santos's re-election, and security is viewed as the most important issue the country faces after unemployment. The president has largely staked his political future on the peace process, which has limited his ability to respond to certain developments. In May 2013, for instance, Venezuelan President Nicolás Maduro accused the Colombian government of conspiring to poison him and threatened to withdraw support for the peace talks. The tough statement was in response to Santos receiving the leader of the Venezuelan opposition, Henrique Capriles. But the Colombian president quickly moved to repair relations with Maduro, chalking the outlandish accusations up to a simple 'misunderstanding'.

However, the real work will begin after an agreement has been reached and approved. Bringing rebel territories back into the government's fold after decades of independent operation will be no small feat. It will require substantial resources and time, and is an inherently destabilising and potentially violent process. As FARC's security structures are dismantled, splinter groups will compete for control. This is particularly true along drug routes, where illicit revenues are highest and state forces are weakest. To avoid creating power vacuums, some assert that FARC must play a role in the process. Police and military forces, for example, could absorb guerrilla fighters and make use of their local knowledge and community ties. However, many Colombians resist the notion of FARC fighters becoming soldiers and police officers. Whatever strategy is chosen, demobilisation alone will not eliminate the countryside's illegal economies, and widespread drug trafficking and other crime will continue for the foreseeable future.

At the same time, an astonishingly high proportion of landowners do not have titles to their property, denying them a means of acquiring credit and increasing their holdings' vulnerability to appropriation by armed groups. The government is trying to rectify this but much remains to be done. Improved infrastructure and land production will also be important in helping to address Colombia's chronic inequality, as well as producing viable alternatives to crime. Providing jobs to ex-combatants, essential for reducing recidivism, remains difficult due to the stigma they face from employers. It is encouraging, therefore, that the peace process has sought to consult the private sector. Another pressing challenge is the assurance that displaced victims can safely return home. Santos's restitution law has been in effect since January 2012, yet safety guarantees have already become a major impediment. Ensuring that those illegally occupying land do not threaten legitimate owners initiating restitution claims will be an important test for the government.

A peace agreement is not a panacea for Colombia. Should an accord materialise, current and subsequent administrations will face the difficult tasks of developing rural areas, reintegrating combatants into society, enhancing citizen security and providing restitution to victims. These are immense undertakings that require resources and political will but, with any luck, will help rectify one of the most acute cases of inequity and insecurity in Latin America.

This process comes as Colombia seeks to position itself as a more influential player in the developing world. Although regional relations were strained under Uribe, the Santos administration has re-engaged with wider Latin America and improved ties with countries such as Ecuador and Venezuela. Notably, the April 2012 Summit of the Americas was held in Cartagena. The summit's main result was the commissioning of a study on illegal narcotics by the Organization of American States (OAS), which was presented to Santos a year later in Bogota. As a member of the Pacific Alliance and an aspiring participant in the Trans-Pacific Partnership (TPP), Colombia has also aligned itself with Latin America's free-market bloc, endearing it to international investors. Nevertheless, the success of the country's foreign-policy initiatives is closely tied to progress on its pressing domestic challenges.

Venezuela: Chávez's legacy

Love him or hate him, for 14 years Hugo Chávez was a rare example of continuity in a rapidly changing region. His popularity among Venezuela's poor, unchecked control of government resources and political deftness made him unbeatable at the ballot box. He was elected to four terms and survived both a recall referendum and an attempted coup. But while Chávez may have been larger than life, he was still mortal. He succumbed to a two-year battle with cancer on 5 March 2013, plunging Venezuela into uncertainty.

Prior to Chávez's death, the country's most significant recent political development occurred during the October 2012 presidential election when the opposition unified behind a single charismatic leader: the governor of Miranda state, Henrique Capriles Radonski. Composed of many different regional and ideological factions, the anti-Chávez coalition had long struggled to present a coherent electoral challenge to the late president. That changed with a presidential primary in February 2012 that nominated the energetic 39-year-old Capriles. The opposition largely coalesced behind the governor, who proved a fierce campaigner and a quick learner. He visited over 300 towns during the campaign and, in a break from the confrontational tactics that Chávez's opponents often used, adopted a conciliatory and high-minded tone.

The opponents were not, however, on even ground. Exploiting laws he pushed through congress, Chávez enjoyed extensive control over the broadcast media, the principal conduit for communicating with poor Venezuelans. The *cadenas* (official broadcasts all television stations are required to air) were frequently used to bolster Chavez's campaign. The government also created a fiscal deficit of 8.5% of GDP after a run of public spending intended to shore up political support. But critics too quick to credit Chávez's election victory to these factors alone risk overlooking an important fact: a large segment of Venezuela has a deep emotional attachment to the late president.

Chávez ultimately beat Capriles by a 10% margin, but the election was hardly a washout for the opposition. In 2000 and 2006, the late president won re-election by 22% and 26% respectively. In just a few months, Capriles reduced that advantage by more than half. Also significantly, over 80% of Venezuelans voted in the 2012 contest, suggesting that the vast majority of the population considers elections to be the primary source of political legitimacy.

Just weeks after Capriles accepted defeat, Chávez made a shocking announcement. In a televised address on 9 December 2012, the late president admitted that his cancer had returned – he had pronounced himself 'cured' just a few months earlier – and that he would return to Cuba for his fourth surgery. In an unprecedented move, Chávez named a successor: the vice-president and former foreign minister, Nicolás Maduro. For two months, Chávez was neither seen nor heard from. Official announcements about his health were characteristically vague, but it was clear that the president's condition was critical. Speculation was rampant that he had actually passed away or was comatose, fuelling political uncertainty. Chávez finally returned to Venezuela on 18 February 2013, and passed away a few weeks later.

While Chávez was in Cuba, Maduro acted as interim president and went about preparing the governing coalition for a change in leadership. His relationship with President of the National Assembly Diosdado Cabello has been a gauge of unity within the chavista camp. Cabello is a former military officer and maintains much stronger ties with the armed forces than Maduro, who represents the more ideological, civilian base of Chávez's support. Despite rumours of a simmering rivalry, the two men presented a unified front following the president's surgery. Maduro, as Chávez had declared, was to lead the 'Bolivarian Revolution'.

The Venezuelan constitution stipulates that should a president step down, elections must be held within a month. Upon the announcement of 14 April 2013 as the date for the vote, both sides immediately embarked on blitz campaigns. Capriles was again the opposition's candidate. This time, however, he pulled no punches and lambasted his opponent for having no clear solutions to the country's acute problems. Maduro proved an inept campaigner and his tactics often verged on the bizarre. Proclaiming himself the 'son of Chávez', Maduro's attempts to channel his predecessor's speech and style amounted to little more than cheap imitation. Rather than present policy ideas, Maduro's rallies were homages to the late president and opportunities to personally attack Capriles. Maduro asserted that Chávez had come to him in the form of a bird, and proceeded to imitate birdcalls, even appearing on stage with a plastic bird on his hat.

Capriles' adept campaigning again paid electoral dividends. Although early polls had Maduro ahead by at least ten points, the final margin was razor-thin: Maduro won with just over 51% of the vote. Instead of ceding defeat, Capriles immediately called for a recount. The government's response was muddled, but it ultimately acquiesced to an audit of the vote. Unsurprisingly, the pro-Chávez electoral council upheld the results in June 2013, ignoring the opposition's calls for a more serious and thorough recount.

The new president now faces a truly daunting set of challenges. His poor showing at the polls further imperilled the prospects for maintaining unity within the governing coalition. As a military officer, pro-Cuba socialist and skilled communicator, Chávez was uniquely capable of incorporating the armed forces into his Bolivarian Revolution and connecting with the poor. Maduro lacks both Chávez's dynamism and his military credentials. Furthermore, while chavista governors, mayors and bureaucrats depended on Chávez's favour for advancement, they owe Maduro next to nothing. In short, the president is governing from a position of weakness and appears to be floundering under the pressure. This makes him unpredictable and more likely to repress his political enemies using force.

Venezuela faces a list of challenges that would overwhelm even the most capable politician. The administration was forced to depreciate its controlled currency by nearly one-third in early 2013, yet the official exchange rate still remains grossly overvalued. Further adjustments are necessary, which will reduce the purchasing power of Venezuelans still further, while the country suffers from acute shortages of basic goods. Inflation, which hits the poor the hardest, exceeded 27% at the end of 2012, the highest such figure in Latin America.

The security situation also deteriorated significantly under Chávez. The homicide rate in Caracas exceeds 100 per 100,000 inhabitants. To put that in context, the World Health Organisation considers ten murders per 100,000 to be an 'epidemic of violence'. In contrast to Mexico and Colombia, Venezuela's violence does not stem from organised crime or an insurgency. Instead, policing and governance in the country's urban areas are so poor that a general state of chaos has become the norm.

It is difficult to predict how this combination of factors will play out. Maduro faces three challenges that he will need to overcome to retain control. Perhaps the most critical test is ensuring unity within his party's ranks. Prior to the election, the regime's vested interests believed that Maduro was their best bet for staying in power. Though no one could match Chávez's political skills, Maduro, as former president of the National Assembly, foreign minister and someone close to the Cuban regime, would be in the strongest position to hold things together within the riven Chávez coalition. If his standing deteriorates, however, the president could be ousted by figures within his government. For the military and many establishment chavistas, retaining influence is much more important than continuing the late president's revolution. A less ideological leader who better guarantees continuity and stability, be it Cabello or another figure, may become a more attractive alternative. Secondly, Maduro does not have Chávez's popular mandate, nor can he count on public sympathy. Should the economic and security situation become even more dire, Venezuelans may take to the streets as they have in the past. Popular protests would further delegitimise an administration that ostensibly represents the country's lower classes. Maduro's final challenge comes from the opposition. Since the election, Capriles has opted for a patient, cool-headed approach. He discouraged demonstrations from his supporters over concerns about violence and has instead pressured the government through institutional means. He has thereby sought to position himself as the democratic counterweight to the chavista regime. Like Maduro, however, Capriles leads a very diverse set of interests. The opposition has splintered in the past, so its success will depend on it maintaining unity, lest the anti-Chávez movement lose its momentum.

This is a crucial moment for Venezuela. Even in the most optimistic scenario, it will take a long time to overcome the governance crisis and begin to heal the country's deep divisions. Venezuelans can only hope that this disunity will not stand in the way of much-needed reforms.

Ecuador: weakening democracy

By the end of his current term in 2017, Ecuadorean President Rafael Correa will have been in office for ten years, the longest tenure in the country's history. This is a remarkable feat, considering that none of the five presidents who preceded him completed a single four-year term. He secured re-election by a wide margin in February 2013 and expanded his control of congress. Ecuador's erstwhile instability has given way to a virtual one-man rule.

To be sure, Correa's power stems in large part from his high popularity among Ecuadoreans. In a country that suffers from crippling poverty, the president has tripled social expenditure and heavily invested in roads, hospitals and schools. Correa has expanded the Bono de Desarrollo Humano (Human Development Bond): a cash-transfer scheme for poor households that reaches nearly 45% of the population, the highest proportion in Latin America. This increase in spending has been financed by taxing oil exports, which constitute over 30% of government revenue. Both record oil prices and the country's large reserves have allowed Correa to pursue his 'Citizens' Revolution' at breakneck speed. Poverty fell by nearly 5% in 2012 alone.

However, there is a darker side to the president's dominance. There are now virtually no checks on presidential authority from within the government. A 2011 referendum allowed Correa to overhaul the judiciary and subject it to executive oversight, and he has manipulated the allocation of congressional seats to his advantage. Although Correa's coalition received less than 55% of the votes for congress in February 2013, it holds over 65% of the national assembly.

Perhaps most troubling is the deterioration of freedom of expression since Correa took office. Fundamedios, a watchdog organisation, documented 172 cases of legal, verbal or physical harassment of journalists in 2012, the highest number since the group started reporting in 2008. The government plays a key role in creating an atmosphere of censorship and has, through the legal system, silenced Correa's critics on many occasions. A 2012 law also prohibits the media from communicating any beneficial or harmful messages about candidates during the run-up to elections, leading commentators to conclude that Ecuador has effectively become a propaganda state.

Correa benefits immensely from facing a fractured opposition. No fewer than seven candidates split the opposition vote in the 2013 general election. Furthermore, Guillermo Lasso, the conservative banker who came in second, spent much of the campaign railing against Correa's popular fiscal policies rather than focusing on the president's weaknesses, such as security and crime. Until the opposition can find a message that resonates with most Ecuadoreans and cease its infighting, Correa has little reason to worry.

Following Chávez's death, there has been speculation over whether Correa will step in and take the Venezuelan leader's place on the regional stage. Correa undoubtedly has a penchant for scorning Western powers, particularly the United States. This defiance was prominently displayed when he granted asylum to Julian Assange, the WikiLeaks founder who has been hiding in the Ecuadorean Embassy in London since August 2012. Assange is wanted in Sweden over allegations of rape, but Correa argues that if he were turned over, he would be extradited to the United States and potentially sentenced to death for releasing sensitive US Department of State cables in 2010. The international press noted the irony of Assange – the world's most prominent information activist – joining forces with a president with such a low tolerance for dissent. Nevertheless, Correa used the episode to rally nationalist support at home against colonial powers.

Rhetoric aside, it seems unlikely that Correa will truly fulfil Chávez's legacy. Ecuador's president is pragmatic, but lacks the desire and capacity to lead a coalition of like-minded governments to counter US influence, as was Chávez's goal. He sought to organise a general boycott of the 2012 Summit of the Americas out of solidarity with Cuba – excluded due to a democratic clause in the conference's charter – but was joined only by Nicaragua. Backed by several other countries, Ecuador has also attempted to curtail the influence of the OAS Inter-American Commission on Human Rights and its special rapporteur for the freedom of expression. The commission was reformed in March 2013, but the majority of OAS members backed away from Ecuador's radical proposals to weaken the body.

Although tensions between Ecuador and Colombia may have eased since 2008, when Uribe authorised a strike on a FARC camp in Ecuadorean territory, the northern border continues to present major challenges to Correa. The armed conflict in Colombia has driven over 50,000 refugees into Ecuador since 2000, the largest such population in Latin America. FARC guerrillas continue to have an active military presence in Ecuadorean territory, but are now just one of many groups transporting cocaine through the country. This is a serious concern for Ecuadoreans, who view the influence of Mexican and Colombian 'narcos' as a pressing threat. Perversely, a peace deal between FARC and the Santos administration may destabilise the regional criminal world and push crime into Venezuela and Ecuador. This case demonstrates the urgent need for interstate cooperation in combatting drug trafficking.

Latin America's Energy Future

Latin America has one of the world's cleanest energy portfolios. This is due to a large hydroelectric sector and the relatively low consumption of fossil-fuels, especially coal. However, there are signs that the region may be moving towards a dirtier energy mix. Although only one-quarter of Latin America's hydroelectric potential is used, environmental and human-rights groups have impeded the construction of large dams. A burgeoning middle class has made the region the fastest growing market for automobiles, increasing demand for fossil fuels. With the development of non-conventional renewable energy sources incipient, for the time being any gaps in energy supply are likely to be filled by more carbon-intensive alternatives.

Although Latin America is unusually energy-rich, Central America and the Caribbean suffer from a scarcity of reserves. Petrocaribe, a scheme initiated under Chávez that allows Caribbean countries to buy heavily subsidised Venezuelan petroleum, has helped relieve that burden. Significantly, Venezuela exported over 100,000 barrels per day to Petrocaribe members in 2012. Yet the future of the project is in doubt. Venezuela's declining production, the country's severe financial challenges and the massive debt owed to Petrocaribe by its members make it unlikely that the initiative will continue in its current form. This bodes ill for a sub-region that already suffers from acute economic problems.

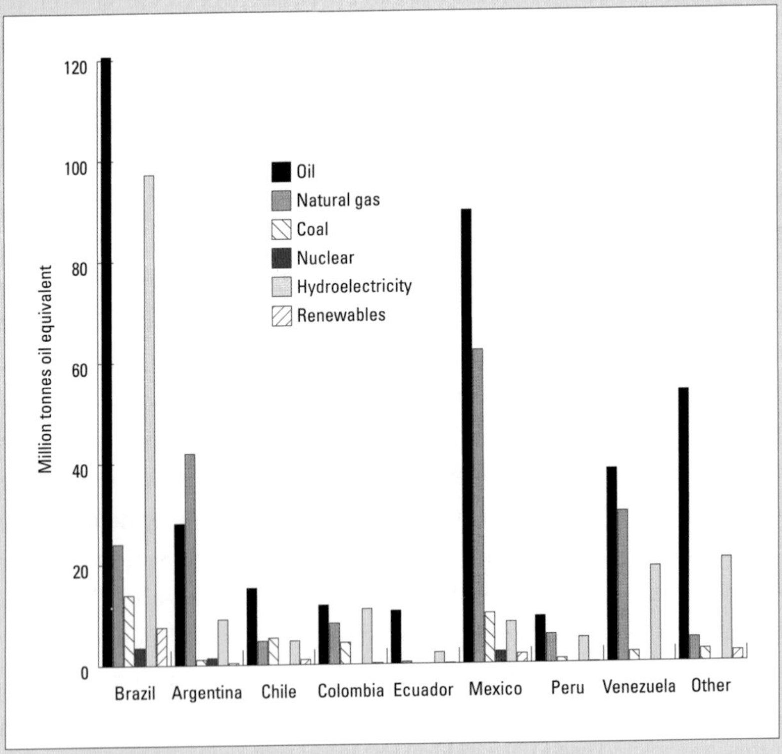

2011 Energy Consumption: Central and South America

Perhaps the most notable development in Ecuadorean foreign policy has been the new dominance of China. Since the Ecuadorean government defaulted on its debts in 2008 – Correa colourfully declaring his country's bonds 'illegal' and their holders 'true monsters' – it has been isolated from international financial markets. This has led the country to increasingly turn to China as a lender of last resort, receiving loans worth over $9bn between 2009 and 2012. The figure amounts to nearly 15% of Ecuador's GDP, raising the question of whether Correa is selling the country's sovereignty. These worries come as the government is increasingly hard-pressed to finance its high levels of public spending: Ecuador's 2013 fiscal deficit is expected to top 8% of GDP. Much of the debt is backed by future oil exports, meaning the country must continue to expand the exploitation of its natural resources, even at the expense of biodiversity and indigenous rights. In March 2013, Ecuador announced that it would auction over 3m hectares of Amazonian rainforest to Chinese companies, more than one-third of the country's wilderness and home to seven native communities.

This latest round of oil auctions typifies the deteriorating relationship between Correa and the country's indigenous population. Despite campaigning as an ally of the environment, the president has enraged leaders who claim resource extraction continues without prior consultation with local communities. Furthermore, Correa has used the military to suppress anti-mining protests and arrested activists on charges of 'terrorism'. An Ecuadorean human-rights group reports that in 2011, 189 indigenous people faced terrorism and sabotage charges due to protests over mining and oil projects. This harsh treatment, like the country's repressive media environment, undermines the democratic credentials of the Citizens' Revolution. Although many Ecuadoreans are less poor than they were five years ago, they have paid for it dearly with their reduced ability to speak freely and openly.

Brazil: Rousseff's threatened popularity

When President Lula left office in 2011, Brazil was the talk of the world. The country had just posted a 7.5% growth rate, the best in a quarter-century, and poverty had fallen by 50% in only eight years. In January 2011, Lula passed the presidential sash to Dilma Rousseff, his protégée and former chief of staff. Although she had never previously held elected office, Rousseff won the presidency by a sizeable margin on a platform of continuity. Despite her considerable popularity, however, replicating the success of Lula's tenure has proven difficult.

Prior to June 2013, when a wave of public protest suddenly swept the country, most of the bad news had been economic. Growth was unimpressive in 2011 and nearly ground to a halt in 2012, after which it failed to gain steam. January 2013 witnessed Brazil's worst trade deficit on record, investment fell, the stock market was down, and droughts raised the possibility of energy rationing (over 80% of the country's electricity comes from hydroelectric dams).

Under Lula, exports were spurred by skyrocketing demand for Brazilian commodities, such as iron ore and soy, while access to credit and a growing middle class accelerated consumerism in the country's massive domestic market. Under Rousseff, however, commodity prices have levelled off and consumption has declined as Brazilians become increasingly indebted. To regain momentum, steps are needed to address Brazil's deep-seated, structural challenges, chief among which is the so-called 'Brazil cost': the combination of strict regulations, poor infrastructure, currency appreciation and high taxes that makes the country uncompetitive globally.

To this end, the administration has opted for piecemeal reforms rather than a more comprehensive approach. This has included slashing interest rates, decreasing industrial payroll taxes, lowering electricity costs and ramping up infrastructure spending. However laudable these measures may be, dealing with each issue separately has injected a degree of uncertainty into the process. The private sector often complains that it is left in the dark about Brasília's next move and criticises the government's heavy-handed interventions. Although Rousseff has in some ways proved to be more pragmatic than her predecessor – for example, she privatised the operation of major airports, ports and roads, which Lula had refused to do – her relationship with the business community has been strained. Moreover, inflation was emerging as a threat, exceeding 6% in 2012 and the early months of 2013. Brazilians are particularly sensitive to this issue as hyperinflation is a not-too-distant memory, and concern over rising prices has permeated the press. Rousseff therefore faces the difficult task of jump-starting the economy without increasing inflationary pressure. In April 2013, Brazil's central bank began raising interest rates again, but some criticised the move as being too little, too late. If prices continue to climb, the government's support, especially among the poor, may begin to look less formidable.

Nevertheless, the president's approval ratings stayed consistently high until mid-2013, thanks to rising wages and low unemployment, and she remained in an enviable position ahead of the 2014 general election – a contest that was already shaping up to be interesting. Likely challengers include green candidate Marina Silva, who surpassed expectations in the 2010 election by securing 20m votes; Aécio Neves, a senator and former governor of Minas Gerais, and Governor of Pernambuco Eduardo Campos. Although they are all dynamic candidates, Silva, Neves and Campos may ultimately compete largely for the same pool of votes rather than cutting into Rousseff's loyal base. The president has already taken steps to shore up support among her 17-party coalition and is the favourite to win.

Protest wave

Discontent with the country's governance, however, remained an important factor. In June 2013, massive protests were sparked by a 20 cent increase in São Paulo's bus fares. Though initial demonstrations were limited, a harsh police crackdown fanned the flames. Soon hundreds of thousands of Brazilians – including many university students protesting for the first time – were demonstrating in major cities across the country against corruption, poor health care and education, and crumbling infrastructure.

The marches took place just months after the supreme court had sentenced dozens of Worker's Party operatives over the largest corruption scandal in modern Brazilian history. The trial, known as the *mensalão* (big monthly payout) because legislators were regularly paid for their votes, originally broke in 2005 and led to the resignation of several top officials. In August 2012, Brazil's high court finally handed down sentences, which were surprisingly tough for a country known for impunity. The proceedings generated a huge amount of interest within the country and reflect the public's growing intolerance of corruption.

Public indignation also stemmed from the massive public spending funnelled into the 2014 World Cup and the 2016 Olympics – money many Brazilians believe would be better spent on high-quality social services. These events, which will cost many billions of dollars, will also

Atlantic vs. Pacific: Economic bifurcation in Latin America

Five hundred years ago, Pope Alexander VI partitioned the Americas along the meridian of Tordesillas, demarcating the Spanish and Portuguese empires. Today, a new division seems to have emerged between the relatively closed economies on the Atlantic coast and those oriented towards commerce in the Pacific. The formal launch of the Pacific Alliance in June 2012 placed this rift in a new light. Comprising Colombia, Peru, Mexico and Chile, the bloc seeks economic integration among its members to increase collective trade with Asia. The organisation formed as the more protectionist Mercosur came under mounting criticism for politicisation and dysfunction. Disagreements between the organisation's two largest members, Brazil and Argentina, have hampered its decisions, which must be made unanimously. Furthermore, the entry of the anti-capitalist Venezuela into the bloc in July 2012 stands to further obstruct the group's ability to negotiate with outside countries.

This competition between economic models became clear during the WTO's search for a new director general in spring 2013. The final candidates hailed from Latin America's two largest economies, which have very different perspectives on global commerce. Herminio Blanco of Mexico espoused a doctrine of free trade, while Brazil's Roberto Carvalho de Azevêdo was considered more sympathetic to the emerging manufacturing and agricultural sectors of the Global South. The showdown was a striking reminder that when it comes to commerce and development, the Americas remain divided in their approach.

To be sure, the Atlantic–Pacific dichotomy is an oversimplification; for instance, Ecuador is slated to become a member of Mercosur and Uruguay is an observer of the Pacific Alliance. Moreover, given that integration between Colombia, Chile, Mexico and Peru is still incipient, the true worth of the Pacific Alliance is yet to be determined. But this does not change the fact that increasing pressure is being placed on the region's economies to open themselves to foreign competition. This is particularly true now that the United States is pursuing a free-trade agreement with the EU, and negotiations continue for the Trans-Pacific Partnership (TPP), which links the most open markets in Asia, Oceania and the Americas. Such developments raise the opportunity costs of countries getting left behind by the rest of the region.

It is not entirely clear what the immediate effects of this tension will be. Despite its protectionist bent, Brazil will surely want to benefit from the dynamism of the TPP or a US–EU agreement. This is especially true as the trade surpluses Brazil traditionally enjoyed within Mercosur diminish. Bolivia and Ecuador are both expected to enter the bloc as well, rendering it even more unwieldy. The size of the organisation, as well as the anti-market attitude of its members, may lead Brasília to push for reforms that allow Mercosur states to enter into bilateral agreements with outside countries. Although this would require Brazil to relax its restrictions, it would make the country's trade policy less beholden to the whims of Caracas and Buenos Aires.

bring intense international scrutiny and a flood of foreign visitors to a country that already suffers from acute congestion problems.

Although Brazil has had years to prepare, it remains woefully behind schedule. Fédération Internationale de Football Association, football's governing body, often reiterates its concern over the delays, which mainly result from onerous bureaucratic requirements that have affected the majority of Brazil's 12 host cities. The massive infrastructure improvements being made to serve tens of thousands of expected tourists are also beset with problems. Travellers leaving São Paulo are currently advised to set off five hours before their flight to accommodate traffic, but a train to the city's main airport will not be operable in time for the tournament. Construction of São Paulo's stadium has also been hamstrung by financing complications, leading to speculation that Brazil's largest city may be dropped as a host site.

Security is another concern. For several years, the government has deployed long-term 'pacification units' in Rio de Janeiro to wrest control of the cities' expansive slums from criminal syndicates. The initiative has seen progress in quelling violence, but gangs such as First Capital Command in São Paulo and Red Command in Rio still pose a very real threat to urban security. In April 2013, the gang rape of a female tourist travelling on a bus in Rio made headlines worldwide and raised safety concerns for women travelling in Brazil's notoriously violent cities.

The scale and intensity of the June 2013 protests caught elected officials off guard. The high expectations of the country's burgeoning middle class have never been more apparent, but whether public discontent can translate into actionable policy remains an open question. The protests stemmed from an amalgam of complaints that no political party is prepared to present as a coherent electoral platform. So while it is clear that many Brazilians are fed up with politics as usual, there is not yet an alternative in sight.

Argentina: combative leadership

The biggest story of the Southern Cone continues to be the increasingly defiant and erratic behaviour of President Cristina Fernández de Kirchner. The strong-willed head of state has sought to silence her critics at the expense of democratic governance, scorned the warnings of economists about the risk of financial ruin and imperilled Argentina's already poor international standing by rebelling against creditors and the IMF. When faced with economic deterioration or political dissent, the administration has responded by tightening its grip. But with the president's tenuous popularity and the country's acute challenges, the situation is looking increasingly uncertain.

Compared to previous years, in which the president had much higher levels of support and Argentina experienced consistently strong growth, this bleak state of affairs is striking. During the presidencies of Fernández and her late husband Néstor Kirchner, Argentina has followed an economic model that, until recently, led to a decade of growth at 7% of GDP. This approach employed fiscal and monetary expansion financed by a drastically higher tax burden. Under the Kirchners, government spending has increased from 30% of GDP to 40%, while government revenues have increased from around 25% to 35%. After a severe crisis in 2002, Argentina had an abundance of idle capacity and reacted strongly to government stimulus. The country's exports were favoured by an undervalued currency and benign external factors, such as strong regional growth and rising commodity prices.

By 2011, however, this model had started to fall apart, and the administration has been left scrambling to respond. As output and commodity prices have levelled off, the peso has become overvalued and years of expansionary policies have led to the region's second-highest inflation rates (around 25%). Yet rather than change course, the Fernández administration has pressured the country's statistical agency, INDEC, to revise its inflation figures to a little over 10% and has implemented strict capital controls. Argentines tolerated rising prices while growth was high, but are now denied access to stable currencies during a period of intense economic uncertainty.

Energy shortages have also become increasingly severe due to a reluctance to bring electricity tariffs to appropriate levels – which would further increase inflation – and declining domestic production. To solve its energy woes, the government in May 2012 expropriated a majority stake in the Argentine energy company YPF, a subsidiary of the Spanish company Repsol, after it discovered major natural-gas reserves. Yet not only has the government declined to pay Repsol the $10bn it seeks in compensation, production is down since the seizure. Indeed, tapping the country's energy deposits will require a level of know-how and investment the government is unable to provide on its own. The manipulation of official data and Fernández's strong hand have provoked both public discontent and condemnation from foreign governments and international institutions, such as the IMF.

Argentina's protracted legal battles with its bondholders are the latest in a series of economic tussles. Following the government's default on $81bn of debt in 2001, it renegotiated some 93% of the debt, with creditors receiving 35 cents on the dollar. The holders of the remaining 7%, the so-called 'vulture funds', have taken the government to court in the United States with the hopes of getting a better deal. In October 2012, a circuit-court judge in New York forbade Argentina from paying the holders of its restructured debt until it starts to reimburse the plaintiffs. Fernández has refused to cooperate, leaving it to the appeals process to determine how to enforce the ruling, and moving the country closer to technical default. Officials in Buenos Aires have sworn that it will continue payments to the holders of its restructured bonds, but the episode has already solidified Argentina's reputation as hostile to foreign investors.

The Fernández administration has been similarly unyielding in dealing with domestic dissent. The president continues her battle against the Clarín Group, the country's largest media conglomerate and main critic. The judiciary had thwarted the government's attempts to break up news companies that were critical of it through a controversial law passed in 2009. But Fernández finally managed to curtail judicial independence in April 2013 with legislation ostensibly designed to 'democratise' the country's courts. In actuality, the move gives the president more control over the body that nominates and disciplines judges, and limits the courts' capacity to stall unconstitutional laws. Large-scale protests erupted across the country in response to these new measures.

Concerns over the economy, crime and the consolidation of executive power have diminished the president's popularity. Although Fernández secured a landslide re-election in 2011, her approval ratings had declined to around 30% by mid-2013. To stoke nationalism, the president has revived the country's claim to the Falkland Islands (which Argentina calls Islas Malvinas), a sparsely populated territory off the Argentine coast controlled by the United Kingdom since 1833. Fernández has taken to regularly invoking the subject in multilateral forums. In a telling parallel, the last time the Argentine government seriously pursued the issue was in 1982, during the end of the country's military dictatorship – a period in which an economic crisis and civil unrest threatened presidential control. On that occasion, a British task force expelled an Argentine invasion force. In March 2013, Argentina's claim was rebuked by the islands' residents in a referendum. Of over 1,500 votes cast, all but three opted to remain under UK control. Fernández has likened the Falklands residents to little more than illegal squatters, and dismissed the results as irrelevant.

That same month, Argentines celebrated the selection of Jorge Mario Bergoglio, former archbishop of Buenos Aires, as the new pope. For Fernández, however, the news was less welcome. As archbishop, Bergoglio had been one of her most strident critics and clashed with the administration over the legalisation of gay marriage and its anti-poverty initiatives. Although Pope Francis will surely have more to worry about than Argentine politics, his papacy may embolden the Argentine church. Debate continues over the church's complicity with Argentina's military dictatorship and Bergoglio's role during the period of government disappearances and torture. Some contend he worked behind the scenes to curtail abuse, while others assert that his actions were less benign.

In what some experts have deemed the most important election since the country returned to democracy, the legislative contests in October 2013 may ultimately determine the future of Fernández's political project. Many assume the president is eyeing a second re-election in 2015, which would require constitutional reform and approval by two-thirds of Argentina's congress. Fernández currently commands a majority in both houses, but faces serious hurdles to regaining her popularity and expanding her control, especially in the senate. An April 2013 poll by Management & Fit found that 40% of those who voted for Fernández would not support her congressional candidates in October. Yet the president's prospects are perhaps not as dim as polling would suggest. The opposition is fractured and lacks a unifying figure, and with no clear successor in the governing coalition's camp, her party may want to keep her in charge. The president's control over the government and economy may be a principal source of discontent for many Argentines but, for now, Fernández seems to be benefitting electorally from calling all the shots.

Contending views

Since 1999, when Chávez came to power, Latin American countries have moved in markedly different directions. Policy divergences among states in the region have become sharper: free trade and liberal democracy are no longer shared goals. And Latin America and the United States have cordially gone their separate ways. Admittedly, generalisations about the region are problematic: for every country that has deviated from democratic norms, another has moved towards them. Chávez was not solely responsible for deflating the collective spirit that prevailed two decades ago but his relentless defiance of Washington and its allies – often accompanied by aggressive, even belligerent, rhetoric – polarised the region.

These divisions were prominently displayed in June 2012, when Paraguay's senate voted to depose Fernando Lugo, the country's leftist president, in a swift impeachment trial. The impetus for the move was a clash between rural protesters and police that left 17 dead, although Lugo's support among his coalition had eroded significantly prior to the incident. Despite its legality, the speed of the vote provoked strong condemnation from Paraguay's neighbours, who deemed Lugo's removal from office a 'parliamentary coup'. With almost the same haste, the member countries of Mercosur voted to suspend Paraguay on the grounds that a 'democratic rupture' had taken place. This temporary revocation of membership prevented the Paraguayan senate from further stalling Venezuela's entry into the bloc. The controversial suspension of Paraguay and Venezuela's rapid admission led many observers to decry the move as overtly political. Indeed, Mercosur's reaction – later replicated by Unasur – contrasted with the more considered response of the OAS, which engaged with the new Paraguayan president to ensure that free and fair elections would take place a few months later.

The proliferation of regional forums in Latin America over the past decade has not corresponded to more effective multilateralism.

CELAC and ALBA have accomplished little since their founding, and the Paraguay episode demonstrated the susceptibility of Unasur and Mercosur to politicisation. In line with this trend, the OAS, which has traditionally been the main body for deliberation among countries in the region, suffers from a lack of funding and attempts to further weaken its reach. Many have hailed the Pacific Alliance as a positive development, but its members might learn from similar initiatives that were founded with fanfare, only to become an afterthought.

Yet regional cooperation has never been more important. Economically, collective action requires more than trade promotion. Political disagreements have hampered joint energy projects, such as electricity grids in Central America, dams in the Southern Cone and deep-water drilling in the Gulf of Mexico. A dearth of skilled labour in Brazil and 11m undocumented immigrants in the United States exemplify the need for a freer flow of labour across the Americas. In a similar vein, to promote mutual understanding and provide young people with employment skills, the United States recently announced initiatives to expand student exchanges with countries such as Mexico and Brazil. These programmes will require a sustained effort to achieve success.

Politically, collective defence of democratic principles has faded from the regional agenda. Although relatively free and fair elections are the norm in Latin America, freedom of expression and checks on presidential power have eroded in a number of countries. Not only are regional human-rights bodies under fire, but leaders are hesitant to criticise encroachment on political freedoms in neighbouring countries. Within this generally permissive atmosphere, a crucial test for Latin American states will be whether they put pressure on those who run roughshod over democratic institutions.

Citizen security is perhaps the area in which cooperation is most sorely needed. Indeed, the wave of democratisation that swept the region in the 1990s has not made Latin Americans safer. Shockingly, the 15 cities with the highest homicide rates – excluding those in war zones – are all in Latin America. The Western Hemisphere is home to 47 of the 50 most violent cities worldwide. The repercussions of this phenomenon for democratic governance are dire. Such violence diminishes trust in institutions and public officials, and has a severe economic impact.

The World Bank estimates that crime, including violent crime, costs Honduras, Nicaragua and El Salvador over 9% of GDP.

The drug trade plays a large role in this surge in violent crime but is by no means exclusively responsible for it. All too often, one country's success in combating illicit commerce is bad news for its neighbours, who may become quickly overwhelmed by displaced criminal activity. This 'balloon effect' demonstrates the importance of developing a comprehensive regional approach to combating transnational organised crime. Given the high demand for drugs, appreciable reductions in the drug trade seem unlikely without significant cost to taxpayers and citizen security. Developing an 'all-of-the-above' approach to mitigate the hazards of narcotics has become a priority on the regional agenda, and will be a principal metric by which to judge Latin American states' ability to cooperate.

The region's challenges are pressing, but not insurmountable. Finding common ground – both within Latin America and globally – will be a critical step in securing a future that is democratic, prosperous and peaceful. Significant progress has been made over the past decade, but it will not sustain itself. It remains to be seen whether the region's leaders will commit to the tough reforms and democratic principles necessary to sustain Latin America's momentum for another ten years, and beyond.

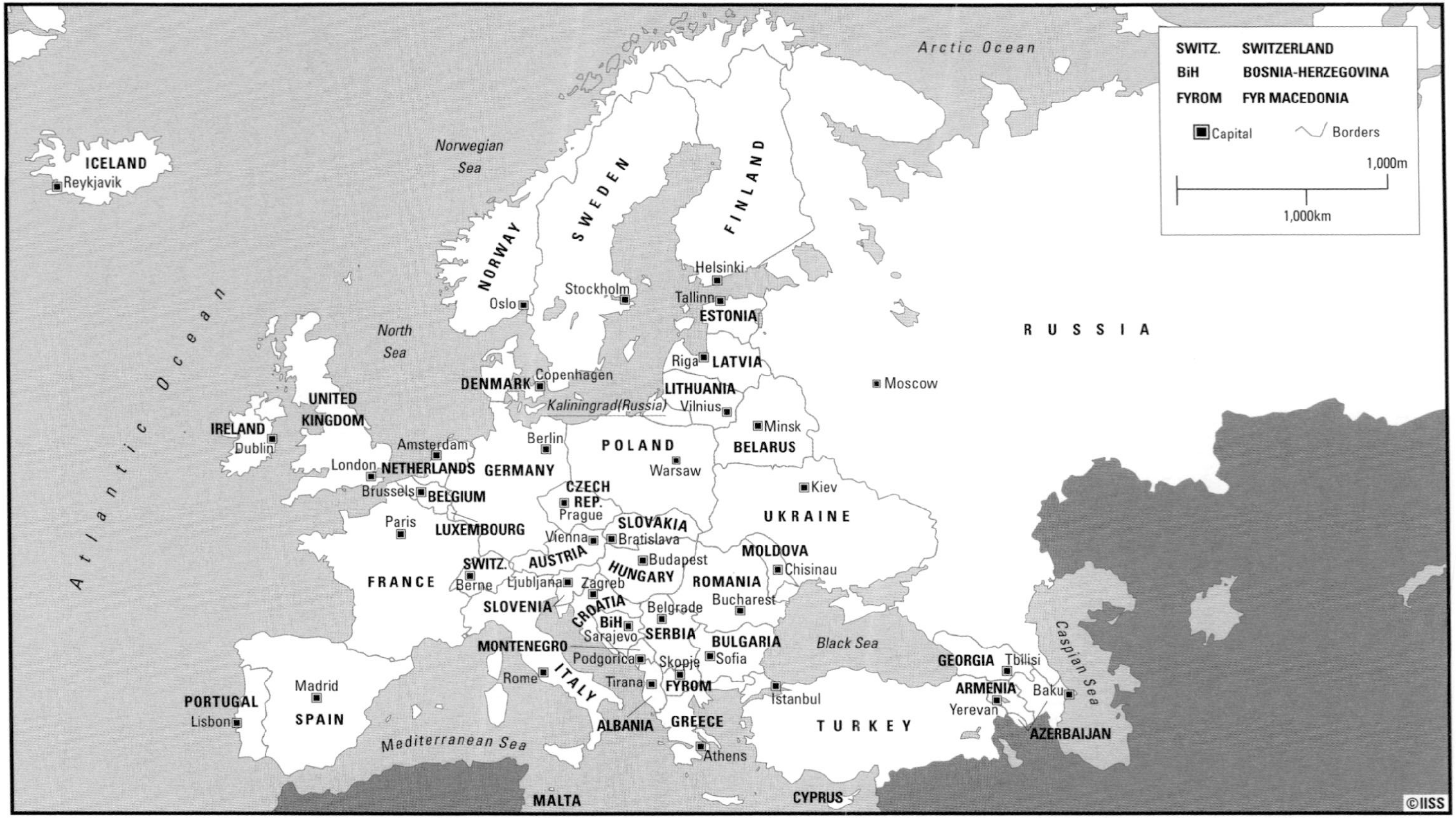
SWITZ. SWITZERLAND
BiH BOSNIA-HERZEGOVINA
FYROM FYR MACEDONIA
Capital
Borders
1,000m
1,000km
Arctic Ocean
Norwegian Sea
North Sea
Atlantic Ocean
Mediterranean Sea
Black Sea
Caspian Sea
ICELAND
Reykjavik
NORWAY
Oslo
SWEDEN
Stockholm
FINLAND
Helsinki
Tallinn
ESTONIA
Riga
LATVIA
LITHUANIA
Vilnius
Kaliningrad(Russia)
RUSSIA
Moscow
DENMARK
Copenhagen
UNITED KINGDOM
London
IRELAND
Dublin
Amsterdam
NETHERLANDS
Brussels
BELGIUM
LUXEMBOURG
Berlin
GERMANY
POLAND
Warsaw
Minsk
BELARUS
Kiev
UKRAINE
CZECH REP.
Prague
SLOVAKIA
Bratislava
Vienna
AUSTRIA
Budapest
HUNGARY
MOLDOVA
Chisinau
ROMANIA
Bucharest
Paris
FRANCE
SWITZ.
Berne
Ljubljana
SLOVENIA
Zagreb
CROATIA
BiH
Sarajevo
Belgrade
SERBIA
MONTENEGRO
Podgorica
BULGARIA
Sofia
Skopje
FYROM
Tirana
ALBANIA
GREECE
Athens
Rome
ITALY
PORTUGAL
Lisbon
Madrid
SPAIN
Istanbul
TURKEY
GEORGIA
Tbilisi
ARMENIA
Yerevan
Baku
AZERBAIJAN
MALTA
CYPRUS
©IISS

Chapter 4

Europe

The most significant development in Europe during the year to mid-2013 occurred shortly after it began, with a declaration from Mario Draghi, president of the European Central Bank (ECB). He said in July 2012: 'Within our mandate, the ECB is ready to do whatever it takes to preserve the euro. And believe me, it will be enough.' While this statement caused a flurry, it would obviously not have been sufficient by itself, after three years in which Europe's authorities had failed to convince the financial markets that the measures they were taking would, indeed, be enough. But two months later, Draghi revealed that the ECB would underpin the debt of any country that undertook satisfactory reform measures, by buying its bonds. The comfort to the markets provided by this guarantee meant that the ECB did not, in fact, have to make any such purchases, because the market interest rates of Spanish and Italian debt fell to such an extent that the need for them to negotiate financial rescues, conditional on economic reforms, receded.

Draghi's action was controversial, especially in Germany. Its central bank, the Bundesbank, continued to argue that bond purchases were an intrusion into fiscal policy, and that central banks should focus only on monetary policy – the setting of interest rates with a view to controlling inflation. The Bundesbank believed that the ECB's plan to purchase government bonds would encourage governments to relax their efforts to reduce fiscal deficits and undertake necessary reforms. This German view was influenced by past periods of fiscal profligacy and runaway inflation. However, most significantly, German Chancellor Angela Merkel sided with Draghi.

That Draghi and Merkel took this common stance was not, however, a result of any feeling on their part that the pressure on governments to restore Europe's economic fortunes should be reduced. Draghi, in fact, took a narrow but logical approach: the ECB, in common with other central banks, had an accommodative monetary policy, keeping interest rates low so as to revive economic growth. But worries about the break-up of the euro, stemming from high sovereign debts, were keeping interest rates high in troubled debtor economies – preventing the policy from achieving its purpose. By removing the risk premium attached to these countries' debts, the central bank could achieve better results through its monetary policy and help kick-start economic growth – which, in turn, would contribute to the reduction of debts.

For her part, Merkel continued to believe that European governments needed to take measures to assure sound finances, and that this would be the foundation for countries – and Europe as a whole – to be competitive in the global economy. She had championed agreement by eurozone governments on the 'fiscal compact' – common targets for fiscal deficits and government debts. Many governments, including Greece, Ireland, Portugal, Spain and Italy, had introduced reform measures with a view to meeting deficit targets. While keeping up that pressure for reform, however, Merkel did, by the autumn of 2012, come to the view that Greece, which had by far the most significant debts relative to the size of its economy and was struggling to reform its economy, should be kept inside the euro and not be ejected – a step that would have had serious long-term consequences for Greece and for Europe as a whole. Greece's exit and a break-up of the euro would have caused major disruption for German businesses just a year before German elections. Thus, Merkel's decision to show overt support for Greece represented another stride towards resolution of the eurozone crisis.

As the crisis had unfolded – since Greece's revelation of a large upward revision to its budget deficit in 2009 – governments had been perceived by the markets to be taking insufficient action. But by 2013, it was clear that the series of steps that had been taken, by individual governments and collectively, had in fact turned the tide. Moreover, governments were persisting with economic reforms that were likely to improve competitiveness, in spite of the inevitable electoral setbacks. The eurozone's problems were not over, as was made clear when Cyprus became the latest country to receive a rescue loan, which was accompanied by an enforced shake-up of its banks. But the atmosphere of constant crisis had subsided. Speculation that Italy and Spain would need to arrange bailouts – the scale of which would have challenged the ability to raise sufficient financing – receded. The tension had eased sufficiently for the EU, in May 2013, to announce that it was relaxing the timetables set for governments to lower their budget deficits, though it could also have been influenced by the persistent debate among economists over whether austerity was really the correct recipe for dealing with debt problems. The balance of that argument was shifting towards those advocating a larger element of Keynesian stimulus.

The years of crisis would leave a legacy. Most obviously, many economies were still stagnant. Only with economic growth could debt burdens be lastingly addressed. But just as important would be the political aftermath. Germany's European dominance had become evident: it was seen as having imposed tough conditions on its European neighbours in return for financial support. In Merkel's view, the country had acted as a good European and preserved European unity. But it now had a much more fractious relationship with France. Much attention was being paid to Merkel herself, and in particular how she had managed to achieve the balance – both in domestic politics and with European counterparts – between toughness and Germany's reluctance to assume the reins of a global power. She was expected to remain at the helm after September 2013 elections.

Whether the preservation of the euro would cement or reduce the chances of closer European unity remained an open question. In both debtor countries and those that had contributed to rescue packages, bad tastes lingered. Some EU members seemed less keen on the prospect of the 'ever closer union' that had been promised in the Treaty of Rome. In the United Kingdom, always unenthusiastic about such a goal, the idea had become increasingly toxic under the Conservative-led coalition of David Cameron. He promised an in-out referendum on EU membership by 2017, and said he would use the interim period to negotiate a better deal for Britain. While other countries would probably feel that the EU was a stronger entity with Britain in it, there was little sign they were willing to engage in such a negotiation. President François Hollande of France certainly had more pressing concerns after a first year in power that he would prefer to forget: after being elected as the pro-growth candidate, he was finding growth elusive, and support for him waned dramatically.

It was left to the United States to make the argument that Britain would be seen as a more significant power inside the EU than outside it, with President Obama telling Cameron in January 2013 that he valued 'a strong UK in a strong European Union'. However, British politicians were not yet making this more strategic case.

France: Hollande's Fraught First Year

A May 2013 *Le Monde* front page summed it up brutally: 'Hollande, l'année terrible'. To mark the first anniversary of President François Hollande's election, the French press indulged in a feast of negativity: electoral promises unfulfilled, domestic and foreign challenges greater than ever, an economy in triple-dip recession, a fractious government, a fractured society and record lows in the polls. On his election in May 2012, 53% had viewed Hollande favourably – hardly an overwhelming vote of confidence. Support thereafter fell constantly, reaching an all-time low for any French president of 26% a year later.

The negative opinion polls reflected popular perceptions rather than actual performance. Given the disastrous economic and social situation that Hollande inherited, his record so far required nuance. By early 2013, his administration had successfully negotiated an employment deal with both moderate unions and employers; crafted a competitiveness pact involving limited, though long-overdue structural reform; helped to turn the European tide of austerity policies, in a trial of strength with Germany; launched a successful military intervention in Mali to the applause of the international community; produced a new defence

White Paper which, contrary to all predictions, temporarily maintained France's strategic posture; embarked on a historic reconciliation with Algeria; and fleshed out the contours of legislation authorising same-sex marriage, possibly the signature act with which his presidency will be historically associated. But Hollande's successes had come at a very high price: the fracturing of his socialist majority, with a disillusioned left wing prepared to vote against the government, and a right-wing opposition seemingly buoyed by the strength of its hatred for the man himself.

Economy: elusive growth

A sense of economic gloom hung like a cloud over Hollande's first year. He had promised to reduce unemployment, the budget deficit and government debt, to restore the health of France's public finances without large cuts in government spending or significant new taxation – and in short to create growth. The government, not surprisingly, failed in each of these objectives. The promise of lower unemployment was constantly reiterated as not only a top government priority but also a feasible one. However, the 10% figure inherited from Nicolas Sarkozy crept higher, nudging 10.8% in November 2012 and 11% in summer 2013. In June, the IMF backed the view of the European Commission (EC) and many economists that unemployment would continue to rise throughout 2014. April 2013 was the 24th consecutive month of rising unemployment, with 3.26 million people out of a job. More worryingly, 900,000 young people between the ages of 15 and 29 were recorded as being neither employed nor in education or training, many of them with little prospect of finding a job.

The picture regarding economic growth was similar, with official predictions steadily revised downwards, as were EC and OECD forecasts, which were less optimistic. On taking office, Hollande predicted growth of 0.5% for 2012, but by August had lowered that forecast to 0.3%. The out-turn for the year proved to be zero. A promise to reduce the budget deficit from 5.3% of GDP in 2011 to 4.5% in 2012 was missed by 0.3 percentage points, but Hollande undertook to meet the EC target of 3% by 2014. In May, the EC, recognising that this was unlikely, extended France's grace period until 2015. However, this would be challenging.

France's economy, subject to less international scrutiny than those of Greece, Spain, Ireland and Portugal, was by some benchmarks in worse shape.

The French fiscal system is highly complex: expensive for the state to manage, difficult for ordinary citizens to understand, and easy for those with highly-paid accountants to manipulate to their advantage. There is a bewildering array of direct and indirect taxes and other fiscal charges, accompanied by a vast range of deductions, allowances, tax credits and exemptions. This is the political bread-and-butter of budget ministers who constantly tinker with the details. France's overall tax rate, one of the highest in the OECD, rose further in 2012 and French households, for the first time in 30 years, found their disposable income dropping. Although Hollande had promised in his campaign to promote growth, in office he charted a course much closer to neo-liberal orthodoxy, insisting that France's credibility with the markets required rapid deficit reduction and belt-tightening. The result was higher taxes, an absence of growth, and mounting popular anger with the government.

The anger rose to fever pitch when Budget Minister Jérome Cahuzac, the main architect and apostle of belt-tightening, and the man responsible for persuading the wealthy to make patriotic fiscal sacrifices, was accused by the media of having a secret Swiss bank account containing €600,000. After outright denials (and warm statements of support from his government colleagues), Cahuzac resigned and later confessed that he had lied. Even worse, it transpired that his tax haven had been established for him in 1992 by a man who, 20 years later, was a main political adviser to the National Front leader, Marine Le Pen. Cahuzac, before becoming a socialist, had flirted with crypto-fascism. A frenzy of enquiries into banking practices revealed that several leading banks arranged tax havens for wealthy and corporate clients, including Hollande's 2012 campaign treasurer Jean-Jacques Augier, who had a nest egg in the Cayman Islands. Hollande had made much political capital out of similar scandals among Sarkozy's entourage, and the Cahuzac revelations rocked his government to the core. Hollande seemed sorely to lack the kind of luck every politician needs.

In two areas however, luck did not desert him. French competitiveness has long been a major hurdle for the overall economy. Labour costs are too high, French goods are too expensive (France accounts for only 13% of eurozone exports, down from 17% in 2011) and imports continue to rise. Hollande commissioned a report on French competitiveness from Louis Gallois, former head of EADS, the aerospace group. The report proposed drastic cuts to employers' social contributions and public spending, along with an increase in VAT. Similar proposals came from the IMF. In November 2012, the government was fortunate in securing the agreement of three moderate unions and the employers' federation for a package of measures – the National Pact for Growth, Competitiveness and Employment – which, while falling short of Gallois's proposals, nevertheless introduced into French labour law much-needed elements, including lower taxes and business costs, greater incentives and support for innovation, and a simplified regulatory environment. The measures will not revolutionise competitiveness, but were an important first step, and one which had eluded Hollande's conservative predecessors.

Hollande also made progress in May 2013 when he and Angela Merkel, the German chancellor, managed to find common ground on future governance of the eurozone. Germany was becoming seriously worried about France's ability to pull out of recession and was prepared to make life slightly more easy for the French president. Merkel agreed to a joint Franco-German approach at a forthcoming EU summit, at which they would jointly propose more regular eurozone meetings and a permanent president of the zone's finance ministers, in what was a German concession to long-standing French proposals.

Fractured domestic politics

The economic gloom was accompanied by a progressive breakdown of the political system. Although the Socialist Party (PS) emerged from the June 2012 elections with almost an absolute majority, with 280 seats in the National Assembly out of 577, Hollande chose to govern in coalition with the Green Party and the Radical Party of the Left. The price of this inclusiveness was vulnerability to the PS's chosen allies. Worse still, the PS itself was ill-disciplined and fractious.

With an idealistic view of politics and their party's cause, France's Socialists have traditionally tended to reject pragmatism and compromise, choosing to ally with political formations to their left rather than the centre. While preserving the party's soul, this makes a Socialist president a hostage to the more extreme factions in government. When, in October 2012, the National Assembly voted on the EU's revised Stability and Growth Pact – the essential rules governing the eurozone's functionality – Hollande's 'allies' in the Green Party and on the left rebelled, with 45 MPs opposing the bill or abstaining. In a similar vein, the PS itself drafted in April 2013 a paper denouncing Germany, and Merkel in particular, the architects of the EU's austerity policy, as 'adversaries' of France. Last-minute edits toned down the more offensive language, but the damage was done. The Franco-German relationship, the cornerstone of Europe, was under attack from the inside.

France's right-wing parties were no more united than the left. France has not had a stable conservative movement similar to the Conservative Party in the United Kingdom or the Republican Party in the United States. Throughout the nineteenth and twentieth centuries, three main strands of right-wing politics – authoritarianism, paternalistic Christian democracy and relatively orthodox liberalism – spent much of their time fighting one another. After the defeat of Sarkozy, the party which he had founded and led, the Union pour une Majorité Populaire (UMP), needed to be redefined. Two candidates for the vacant leadership, former prime minister François Fillon and party secretary-general Jean-François Copé, fought a contentious battle, which Copé won by only a handful of votes. Fillon, crying fraud, threatened to split the UMP to form his own centre-leaning party. The assumption was that Copé, representing the authoritarian side of the party, would seek to attract voters from the right-wing National Front and perhaps even do a deal with its leader, Marine Le Pen. In the event, a temporary truce was called, but nothing was resolved.

Under the Fifth Republic, the system has tended to be shaped by what has been called 'bipolarisation', whereby the mainstream parties of left and right each form political coalitions with parties from their own side of the spectrum. This tends to squeeze the centre and push politics towards the extreme. Just as the PS prefers to govern in coalition with parties to its left, so the main right-wing party (its name has changed many times since 1958) knows that it has to accommodate the National Front, or risk losing the election. In recent years, bitter divisions within both left and right have made the system dysfunctional. Constitutional experts, in desperation, are beginning to call for a return to the proportional representation system of the Fourth Republic (1944–1958).

Same-sex marriage

In domestic politics, the most explosive issue was legislation on same-sex marriage, which passed the National Assembly in April by 331 votes to 225. The debate on the bill began in January when the right embarked on an all-out filibuster, tabling no fewer than 2,439 amendments, each of which required a vote. For the left, the measure was an indication that France was entering the twenty-first century. For the right, it became a crusade to defend French civilisation and its norms and values.

At issue was not just the right to same-sex marriage (as opposed to civil unions, which had been available since the 1990s) but also, more controversially, the right of lesbian, gay, bisexual and transgender (LGBT) people to be parents, whether through adoption or surrogate arrangements. LGBT parenting had less popular support than same-sex marriage, and those with strong views outnumbered those with less firm opinions. There were mass demonstrations against the bill between January and May. Both Fillon and Copé spoke of a profound rupture between the president and the French people, trying to create the image of a systemic crisis in an overt attempt to question the government's very legitimacy. Initially, these mainstream politicians took a hands-off approach to the demonstrations, which were strongly supported by the Catholic Church and right-wing extremists. But as the crowds grew larger, the UMP leaders were induced to make common cause with the National Front, marching, arms linked, with extreme-right leaders with whom they had vowed publicly never to associate. As the bill passed into law, its opponents vowed to continue demonstrating throughout the summer and to repeal it when they returned to power. But pollsters recorded in May that people were tiring of the issue: 67% felt that the demonstrations should stop. Any move from a subsequent right-wing government to repeal the measure would be likely to open a Pandora's box of social crisis and litigation. Same-sex marriage is legal in 14 other countries, including seven in Europe, and in 12 American states. But nowhere did it produce the fissuring of society that France experienced in early 2012.

Mali: *Opération Serval*

Hollande came to power with no foreign-policy experience at all. It was therefore paradoxical that perhaps his greatest success so far came with his January 2013 decision to deploy military force to Mali (see West Africa, pp. 248–257). The large West African state had suffered severe destabilisation in the wake of the revolution in Libya, when thousands of former mercenaries hired by Muammar Gadhafi, many of them Tuareg nomads from the vast north of Mali, returned home, bringing weapons with them. Joined by Islamist jihadists linked to al-Qaeda in the Islamic Maghreb (AQIM), they declared the independence of an area of northern Mali the size of France. The Tuareg separatists were then marginalised by the radical Islamists, who imposed a brutal regime of sharia law. While the United Nations prepared a resolution authorising an African intervention force, the Islamists in January 2013 descended in massed columns of armoured pick-ups on the two strategic towns of Mopti and Ségou, the fall of which would have left open the route to Bamako, home to 12,000 Europeans including 6,000 French. The interim president of Mali, Dioncounda Traoré, asked the French president for air support for beleaguered Malian troops vainly trying to defend the two towns. Hollande, on the strong advice of his defence minister Jean-Yves Le Drian, immediately gave the order.

The next day, combat helicopters from French special-forces bases in Burkina Faso, followed by *Mirage* 2000D fighters based in Chad, thwarted the Islamist drive south. One day later, light armour from the French base in Côte d'Ivoire rolled into Bamako. Over the next two weeks, 4,500 French troops were airlifted to Mali to drive the rebels back to their northern desert hideouts. By the end of January, the major towns in the North – Gao, Timbuktu and Kidal – had all been cleared of their Islamist occupiers and a semblance of stability was restored, pending the arrival of a UN peacekeeping mission. Stability was precarious and deep political divisions between the Arab north and the

African south remained. But the French operation, which benefitted from massive airlift and air-refuelling support (but no combat troops) from allies, was widely seen as an impressive feat of French military planning. The glory redounded to Hollande. For a month, his polling numbers stabilised.

The mission had actually been long in the planning. As early as May 2012, Hollande had been briefed by his predecessor on the situation in Mali, where lawlessness had resulted in the kidnapping of French citizens. Paris decided to prepare a military operation, and attempted – in vain – to persuade the United States to join it in military planning. As the UN moved towards forming an African peacekeeping mission, Hollande was asked by African leaders in states adjacent to Mali to prepare a robust air-support operation. The decision to do so was taken in October 2012, even while, mindful of the fate of French hostages, Hollande strenuously denied the existence of any such plans. The precise details were worked out in December at the French planning headquarters, initially for air support only. After the launch of *Opération Serval*, when France realised how poorly trained the regular Malian army was, a quick decision was taken to deploy combat troops.

One consequence of the French operation was that further questions were raised about the capability and the credibility of the European Union's Common Security and Defence Policy (CSDP). As early as March 2011, conscious of the growing activities of AQIM in North Africa, the EU had published a 'Strategy for Security and Development in the Sahel'. In July 2012, it began to examine the possibility of a CSDP mission to train the Malian army, which received the green light from the European Council in December and which finally set up camp at Koulikoro, 45 miles north of Bamako, in late March, just as the first French troops from *Opération Serval* were already being repatriated. As with the Libyan crisis in 2011, the EU had demonstrated the ineffectiveness of its collective efforts to emerge as a security actor.

For *Opération Serval,* Paris was fortunate that the Algerian government opened its skies to French aircraft, authorisation which had been refused during the Libyan operation in 2011. In the context of the 50th anniversary of Algerian independence in summer 2012, Hollande had gone further than any previous French leader in acknowledging the suffering of the Algerian people under France's 'brutal' colonialism, although he declined to offer a formal apology. On a visit to Algiers in December, he reached significant new trade deals, including the installation of a Renault plant, and formed a rapport with President Abdelaziz Bouteflika who in April 2013 flew to Paris for medical treatment following a stroke.

Defence strategy

A long-awaited defence White Paper, published in April 2013, proved in essence to be a holding operation, pending the adoption of longer-term choices for France's armed forces. The choices facing the Hollande government, given the need for drastic fiscal consolidation, were unpalatable. One was to sacrifice an entire major type of equipment, such as the aircraft-carrier or main battle tanks. The other was to reduce the numbers of all types across all three services, thereby maintaining a little of everything.

The Finance Ministry, looking for significant savings, was pressing for downsizing. In the event, Defence Minister Le Drian persuaded Hollande to hold the defence budget steady at €31.4 billion over a three-year period, though this meant that it would fall in inflation-adjusted terms. Although, in the context of the fiscal crisis, this was an achievement, the White Paper was in reality a decision not to decide. France's defence spending was set to fall over the next three years from 1.6% of GDP to 1.2%. The precise consequences of the White Paper in terms of procurement plans for weapons systems and military platforms would be spelled out later in 2013.

The White Paper envisioned three types of threat. Firstly, power-based threats (*menaces de la force*) emanating probably from Asia or from WMD proliferation. Secondly, risks, such as migratory flows emanating from weak or failing states: Africa emerged from the Paper as an area of ever-increasing strategic importance. Thirdly, risks deriving from globalisation: terrorism, cyber attacks and access to and free flow of resources. A major cyber attack would henceforth be considered an act of war and considerable new resources would be committed to an 'offensive cyber capacity'.

These threats called forth four strategic priorities. The first was territorial protection, involving defence against external aggression and counter-terrorism, and protection of French citizens around the world. The second priority was collective guarantees for the security of Europe and the North Atlantic area, which were presented as inseparable from national defence. France intended to play a leading and active role in NATO. As for the EU's CSDP, a very strong pitch was made for the re-launch of the EU's defence and security project, portrayed as having run out of steam. The Paper stressed it was both 'possible and urgent' to increase 'pooling and sharing' of defence capabilities, and called for an EU defence White Paper.

The third strategic priority was stabilisation of Europe's neighbourhood. In the context of the US pivot to Asia, Paris considered that Europeans no longer had any alternative but to consider their entire neighbourhood as a strategic priority which they must manage. The fourth priority therefore was a French (and European) contribution to the stability of the Middle East and the Gulf. France intended to prioritise this area, in partnership with other powers.

The White Paper highlighted five areas that would support these priorities. France would retain a capacity for intervention, to manage a similar crisis to Mali, by projecting force to 'priority zones' in the Mediterranean, Africa, the Gulf and the Indian Ocean. But these forces would be cut by half from 30,000 to 15,000. The nuclear arsenal, comprising both airborne and submarine-launched components, would be retained. There would be 24,000 job losses, mostly in the army, but some expansion in intelligence, which would be beefed up through drones and an increased space budget, and in cyber defence. Special forces, so crucial in Mali and Libya, would be prioritised.

The White Paper was criticised from both the left, which deplored the importance attached to NATO, and the right, which attempted to make political capital out of budget cuts. Expert comment was unanimous in judging that the document avoided making painful choices that would be inevitable, sooner rather than later. The can had been kicked down the road. For Hollande, given his overall situation, that in itself was an achievement. However, nothing could conceal the fact that the president's first year in office was indeed a terrible experience. There were, at mid-2013, few signs that matters would improve much over the following 12 months.

Germany: Merkel's Strong Position

With Germany heading towards a general election on 22 September 2013, opinion polls suggested Chancellor Angela Merkel would hold on to power and govern for a third term. Her approval ratings remained above those of other German politicians, even though she was frequently criticised for a failure to innovate and for missing opportunities to modernise the political platform of her party, the Christian Democratic Union (CDU).

There was uncertainty regarding the likely coalition partner of the CDU/CSU grouping (the CDU is allied with Bavaria's Christian Social Union), which was polling at 38–42% in June 2013. The existing partner, the Free Democratic Party (FDP), was hovering around 5%, the minimum share of the vote required to be represented in the German parliament, the Bundestag. The main opposition Social Democratic Party (SPD), under the leadership of Peer Steinbrück, a former finance minister in Merkel's first cabinet, failed to make inroads into the CDU/CSU lead and was stuck at 22–28% in the polls. Steinbrück struggled to run a gaffe-free campaign, contributing to the SPD's inability to generate support. The Green Party, with a comparatively strong showing, polling at 13–15% of the vote, kept hopes alive among SPD supporters that a centre-left coalition remained a possibility. The Left Party had 6–8% support, but Steinbrück ruled out a coalition with it. The Pirate Party, which has a platform of government transparency and Internet freedom, fell back from over 10% support in 2012 to 2–3%, making it unlikely that it would be represented in the Bundestag.

The government did face some political difficulties. Defence Minister Thomas de Maizière, a close confidant of Merkel and a respected member of her cabinet, ran into controversy in May 2013 when he cancelled plans to procure *Euro Hawk* reconnaissance drones, citing problems with their integration into civilian airspace and cost increases relating to certification. De Maizière said it was necessary to end a programme that would require additional spending of €600m with no guarantee of success. However, the media and opposition parties focused on the funds that had already been spent on development and testing phases, and asked why the problems had not been addressed earlier. However, while the decision did damage de Maizière's personal standing, it had not yet affected support for the CDU as a whole.

By June 2013 the electoral arithmetic suggested that a repeat of the 2005–09 'grand coalition' between CDU/CSU and SPD was the most likely election outcome, though Steinbrück suggested the SPD would not enter such an arrangement under his leadership. The SPD had suffered from a blurring of its image amongst voters during the previous grand coalition, with Merkel claiming the government's successes for the CDU/CSU. With an SPD–Greens coalition only a remote possibility unless the fortunes of the SPD improved, much depended on whether the FDP would manage to cross the 5% threshold to enter parliament, a result that would enable Merkel to extend the existing arrangement.

Merkel, a political phenomenon

Merkel's performance as chancellor and the political positions she has taken have been the subject of intense debate. Several books were published that sought to understand her popularity and examine her style of governing. While some analysts argued that a third term under Merkel's leadership was unlikely to be dynamic and criticised her for being overly cautious, indecisive and driven by events, most assessments saw her as possessing considerable political acumen. She remained popular with voters: if the German head of government were elected in a direct vote instead of via the majority in parliament, she would almost certainly win.

Many attempts to understand Merkel's political prowess and style of governing start with her personal history and experience. A physicist by training, she brought a scientist's approach to politics, which would help explain her gradual, step-by-step approach to reach solutions to problems. The fact that Merkel grew up in East Germany – and thus under a regime that put significant parts of the population under close scrutiny and surveillance – is often advanced to explain her risk-averse method and her reliance on a small circle of trusted advisers. However, this account fails to explain the fact that, at times, Merkel has shown herself to be utterly pragmatic, even opportunistic. Examples include her turnaround on energy policy after the 2011 Fukushima nuclear accident in Japan, which committed Germany to radically alter its energy mix at great financial cost and risk. In the domestic realm, Merkel in 2013 adopted a campaign proposal popular in the SPD, but initially shunned in her own party, for government-controlled ceilings on rent increases in order to rein in the rising cost of housing.

Another strand of analysis sees Merkel as the embodiment of German political culture. In this picture, just as Germany struggles to put the power it has gained economically to effective political use for fear of negative reactions from partners, Merkel – though repeatedly topping the *Forbes* list of the world's most powerful women – is seen as hesitant and cautious because she refrains from ruthlessly applying the political power she has. This produces, in the words of the writer and commentator Judy Dempsey, a legacy of 'unfinished business'. This view of Merkel's political career will rankle with political rivals, including several within her own party, who have been discarded with efficiency and, arguably, ruthlessness.

Merkel has stuck determinedly to the need for fiscal discipline and ever-increasing competitiveness, even as other European governments, struggling under the weight of low economic growth and high budget deficits, have looked to Germany to provide some stimulus. German economic growth slowed to 0.7% of GDP in 2012 and estimates for 2013 were for growth of 0.3–0.5%. However, the government was keeping a tight fiscal stance, aiming for a balanced budget in 2014, with surpluses in the following years. Berlin's continued insistence on austerity measures to deal with the debt crisis in Europe led to very critical reactions in countries affected by these policies. A poll commissioned by the *Financial Times* in June 2013 showed that almost 90% of Spaniards and more than 80% of Italians believed Germany's influence on the EU had become too strong.

Germany, however, continued to argue for cuts in government spending as the recipe for the heavily indebted countries of the eurozone. This was paired with a drive to increase economic competitiveness based on the German experience of the past decade, which saw labour market reform and wage restraint. While this approach remained popular in Germany, governments and economists across Europe pointed to the significant social costs of these policies and criticised the lack of focus on economic growth. The German approach was condemned for unrealistically expecting others simply to become more like Germany.

Merkel went to some length to explain that her policies were based on the assumption that countries in Europe were mutually dependent. In an interview with the German weekly *Der Spiegel* published in June 2013 she argued 'no European country can be strong in the long run if the others do not do well'. Referring to the financial commitments that Germany and others had made, she noted that 'budget consolidation and reform requirements were negotiated with the countries [under financial strain] and have to be seen alongside the solidarity these countries receive from Europe and all of us.'

German policy in the eurozone crisis was based on the assumption that Germany's own belt-tightening of previous years, actually initiated by Merkel's predecessor Gerhard Schröder, was the backbone of its recent economic strength. However, economists pointed out that Germany's growth had been heavily dependent on exports and thus on international demand, much of it financed through debt. Consumer spending in Germany itself remained weak. Secondly, the reforms initiated by the Schröder government had not taken place in a context of budget consolidation – in fact, the federal budget deficit had risen quickly through the EU limit of 3% of GDP. Under Merkel, Germany's focus had shifted from structural reform to budget consolidation. Thus, Germany had actually never managed the twin approach it was now asking of others: to undertake deep reforms of labour markets and welfare systems while at the same time curbing government spending.

When Greece and other countries ran into problems, Merkel's approach developed as one of gradual steps rather than bold choices. She told *Der Spiegel*: 'I do indeed believe that it is sensible and promising to work ourselves out of the crisis step-by-step because the all-decisive coup does not exist.' This was interpreted by some as proof that Merkel had lacked a plan for Europe and was making ad hoc policy decisions. But the German journalist Stefan Kornelius offered a different explanation, suggesting that, for Merkel, the basic policy choice boiled down to two options. Convinced that the European project needed to be strengthened, she opted for more cooperation among member-state governments, including contractual obligations such as the 'fiscal compact' agreed by most EU members in December 2011. This choice represented an explicit rejection of the transfer of more authority from the national level to Brussels-based institutions. Merkel said she wanted 'better coordination in policy areas that are decisive for improving our competitiveness ... Economic coordination in Europe is not developed enough, it needs to be strengthened, but that is different from more competencies for Brussels.' The fiscal compact, establishing limits on budget deficits and other measures, followed this logic. The fact that this cooperation would also reduce the autonomy of participating governments was viewed as a necessary cost.

Many analyses of Germany's policies under Merkel's leadership put extraordinary emphasis on the chancellor herself. However, her capacity as an individual leader to make choices was easily overstated. Like other European leaders, she faced important structural constraints which limited her options. Chief among them was limited popular willingness in Germany to make financial transfers to indebted countries in southern Europe. Another limiting factor was that Merkel, for all her influence, did have to maintain the ability to cut deals with fellow European leaders who continued to pursue different policy preferences. For example, French President François Hollande and Merkel reached an agreement on financial-sector oversight in October 2012 which charted a course to common banking oversight – a preference of Hollande – but left implementation for later and with a murky timetable – a preference of Merkel. In June 2012, Merkel agreed to a fiscal stimulus package in a move seen as an early concession to Hollande, as well as Italian and Spanish leaders, even though the €130bn package did largely consist of funds already committed. Like other policymakers, the German chancellor had to engage in two-level diplomacy, balancing the demands of the domestic political arena with those of international and European relationships. Arguably, Merkel did well to mesh these competing arguments, both foreign and domestic. She began to temper the financial conditions imposed on indebted countries without being seen as overtly contradicting the preferences of German voters. What looked hesitant and overly cautious often turned out to be good politics for the chancellor.

United Kingdom: Anti-Europe Sentiment Grows

An atmosphere of gloom pervaded Britain in the year to mid-2013, punctuated by the uplifting experience of the London Olympic and Paralympic Games. Five years after the financial crisis of 2008, economic activity was still failing to shake off the shackles of the austerity policies that the Conservative-led coalition had introduced to restore fiscal discipline.

With less than two years to go before elections due by May 2015, the stagnation of the economy – neither growing nor contracting – was beginning to threaten the chances that Prime Minister David Cameron could win a second term. But his prospects were helped by the lacklustre approach of the opposition Labour Party and its leader, Ed Miliband. Surprisingly, the government's tight fiscal policy and spending cuts, though heavily criticised by economists, met little political opposition.

The Conservatives' coalition with the Liberal Democrats, led by Nick Clegg, deputy prime minister, held together in spite of some awkward moments, and seemed set – barring accidents – to last the full five-year parliamentary term. But Cameron's biggest struggle was to keep support within his own party, which was increasingly dominated by Eurosceptics and right-wingers who sought to heal the country's supposed ills by forcing its departure from the EU. Thus, the dominant theme of the year became the UK's relationship with the rest of Europe. A debate on the country's membership of the EU was set to come to a head in 2017 – if the Conservatives remain in government – with an 'in-out' referendum promised by Cameron in an attempt to appease his party's right wing.

A decision to quit the EU would be a fundamental strategic choice. But another decision affecting the country's very nature was looming more imminently: Scotland's referendum in September 2014 on whether to remain part of the United Kingdom. While opinion polls suggested that voters would reject independence, a decision to leave the union would pose profound questions not only about Scotland's future as an independent nation, but also about the identity and structure of the remaining countries: England, Wales and Northern Ireland.

Meanwhile, the brutal murder of a British soldier on a London street showed that violent Islamism remained a problem.

Mounting euroscepticism

For decades, Britons have had mixed feelings about being part of Europe. Two years after Prime Minister Edward Heath took the country into what was then the European Economic Community in 1973, his successor, Harold Wilson, held a referendum on staying in, which was passed with 67% support. Nevertheless, the UK did not sign on with all its heart to the visionary goal of an 'ever-closer union' foreseen in the 1957 Treaty of Rome. Rather, it has tended to view its participation on a transactional basis, as was seen most starkly in 1984 when Prime Minister Margaret Thatcher demanded and won a rebate on UK contributions to the EU budget, arguing that 'we are simply asking to have our own money back'. Since then, sentiment has grown in the Conservative Party about spreading EU bureaucracy and its perceived tendency to impose unnecessary, costly and invasive regulation. Among bugbears is the Working Time Directive, which sets a maximum working week of 48 hours. This was, for example, seen as inhibiting the training of junior hospital doctors who were frequently on call for longer periods – though in fact the UK obtained a derogation under which workers could agree to longer hours. More generally, sceptics have painted a picture of national sovereignty steadily seeping away to bureaucrats in Brussels, even if hard evidence for such a trend could be difficult to find.

In the 1990s, the Conservative Party became bitterly divided on the issue, as eurosceptics undermined Prime Minister John Major, who was attempting to govern with a small majority. After losing a parliamentary vote on the Maastricht Treaty – he had negotiated an opt-out on the single-currency project which the treaty set in train – he was unwittingly recorded describing three eurosceptic cabinet colleagues as 'bastards'. Though Britain was not part of the euro, the eurozone debt crisis that began in 2010 was seen by sceptics as fuelling the arguments for departure, since it bound financially strong and weak countries together in what they saw as a fatal embrace, the former having to rescue the latter purely to hold together the artificial construct of a single currency. British critics believed that over the longer term, eurozone members would need to tie their economies much closer together, since the failure to harmonise fiscal policies had contributed to the crisis. To them, the 'fiscal compact' agreed by most EU members in 2011 was the beginning of such a trend, and they believed

Britain, as an EU member, even though not part of the fiscal compact or the currency, would over the long term be affected by it. In their opinion, Britain would be better off if it were free to determine its own policies: its priorities would increasingly diverge from those of its European partners.

The country's – but especially the Tories' – chronic ambivalence on the issue of Europe spawned the rise of the right-wing UK Independence Party (UKIP), led by an anti-Europe member of the European Parliament, Nigel Farage. A man with a liking for being photographed in a pub with a lunchtime pint of beer, he found a ready audience in attacking EU regulations said to impinge on British freedoms, and in railing against immigration. As a result, UKIP ate into the Conservative vote in May 2013 local elections, gaining a significant number of seats on local councils. Its support came mostly from the affluent 'home counties' around London and in eastern England – for example, it became the second-largest party on county councils in Kent, Lincolnshire and Norfolk. However, the fact that it was striking a chord across England was shown by the result of a by-election in the staunch Labour parliamentary constituency of South Shields, in northeast England, in which UKIP came second to Labour, winning 24.2% of the vote and taking large numbers of votes from the Conservatives, who won only 11.5% and the Liberal Democrats, whose share slumped to 1.4%. While by-election results are very poor indicators of the outcome of general elections, the South Shields vote showed a high level of dissatisfaction with the coalition's performance and a willingness to embrace anti-European, anti-immigration policies in order to generate jobs and growth.

The rise of UKIP strengthened the hand of like-minded eurosceptics within the Conservative Party, forcing Cameron to shift in their direction. Several times since 2010, he had sought to draw a line on the Europe issue by making concessions to them: for example, he promised a referendum if there was any threat in the future of further loss of sovereignty to Brussels. In December 2011, he vetoed the proposed adoption of the 'fiscal compact' – budget regulations intended to strengthen the functioning of the eurozone and address the crisis then surrounding the common currency – as an EU treaty. This late-night summit move won loud praise from eurosceptics, but had little practical import, as 25 out of 27 EU members proceeded to sign a separate treaty.

Cameron's efforts at appeasement did not halt right-wing clamour for steps to resolve the issue once and for all. He was in a weak position since several senior members of his cabinet were eurosceptics, and his own leadership of the party, while not under any immediate threat, was not completely secure – he was still blamed, for example, for not winning the 2010 election outright. Moreover, opinion polls showed that, if a referendum was held immediately, about half of Britons would vote to leave the EU – though many of them would reconsider this choice if the government was able to negotiate a new accommodation with Brussels. Again, Cameron sought to prevent the issue from damaging electoral prospects by making what was intended to be a definitive speech in January 2013.

Cameron noted that the British came to the EU 'with a frame of mind that is more practical than emotional'. It was not an end in itself. Europe was facing serious problems, such as a decline in competitiveness in the face of the rise of emerging nations, because of excessive regulation and 'complex rules restricting our labour markets'. He saw a lack of EU democratic accountability, and 'a growing frustration that the EU is seen as something that is done to people rather than acting on their behalf'. Cameron wanted an EU that was more competitive, with the extension of the single market to services and digital products; less bureaucratic; and more flexible, so that members could choose which areas to take part in and which not. 'We cannot harmonise everything,' he said. A new settlement was needed, 'where member states combine in flexible co-operation, respecting national differences, not always trying to eliminate them and in which we have proved that some powers can in fact be returned to member states.' From the UK point of view, some elements had already been achieved, such as staying out of the fiscal compact and safeguards on banking union. But in any case, the Conservatives would seek in the next parliament to negotiate a new settlement and would hold an in-out referendum in 2017.

Though Cameron did mention the benefits of the single market, such as the freedom of Britons to live and work across Europe, the approach that he spelled out risked a drift towards the exit, simply because UK membership of the EU lacked strong advocates. While eurosceptics tended to be obsessed by the issue, non-eurosceptics were concerned mostly with what they saw as more pressing matters, such as economic revival. It was difficult for them to grasp the purported need for a new settlement in which the UK might, for example, win back powers from Brussels in the realms of justice and home affairs. They saw that Britain would not be in a strong position to negotiate such a settlement. Herman Van Rompuy, President of the European Council, asked in London: 'How do you convince a roomful of people, when you keep your hand on the door handle?'. Earlier, Radek Sikorski, Poland's foreign minister, had said: 'Please don't expect us to help you wreck or paralyse the EU.' Angela Merkel, German Chancellor, appeared not to want British departure, because Germany was uncomfortable with the unpopular leadership role that it had assumed in imposing conditions on ailing eurozone countries. But it was not clear how far she would go to prevent it. French President François Hollande noted that 'Europe existed before Britain joined it,' and said his priority was the strengthening of the eurozone. Meanwhile, Washington viewed with concern the prospect of Britain's departure from the EU. Philip Gordon, a US State Department official, said it was in America's interest to see a strong British voice in the EU. Later, President Barack Obama, standing alongside Cameron at a press conference in Washington, said it made sense to try to 'fix' the relationship before breaking it off. 'The UK's participation in the EU is an expression of its influence and its role in the world as well as obviously a very important economic partnership,' he said.

Cameron's speech did not silence his right wing as he had hoped. Some present and former Tory cabinet members, sensing the public mood, said they would vote to quit the EU. An important subtext of the eurosceptic argument was xenophobia – a feeling, common to many countries, that foreigners were taking British jobs and welfare benefits. The EU was supposedly to blame because it had caused an influx of people from eastern Europe. Polish had become the second-most spoken language in Britain (although put together, the languages of the Indian subcontinent far surpassed it). However, there was strong evidence that this influx had made a net contribution to economic growth and tax payments, and that the jobs tended to be those that British people did not want. The government had introduced measures to curb immigration, but the main effect appeared to be a fall in the number of foreigners studying in some types of colleges and language schools, though not in universities.

Announcement of the referendum plan did have the salutary effect of stirring more thoughtful debate about the value of British EU membership. It was noted, for example, that Britain (as well as other EU members) regularly scored near the top of global rankings for the openness and competitiveness of its economy, and attracted substantial foreign investment, in spite of the alleged burden of EU regulation. Arguments began to be made that membership brought tangible benefits, and that exit would impose costs – and these would no doubt be developed in coming years. The Labour Party kept quiet, but it was possible that it too might see political advantage in committing itself to a referendum.

Economic conundrum

Cameron and his finance minister, George Osborne, stuck to their 2010 plan to cut public spending so as to reduce government borrowing and debt. They had done this originally to avoid the risk that the markets would treat Britain, with its high budget deficit, in the same way that they were treating Greece. Tough fiscal discipline, it was argued, was needed to ensure British credibility. However, the price has been the strangulation of economic growth.

Many economists argued that credibility had been won: the government was still able to borrow at very low interest rates, and would very likely continue to be able to do so. Stimulation of the economy had become the much more pressing need, they said. The government could afford to relax its tight fiscal stance, and the economic growth that would result would generate tax payments and so would not damage the fiscal position. However, this Keynesian approach still fell on deaf ears. Indeed, Osborne sensed that his continued cutting of public-sector jobs and welfare benefits was to the government's political advantage: the Conservatives would campaign on it in the 2015 election. For its part, Labour, fearful of being painted as the party of profligate hand-outs and excessive borrowing, curtailed its criticism and, in fact, explicitly accepted the government's spending plans up to 2015.

The government relied on the Bank of England, the central bank, to pump money into the economy through so-called 'quantitative easing' to counteract the effects of fiscal austerity and to stimulate bank-lending to companies and individuals. However, this had limited effect, and Mervyn King, the outgoing central bank governor, was critical of several aspects of government policy. At mid-2013, a new factor entered the equation in the form of Mark Carney, the highly praised head of the Canadian central bank, who became the first foreigner to head the Bank of England since its foundation in 1694. Markets would be watching closely for changes in the Bank's approach.

In terms of economic policy, there seemed little that fundamentally distinguished the three main parties from each other. But the explosion of emotion that followed the death of Margaret Thatcher in April 2013 at the age of 87 indicated that, amongst the British people, deep divisions were not far from the surface. Thatcher, Conservative prime minister from 1979 to 1990, had overseen the imposition of monetarist policies to curb inflation, and a drastic reduction of the public sector through privatisation. In a high confrontation, she took on the striking miners and defeated them. The economy recovered from chronic weakness and boomed, but her tenure also saw a switch towards services and away from manufacturing. Credited by some with having rescued the country from shambolic socialism and trade-union domination, Thatcher was popularly blamed for destroying the country's manufacturing heartland and causing the 'casino' banking excesses that were exposed, much later, in the 2008 financial crisis. A north–south divide can still clearly be seen in prosperity and employment, with southern England much more affluent and forming the Conservatives' political base. Amidst the emotions roused by Thatcher's death, Cameron was careful to salute her achievements – she is revered by right-wingers – but to indicate that present-day issues were different from those that she had confronted.

Continuing challenges

Three other issues were prominent in the year to mid-2013. Firstly, in spite of the end of the war in Iraq and the planned withdrawal of British combat forces from Afghanistan in 2014, Britain's military ventures continued to stir violent responses from Islamist extremists. In May 2013, an off-duty soldier, Drummer Lee Rigby, was hacked to death in a street near his east London barracks. The attackers, two Britons of Nigerian descent, waited at the scene and were then shot when running towards arriving armed police. In June 2013, they were awaiting trial. During the year several other groups were convicted of terrorist offences. Questions were raised about why intelligence agencies had failed to prevent Rigby's murder when at least one of the suspects was known to them. But the number of people who might commit offences clearly exceeded the agencies' surveillance capacity, and there were limits on their powers to track people without clear evidence of violent intent.

Secondly, a judge-led inquiry, set up by the government into intrusive media practices and corrupt collusion between journalists and police, recommended statutory regulation of the press. Cameron rejected this as too dangerous to free speech, but an awkward political compromise was subsequently reached. The controversy had been sparked by journalists' hacking of the mobile telephones of thousands of people, many details of which emerged during the inquiry. Separate police investigations were under way, and a large number of journalists and police personnel were arrested and awaited trial. It was unclear whether the affair – which triggered a reshaping of the global media empire of Rupert Murdoch, owner of most of the newspapers involved – would have any lasting impact on media practices.

Thirdly, the referendum on Scottish independence was looming. The vote would be the climax of a campaign led by Alex Salmond, head of Scotland's semi-autonomous government and leader of the Scottish National Party. Opinion polls indicated that about a third of Scots would vote for independence, and nearly half would vote against it, with the remainder undecided. Among the issues was whether Scotland would be able automatically to join NATO and the EU – Salmond said yes, but the official line from Brussels appeared to be no. In addition, British defence arrangements would need substantial revision because many significant assets were located in Scotland, such as the base for Trident nuclear deterrent submarines and naval shipyards. Independence would create more mundane headaches: how would Scots see their favourite television programmes, given that many of them were broadcast by the state-chartered British Broadcasting Corporation? South of the border, Scotland's exit from the union could prompt extensive readjustment at

Westminster, and a debate about how the government of England itself should be structured.

Just as in the EU debate, the case for the status quo was not yet being powerfully and convincingly made. Unless politicians began to do so, there was danger of drift into a much-changed future.

European Defence: Budget Cuts

Budgetary constraints have for several years dominated defence policy-making for most if not all members of the European Union and NATO. In the year to mid-2013, senior defence policymakers continued to call for closer cooperation among nations to address the growing mismatch of ambitions and capability. Both NATO and the EU have launched initiatives to generate greater cooperation under the rubrics of 'Smart Defence' and 'pooling and sharing'. Projects are now under way to achieve greater value in European defence, in terms of both efficiency and effectiveness (see Strategic Policy Issues, pp. 44–58). However, progress has been slow and uneven due to concerns about erosion of national sovereignty, differing national strategic cultures, and possible defence-industrial implications.

The recent focus on defence economics and defence cooperation has diverted attention from other trials that both NATO and the EU are facing. NATO will be profoundly challenged by the transition from operations to contingency planning that is likely to ensue – bar major unforeseen events – when its International Security Assistance Force (ISAF) mission in Afghanistan ends in 2014. NATO's secretary-general, Anders Fogh Rasmussen, will have to address renewed debate about the Alliance's relevance as many of its members – and their electorates – do not regard defence as a high priority at a time of extreme pressure on budgets.

The EU, on the other hand, will need a coherent, credible, and comprehensive Common Security and Defence Policy (CSDP) if it is to expand its zone of peace and prosperity. When it was awarded the Nobel Peace Prize on 12 October 2012 – a decision that provoked puzzlement and even ridicule – Herman Van Rompuy, President of the

European Council, declared, 'the European Union is really the biggest peacemaking institution ever created in world history, and we still have a mission of promoting peace, democracy, human rights – in the rest of the world.' He placed the issue of defence cooperation on the agenda of the European Council summit meeting in December 2013, setting off a flurry of discussion about possible revamping of the CSDP and of the EU's defence role.

New EU operations

Despite questions regarding the CSDP's ambition and viability, the year to mid-2013 witnessed substantial operational activity for the EU. All of the new missions undertaken were relatively small and focused on capacity-building in Africa – a trend noted in *Strategic Survey 2012* (pp. 158–159) that has solidified. A regional maritime capacity-building mission in the Horn of Africa and Western Indian Ocean – EUCAP NESTOR – was established on 16 July 2012. It is a civilian mission augmented with military expertise for a total of 175 personnel. *Nestor* has a two-year mandate and reached its full operational capability in February 2013. It is coordinated with the EU counter-piracy operation *Atalanta* and the EU training mission for Somali security forces in Uganda. A key objective is to improve the capacity of governments in the region to effectively control their territorial waters with a view to fighting piracy. In the case of Somalia, this will include training for a coastal police force, and the training and protection of judges. Other countries to be included in *Nestor's* activities are Djibouti, Kenya, Tanzania, Mozambique, the Seychelles, Mauritius and Yemen.

A second new operation, EUCAP SAHEL Niger, was launched in August 2012 in the Sahel region. This civilian-assistance mission aims to help local police forces improve their inter-operability and strengthen their capacity to counter terrorist activities and organised crime. The EU hopes these activities will in turn facilitate development projects as local authorities gain greater control of their territory. Deployment, with a focus on Niger, began in late 2012 and a possible extension of the mission to Mauritania and Mali has been discussed.

A third mission, EUAVSEC South Sudan, was approved by the Council on 18 June 2012 after South Sudan requested assistance to strengthen security at Juba international airport. The overall goal is to prevent its use by criminal and terrorist networks and create conditions where the airport can contribute to economic development. The EU's advisory, mentoring and technical assistance mission began in September 2012 with 65 staff and a mandate of up to 19 months.

While the EU had been discussing engagement in Mali for some time, the deteriorating situation in that country (see West Africa, pp. 248–257) prompted the EU to launch a training mission on 18 February 2013, following French military intervention to counter a rebel advance. EUTM Mali has a 15-month mandate, contributions from 22 EU member states and 500 personnel in total. Its core objective is to train and advise the Malian armed forces (under the control of legitimate civilian authorities) with a focus on unit capabilities, command and control, logistics and human resources. Training will also cover international humanitarian law and the protection of civilians and human rights.

In early 2013, the Council also approved the concept of a border assistance mission to Libya, EUBAM Libya. This civilian mission is designed to build capacity for border management in Libya and has a two-year mandate. Local authorities will be supported in their efforts to enhance the security of air, land and sea borders. This will include border surveillance, airport and harbour security, and coast guard training. Full deployment of EUBAM Libya was expected by mid-2013.

The EU was keen to emphasise that the new missions were building blocks in a comprehensive approach to security, which involved the use of development, economic, diplomatic and military instruments. Nonetheless, these modest ventures seemed small steps towards achieving the grander ambitions of the CSDP, which amount to an autonomous global crisis-management role for the EU. The level of EU missions under way – a far cry from any exercise of 'hard power' – raised the question of whether the level of ambition should be adjusted downwards so as to focus more on the kind of activities the EU was actually willing and able to conduct. For example, EU members have since 2007 formed battlegroups that are kept on standby for six-month rotations, ready to be deployed at short notice to deal with sudden contingencies. But no battlegroup has yet been deployed – even though EU member countries have several times deployed troops to deal with such contingencies in Africa.

Political momentum

The primary venue for such discussion will likely be the European Council meeting in December 2013. EU leaders tasked Catherine Ashton, High Representative for Foreign and Security Policy, and the European Commission (EC) to develop ideas on how to strengthen CSDP, with three broad objectives in mind: increasing its effectiveness, visibility and impact; enhancing defence capabilities; and strengthening Europe's defence industry. The summit's support for significant changes would provide renewed impetus at the highest levels of governments for a revamped EU defence role. But if support is weak and changes minor, the opportunity will likely be lost for quite some time.

The Council meeting may see the adoption of a revised battlegroup concept. At an EU defence ministers' meeting in April 2013, German minister Thomas de Maizière renewed discussion of battlegroups, explaining that 'there are many situations in which the European Union needs to act rapidly in a different way' than was previously envisioned. To increase their flexibility, he proposed that they focus on 'rapid training missions'. This would be done by building the necessary force elements into one of the two battlegroups on standby, which would then be earmarked for appropriate missions. The thrust of de Maizière's proposal was well-received, not least because other defence ministers and EU officials interpreted it as adding to the existing concept rather than questioning its overall utility.

In recognition of the growing importance of cyberspace, Ashton and the EC published the EU's cyber-security strategy, 'An Open, Safe and Secure Cyberspace', in February 2013. The strategy outlined five priorities to address cyber threats: achieving cyber resilience; reducing cyber crime; developing cyber-defence policy and capabilities (such as detection, response and recovery); developing the industrial and technological base for cyber security; and establishing a coherent international cyberspace policy for the EU. The paper noted that cyber attacks 'can have different origins – including criminal, politically motivated, terrorist or state-sponsored attacks as well as natural disasters and unintentional mistakes'. Although the main responsibility for cyber security lay with national governments, the EU was seeking to add an additional layer of activity across the pillars of network and information security law enforcement and defence. The EU would add value by facilitating collaboration and coordination among member states in these areas.

NATO in transition

By mid-2013 Afghan forces had responsibility for security in every district in Afghanistan, as NATO prepared to withdraw combat forces by end-2014. While a smaller NATO mission would probably stay to train and assist Afghan security forces, the logistical challenge of withdrawing personnel and equipment was already the focus for most Allies. The end of ISAF will mark the end of a two-decade era of large-scale deployments on operations out of area. While unforeseen events could require yet another significant crisis-management effort, mixed results in the Balkans and Afghanistan (and for some NATO members, Iraq) have discouraged Alliance leaders from pursuing demanding, open-ended operations in the future. A shift will likely occur from deployments and operations to exercises and contingencies, requiring careful management, both politically and militarily.

The transition is made more complex by three interrelated issues. Firstly, financial pressure on defence budgets may widen an intra-European gap, with only a small number of European Allies able to acquire modern deployable capabilities. France, Germany and the UK account for more than 50% of non-US defence spending in the Alliance. Secondly, the transatlantic gap continues to grow. In 2012, European NATO members' defence spending was, in real terms, about 11% lower than in 2006. While this problem will be somewhat mitigated by planned significant decreases in US defence spending over the coming decade, the US has initiated a shift towards the Asia-Pacific region which will reduce its willingness to carry a disproportionate share of the burden in NATO. Thirdly, while defence spending in the West is on a downward trajectory, it continues to grow in other regions of the world, notably in Asia. As the IISS *Military Balance 2013* showed, Asian defence spending overtook that of NATO European states in 2012 for the first time.

To help manage future challenges, NATO has developed the 'NATO Forces 2020' concept, which includes elements of its 'Smart Defence' project and the Connected Forces Initiative (CFI). As Rasmussen outlined in his annual report, released in January 2013, 'the objective [of

NATO Forces 2020] is to have a coherent set of deployable, interoperable and sustainable forces that are equipped, trained, exercised and commanded so as to be able to meet the targets the Alliance has set itself. These Allied forces should be able to operate together, and with partners, in any environment.' Smart Defence, with its principles of prioritisation, cooperation and specialisation, will be a core component (see *Strategic Survey 2012*, pp. 155–157). At the 2012 Chicago Summit, NATO heads of state and government agreed an initial package of 22 projects covering, for example, the pooling of maritime patrol aircraft and improving the availability of precision weapons. Each project will be taken forward by a volunteering lead nation and the list of active projects is slowly growing as proposals in a pool of some 150 potential projects develop.

The track record so far suggests that NATO member states will continue to focus on projects in the areas of support and logistics or training and education, as these are considered less politically sensitive. Two out of three Smart Defence projects currently under way fall into these categories. Smart Defence also provides an opportunity for European Allies to address the transatlantic gap in capabilities. Two-thirds of the projects under way have a European lead nation and one-third of the projects have no North American involvement.

CFI, an endeavour introduced by the secretary-general in 2012, is gaining traction as plans for its implementation develop. The goal is to maintain the level of inter-operability already achieved among NATO militaries on operations, but in the context of a much-reduced operational tempo. Attempts to revitalise the NATO Response Force and a renewed focus on high-visibility live exercises will play a key part in CFI implementation. Thus in the post-ISAF environment, CFI is likely to concentrate on combat effectiveness, in particular by focusing on training and exercises.

NATO's deployment of six *Patriot* missile batteries to Turkey's border with Syria, underlined that NATO cannot afford to simply prepare for the missions that are most likely. Yet Allies cannot prepare for everything, because doing so would be too expensive. It is likely then that the post-Afghanistan transition will not only see a sustained effort in terms of closer defence cooperation among EU and NATO member states, but will also trigger renewed discussion about the appropriate levels of ambition and the division of labour between the two organisations.

Turkey: Contentious Transition

Turkey's political and cultural life was in transition at mid-2013. After ten years in power, the ruling Justice and Development Party (AKP) continued to dismantle the secular, Western-oriented state created by Mustafa Kemal Ataturk, who founded the modern republic from the ruins of the Ottoman Empire in 1923. In its place, the AKP was crafting a more conservative society, shaped by Islamic values and traditions. Though mindful of the need to maintain good relations with its traditional allies in the West, Turkey now looked primarily to its own region and to other Muslim countries in the Middle East and North Africa. This shift, viewed by many in the AKP as a return to the country's roots, was accompanied by a wave of Ottoman nostalgia, evident in political decision-making as well as in Turkish film, television and fashion.

There was talk, too, of change in the political system. Prime Minister Recep Tayyip Erdogan was known to be preparing his candidacy for the presidential elections in summer 2014. The presidency is considered a ceremonial office, but Erdogan made no secret of his desire to introduce a new constitution and replace Turkey's parliamentary system with a presidential one, with increased powers for the president. Indeed, through 2012 and into 2013, many government policies seemed to be designed, directly or indirectly, to serve Erdogan's presidential ambitions, including his efforts to end the 29-year-old Kurdish insurgency.

Among Erdogan's initiatives was a series of ambitious infrastructure projects, including the redevelopment of the Taksim Square area of Istanbul and neighbouring Gezi Park. A police raid on 31 May 2013 on a makeshift camp set up by environmentalists in the park triggered mass protests that indicated popular disquiet at Erdogan's growing authoritarianism. The prime minister refused to accept that the protests could be caused by his policies, and blamed them on a Western conspiracy.

The Syrian imbroglio

Erdogan's dreams of making Turkey a more powerful and influential regional actor appeared in disarray, and nowhere was this more evident than in the Syrian conflict. In November 2011, when Erdogan first publicly called on Syrian President Bashar al-Assad to step down, he had expected the Syrian civil war to be relatively brief. He sought to position Turkey as the leading supporter of the coalition of forces fighting Assad, opening its border to refugees and serving as a conduit for supplies of arms, mostly bought with Qatari and Saudi Arabian funds, to the rebels. Erdogan's expectation was that the predominantly Alawite regime in Damascus would soon be replaced by a Sunni-led government that would look to Turkey for leadership, and that Turkey would be able to take some of the credit for the fall of Assad and boost its claim to regional prominence.

As the civil war continued, Turkish frustration began to mount. On 22 June 2012, Syria's air defences shot down a Turkish F-4E *Phantom* reconnaissance aircraft, which it claimed had violated Syrian airspace. Turkey denied this and vowed retribution, but then merely increased its military presence along the Syrian border. However, after a shell from Syria killed five civilians in the Turkish border town of Akcakale on 5 October 2012, Turkish artillery retaliated by targeting Assad's forces inside Syria. There were further sporadic clashes through the rest of October and into November 2012.

The war resulted in a steady flow of refugees into Turkey. By May 2013, 195,000 Syrian refugees – up from 20,000 in mid-2012 – were being housed in 17 camps inside Turkey. Another 100,000 refugees were scattered through towns and cities close to the border, causing friction with the local population.

After a car bomb in February 2013 at the Cilvegozu border gate killed 14 people, twin car bombs in the border town of Reyhanli killed 46 Turks and five Syrians on 11 May. The identity of the perpetrators was unclear, but Ankara blamed Assad. The local population in Reyhanli staged a series of angry demonstrations against the government for pursuing policies that brought Syria's violence into their community. The bombings prompted a renewal of Turkish calls for international military support.

Sectarian sympathies

In mid-2013, the Syrian civil war appeared both to have deepened the sectarian fault lines in the Middle East and to have sharpened the AKP's own sectarian focus, pitting Turkey against not just Assad but also Iran, the Shia-dominated Iraqi central government in Baghdad and the Lebanese Hizbullah. Public statements by Turkish government officials condemning Assad started to include regular references to his Alawite beliefs. Erdogan even accused members of Turkey's own Alevi minority, who constitute around 10% of the Turkish population and hold similar beliefs to the Alawites of Syria, of sympathising with the Assad regime.

A sense of sectarian solidarity facilitated the growing rapprochement between Ankara and the Sunni-dominated Kurdistan Regional Government (KRG) in northern Iraq. After the 2003 Iraq War, Turkey had avoided direct contact with the KRG for fear that acknowledging it would encourage Turkey's own restive Kurds to push for autonomy. However, starting in 2007, estrangement had begun to give way to engagement, particularly through strengthening economic ties. By mid-2013, despite its relatively small size, the KRG had become Turkey's second-largest export market after Germany, and Turkish firms accounted for over half of all the foreign companies active in northern Iraq.

The two sides had also begun to explore ways of reinforcing the relationship through closer energy ties. The KRG was negotiating with foreign energy companies for licence deals for the extraction of oil and natural gas in northern Iraq, despite furious protests from Baghdad that the KRG was usurping the central government's prerogatives. The KRG also started meetings with Turkish officials to discuss exporting oil and gas via Turkey to international markets. The resulting tensions peaked in December 2012 when the government in Baghdad prevented Turkish Energy Minister Taner Yildiz from attending an energy conference in Arbil, the KRG capital, by refusing to allow his plane to enter Iraqi airspace. In January 2013, Genel Energy, which is listed on the London Stock Exchange but headquartered in Ankara, announced that it had begun to export small quantities of oil from the KRG via the Turkish Mediterranean port of Mersin.

Relations with the West: flexible or fraying?

Ankara's Middle East focus meant that its policies towards the region began to play a larger role in shaping its relations with traditional allies in the West, particularly the United States. As a result, its ties with the West seemed at times to wear dangerously thin, while at others Ankara favoured cooperation.

Turkey's cultivation of closer economic and political ties with the KRG alarmed Washington as much as it did the Iraqi government in Baghdad. The United States repeatedly pressed Turkey not to allow the relationship to develop into a strategic partnership, which could encourage the KRG to push for full independence and trigger the break-up of Iraq. But Turkey remained defiant, arguing that it needed to diversify its energy supplies, particularly given that US pressure had forced it to reduce its oil imports from Iran. Some Turkish officials even argued that the breakup of Iraq would increase the KRG's dependence on Ankara, which would eventually bring it into a Turkish sphere of influence.

The impact of the civil war in Syria was more complex. Turkey and the United States agreed that Assad must step down, but disagreed on how to achieve this. Turkish officials frequently expressed their frustration at Washington's reluctance to become militarily involved in the conflict, either by supplying arms to the rebels or by supporting Ankara's calls for the establishment of a no-fly zone over northern Syria and the creation of a safe haven in Syria for refugees. In turn, the United States complained that Turkey was failing to stem the flow of militant Islamists into the rebel forces fighting to overthrow Assad, and allowing organisations such as Jabhat al-Nusra, which in April 2013 publicly pledged allegiance to al-Qaeda in Iraq, to operate openly in areas along the Turkish–Syrian border. Turkey's refusal to act on US concerns and clamp down on the activities of such groups made Washington more wary of supplying the rebels with arms, lest they found their way into the hands of militant Islamists.

Despite its aspirations for regional pre-eminence, Turkey baulked at intervening in Syria on its own. Significantly, although the government's rhetoric distanced Turkey from the West, when it felt that its security was threatened it turned to its NATO Allies for assistance. In June 2012, four days after the Turkish F-4E *Phantom* was shot down, Turkey invoked

Article 4 of the North Atlantic Treaty to call a meeting in Brussels in the hope of securing a condemnation of Syria's actions. In November, amid growing concerns in Ankara about border security, Turkey formally asked NATO for the deployment of additional air defences. NATO approved the request, and by February 2013 six *Patriot* missile batteries, operated by Dutch, German and US personnel, were operational.

Stalled EU accession

By May 2013, Turkey's EU accession process seemed to have stalled. Three years had passed since any new chapters in the process had been opened, and although the EU and Turkey continued to issue statements reaffirming their commitment to Turkish membership, the prospect seemed to be fading. In early 2013, opinion polls suggested that less than 30% of Turks still supported joining the EU, down from 75% in 2004.

In July 2012, Turkey suspended all contacts with the EU for the six months of the presidency of the Republic of Cyprus. Privately, AKP officials admitted that they were no longer interested in membership and saw Turkey's future in the Middle East. But they were reluctant to withdraw from the process, not least for fear that such a move would send a negative signal to the international financial community at a time when the Turkish economy was still heavily dependent on foreign funding.

The waning of Turkey's enthusiasm for the EU reduced the incentive to break the long-running impasse over Cyprus, which has been divided on ethnic lines since 1974. The Turkish Cypriots withdrew from UN-brokered reunification negotiations when Cyprus assumed the rotating EU presidency for the second half of 2012, arguing that it gave the Greek Cypriots an unfair advantage. Talks were expected to resume in March 2013, after Cyprus had handed over the EU presidency to Ireland and had held its own presidential elections. However, the deepening of the financial crisis in Cyprus in early 2013 postponed the negotiations again, this time at the behest of the Greek Cypriots. At mid-2013, talks were expected to resume in October.

There were also concerns that Cyprus' plans to exploit undersea natural gas fields off its southern coast – even more crucial after the financial collapse of early 2013 – could escalate tensions with Turkey, which insisted that the breakaway Turkish Republic of Northern Cyprus

(TRNC) also had rights to the reserves. The stand-off threatened further deterioration in Turkey's already troubled relationship with Israel, which had plans to develop natural gas fields off its own coast and was exploring possible cooperation with Cyprus. In March 2013, Israel issued a formal apology to Turkey and offered to pay compensation for the deaths of nine Turks who had been killed in an Israeli commando raid on a Gaza-bound aid flotilla in May 2010. However, even without possible tensions over natural gas, there appeared little prospect of Israel's apology leading to a rapprochement. Ankara remained almost instinctively hostile to Israel. Perhaps more critically, because Erdogan has frequently used his willingness to criticise Israel as a way of enhancing Turkey's credibility in the Middle East, a thaw in relations could be regarded as damaging to Turkey's regional ambitions.

Conservative authoritarianism

Coinciding with a period of sustained economic growth, Erdogan's bold visions for Turkey's future and his willingness to assert himself on the global stage generated pride in being Turkish which even his political opponents expressed. But he remained a polarising figure: while his supporters lauded his boldness, there was growing alarm among his detractors at his authoritarian bent, particularly his ambitions to introduce a presidential system and succeed Abdullah Gul as president in August 2014.

Erdogan exercised more political power than any Turkish politician in decades. He extended his mandate into Turkey's cultural life, and increasingly appeared to regard himself as the arbiter of public taste. In November 2012 the producers of a popular television series set in the Ottoman period were forced to change its script and costumes after Erdogan publicly complained that it neglected the era's military conquests in favour of palace intrigues. In April 2013, without consultation he pronounced *ayran,* or buttermilk, Turkey's 'national drink'.

In September 2012, Erdogan introduced comprehensive educational reforms, lowering the age of entry for Sunni Islamic religious training schools and increasing compulsory lessons in Koranic studies throughout the education system. The protests of Turkey's Alevi minority were ignored, and there were alarming signs of a decreasing tolerance for opposition. By mid-2013, more than 60 journalists were in prison and many more had been dismissed by their editors under pressure from the government. Access to over 20,000 websites had been blocked by court orders on the grounds that they were incompatible with national values.

Concerns about the politicisation of the judicial system were reinforced in September 2012 when 331 serving and retired military personnel were sentenced to lengthy jail terms on charges that they had plotted to stage a coup in 2003. The evidence against them was based solely on digital documents on a single CD, which prosecutors claim had been last saved on 5 March 2003, even though forensic analysis showed that the documents had all been written using Microsoft Office 2007. In mid-2013, over 700 other suspected government opponents and critics were being tried in other highly politicised cases. More than 50 of the defendants had already spent more than five years in prison awaiting the completion of their trial.

At the end of May 2013, a violent police crackdown on a protest by a small group of environmentalists against the construction a new shopping mall in Istanbul's Gezi Park triggered a wave of demonstrations across the country, with hundreds of thousands of people taking to the streets in a spontaneous eruption of frustration and resentment at what was seen as Erdogan's growing authoritarianism and didactic conservatism. Erdogan responded by organising mass rallies of his supporters, claiming that the anti-government protests were being orchestrated by what he described as foreign dark forces desperate to halt Turkey's rise to greatness under his leadership. The protests were leaderless and mostly involved young members of Turkey's previously apolitical middle class. By late June 2013, they had begun to evolve and diversify into individual acts of civil disobedience as well as mass confrontations with the police. Although Erdogan continued to vow to crush the protests through the use of force, they retained considerable momentum and Turkey appeared set for a period of sustained political instability.

Kurdish insurgency: peace at last?

In July 2012, the military Kurdistan Workers' Party (PKK) stepped up its armed campaign for greater political and cultural rights for Turkey's

Kurds. The PKK not only increased its attacks against the Turkish security forces but, for the first time since the early 1990s, sought to hold territory. By mid-August 2012, the PKK had asserted its authority over large swathes of the mountainous district of Semdinli close to Turkey's border with Iraq. By October 2012, when the first winter snows put an end to the campaigning season, the Turkish military had reduced the area under PKK control and inflicted heavy casualties. Nevertheless, the PKK had demonstrated the limitations of the state's authority and vowed to return to the offensive in the spring.

Erdogan was mindful that a successful 2014 presidential campaign would depend on his record as prime minister and that a repeat of 2012, during which more than 500 people were killed in PKK-related violence, would be regarded as a serious failure. He risked losing votes from Turkish nationalists for not eradicating the PKK, and from liberals and Kurds for not addressing the issue of Kurdish rights that was fuelling the insurgency. Thus, in December 2012, he instructed members of the Turkish National Intelligence Organization (MIT) to begin a dialogue with Abdullah Ocalan, a prominent PKK leader who had been incarcerated since 1999 but still enjoyed iconic status amongst Kurdish nationalists.

In March 2013, Ocalan called on the PKK to announce a ceasefire while he negotiated with MIT, and in May 2013 the PKK began withdrawing its units in Turkey to its main bases in northern Iraq, a process that was expected to last for several months.

At mid-2013, the negotiations remained opaque. But Erdogan appeared unlikely to accede to the main PKK demands, such as full political and cultural rights and a large measure of autonomy for predominantly Kurdish areas. Instead, he seemed likely to extend the negotiating process through the summer, which would make it impossible for the PKK to re-infiltrate its militants into Turkey and resume its insurgency before the end of the 2013 campaigning season. It was unclear what concessions he would eventually offer. But if they were insufficient to persuade the PKK to abandon its insurgency, Erdogan would still be able to go into the presidential election campaign claiming that he had tried to resolve the issue peacefully, without the potential repercussions of a Turkish nationalist backlash over any concessions that he might have made.

A power struggle at home, uncertainty abroad

The main opposition parties in the Turkish parliament remained weak. As Erdogan pushed ahead with his presidential ambitions, the main opposition came not from secularists, but from within the Turkish Islamist movement in which he had begun his political career. Gul, a former foreign minister in Erdogan's first government and a founding member of the AKP, had already made it clear that he was reluctant to relinquish the presidency in 2014 unless the current system was maintained. This would allow him to re-enter parliament and form a new government as prime minister. Yet the rivalry between Erdogan and Gul was about power rather than ideology. Although Gul appeared less authoritarian and more tolerant than Erdogan, they shared a similar conservative social agenda. As a result, although the outcome of the growing power struggle between the two men – which appeared likely to be the dominant feature of Turkish domestic politics in the coming months – remained unclear, it appeared unlikely to reverse the increasingly conservative nature of Turkish society, and the growing emphasis on Islamic values.

Of more immediate concern was the possible impact of Erdogan's presidential ambitions on Turkey's policies towards Syria. For a politician who owed much of his popular appeal to his bold rhetoric and efforts to transform Turkey into a regional power, Assad's continued defiance of Erdogan's calls for him to step down was a humiliating demonstration of Turkey's limits on the regional stage, which he feared would damage his presidential prospects.

Although a full-scale Turkish military intervention in Syria appeared unlikely, it was possible that, if Assad remained in power in autumn 2013, Erdogan would seek to raise tensions to the point where the international community would be forced to intervene. But there was no sign that Erdogan had formulated a policy to deal with what – regardless of Assad's fate – appeared likely to be a sustained period of uncertainty and instability along Turkey's southern border.

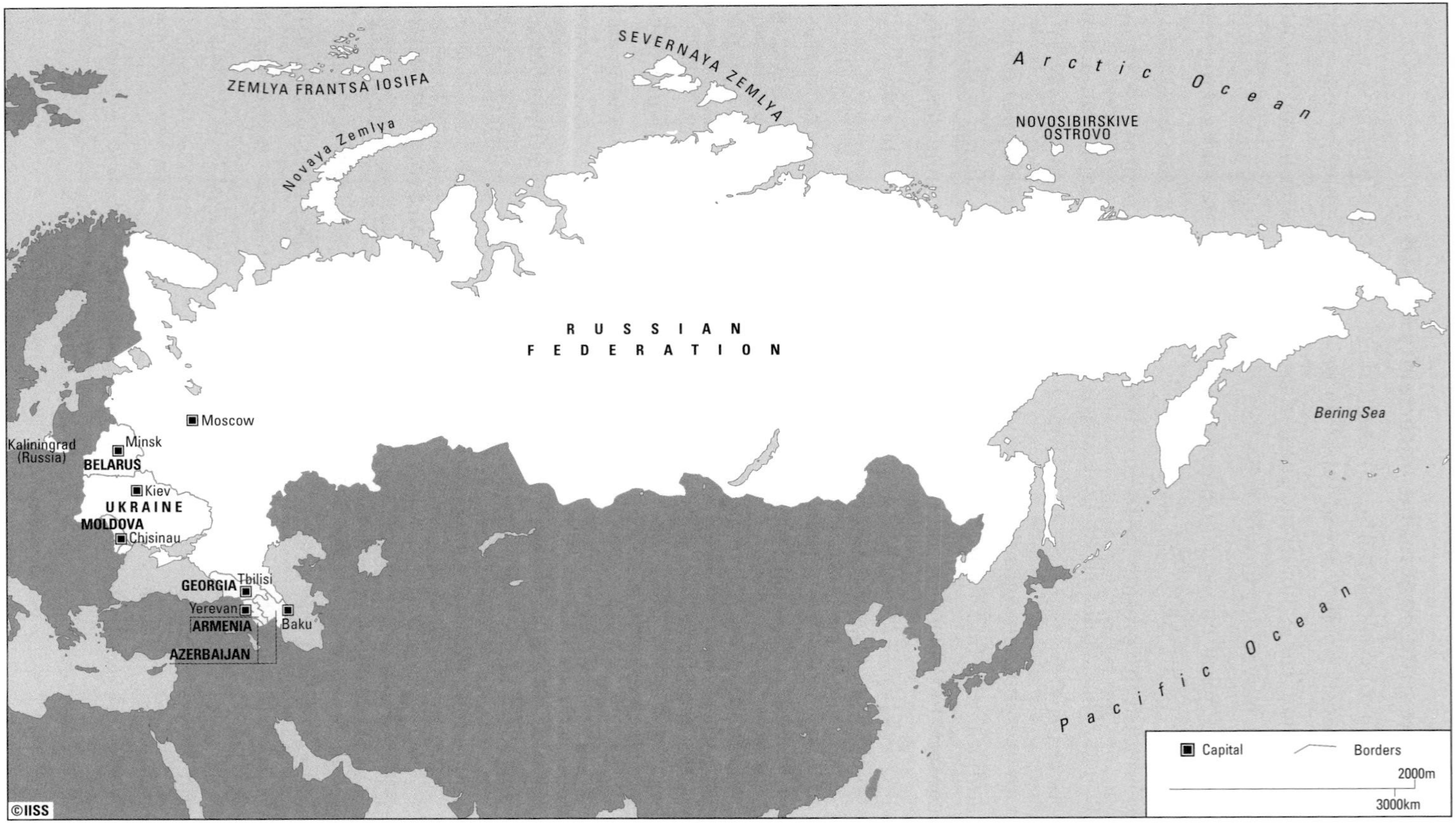
ZEMLYA FRANTSA IOSIFA
SEVERNAYA ZEMLYA
Arctic Ocean
NOVOSIBIRSKIVE OSTROVO
Novaya Zemlya
RUSSIAN FEDERATION
Moscow
Kaliningrad (Russia)
Minsk
BELARUS
Kiev
UKRAINE
MOLDOVA
Chisinau
GEORGIA
Tbilisi
Yerevan
ARMENIA
Baku
AZERBAIJAN
Bering Sea
Pacific Ocean
Capital
Borders
2000m
3000km
©IISS

Chapter 5

Russia and Eurasia

Russia's Rising Conservatism

Russia's political turbulence continued unabated in the year to mid-2013, as Vladimir Putin embarked on his third presidential term. Although Putin has come to personify conservation of the past, there has already been significant change. After making some liberalising concessions to the opposition, the government took a range of reactionary steps to neutralise the threat represented by the wave of protests that had begun in late 2011. Though these moves succeeded in blunting the momentum of the organised opposition, it appeared that the previous social contract between middle-class Russians and those who governed them – the former got prosperity, the latter, a free hand – had been irrevocably breached.

Putin sought to re-establish a contract on similar terms. However, the politically awakened middle class was no longer interested in such an arrangement. Some kept up organised opposition to the government, on the street, online and in local elections. Others, including some of Russia's most talented rising professionals, such as Sergei Guriev, prominent economist and rector of the New Economic School, left the country. Many went into 'internal emigration' – a neologism that seemed to imply withdrawal from public life. It was unclear how wide the chasm between the government and such a key elite group could grow before the sustainability of the political system was called into question.

Increasingly, signs emerged that Putin could not, in any case, sustain his end of the contract. Russia's GDP was projected to grow at or just below 3% in 2013 – not bad by comparison with the crisis-ridden West, but nowhere near Russia's pre-2008 growth rates. Meanwhile, the new deal Putin struck with his core electorate – pensioners, state officials, government-salaried workers – in the form of promised increased total budgetary outlays amounting to 1.5% of GDP by 2018 could pose a medium- to long-term threat to Russia's macroeconomic stability.

Putin's return

This budgetary largesse – something Putin and his team had previously avoided – was one of several steps taken in reaction to the tectonic shift that has been taking place in Russian politics. Over the previous 18–24 months, the foundational pillar of the political system Putin constructed – consistently very high levels of popular support for the leadership – had begun to crumble. Some analysts, particularly Mikhail Dmitriev and his colleagues at the Centre for Strategic Research, had seen the trend in focus groups as early as three years ago, but the problem only became obvious when Putin announced in September 2011 that he had decided to run for the presidency for a third term, replacing his one-term successor and protégé, Dmitry Medvedev, whom Putin in turn appointed prime minister. This was dubbed by Russians a *rokirovka,* the castling move in chess.

That decision marked the personalisation of Russian politics, and, correspondingly, the further weakening of Russia's post-Soviet political institutions. For many in the urban middle class, Putin's return, and the way in which it was announced and implemented, undermined the legitimacy of the entire political system. These Russians thought of themselves as Europeans, not as subjects of a personalised kleptocracy, and the *rokirovka* seemed to be leading to precisely that. To them, Medvedev's presidency had represented the possibility of evolutionary change in the system.

The *rokirovka* was intended to boost political stability; Putin was said to be convinced that Medvedev could not command the respect of all the key elite groups. But instead, his return had the opposite effect. It transformed the so-called Putin majority – a coalition of middle-class, economically dynamic Russians, on the one hand, and government employees, state beneficiaries such as pensioners, and rural heartland voters on the other – into a narrower, more reactionary political base consisting only of the latter. Putin's approval ratings dropped consistently as the year progressed, plateauing at about 60%, well below the peak of 79% reached in the period after the 2008 global financial crisis.

Assisted by his domestic security chiefs and political strategists – particularly Investigative Committee head Aleksandr Bastrykhin and hardline Kremlin Deputy Chief of Staff Vyacheslav Volodin – Putin responded with a more divisive approach, mobilising his core supporters with a new conservative identity politics. During and after the campaign, Putin mocked protesters as spoiled, rich cosmopolitans who took their marching orders from the US State Department. In May 2012, he rewarded a tank-factory foreman who had offered to round up his workers, head to Moscow and break up the protests by appointing him as special envoy to the Urals, a powerful post. 'People's brigades', which included Cossack groups and were empowered to patrol neighbourhoods, raided edgy art exhibitions and plays. They often claimed to act in the name of the Russian Orthodox Church, which gained significant attention after Patriarch Kirill I firmly allied it with Putin and the authorities. In June, the Duma, the lower house of parliament, approved a bill outlawing the promotion of 'homosexual propaganda' among minors with a vote of 436 to nil. Violations of the new law were punishable by fines of around $150 for private individuals, $1,600 for officials and $30,000 for businesses and schools.

Putin vocally supported a new nationalism. In September 2012, he chaired a meeting that started a drive for 'patriotic education', remarking that the struggle over 'cultural identity, spiritual and moral values, and moral codes … [is] at least one of the forms of competitive battles that many countries encounter, just like the battle for mineral resources. Distortion of the national, historic and moral consciousness more than once led the whole state to weakness, collapse and loss of sovereignty.' In contrast to his first two presidential terms, during which he often spoke of Russia's European identity, Putin regularly highlighted the alleged cultural distinctness of Russia from Europe, particularly regarding issues such as gay marriage.

The government also launched a comprehensive effort to marginalise its opponents and discourage the middle class from participating in public life. In June 2012, a new law was enacted that made participating in illegal protests (those that did not have a permit from local authorities) a felony punishable by heavy fines. The definition of treason was also changed to include any behaviour the authorities deemed to have undermined 'the constitutional system, sovereignty, and territorial integrity'. The media came under increased pressure, including through a new law that once again outlawed slander, just two years after Medvedev had decriminalised it.

In July, Putin signed into law a new requirement for NGOs that were engaged in 'political activity' and received funding from non-Russian sources to register as 'foreign agents' and to comply with a host of new oversight measures. This term is perhaps even more loaded in Russian than it is in English, implying a clear connection to intelligence and espionage. However, Putin and other senior officials claimed it was chosen to mirror the United States' 1938 Foreign Agents Registration Act and the new rules were defended with reference to the American statute. Beyond the title, this analogy was at best questionable; the US law applied to organisations that acted as 'agent of a foreign principal' and worked on behalf of that foreign principal. The Russian law, in contrast, used only the source of funding to classify 'foreign agents'. As of mid-2013, it had been applied to several prominent international NGOs, including the election monitor Golos, the independent polling organisation the Levada Center and the human-rights group Memorial, Russia's oldest and most respected body of this kind. All three organisations appealed the designation in court, stating that they would close their operations in the country rather than accept the label.

There have been similar periods in which the government increased pressure on NGOs, particularly those with foreign ties, since Putin first took office in 2000. But there was a consensus that this time was different. The authorities seemed determined to assert much greater control over public life and either eliminate or discredit those groups that refused to be controlled. Despite outrage from Western governments, Russian opposition figures and international NGOs, this effort was supported within Russia. In an April 2013 nationwide poll – ironically, one conducted by the Levada Center – 66% of respondents believed that Russian NGOs which defend civil rights and criticise the government should not be allowed to receive foreign funding; 52% said they were unaware of the ongoing raids on Russian NGOs by authorities under the new law and only 19% of respondents believed that NGOs generally played a positive role in society.

Lawmakers from the 'systemic' opposition parties (those represented in the Duma) who allied themselves with the protest movement also came under fire. Gennady Gudkov, an MP from the Just Russia party and former KGB officer, was expelled from the Duma, nominally on ethical grounds. His son Dmitry, also an MP from the party, was censured for having publicly criticised Putin's government while in Washington. The Investigative Committee launched a criminal inquiry into Ilya Ponomarev, another prominent Just Russia MP with connections to the protests, for allegedly embezzling funds from the Skolkovo Innovation Centre.

Co-opting the protesters' narrative

Russia's rampant corruption was often a rallying point of the mass protests in 2011–12. The World Economic Forum, in its 2012 global competitiveness survey, found that the country fell towards the bottom of international rankings in terms of property rights, judicial independence, bribery and reliability of government and police services. Indeed, opposition leader Alexei Navalny became Russia's most prominent anti-corruption activist through muckraking investigations that exposed the machinations of government officials. As well as taking active measures against Navalny and others, the government attempted to undermine the protesters' narrative through a purported anti-corruption drive of its own.

The drive began with the sensational firing of Defence Minister Anatoly Serdyukov in November 2012, following the initiation of a criminal case against one of his top deputies. The case centred on Oboronservis, a contractor that was created in 2008 to handle real-estate sales and transactions for the Ministry of Defence. Top Oboronservis employees were alleged by investigators to have undervalued the ministry's holdings, sold this property to Oboronservis-linked companies and embezzled the profits. In late October 2012, investigators raided the apartment of Yevgeniya Vasilieva, the director of the ministry's financial department, who had been appointed by Serdyukov and was responsible for the Oboronservis contract. Russian television widely reported Serdyukov's presence at Vasilieva's home during the early morning raid, creating an impression of a strong link between him and the alleged corruption. It also meant that Serdyukov had publicly disgraced his wife Yulia, the daughter of Viktor Zubkov, a member of Putin's inner circle, chairman of the energy company Gazprom and a former prime minister.

The defence minister's firing was quickly followed by more corruption investigations. Roman Panov, prime minister of Perm region, was arrested on suspicion of embezzling over $3 million from an Asia-Pacific Economic Cooperation (APEC) forum fund. An investigation was opened into contractors used by Elena Skrynnik, the former minister of agriculture. Officials involved in the 2014 Winter Olympics, to be held in Sochi, were also pursued on graft allegations.

In reaction to the Sergei Magnitsky Rule of Law Accountability Act, passed by the US Congress in 2012 to sanction Russian officials suspected of corruption, and revelations about senior government officials' foreign assets by bloggers, Putin proposed several measures intended to 'nationalise' the elite. The government enacted a law banning officials and their immediate families from owning foreign assets and compelling them to report their income and spending in greater detail. Much like Serdyukov's firing, these steps allowed the government to co-opt the opposition's anti-corruption narrative. The three state-run nationwide television stations amplified the effect of the arrests, with pro-government talk-show hosts excoriating the accused. Opposition leaders lacked access to these stations, which dominate the media landscape in Russia, and therefore had only a fraction of the government's media reach. Putin thus reinforced his support base by distancing himself from the corruption that Russians see as pervasive.

Show trials

Several highly publicised trials typified the Kremlin's new political strategy. The first of these stemmed from the filming of a music video by punk performance group Pussy Riot at Moscow's Christ the Saviour

Cathedral in February 2012. Instead of fining the three women for trespassing, the authorities charged them with hooliganism and inciting religious hatred. After a trial in which the prosecutor invoked a fourth-century Orthodox church ruling, they were sentenced to two years in prison in August 2012. (One of the group members, who was not present at the performance, was released the following October.) The lyrics of the song were harshly critical of both Putin and Kirill, and the Western media saw the trial as an attack on free speech. In fact, it was a demonstration of the authorities' solidarity with the church and with the conservative values of Russia's rural heartland.

Whereas the Pussy Riot trial furthered the government's new identity politics, the trial of Navalny, who led the protest movement, was clearly intended to undermine his image and make him seem no different to the government he so often critiqued. Navalny was charged with embezzlement and fraud in a case that dated from 2009, when he served as an unpaid adviser to the governor of the Kirov region. After he cooperated with investigators, the original charges were dropped in 2011, only to be reinstated in June 2012. Navalny was accused of planning the embezzlement of around $490,000 from the Kirov budget.

Opposition activists, including Navalny himself, accused the government of carrying out a political vendetta; the charges came at a time when he had established himself as the leader of the opposition's Coordinating Council. Navalny used the Internet to plead his case, posting all the court documents and prosecutor's statements online. The charges could carry a ten-year sentence if Navalny is convicted, but even a suspended sentence would prevent him from running for office – although Moscow Mayor Sergei Sobyanin's last-minute decision to call elections for autumn 2013 allowed Navalny to attempt to register as a candidate for that office before any verdict was handed down.

A third trial, which began in 2013, related to the events of 6 May 2012. On the night before Putin's third inauguration, an estimated 20,000 protesters congregated in Bolotnaya Square, in what was called the 'March of Millions'. They were met by underprepared riot police, and violent clashes began when unidentified individuals attempted to access the square after police had cordoned it off, along with the surrounding metro stations. Dozens of protesters were injured and over 400 were detained, including Navalny and Sergei Udaltsov, another opposition leader. They were both imprisoned for 15 days for taking part in an unauthorised demonstration and for failing to follow police orders.

The Investigative Committee began a wide-ranging inquiry into the violence and made dozens of arrests under articles of the criminal code barring organised mass disturbances. On 22 May 2013, 12 people were indicted for inciting the riots, including youth opposition leader Alexei Gaskarov. More opposition activists – possibly as many as 86 – were expected to be indicted in the following months. Whereas such activists had previously been fined or charged with misdemeanours, they now faced criminal charges that could lead to 13-year jail sentences.

Selective liberalisation

Along with these repressive moves, the authorities made a number of concessions following the protests that provided new avenues for opposition participation in politics. Though important, they were done in such a way as to ensure that they did not pose a threat to the status quo.

A law signed by Medvedev in May 2012 restored gubernatorial elections and ended the system of presidential appointments established in 2004. The first elections were held in five regions in October 2012. However, the new rules allowed the authorities to screen candidates, which often ruled out or deterred strong opposition contenders. Pro-Kremlin incumbents from ruling party United Russia won all five elections. The party also won the vast majority of the municipal and regional elections held the same day.

Medvedev also signed into law provisions drastically liberalising the requirements for registration of political parties. Dozens of new parties were registered, including opposition groups. However, this had the effect of further weakening the government's opponents by facilitating their long-standing aversion to working together.

Under the same banner of liberalising concessions to the opposition, the government passed a bill reverting the electoral system of the Duma to that used in the 1995, 1999 and 2003 elections. Under the older system, half of the Duma's 450 seats were allocated on a proportional basis using party lists, and the other half were assigned to single-mandate districts. In contrast, the post-2003 system used only proportional representation based on lists of parties that received at least 7% of the vote. At the time, the change was justified by the need to strengthen the major parties, particularly United Russia. Many alleged that the latest change was a ploy to compensate for United Russia's declining popularity and ensure de facto pro-government majorities, as it enabled non-partisan loyalist candidates to win districts in which its support was weak.

Putin's imperfect recovery

Putin was able to contain threats to the political system he led, mobilise his core supporters and stabilise his approval rating at around 60%. But his political standing was clearly weakened: 41% of Russians did not want Putin to run for president when his term ends in 2018, whereas only 28% did. Approval ratings of the ruling United Russia party fell from 34% to 24% between July 2012 and May 2013. However, the number of Russians who said they would refuse to vote in future parliamentary elections increased by around the same amount. This meant the authorities would need to rely on the apathy of ordinary Russians in the next round of national elections in 2015.

Although Putin was able to recover momentum in the short term and contain the immediate threat to his leadership, the *rokirovka* added an element of systemic uncertainty to Russian politics not seen in years. Intense coverage of Putin's alleged health troubles in late 2012, both in Russia and abroad, underscored the fragility of a system that relied on one man's authority and lacked robust institutions. In the long term, the political system will struggle to cope when the urban middle class and the government's priorities diverge so spectacularly. In the short term, elite discord reached levels not seen since the 2007–08 search for Putin's successor.

This tension led to the kind of 'elite splits' often seen as a feature of political transitions. In May 2013, for example, Putin issued an extraordinary public reprimand of the government for failing to implement his decrees, making a series of remarks that were widely covered by the Russian media. The next day, Deputy Prime Minister Vladislav Surkov resigned. He was the third leading cabinet official to leave Medvedev's year-old government. Surkov's departure was a remarkable development in that he had served as Putin's chief political strategist from the beginning of his presidency. Although his appointment as deputy prime minister when Medvedev and Putin swapped roles was seen as a demotion, Surkov had remained a central figure in Russian politics. Despite his reputation as the grey cardinal of Putin's Kremlin, Surkov was actually part of the liberal-technocratic wing of the governing elite. His departure represented another blow to the group, which took several other hits after Putin returned to the presidency – mostly to the benefit of the *Siloviki* (officials with law enforcement, military or intelligence backgrounds). Surkov did not, however, show any sign of joining the opposition, and it would be unwise to interpret any one change in personnel as a sign of systemic transformation.

Worsening US relations

High-profile disputes between Washington and Moscow, such as Russia's expulsion of the US Agency for International Development in autumn 2012 and a May 2013 televised arrest and subsequent expulsion of a US diplomat alleged to be a spy, marked a significant deterioration of the US–Russia relationship over the past year.

At the beginning of Putin's third presidential term, the negative effects of his return on US–Russia relations were indirect. At that point, Putin had not taken deliberate steps to worsen the relationship, and merely demonstrated no interest in investing in it. He signalled that relations with the United States were not one of his foreign-policy priorities in several ways, most noticeably by failing to attend the Camp David G8 meeting in May 2012. Although Putin's history of working with George W. Bush, especially after 9/11, showed that he was not ideologically opposed to US–Russia cooperation, the Russian president over time became fed up with certain aspects of US foreign policy. These included perceived meddling in Russian domestic politics and what he saw as Washington's habit of toppling sitting governments that disagreed with it. Accordingly, Putin displayed a clear intent to signal his frustration to Washington.

But if his return initially worsened only the atmosphere in bilateral relations, the steps he took towards the end of 2012 – particularly a ban on American adoptions of Russian children and his apparent sanctioning of the state media's virulent anti-Americanism – caused significant damage. Putin's actions to crack down on the opposition also dragged down the relationship. Under such circumstances, it becomes more complicated for any US administration to do business with Russia.

The decline in relations followed the most productive period of cooperation between the two countries since the Soviet Union's collapse. That 'reset', which ran from 2009–11, took its name from US Vice President Joe Biden's use of the term at the Munich Security Conference in February 2009. Key developments of that period included the landmark New START strategic arms reduction agreement; the 123 agreement on civil nuclear cooperation; accords regarding transit to Afghanistan, including the rail-based Northern Distribution Network and an overflight arrangement that, as of January 2013, allowed for over 2,500 US flights to cross Russian airspace, carrying over 460,000 US military personnel; and an amendment to the Plutonium Management Disposition Agreement that provided for the safe disposal of enough weapons-grade plutonium for 17,000 nuclear warheads. Moscow and Washington also closely cooperated on reining in Iran's nuclear ambitions, including through agreement on uniquely comprehensive sanctions at the UN Security Council, and Russia's cancellation of the sale of an S-300 air-defence system to Tehran. During the period, Russia was granted WTO membership – 18 years after its bid was launched – as a result of a significant bilateral push on trade issues. The two sides also came to a deal on facilitating visas that made it easier for Americans and Russians to visit, and do business in, each other's countries.

Cooperation also increased across a wide range of issues addressed by the 19 working groups of the Bilateral Presidential Commission, which was created in mid-2009 and covered issues such as counter-terrorism (including a summer 2010 joint exercise simulating a plane hijacking over the Bering Strait), global health, energy efficiency and counter-narcotics. Moscow also cooperated with Washington to provide helicopters for both the Afghan National Army and for peacekeeping in Sudan and the two sides took part in the first bilateral Antarctic inspections.

Commentators and policymakers in both the United States and Russia continued to use such achievements to gauge the strength of bilateral ties. But these often belied the underlying fragility of the relationship. When Washington and Moscow were not working towards specific goals, they had to reckon with several serious problems in the relationship. These resurfaced after the achievements of the reset period faded and new ones were not forthcoming.

The most corrosive problem remained the fact that elements within both countries' national security establishments still viewed each other as an adversary, almost 25 years after the end of the Cold War. Such attitudes were most clearly seen in the persistence of mutually assured destruction as the paradigm governing the US–Russia nuclear relationship. Mistrust created by the worst-case-scenario assumptions associated with this paradigm severely limited the scope for security dialogue. The lack of substantive cooperation between the countries' intelligence agencies regarding the suspects in the April 2013 bombing of the Boston marathon underscored the tragic consequences of this lack of trust.

The second problem was the yawning gap between reality and Washington's expectations for Russia's post-Soviet political development. Many countries with which the United States had important relationships, such as Saudi Arabia and China, had poor human-rights records and no democratic processes. But Russia's democratic shortcomings had a greater impact on its relations with the United States due to international commitments made by Moscow in the 1990s, particularly its membership of the OSCE and the Council of Europe. Joining these organisations created additional obligations to protect human rights and strengthen democratic institutions, and intensified oversight of Russia's progress in these areas. Washington's expectations were further raised by the 'transition' model of post-communist development that posited a smooth shift from the party-state to market democracy.

The third problem was rivalry in post-Soviet Eurasia. Some US discomfort with Russia's relationships in the region was certainly warranted as, since 1991, Moscow's actions had often been heavy-handed. But by the end of the 1990s, Washington's nightmare scenario of Russia's reintegrating the other former Soviet republics and forming a new anti-Western bloc had been avoided. The US aim of bolstering the sovereignty of these states at times turned into outright paranoia about any degree of Russian influence in the region. Many in Moscow were convinced that Washington's exclusive goal in the region was to contain Russia, and that it acted accordingly.

Although the reset did not address these fundamental problems, it was remarkable in that it demonstrated the capacity of the US–Russia relationship to achieve a large number of important global policy goals even without an attempt at reconciliation. The lack of such a reconciliation effort on Capitol Hill became clear in late 2012, when in a 'lame duck' session of Congress, both chambers voted overwhelmingly in favour of linking the Magnitsky legislation to a bill granting Russia permanent normal trade relations. Washington was compelled to grant Russia this status following its membership of the WTO, as failing to do so would have violated the organisation's rules, to the detriment of US businesses.

Magnitsky was a lawyer who died in pre-trial detention in a Moscow prison in November 2009 after uncovering a fraud allegedly perpetrated by the police and tax officials. The Magnitsky Act, which US President Barack Obama opposed but was in effect forced to sign because of Congress' actions, barred those allegedly responsible for Magnitsky's death and other human-rights abuses from entering the United States, seized their assets in US banks and compelled the State Department to publish a list of their names. The Russian reaction was swift. As well as publishing its own list of Americans barred entry to Russia, the Duma passed a law banning Americans from adopting Russian children and restricting the roles of US citizens working in Russian NGOs. The Russian list included Americans responsible for investigating and prosecuting Russian citizens in US courts, including the arms dealer Viktor Bout, and prominent officials in the George W. Bush administration who

Asia-Pacific Economic Cooperation (APEC) summit

Russia's extravagant hosting of the Asia-Pacific Economic Cooperation (APEC) summit in September 2012 was intended to demonstrate Russia's commitment to the Asia-Pacific region and the development of the Russian Far East. First Deputy Prime Minister Igor Shuvalov said $20.4 billion was spent on preparations for the event, including a facelift for the Pacific port city of Vladivostok, which gained new luxury hotels, a university and the world's longest cabled bridge from the city to the island on which the summit took place. At the meeting, Putin and other senior Russian officials declared Russia's focus on the Asia-Pacific region. However, the event did not match press reports of a 'Russian pivot'. Few agreements were signed. Moreover, the summit highlighted several of Russia's problems. Corruption allegations swirled around officials involved in the Vladivostok renewal projects and delegates complained of difficulty in procuring visas. Several infrastructure projects were not finished on time.

were involved in establishing and legally justifying post-9/11 detention practices.

Problems in the relationship intensified when the agenda shifted away from the familiar ground of strategic arms control to more divisive issues, particularly missile defence. Moscow and Washington had been fitfully trying – and failing – to find common ground on the issue since the late Reagan era. The fundamental problem remained the Soviet Union's, and latterly Russia's, insecurity about the effects of planned US missile-defence systems on their capacity to retaliate after a disarming first strike. In April 2013, Obama reportedly wrote a letter to Putin, delivered by US National Security Advisor Thomas Donilon, in another attempt to assuage these concerns through an offer of a legally binding transparency and missile-defence cooperation arrangement. Putin's response the next month reportedly left little hope for an agreement: Russia's position remained that it would not cooperate until Washington agreed to limit its missile-defence plans – through an accord similar to the Anti-Ballistic Missile Treaty, which Washington abrogated in 2001. Such an agreement was both strategically undesirable to the US defence establishment, which wanted to develop missile defence to hedge against proliferation in other countries, and politically unthinkable.

Despite the deterioration in relations, bilateral ties were still a far cry from their near-hostile state in late 2008. During the conflict in Georgia that August, the US National Security Council's Principals Committee, which includes the president, vice-president and other senior national security officials, reportedly considered using military force to prevent Russia from continuing its assault on Georgia. Such a conversation was far removed from more recent US–Russia relations, which featured 17 joint military exercises in 2012. And it seemed highly unlikely that there would be a return to the tensions of 2008 in Obama's second term. Key foreign-policy goals of the Obama administration required Russian cooperation, and Russia and the United States shared several security aims. The most prominent of these were Iran's nuclear programme and stabilising Afghanistan before the NATO withdrawal in 2014. At their meeting during the June 2012 G20 summit at Los Cabos, Mexico, both presidents also committed to boosting trade and investment, an initiative that would be to their mutual benefit. However, there was an acute divergence in approaches to dealing with the Syrian civil war.

For the Obama administration, advancing the nuclear agenda the president laid out in his April 2009 speech in Prague remained a priority. It was therefore likely that there would be a US offer regarding one or more of the three categories of nuclear weapons Obama referred to in a letter to the Senate following the ratification of New START: deployed strategic weapons, non-deployed strategic weapons and non-strategic nuclear weapons. In June 2013, Obama proposed that the two countries cut their deployed strategic arsenals by a third. Russia continued to make it clear that a resolution to the missile-defence dispute was essential for further reductions.

In any case, a new bilateral arms-control deal could be significantly harder to negotiate than New START, which itself was by no means easy, as the presidents reportedly had to resolve several issues themselves in direct talks. The expiration of START I in December 2009, which ended the mutual verification regime, had been a powerful incentive for both sides to reach a deal. With New START's verification regime being fully implemented, the Russians were at best lukewarm about another bilateral deal in the short term. However, such an agreement was not unimaginable, as moving from the New START limit of 1,550 deployed strategic warheads to 1,100 – the number implied in Obama's June 2013 speech in Berlin – would not require a major change in doctrines.

Moscow's Syrian position

Syria remained a bone of contention in Russia's relations with the United States, other Western nations and Gulf Arab countries. Russia suggested it would honour its contracts with Syria's government for sophisticated air- and sea-defence systems, and steadfastly refused to join in calls for the departure of President Bashar al-Assad. In April–May 2013, new US Secretary of State John Kerry sought to co-sponsor a US–Russia peace conference, but with small chance of success. Russia was unwilling to help resolve the crisis on terms that the West and the Syrian opposition could accept. Senior Russian officials often made this clear, even if some in the international community seemingly refused to believe them.

This apparent disbelief stemmed from a misunderstanding of the Russian position. The focus in the West was on the ties – including military, military-industrial, intelligence-sharing and cultural links – that supposedly bound Russia to Assad's Syria. A less noted but significant factor was Russian anxiety about Sunni Islamist governments displacing secular autocrats in Syria and other Arab countries following the Arab Spring. Russia borders several South Caucasian and Central Asian countries in which such a scenario could not be excluded. There are over 20m Russian Muslims, the majority of whom are Sunni and live in the regions of the North Caucasus where Russia has fought two civil wars and continues to battle the Caucasus Emirate, a group of armed extremists. Decision-makers in Moscow were quick to point out that this militant group and its predecessors were directly supported by entities in some of the Arab countries leading the call for Assad's removal.

While these factors played a role in Moscow's thinking regarding Syria, they did not explain Russian policy on international intervention in the crisis. The Kremlin's actions – including three UN Security Council vetoes – were taken not because of its interests in Syria, its fear of extremist spillover or because it backed Assad. In fact, Moscow persistently signalled that it cared nothing for Assad's fate. As early as the summer of 2011, Medvedev warned that, barring immediate reforms, 'a sad fate awaits [Assad]'.

Instead, the tragedy in Syria brought to the surface a fundamental divergence between Russia's approach to international intervention and that of much of the rest of the world, particularly the United States and the EU. Moscow did not believe the UN Security Council should implicitly or explicitly endorse the removal of a sitting government. Many in the Moscow foreign-policy establishment believed that the string of US-led interventions resulting in regime change since the end of the Cold War – Kosovo, Afghanistan, Iraq and Libya – were a threat to the stability of the international system and, potentially, to the Russian government itself. Russia did not let the Security Council give its imprimatur to such interventions if it suspected the motive was removal of a sitting government. Its regret for abstaining from the vote on UN Resolution 1973 authorising intervention in Libya underscored the point. NATO's implementation of the resolution irked Russian decision-makers not only because of the impact on the ground in Libya. It also convinced them that humanitarian intervention under the rubric of the Responsibility to Protect was an elaborate cover for regime change.

The notion that Russia could eventually be the target of such an intervention might seem absurd in the West but suspicion, bordering on paranoia, of US intentions runs deep in Moscow. Regarding Syria, Russia therefore used what power it had, particularly its permanent seat on the UN Security Council, to avoid creating a precedent that could eventually be used against it.

Moscow could not be convinced that US policy on Syria was purely driven by the humanitarian calamity that Assad created. Instead, it saw Washington as having the sinister motive of removing a government whose foreign policy had long contradicted US interests, particularly by aligning with Iran. So when Obama proclaimed that 'the time has come for President Assad to step aside' on 18 August 2011, thereby making regime change an official US aim, the opportunity to find common ground with Russia at the UN was lost. The fact that the proposed UN resolutions did not reflect this aim was irrelevant, given what Moscow saw as the United States' openly stated ultimate goal.

Energy shifts

Despite political turbulence and slowing GDP growth, Russia's macroeconomic balances were strong. Foreign-exchange reserves remained the world's third-largest. The balance of payments was in surplus, the budget was more or less balanced, and debt was low. Inflation was 7% in 2012, modest by historical standards. But on the microeconomic level, and from a longer-term perspective, the picture looked much less rosy. Approximately 300,000 non-incorporated individual-owned businesses formally closed in early 2013 due to a hike in social-security taxes – they most likely entered the shadow economy. And in mid-2013 the Russian stock market was down to levels not seen since the height of the financial crisis. Investors' doubts about economic growth in the medium term stemmed from stagnation of structural reform measures, a halt to the privatisation programme and uncertainty created by the growing role of the state in the economy.

The absence of structural reform meant that the economy continued to be dominated by energy production and exports. However, the global 'revolution' in unconventional oil and gas continued to create shockwaves in Russian hydrocarbon markets, though its impact has been mixed. On the one hand, after years of international negotiations with potential partners and exploratory work, in August 2012 Gazprom announced that it would indefinitely postpone development of the mammoth Shtokman gas field under the Barents Sea. This decision, although partly stemming from the earlier withdrawal of Norway's Statoil from the project, was largely precipitated by the global gas glut caused by the saturation of the US market with domestically produced shale gas. Another change came with Rosneft's purchase of TNK-BP, which had been jointly owned by a Russian consortium and BP of the UK. Rosneft emerged as the world's largest listed oil company by production. In addition to cash payments resulting from the sale, BP was left with a 19.75% stake in Rosneft, which in turn acquired BP technologies to prolong the life of its West Siberian oil fields.

Meanwhile, the drastic decline in the price of the technology for extracting hydrocarbons from shale also represented an opportunity for Russia. The shale-oil potential of Russia's brownfields – the massive Western Siberian oil deposits that Moscow has relied upon for export revenue since the 1970s – was widely trumpeted by Rosneft, the state-controlled oil company. A June 2013 US Energy Department estimate put Russia's shale oil reserves at 75m barrels, the largest in the world. Shale oil development could displace the more expensive Arctic and Eastern Siberian projects that made headlines in recent years.

Georgia's New Pluralism

Parliamentary elections in October 2012 marked a sea change for the Republic of Georgia. The entry of Bidzina Ivanishvili, the country's richest man, into politics and a prison abuse scandal led to a surprise electoral loss for the United National Movement (UNM), the party of President Mikheil Saakashvili. Contrary to concerns about possible civil strife, the elections and their aftermath proceeded peacefully. Georgia entered a fundamentally new period in its development: for the first time, its politics could genuinely be called pluralistic.

Before 2011, Saakashvili and the UNM had dominated the executive branch, parliament, the courts and the media. Georgian opposition parties had long been poorly financed and riven by personal rivalries and ideological differences. Although Saakashvili and the UNM suffered from declining approval ratings in recent years, there seemed to be no cohesive opposition to challenge either the president or his parliamentary bloc. The main TV stations, the source of news for the vast majority of Georgians, kept faithfully to the UNM party line.

Ivanishvili's arrival in politics resulted in major changes. Having made billions in 1990s Russia, he declared his intent to use his personal wealth – which amounted to about half of Georgia's GDP – to effect political change. With this infusion of cash, the five main opposition parties were convinced to merge into a coalition called the Georgian Dream (GD) in April 2012. It ran on an anti-Saakashvili platform, vowing to investigate alleged UNM wrongdoing and deal with excesses, in addition to promises to pursue a more balanced foreign policy and address rural poverty through government programmes. Such social initiatives were anathema to the UNM government's libertarian ideology but appealed to many in Georgia, which remained a largely agrarian, relatively poor country.

These developments caused Saakashvili and his allies to panic and use the administrative resources at their disposal to undermine GD's activities, a tactic that ultimately proved self-defeating and caused major tensions during the campaign. The president stripped Ivanishvili of his Georgian citizenship, claiming he had forfeited it after accepting French citizenship in 2010. This prevented Ivanishvili from standing as a candidate in the election. It also served to reinforce the government's narrative about him, which questioned his patriotic credentials and portrayed him as a Russian agent. GD candidates were also subjected to fines and activists were detained. But Ivanishvili's resources, including a TV station owned by his wife, allowed GD to overcome these obstacles and reach voters throughout the country. Such reach was unprecedented for the opposition in any former Soviet republic.

Ivanishvili's activities caused the UNM's dominance of the electorate to wane, with polls putting the GD in a competitive position in the months leading up to the elections. The contest appeared likely to be a dead heat until the balance shifted decisively a mere ten days before the election, when a graphic video of guards assaulting prisoners in Georgian jails was widely broadcast. The abuses seemed to exemplify the government's overreach and turned undecided voters strongly against the UNM, which previously campaigned on prison reform. The president's first reaction was to blame opposition activists for fabricating the video. However, within 24 hours, a contrite Saakashvili apologised on television, the minister in charge of Georgia's prisons was sacked and the officials in charge of the facilities featured in the videos were arrested.

The elections themselves only involved a few incidents of violence and sporadic reports of vote tampering by the UNM. Even if Saakashvili had wanted to alter the result, he was not given the opportunity to do so, having invited hundreds of international election observers to the country before Ivanishvili became a credible threat. The GD carried the day with 54% of the vote.

In an important step, Saakashvili conceded defeat the next day and took steps to ensure that a new government would be formed that reflected the election outcome, including by reinstating Ivanishvili's Georgian citizenship, which allowed him to become prime minister. This unprecedented power-sharing arrangement took place in a political environment further complicated by a strange quirk of constitutional reforms enacted in 2010. The new constitution, which transfers a wide range of functions from the president's office to the prime minister and the parliament, will come into effect after a new president is inaugurated following elections in October 2013. (Saakashvili is barred from running again due to term limits.) Although the GD government came to power under the old system, in which the president still had wide-ranging control, in the months following the 2012 election Saakashvili voluntarily ceded certain powers and was stripped of others through constitutional amendments. The GD government complained that Saakashvili complicated the transfer of power by failing to sign certain documents, but on the whole the president behaved largely as if he, and not just his party, had been voted out of office.

The new coalition made several missteps after assuming office. While following through on its campaign pledge to investigate and curb alleged government wrongdoing in the Saakashvili era, GD at times crossed the line between pursuing justice and exacting revenge. Investigations were launched into top UNM figures, including former Prime Minister Vano Merabishvili, who was also the chairman of the UNM, and Tbilisi Mayor Giorgi Ugulava. In response to a sharp reaction from the West, the new government toned down the zeal with which it investigated the alleged wrongdoing of its predecessor. Still, more nationalistic elements of the government stirred up racial tensions and other forms of intolerance, as demonstrated by a brutal attack on gay-rights protesters in May 2013. The GD government remained an uneasy coalition of these groups with mainstream, pro-Western parties such as the Republican Party and the Free Democrats, led by Minister of Defence Irakli Alasania.

Although he became more polished after taking office, Ivanishvili proved to be anything but a natural politician. He remained prone to public gaffes and too often seemed driven by animosity towards Saakashvili. For example, in the aftermath of the GD victory, Ivanishvili declared his intention to force Saakashvili to step down from the presidency. He also repeatedly said that he planned to step down as prime minister well before the next elections, and that he expected the coalition to dissolve at that point.

Ivanishvili's stated lack of interest in staying in power even for one full term was unusual, but it underscored a key distinction between him and the vast majority of political leaders in post-Soviet Eurasia (including his predecessors): he did not need his office to ensure his livelihood. Politics in the region had been a winner-take-all affair largely because of the interdependence of power and money. In other words, losing an election could mean losing assets, rents and even freedom – as happened to former Ukrainian Prime Minister Yulia Tymoshenko. That Ivanishvili did not depend on his office for financial security may have helped depersonalise Georgia's politics and cement pluralism. Indeed, this could be seen in the UNM's strong parliamentary opposition to the government and the variety of viewpoints encountered in the major media outlets. The government's actions were scrutinised by the opposition at parliamentary hearings and, despite heated rhetoric, both sides worked together to compromise on key issues. In this context, the UNM's strong second-place finish in the parliamentary elections was as important as the GD's victory.

In terms of policy shifts, the new government's approach to Russia received the most international attention. The two countries had not had diplomatic relations since the August 2008 war and Moscow's subsequent recognition of Abkhazia and South Ossetia, breakaway regions of Georgia, as independent states. During the 2012 electoral campaign, Ivanishvili rightly critiqued Saakashvili's needlessly antagonistic approach to Russia and pledged to improve ties. He made clear that this pledge would not come at the expense of Georgia's EU and NATO membership ambitions or its territorial integrity. After the new government took office, tensions between Russia and Georgia eased and progress was made on some bilateral issues. Ivanishvili appointed Zurab Abashidze, the widely respected former Georgian ambassador to Moscow, as his special envoy for relations with Russia. Abashidze began quarterly meetings with Russian Deputy Foreign Minister Grigory Karasin, which resulted, inter alia, in Georgian wine and mineral water returning to the Russian market for the first time since Moscow banned them, as relations worsened, in 2006.

Abashidze's mandate specifically excluded the conflict-related issues covered by the Geneva Discussions, the forum that emerged following the 2008 war. On those issues, Russia's position had hardened, as was demonstrated by May 2013 reports of the 'borderisation' of the South Ossetia administrative boundary line, where Russian guards put up barbed wire fences that cut into Tbilisi-administered territory. In several cases, Georgian villagers woke up to find themselves on the other side of the fence. It seemed likely that this stance reflected the Russian military and intelligence services' preparations for the 2014 Sochi Winter Olympics, which will take place just 8 kilometres north of Abkhazia. Although Russia's hardline approach caused GD problems domestically, a foreign-policy document agreed by both political sides in March 2013 included a goal of improving ties with Russia within the framework of long-held Georgian positions on NATO and EU membership and territorial integrity.

Strategic Geography 2013

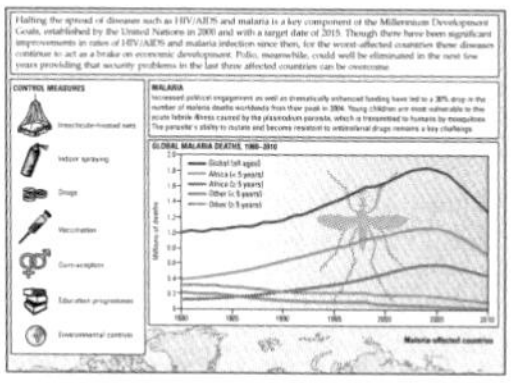

II
Reasons for hope in the fight against global disease

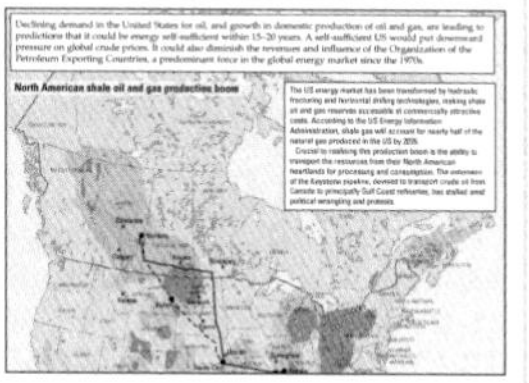

IV
The shifting dynamics of world oil markets

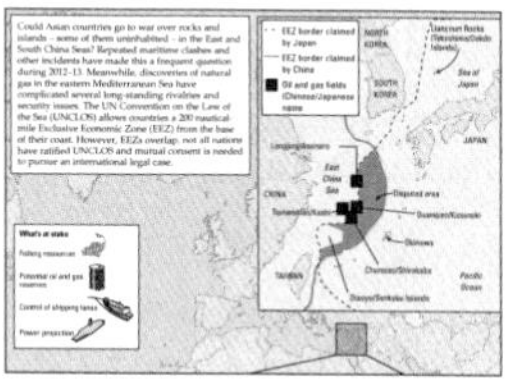

VI
Maritime disputes in focus

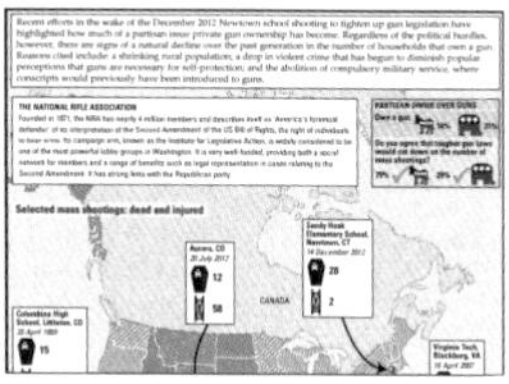

VIII
The United States' gun debate rumbles on

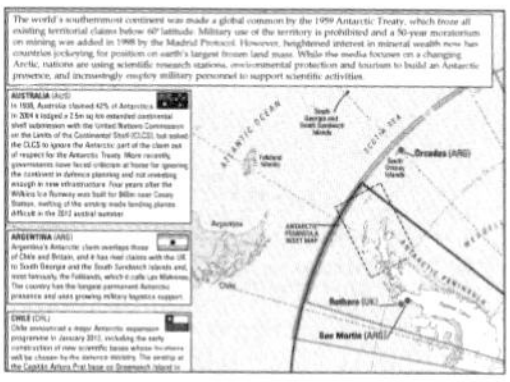

X
Antarctica: the quiet race for national influence

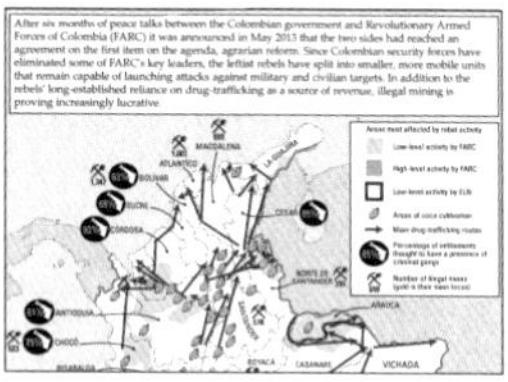

XII
Colombia: FARC rebels' changing tactics

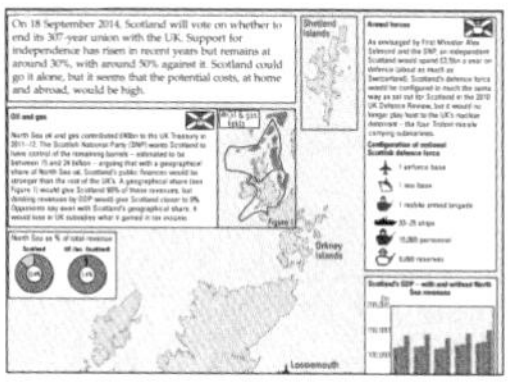

XIII
Could Scotland go it alone?

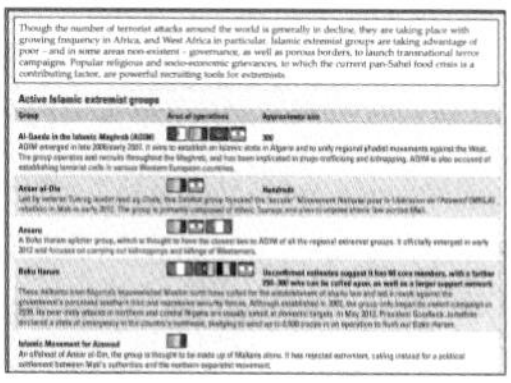

XIV
Islamic extremism in West Africa

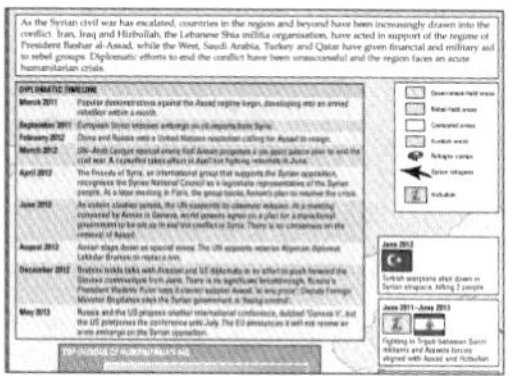

XVI
Syria's increasingly internationalised civil war

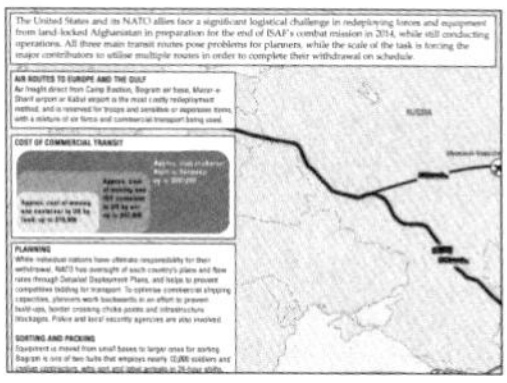

XVIII
Afghanistan: the long drawdown

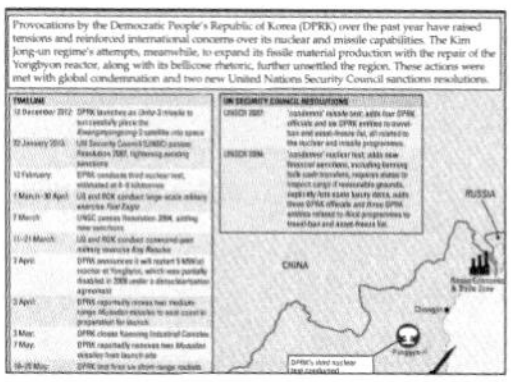

XX
North Korea does it again

Reasons for hope in the fight against global disease

Halting the spread of diseases such as HIV/AIDS and malaria is a key component of the Millennium Development Goals, established by the United Nations in 2000 and with a target date of 2015. Though there have been significant improvements in rates of HIV/AIDS and malaria infection since then, for the worst-affected countries these diseases continue to act as a brake on economic development. Polio, meanwhile, could well be eliminated in the next few years providing that security problems in the last three affected countries can be overcome.

CONTROL MEASURES

MALARIA

Increased political engagement as well as dramatically enhanced funding have led to a 30% drop in the number of malaria deaths worldwide from their peak in 2004. Young children are most vulnerable to this acute febrile illness caused by the plasmodium parasite, which is transmitted to humans by mosquitoes. The parasite's ability to mutate and become resistant to antimalarial drugs remains a key challenge.

GLOBAL MALARIA DEATHS, 1980–2010

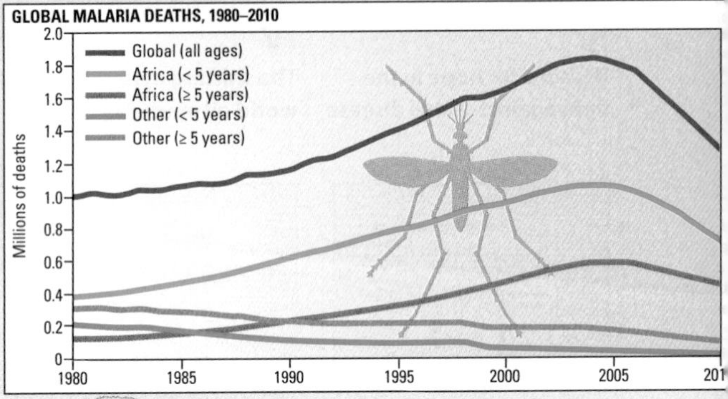

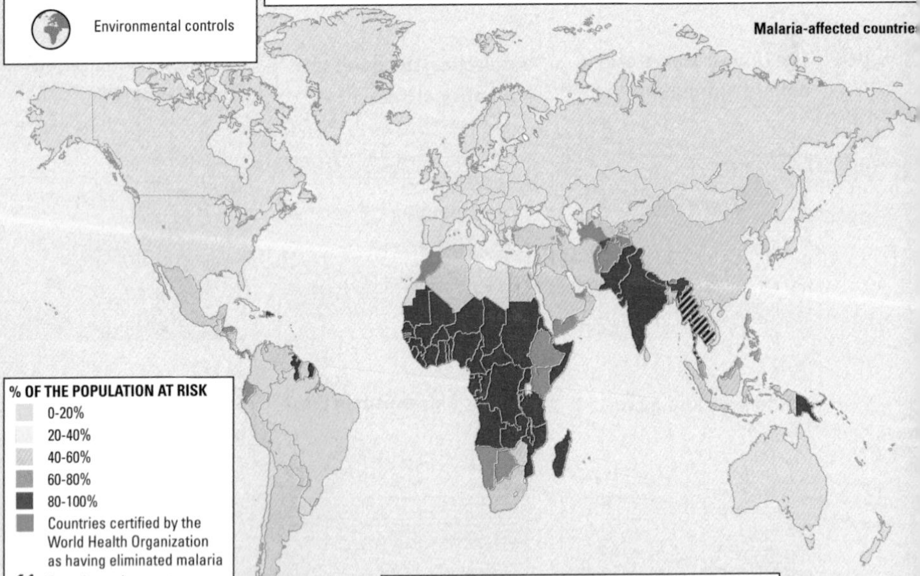

% OF THE POPULATION AT RISK

- 0-20%
- 20-40%
- 40-60%
- 60-80%
- 80-100%
- Countries certified by the World Health Organization as having eliminated malaria
- Parasite resistance to artemisinin (currently the most effective antimalarial) detected

NUMBER OF DEATHS ATTRIBUTED TO MALARIA IN 2010	
1. Democratic Republic of the Congo	21,168
2. Côte d'Ivoire	18,156
3. Angola	10,530
4. Burkina Faso	7,982
5. Nigeria	7,522

CONTROL MEASURES AGAINST MALARIA

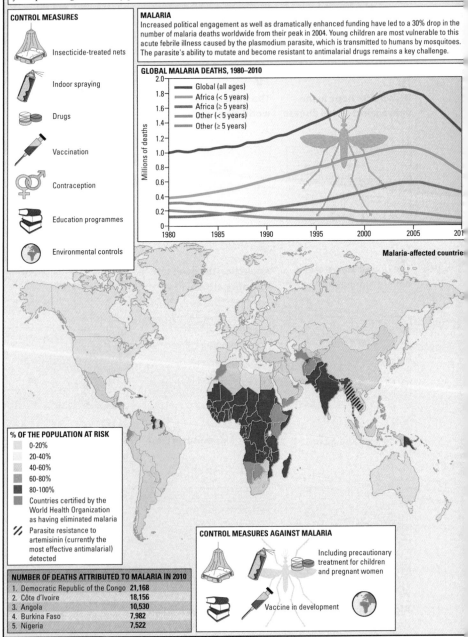

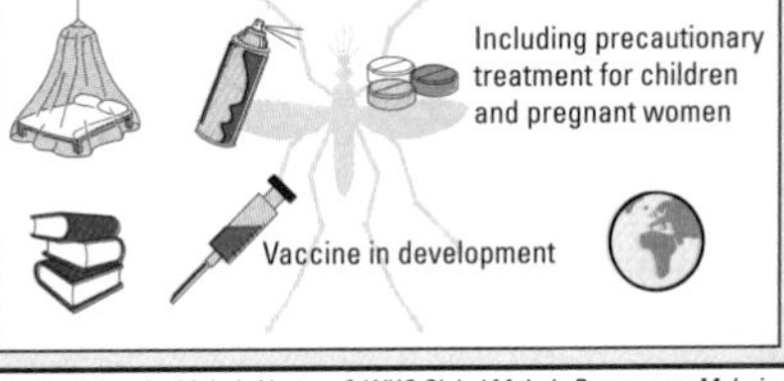

Sources: AIDSinfo; Associated Press; Daily Telegraph; Global Malaria Mapper by Medicines for Malaria Venture & WHO Global Malaria Programme; Malaria Atlas Project; Murray et al., 'Global malaria mortality between 1980 and 2010: a systematic analysis', The Lancet, vol. 379, no. 9814, 4 February 2012; Time; UNAIDS; World Health Organization.

LIO – END IN SIGHT

or governance, security problems and mistrust on the part of conservative Islamic clerics in certain provinces of Afghanistan, Pakistan and Nigeria an that these are the last three countries in the world where polio is prevalent. The leaders of all three countries have pledged to take further steps help eradicate this virus that attacks the body's motor neurons leading to paralysis in the arms or legs.

GHEST PREVALENCE OF POLIO

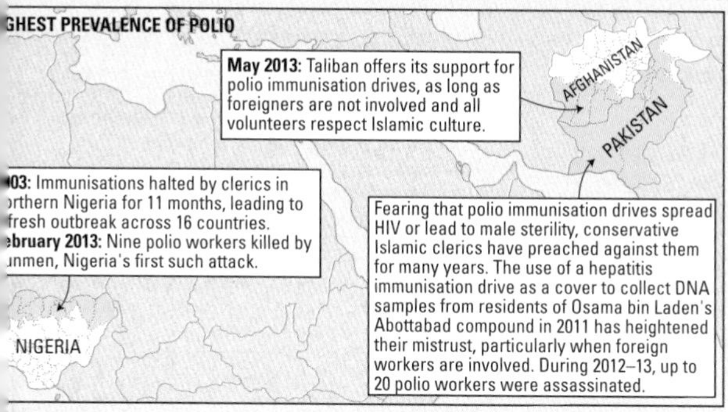

May 2013: Taliban offers its support for polio immunisation drives, as long as foreigners are not involved and all volunteers respect Islamic culture.
AFGHANISTAN
PAKISTAN
03: Immunisations halted by clerics in rthern Nigeria for 11 months, leading to fresh outbreak across 16 countries.
bruary 2013: Nine polio workers killed by nmen, Nigeria's first such attack.
NIGERIA
Fearing that polio immunisation drives spread HIV or lead to male sterility, conservative Islamic clerics have preached against them for many years. The use of a hepatitis immunisation drive as a cover to collect DNA samples from residents of Osama bin Laden's Abottabad compound in 2011 has heightened their mistrust, particularly when foreign workers are involved. During 2012–13, up to 20 polio workers were assassinated.

CONTROL MEASURES AGAINST POLIO

Salk vaccine – an injection that relies on a dead virus. It costs circa $3 and is highly effective.

Sabin vaccine – oral drops consisting of a live but weakened virus. It costs <20¢, but the virus can occasionally mutate and become active as it passes through a recipient's body. The Salk vaccine is used as a further treatment in these cases.

/AIDS

e number of new cases of the human immunodeficiency virus (HIV) is thought to have reached its peak in 1997. The number of deaths from esses related to acquired immunodeficiency syndrome (AIDS), the final stage of HIV infection, subsequently began to decline in the mid-2000s. b-Saharan Africa still has the largest population living with HIV, but greater political engagement over the past decade and the increased ailability of affordable antiretroviral drugs have brought about a significant reduction in the number of new infections.

IMBER OF NEW HIV FECTIONS, 2001–2011

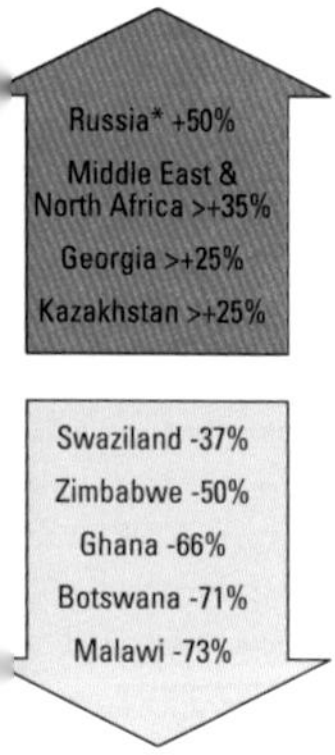

igure for Russia is an timate, for the period tween 2006–2011

Population living with HIV and AIDS-related deaths in 2011, by region

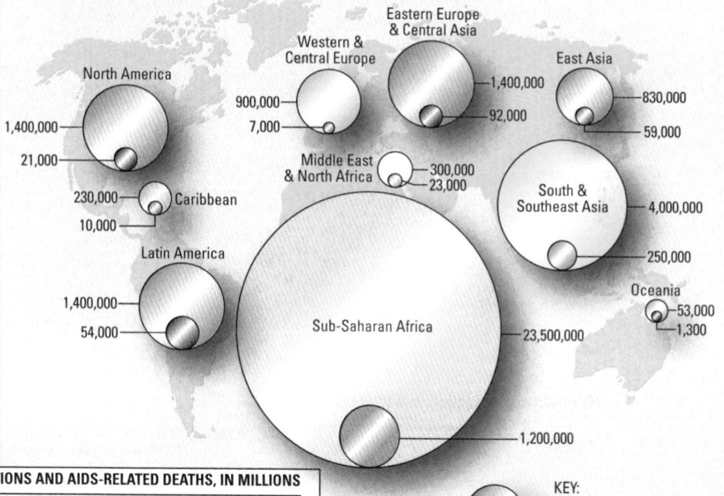

OBAL RATES OF HIV INFECTIONS AND AIDS-RELATED DEATHS, IN MILLIONS

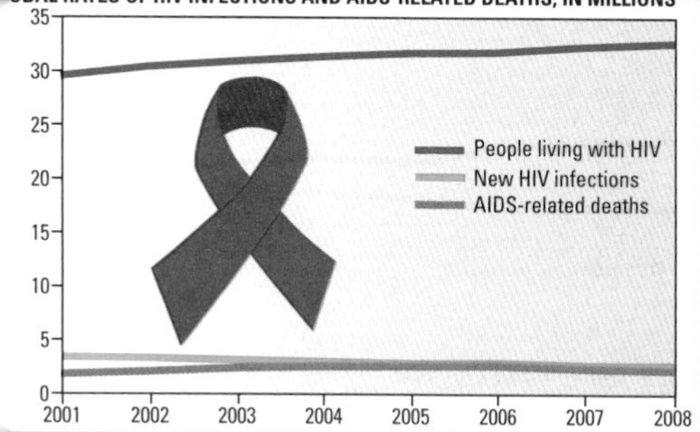

HIGHEST RATES OF HIV INFECTION AMONG 15–49 YEAR OLDS	
1. Swaziland	**26%**
2. Botswana	**23.4%**
3. Lesotho	**23.3%**
4. South Africa	**17.3%**
5. Zimbabwe	**14.9%**

CONTROL MEASURES AGAINST HIV/AIDS

The shifting dynamics of world oil markets

Declining demand in the United States for oil, and growth in domestic production of oil and gas, are leading to predictions that it could be energy self-sufficient within 15–20 years. A self-sufficient US would put downward pressure on global crude prices. It could also diminish the revenues and influence of the Organization of the Petroleum Exporting Countries, a predominant force in the global energy market since the 1970s.

North American shale oil and gas production boom

The US energy market has been transformed by hydraulic fracturing and horizontal drilling technologies, making shale oil and gas reserves accessible at commercially attractive costs. According to the US Energy Information Administration, shale gas will account for nearly half of the natural gas produced in the US by 2035.

Crucial to realising this production boom is the ability to transport the resources from their North American heartlands for processing and consumption. The extension of the Keystone pipeline, devised to transport crude oil from Canada to principally Gulf Coast refineries, has stalled amid political wrangling and protests.

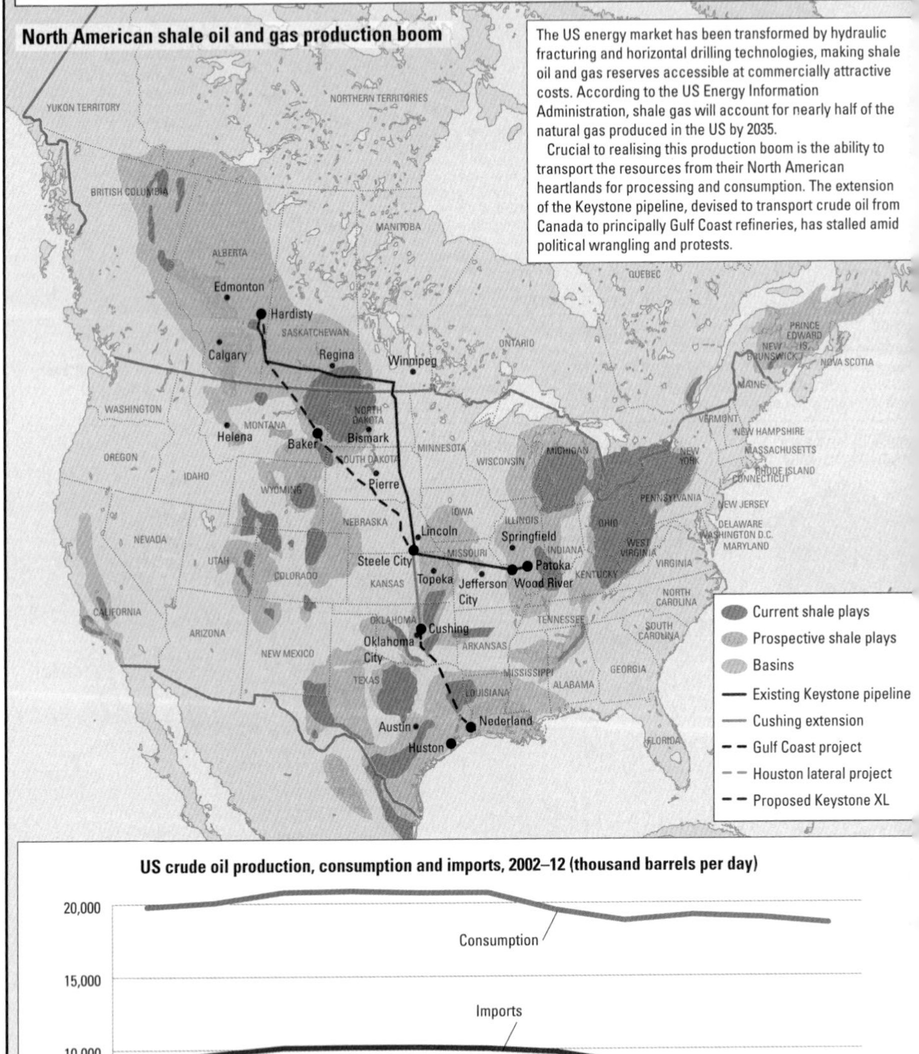

US crude oil production, consumption and imports, 2002–12 (thousand barrels per day)

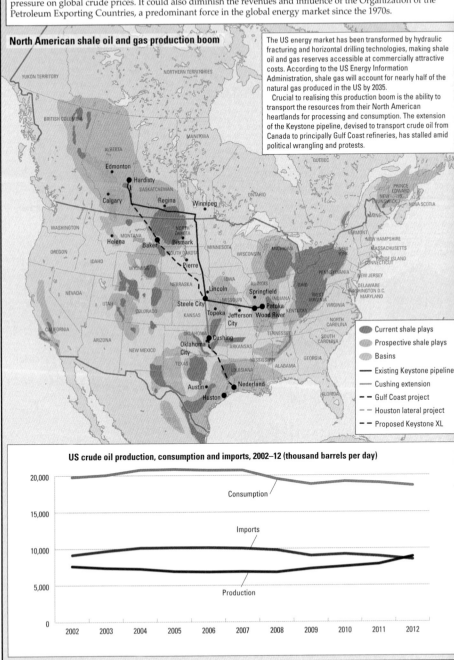

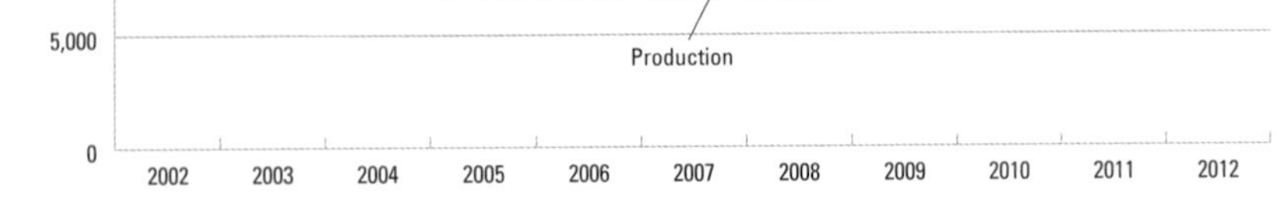

Sources: BP Statistical Review of World Energy 2013; International Monetary Fund; Qatar National Bank; TransCanada; US Energy Information Administration.

Dynamics of energy markets in the Gulf

Impact of sanctions on Iran:
Iran has the fourth-largest proven oil reserves and the second-largest natural gas reserves in the world. As a result of international sanctions, its crude oil exports fell by 20% in 2012, to 1.5 million b/d. The sanctions have prompted Iran to export oil products as opposed to crude shipments; in February 2012, it announced that it would begin to trade oil in currencies other than the dollar. The majority of its oil exports are destined for China, South Korea, Japan and India.

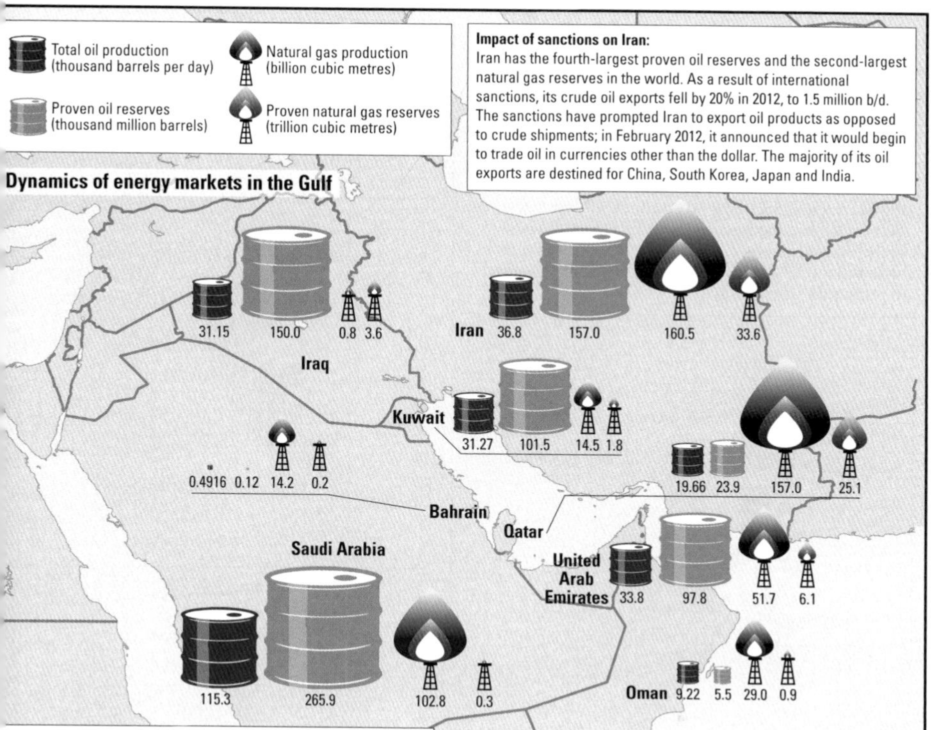

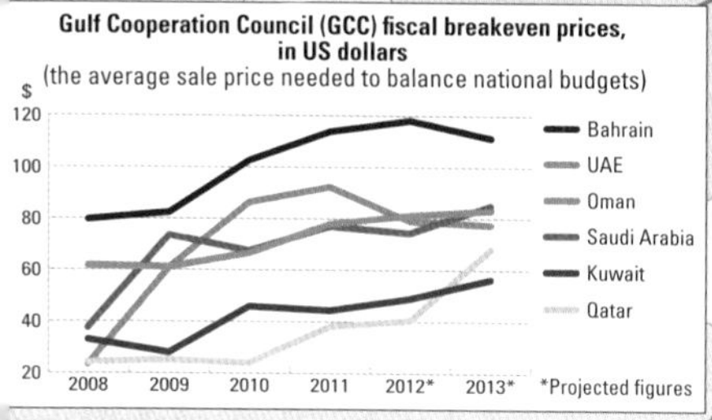

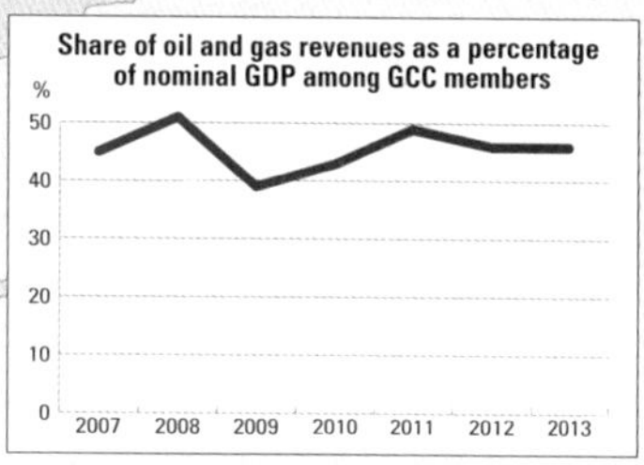

World oil consumption in 2011, million barrels per day (b/d)

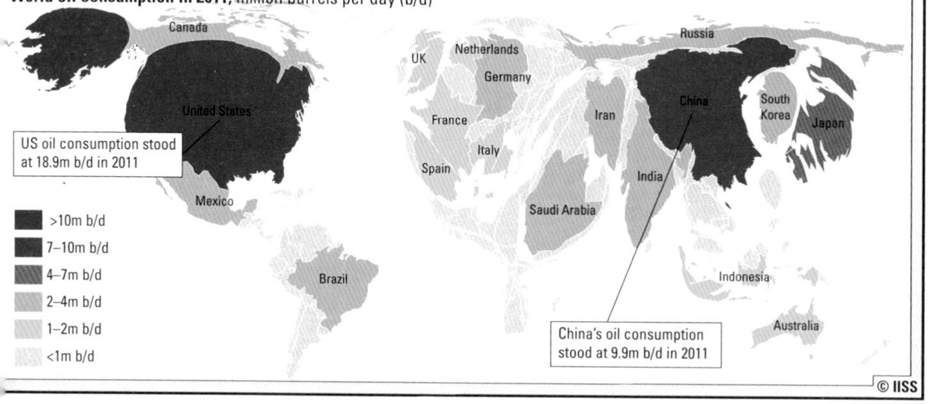

Maritime disputes in focus

Could Asian countries go to war over rocks and islands – some of them uninhabited – in the East and South China Seas? Repeated maritime clashes and other incidents have made this a frequent question during 2012–13. Meanwhile, discoveries of natural gas in the eastern Mediterranean Sea have complicated several long-standing rivalries and security issues. The UN Convention on the Law of the Sea (UNCLOS) allows countries a 200 nautical-mile Exclusive Economic Zone (EEZ) from the base of their coast. However, EEZs overlap, not all nations have ratified UNCLOS and mutual consent is needed to pursue an international legal case.

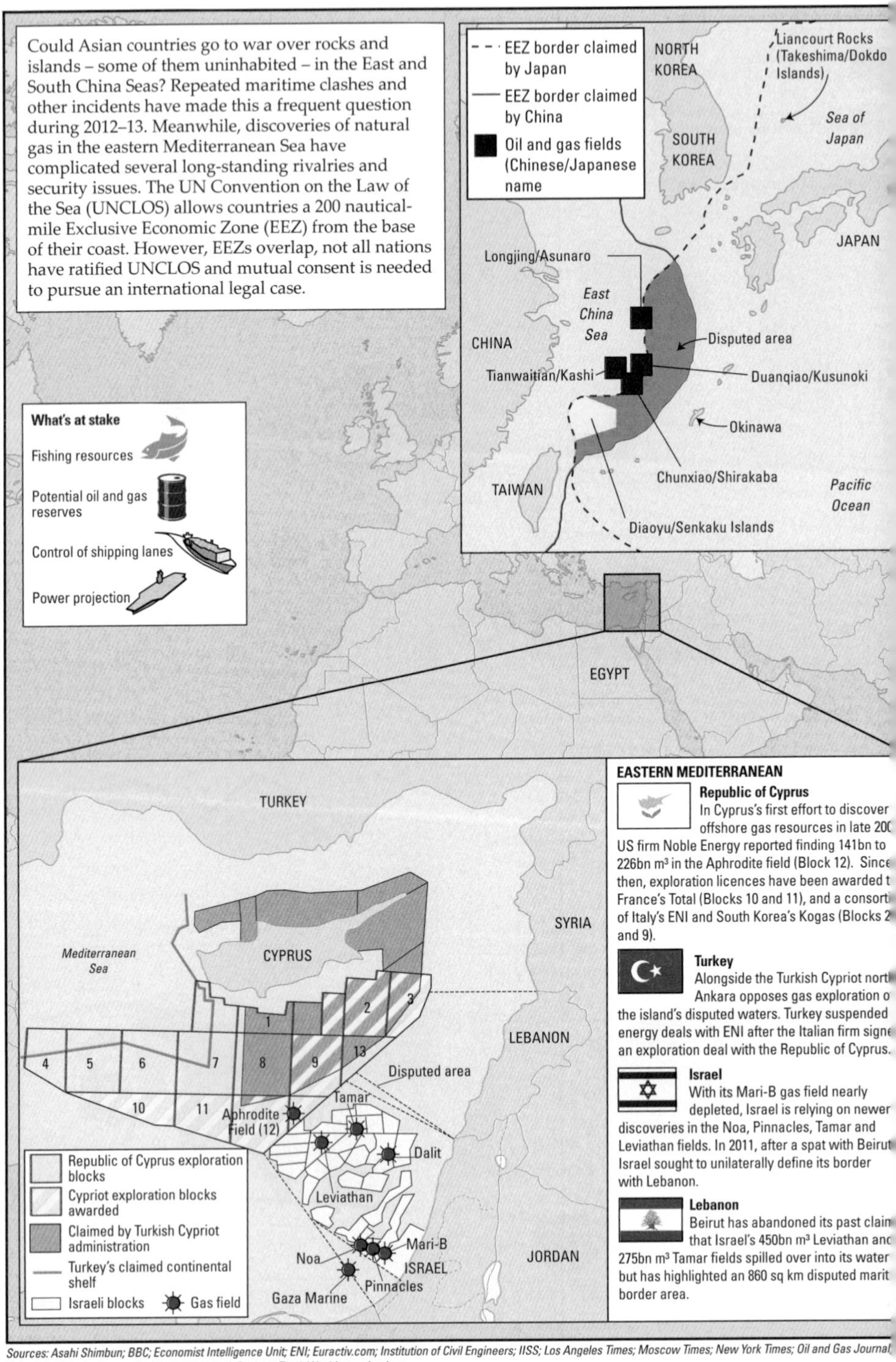

EASTERN MEDITERRANEAN

Republic of Cyprus

In Cyprus's first effort to discover offshore gas resources in late 20[…] US firm Noble Energy reported finding 141bn to 226bn m³ in the Aphrodite field (Block 12). Sinc[…] then, exploration licences have been awarded t[…] France's Total (Blocks 10 and 11), and a consorti[…] of Italy's ENI and South Korea's Kogas (Blocks 2[…] and 9).

Turkey

Alongside the Turkish Cypriot nort[…] Ankara opposes gas exploration o[…] the island's disputed waters. Turkey suspended energy deals with ENI after the Italian firm sign[…] an exploration deal with the Republic of Cyprus.

Israel

With its Mari-B gas field nearly depleted, Israel is relying on newer discoveries in the Noa, Pinnacles, Tamar and Leviathan fields. In 2011, after a spat with Beiru[…] Israel sought to unilaterally define its border with Lebanon.

Lebanon

Beirut has abandoned its past clai[…] that Israel's 450bn m³ Leviathan an[…] 275bn m³ Tamar fields spilled over into its water[…] but has highlighted an 860 sq km disputed marit[…] border area.

Sources: Asahi Shimbun; BBC; Economist Intelligence Unit; ENI; Euractiv.com; Institution of Civil Engineers; IISS; Los Angeles Times; Moscow Times; New York Times; Oil and Gas Journal; Oxford Institute for Energy Studies; RIA Novosti; Reuters; Total; Washington Institute

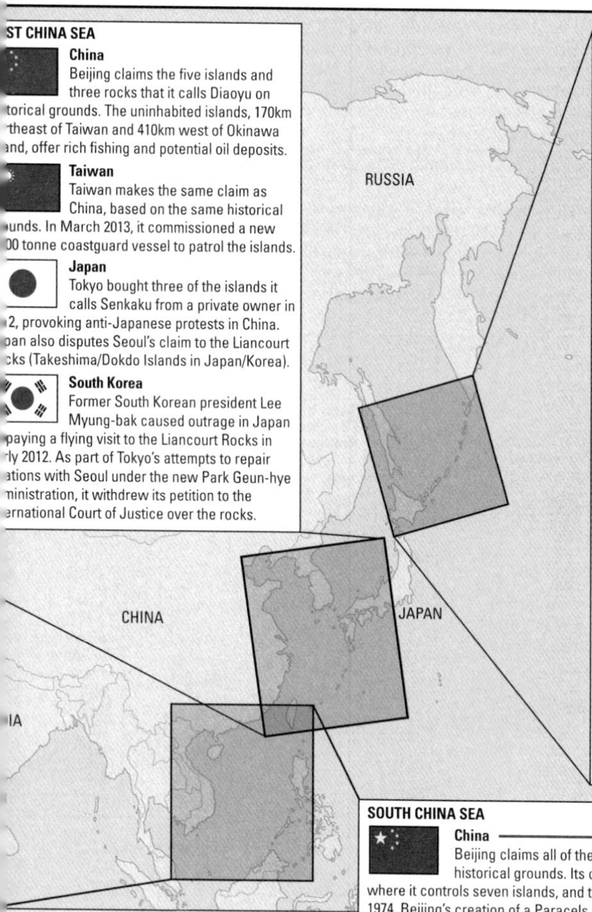

ST CHINA SEA

China
Beijing claims the five islands and three rocks that it calls Diaoyu on
torical grounds. The uninhabited islands, 170km
theast of Taiwan and 410km west of Okinawa
ınd, offer rich fishing and potential oil deposits.

Taiwan
Taiwan makes the same claim as China, based on the same historical
unds. In March 2013, it commissioned a new
00 tonne coastguard vessel to patrol the islands.

Japan
Tokyo bought three of the islands it calls Senkaku from a private owner in
2, provoking anti-Japanese protests in China.
pan also disputes Seoul's claim to the Liancourt
cks (Takeshima/Dokdo Islands in Japan/Korea).

South Korea
Former South Korean president Lee Myung-bak caused outrage in Japan
paying a flying visit to the Liancourt Rocks in
ly 2012. As part of Tokyo's attempts to repair
ations with Seoul under the new Park Geun-hye
ninistration, it withdrew its petition to the
ernational Court of Justice over the rocks.

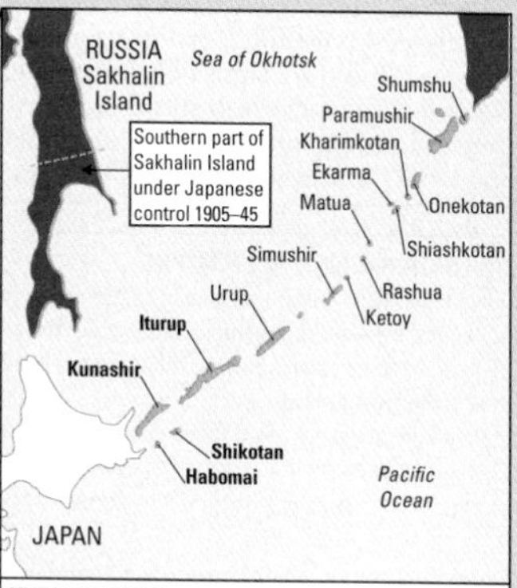

KURIL ISLANDS

Russia
Russia took control of the Kurils and southern Sakhalin during the Second World War, formalising this in a 1951 treaty. It has spent millions on island infrastructure and is interested in offshore fishing and potential oil resources. But the dispute has prevented Moscow and Tokyo signing a WWII peace treaty and new talks began in April 2013 on returning some islands. With nuclear submarines in the area, Moscow might wish to prevent Tokyo installing sonar or radar if Kunashir or Iturup were ever returned to Japan.

Japan
Tokyo says the four southern Kuril islands, or 'Northern Territories' of Habomai, Kunashir, Iturup and Shikotan, were not included in the 1951 treaty. Experts believe the Japanese public is unlikely to accept any proposal by Moscow to return just Habomai and Shikotan.

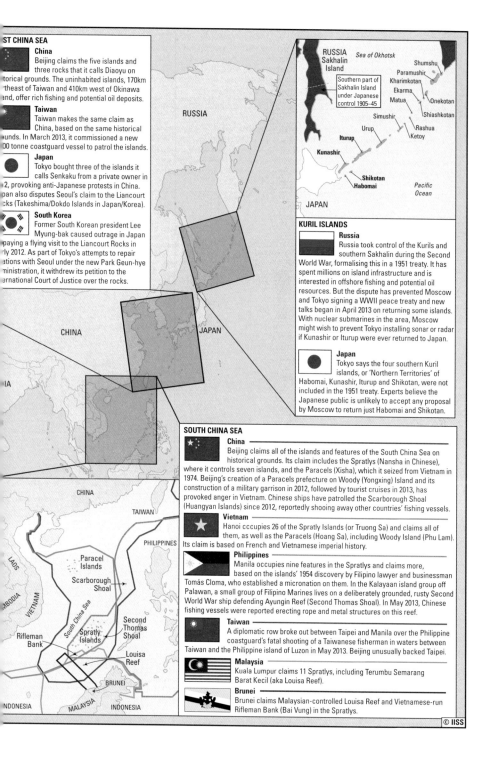

SOUTH CHINA SEA

China
Beijing claims all of the islands and features of the South China Sea on historical grounds. Its claim includes the Spratlys (Nansha in Chinese), where it controls seven islands, and the Paracels (Xisha), which it seized from Vietnam in 1974. Beijing's creation of a Paracels prefecture on Woody (Yongxing) Island and its construction of a military garrison in 2012, followed by tourist cruises in 2013, has provoked anger in Vietnam. Chinese ships have patrolled the Scarborough Shoal (Huangyan Islands) since 2012, reportedly shooing away other countries' fishing vessels.

Vietnam
Hanoi cccupies 26 of the Spratly Islands (or Truong Sa) and claims all of them, as well as the Paracels (Hoang Sa), including Woody Island (Phu Lam). Its claim is based on French and Vietnamese imperial history.

Philippines
Manila occupies nine features in the Spratlys and claims more, based on the islands' 1954 discovery by Filipino lawyer and businessman Tomás Cloma, who established a micronation on them. In the Kalayaan island group off Palawan, a small group of Filipino Marines lives on a deliberately grounded, rusty Second World War ship defending Ayungin Reef (Second Thomas Shoal). In May 2013, Chinese fishing vessels were reported erecting rope and metal structures on this reef.

Taiwan
A diplomatic row broke out between Taipei and Manila over the Philippine coastguard's fatal shooting of a Taiwanese fisherman in waters between Taiwan and the Philippine island of Luzon in May 2013. Beijing unusually backed Taipei.

Malaysia
Kuala Lumpur claims 11 Spratlys, including Terumbu Semarang Barat Kecil (aka Louisa Reef).

Brunei
Brunei claims Malaysian-controlled Louisa Reef and Vietnamese-run Rifleman Bank (Bai Vung) in the Spratlys.

The United States' gun debate rumbles on

Recent efforts in the wake of the December 2012 Newtown school shooting to tighten up gun legislation have highlighted how much of a partisan issue private gun ownership has become. Regardless of the political hurdles, however, there are signs of a natural decline over the past generation in the number of households that own a gun. Reasons cited include: a shrinking rural population; a drop in violent crime that has begun to diminish popular perceptions that guns are necessary for self-protection; and the abolition of compulsory military service, where conscripts would previously have been introduced to guns.

THE NATIONAL RIFLE ASSOCIATION

Founded in 1871, the NRA has nearly 4 million members and describes itself as 'America's foremost defender' of its interpretation of the Second Amendment of the US Bill of Rights, the right of individuals to bear arms. Its campaign arm, known as the Institute for Legislative Action, is widely considered to be one of the most powerful lobby groups in Washington. It is very well-funded, providing both a social network for members and a range of benefits such as legal representation in cases relating to the Second Amendment. It has strong links with the Republican party.

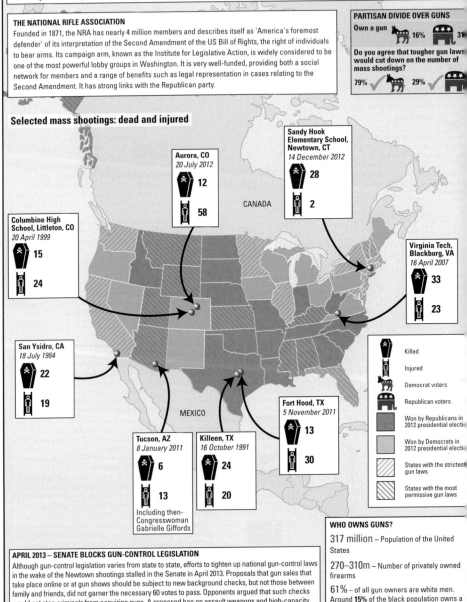

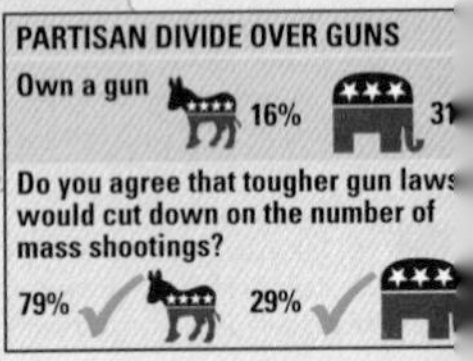

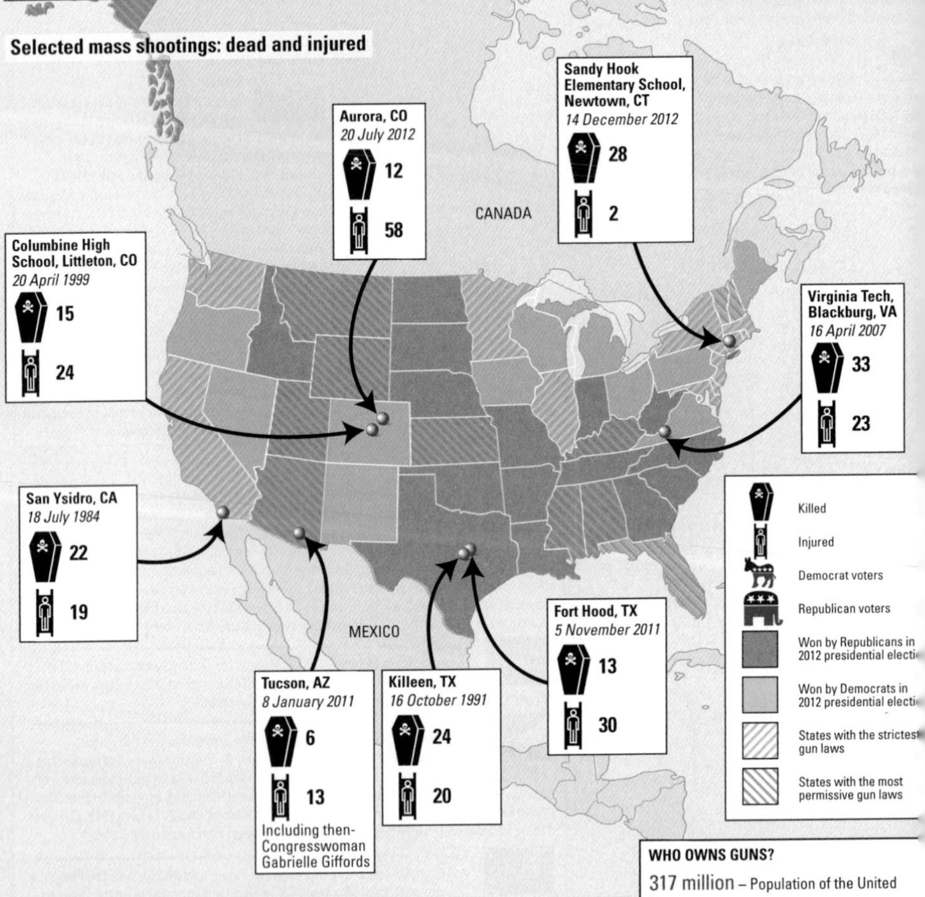

APRIL 2013 – SENATE BLOCKS GUN-CONTROL LEGISLATION

Although gun-control legislation varies from state to state, efforts to tighten up national gun-control laws in the wake of the Newtown shootings stalled in the Senate in April 2013. Proposals that gun sales that take place online or at gun shows should be subject to new background checks, but not those between family and friends, did not garner the necessary 60 votes to pass. Opponents argued that such checks would not stop criminals from acquiring guns. A proposed ban on assault weapons and high-capacity magazines, and measures to criminalise purchases made by proxy were also defeated.

WHO OWNS GUNS?

317 million – Population of the United States

270–310m – Number of privately owned firearms

61% – of all gun owners are white men. Around **15%** of the black population owns a gun; **11%** of Hispanics own a gun

Sources: Business Insider; GunPolicy.org; Guns & Ammo; Mother Jones; National Rifle Association; New York Times; Pew Research Center; Small Arms Survey; UNODC; US Bureau of Alcohol, Tobacco, Firearms and Explosives.

SIGNS OF DECLINE IN US GUN OWNERSHIP

nducted almost every two years since 1972, the General Social Survey asks:
you happen to have in your home (or garage) any guns or revolvers?'

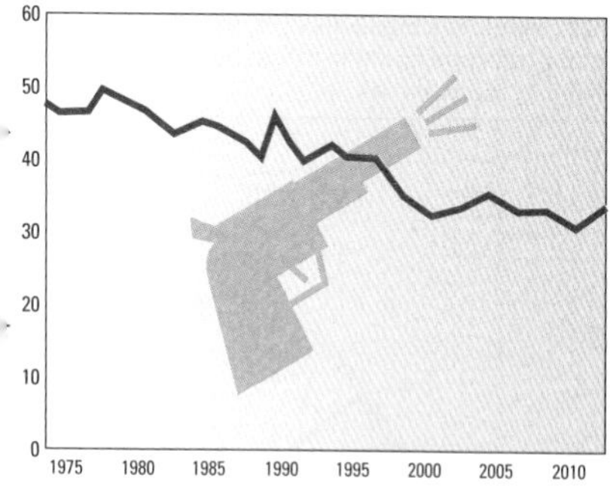

TOTAL NUMBER OF FIREARMS MANUFACTURED IN THE US, IN MILLIONS

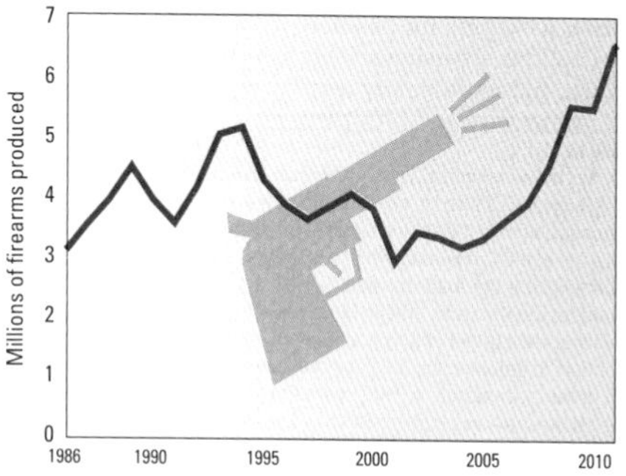

MICIDE BY FIREARM RATE PER 100,000 POPULATION, AS CALCULATED BY THE UNITED NATIONS OFFICE ON DRUGS AND CRIME (UNODC)

R 2010 *(unless otherwise stated)*

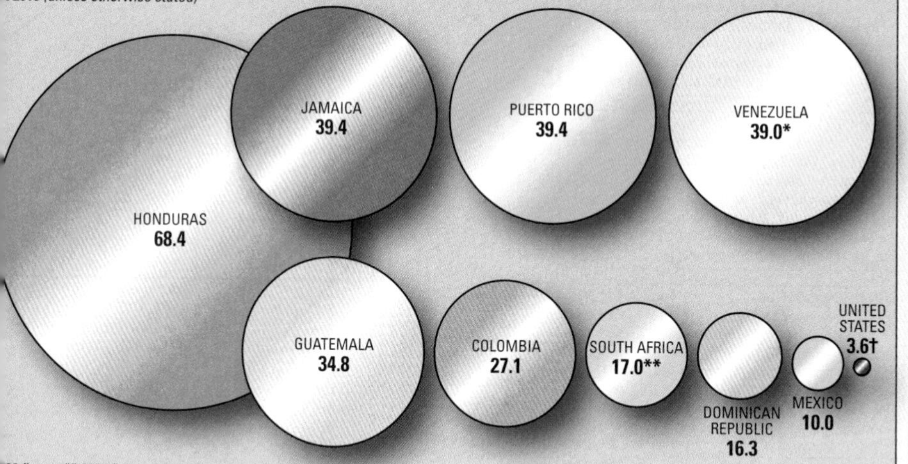

09 figure, ** 2007 figure, † 2011 figure

MBER OF PRIVATELY OWNED FIREARMS, IN MILLIONS

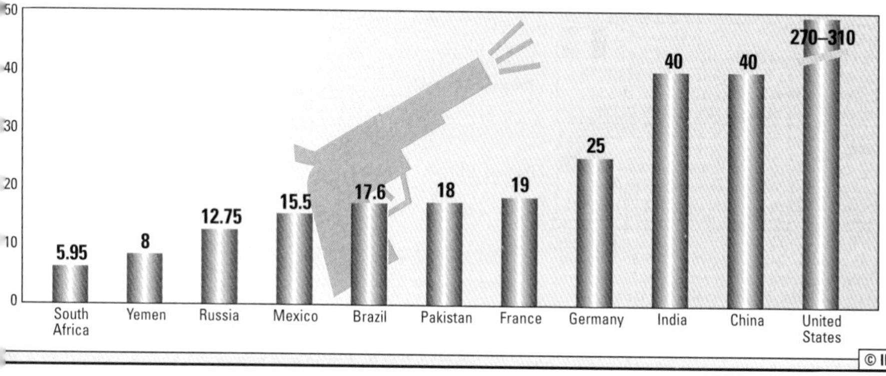

Antarctica: the quiet race for national influence

The world's southernmost continent was made a global common by the 1959 Antarctic Treaty, which froze all existing territorial claims below 60° latitude. Military use of the territory is prohibited and a 50-year moratorium on mining was added in 1998 by the Madrid Protocol. However, heightened interest in mineral wealth now has countries jockeying for position on earth's largest frozen land mass. While the media focuses on a changing Arctic, nations are using scientific research stations, environmental protection and tourism to build an Antarctic presence, and increasingly employ military personnel to support scientific activities.

AUSTRALIA (AUS)
In 1936, Australia claimed 42% of Antarctica. In 2004 it lodged a 2.5m sq km extended continental shelf submission with the United Nations Commission on the Limits of the Continental Shelf (CLCS), but asked the CLCS to ignore the Antarctic part of the claim out of respect for the Antarctic Treaty. More recently, governments have faced criticism at home for ignoring the continent in defence planning and not investing enough in new infrastructure. Four years after the Wilkins Ice Runway was built for $40m near Casey Station, melting of the airstrip made landing planes difficult in the 2012 austral summer.

ARGENTINA (ARG)
Argentina's Antarctic claim overlaps those of Chile and Britain, and it has rival claims with the UK to South Georgia and the South Sandwich Islands and, most famously, the Falklands, which it calls Las Malvinas. The country has the longest permanent Antarctic presence and uses growing military logistics support.

CHILE (CHL)
Chile announced a major Antarctic expansion programme in January 2012, including the early construction of new scientific bases whose locations will be chosen by the defence ministry. The airstrip at the Capitán Arturo Prat base on Greenwich Island in the South Shetlands – already able to welcome C-130 *Hercules* aircraft – is to be upgraded.

UNITED KINGDOM (UK)
For the Queen's Diamond Jubilee in 2012, Britain named a 437,000 sq km area of Antarctica 'Queen Elizabeth Land'. This prompted a formal protest from Argentina, which also claims the territory. There was an outcry in October 2007, when the UK proposed claiming 1m sq km of Antarctic seabed. No claim was lodged, but the UK reserves the right to do so.

NEW ZEALAND (NZ)
When the New Zealand Defence Force left Afghanistan in April 2013, Antarctica became its biggest annual mission. It provides military airlift, sea cargo, engineering and rescue services.

FRANCE (FRA)
France, the EU, Australia, the US and NZ have proposed Ross Sea sanctuaries to stem illegal fishing in the Southern Ocean. A July 2013 US–NZ attempt failed, with Russia raising doubts about its legality.

NORWAY (NOR)
First to the South Pole when Roald Amundsen won the race in 1911, Norway is now a minor Antarctic player. Its 2013–22 plan is to step up research activities.

UNITED STATES (US)
The US made no claim to Antarctica in 1959, but reserved its right to do so, and its Amundsen-Scott base sits at the South Pole, astride all rival claims. In 2011, Washington signed a $2bn deal with defence firm Lockheed Martin for Antarctic logistics (taking over from Raytheon). Its McMurdo base is Antarctica's largest.

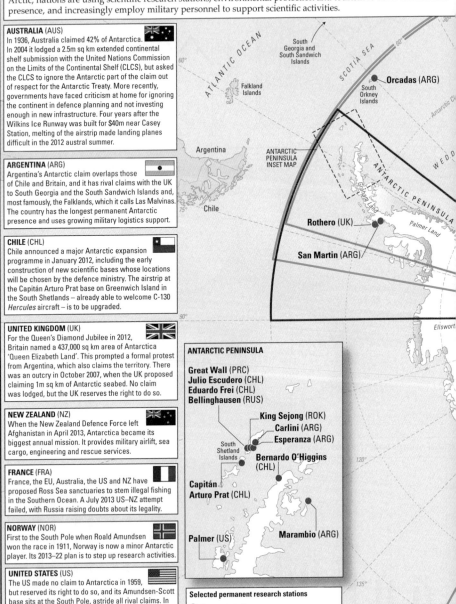

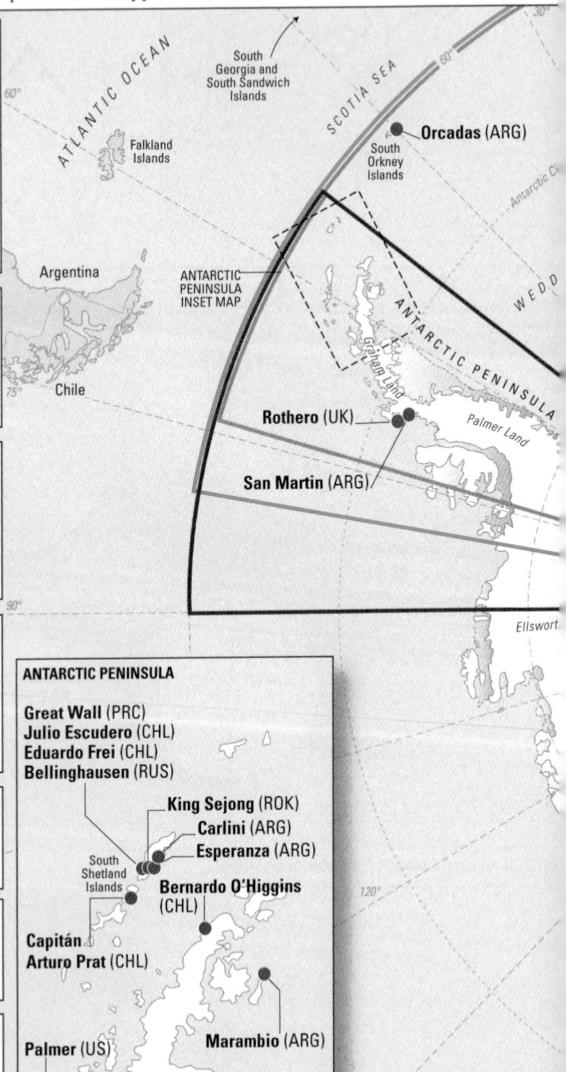

Sources: the Age; Agence France Presse; the Australian Antarctic Data Centre; the Australian Strategic Policy Institute; Canterbury University (New Zealand); Chosun Ilbo; the Conversation (Australia); the Global Post; the Guardian; Hindustan Times; IANS Indo-Asian News Service; Lockheed Martin; Lowy Institute; Mercopress; News.com.au; New Zealand Defence Force; The Scientific Committee on Antarctic Research; Sydney Morning Herald; UPI; US National Science Foundation; Zee News (India).

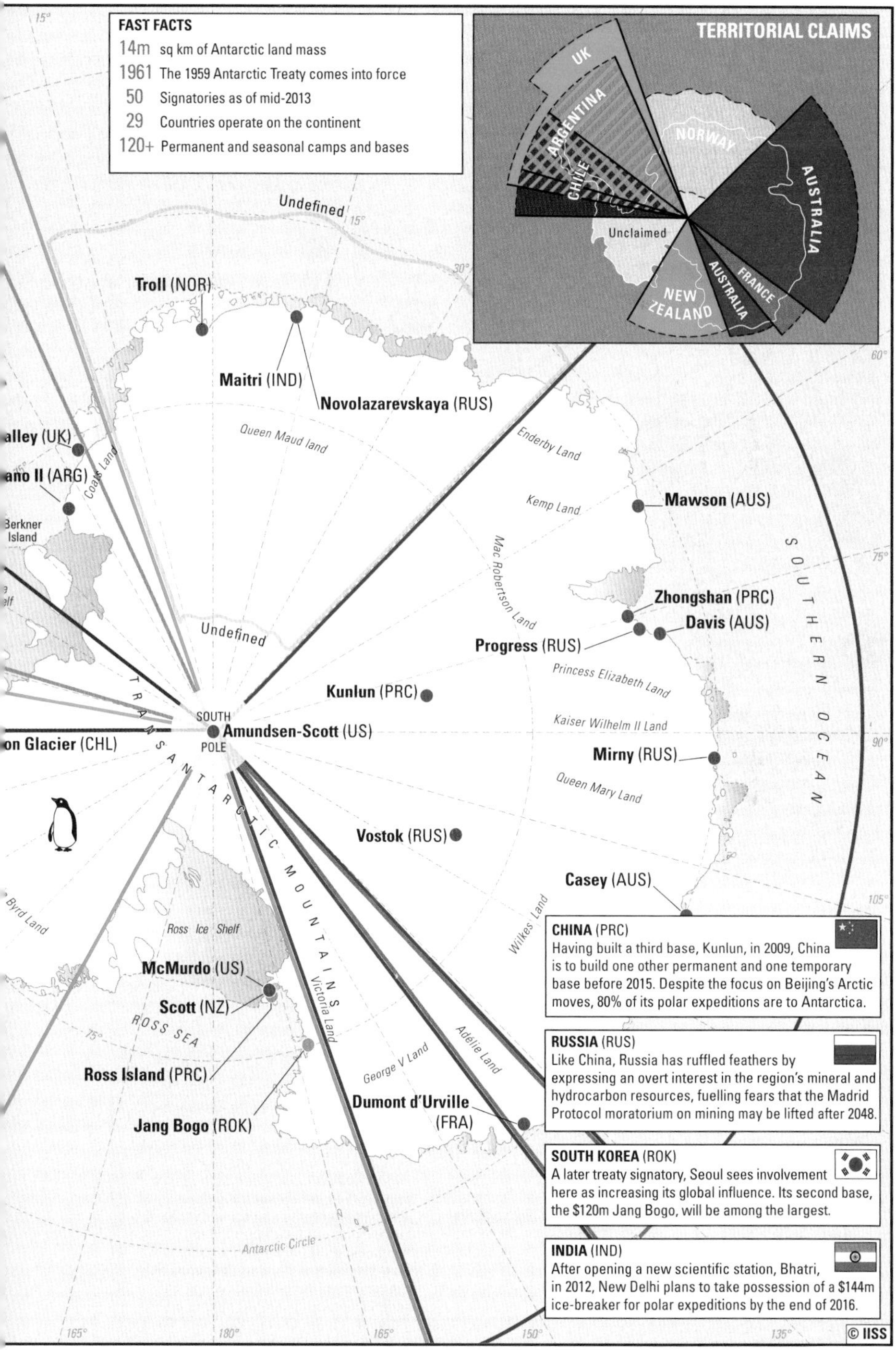
FAST FACTS
14m sq km of Antarctic land mass
1961 The 1959 Antarctic Treaty comes into force
50 Signatories as of mid-2013
29 Countries operate on the continent
120+ Permanent and seasonal camps and bases
TERRITORIAL CLAIMS
UK
ARGENTINA
CHILE
NORWAY
AUSTRALIA
Unclaimed
NEW ZEALAND
AUSTRALIA
FRANCE
Undefined
Troll (NOR)
Maitri (IND)
Novolazarevskaya (RUS)
Queen Maud land
Enderby Land
Kemp Land
Mawson (AUS)
Mac Robertson Land
Zhongshan (PRC)
Davis (AUS)
Progress (RUS)
Princess Elizabeth Land
Kunlun (PRC)
Kaiser Wilhelm II Land
SOUTHERN OCEAN
alley (UK)
ano II (ARG)
Coats Land
Berkner Island
Undefined
TRANSANTARCTIC MOUNTAINS
SOUTH POLE
Amundsen-Scott (US)
on Glacier (CHL)
Mirny (RUS)
Queen Mary Land
Vostok (RUS)
Casey (AUS)
Wilkes Land
Byrd Land
Ross Ice Shelf
McMurdo (US)
Scott (NZ)
ROSS SEA
Victoria Land
Ross Island (PRC)
Jang Bogo (ROK)
George V Land
Adélie Land
Dumont d'Urville (FRA)
Antarctic Circle
CHINA (PRC)
Having built a third base, Kunlun, in 2009, China is to build one other permanent and one temporary base before 2015. Despite the focus on Beijing's Arctic moves, 80% of its polar expeditions are to Antarctica.
RUSSIA (RUS)
Like China, Russia has ruffled feathers by expressing an overt interest in the region's mineral and hydrocarbon resources, fuelling fears that the Madrid Protocol moratorium on mining may be lifted after 2048.
SOUTH KOREA (ROK)
A later treaty signatory, Seoul sees involvement here as increasing its global influence. Its second base, the $120m Jang Bogo, will be among the largest.
INDIA (IND)
After opening a new scientific station, Bhatri, in 2012, New Delhi plans to take possession of a $144m ice-breaker for polar expeditions by the end of 2016.
© IISS

Colombia: FARC rebels' changing tactics

After six months of peace talks between the Colombian government and Revolutionary Armed Forces of Colombia (FARC) it was announced in May 2013 that the two sides had reached an agreement on the first item on the agenda, agrarian reform. Since Colombian security forces have eliminated some of FARC's key leaders, the leftist rebels have split into smaller, more mobile units that remain capable of launching attacks against military and civilian targets. In addition to the rebels' long-established reliance on drug-trafficking as a source of revenue, illegal mining is proving increasingly lucrative.

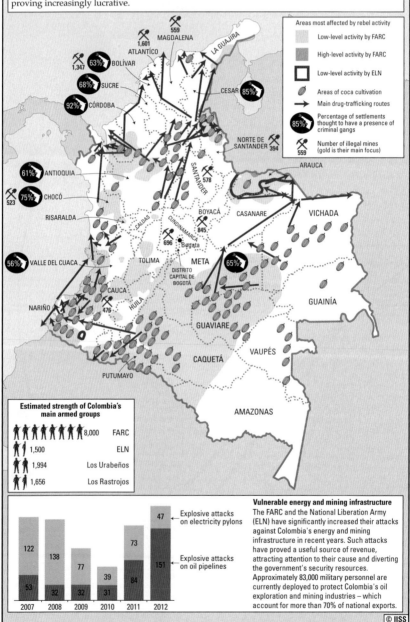

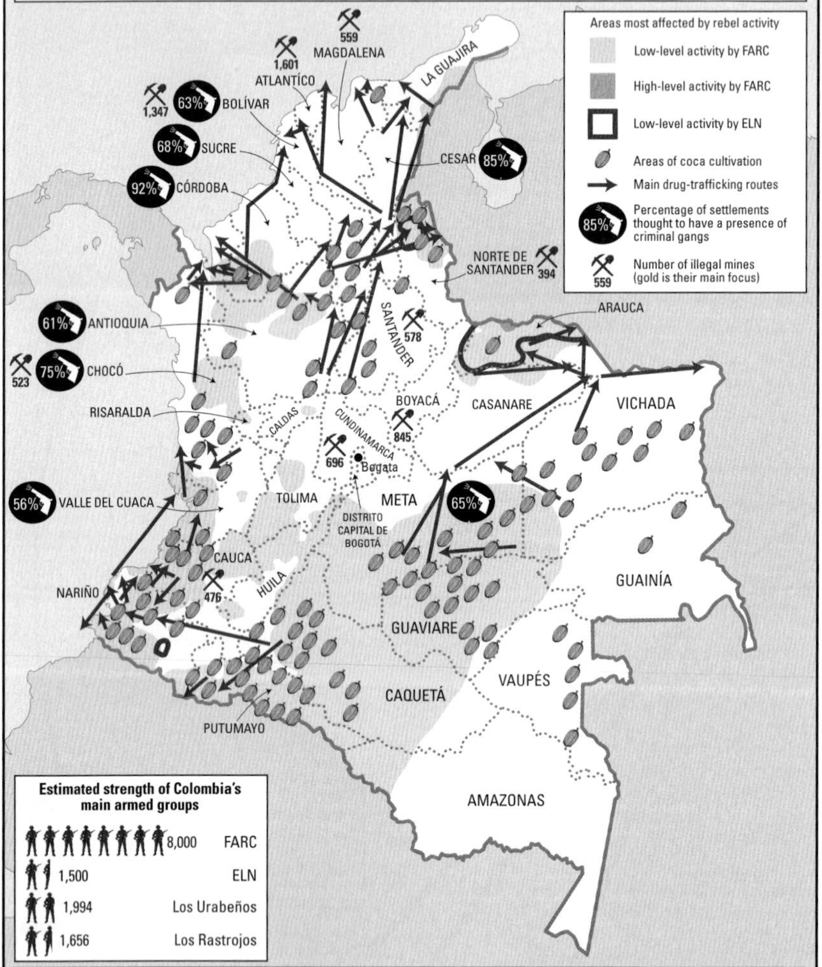

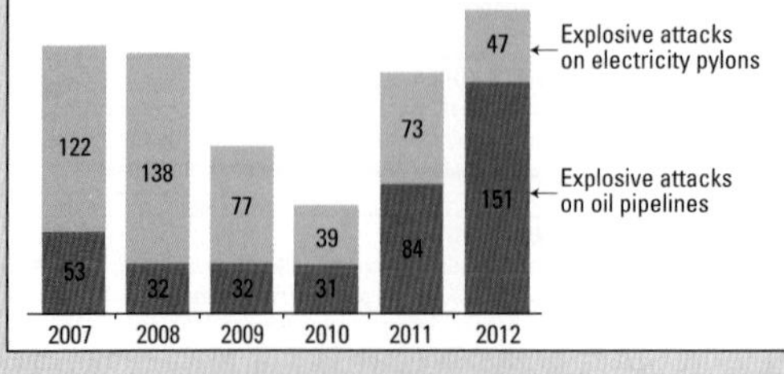

Vulnerable energy and mining infrastructure
The FARC and the National Liberation Army (ELN) have significantly increased their attacks against Colombia's energy and mining infrastructure in recent years. Such attacks have proved a useful source of revenue, attracting attention to their cause and diverting the government's security resources. Approximately 83,000 military personnel are currently deployed to protect Colombia's oil exploration and mining industries – which account for more than 70% of national exports.

Sources: Colombian Ministry of Mining and Energy; Colombian National Ministry of Defence; Colombian Presidential Programme for Human Rights; Fundación Ideas para la Paz; United Nations Office on Drugs and Crime.

Could Scotland go it alone?

On 18 September 2014, Scotland will vote on whether to end its 307-year union with the UK. Support for independence has risen in recent years but remains at around 30%, with around 50% against it. Scotland could go it alone, but it seems that the potential costs, at home and abroad, would be high.

Shetland Islands

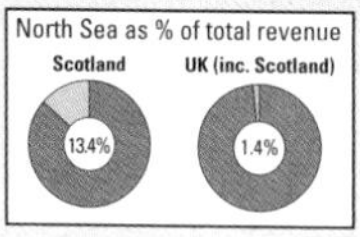

Armed forces

As envisaged by First Minister Alex Salmond and the SNP, an independent Scotland would spend £2.5bn a year on defence (about as much as Switzerland). Scotland's defence force would be configured in much the same way as set out for Scotland in the 2010 UK Defence Review, but it would no longer play host to the UK's nuclear deterrent – the four Trident missile carrying submarines.

Configuration of national Scottish defence force

- 1 airforce base
- 1 sea base
- 1 mobile armed brigade
- 20–25 ships
- 15,000 personnel
- 5,000 reserves

Oil and gas

North Sea oil and gas contributed £40bn to the UK Treasury in 2011–12. The Scottish National Party (SNP) wants Scotland to have control of the remaining barrels – estimated to be between 15 and 24 billion – arguing that with a geographical share of North Sea oil, Scotland's public finances would be stronger than the rest of the UK's. A geographical share (see Figure 1) would give Scotland 90% of these revenues, but dividing revenues by GDP would give Scotland closer to 9%. Opponents say even with Scotland's geographical share, it would lose in UK subsidies what it gained in tax income.

Oil & gas fields

Figure 1

North Sea as % of total revenue

Scotland — 13.4%
UK (inc. Scotland) — 1.4%

Orkney Islands

Scotland's GDP – with and without North Sea revenues

£m
200,000
150,000
100,000
50,000
0

07–08 08–09 09–10 10–11 11–12

- Now, exc North Sea
- Inc. per capita share of North Sea
- Inc. geographic share of North Sea oil

Lossiemouth

Inverness

North East

Aberdeen

Highlands & Islands

Mid & Fife

Dundee

Central

Perth

HMNB Clyde (Faslane)

RNAD Coulport

Edinburgh

Lothians

Glasgow

Glasgow

Trident

West

South

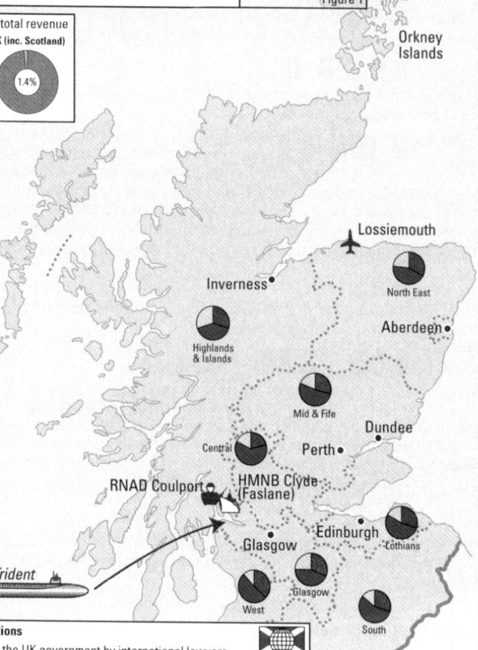

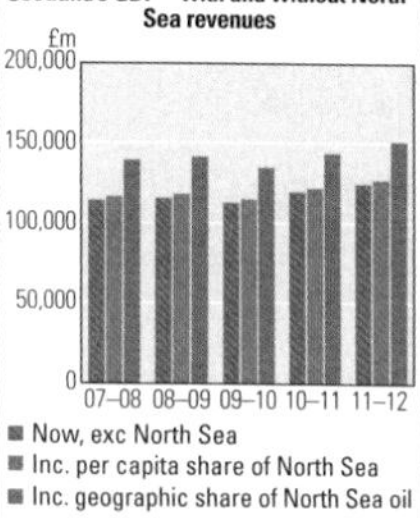

Economy

In 2011–12, with a geographical share of North Sea oil and gas revenues, Scotland generated 9.9% of total UK revenues while accounting for 9.3% of total UK spending. But opponents warn that relying on this revenue is too risky in the long term: in the last 15 years, even with a geographical share of oil and gas revenues, Scotland's net fiscal deficit varied from a low of -2.6% to a high of -10.7%, or £14.5bn.

Total managed expenditure per capita
(2011/12 prices) – Scotland and UK

13,000
12,000 — Scotland
11,000 — UK
10,000
9,000
8,000
7,000
6,000
5,000
4,000

1984–5 89–90 94–95 99–00 04–05 09–10

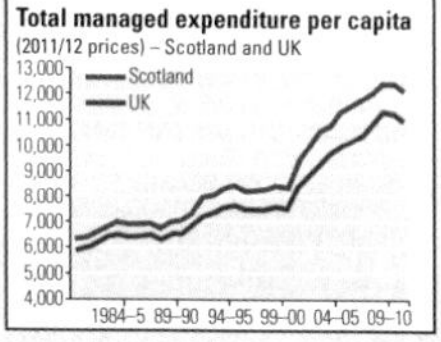

International relations

A legal opinion for the UK government by international lawyers indicated that by far the most likely outcome of Scottish independence is that the UK would become a 'continuator state', retaining its memberships and status under international law, and that Scotland would form a new state, meaning that its membership of international organisations and institutions, such as the United Nations and European Union, would not be automatic.

Regional results of April 2013 poll

- Yes
- No
- Don't know

Polls on independence

Do you agree that Scotland should be independent?

- Yes
- No
- Don't know

April 2013 — 19% / 30% / 51%

By gender

Male — 17% / 36% / 47%
Female — 21% / 25% / 55%

Percentage of 'yes' votes in polls: historical trend

%
60
SNP form majority government
50 — Poll tax introduced in Scotland
Scottish parliament opens
40
30
20
Devolution referendum
10
SNP form majority government
Edinburgh Agreement signed
0

1980 1985 1990 1995 2000 2005 2010

18 Sept 2014 referendum

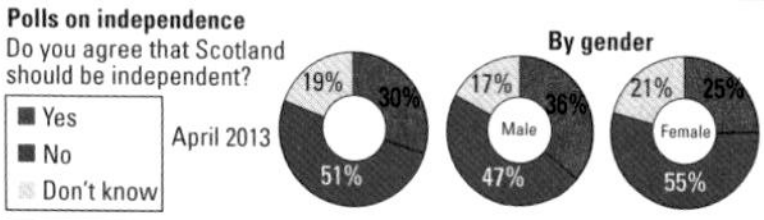

Demographics

GDP: £124,676 billion. Population: 5.3 million (2011 census)

Likely to vote 'yes'

Composition of parliament

Government	Opposition Parties
SNP (64) ○	Labour (37) ●
	Conservative (15) ●
	Liberal Democrats (5) ●
	Green (2) ●
	Independent (4) ○
	Presiding Officer ●

© IISS

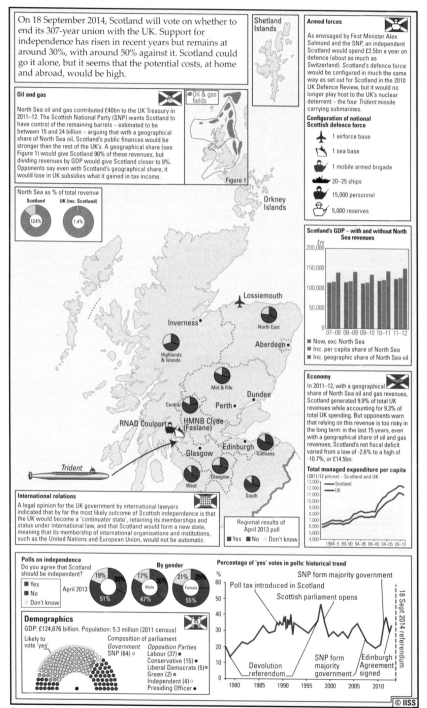

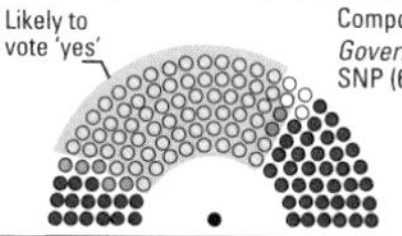

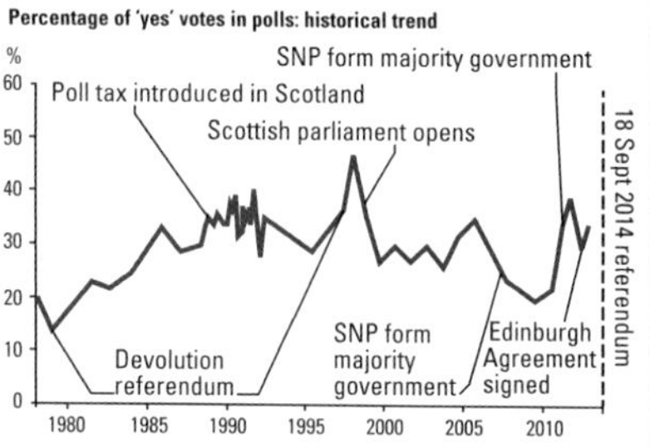

Sources: BBC; Better Together; GERS; Guardian; HM Government; Icas; Institute for Fiscal Studies; Ipsos MORI; Office for National Statistics; UK government, Scotland analysis: Devolution and the implications of Scottish independence – Annex A: Opinion; Scottish government; Scottish Marine Government Directive; Scottish National Accounts Project; TNS BMRB; University of Aberdeen/Professor Alex Kemp; Yes Scotland; YouGov.

Islamic extremism in West Africa

Though the number of terrorist attacks around the world is generally in decline, they are taking place with growing frequency in Africa, and West Africa in particular. Islamic extremist groups are taking advantage of poor – and in some areas non-existent – governance, as well as porous borders, to launch transnational terror campaigns. Popular religious and socio-economic grievances, to which the current pan-Sahel food crisis is a contributing factor, are powerful recruiting tools for extremists.

Active Islamic extremist groups

Group	Area of operations	Approximate size
Al-Qaeda in the Islamic Maghreb (AQIM)		**300**
AQIM emerged in late 2006/early 2007. It aims to establish an Islamic state in Algeria and to unify regional jihadist movements against the West. The group operates and recruits throughout the Maghreb, and has been implicated in drugs-trafficking and kidnapping. AQIM is also accused of establishing terrorist cells in various Western European countries.		
Ansar al-Din		**Hundreds**
Led by veteran Tuareg leader Iyad ag Ghaly, this Salafist group hijacked the 'secular' Mouvement National pour la Libération de l'Azawad (MNLA) rebellion in Mali in early 2012. The group is primarily composed of ethnic Tuaregs and aims to impose sharia law across Mali.		
Ansaru		
A Boko Haram splinter group, which is thought to have the closest ties to AQIM of all the regional extremist groups. It officially emerged in early 2012 and focuses on carrying out kidnappings and killings of Westerners.		
Boko Haram		**Unconfirmed estimates suggest it has 60 core members, with a further 250–300 who can be called upon, as well as a larger support network**
These militants from Nigeria's impoverished Muslim north have called for the establishment of sharia law and led a revolt against the government's perceived southern bias and repressive security forces. Although established in 2002, the group only began its violent campaign in 2009. Its near-daily attacks in northern and central Nigeria are usually aimed at domestic targets. In May 2013, President Goodluck Jonathan declared a state of emergency in the country's northeast, pledging to send up to 8,000 troops in an operation to flush out Boko Haram.		
Islamic Movement for Azawad		
An offshoot of Ansar al-Din, the group is thought to be made up of Malians alone. It has rejected extremism, calling instead for a political settlement between Mali's authorities and the northern separatist movement.		
Mouvement pour l'unicité et le jihad en Afrique de l'Ouest (MUJAO)		**Hundreds**
MUJAO is an AQIM splinter group that emerged in mid-2011; it aims to spread Salafist doctrine throughout West Africa, rather than just the Maghreb and Sahel regions. It teamed up with Ansar al-Din in June 2012 to defeat the MNLA in a battle for the Malian city of Gao, facilitating Ansar al-Din's rapid takeover of Timbuktu and Kidal. MUJAO also kidnapped three aid workers from the Tindouf Western Saharan refugee camp in Algeria in October 2011, only releasing them in July 2012 in exchange for Islamists held in Mauritania (and an unconfirmed ransom). It is thought to have carried out two suicide attacks in Niger in May 2013 on the orders of Mokhtar Belmokhtar.		
Signed-in-Blood Battalion (SIBB)		
Led by Mokhtar Belmokhtar, this AQIM splinter group formed in late 2012 and gained notoriety for its January 2013 attack on Algeria's In Amenas gas plant that left 38 civilians and 29 militants dead. Belmokhtar is also thought to have instructed MUJAO to carry out two suicide attacks in Niger in May.		

Relationships between the main regional extremist groups

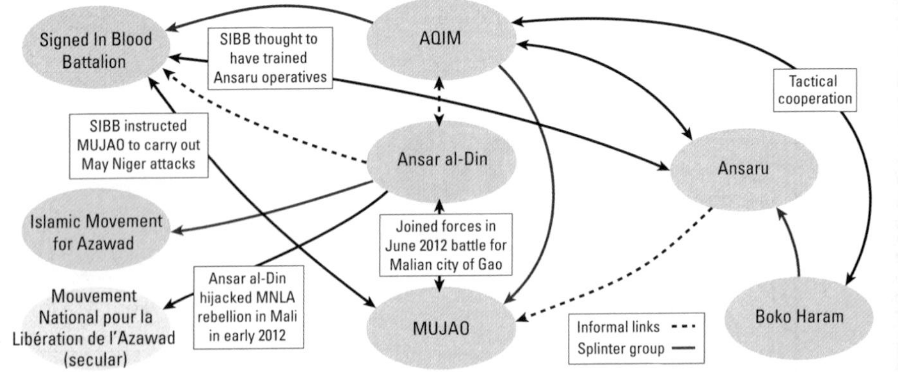

Sources: Guardian; IISS; New York Times; Transparency International; United Nations Office for the Coordination of Humanitarian Affairs (UNOCHA); US Department of State; US National Counterterrorism Center; World Bank.

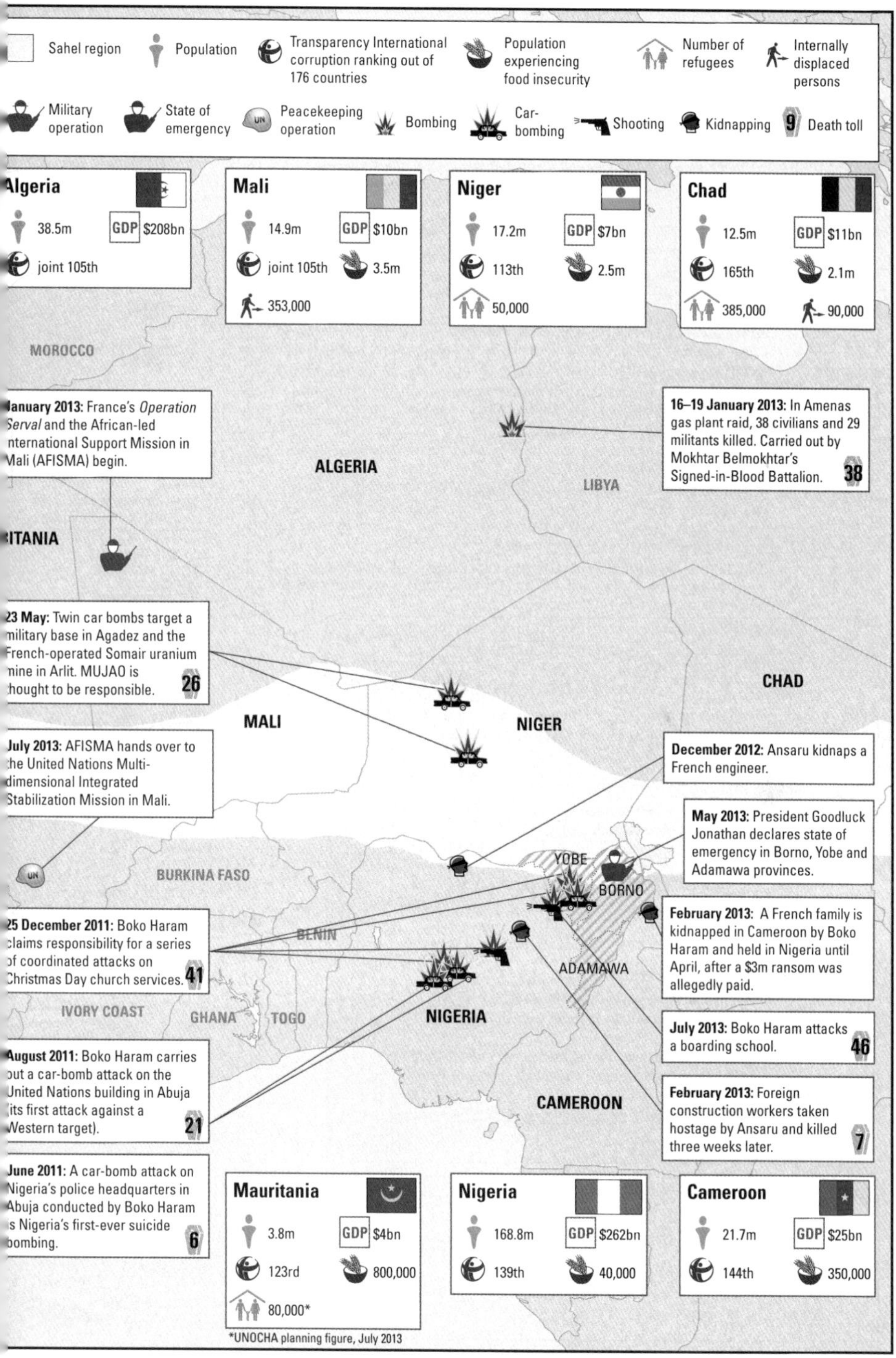
Sahel region
Population
Transparency International corruption ranking out of 176 countries
Population experiencing food insecurity
Number of refugees
Internally displaced persons
Military operation
State of emergency
Peacekeeping operation
Bombing
Car-bombing
Shooting
Kidnapping
9 Death toll
Algeria
38.5m
GDP $208bn
joint 105th
Mali
14.9m
GDP $10bn
joint 105th
3.5m
353,000
Niger
17.2m
GDP $7bn
113th
2.5m
50,000
Chad
12.5m
GDP $11bn
165th
2.1m
385,000
90,000
MOROCCO
January 2013: France's Operation Serval and the African-led International Support Mission in Mali (AFISMA) begin.
ALGERIA
16–19 January 2013: In Amenas gas plant raid, 38 civilians and 29 militants killed. Carried out by Mokhtar Belmokhtar's Signed-in-Blood Battalion. 38
LIBYA
ITANIA
23 May: Twin car bombs target a military base in Agadez and the French-operated Somair uranium mine in Arlit. MUJAO is thought to be responsible. 26
CHAD
MALI
NIGER
July 2013: AFISMA hands over to the United Nations Multi-dimensional Integrated Stabilization Mission in Mali.
December 2012: Ansaru kidnaps a French engineer.
May 2013: President Goodluck Jonathan declares state of emergency in Borno, Yobe and Adamawa provinces.
YOBE
BURKINA FASO
BORNO
25 December 2011: Boko Haram claims responsibility for a series of coordinated attacks on Christmas Day church services. 41
BENIN
February 2013: A French family is kidnapped in Cameroon by Boko Haram and held in Nigeria until April, after a $3m ransom was allegedly paid.
ADAMAWA
IVORY COAST
GHANA
TOGO
NIGERIA
July 2013: Boko Haram attacks a boarding school. 46
August 2011: Boko Haram carries out a car-bomb attack on the United Nations building in Abuja (its first attack against a Western target). 21
CAMEROON
February 2013: Foreign construction workers taken hostage by Ansaru and killed three weeks later. 7
June 2011: A car-bomb attack on Nigeria's police headquarters in Abuja conducted by Boko Haram is Nigeria's first-ever suicide bombing. 6
Mauritania
3.8m
GDP $4bn
123rd
800,000
80,000*
Nigeria
168.8m
GDP $262bn
139th
40,000
Cameroon
21.7m
GDP $25bn
144th
350,000
*UNOCHA planning figure, July 2013

Syria's increasingly internationalised civil war

As the Syrian civil war has escalated, countries in the region and beyond have been increasingly drawn into the conflict. Iran, Iraq and Hizbullah, the Lebanese Shia militia organisation, have acted in support of the regime of President Bashar al-Assad, while the West, Saudi Arabia, Turkey and Qatar have given financial and military aid to rebel groups. Diplomatic efforts to end the conflict have been unsuccessful and the region faces an acute humanitarian crisis.

DIPLOMATIC TIMELINE

March 2011	Popular demonstrations against the Assad regime begin, developing into an armed rebellion within a month.
September 2011	European Union imposes embargo on oil imports from Syria.
February 2012	China and Russia veto a United Nations resolution calling for Assad to resign.
March 2012	UN–Arab League special envoy Kofi Annan proposes a six-point peace plan to end the civil war. A ceasefire takes effect in April but fighting resumes in June.
April 2012	The Friends of Syria, an international group that supports the Syrian opposition, recognises the Syrian National Council as a legitimate representative of the Syrian people. At a later meeting in Paris, the group backs Annan's plan to resolve the crisis.
June 2012	As violent clashes persist, the UN suspends its observer mission. At a meeting convened by Annan in Geneva, world powers agree on a plan for a transitional government to be set up to end the conflict in Syria. There is no consensus on the removal of Assad.
August 2012	Annan steps down as special envoy. The UN appoints veteran Algerian diplomat Lakhdar Brahimi to replace him.
December 2012	Brahimi holds talks with Russian and US diplomats in an effort to push forward the Geneva communiqué from June. There is no significant breakthrough. Russia's President Vladimir Putin says it cannot support Assad 'at any price'; Deputy Foreign Minister Bogdanov says the Syrian government is 'losing control'.
May 2013	Russia and the US propose another international conference, dubbed 'Geneva II', but the US postpones the conference until July. The EU announces it will not renew an arms embargo on the Syrian opposition.

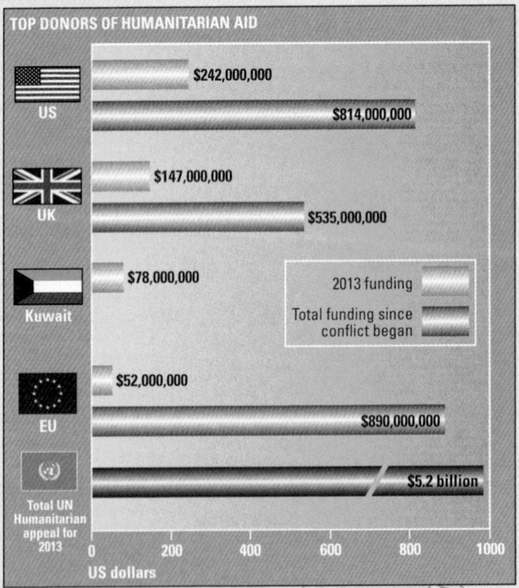

Government-held areas
Rebel-held areas
Contested areas
Kurdish areas
Refugee camps
Syrian refugees
Hizbullah
June 2012
Turkish warplane shot down in Syrian airspace, killing 2 people.
June 2011–June 2013
Fighting in Tripoli between Sunni militants and Alawite forces aligned with Assad and Hizbullah.
June 2013
Clashes in Bekaa Valley between Syrian rebels and Hizbullah fighters after Syrian rockets hit Baalbek, a Hizbullah stronghold.
May 2013
Exchange of fire between Israeli and Syrian forces across the ceasefire line in Golan Heights.
January–May 2013
Israeli air-strikes target Iranian-supplied Fateh-110 missiles, Russian SA-17 anti-aircraft missiles and Syria's main scientific research centre near Damascus.
ISRAEL
EGYPT
95,364

CONFLICT IN FIGURES

Number of deaths since March 2011:	Number of refugees as of 17 July 2013:	Number of IDPs as of 16 April 2013:
93,000–100,000	1,811,867	4,254,500

Sources: al-Arabiya; al-Jazeera; BBC News; CNN; Department for International Development; European Commission Humanitarian Aid Office; Financial Times; Guardian; New York Times; ReliefWeb; Syria Needs Analysis Project; Syrian Observatory for Human Rights; UNHCR; UNOCHA; United States Agency for International Development; VOA News; Washington Post

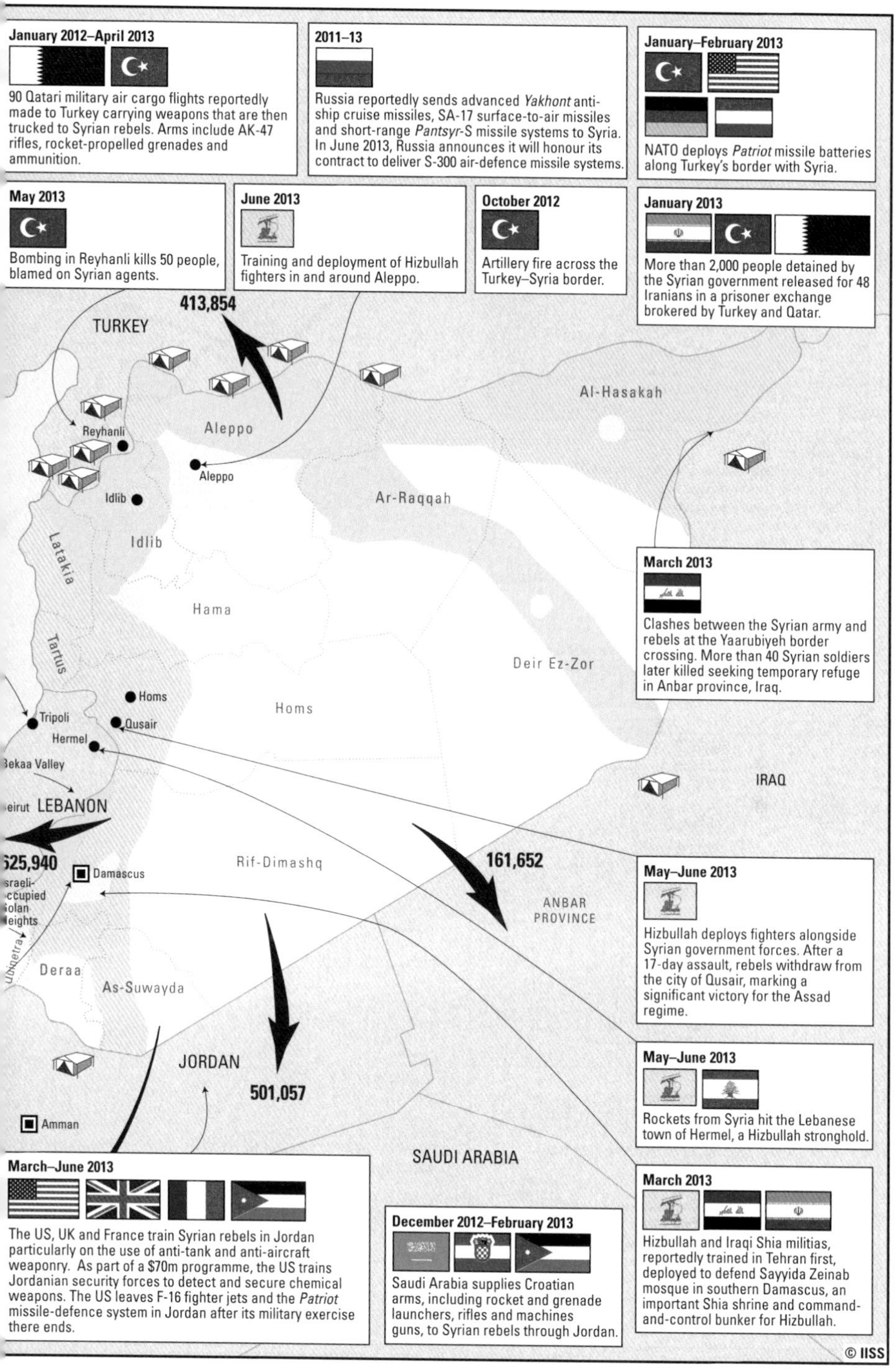
January 2012–April 2013
90 Qatari military air cargo flights reportedly made to Turkey carrying weapons that are then trucked to Syrian rebels. Arms include AK-47 rifles, rocket-propelled grenades and ammunition.
2011–13
Russia reportedly sends advanced Yakhont anti-ship cruise missiles, SA-17 surface-to-air missiles and short-range Pantsyr-S missile systems to Syria. In June 2013, Russia announces it will honour its contract to deliver S-300 air-defence missile systems.
January–February 2013
NATO deploys Patriot missile batteries along Turkey's border with Syria.
May 2013
Bombing in Reyhanli kills 50 people, blamed on Syrian agents.
June 2013
Training and deployment of Hizbullah fighters in and around Aleppo.
October 2012
Artillery fire across the Turkey–Syria border.
January 2013
More than 2,000 people detained by the Syrian government released for 48 Iranians in a prisoner exchange brokered by Turkey and Qatar.
413,854
TURKEY
Reyhanli
Aleppo
Aleppo
Al-Hasakah
Idlib
Ar-Raqqah
Idlib
Latakia
Hama
Tartus
Deir Ez-Zor
March 2013
Clashes between the Syrian army and rebels at the Yaarubiyeh border crossing. More than 40 Syrian soldiers later killed seeking temporary refuge in Anbar province, Iraq.
Homs
Homs
Tripoli
Qusair
Hermel
Bekaa Valley
LEBANON
IRAQ
Beirut
525,940
Damascus
Rif-Dimashq
161,652
ANBAR PROVINCE
Israeli-occupied Golan Heights
May–June 2013
Hizbullah deploys fighters alongside Syrian government forces. After a 17-day assault, rebels withdraw from the city of Qusair, marking a significant victory for the Assad regime.
Deraa
As-Suwayda
Quneitra
JORDAN
501,057
May–June 2013
Rockets from Syria hit the Lebanese town of Hermel, a Hizbullah stronghold.
Amman
SAUDI ARABIA
March–June 2013
The US, UK and France train Syrian rebels in Jordan particularly on the use of anti-tank and anti-aircraft weaponry. As part of a $70m programme, the US trains Jordanian security forces to detect and secure chemical weapons. The US leaves F-16 fighter jets and the Patriot missile-defence system in Jordan after its military exercise there ends.
December 2012–February 2013
Saudi Arabia supplies Croatian arms, including rocket and grenade launchers, rifles and machines guns, to Syrian rebels through Jordan.
March 2013
Hizbullah and Iraqi Shia militias, reportedly trained in Tehran first, deployed to defend Sayyida Zeinab mosque in southern Damascus, an important Shia shrine and command-and-control bunker for Hizbullah.
© IISS

Afghanistan: the long drawdown

The United States and its NATO allies face a significant logistical challenge in redeploying forces and equipment from land-locked Afghanistan in preparation for the end of ISAF's combat mission in 2014, while still conducting operations. All three main transit routes pose problems for planners, while the scale of the task is forcing the major contributors to utilise multiple routes in order to complete their withdrawal on schedule.

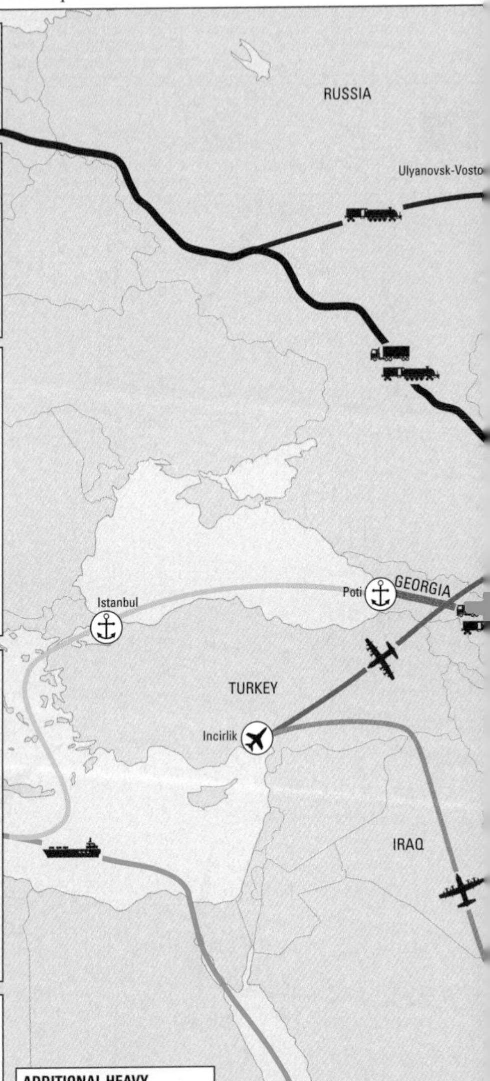

AIR ROUTES TO EUROPE AND THE GULF

Air freight direct from Camp Bastion, Bagram air base, Mazar-e-Sharif airport or Kabul airport is the most costly redeployment method, and is reserved for troops and sensitive or expensive items, with a mixture of air force and commercial transport being used.

COST OF COMMERCIAL TRANSIT

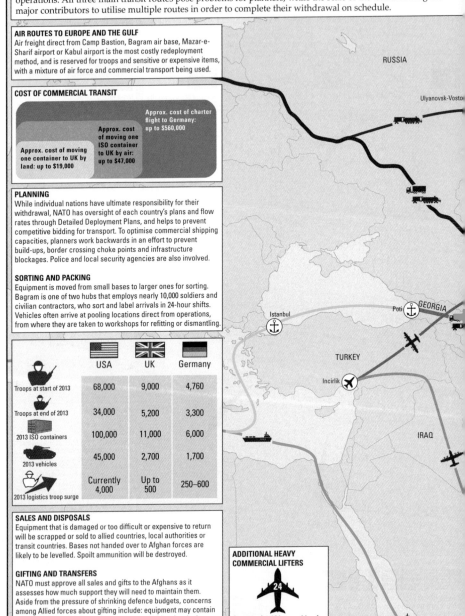

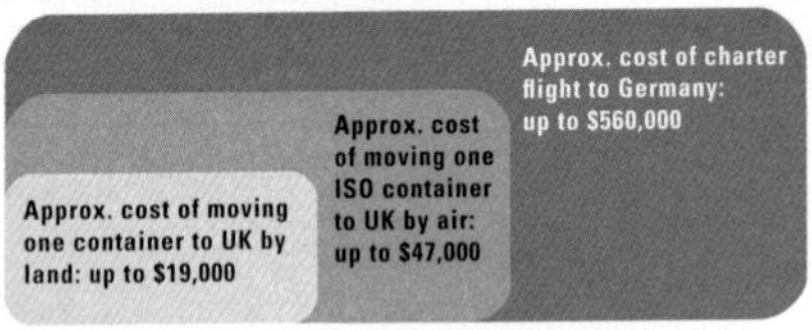

PLANNING

While individual nations have ultimate responsibility for their withdrawal, NATO has oversight of each country's plans and flow rates through Detailed Deployment Plans, and helps to prevent competitive bidding for transport. To optimise commercial shipping capacities, planners work backwards in an effort to prevent build-ups, border crossing choke points and infrastructure blockages. Police and local security agencies are also involved.

SORTING AND PACKING

Equipment is moved from small bases to larger ones for sorting. Bagram is one of two hubs that employs nearly 10,000 soldiers and civilian contractors, who sort and label arrivals in 24-hour shifts. Vehicles often arrive at pooling locations direct from operations, from where they are taken to workshops for refitting or dismantling.

	USA	UK	Germany
Troops at start of 2013	68,000	9,000	4,760
Troops at end of 2013	34,000	5,200	3,300
2013 ISO containers	100,000	11,000	6,000
2013 vehicles	45,000	2,700	1,700
2013 logistics troop surge	Currently 4,000	Up to 500	250–600

SALES AND DISPOSALS

Equipment that is damaged or too difficult or expensive to return will be scrapped or sold to allied countries, local authorities or transit countries. Bases not handed over to Afghan forces are likely to be levelled. Spoilt ammunition will be destroyed.

GIFTING AND TRANSFERS

NATO must approve all sales and gifts to the Afghans as it assesses how much support they will need to maintain them. Aside from the pressure of shrinking defence budgets, concerns among Allied forces about gifting include: equipment may contain sensitive technological components; arms could end up in the wrong hands; and leaving behind more potent weapons might not be compatible with arms-export guidelines or United Nations regulations.

ADDITIONAL HEAVY COMMERCIAL LIFTERS

24

Antonov An-124s capable of carrying oversized equipment ready to charter, but 12+ NATO nations bidding to hire them.

Sources: Aviation Week, Christian Science Monitor, Defense News, en.apa.az, EurasiaNet.org, Guardian, Hansard, isn.ethz.ch, Jane's Defence Weekly, nato-russia-council.info, NBCnews.com, parliament.gov.uk, RUSI, Spiegel Online, Time.

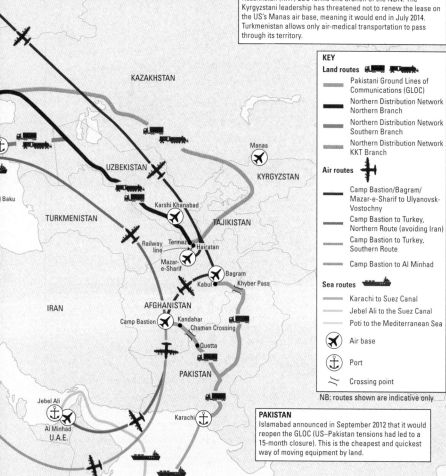

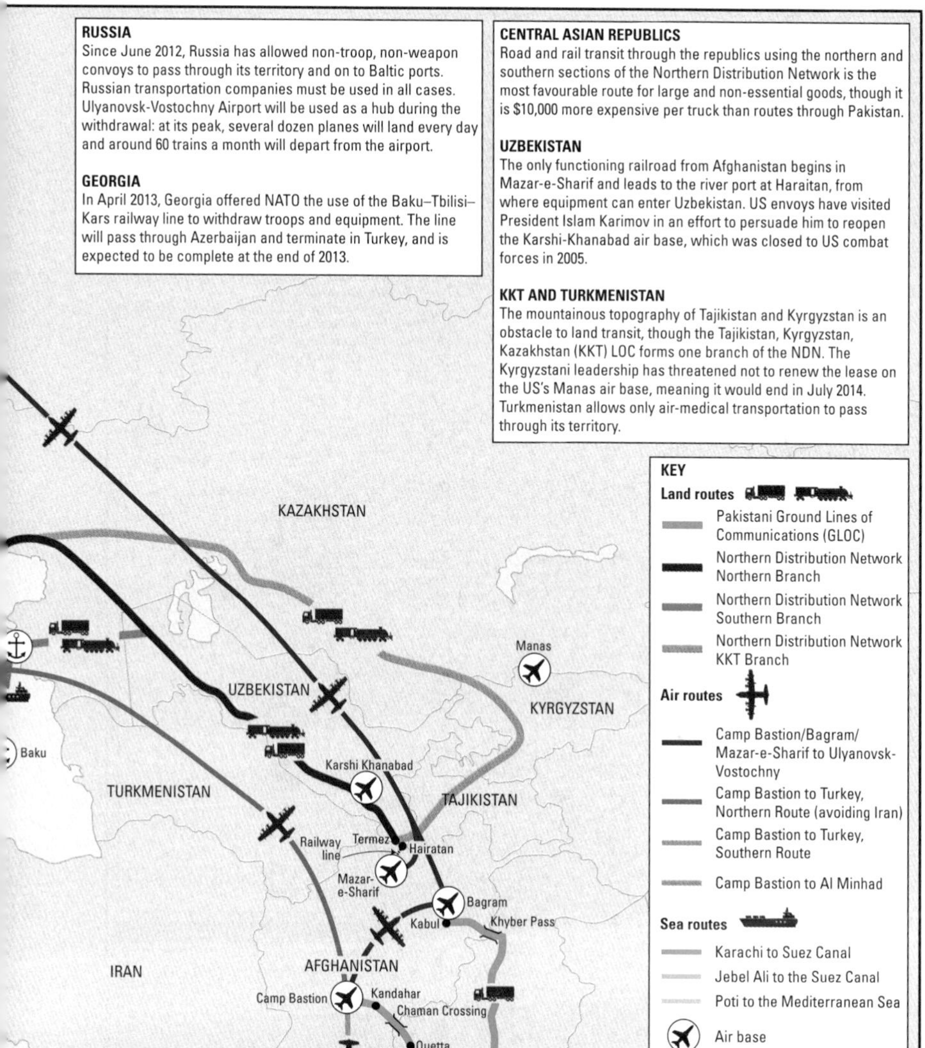

RUSSIA
Since June 2012, Russia has allowed non-troop, non-weapon convoys to pass through its territory and on to Baltic ports. Russian transportation companies must be used in all cases. Ulyanovsk-Vostochny Airport will be used as a hub during the withdrawal: at its peak, several dozen planes will land every day and around 60 trains a month will depart from the airport.

GEORGIA
In April 2013, Georgia offered NATO the use of the Baku–Tbilisi–Kars railway line to withdraw troops and equipment. The line will pass through Azerbaijan and terminate in Turkey, and is expected to be complete at the end of 2013.

CENTRAL ASIAN REPUBLICS
Road and rail transit through the republics using the northern and southern sections of the Northern Distribution Network is the most favourable route for large and non-essential goods, though it is $10,000 more expensive per truck than routes through Pakistan.

UZBEKISTAN
The only functioning railroad from Afghanistan begins in Mazar-e-Sharif and leads to the river port at Haraitan, from where equipment can enter Uzbekistan. US envoys have visited President Islam Karimov in an effort to persuade him to reopen the Karshi-Khanabad air base, which was closed to US combat forces in 2005.

KKT AND TURKMENISTAN
The mountainous topography of Tajikistan and Kyrgyzstan is an obstacle to land transit, though the Tajikistan, Kyrgyzstan, Kazakhstan (KKT) LOC forms one branch of the NDN. The Kyrgyzstani leadership has threatened not to renew the lease on the US's Manas air base, meaning it would end in July 2014. Turkmenistan allows only air-medical transportation to pass through its territory.

PAKISTAN
Islamabad announced in September 2012 that it would reopen the GLOC (US–Pakistan tensions had led to a 15-month closure). This is the cheapest and quickest way of moving equipment by land.

North Korea does it again

Provocations by the Democratic People's Republic of Korea (DPRK) over the past year have raised tensions and reinforced international concerns over its nuclear and missile capabilities. The Kim Jong-un regime's attempts, meanwhile, to expand its fissile material production with the repair of the Yongbyon reactor, along with its bellicose rhetoric, further unsettled the region. These actions were met with global condemnation and two new United Nations Security Council sanctions resolutions.

TIMELINE

12 December 2012:	DPRK launches an *Unha*-3 missile to successfully place the *Kwangmyongsong*-3 satellite into space
22 January 2013:	UN Security Council (UNSC) passes Resolution 2087, tightening existing sanctions
12 February:	DPRK conducts third nuclear test, estimated at 4–8 kilotonnes
1 March–30 April:	US and ROK conduct large-scale military exercise *Foal Eagle*
7 March:	UNSC passes Resolution 2094, adding new sanctions
11–21 March:	US and ROK conduct command-post military exercise *Key Resolve*
2 April:	DPRK announces it will restart 5 MW(e) reactor at Yongbyon, which was partially disabled in 2008 under a denuclearisation agreement
3 April:	DPRK reportedly moves two medium-range *Musudan* missiles to east coast in preparation for launch
3 May:	DPRK closes Kaesong Industrial Complex
7 May:	DPRK reportedly removes two *Musudan* missiles from launch site
18–20 May:	DPRK test fires six short-range rockets

UN SECURITY COUNCIL RESOLUTIONS

UNSCR 2087:	'condemns' missile test; adds four DPRK officials and six DPRK entities to travel-ban and asset-freeze list, all related to the nuclear and missile programmes.
UNSCR 2094:	'condemns' nuclear test; adds new financial sanctions, including banning bulk cash transfers, requires states to inspect cargo if reasonable grounds, explicitly lists some luxury items, adds three DPRK officials and three DPRK entities related to illicit programmes to travel-ban and asset-freeze list.

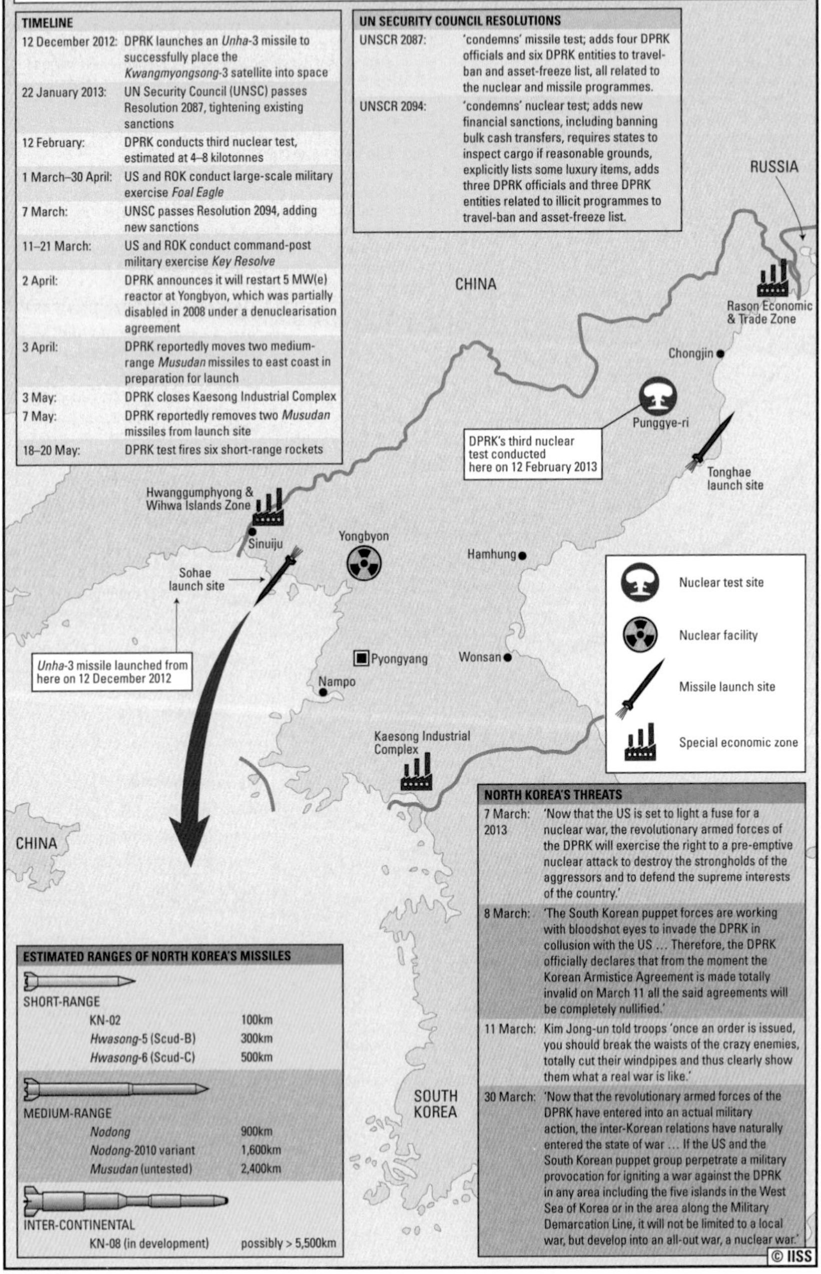

NORTH KOREA'S THREATS

7 March: 2013	'Now that the US is set to light a fuse for a nuclear war, the revolutionary armed forces of the DPRK will exercise the right to a pre-emptive nuclear attack to destroy the strongholds of the aggressors and to defend the supreme interests of the country.'
8 March:	'The South Korean puppet forces are working with bloodshot eyes to invade the DPRK in collusion with the US ... Therefore, the DPRK officially declares that from the moment the Korean Armistice Agreement is made totally invalid on March 11 all the said agreements will be completely nullified.'
11 March:	Kim Jong-un told troops 'once an order is issued, you should break the waists of the crazy enemies, totally cut their windpipes and thus clearly show them what a real war is like.'
30 March:	'Now that the revolutionary armed forces of the DPRK have entered into an actual military action, the inter-Korean relations have naturally entered the state of war ... If the US and the South Korean puppet group perpetrate a military provocation for igniting a war against the DPRK in any area including the five islands in the West Sea of Korea or in the area along the Military Demarcation Line, it will not be limited to a local war, but develop into an all-out war, a nuclear war.'

ESTIMATED RANGES OF NORTH KOREA'S MISSILES

SHORT-RANGE	
KN-02	100km
Hwasong-5 (Scud-B)	300km
Hwasong-6 (Scud-C)	500km
MEDIUM-RANGE	
Nodong	900km
Nodong-2010 variant	1,600km
Musudan (untested)	2,400km
INTER-CONTINENTAL	
KN-08 (in development)	possibly > 5,500km

Source: IISS

Chapter 6

Middle East/Gulf

Two years after the Arab uprisings shook the regional landscape and political culture, there remained an acute sense of uncertainty and disorder throughout the region, with the intensification of the civil war in Syria, enduring Iran-centred tensions, political violence in Iraq and growing unrest in Egypt that led to the sudden removal of President Muhammad Morsi.

Although the balance of power in the Middle East remained essentially intact in the year to mid-2013, the unfolding conflict in Syria was expected to shape the future of the Levant, and by extension the regional order. Indeed, it drew in every neighbouring country and destabilised its vicinity: in terms of both spillover effects and regional competition, it quickly surpassed the Iraq War. The Sunni-Shia divide, still brewing in neighbouring Lebanon and Iraq, found a new arena, as did the rivalry between Iran and Saudi Arabia. Major powers, notably Saudi Arabia, Turkey and Iran, saw their regional influence as being tied closely to the outcome of the struggle over Syria. The war cemented a convergence of interests and sectarian solidarity between the regime of President Bashar al-Assad, Iran, Iraq and Hizbullah. Al-Qaeda affiliates and Hizbullah, the Lebanese Shia militant party, faced each other directly on the Syrian battlefield – adding a distinctly sectarian jihadist dimension. The anti-regime camp was, however, beset by rivalries, notably between Saudi Arabia and Qatar but also between pro-Muslim Brotherhood Turkey and

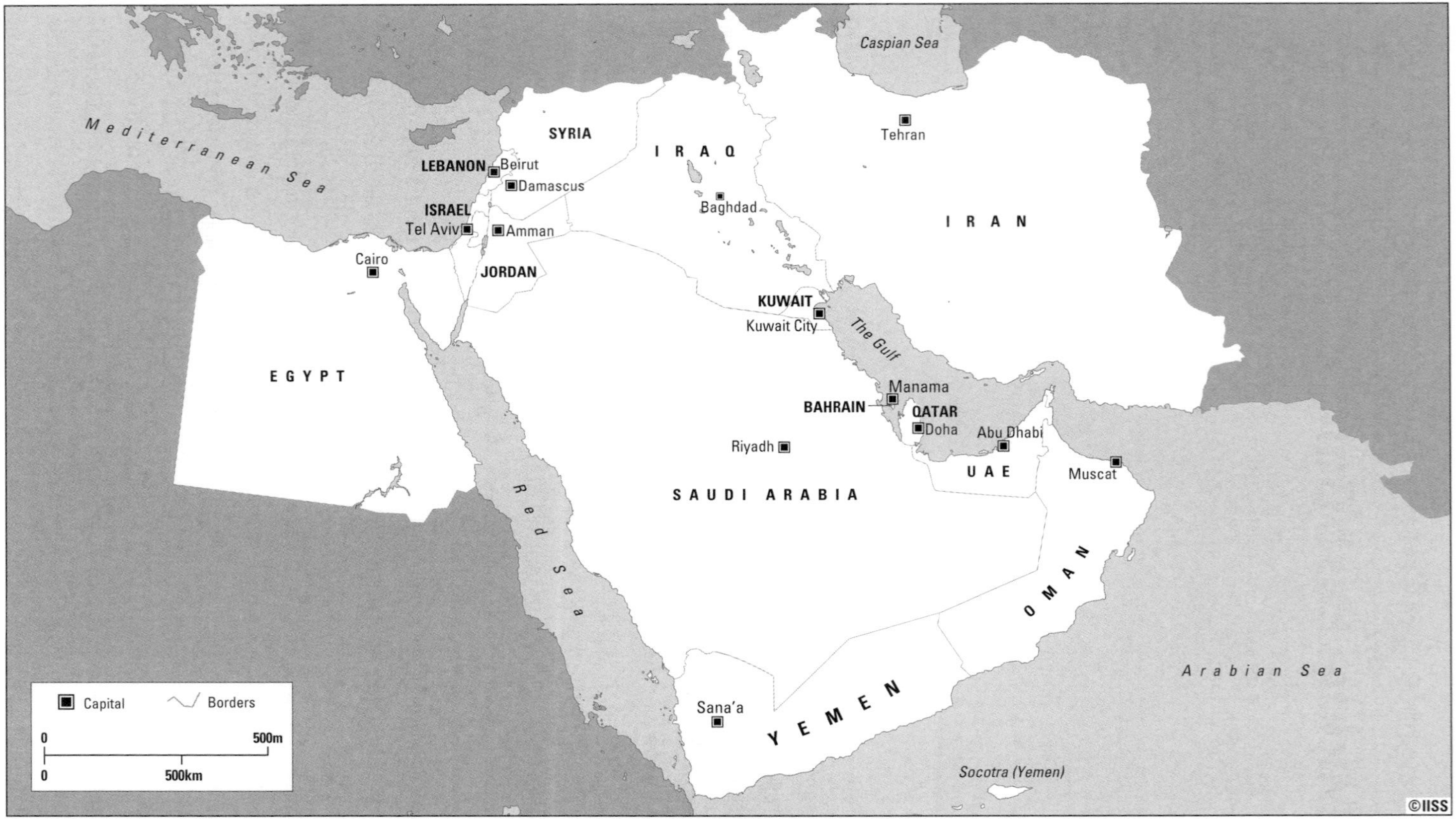
Mediterranean Sea
Caspian Sea
SYRIA
IRAQ
IRAN
Tehran
LEBANON
Beirut
Damascus
ISRAEL
Tel Aviv
Amman
Baghdad
Cairo
JORDAN
KUWAIT
Kuwait City
The Gulf
EGYPT
Manama
BAHRAIN
QATAR
Doha
Abu Dhabi
Riyadh
UAE
Muscat
Red Sea
SAUDI ARABIA
OMAN
Arabian Sea
Sana'a
YEMEN
Socotra (Yemen)
Capital
Borders
0
500m
0
500km
©IISS

Qatar and anti-Muslim Brotherhood countries, all of which were compounded by US hesitancy and reluctance to coordinate and harmonise the opposition's activities.

Egypt, meanwhile, struggled to exert regional influence. Morsi, who took office on 30 June 2012 after being elected as the candidate of the Muslim Brotherhood, managed to play a key role in ending the conflict between Israel and Hamas in November and started a rapprochement with Iran. But the country was steadily engulfed by protests against the president's style of leadership and the government's poor administration. Discontent with the perceived power play of the Muslim Brotherhood and worsening economic and social conditions spread to key segments of society, including the judiciary, the military, the revolutionary youth and the secular opposition. By mid-2013, these constituencies coalesced against Morsi and mounted a popular challenge which peaked on 3 July with the removal of Morsi and a crackdown on the Brotherhood. The acrimonious and polarising dismissal of Egypt's first democratically elected president ended a volatile experiment in Islamist government, at the risk of alienating Islamist movements from mainstream politics. It also marked the ascendancy of anti-Brotherhood Gulf nations, notably Saudi Arabia and the United Arab Emirates (UAE), over Qatar and Turkey, which had so far positioned themselves as the mentors of the Arab world's transitioning countries.

The war in Syria created new risks for Israel, which was drawn into the conflict: its air force repeatedly struck Syrian targets to destroy weapons allegedly destined for Hizbullah, raising concerns of a regional war. The regional upheaval troubled an already difficult landscape for Israel, which had lost in 2011 a reliable partner in Egypt's Hosni Mubarak. The short conflict with Hamas in late 2012, turmoil on the Sinai Peninsula, the frailty of Jordan, the weakening of the Assad regime and Hizbullah's desire to acquire game-changing weapons – notably anti-aircraft missiles – meant that each of Israel's neighbours now posed a threat.

The Syrian conflict also exposed divisions in the Arab world. Qatar, in cooperation with Turkey, emerged as a key provider of political and material assistance to the Syrian Muslim Brotherhood and promoted the group regionally and internationally. Saudi Arabia and the UAE, however, supported other components of the Syrian opposition to balance Qatar's ambitious power play and the regional rise of the Brotherhood.

The vulnerability of Jordan and Lebanon to the Syrian conflict became more pronounced. Both countries hosted growing numbers of Syrian refugees, had their territory used to send weaponry and fighters to Syria, and were directly exposed to the military repercussions of the civil war. The Lebanese prime minister, Najib Mikati, who had tried to adopt a policy of neutrality, had to resign after being abandoned by his centrist allies. Jordan held elections in January 2013 to relieve the tension building up against the government, but the Islamic Action Front, its main opposition party, chose to boycott them. Iraq too was affected. The Shia-dominated government of Nuri al-Maliki feared that a Sunni victory in Syria would rekindle the hopes of its own Sunni minority. It proceeded to contain Sunni protest movements, often using deadly force, and moved against key Sunni politicians, only inflaming passions in the process.

The growing radicalisation of the Syrian opposition and the emergence of Salafist groups threatened to provide a foothold for jihadism at the heart of the Arab world. There were signs of jihadist re-emergence in Jordan and Lebanon too, heightening fears that returning fighters would bring the conflict home. The influx of foreign fighters from not only the Middle East but also Western and Asian countries raised the prospect of terrorist activities beyond Syrian borders.

Iran's perceived ambitions remained a central element of regional politics. Tehran's escalating support for Assad, alongside Iraq's Shia-dominated central government, amplified geopolitical rivalries just as questions about US commitment to Gulf security were raised. The US decision in February 2013 to withdraw an aircraft carrier group from the Gulf as a result of budgetary constraints, inconclusive talks with Iran over its nuclear programme and cyber attacks on Aramco, the Saudi oil giant, and RasGas, Qatar's main gas company, further alarmed the Gulf states. To reassure their Gulf allies, the US, French and British governments maintained a military presence in the region and pushed arms sales.

By mid-2013, the situation in the Arab world appeared bleak, with post-revolutionary transitions gone awry in North Africa and a civil war being fought in the heart of the Levant. The Gulf states, which had managed to counter dissent, faced daunting social and economic challenges that required new policy responses in a tense regional environment.

Spreading Conflict in the Levant

Syria: regime fights back

Syria's deepening civil war dislocated society, caused enormous human suffering and affected the country's immediate neighbourhood. The struggle acquired an overt sectarian character. It extended to all corners of the country, and increasingly involved foreign actors on the sides of both the regime and the rebellion. By mid-2013, a stalemate had developed to the short-term advantage of Bashar al-Assad's regime.

As the death toll increased, calls for foreign intervention grew louder, to no avail. By mid-2013, 100,000 Syrians had been killed in the violence; more than 1.5 million Syrians had sought refuge in neighbouring countries, while more than 5 million were internally displaced. Sectarian massacres, overwhelmingly by regime forces and affiliates, reinforced the communal nature of the conflict. Tentative UN-led diplomacy to bring the main global, regional and local players together faced major hurdles.

Stalemate reached

The second half of 2012 witnessed significant rebel momentum and a shift from a war of attrition in the rural areas to attempts to capture urban centres. During the summer, a bomb inside the national security headquarters killed senior regime figures, a top confidant of Assad defected, as did his prime minister, and rebel groups launched an attack on Aleppo, the country's largest city and commercial centre. The battle for Aleppo proved considerably harder; after securing much of the city's eastern side in the fighting's early weeks, the rebel offensive stalled as the regime, backed by militias composed of various minorities, defended loyalist neighbourhoods. The transformation of the conflict into urban warfare came at a huge humanitarian cost and induced negative perceptions of the rebels among many civilians.

In March 2013, rebels finally captured the northeast city of Ar-Raqqah and much of the north, including oilfields and agricultural areas. A push on Damascus from the east and the south in late 2012 and early 2013 also mobilised large numbers of rebels.

By mid-2013, however, it was clear that their efforts elsewhere were being frustrated by the regime's military and political resilience. Indeed, Assad forces maintained military dominance and had adapted to shrinking resources and new combat conditions. The regime focused on securing the central corridor running from Damascus to Aleppo and to the coastal regions, including the cities of Homs and Hama. In several areas, rebel advances, made possible by an influx of weaponry, were reversed as foreign assistance proved inconstant and rebel ranks fragmented. As important was the regime's use of its full range of conventional capabilities, including air power and missiles. In spring 2013, it also used limited amounts of chemical agents. Alongside regime forces, an array of popular militias was deployed, as well as Shia Lebanese and Iraqi fighters.

The expansion of the rebellion sharpened existing divides within Syrian society. Clashes between Kurdish and Arab factions in the northeast multiplied; urban dwellers in Aleppo and Damascus proved extremely distrustful of the mostly rural fighters in the insurgency; many minorities, middle- and upper-class secularists and public-sector employees sided with the regime or withdrew in an effort to preserve neutrality and ensure survival.

Assad sought to capitalise on such feelings, as well as on rebel mistakes and the lack of opposition leadership. In a series of public speeches, he adopted an uncompromising stance, portraying the uprising as criminal, terrorist and Islamist in nature and as foreign-inspired. By defining more realistic goals, the regime managed to allocate its resources to meet them: the development of a war economy and economic assistance from Iran and Iraq worked to its advantage, though living conditions in the territories it controlled deteriorated.

Opposition seeks legitimacy

The fragmentation of rebel ranks and their lack of resources proved major impediments to military performance and to their ability to govern liberated territories and expand their appeal. The Free Syrian Army (FSA) suffered from a lack of leadership and command-and-control which made foreign assistance less effective and deterred Western powers from providing weapons and other types of military aid. To remedy this problem, rebel commanders and military defectors formed command structures, several of which were stillborn.

In December 2012, the Supreme Military Council (SMC), headed by General Salim Idriss, was established in an effort to coordinate logistics, intelligence and operations. The SMC became the principal interlocutor with Western powers that were considering arming Syrian rebels, but its real authority over FSA units and other rebel groups was limited. Its image was eroded by its inability to govern liberated areas, provide essential goods and services to other opposition groups, and rein in rebel units.

The concomitant radicalisation of large parts of the insurgency fed the growth of Islamist factions and led to the imposition of various versions of Islamic law in liberated territories. The military performance, discipline and resourcefulness of Salafist factions, notably Jabhat al-Nusra and Ahrar al-Sham, contributed to their popularity among Syrians, though their embrace remained more opportunistic than ideological. In December 2012, the United States designated Jabhat al-Nusra as a foreign terrorist organisation for its links to al-Qaeda. The Salafist groups remained largely outside the umbrella of the FSA, the franchise under which most rebel groups operated, and chose to form separate alliances, most notably the Syrian Islamic Front and the Syrian Islamic Liberation Front.

Syria's main opposition umbrella group, the Syrian National Council (SNC), struggled to establish legitimacy and credibility, and to create a presence inside zones where rebels had control. As a result of internal disputes over politics and resources, and of a perceived power-grab by the Muslim Brotherhood (backed by Qatar and Turkey), a number of secular-leaning members resigned from the SNC, leaving it weakened and complicating foreign patrons' support. The SNC's internal divisions and poor performance alienated a number of Western and Arab powers, leading to a revamp in November 2012. The newly formed National Coalition was a broader representation of the Syrian revolutionary movement, including local activist groups and military councils. It received full recognition by key Western powers and Arab countries, and was handed the Syrian seat at the Arab League, angering the regime.

The coalition, however, suffered from similar problems to the SNC. It chose as leader a moderate cleric, Moaz al-Khatib, who struggled to impose his authority. A general lack of resources and capability was compounded by disagreements within the coalition about the merits and modalities of a dialogue with the regime, as well as about the nature of the armed struggle, external alliances and local administration of liberated areas. The coalition moved to appoint an interim prime minister, Ghassan Hitto, to supervise local governance and conduct post-conflict planning, but his authority remained illusory. While the influence of the Muslim Brotherhood was diluted in the new alliance, tense internal politics over its role led to Khatib's resignation after only five months. This dysfunction drove a number of anti-Assad countries to shift their attention to the SMC.

Regional actors mobilise

The regionalisation of the crisis took two forms: spillover into neighbouring countries and greater involvement of regional powers inside Syria. Lebanon and Jordan, Syria's most vulnerable neighbours, were overwhelmed with refugees, and both suffered direct security repercussions. Jordan dismantled jihadist groups intent on striking on its soil while Lebanon struggled with low- and mid-level violence between pro-Assad and anti-Assad factions across the country. While Jordan received US military assistance (including air- and missile-defence systems) and Gulf financial aid, Lebanon's frail security forces and weak government came under enormous stress.

Regional competition over Syria pitted countries against one another along sectarian and strategic fault lines, deepening the Sunni-Shia divide. Across the Arab world, clerics on both sides stirred sectarian passions and called for mobilisation while satellite channels propagated increasingly strident editorial lines. Iran increased its involvement in Syria, as evidenced by the deployment of military advisers, financial aid and provision of weapons and ammunition. Iraq, where Maliki's Shia-dominated government feared that the Syrian struggle would revive

Sunni opposition at home, sided with Iran and Assad, facilitating transit of weapons and allowing Shia militiamen to deploy in Syria.

The Gulf states, on the other hand, mobilised against Assad, hoping to check Iran's power in the process, but did so in uncoordinated and often conflicting ways. Qatar worked primarily through the Muslim Brotherhood, while Saudi Arabia preferred to support other Islamist groups as well as more secular factions. These two countries emerged as the primary supporters of the rebellion, providing funding, weaponry and media coverage – Qatar mostly to groups in the north and Saudi Arabia to those in the south. The UAE, distrustful of the Muslim Brotherhood and Salafist elements of the opposition, remained comparatively disengaged.

Despite Turkey's vocal condemnation of Assad, its diplomatic role was limited by the underperformance of the Syrian opposition. A series of incidents provoked domestic criticism of the Syrian policy of Turkish Prime Minister Recep Tayyip Erdogan. Turkish demands for NATO support following the downing of a Turkish jet led to the deployment of anti-missile *Patriot* batteries. In May 2013, a car bombing in the border town of Reyhanli killed 50 people and laid bare the tensions between Syrian refugees and Turkish residents.

For its part, Israel shored up its intelligence capabilities and military readiness, intervening three times in Syria to destroy anti-aircraft and other advanced weaponry destined for Hizbullah. The Golan Heights were also affected by the instability in Syria; in June, Syrian rebel groups seized Filipino soldiers belonging to the United Nations monitoring mission.

Diplomacy interrupted

A six-point transitional plan adopted in June 2012 by global and regional powers, under UN auspices, became the focus of international diplomacy. The Geneva plan did not, however, directly address the matter of Assad's fate, which made the fragmented opposition uneasy.

Diplomacy proved a frustrating process. Kofi Annan, the first joint UN–Arab League envoy, resigned, blaming foreign powers for complicating a political solution. His successor, Lakhdar Brahimi, hoped that changing conditions on the ground, converging views between Russia and the United States and a sense of doom should diplomacy fail, would work in his favour. The taboo over negotiations with the regime was removed after Khatib, the short-lived head of the National Coalition, offered conditional talks.

Brahimi's efforts received a boost from John Kerry, the new US secretary of state, who agreed on a resumption of diplomacy with Russia and sought to mobilise opposition support. The merit and the timing of this push, which coincided with regime victories, exposed divisions within the opposition, while the Assad government agreed in principle to attend without demonstrating serious commitment to a political solution. Russia itself showed no sign of reducing its support for Assad, mentioning at times that it would provide an advanced anti-aircraft missile system to counter a possible US-led intervention in the form of a no-fly zone or a safe zone inside Syria.

Lebanon: mirroring Syria's crisis

Lebanon struggled to contain the ripple effects of the Syrian civil war. The country found itself increasingly vulnerable as political and sectarian tensions grew. Security forces struggled to respond to localised violence inspired by events in Syria and to secure the country's porous borders.

The northern part of the country and the eastern Bekaa Valley became prime conduits for the movement of fighters and weapons to Syria, as well as recipients of Syrian refugees. These two regions witnessed regular clashes between Sunni forces sympathetic to the Syrian rebellion and local allies of the Syrian regime. In particular, the northern city of Tripoli saw sporadic clashes between Sunni militiamen and Alawite fighters allied with Assad, necessitating an intervention by the Lebanese military. In order to cut rebel supply lines, the Syrian military occasionally shelled and intervened on Lebanese soil, meeting mild protests from the Lebanese government. In August 2012, security services uncovered a plot by a prominent Assad supporter, Michel Samaha, to kill prominent religious figures and spread sectarian infighting. The security chief behind his arrest, General Wissam al-Hassan, was killed in a car bombing three months later.

The Syrian struggle's sectarian turn exacerbated Lebanon's own divisions. The assertiveness of Salafist factions, until then politically marginalised, translated into radicalisation, street mobilisation and recruitment of fighters, which embarrassed the mainstream Sunni leadership. The Shia militant group Hizbullah decisively upped its involvement to support Assad even at the risk of a confrontation inside Lebanon with Sunni groups that it had previously been keen to avoid; to justify this objective, it played on the fears of the Shia community by echoing Assad's portrayal of the rebellion as foreign-inspired and Salafist-dominated. The Christian community, divided between pro- and anti-Assad factions, was alarmed by the twin rise of Sunni and Shia fundamentalism.

The Syrian refugee crisis particularly affected Lebanon. By mid-2013, more than one million refugees constituted one-fifth of the country's population. Political tensions and financial problems prevented the state from articulating an adequate strategy. In particular, fear that refugees would settle in Lebanon provoked resistance to any plan to create camps administered by the state and UN agencies. The spread of refugees created local tensions with residents and became a source of political discord.

Hizbullah was pivotal in involving Lebanon in the Syrian crisis. As a result of the expansion of the conflict, the radicalisation of the rebellion and the increased threat to its supply lines from Iran, the Shia group gradually increased its military support for Assad. Its leader, Hassan Nasrallah, hardened his discourse in a series of speeches in the spring, including one from Iran, in which he likened the fight in Syria to the resistance against Israel. Hizbullah provided assistance in the form of military expertise, operations against Syrian rebels and their sympathisers on Lebanese soil, and help in organising pro-Assad militias. Its support culminated with the deployment of fighters to reclaim the strategic town of Qusair from the Syrian rebels in June 2013.

Despite international support, Prime Minister Najib Mikati's policy of neutrality came under assault from both his pro-revolution political rivals and his own ministers affiliated with pro-Assad parties. The economic toll of the Syrian crisis proved considerable, with tourism and trade hit hard. The Gulf states warned their citizens against travelling to Lebanon; they also pressured the government over the alliance between Hizbullah and Assad.

Mikati came under other pressures. With elections scheduled for the summer of 2013, the various political factions proved unable to agree on an electoral law, driving parliament to extend its own mandate for another year. The debate over the electoral law was particularly divisive: Christian and Shia factions pushed for the election of parliamentarians only by the members of their own sect, which Sunni, independent, leftist and liberal politicians condemned as institutionalising sectarianism even more.

The performance of the cabinet also came under criticism. Although dominated by the pro-Assad March 8 faction, it failed to pass any substantive legislation while many of its ministers operated beyond the prime minister's purview. Growing energy woes, economic paralysis, discontent in the public sector, allegations of corruption and issues surrounding the development of the country's newfound gas holdings in the Mediterranean all affected its image and credibility. Tensions peaked over the fate of Ashraf Rifi, the internal security chief who was aligned with an anti-Hizbullah faction. Mikati wanted to retain him although he had reached retirement age, but the cabinet refused to do so. In March 2013, Mikati offered his resignation, hoping to force coalition partners into renewing their support. However, political shifts and interference from Saudi Arabia led to the nomination of Tammam Salam, a Beirut politician allied with the anti-Assad March 14 faction. By mid-2013, with Salam struggling to put together a cabinet, Lebanon had a weakened acting cabinet, a prime minister-in-waiting, a parliament that had extended its own term and an overstretched military.

Jordan: between Syria and a hard place

Jordan's fragile economic situation and contentious politics were exacerbated by looming threats from Syria, a decrease in foreign aid and energy shortages. The monarchy's attempts to counter mounting domestic discontent succeeded, at least for the time being, in co-opting and dividing the various segments of the opposition.

King Abdullah adopted a progressive tone, introduced minor political reforms and appointed, in October 2012, a new prime minister, Abdullah Ensour, to address the calls for change. Early legislative elections were held in January 2013, and proved controversial and divisive. Ahead of the elections, the main Islamist faction, the Islamic Action Front (IAF), set conditions for participation: modifications to the electoral law, which was designed to weaken the opposition by giving rural districts greater representation than urban centres; and an increase in the powers of parliament, which remained limited. When its demands were not met, the IAF chose to boycott the elections. The rest of the opposition and civil-society groups were split over the decision, with many choosing to part ways with the party.

Despite accusations of bribery and government meddling, independent monitors validated the election results as mostly free and fair. There was a sense among voters that the opposition was too extreme and fragmented, and that such political wrangling was dangerous at a time of gathering external threats. A reported 56% turnout and the victory of pro-government conservative and tribal candidates seemed to give the king the upper hand, if only momentarily. Even then, protests rocked several cities, such as Karak and Irbid, over social and political grievances.

King Abdullah pledged that the new government – headed once again by Ensour and comprising more technocratic figures – would introduce more reforms, but his room for manoeuvre remained limited. Jordan's financial situation worsened, partly due to the influx of Syrian refugees and energy issues linked to unstable gas supply from Egypt. Reforms to the fuel-subsidies system, which weighed heavily on the government budget, led to protests and Ensour became a target of the opposition's criticism. Public discontent also rose after the government decided to introduce new Internet regulations that could affect many news websites. A surprisingly candid interview with King Abdullah in *The Atlantic* magazine (later denounced as inaccurate by the royal court) shook Jordanian politics in spring 2013; the monarch came across as detached, condescending and lacking purpose and energy.

While the king struggled to maintain his standing at home, the prospects of a renewed US-led peace process between Israelis and Palestinians put Amman at the centre of regional diplomacy. His international profile received a boost during US President Barack Obama's visit in March but Jordan's role was made more difficult by growing popular and parliamentary criticism of Israel, especially after the Israeli attack on Gaza in November and an Israeli incursion into the al-Aqsa mosque.

The widening conflict in Syria shaped Jordan's security outlook. It led to several serious border incidents that called for greater monitoring. The influx of refugees and the cost of humanitarian relief put a major burden on the government's budget. The refugee camp of al-Zaatari became the world's largest, according to the UN. At times, Jordan restricted entry of Syrian refugees.

The rise of the Muslim Brotherhood regionally and within the Syrian opposition emboldened its affiliate, the IAF. In addition, the growing role in Syria of Salafist jihadists, several of whom were either Jordanians (notably, commanders of Jabhat al-Nusra) or transited through Jordan, augured possible attacks within Jordan. Security services dismantled several jihadist cells allegedly planning bombings in Amman, the capital.

The Jordanian government struggled to define a policy toward Syria. While it officially subscribed to Assad's ouster through a managed process, it provided an entry point and logistical support for weapons deliveries to Syrian rebels from Saudi Arabia. It allowed Syrian rebels (notably the Deraa Military Council), defectors (such as Prime Minister Riad Hijab) and oppositionists to base themselves on its soil, and hosted meetings of the Friends of Syria group. Notably, Jordan increased cooperation with the US military, which deployed advisers tasked with designing responses to the potential use, loss or transfer of Syrian chemical weapons and upgraded Jordan's air- and missile-defence systems. Alongside the Israeli-Palestinian peace process, the ripple effects of Syria figured prominently during King Abdullah's visit to Washington in May; there he painted a daunting picture of the consequences of the Syrian conflict to a US administration still reluctant to get more involved. The United States did, however, donate $200m to the kingdom's treasury.

North Africa's Difficult Transitions

Morsi's removal by the Egyptian army, following months of popular protests against his government, underlined the challenges that were being faced by countries that had overthrown long-standing dictatorships in 2011. In Egypt, Tunisia and Libya, partisan infighting, institutional resistance and questions of legitimacy plagued political processes and paralysed policymaking. Accusations of monopolisation of power, betrayal of revolutionary ideals and subversion of democracy infused political debates. The Muslim Brotherhood, in power in Egypt, found itself at odds with the very forces that had carried the revolution. Its relations with more conservative factions, including the military and judiciary, also became crucially damaged. In Libya, worries about a betrayal of revolutionary ideals prompted a controversial law that excluded from political office people who had worked for the regime of Muammar Gadhafi, even if they had defected or served at a low level. In all three countries, legitimacy gained from electoral victories conflicted with ill-defined revolutionary demands, conservative institutional interests and the unrealistic expectations of large segments of society.

Transitional processes, including the drafting of new constitutions, took longer than had been intended, and were highly controversial and convoluted. Egypt's Islamists rushed the adoption of a constitution that was regarded as flawed by many and endorsed by a low-turnout referendum; Tunisia's constituent assembly issued, after several delays and intense internal disputes, a draft constitution in April 2013, with new elections expected in December; Libya's constitutional process suffered from delays, with a draft constitution planned for late 2013.

In each of these countries, the role of Islam in public life became a central question. Secularists and minorities struggled to contain the push for Islamisation, while Islamist parties differed on the manner and extent of it. Differences about strategy and tactics led to greater fragmentation among revolutionary movements and secular forces, though perceived abuses of power by the Brotherhood-led governments in Cairo and Tunis at times compelled better coordination.

Nevertheless, the slide into identity politics benefitted the more radical forms of political Islam at the expense of the more mainstream Muslim Brotherhood, forcing the latter to try to prove its Islamist credentials. The rise of Salafist parties throughout North Africa resulted in a more aggressive Islamist presence in political and social life, and in the media. Consequently, the debate over religion coloured policy issues and delayed any serious political action to address the structural challenges that had prompted the uprisings.

As a result, economic conditions in Egypt and Tunisia continued to worsen. Turmoil and uncertainty obstructed job creation and foreign investment. The tourism and service industries particularly suffered. Both countries requested foreign assistance through bilateral and multilateral loans, but the political tumult limited the capacity of their governments to introduce reforms, making loans more difficult to obtain.

All three countries struggled to maintain border security and faced armed challenges: militias tried to obtain concessions from the Libyan authorities by force; mass protests inflamed Egyptian cities, while instability persisted in the Sinai; and Salafist-inspired assassinations in Tunisia followed by demonstrations led to the resignation of Prime Minister Hamadi Jebali. Examples of weakening central authority included the September 2012 assault on the US consulate in Benghazi, in which Ambassador Christopher Stevens was killed, and the January 2013 capture of a large gas facility in Algeria by jihadist groups associated with al-Qaeda.

Inevitably, the travails of Egypt, Libya and Tunisia echoed throughout the region. Jihadists from all three countries joined the struggle in Syria, where minorities and secularists were caught between the Assad Alawite regime and an increasingly Islamist rebellion.

Egypt: from transition to coup

The year to mid-2013 saw massive political and popular shifts that shook Egypt's transition and increased polarisation between the competing segments of Egyptian society. The fortunes of Egypt's main political actors (the Muslim Brotherhood, Salafist factions, the fragmented liberal and leftist opposition, revolutionary youth, bureaucracy, judiciary and military) fluctuated heavily as relationships among these players underwent adjustments that reshaped the political scene.

By mid-2013, discontent with the ruling Muslim Brotherhood among large segments of society threatened to throw the country into limbo. Debates over electoral legitimacy and allegations of subversion of democratic principles marred political discourse. Tensions peaked in June with the emergence of a movement named Tamarod calling for early presidential elections and later for the removal of Morsi. Massive popular mobilisation and dissatisfaction in senior military ranks about the sitting president posed a formidable challenge to Morsi that resulted, on 3 July, in his removal from office and his replacement by an army-nominated transitional president. The Muslim Brotherhood's fall from power heralded a turbulent period ahead.

Muslim Brotherhood in power

The victory of Muhammad Morsi in the June 2012 presidential election by a narrow margin marked the zenith of the Muslim Brotherhood's participation in electoral politics. Despite profound misgivings – the Brotherhood's political arm, the Freedom and Justice Party, had reneged on its original pledge not to field a candidate – various opposition and revolutionary groups supported Morsi in the run-off against Ahmed Shafiq, a former military officer and a senior figure in the Mubarak regime.

Initially, Morsi seemingly sought accommodation with other groups, and made overtures. He promised, for example, to appoint vice-presidents and aides from outside the Brotherhood, including women and Christians. However, he quickly recanted on such promises and relied primarily on a closed circle of advisers and the guidance bureau of the Brotherhood. This secretive decision-making process heightened other factions' concerns about a Brotherhood power grab. Appointments of Muslim Brotherhood members and allies in the bureaucracy, the judiciary and the government (including a cabinet reshuffle in May 2013) validated this fear. At times, Morsi displayed an incredible lack of sensitivity; for example, he appointed as governor of the province of Luxor a member of Gamaa Islamiya, a radical Islamist group that had killed scores of foreign tourists in the city in 1997 – a decision that was later reversed.

Morsi sought to impose his authority on the military and the judiciary, both of which had historically been at odds with the Brotherhood. In August 2012, he used a serious security breakdown in the Sinai Peninsula to force the retirement of Defence Minister Field Marshal Mohammed Hussein Tantawi (Egypt's interim head of state from the 2011 revolution until Morsi's election) and Chief of Staff General Sami Anan, the two officers at the helm of the Supreme Council of the Armed Forces (SCAF). Tantawi was immediately replaced by General Abdel Fattah al-Sisi, who was seen as less prone to involving the military in politics.

The president, who later removed several judges and the prosecutor general, justified these moves as necessary to protect revolutionary gains and prevent the judiciary, suspected of sympathies with the old regime, from interfering in the transitional process. Indeed, the courts had voided several elections, including that of the Brotherhood-dominated parliament, and dissolved the Constituent Assembly, which was due to draw up a draft constitution, before Morsi took office. In November 2012, Morsi issued executive decrees granting himself additional authority and his decisions legal immunity, to pre-empt any further judicial move against him. Public outrage forced him to rescind these orders, but the move further ingrained fears of a hurried political takeover by the Brotherhood.

Political impasse

The drafting of Egypt's constitution proved very controversial. Many secularists were alienated by the composition of the drafting committee, in particular the domination of Islamist-leaning members, by the manner in which internal discussions were conducted and by the rushed finalisation of the document. So too were constitutional experts who resigned en masse from the committee. The final document included many provisions strengthening the role of religion and clerical institutions in public affairs, such as an article stating that the principles of Islamic sharia law would be the main sources of legislation. The document also omitted any serious attempt to improve civilian oversight of the security sector and even allowed for the prosecution of civilians in military courts: two issues that pitted revolutionaries against the SCAF. As a result, the referendum on the constitution, held in December, suffered from a low turnout of 33% and heavy criticism from the opposition.

The tension between the Muslim Brotherhood, which claimed democratic legitimacy after winning several elections (though with decreasing margins of victory), and other segments of Egyptian society, which blamed Morsi and his government for incompetence, monopolisation of power and subversion of democracy, drove Egyptian politics. Discontent took the form of regular street demonstrations, polarising discourse and cultural protest, such as the wildly popular comedy television shows of Bassem Youssef. Several of Morsi's advisers quit in protest, and even the

Salafist al-Nour Party denounced the performance of the government and the Brotherhood's tactics. Several journalists critical of the government were jailed despite Morsi's promise to protect press freedom. Sporadic clashes between Morsi supporters and opponents occurred, including outside the presidential palace, after which opposition members alleged that the Brotherhood had formed a militia.

The polarisation seriously impeded the processes of government and democracy. The Supreme Constitutional Court (SCC), for instance, rejected in February an electoral law drawn up by the Upper House (Shura Council) that was meant to govern legislative elections scheduled for April 2013. Elections were eventually postponed, which left Egypt without a legislative body, as the SCC had already invalidated the lower house of parliament. The prime minister, Hisham Kandil, and many cabinet members were harshly criticised for poor public administration; the Brotherhood argued that Egypt's decline had preceded its rule and that it had been given little time and room to advance reforms.

Decay of the state

Morsi's election coincided with the erosion of state authority across the country. Dejection among policemen and a lack of meaningful security-sector reform compounded lingering popular distrust of the police and complex relations between the interior ministry and the presidency. As a result, a sense of lawlessness developed across the country, with an increase in crime and violence.

The Sinai Peninsula, rife with disgruntled tribes and smugglers, witnessed several incidents in which military personnel were killed; a military campaign was launched in August 2012. In early 2013, following a verdict in the case of deadly clashes involving football fans and policemen, unrest developed in the cities of Port Said, Suez and Ismailia. This forced Morsi to declare a state of emergency and a curfew to restore state authority. State control over the borders with Libya and Sudan also weakened, stoking fears that weapons could reach various radical groups inside Egypt.

Sectarian violence grew. Several instances of clashes between Muslims and Copts were recorded. The release of an online video in September 2012 insulting Islam by a radical Copt living in the United States served as a pretext for more anti-Christian violence; it also led to a brief storming of the US Embassy in Cairo. In April 2013, violent clashes outside St Mark's Cathedral in Cairo and the slow police response heightened Christian fears. Sectarian passions over Syria and anti-Shi'ite incitement grew in Egyptian media and mosques, escalating in June with the mob lynching of four Shi'ites near Cairo.

Domestic instability led General Sisi to make a dramatic statement in January 2013: 'Disagreement [between political factions] on running the affairs of the country may lead to the collapse of the state and threatens the future of the coming generation.' This suggested that the military, whose political role had ostensibly diminished in previous months, could intervene to force a compromise or broker a new political road map. Distrust of the military ran deep among both Islamists and revolutionaries.

A rise in food prices, energy and gasoline shortages, capital flight and low tourism receipts all crippled the Egyptian economy. Attempts at economic reform were complicated by domestic tensions and fears that such reforms would only exacerbate popular discontent. This was a prime concern in negotiations between the IMF and Egyptian government over a $4.8 billion loan. A deal was seen as crucial to restoring confidence in the Egyptian economy and attracting much-needed foreign investment, but the IMF's insistence on slashing subsidies and on better allocation of resources proved a major hurdle.

Foreign-policy moves

Morsi attempted to conduct a more autonomous foreign policy than that of Mubarak. However, he was constrained by Egypt's dependence on the Gulf states and economic and political weakness. Though his first trip was to Saudi Arabia to assuage tensions that could affect Egyptian workers in the kingdom, Saudi distrust of the Muslim Brotherhood remained considerable. Relations with the UAE, which saw the Brotherhood as both a domestic and regional threat, also soured.

Morsi's attempts to improve relations with Iran further damaged his ties with the Gulf states. In August 2012, he attended the Non-Aligned Movement summit in Tehran, and later he hosted Iranian President Mahmoud Ahmadinejad in Cairo. He welcomed Iran's attempts to involve Egypt in a regional mechanism to reach a political settlement in Syria. While this rapprochement appeared tentative at best and was not grounded in economic or strategic interests, Western and Arab states feared that Islamist affinity would bring Iran and Egypt closer and upset the regional order. Eventually, the growing sectarian character of the Syrian conflict constrained Morsi's rapprochement with Iran; in June 2013, to the dismay of the military and opposition, he condoned a meeting of senior Sunni figures who preached jihad against the Assad regime.

Morsi did benefit from continued financial support from Qatar, whose alliance with the Brotherhood remained strong. This support and the perceived bias of the Qatar-based Al Jazeera television network towards the Brotherhood, however, enraged the Egyptian opposition, which accused Qatar of ulterior motives.

The brief but violent escalation between Israel and Hamas in the Gaza Strip in November gave Morsi an opportunity to gain international legitimacy by overseeing mediation. His role won praise from a US administration struggling to adapt to Egypt's new dynamics. Indeed, while the United States was broadly criticised for its perceived embrace of the Muslim Brotherhood, Washington remained worried that instability and polarisation in Egypt would threaten regional stability, including relations with Israel, and erode the capacity of the state to combat terrorist threats and strengthen its economy. The US government settled on a policy of support (notably financial) to the Egyptian government while privately counselling outreach to non-Brotherhood factions and also maintaining its relations with the Egyptian military.

Opposition turns to the military

Egypt's fragmented opposition struggled over the year to elaborate a political strategy to confront the Muslim Brotherhood. Divisions over strategy, tactics and personal interests prevented the articulation of a unified message.

Opposition members, working under the umbrella of the National Salvation Front (NSF), differed on whether to boycott elections, how to force constitutional revisions, and whether to appeal to the military to extract compromises from Morsi. The NSF grouped the liberal Mohamed

ElBaradei, the nationalist leftist Hamdeen Sabahi and the establishment figure Amr Moussa, as well as several political parties. Meanwhile, the al-Nour Party separately continued to urge Morsi to make political concessions.

The Brotherhood's uncompromising stance – despite repeated, if half-hearted, attempts at dialogue – led to a convergence of interests between Tamarod, opposition politicians, remnants of the Mubarak regime and the military. Massive demonstrations across Egypt on 30 June and on following days resulted in the army-induced removal of Morsi as president and his replacement by Adly Mansour, head of the SCC. General Sisi played the decisive role: in days prior to the ouster he attempted to convince Morsi to form a government of national unity and met with opposition and Tamarod representatives. Sisi associated figures representing a broad spread of Egyptian society, including Sheikh al-Azhar, the Coptic Patriarch, opposition politicians, and representatives of the al-Nour Party, with his announcement that Morsi had been removed.

The manner of Morsi's ouster, through a combination of popular mobilisation and military intervention, created a debate over whether a revolution or a coup had occurred; in reality, the complexity of Egyptian politics suggested a hybrid. The army had remained powerful behind the scenes all along, and Morsi's presidency had lacked institutional checks and balances.

The subsequent crackdown on the Brotherhood, including the arrest of Morsi and other senior leaders, and the bloody dispersal of pro-Morsi gatherings outside army barracks, ignited concerns that the political exclusion of the Brotherhood would weaken any new transitional process and lead to further polarisation and violence. A notable worry was that it would validate views among Islamists, in Egypt and beyond, that participation in mainstream politics and elections was useless and that they would constantly be victims of conspiracies by secularists and the military – and that such dejection would result in a new wave of Islamist violence.

The new president announced a timetable for a rapid transition, including the drafting of a new constitution and the holding of presidential and legislative elections. The revolution-cum-coup nevertheless left revolutionaries and liberals uncomfortable. The pro-Morsi media was muzzled, the army and police were using violence, and the dominant role of the military – which the revolutionaries had previously denounced – was once again made clear. The concentration of power in the hands of Mansour provoked criticism. Political difficulties soon arose with the Salafists blocking the nomination of ElBaradei as prime minister and confusion about the formation of a government.

The external dimension of the Egyptian crisis was notable. Within hours of Morsi's ouster, Saudi Arabia and the UAE made strong statements of support to the new president and promised significant packages of economic assistance – $12bn, including Kuwait's contribution. Qatar, once Morsi's closest external supporter but now in the midst of its own transition, adopted a low official profile, congratulating the military but also allowing the Al Jazeera television network to broadcast messages of support for Morsi. The United States was left in a difficult position. Decried before the protests for its perceived support of Morsi, it was later accused by Islamists of having condoned his removal. Nevertheless, Washington stood by its main Egyptian ally, the military, and dithered about calling Morsi's removal a coup because of the legal implications this would have had for US military assistance.

Libya: mounting instability

Instability remained a major challenge in post-Gadhafi Libya. The authority of the central government was challenged by militias which refused to hand in their weapons and disband. Authorities sought, with limited success, to integrate militias and armed groups into the police and military forces so as to contain the proliferation of weapons and outbreaks of violence between rival groups. At the same time, they began to implement stricter measures on armed groups that were operating illegally. The murder of the US ambassador, and other attacks on foreign targets, raised concerns about the threat of radical Islamist groups.

Libya held its first legislative elections for the General National Congress (GNC) in July 2012. The National Forces Alliance, a centrist-leaning coalition, secured a plurality of seats, setting Libya apart from Tunisia and Egypt, where elections had brought Islamists to power. The country's more homogeneous fabric neutralised identity politics to a large extent, weakening the power of Islamist parties. In August the GNC took over power from the National Transitional Council, naming

Mohammed Magarief as its president. In October, it appointed Ali Zaydan as prime minister.

In April 2013, the GNC put in motion a complex process to draft a new constitution of which the first step would be the election of a constituent assembly by the end of 2013. This followed a tense debate over the best mechanism to adopt a constitution, with factions opposed to the National Forces Alliance advocating an appointed rather than an elected committee. There were other disruptions to parliamentary work; in May, armed demonstrators surrounded ministries, stormed parliament and held members hostage to demand the adoption of the 'political isolation' draft law. The law, which was eventually adopted, effectively bans anyone who served in the Gadhafi regime from working in the post-revolution government. This would arguably affect Zaydan, who was a diplomat prior to his defection, as well as other important figures.

Marches and sit-ins were held by different interest groups, and armed protesters often stormed public offices and media networks' headquarters. Protesters voiced their dissatisfaction with the political transition and the deteriorating security situation. In July 2012, over 1,000 people occupied a building hosting the election commission in Benghazi, demanding more seats for the eastern district, ahead of the GNC election. After armed men stormed two ministries' buildings in March, defence minister Mohammed al-Barghathi resigned, only to retract his resignation a few hours later. In April 2013, hundreds of armed Libyans stormed the ministries of interior and foreign affairs as well as the state-owned al-Wataniya television channel, demanding employment for former rebels.

The gradual deterioration of the security situation was highlighted in May 2013 when a car bomb exploded in the centre of Benghazi. Militants attacked several police stations in the city and assassination attempts and politically motivated abductions increased nationwide; a former commander of the military council of Tarhuna was abducted in June and a group affiliated with the fallen Gadhafi regime kidnapped a prosecutor in the town of Bani Walid. An investigator in the controversial assassination case of rebel General Abdel Fattah Younes in 2011 was killed in June 2012, while Magarief, the GNC's president, escaped assassination attempts in January and March.

The rise of jihadist factions was highlighted by the September 2012 attack on the US consulate in Benghazi, in which US Ambassador Christopher Stevens and three other Americans were killed. Initially the attack was presumed to be in response to an anti-Islamic video, but later reports revealed that radical Islamist groups, including Ansar al-Sharia and al-Qaeda in the Islamic Maghreb (AQIM), had assisted in the operation. European embassies were also targeted. A British diplomatic convoy was attacked in Benghazi in June 2012, followed by the Italian consulate in January, and a car bomb exploded outside the French Embassy in April 2013.

Clashes between supporters of the fallen regime and security forces continued, especially in the pro-Gadhafi town of Bani Walid. Tensions resurfaced after a rebel who had helped capture Gadhafi was killed by suspected loyalists. Libyan security forces, with the help of militias, launched an offensive and gained control of the area in October. Other Gadhafi loyalists remained in limbo, including 60,000 displaced former fighters and their families, half of whom were from the town of Tawergha. Residents of Tawergha have come under sustained repression for alleged crimes committed against rebels during the 2011 revolution.

Tribal clashes highlighted another dimension of Libya's security failures. Fighting in the town of Kufra between the rival Toubou and Zwai tribes killed almost 200 people in 2012. Authorities attempted to mitigate tribal tensions by integrating Toubou fighters into Libya's public institutions and police force. Meanwhile, the decaying rule of law enabled the easy flow of smugglers, illegal immigrants and radical Islamists, as well as the flow of weapons, from Libya to other conflict zones in Syria and Mali.

The International Criminal Court (ICC) persistently demanded the extradition of Saif al-Islam Gadhafi, son of the late dictator, and other members of the fallen regime, including former intelligence chief Abdullah al-Senussi, to be tried in The Hague for crimes against humanity. These requests were rejected by Libyan authorities, however, who insisted that Saif al-Islam be tried in Libyan courts. In January 2013, he appeared in court to face charges relating to 'trading information threatening national security'. After the case was postponed due to lack of legal representation, he reappeared in May only to have it put back to

September. Gadhafi's widow, daughter and another son sought asylum in Oman, pledging that they would not conduct political activity there.

Libya contributed weapons, fighters and funding to the Syrian rebellion, including $20m to the Syrian National Council. Libyan-Egyptian diplomatic relations, on the other hand, worsened following the arrest in Libya of Egyptian Christians on charges of proselytism. The death of an Egyptian Copt in prison, which Egypt's Christian minority believed to be due to mistreatment, sparked protests in front of Libya's consulate in March. There were also protests at the border after Libyan authorities revised visa requirements for Egyptians. The two countries decided to establish consulates at the border to ease the movement of people.

Tunisia: contentious politics

While Tunisia's transitional process proved smoother than those of its neighbours, the country was affected by political polarisation and Salafist-driven violence. The Islamist An-Nahda-led government, which includes two secular partners, faced accusations of incompetence and cronyism from secular factions. Concerns grew of Islamisation in state bureaucracy and public bodies. Deepening economic woes eroded public confidence in the government. The Muslim Brotherhood affiliate also had to contend with the rise of Ansar al-Sharia, a Salafist movement.

Drafting of a new constitution was contentious. Thousands protested against moves to reduce women's rights; the first draft referred to women as 'complementary to men', whereas the 1956 constitution had granted women full equality. After intense public pressure, the language was changed. The draft stated that Islam was the religion of the state, but made no explicit reference to sharia law. It gave the president authority over foreign affairs and defence, thus weakening the power of the prime minister. An-Nahda was pushing for a strong parliamentary system while secularists preferred a strong presidency. The draft was expected to be voted on by late 2013. The document would require a referendum if it was not approved by two-thirds of the Constituent Assembly, the drafting body. The lengthy drafting process delayed the holding of legislative elections to form a national assembly.

Clashes continued on the streets of Tunis between Salafist fundamentalists and the security forces over adherence to sharia law.

Increasing violence prompted the authorities to impose an overnight curfew in several areas following Islamist riots against alcohol sellers and art exhibitions. Tensions peaked with the assassination in February 2013 of Chokri Belaid, an opposition anti-Islamist leader, prompting widespread and violent protests. An-Nahda denounced opposition allegations of complicity. The assassination, combined with dwindling popular support and political upheaval, led Prime Minister Hamadi Jebali to resign in February 2013, after An-Nahda rejected his proposal to form a non-partisan government of technocrats. The newly selected prime minister, Ali Larayedh, former minister of the interior, promised the country was 'entering a new era of forming a new government for all Tunisians, men and women'.

Such a promise was dependent on the recovery of the Tunisian economy, which had been badly hurt by political instability and the European economic crisis. Foreign exchange reserves ran low, prompting the IMF to issue a much-needed $1.8bn standby loan. Qatar too provided financial and material support.

Despite some pessimism about its democratic future, Tunisia showed signs of an emerging political maturity evidenced in constructive sessions of a national dialogue involving politicians from all sides, and in the vigour of its civil society – though some leftist groups boycotted the dialogue over An-Nahda's perceived monopoly of power.

Morocco: unsteady path to reform

Since Morocco's moderate Islamist Justice and Development Party (PJD) won the legislative elections in late 2011, the performance of the government has been undermined by internal tensions, the party's limited experience in office, and opaque power struggles between King Mohammed VI and ministers.

The government introduced several social reforms. Under public pressure, legislators amended laws concerning rape and passed laws to guarantee gender equality, though implementation in Morocco's conservative society remained a challenge. Reforms were also introduced to protect the Berber identity, including the incorporation of the Amazigh language into the constitution, the media, school curricula and public administration.

The youth-led February 20 movement resumed its drive for political reforms and greater democracy with street demonstrations. Public-sector pay disputes and the increasing cost of living prompted protests. A stand-off between the government and young, unemployed graduates continued to escalate, with youth movements occupying the offices of the ruling party in Rabat. With unemployment, poverty and corruption still high, the PJD's room for manoeuvre was limited. The perception that the party was in control, rather than the king and his court (Makhzen), which retained significant power, only increased the pressure.

To contain the deteriorating financial situation, Prime Minister Abdelilah Benkirane announced structural reforms and secured a $6.2bn IMF credit line. Proposed reforms include lowering business taxes, which attracted criticism for favouring large businesses and the network of Makhzen allies of the king, to the detriment of lower classes. In a further attempt to restore finances, the government cut subsidies in June 2012, causing a 20% rise in gas prices and higher increases in other commodity prices. A drought and a 12% decrease in tourism receipts also contributed to low 2.6% GDP growth. However, Morocco, which imports 95% of its oil, introduced a fuel-subsidy system which was criticised by the IMF.

The monarchy looked to deepen political and economic ties with sub-Saharan Africa. The king announced plans to rejoin the African Union after years of absence due to tensions with Algeria over border issues and the Western Sahara. However, the Western Saharan conflict between Morocco and the Algeria-backed Polisario Front of the Sahrawi people remained one of the world's longest-running post-colonial territorial disputes. The Moroccan government allowed the UN special rapporteur on torture a rare inspection of the Western Sahara in September. But this was overshadowed by UN Secretary-General Ban Ki-moon's rejection of Mohammed VI's demand to replace Christopher Ross, the UN envoy, on the grounds that he was 'unbalanced and biased' towards the Sahrawi position. Morocco remained at odds with the UN when the Security Council voted unanimously to keep a UN peacekeeping force in Western Sahara for another year. To the dismay of Sahrawis, a US proposal to extend the mandate of the peacekeepers to monitor human rights in the disputed territory was abandoned after strong opposition from Rabat, increasing the possibility that the conflict would intensify.

Algeria: growing discontent

After President Abdelaziz Bouteflika suffered a stroke in April 2013, there was uncertainty about whether he would run for a fourth term in the 2014 presidential elections. Algeria had so far managed to avoid the kind of unrest that hit neighbouring North African states, but the absence of reform and discontent with the military's role threatened future instability. With a growing population, high unemployment and heavy subsidies, the government failed to enact effective economic and social reform, in spite of oil and gas revenues.

Demand for development sparked protests by unemployed young people, and waves of strikes, for example by teachers and paramedics. Demonstrators called for justice, the rule of law and more political rights. Though police managed to contain the protests, Algeria's ageing regime proved unresponsive and unable to deal with corruption and soaring unemployment. This adversely affected the economy, with major foreign investments held up because of the government's slow decision-making. Raising funds for a promised five-year, $286bn programme in housing, infrastructure and other social investments was another challenge, especially after oil and gas earnings dropped by 9% in the first quarter of 2013 due to increases in shale oil production in the United States, traditionally a major importer from Algeria.

Following months of political wrangling after controversial legislative elections in May 2012, which were boycotted by several opposition parties and marred by accusations of fraud, Abdelmalek Sellal, a member of the victorious National Liberation Front (FLN), was tasked with forming a government in September. In preparation for possible constitutional amendments in 2014, Islamist parties decided in March 2013 to unify politically and push for joint demands. Nevertheless, as the 2014 presidential elections approached, Islamist blocs had yet to designate a common candidate.

Algeria was affected by instability in neighbouring Mali, Libya and Tunisia. Islamists in northern Mali reportedly executed an Algerian diplomat in September 2012. Smuggling increased, and the Western Saharan dispute with Morocco continued. Cooperation between Tunisian and Algerian forces against jihadist militants linked to AQIM suffered from disagreements over security procedures. In particular, the French-led international military intervention against Islamist insurgents in Mali in early 2013 had direct implications. While Algeria was at first ambivalent about the French initiative, its intelligence services cooperated to prevent a revival of its own jihadist movement and to contain the rapid increase of weapons and jihadists fleeing Mali and seeking refuge across the long Algerian border.

The most serious incident occurred in January 2013 when a group of jihadist fighters linked to an Algerian jihadist and smuggler, Mokhtar Belmokhtar, seized the Tiguentourine gas facility near the southeastern town of In Amenas, close to the Libyan border. Over 800 people, including more than 100 foreigners, were taken hostage. A four-day crisis culminated in an Algerian military assault in which nearly 40 foreign hostages and about 30 militants were killed.

This led to a more aggressive effort to combat Islamist militancy. In February, the Algerian government pushed for the punishment of those facilitating and financing terrorism at an Organisation of Islamic Cooperation summit in Cairo. Algeria's Ministry of Religious Affairs and Endowments warned against the rise of religious extremism, including rising home-grown Takfiri Salafism in the centre of the country. The government also released a draft law to bring Algeria's religious institutions under the aegis of a single legal body.

Gulf States: Containing Change

The painful transitions that were occurring in countries that had ousted dictators provided many other governments across the region with an excuse to warn their own populations against acting on similar revolutionary yearnings. Gulf states, in particular, continued their strategy to reward their populations in exchange for loyalty and relative stability. They did experience political dissent, but at a much lower level than elsewhere. In Saudi Arabia, small demonstrations took place while online activism boomed. There was tension in the Eastern Province, where the disenfranchised Shia community organised protests and clashed with police forces. Discontent with the Kuwaiti government escalated into mass protests and unprecedented public criticism of the emir. Bahrain, which adopted very limited reforms, witnessed continued mobilisation of political and Shia activists.

The conservative Sunni monarchies of the Gulf approached the new governments in North Africa divided. Qatar sought political influence through its support for the Muslim Brotherhood, by for example extending financial assistance to Egypt. Saudi Arabia and the UAE, on the other hand, saw the Islamist movement as both an ideological and strategic challenge that could exacerbate their internal oppositions. The six Gulf states agreed in December 2012 to strengthen security coordination and expand the scope of collective security, making it easier for one of the countries to request assistance from the others. Such cooperation heightened concerns about further restrictions on political freedoms.

Saudi Arabia: lingering unrest

With nearby Bahrain and the Levant embroiled in tense sectarian politics, unrest in the predominately Shia Eastern Province posed a gathering threat to the Saudi authorities. After Sheikh Nimr al-Nimr, a prominent Shia cleric, was arrested in July 2012 on charges of instigating unrest and backing foreign meddling in Saudi affairs, protesters marched in the city of al-Qatif demanding his release. Unrest escalated again in August after a Saudi policeman and a Shia gunman were killed in clashes in al-Qatif. The removal in January 2013 of Prince Mohammed bin Fahd, the long-time governor of the Eastern Province, was reportedly partly due to his heavy-handedness toward the Shia population. In March, the government announced the arrest of 18 Shias across the country, including an Iranian and a Lebanese, on suspicion of spying for a foreign country.

Following a clampdown on political activists and human-rights observers, over a hundred Saudi clerics wrote to King Abdullah asking him to release detainees, warning that protests would otherwise grow; the prominent Sunni cleric Salman al-Odah issued a letter in March demanding political and security reforms. Families of detained activists staged unprecedented protests and sit-ins, demanding their release. In

March, a sit-in in al-Qassim province in front of a local police headquarters led to the arrest of over 170 people, including 15 women. Mohammed al-Qahtani and Abdullah al-Hamid, founders of the Civil and Political Rights Association (ACPRA), a leading civil society NGO that advocates greater representation and political reforms, were sentenced to jail terms for sedition and falsifying information.

Positive steps were, however, taken to enhance the status of Saudi women. The king signed a decree that required 20% of the people on the Shura Council, an advisory body on legislation, to be women. For the first time, 30 women were appointed to the council, including Shia women and a former UN official. Despite fundamentalist criticism, there was female representation at the 2012 Summer Olympics in London, easing of work and recreational rules, and discussion of integrating policewomen into the kingdom's religious police force.

Regionally, Saudi Arabia had to contend with the impact of the turmoil in Egypt and Syria. After tensions rose over the arrests of Egyptian expatriates in the kingdom, Morsi conducted his first foreign trip to Saudi Arabia to improve relations. Saudi Arabia began to deliver financial aid to Egypt as promised after the 2011 revolution, and in November 2012 the two states signed agreements over funding support for Egypt's central bank and development projects. However, tensions lingered, especially over the perceived rapprochement between Iran and Egypt. As a result, Riyadh maintained ties with anti-Muslim Brotherhood factions and supported Morsi's removal.

Saudi Arabia faced complex calculations regarding Syria. It had to balance its stated objective of ousting Assad and checking Iran's influence in the Levant with concerns about the revival of jihadism and the spillover into countries such as Lebanon and Jordan, whose stability Saudi Arabia considered vital to its own. The kingdom, which had until late 2012 let Qatar lead diplomacy over Syria, played an increasingly active role as Iran, Iraq and Hizbullah stepped up support for Assad. It emerged in late 2012 that Saudi Arabia had provided Croatian weaponry to rebels in southern Syria through Jordan. Riyadh intensified contacts with the Syrian opposition to balance the perceived rise of the Muslim Brotherhood and expand the representation of other factions within the Syrian National Coalition. Although officials warned Saudis – and state-controlled clerics issued fatwas – not to fight against Assad, there was evidence that Saudi fighters had joined extremist factions in Syria and were obtaining funding from individual Saudis and religious charities.

The Saudi Arabian Oil Company (Aramco) was the target of a large cyber attack in August 2012. Aramco initially stated that the virus used in the attack, known as Shamoon, disabled 30,000 workstations and replaced screens with an image of a burning American flag. Following internal investigations, it revealed that the attack was also aimed at halting production and destabilising the energy market. Even though Aramco avoided permanent damage to its networks, the incident heightened concerns about the vulnerability of the energy markets to such attacks.

Meanwhile, the issue of succession to the monarchy gained attention with reports of the declining health of King Abdullah and Crown Prince Salman. New government appointments raised speculation, particularly the elevation of Prince Mohammed bin Nayef to interior minister in November 2012. An important official behind the kingdom's counter-terrorism strategy and an interlocutor of Western intelligence agencies, Prince Mohammed, in his fifties, was the first of the younger generation to hold such a senior position. Prince Bandar bin Sultan, previously head of the National Security Council, replaced Prince Muqrin bin Abdulaziz as director general of the General Intelligence Directorate in July 2012. Initially, this was interpreted as Muqrin's relegation as a candidate for the throne, but his appointment in February 2013 as second deputy prime minister suggested that he remained a contender.

United Arab Emirates: crackdown continues

Amid regional upheaval, the UAE sought to contain the rise of Islamist movements. The government embarked on a campaign against Islamist activists: 94 members of al-Islah, an Emirati group tied to the Muslim Brotherhood, were tried for illegal political activities and plotting to overthrow the government. Detainees included prominent lawyers, judges, students, academics and even a member of the ruling family of the emirate of Ras al-Khaimah. Human-rights organisations criticised UAE authorities for failing to ensure the rights of the defendants and for restricting media access to the trials. To placate internal discontent, the government launched several infrastructure and social projects in the comparatively poor northern emirates, where support for al-Islah was greatest.

The perceived threat from the Muslim Brotherhood strained UAE–Egypt relations. In January 2013, UAE security forces arrested 11 Egyptian members of a Muslim Brotherhood cell that was allegedly recruiting Egyptians while establishing companies that funded the Brotherhood both locally and in Egypt. Efforts by other Islamist groups to recruit young Emiratis and Arabs residing in the UAE to join the fight against Assad were also disrupted. A terror cell composed of Saudi and Emirati nationals and another belonging to al-Qaeda were dismantled in December 2012 and April 2013 respectively.

In this tense environment, the UAE enforced stricter oversight of online activism. A new cyber-crime law was passed to allow government authorities to prosecute Internet users deemed to have undermined the state, its institutions and its officials. The broad mandate of the law led to arrests of cyber activists and bloggers, including relatives of the al-Islah detainees. As part of the crackdown on internal dissent and external criticism, UAE authorities closed down local offices of several international NGOs, including the Abu Dhabi office of the US-based RAND Corporation.

At the same time, the UAE reinforced ties with Western partners, enhancing defence relationships with the United Kingdom, France and the United States so as to counter the perceived threat from Iran. Another element of the UAE's contingency planning was the opening of an overland pipeline bypassing the Strait of Hormuz and linking Abu Dhabi's oilfields to a port in Fujairah on the Arabian Sea.

Bahrain: dialogue stalls

Bahraini authorities tried to project normality amid continued public discontent since the quashed 2011 uprising. The security situation had been largely contained, but the country's youth continued to mobilise in Shia villages and to clash with security forces. Crown Prince Salman al-Khalifa, the ruling family's presumed leading reformist, re-emerged on the political scene and renewed his call for political dialogue at the IISS Manama Dialogue in December 2012. In March 2013, his father King

Hamad nominated him to the newly-created position of First Deputy Prime Minister, giving him executive powers. This raised hopes for a breakthrough in Bahrain's lingering political crisis.

In January 2013, Justice Minister Sheikh Khalid bin Ali al-Khalifa invited political societies and independents to a national dialogue that, unlike its predecessor in 2011, would only discuss political affairs. The first session took place in February; participants included loyalist parliamentarians and members of the opposition. The government was represented by the ministers of justice, education and works, though not the Crown Prince, who said the timing was not yet suitable. The opposition disputed the format, which seemingly pitted Sunni and Shia factions against each other while making the government an arbiter rather than a full participant.

The government was criticised at home and abroad for its response to unrest in Shia areas and the slow and limited reforms. In October 2012, the interior ministry issued a ban on protests, citing 'repeated abuse', though the ban was lifted in December, while the ministry proposed amendments to the law. Following up on the findings of the 2011 Bahrain Independent Commission of Inquiry (BICI), the government began to prosecute security officers implicated in cases of torture. Two policemen were sentenced to seven years in prison for causing the death under torture of Karim Fakhrawi, founder of a pro-opposition newspaper. However, verdicts were criticised as too lenient and for whitewashing the responsibility of senior commanders. Human-rights groups and activists claimed that the government had only implemented BICI recommendations selectively. In January 2013, Bahrain's highest court upheld verdicts against 20 opposition leaders, including life imprisonment for prominent activists. The government stripped 31 activists of their citizenship and arrests continued, including that of Nabeel Rajab from the Bahrain Center for Human Rights.

The country faced growing security challenges. In November, five home-made devices exploded in the capital, Manama, killing two foreign workers. The use of Molotov cocktails and other violent tactics became common in daily clashes between young people and police in Shia villages. The Peninsula Shield Force, the Gulf Cooperation Council's (GCC) military arm, announced the establishment of a permanent base in Bahrain, a move widely interpreted as providing an additional security cushion to the ruling family. GCC states also assisted Bahrain's ailing economy. In December 2012, Saudi Arabia signed agreements amounting to $448m to fund infrastructure and housing projects, and Kuwait also agreed to finance housing projects. The UAE followed suit in February, committing $2.5bn over the next ten years.

Kuwait: political turmoil

Kuwait faced unprecedented political upheaval. The election of an opposition-dominated parliament in February 2012 had raised tensions between the government and opposition factions. A constitutional court ruling that dissolved parliament over a legal technicality in June 2012 then further complicated the situation. The government attempted to seize this opportunity to introduce a new electoral law to weaken the opposition, but the constitutional court surprisingly ruled against the government and left electoral districts intact.

The jockeying between government and opposition continued in October when the emir issued an emergency decree reducing the number of votes per citizen from four to one. The move prompted protests by 50,000 people in Kuwait City, who chanted unprecedented slogans directed at the emir. Nevertheless, the movement failed to block electoral changes and new elections were scheduled for December 2012.

All opposition factions boycotted the elections and turnout dropped from 60% to 43%, according to official estimates. Parliamentary candidates were all pro-government. Kuwait's Shia minority won an unprecedented 17 seats, as did three women, including a tribal candidate. The pro-government parliament ratified the contested emergency decree, but as part of an effort to placate citizens and retain their loyalty, it also approved a law to forgive interest on loans taken out by Kuwaiti citizens from commercial banks, costing the government $2.6bn.

The opposition tried to unify its different factions under one umbrella. In March 2013,the Etilaf al-Mu'aratha (the Opposition Coalition) brought under its wing NGOs as well as trade and student unions. However, as in previous coalition-building attempts, the Etilaf was unable to attract liberal groups such as the Democratic Tribune and the National

Democratic Coalition, or conservative Salafist groups. Meanwhile, several opposition figures, former parliamentarians and activists were facing charges of 'offending the emir'. In April, a former prominent parliamentarian, Musallam Al-Barrak, who won a seat in the February elections by a sweeping 30,000 votes, was handed a five-year sentence for insulting the emir and challenging his authority. A hardening of the government's position was also reflected in a proposed media law which could impose fines of up to $1m for insulting the emir and members of the royal family.

The country's bedoun (stateless) population staged protests despite a Ministry of Interior ban. In October, authorities detained several individuals for participation in bedoun-rights protests, but later released them on bail. The bedoun population numbers 100,000–180,000, but officials insisted that only 34,000 could qualify for citizenship. Parliament passed a bill granting citizenship to 4,000 foreigners in 2013. It initially used the term 'stateless', but this was changed to 'foreigners' under government pressure.

In the face of domestic and regional upheaval, Kuwait moved to strengthen security cooperation with other GCC states. During a GCC summit held in Bahrain in December, it finally signed the GCC security pact which it had resisted for almost two decades due to constitutional concerns. This surprise move sparked suspicions in Kuwait over whether the government was moving towards further security integration with GCC states to counter domestic unrest.

Relations with Iraq improved. In January 2013, the Kuwaiti parliament ratified a $500m deal between Iraqi Airways and Kuwait Airways to settle a financial dispute. A month later, an Iraqi Airways flight landed in Kuwait for the first time since the 1990 invasion. In March, the UN secretary-general's special representative for Iraq, Martin Kobler, announced that the prolonged Kuwaiti-Iraqi border dispute over land demarcation had finally been resolved.

While adopting a relatively passive approach toward the Syrian crisis, the Kuwaiti government hosted a UN-sponsored donors' conference in January to raise $1.5bn in humanitarian funds, with Kuwait itself pledging $300m. It also emerged as a platform for the financing of Islamist rebel groups in Syria.

Qatar: leadership change

In a surprise move, the emir, Sheikh Hamad bin Khalifa al-Thani, stepped down in June 2013, handing power to his 33-year-old son, Sheikh Tamim bin Hamad al-Thani. The cabinet was reshuffled, ending the tenure of Prime Minister and Foreign Minister Sheikh Hamad bin Jassim al-Thani. While Qatar's domestic and foreign policies were not expected to change dramatically, setbacks in Egypt and Syria, and a failed attempt to facilitate talks between the United States and the Afghan Taliban, suggested that Qatar's regional ventures would have reduced importance under the new ruler.

During the year to mid-2013, Qatar continued to use its wealth to expand its regional and global influence, while largely avoiding domestic unrest. It kept up its involvement in Syria, providing political and financial support to the Syrian opposition, estimated at $1–3bn since 2011. Qatar was a key weapons provider to various rebel factions in Syria, but differences with Saudi Arabia and Turkey over strategy, and particularly over which rebel groups to support, complicated supplies. Its close relations with the Syrian Muslim Brotherhood and alleged support for radical Islamist factions created tensions with other elements of the Syrian opposition and key allies, including the United States. However, even after the SNC – deemed too close to Qatar and the Muslim Brotherhood – was re-formed into the National Coalition, Qatar remained at the diplomatic forefront, pushing for recognition of the coalition as the only representative of the Syrian people. At the Arab League Summit, hosted in Doha in March 2013, the emir, Sheikh Hamad, invited the head of the National Coalition, Moaz al-Khatib, to take the seat reserved for Syria.

Qatar also increased its involvement in post-revolutionary Egypt. In September 2012, it announced investments worth $18bn, primarily in the tourism and energy sectors, to assist economic recovery. In January, it pledged $5bn in financial aid and, four months later, offered to buy Egyptian treasury bonds worth $3bn. Here too, Qatar's close ties to the ruling Muslim Brotherhood – which was later ejected from government in July 2013 – were criticised by many Egyptian opposition figures and other Arab states, particularly as its assistance came with no clear conditions for reform. Diplomatic outreach to Arab countries in transition and to the Muslim Brotherhood strained relations with other GCC states, particularly the UAE.

Qatar's diplomacy also extended to Palestine. After Hamas parted ways with Assad, the Qatari emir conducted an official visit to Gaza in October 2012 – the first by a head of state since Hamas seized the strip in 2007. He pledged $400m for housing, main roads and other infrastructure projects. The visit, however, alienated the rival leadership in the West Bank, with a spokesperson for the Palestinian Authority declaring that the 'legitimate representation of the Palestinian people' should be respected. To deflect further criticism, Qatar called for the creation of a billion-dollar fund and pledged $250m in March 2013 to assist Palestinians residing in East Jerusalem.

Qatar looked to expand its foreign investments. Its acquisitions in Western Europe included real estate and football clubs. Its sovereign wealth fund, the Qatar Investment Authority (QIA), allocated $5bn to China, making Qatar the biggest foreign investor in Chinese capital markets. The QIA also acquired 22% of the Chinese investment firm CITIC Capital Holdings, which is partly owned by China's sovereign wealth fund, China Investment Corporation.

A notable exception to domestic calm was the case of Ibn al-Dheeb al-Ajami, a poet sentenced to life in prison in late 2012 for insulting the Qatari emir and calling for the overthrow of the ruling family. The case attracted international attention, and in February a Qatari court reduced al-Ajami's sentence to 15 years.

Oman: protests and pardon

Oman sought to contain discontent in March 2013 when its ruler, Sultan Qaboos, extended a royal pardon to activists convicted of insulting the ruler and participating in illegal demonstrations. Omani authorities had been criticised by international organisations following a June 2012 decision to take legal action against people who had allegedly made inflammatory remarks under 'the pretext of freedom of speech'. Close to 50 activists, lawyers, writers and online bloggers had been arrested by late 2012.

Activists sought better economic conditions, judicial-sector reform and greater political representation. In 2011, Oman had managed to contain unrest during the Arab uprisings with limited political and economic reforms and a cabinet reshuffle. However, dissent deepened in June 2012 after three activists were arrested for showing solidarity with oil-company workers who had gone on strike for better pay. Their arrests led to a protest calling for their release in front of a Muscat police station. Security forces detained 22 demonstrators.

Oman's elected Shura Council advised the government to speed up labour reforms to improve conditions for private-sector workers, especially those in the oil industry. Unemployment remained a pressing issue. According to IMF estimates, the unemployment rate was close to 24%. In September, authorities announced an ambitious scheme to create 56,000 jobs in the public and private sectors in 2013, and the 2013 state budget was increased by 30% to finance large development projects. However, the budget deficit deepened and the country remained a recipient of funds from other Gulf states, including Kuwait and the UAE.

Yemen: troubled transition

Yemen's long-awaited National Dialogue Conference was launched in March 2013 amid heightened tensions. The country continued to grapple with the growing threat from al-Qaeda in the Arabian Peninsula (AQAP) insurgents, political turmoil between the central government and southern secessionists, and the Houthi insurgency in the north. Yemen's structural problems – including water shortages, food insecurity and unemployment – remained acute.

Despite a boycott by southern separatist hardliners, an internationally backed national dialogue commenced in Sana'a, where more than 500 delegates represented a wide array of the country's political factions, civil-society organisations and regional groups, including the Houthi movement and some southern delegates. The dialogue aimed to draft a constitution ahead of general elections in February 2014 to replace interim President Abd Rabbuh Mansour Hadi. It also planned to address the status of the south, the Houthi movement and political reform.

The optimism that accompanied the launch of the dialogue soon flagged as tensions escalated between southern delegates and other representatives, prompting withdrawals and accusations of duplicity by all sides. The slow pace led some to argue that the timeline was unrealistic and should be extended, which could extend Hadi's term.

Crucially, Yemen tried to restructure its security sector and move away from remnants of the old regime. Political and civil-society activists demanded that former President Ali Abdullah Saleh's supporters and relatives be stripped of their military posts ahead of the national dialogue. In December 2012, Hadi issued a decree to restructure the military and rein in internal rivalries and factional loyalties. The decree effectively brought the Yemeni Republican Guard and the First Armoured Division under the wing of the Ministry of Defence, thus removing two prominent feuding leaders, General Ahmed Ali Saleh (son of the former president) and General Ali Mohsen al-Ahmar.

Meanwhile, the government faced a deteriorating security situation. Killings of security personnel by radical Islamists grew. In May 2012 a suicide attack at a rehearsal for a military parade in Sana'a killed more than 90 people. The bombing, for which the AQAP affiliate Ansar al-Sharia claimed responsibility, was an act of revenge against a military offensive in the southern province of Abyan, an al-Qaeda stronghold. Foreign embassies were also targeted: in November a Saudi diplomat and his bodyguard were shot dead in Sana'a. A month earlier, a Yemeni security official working for the US Embassy was killed.

Houthi insurgents carried out attacks. In March 2013 landmines killed over 30 people. In May, Houthis seized control of several Sunni mosques in the northern city of Sa'dah. Suspicions of the Houthis' links to Iran resurfaced when Yemeni and US naval forces intercepted a large weapons shipment, believed to be from Iran for the rebels. A meeting between Houthi leader Saleh Habra and the Iranian ambassador to Yemen provoked criticism of suspected Iranian interference.

The United States continued its use of drones to target suspected terrorists in Yemen, particularly AQAP members. Media reports revealed a secret drone air base operated by the CIA in Saudi Arabia, used to carry out targeted killings including that of American national Anwar al-Awlaki in September 2011. As drone attacks claimed more lives, Yemenis attempted to raise awareness of their humanitarian implications. In April 2013, a Yemeni writer whose village was attacked by a drone testified before a US Senate committee, arguing that the strikes fuelled extremism.

Yemen's economy experienced a slight recovery following its near collapse after the 2011 uprising. The IMF predicted the economy would grow by 4.4% in 2013, up from 0.1% in 2012. However, the population suffered from malnutrition, poverty, water shortages and rising unemployment. In July 2012, the UN World Food Programme warned that close to one million Yemeni children were undernourished as food prices had risen almost 60% since the 2011 uprising. At a Friends of Yemen donors' conference hosted by Saudi Arabia in September, international donors pledged over $6.4bn in financial aid. Saudi Arabia had previously pledged $3.3bn and deposited $1bn in Yemen's central bank. However, by March 2013, with the exception of Saudi Arabia, donors had only disbursed $500m.

Israel and Palestine: Status Quo Amidst Regional Upheaval

Negotiations between Israel and Palestine stalled amidst upheaval in both their political systems, regional turmoil and increased strain on the US–Israel relationship. However, newly appointed US Secretary of State John Kerry engaged in energetic diplomacy.

Complex coalition

Israel held early legislative elections in January 2013, prompted by the failure of Prime Minister Benjamin Netanyahu's coalition government to agree on a budget. The disagreement stemmed partly from fissures in the Knesset, Israel's parliament, over the Tal Law, which exempted some religious groups from military service and expired in August 2012, and attempts to pass laws creating more equal participation in military service.

Political divisions surrounding the role of ultra-orthodox Jews in society, as well as unprecedented protests in 2011 over the rising cost of living, led to the formation of new political parties and electoral alliances. Netanyahu's centre-right Likud party allied with the secular nationalist Yisrael Beiteinu ('Israel is Our Home'), a right-wing nationalist party popular with citizens of Russian origin. In November former foreign minister Tzipi Livni announced the formation of the liberal party

Hatnuah ('The Movement') which attracted disgruntled members of the liberal centrist Kadima Party and ran on a platform advocating a two-state solution and a peace settlement with the Palestinians. Many other parties competed in the poll: opposition party Avodah (Labor), led by Shelly Yachimovich; Habayit HaYehudi ('The Jewish Home'), a right-wing ultra-nationalist party led by Naftali Bennett; new centrist party Yesh Atid ('There is a Future'); ultra-orthodox parties Shas and United Torah Judaism; secular-left Meretz; and Arab parties Hadash, Balad and Ra'am Ta'al ('United Arab List').

The election results were remarkable both in the resulting shakeup of key players and in the issues voters prioritised. Though it won 31 seats and was the largest party, Likud Beiteinu's margin of victory was considerably slimmer than predicted. Newcomer Yesh Atid came second with 19 seats, turning Yair Lapid, the journalist and media personality who had formed the party, into a potential spoiler to Netanyahu's coalition-building plans. The success of Yesh Atid – which championed social and economic liberalisation as well as mandatory national service – demonstrated a shift from national security to socio-economics as the decisive issue for voters. Labor enjoyed resurgent popularity with 15 seats, becoming the main opposition force. The traditional blocs within the Knesset were evenly divided; the right-wing and religious parties received 60 seats, as did the centre, left and Arab parties.

As leader of the largest bloc, Netanyahu was charged with forming a government. Complex horse-trading followed. Early overtures to Labor, Yesh Atid and Habayit HaYehudi – considered the most likely partner for Likud Beiteinu due to its religious nationalist platform – failed. For its part, Labor attempted to build a centre-left coalition excluding Likud Beiteinu, but this attempt fell flat when Yesh Atid refused to join. Yisrael Beiteinu leader Avigdor Lieberman's indictment for fraud complicated negotiations, as Netanyahu decided to hold the foreign minister position open for him.

In February 2013, Netanyahu secured a deal with Hatnuah under which Livni would be named justice minister and would lead negotiations with the Palestinians. Even with the addition of Hatnuah, Netanyahu was still short of the requisite number of seats to form a government, while the presence of pro-peace Livni complicated the inclusion of Habayit HaYehudi and the ultra-orthodox parties in the coalition. As negotiations went on, Habayit HaYehudi and Yesh Atid teamed up to increase their negotiating power, stating that neither would join the government without the other party. This move was surprising as the two parties had serious political differences, including over the Tal Law and the annexation of the West Bank, and had different constituencies with often competing priorities.

Netanyahu finally reached a compromise that involved relinquishing control over the majority of the domestic ministries to Yesh Atid and Habayit HaYehudi, including those for education, economy and housing and construction. A formal coalition of Likud Beiteinu, Yesh Atid, Habayit HaYehudi and Hatnuah was announced on 14 March 2013. Notably, the government excluded the ultra-orthodox parties, usually major power brokers in Israeli politics.

Palestinian infighting

Palestine had an equally complex political situation, but made progress towards greater recognition at the UN. In November 2012, and despite active lobbying by the United States, more than 130 countries voted to upgrade Palestine's status to 'non-member observer state'. The new status provided greater leeway for Palestine to challenge Israel in international fora on issues such as human rights and settlement expansion. It also meant that the 'State of Palestine' could be used in official documents. The vote was a diplomatic setback for the United States and Israel.

However, Palestine's own political scene was fraught with infighting. Fatah and Hamas had moved toward reconciliation in early 2012, when an agreement was signed in Doha that placed Palestinian Authority (PA) President Mahmoud Abbas as head of an interim government and charged him with scheduling elections in 2012. In May 2012, Hamas and Fatah signed an additional agreement promising to hold elections and form a unity government. However, in spite of Egyptian supervision, steps toward reconciliation stalled and elections were indefinitely delayed, highlighting the enduring rift between the two movements, primarily over negotiations with Israel and power-sharing.

Hamas itself was divided over reconciliation: the Gaza-based leadership proved more hardline than the leadership abroad, now based in

Qatar. Steps to further Islamise Gaza and to secure funding by taxing trade from Egypt led to tensions with the local population and accusations of overreach and mismanagement on the part of Hamas.

Tensions between Abbas and Prime Minister Salam Fayyad, the main interlocutor of Western countries, reached boiling point over personnel and policy differences. In April 2013 Fayyad resigned, complicating Kerry's efforts to restart US-Israeli-Palestinian negotiations. This compounded economic problems in the West Bank. As foreign aid decreased, Palestinian unemployment rose to almost 25% in 2013. Israel withheld tax revenues in response to the Palestinian UN bid, delaying public-sector salary payments.

Israeli-Palestinian tensions

While Israel–PA security cooperation continued, Israel saw Gaza as a mounting threat and feared that Hamas was taking advantage of turmoil in Egypt to re-arm. These tensions culminated in military operations in November 2012. In response to increased rocket attacks from Gaza and an attack on the Israel Defense Forces (IDF), the Israeli Air Force killed Ahmed Jabari, chief of Hamas's military wing, and struck several Hamas targets in Gaza. Gaza-based militants from Hamas, Islamic Jihad and several Salafist groups retaliated, firing over 1,000 rockets toward cities in southern Israel. Israel's *Iron Dome* missile-defence system was used to intercept rockets and the IDF struck more than 1,500 targets within the Gaza Strip. Approximately 130 Palestinians were killed and nearly 800 were wounded. In November, an explosive device was detonated on a passenger bus in central Tel Aviv, the first mass-casualty attack there since 2006. An Egyptian-mediated ceasefire was announced in November.

The continued expansion of Israeli settlements in East Jerusalem and the West Bank raised tensions. In November 2012, in retaliation against the UN vote to upgrade the Palestinian's status, Israeli officials announced plans to develop settlements that would severely hinder the movement of people and goods between East Jerusalem and the West Bank. This move complicated efforts to map a future contiguous Palestinian state and raised tensions between Israel and the United States, which condemned settlement expansion. In January 2013, Palestinians set up a tent city in the area in protest; however, several days later, Israeli security forces evicted the protesters in a pre-dawn operation. A UN panel of experts found that Israeli settlements violated international law and called for an immediate halt to all settlement activity. However, Israel continued settlement expansion and retroactively legalised three settlement outposts in the West Bank.

Israel and its neighbours

Israel contended with the destabilisation of Syria and the increased threats from Hizbullah and other militant groups operating on Syrian territory. In January 2013, it conducted an air-strike on a convoy at a scientific research centre near Damascus as well as a nearby munitions building which Israel believed contained advanced anti-aircraft weaponry for Hizbullah. The air raid demonstrated Israel's greater willingness to violate Syria's sovereignty to counter the risk posed by Hizbullah and signal to the group's allies, Assad and Iran, not to alter the military balance. Two similar strikes followed.

While the Morsi government remained committed to the Egypt–Israel Peace Treaty, following the attack on the Israeli Embassy in Cairo in 2011, relations were troubled by the entry of Egyptian tanks into Sinai in August 2012 and growing discussion in Egypt about the need for changes to the Camp David agreement. Weak Egyptian control over Sinai and the border deepened Israeli fears. In August 2012, militants entered Israel through Egypt and engaged in a firefight with IDF troops. Israel intensified border patrols and finished building a fence.

Israel resolved a three-year feud with Turkey, stemming from the killing of nine Turks when Israeli commandos boarded a ship in 2010. It apologised for 'operational mistakes' made during the attack on pro-Palestinian activists. Both sides agreed to return envoys to each other, having recalled them shortly after the flotilla incident.

US–Israel relations

The interlinked nature of Israeli and US politics was displayed during their respective electoral campaigns. Netanyahu and Obama had clashed on numerous issues, notably on Israel's settlement activity and Iran's nuclear programme, and there was a sense that the former privately rooted for Obama's Republican challenger Mitt Romney, who visited Israel in July 2012 to court the conservative and pro-Israel vote.

The two governments' differing approaches to the Iranian nuclear programme were shown in sharp relief. Israeli scepticism about US diplomacy with Iran, conflicting assessments of Iran's nuclear capabilities, differing US and Israeli red lines, and tension over the kind of action to take should these red lines be crossed, complicated US-Israeli cooperation. Obama stated that it would take Iran at least a year to develop a nuclear weapon; but in a dramatic presentation at the UN in September 2012, Netanyahu stated that Iran would cross a critical threshold in its nuclear capacity by summer 2013. As these differences played out in public, the strain on Netanyahu and Obama's relationship was clear.

However, the re-election of both leaders forced renewed cooperation. In April 2013, they agreed on a multi-billion dollar arms deal to strengthen Israel's military edge as the US finalised arms sales to several Gulf nations. Air-refuelling capabilities, essential for an Israeli strike on Iran, were included in the package, though other items – such as 'bunker buster' bombs to destroy Iran's well-protected nuclear infrastructure – were not. Joint planning took place to deal with the fallout of the Syrian civil war, especially the risk of chemical weapons and advanced weaponry falling into the hands of radical rebel groups, and Hizbullah obtaining surface-to-air and advanced rockets. Obama's March 2013 trip to Israel served to reset his relationship with Netanyahu, reach out to the Israeli and Palestinian publics and reinvigorate the Kerry-led peace process. Iran was the paramount issue on the leaders' agenda.

Iran: Persistent Confrontation

The stand-off over Iran's nuclear programme further escalated in the year to mid-2013. Tehran increased both the quantity and quality of the centrifuges used to produce enriched uranium while the United States and its allies tightened their sanctions squeeze. The hard-hit Iranian economy saw oil revenues halved, the currency at one-fifth of its previous value, and inflation and unemployment rising sharply. Talk of an Israeli unilateral air-strike against Iran's nuclear facilities abated in autumn 2012 as a result of US pressure and an Iranian tactical effort to keep below Israel's declared red line for attack.

A de-emphasis on military options bought time for diplomacy but it was not well spent. Iran and its six negotiating partners met only twice during this time and made no progress toward a solution. In early 2013, an adjustment in the proposal by the E3+3 (the United Kingdom, France and Germany, plus China, Russia and the United States) to offer slightly more and demand slightly less was not reciprocated by Iran. It appeared that compromise by Iran would be impossible at least until after the election in June, when the tenure of controversial President Mahmoud Ahmadinejad would end, as would the bitter power struggle between the president and Supreme Leader Ayatollah Ali Khamenei, which had impeded compromise on almost any policy matter. When the 14 June presidential election produced a surprise victory by centrist cleric Hassan Rouhani, hopes emerged both inside and outside Iran that the nuclear crisis might be solved diplomatically. Rouhani had yet to say, however, how he would handle the issue, other than that he would engage the major powers more skilfully in order to remove sanctions. Even if he were inclined to seek compromise, there was no certainty that the Supreme Leader, who is in charge of the nuclear issue, would allow it. If Iran does not accept some limits on the nuclear programme, it could be on a trajectory that would cross Israeli – and even American – red lines some time in 2014.

Nuclear progress

In the year to mid-2013, Iran steadily increased its stockpile of low-enriched uranium (LEU). By May, it had produced 8,960 kilogrammes of LEU of 3.5–5% purity – the level needed to fuel most nuclear power plants. Over one-quarter of this amount had been used to produce 324kg of 19.75% enriched uranium, the level needed to fuel the Tehran Research Reactor (TRR). If Khamenei were to change his religious edict against nuclear weapons and the nation chose to break out of the Nuclear Non-Proliferation Treaty (NPT), the stockpile of LEU would be sufficient for up to six bombs when further enriched.

The time it would take Iran to produce a nuclear weapon was a matter of keen interest. In March 2013, President Obama said it would take at least a year if Iran made that decision. It was understood that this would include both the time to produce enough highly enriched uranium and the time to design and fashion it into a weapon. Making a bomb small enough to fit one of Iran's ballistic missiles would take additional time, as would developing the missiles themselves. Although Iran has a range of nuclear-capable short- and medium-range missiles, including the *Ghadr*-1, their restricted range and reliance on liquid fuel makes them sub-optimal as nuclear delivery vehicles. Iran's most potent missile, the solid-fuelled *Sajjil*-2, remained under development, untested since February 2011, possibly because of lack of reliable access to foreign ingredients for the fuel, due to sanctions. Nuclear weapons can be delivered by other means, however, including by ship.

Making weapons-grade highly enriched uranium might take as little as two months if Iran started with medium-enriched feedstock. In a September 2012 speech to the UN General Assembly, Israeli Prime Minister Benjamin Netanyahu displayed a cartoon bomb and declared that Iran's production of enough near-20% enriched uranium for a bomb – believed to be 240–50kg – should be considered a red line for military action, and that Iran was on a trajectory to reach this point by the following spring or summer.

Netanyahu's speech effectively signalled that, contrary to what he and Defence Minister Ehud Barak had been saying throughout the summer, Israel was not considering immediate military action. The change in message was the result of an extraordinary public debate in Israel over the wisdom of a unilateral military strike. For months, US officials had counselled that Israeli air-strikes would be destabilising and ineffective, not delaying Iran's ability to produce nuclear weapons by more than 1–3 years. Senior members of the Israeli security establishment agreed, adding that a unilateral attack would damage Israeli-US relations. Although Netanyahu continued to argue that diplomacy would not succeed unless Iran faced a credible military option, he could not discount these views, especially when Israeli President Shimon Peres himself came out publicly against an attack in August 2012.

Netanyahu reluctantly accepted America's message that a premature strike on Iran's nuclear facilities would be counter-productive, but differences remained over what should constitute the red line. Israel wanted the United States to set a firm deadline for a diplomatic solution, after which the military option should come into play. For Obama, the tripwire for US military action would be Iranian nuclear-weapons acquisition. He deviated slightly from this, however, in the third presidential debate in October when he said, 'We're not going to allow Iran to perpetually engage in negotiations that lead nowhere ... we have a sense of when they would get breakout capacity, which means that we would not be able to intervene in time to stop their nuclear programme, and that clock is ticking.' In other words, even if Iran did not purposely cross Obama's red line of weapons acquisition, a US military option could come into play if Iran's enriched-uranium stockpile and growing enrichment capability made it possible to enrich to weapons grade before such a step could be detected.

This point, described by some as a 'critical capability', could come by mid-2014. An additional red line has been suggested: any Iranian production of highly enriched uranium – that is, over 20%. In October, a senior parliamentarian in Iran implied that the country might do just that, saying 60% enrichment would be justified in order to produce fuel for future nuclear-powered submarines.

Netanyahu and Barak justified postponing military action on grounds that Iran had converted a portion of the near-20% enriched uranium hexafluoride (UF_6) to a solid oxide form that could not be immediately further enriched. Oxide conversion is a step in the fabrication of TRR fuel. Although the process can be reversed in a few weeks' time, Iran's decision to continue converting a portion of the UF_6 throughout the year was praised as a useful step to keep the military option at bay.

Iran may have also made a tactical decision not to operate most of the 2,700 centrifuges installed at the deeply buried underground enrichment facility at Fordow. Throughout the year, only one-quarter of them were operating, producing 19.75% enriched uranium. Whether this was for technical or political reasons was unclear. Meanwhile, however, Iran sharply increased the number of centrifuges installed and operating at the larger underground facility at Natanz. By May, 14,244 were in place, up from 9,330 a year earlier. About 690 of the centrifuges were of a second-generation model, the IR-2m, which is 2–4 times more efficient than the first-generation models used by Iran to date. Iran started employing them at the Natanz facility in February, and announced that 3,000 in total would be installed. This news came as a setback to Western governments which had hoped that sanctions and export controls would prevent Iran from obtaining the high-quality carbon fibre and maraging steel needed to produce the faster-spinning IR-2m models.

Iran made further progress at another nuclear facility; most of the components for a 40MW heavy-water-moderated research reactor at Arak had been produced and delivered to the site. Although Iran seemed to have trouble making the fuel for the reactor, it said the facility was on track to become operational during the third quarter of 2013. This schedule introduced a second timeline into the discussion of weapons capability and military options because once the reactor is operational it could, if Iran so desired, produce a bomb's worth of weapons-grade plutonium in a year. Iran vowed to use the reactor only for isotope production and other peaceful purposes, and it does not have a reprocessing capability to extract plutonium from spent fuel. Yet two factors about Arak sparked concern. Firstly, it would provide a potential second path to a nuclear weapon. Secondly, once Arak begins irradiating fuel, any military attack on it could spew deadly radiation into the atmosphere. If a military strike became increasingly probable due to the failure of diplomacy, the date for Arak's start-up would provide a deadline for military strikes without radioactive fallout.

The schedule for Arak may well be set back, however, in light of problems at Iran's nuclear power plant. Bushehr became operational in September 2011, but has been repeatedly shut down since. In October 2012, the fuel at Bushehr had to be unloaded because stray bolts were discovered under the fuel cells. Iran was meant to take over operational control of the Russian-built reactor in December but this was postponed. In February, visiting IAEA inspectors found the reactor to be shut down again, for unexplained reasons. Two earthquakes that struck southern Iran in April 2013, including one with a magnitude of 6.3 on the Richter scale and an epicentre 78 kilometres from the nuclear power plant resulted in no radiation leak, though later it was revealed that several cracks had been discovered in one part of the plant. Iran's Gulf neighbours, most of whose capitals are closer to Bushehr than is Tehran, voiced strong concerns about the potential danger. This was compounded by

Iran being the only country with a nuclear power plant not to be party to the IAEA Convention on Nuclear Safety.

Lack of transparency characterised other aspects of Iran's nuclear programme. In May 2013, IAEA inspectors were allowed to visit Arak for the first time in almost two years, but Iran still refused to provide updated design information as required by safeguards rules that Iran has unilaterally opted out of since 2007 and without which the IAEA said it would have difficulty implementing an effective safeguards approach.

The IAEA was also frustrated by Iran's refusal to allow investigation into allegations that Iran had conducted various nuclear activities of a 'possible military dimension'. Reports of nuclear-weapons-related high-explosive testing at the Parchin military complex garnered particular attention. Because overhead imagery indicated that clean-up and landscaping were under way that might eliminate any remaining traces of such experimentation, the IAEA put a priority on gaining access to Parchin. Iran indicated that it would allow a visit there if agreement could be reached on a 'structured approach' for addressing all of the allegations about military-related nuclear activities. But repeated efforts to negotiate such an agreement failed, as Iran sought to use transparency with the IAEA as leverage in talks with the E3+3. In June, IAEA Director General Yukiya Amano said talks with Tehran had been 'going around in circles' for some time. The United States and other board members threatened to send the issue to the Security Council for possible enforcement action, but decided to wait until after the Iran presidential election in order not to detract from diplomatic efforts.

Diplomacy stalled

E3+3 talks with Iran resumed in Almaty, Kazakhstan, in February 2013, eight months after the previous round in Moscow in June 2012. At the June meeting, Iran had presented a five-step proposal asking for all sanctions to be lifted and its 'right to enrichment' acknowledged, in exchange for which Iran would halt near-20% enrichment. In September, EU foreign-policy chief Catherine Ashton, who leads the talks on behalf of the E3+3, met Saeed Jalili, Iran's nuclear negotiator, but he said Iran had not budged from its June position.

The long hiatus was initially blamed on the November US presidential election, on the assumption Tehran would want to know if Obama would continue to occupy the White House before it could offer any concessions. Press reports that talks would resume shortly after the election proved false, however. Likewise, there was no substantiation to reports of secret US–Iran bilateral meetings. A message from the White House to Tehran after the election elicited no response. Ashton's repeated attempts in December to set up a full director-level meeting were met with a fictitious debate over the appropriate venue. At the Munich Security Conference in February, both US Vice President Joe Biden and Iranian Foreign Minister Ali Akbar Salehi spoke positively about the prospects for bilateral talks, but Khamenei immediately rejected the idea. Claiming the United States was proposing talks while 'pointing a gun at Iran', he said 'some naive people like the idea of negotiating with America, [but] negotiations will not solve the problem'. Later, he clarified that he was not opposed to direct talks with Washington, but said they would not yield results unless sanctions were lifted. Several months later, it emerged that he had grudgingly approved a January written request by Salehi for bilateral engagement with the United States, yet nothing came of the idea.

At the first round of talks in Almaty on 26–27 February, the E3+3 put a revised proposal to Iran for confidence-building measures focused on the nuclear activities of most immediate concern. In talks the previous spring and summer they had asked Iran to suspend production of near-20% enriched uranium, ship the accumulated 20% stockpile out of the country and shut down the Fordow facility. In exchange, they offered to provide fuel for the TRR, along with nuclear-safety assistance and spare parts for civilian aircraft. No additional sanctions would be lifted, but no new measures would be imposed if negotiations were successful. At Almaty, this proposal was adjusted in two ways: rather than completely shutting down Fordow, Iran was asked to temporarily suspend operations at Fordow but not to dismantle the facility as previously demanded. The quid pro quo was also increased, by offering to lift sanctions on trade in gold and precious metals, and petrochemical sales, which had been imposed in early February.

The Iranians said the proposal was welcome, though not enough, and that they would respond soon. When the second round of talks in

Almaty took place on 5–6 April, it was widely expected that Iran would offer slight modifications to its own plan. However, Iran stuck to its maximalist position and spoke instead about a comprehensive solution to various issues of concern, including the situation in Syria and Bahrain. A senior US official said it was 'neither a breakdown nor a breakthrough'. An extended back and forth between Jalili and Wendy Sherman, the US chief negotiator, was seen as a positive indication of Iran's willingness to discuss substance, but no further meetings were scheduled.

Sanctions squeeze

With diplomacy stalled, the policy pursued by the West toward Iran relied even more on sanctions. In July 2012, Obama expanded the scope of measures aimed at reducing Iran's oil exports. Second-tier sanctions that previously sought to limit oil sales financed through the Central Bank of Iran were extended to oil sales conducted through any bank. Sanctions were also extended to Iranian petrochemical products. As of February 2013, Iran would not be able to repatriate money from foreign oil sales; instead, oil payments to Iran would have to be kept in the purchaser country and spent on local products. Foreign entities that did not abide by these measures would face penalties in the United States.

In January, Obama signed the Iran Freedom and Counter-Proliferation Act of 2012, passed by Congress with a huge majority. The measure blacklists any party that operates a port in Iran or is part of its energy, shipping or shipbuilding sectors. This affects whole sectors of the economy rather than specified entities, making it harder for Iran to evade sanctions by simply switching business to newly named companies. The provision of precious metals to Iran would also be penalised – intended to stop the gold-for-oil trade through which Iran was conducting much of its oil sales to Turkey.

Many of the Iranian entities that have come under European sanctions have challenged the legality of the designations. In early 2013, Iran's Bank Mellat and Bank Saderat persuaded the EU General Court in Luxembourg to annul their designation, although the measures remain in place pending appeal. Bank Mellat also won its case in the UK High Court, which held an unprecedented secret session to review government evidence of the bank as an agent of proliferation.

Notwithstanding these challenges, the EU imposed new sanctions measures against Iran in October 2012, restricting financial transactions and banning the purchase of natural gas from Iran by its member states. Previously, the EU had allowed business with Iran that was not explicitly prohibited. Reversing this approach, the new rules declared that all financial transactions between European and Iranian banks were banned except those that were expressly allowed, mostly for humanitarian purposes. A ban on importing Iranian gas stopped what had been a significant European brokerage trade in that commodity, even though Europe itself did not import much natural gas from Iran. No longer could sanctions be described as targeted. By 2012, the sanctions measures were wholesale efforts to squeeze the Iranian economy, affecting not just the government and organisations associated with the nuclear programme, but the Iranian people as a whole. By April 2013, oil exports dropped to 750,000 barrels per day, in contrast to 2.5 billion barrels per day in 2011. High oil prices partly offset the reduced sales, but oil revenues overall dropped by 45%, costing the economy about $150 million per day in lost earnings. According to the Iranian parliament's research centre, industrial production fell 40% in the year to October 2012, unemployment grew by 36% and consumer prices rose by 87%. In March, the government reported the inflation rate to be 31.5%, although many private economists argued that the real inflation rate could be at least double this figure.

In October, the exchange rate dropped sharply, as panicked consumers exchanged rials for dollars or gold on the black market. Combined with a similar plunge in January 2012, the rial lost nearly 80% of its value in the course of a year. To stem the currency free fall, the government imposed a trading holiday for currency exchanges, which led to a one-day protest in Tehran's Grand Bazaar. Some Western analysts and policymakers saw this limited protest – the only one of its kind reported during the entire year – as evidence that the sanctions were achieving their intended impact of causing internal pressure on the government.

Although the sanctions exempted humanitarian goods, Iran experienced a widespread shortage of speciality medicines because many foreign banks, shipping companies and trading firms found it prudent to cut off all dealings with Iran lest they inadvertently run afoul of the increasingly complex set of restrictions imposed by the United States in particular.

In response to the sanctions, the government proclaimed a 'resistance economy', to stimulate domestic substitutes for foreign imports and a diversified export base less dependent on oil sales, with mixed results. A variable exchange rate benefitted consumers and enterprises affiliated with the state but contributed to corruption, and subsidy stipends contributed to inflation. Middle-class consumers and independent businesses bore the brunt of the sanctions though the Iranian economy was 'limping along' by keeping both the balance of trade and government balance of payments positive. Trade patterns shifted to China, India and other Asian partners, with barter arrangements increasingly the norm.

Sanctions advocates argued that additional penalties had to be imposed in order to keep up the pressure. In May, Canada cut all non-humanitarian trade with Iran. In June, the United States imposed sanctions on foreign financial institutions that conduct or facilitate significant transactions in the rial in an effort to make it 'as unusable a currency as possible'. From July 2013, sanctions were applied against entities that do business with Iran's auto sector. In the spring and summer, Congress was considering additional sanctions, including a measure to deny the Iranian government access to an estimated $100bn of its foreign-exchange reserves that are held in foreign banks. Although US Secretary of State John Kerry sought to delay additional measures while diplomacy was still being pursued, the message from Washington was that unless Iran accepted limits on its nuclear programme, the economic pressure would continue to increase.

Iran's domestic politics

The worsening economy contributed to intensifying internal disputes, manifest most clearly in the ongoing power struggle between President Ahmadinejad and the Supreme Leader. In a message marking the Iranian new year in March, Khamenei implicitly held the president's cabinet responsible for the nation's economic woes, saying 'some people were short in their efforts and inconsiderate in their measures, all of which helped the enemy's plan.' Ahmadinejad responded by saying that the

Supreme Leader had only one vote in the upcoming election and that 'the country must be governed by the will of the people and the whole nation must decide.'

In September, while Ahmadinejad was making his final appearance at the UN General Assembly in New York, his press adviser and close ally, Ali Akbar Javanfekr, was jailed for six months by the Tehran prosecutor's office on charges of 'insulting the leader'. He allegedly had allowed a state newspaper to question the custom of women wearing the chador, a head-to-toe black veil. These charges had a political underpinning. As managing director of the Islamic Republic News Agency, Javanfekr was well positioned to manipulate the pre-election debate on topics and candidates. Ahmadinejad was barred from visiting Javanfekr in the infamous Evin Prison.

The president struck back, publicly accusing the head of the judiciary, Ayatollah Sadegh Larijani, of protecting individuals including his brother, the speaker of the Majles (parliament), from prosecution for corruption. The public attack on the Larijani brothers, the first of many to come, indicated a failure of Khamenei's efforts to re-establish unity amongst the regime leadership.

In November, the Majles summoned Ahmadinejad for the second time that year for questioning over the burgeoning economic and currency crisis. This time, the Supreme Leader stepped in and demanded that the fracas not continue. Despite his differences with Ahmadinejad, Khamenei recognised the importance of perceived unity. 'The country needs tranquillity,' he said, and summoning the president was 'what the enemy seeks'. But Ahmadinejad paid little heed to these words. In February 2013, during a parliamentary debate that was being broadcast live on the radio, Ahmadinejad played a video incriminating the Larijani brothers in a corruption and nepotism scandal. In the ensuing uproar, 192 out of 272 Majles members voted to impeach the president – an unprecedented move.

Ahmadinejad's persistence in stirring trouble during his last year in office was likely intended to secure support amongst the masses as he lost support within the regime. In an effort to remain relevant after his mandate and boost his top aide, Esfandiar Rahim Mashaei, as a successor in the upcoming presidential election, his actions sought to divert attention away from his economic failures in favour of his campaign to purify the regime of corruption.

As it transpired, Mashaei's candidacy was not approved by the 12-jurist Guardian Council, which vets all political candidates on the stated basis of belief in God and loyalty to the constitution, plus various unstated qualifications. Of the 680 individuals, including 30 women, who registered as potential candidates, only eight men passed this vetting process. Mashaei's disqualification was no surprise; he had been accused by hardliners as being 'deviant' because he advocated direct relations with God, instead of through clerical intermediaries. It was more surprising, however, that Akbar Hashemi Rafsanjani, former president and Iran's best-known politician, was also disqualified, on grounds of old age (at 78, he was eight years younger than the head of the Guardian Council). Many thought the real reason was that he was too closely associated with reformists and was too popular.

Among the eight qualifying candidates, Jalili, chairman of the National Security Council, appeared to emerge as the front-runner because he was deemed to be the most conservative and loyal to Khamenei. However, another conservative, Tehran Mayor Mohammad Baqer Qalibaf, was more popular. It appeared that no candidate would achieve a majority in the 14 June election and that either Jalili or Qalibaf would emerge victorious in the prospective second round of voting on 21 June.

One candidate did win in the first round, however, and not one of the conservatives. Hassan Rouhani, former foreign minister, former nuclear negotiator and a centrist, was elected the seventh president of the Islamic Republic, with an announced total of 50.7% of the votes. Qalibaf garnered 16.5% and Jalili came in a distant third with 11.3%. The results were surprising as many believed they would be rigged, in light of Rafsanjani's disqualification, the near shutdown of the Internet during the campaign and the many arrests of journalists and other forms of intimidation in the months leading up to the election. One curious and unexplained incident, for example, was the March arrest of a senior diplomat, Bagher Asadi, apparently because he had previously been associated with the reformist camp. In addition, the two reformist candidates from 2009, seen as leaders of the Green Movement, remained under extra-judicial house arrest. But instead of manipulating votes, the regime focused on ensuring legitimacy by encouraging high voter turnout. Two days before the election, Khamenei said: 'Some people, for whatever reason, do not want to support the Islamic Republic establishment but they do want to support their country. They should also come to the polls. Everyone should come to the polls.' According to the interior ministry, voter turnout was 72.7%.

The result was announced in the evening of 15 June, almost 24 hours longer than it had taken to announce Ahmadinejad's re-election in 2009. That announcement four years ago had provoked mass protests and accusations of fraud. This time there were no protests, only large-scale street demonstrations of joy. Conservatives blamed the loss on their failure to settle on one candidate. Although one conservative had pulled out a few days before the election, three had remained in the race. By contrast, the only other centrist had withdrawn, leaving reformists and the pragmatically inclined voters to unite behind Rouhani.

A long-time regime insider, Rouhani was not considered to be a reformist himself. In his vigorous campaign appearances, however, he appealed for moderation and pragmatism. He also challenged the government's handling of foreign policy. In electing him, voters repudiated the isolation that was being heightened by Jalili's policy of resistance to Western demands. Rouhani made clear that he supported the nuclear programme, and boasted that, under his watch before mid-2005, it had made considerable progress, even as he made a tactical deal in 2003 to temporarily suspend some parts of the programme in order to forestall sanctions. Criticising Jalili's handling of the nuclear issue, he said in a television debate: 'All of our problems stem from this – that we didn't make an utmost effort to prevent the (nuclear) dossier from going to the Security Council.' He added that 'it is good to have centrifuges running, provided people's lives and livelihoods are also running.' During his first press conference as president-elect, Rouhani called for greater transparency in Iran's nuclear programme and the need to build trust between the two sides in the negotiations. Although he made no mention of compromise, this more moderate tone led to optimism about a diplomatic solution. The next round of talks was being mooted for some time after he would take office in August.

Foreign relations worsen

Iran's confrontation with the West and Gulf states was exacerbated by the ongoing conflict in Syria, as Iran increased its materiel and personnel support for the Assad regime. In August 2012, the Free Syrian Army (FSA) captured 48 Iranians near Damascus. The Iranian government initially claimed they were religious pilgrims, but the FSA said documentation on some of the men showed they were Iran Revolutionary Guard Corps (IRGC) officers. Salehi then admitted that some were retired IRGC and military personnel. Five months later, Turkey and Qatar brokered their release in exchange for 2,130 FSA prisoners held by the Assad regime. After this incident, it was difficult for Iran to hide its involvement in Syria. In September 2012, the head of the IRGC, Commander Mohammad Ali Jafari, confirmed that 'a number of the Quds force are present in Syria, but this isn't the same as a military presence in this country,' adding that they were providing 'intellectual and advisory help'. In addition to opening credit lines worth several billion dollars to Syria, Iran stepped up shipment of weapons to Assad via Iraqi airspace, creating tension between Iraq and the United States.

Iran's support for Assad complicated its efforts to appeal to the Arab street. Many Arabs had previously considered Iran to be an example of leadership, defiance and resistance. In a March 2013 poll conducted by Zogby Research Services, however, Iran was viewed unfavourably in 14 out of 20 Arab and Muslim countries, largely due to its involvement in Syria. Iran's popularity among Turks also fell; 57% viewed the country unfavourably.

Some traditional allies questioned their ties with Iran, but not to the point of severing them. In November 2012, Khaled Mashal, the leader of the political wing of Hamas, admitted that the relationship with Iran was 'affected and harmed' by disagreements over Syria. Yet Iran continued to supply weapons to Hamas during the November exchange of rocket fire between Hamas and Israel. The commander of the IRGC Aerospace Force publicly admitted that his forces had supplied Hamas with the know-how to develop *Fajr*-5 rockets capable of reaching Tel Aviv. Although Egypt sided with the Sunni rebels, President Muhammad Morsi included Iran in the quartet of regional states that he proposed should try to solve the Syrian issue, echoing sentiments expressed by UN envoys Kofi Annan and Lakhdar Brahimi that Iran could be part of the solution.

Morsi in various ways showed interest in improving relations with Iran, but with caution. He visited Tehran in August for the Non-Aligned Movement (NAM) summit, but spent as little time as possible in the country and used his speech there to express solidarity with the 'struggle of those who are demanding freedom and justice in Syria'.

Meanwhile tensions between the GCC and Iran remained high. The GCC continued to express concerns over Iran's advancing nuclear programme and its 'unacceptable' interference in regional affairs. In December 2012, Bahrain Foreign Minister Sheikh Khalid Bin Ahmed al-Khalifa announced the GCC would coordinate air, land and marine forces under one structure and called Iran's nuclear programme a 'very serious' threat, implying that this closer cooperation was directed at containing Iran.

Iran's involvement in Yemen was another source of concern. In January, Yemeni Coast Guard and US Navy vessels seized an Iranian vessel carrying Chinese-origin anti-aircraft missiles, *Katyusha* rockets, rocket-propelled grenades and C4 explosives, which was reportedly bound for Houthi rebels. Although a UN investigative panel was split over Iranian government complicity, the attempted supply of anti-aircraft missiles led US Defense Secretary Leon Panetta to accuse Iran of intensifying a campaign to destabilise the Middle East. The United States cited the case as another reason to supply arms to Iran's adversaries.

Although talk of pre-emptive attack abated in late 2012 and Rouhani's election renewed hopes for a diplomatic solution, Iran's steadily increasing nuclear capabilities may yet prompt consideration of a military option. In some ways, Iran and the West are already at war. The widespread sanctions imposed on Iran are often described as economic warfare and cyber attacks have escalated. After repeated targeting of its nuclear programme, Iran apparently responded, in the latter half of 2012, with denial-of-service attacks on major US and international banks, as well as on Saudi Aramco, damaging some 30,000 computers.

Another form of conflict took place in the skies. In November, two Iranian Air Force planes targeted a US unmanned drone that the US Department of Defense said was conducting surveillance operations outside Iran's territorial waters. In March, an Iranian fighter jet similarly targeted a US *Predator* drone over the Persian Gulf. No shots were fired in either case, but the incidents prompted concern that hostilities could be unintentionally triggered. Similarly, although Iran is unlikely overtly to cross Obama's red line of nuclear-weapons acquisition, it might do so inadvertently through uncontrolled expansion of the uranium-enrichment programme, especially if the hopes for diplomatic progress following Rouhani's election prove to be false.

Iraq: Political Deadlock

The year to mid-2013 witnessed a political crisis that caused governmental deadlock, rising tension across the country and a steep increase in politically motivated violence. The crisis was indicative of the failings of political institutions built in the period following the 2003 regime change and subsequent insurgency, and also underlined the increasing instability of the country since US troop withdrawal in December 2011.

The crisis was triggered by raids on the houses of two senior Iraqiyya politicians by Iraqi security forces. The Iraqiyya coalition, which had won 91 seats in the March 2010 elections, and the State of Law coalition of Prime Minister Nuri al-Maliki, which had won 89 seats, had formed a government of national unity after 10 months of negotiations, with Maliki remaining as prime minister. In December 2011, Vice President Tariq al-Hashemi and his bodyguards were arrested. Hashemi fled the country but his bodyguards confessed to terrorism offences and Hashemi was sentenced *in absentia* to execution. In December 2012, the house of Finance Minister Rafi al-Issawi was raided and his bodyguards were taken into custody. Hashemi was not a particularly effective or popular politician and his arrest resulted in little popular protest. Issawi, however, had a strong political constituency in his home province of

Anbar and had won international respect for his effective and non-partisan management of the country's finances.

Spreading protests

The raid on Issawi's house and his subsequent resignation in March 2013 triggered mass protests across the Sunni-dominated northwest. Sunnis had felt increasingly excluded from national politics since the 2010 elections, cut off from the benefits of oil wealth and discriminated against by the security forces.

From December 2012 to April 2013, tens of thousands of people demonstrated in Anbar's two biggest cities, Fallujah and Ramadi. Protests quickly spread into the neighbouring provinces of Diyala and Nineveh. Demonstrators blocked the main highways to Jordan and Syria. What began as spontaneous protests became sustained and coordinated weekly demonstrations, organised by the political party of a senior Iraqiyya politician, Osama al-Nujaifi, speaker of the Iraqi parliament. By the beginning of January, an organising committee based in Ramadi had issued a list of 13 demands for the government to meet before they would call off the protests.

Maliki was clearly surprised by the extent and longevity of the protests. At first he sought to dismiss them as irrelevant. However, once their significance became apparent, he attempted to defuse them by making a series of concessions. First, a number of prisoners, many held without trial, were released. Then a cabinet committee was set up to examine issues surrounding widespread abuse of prisoners. Finally, Maliki negotiated a deal with the deputy prime minister and al-Iraqiyya politician, Saleh al-Mutlaq, that sought to deal with the protesters' demands by reforming the de-Ba'athification laws, reversing punitive economic measures against former members of the old regime and reforming the way in which detainees were prosecuted. However, Mutlaq's ability to mediate between the government and protesters proved limited. On 30 December 2012, he and his bodyguard were driven out of Ramadi by demonstrators who condemned him for being too close to the prime minister.

When indifference and then conciliation did not work, the army was brought in to break up the demonstrations, resulting in the deaths of nine people at the end of January 2013 and a further 40 in April. The size and frequency of anti-government demonstrations began to decline, but the use of state-sponsored violence to break up popular protests left a legacy of resentment and feelings of alienation amongst Iraq's Sunni population. The steady rise in politically motivated violence during 2013 can be seen as a direct result of the suppression of the protest movement, as well as of the underlying grievances that initially triggered the demonstrations.

The raid on Issawi's house and the mass protests it sparked indicated major failings within the political system. Maliki had remained prime minister after lengthy negotiations by promising to abide by strict rules designed to constrain his increasingly authoritarian behaviour. However, he made a concerted effort to escape the limits placed upon him. For example, in October 2012, after falling out with the prime minister over the independence of the central bank, Sinan al-Shabibi, its widely respected head and his deputy, Mudher Saleh, were indicted on corruption charges. Shabibi was then forced into exile and replaced by Abdel Basset Turki, who had previously been appointed by Maliki as head of the anti-corruption organisation, the Board of Supreme Audit. The removal of Shabibi meant that the central bank was no longer independent from the prime minister's office.

Dissatisfaction with the prime minister amongst the rest of Iraq's ruling elite reached a peak in the summer of 2012 when Iraqiyya, in alliance with the Kurdistan Democratic Party (KDP) and Moqtada al-Sadr, the radical Shia Islamist and leader of the Jaish al-Mahdi militia, attempted to pass a vote of 'no confidence' against him in parliament. In response, President Jalal Talabani forged an alliance with Maliki and successfully blocked the vote, arguing that the prime minister's opponents did not have the 163 votes needed to gain a majority. However, in January 2013 Talabani suffered a stroke that prevented him from playing a role in politics. In his absence, parliament proved more coherent in mobilising support to limit Maliki's power, and passed a law restricting any prime minister from serving more than two terms in office. Maliki dismissed this as unconstitutional: firstly, because the constitution did not mention term limits for ministers; and secondly because the Higher Judicial Council – in a ruling that appeared to show a lack of autonomy – had curtailed the power of parliament by ruling that only the cabinet, not parliament, had the power to introduce legally binding legislation.

Maliki's ability to survive these attempts to limit his power illustrated his skills as a political operator but also revealed the weakness of constraints on the actions of politicians, as well as the chronic disunity of the forces arrayed against him. Since his appointment in 2006, Maliki had gradually centralised power and influence within his own private office, cultivating a network of loyalists throughout the civil service, judiciary and armed forces. He used these functionaries to obstruct moves against him from within the wider ruling elite. He also used the power and patronage of office to break the coherence of parties and coalitions opposed to him. This tactic was most successful when deployed against Iraqiyya, which won the largest number of seats in the 2010 election, but three years later had fractured into a number of splinter groups.

Disunity amongst his opponents left Maliki free to further constrain political freedoms. In April 2013, for example, ten Arab satellite channels, including Al Jazeera, had their licences to operate withdrawn and their journalists thrown out of the country for 'misleading and exaggerated coverage' which 'promoted violence'.

Finally, when faced with the difficulties of ruling through a government of national unity, Maliki made it clear that he would attempt to move to a majoritarian government after the next national elections in 2014. This would in effect see his coalition, State of Law, either ruling on its own or more likely in alliance with the other Shia Islamist parties – excluding the two dominant Kurdish parties, the Patriotic Union of Kurdistan and the KDP, along with Iraqiyya. Maliki said this would lead to more efficient government, with the other parties providing oversight from the opposition benches.

The three governments that have run Iraq since its first democratic elections in 2005 have contributed importantly to the creation of a weak and profoundly corrupt state. However, a move to a majoritarian government led by Maliki would further alienate the Kurdish and Sunni populations, and exacerbate their fears that the country was moving back towards authoritarianism, further increasing the sectarian bias of the state.

Provincial elections

The first step in Maliki's move towards a majoritarian government began with the campaign for provincial elections held on 20 April 2013. The Independent High Electoral Commission (IHEC) was set up under American occupation to oversee free and fair elections. Its independence has been fought over by political parties, each seeking to maximise their influence. Maliki blamed it for his inability to gain a majority of seats in the 2010 national elections when, with UN support, the commission oversaw a recount of ballot papers and certified the results unchanged. In June 2011, Maliki ordered the IHEC to suspend its work so it could be 'reformed', but its head, Faraj al-Haidari, refused, saying it was an independent body answerable only to parliament. In April 2012, Haidari was arrested on minor charges of corruption and given a one-year suspended sentence, though the conviction was thrown out on appeal. In a comparable way to the treatment of the former head of the central bank, the Iraqi judiciary appeared to have been used to intimidate civil servants whose job it was to oversee the independent functioning of state institutions.

The IHEC's mandate expired in April 2012, but was extended for three months while parliament debated how new members would be chosen. The political affiliations of nine members who had made up the board were thought to approximate the balance of political power, thus guaranteeing a rough-and-ready equilibrium in its rulings. Maliki proposed an expansion to 15 members. Parliamentary opponents feared that this would give him more power to influence the commission's work by nominating board members aligned to his own party. In September 2012, parliament voted against the prime minister's proposals and moved to appoint another nine-member board.

The new IHEC head, Sarbas Mustafa Rashid, is a member of Masoud Barzani's KDP, and an implacable foe of the prime minister. Four members of the board are members of Shia Islamist parties but only two are from Maliki's Islamic Dawa Party. These are counterbalanced by two representatives from Iraqiyya. The rejection of Maliki's proposal to expand the board and the election of Rashid as its new head showed that, when faced with a direct threat, parties opposed to Maliki's increasing power could occasionally find the unity of purpose needed to block him.

In March 2013, the IHEC asserted its independence by announcing changes to the rules under which provincial election seats would be allocated. They moved away from a system that favoured the largest parties, which was deemed unconstitutional, to one which allocated seats in closer proximity to the actual vote, thus favouring a myriad of smaller parties contesting the elections.

The campaign itself got off to an unpromising start. A month before voting took place, the government announced that due to the demonstrations it was postponing the election in the Sunni-majority northwestern provinces of Anbar and Nineveh. Security concerns then led to the suspension of voting in the northeastern city of Kirkuk. The delay in what had been two of Iraqiyya's main provincial voting blocs gave rise to concerns that the government was using security issues to fracture its election campaign. However, 14 candidates, most of them Sunni, were killed during the campaign, Saleh al-Mutlaq claiming his party alone had lost six election workers.

On the day of the election, 12 of Iraq's 18 provinces voted – the three provinces that make up the Kurdish Regional Government (KRG) vote on a different electoral timetable. In the third set of local elections since regime change, 12 provincial governorships and 378 provincial councillor's seats were contested. These were fought over by 8,100 candidates, largely organised into 50 coalitions. In the competition for 16 million potential votes, most coalitions sought to maximise their count by stressing the religious identity of their candidates. The stakes were highest for Maliki's State of Law coalition, which in 2009 had won a landslide victory in the Shia majority provinces of southern Iraq and Baghdad itself.

Turnout, at 50%, was comparable to the 2009 provincial elections. Maliki's coalition won the most seats, with a majority in seven provinces (Baghdad, Basra, Babil, al-Qadisiyah, Dhi Qar, Karbala and al-Muthanna) and was tied with another Shia party, the Islamic Supreme Council of Iraq (ISCI) in an eighth (Wasit). While this represented a victory, Maliki had wanted to use the provincial elections as a springboard to victory in the 2014 national elections and the results indicated this would be difficult. Firstly, in 2013 the State of Law coalition had many more parties within it than in 2009 but saw a reduction in the council seats it took.

Secondly, after the vote itself, when negotiations began to form provincial councils, the two main rivals for the Shia vote, the Sadrists and ISCI, put aside long-standing rivalries to collaborate and block State of Law candidates for provincial governorships. This meant that, in spite of winning the most seats generally across the south, State of Law only managed to secure governorships for its favoured candidates in Najaf and Dhi Qar.

Even though Maliki and State of Law showed they had the ability to win votes across Baghdad and the south of Iraq, they did not win enough votes to secure an outright majority, leaving their Shia opponents the space to unite against Maliki and constrain his influence. If this result is mirrored in the 2014 elections, the prime minister will do well in terms of voting numbers from the Shia majority, but will be far from securing a parliamentary majority. It will then be up to the Sadrists and the ISCI – the election saw a dramatic drop in Iraqiyya's seats, possibly rendering them no threat – to decide to back him as the most plausible Shia candidate (as they did in 2010) or to unite to remove him as a threat to democracy and ensure their long-term survival.

Growing violence

The crisis triggered by the security forces' moves against Hashemi and Issawi, and the violent suppression of the demonstrations that followed, created a widespread feeling of alienation amongst the minority Sunni population. Radical jihadist groups organised under the banner of al-Qaeda in Mesopotamia (AQM) sought to exploit this by recruiting more Iraqis, creating a rising tide of politically motivated violence.

Gauging the extent of the violence was difficult. The Iraqi government, the UN and the independent non-governmental organisation Iraq Body Count collate casualty figures. Though they use different techniques, analysis points to a steady rise in civilian casualties. In 2013, Iraq Body Count recorded 561 people killed in March, the highest monthly figure since 2009. The UN estimated that 712 people had been killed in April and 1,041 in May.

In July 2012, AQM's leader, Abu Bakr al-Baghdadi, announced the start of a new campaign: 'Breaking Down the Walls'. Its aim was to take back the areas it had been driven out of during the US-led 'surge' that started in 2007, free its members from prison and unite its struggle in Iraq with the civil war in Syria. It was soon openly skirmishing with government forces. By October, US and Iraqi government sources estimated that it had doubled the number of its fighters over the previous 12 months to as many as 2,500. AQM and the second-largest Sunni insurgent group, Jaish Rijal Tariqah al-Naqshabandi, sought to capitalise on violent government suppression of protests, claiming to offer protection to the whole of the Sunni population.

Of greater concern, and mirroring Iraq's descent into inter-communal violence in 2004–05, there were reports in June 2013 that the radical Shia militia Asa'ib Ahl al-Haq had set up roadblocks in Baghdad and had started to kidnap and murder innocent Sunnis in retaliation for AQM's campaign of car-bomb attacks in the capital.

Future stability depended on the ability of Iraq's security forces to stay neutral and united, target terrorists working on both sides of the sectarian divide and contain the escalating conflict. The military received significant investment over the past year, with $12bn worth of purchases from the United States, including 36 F-16 aircraft and 140 M1A1 Abrams tanks. It also sought to diversify weapons suppliers by signing a $4.2bn arms deal with Russia. However, allegations of corruption surrounding the Russian arms deal, reported to involve very senior Iraqi officials, indicated that the armed forces faced serious problems. These were compounded by reports in June 2013 that 1,070 Kurdish members of the Iraqi army's 16th Brigade had defected to the Peshmerga forces of the KRG. This suggested that the centralisation of command and control in the prime minister's office had broken the managerial coherence of the army and undermined its *esprit de corps* by politicising senior ranks.

Oil-sector problems

The government's programme of arms purchases indicated a hope that military and political weaknesses could be overcome, or at least minimised, by dramatically increasing state income and expenditure. During 2012, Iraq earned on average $7.8bn per month from the sale of crude oil. Ambitious plans were announced to create 5 million jobs over the next five years by spending $275bn. The International Energy Agency's (IEA) assessments supported the spending plans, estimating that Iraq could export 3 million barrels of oil per day by 2020 compared with 2.48 million in May 2013, rising to 8 million by 2035. With average yearly export earnings rising to $200bn, Iraq would certainly have the resources needed to placate its population with high levels of state spending. However, the IEA tied its optimistic estimates to the need for $530bn of extra investment in the energy sector, including significant amounts from international oil companies.

Iraq's relations with foreign oil companies suggested it would face difficulties in attracting sufficient external investment. In 2012, the Norwegian oil company Statoil sold its stake in the West Qurna-2 oilfield to Lukoil of Russia. This was followed by ExxonMobil's announcement that it too wanted to disinvest from Iraq's southern oilfields. The companies' desire to leave was driven by logistical problems linked to the government's inability to deliver required infrastructure. The government was also slow in paying them for work already done. Most importantly, both companies felt the contracts they signed when they entered the Iraqi market were not lucrative enough given the difficulties involved.

To add to Baghdad's problems, the KRG set about offering more commercially advantageous contracts to companies wishing to invest in Iraqi Kurdistan. Under the KRG's interpretation of the Iraqi constitution, it had the right to sign independent contracts with companies wishing to develop new oilfields.

Kurdistan and Turkey

Several companies, including ExxonMobil, Chevron, Total and Gazprom signed contracts with the KRG. Faced with the undermining of its own oil policy by a more commercially attractive approach, Baghdad threatened to exclude companies with KRG contracts from any business in southern and central Iraq. It then threatened to reduce the KRG's share of the central Iraqi budget. This rising tension led to a small number of clashes between KRG forces and the Iraqi army in 2012 and 2013.

As relations continued to deteriorate, the Kurds looked to Turkey, by far the biggest investor in Iraqi Kurdistan, to help them become more economically independent of Baghdad. Although Ankara agreed to buy Kurdish oil and gas, it did not commit to building a pipeline that would allow the KRG to export large quantities directly into Turkey. Such a move would herald a step change in the relationship between the KRG and the Iraqi government, but would also signal a big change in Turkish foreign policy, which had sought to constrain the KRG's autonomy from Baghdad because of its own domestic problems with the Kurdish population.

Relations between Turkey and Iraq declined because of their very different policies towards the civil war in Syria. Ankara was explicitly backing moves to remove President Bashar al-Assad from power in Damascus, while Baghdad committed itself to no interference in Syrian affairs. Iraq's policy of constructive ambiguity towards Syria gradually hardened into support for the Assad regime. This contributed to further deterioration of inter-communal relations in Iraq. As the government aligned itself with both Syria and Iran, the Sunni population made clear its support for the Syrian rebels. When combined with Iraq's political troubles, this meant that tensions and violence were destined to continue for the foreseeable future.

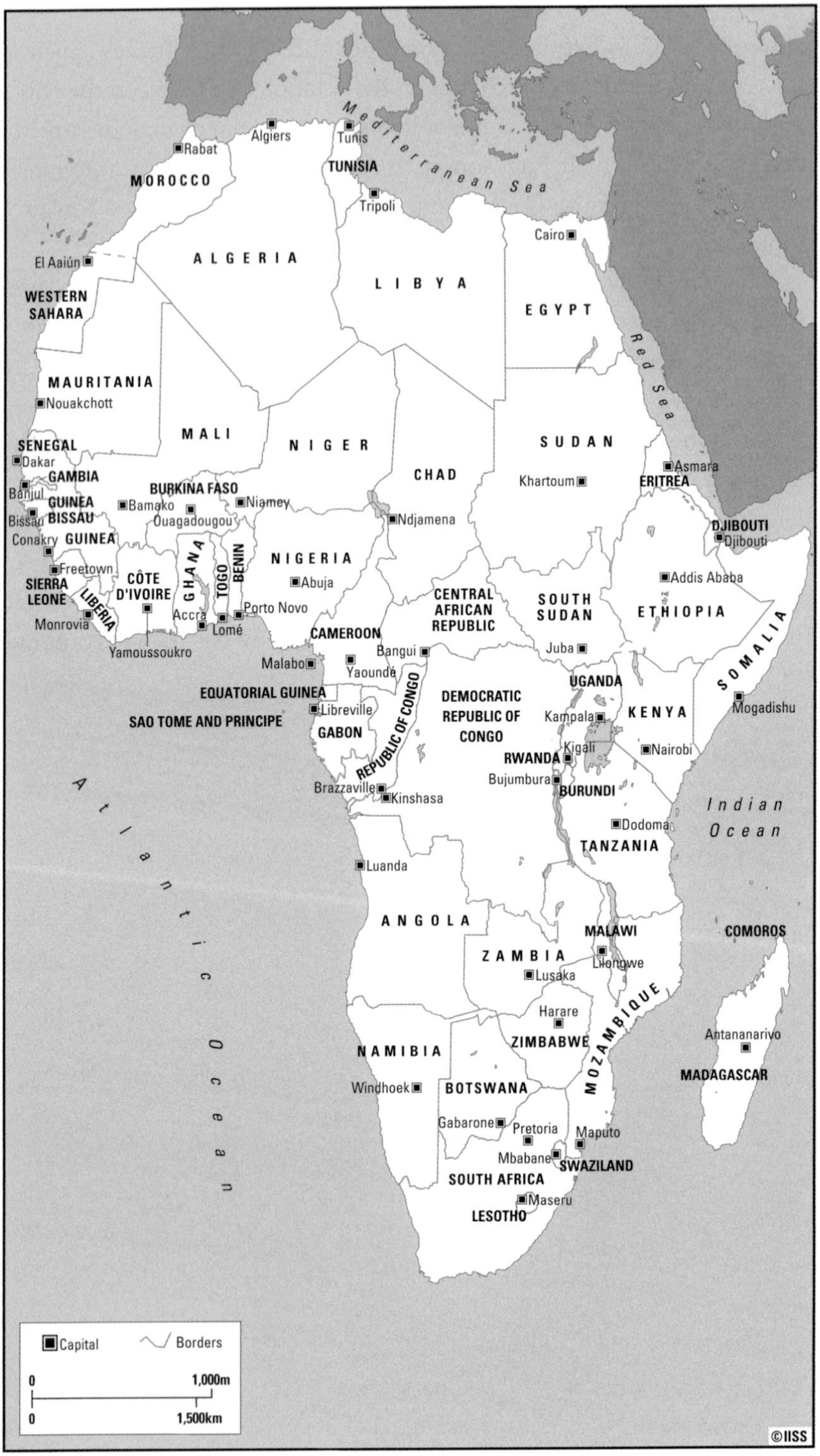

Mediterranean Sea
Algiers
Tunis
Rabat
TUNISIA
MOROCCO
Tripoli
Cairo
El Aaiún
ALGERIA
LIBYA
WESTERN SAHARA
EGYPT
Red Sea
MAURITANIA
Nouakchott
MALI
NIGER
SUDAN
SENEGAL
Dakar
GAMBIA
Banjul
CHAD
Asmara
Khartoum
ERITREA
BURKINA FASO
GUINEA BISSAU
Bamako
Niamey
Bissau
Ouagadougou
Ndjamena
DJIBOUTI
Djibouti
Conakry
GUINEA
Freetown
GHANA
TOGO
BENIN
NIGERIA
Addis Ababa
SIERRA LEONE
CÔTE D'IVOIRE
Abuja
CENTRAL AFRICAN REPUBLIC
SOUTH SUDAN
ETHIOPIA
LIBERIA
Porto Novo
Monrovia
Accra
Lomé
CAMEROON
Bangui
Juba
Yamoussoukro
Malabo
SOMALIA
Yaoundé
UGANDA
EQUATORIAL GUINEA
Libreville
REPUBLIC OF CONGO
DEMOCRATIC REPUBLIC OF CONGO
Mogadishu
SAO TOME AND PRINCIPE
Kampala
KENYA
GABON
Kigali
Nairobi
RWANDA
Bujumbura
Atlantic Ocean
Brazzaville
Kinshasa
BURUNDI
Indian Ocean
Dodoma
TANZANIA
Luanda
ANGOLA
MALAWI
COMOROS
ZAMBIA
Lilongwe
Lusaka
MOZAMBIQUE
Harare
Antananarivo
NAMIBIA
ZIMBABWE
MADAGASCAR
Windhoek
BOTSWANA
Gabarone
Pretoria
Maputo
Mbabane
SWAZILAND
SOUTH AFRICA
Maseru
LESOTHO
Capital
Borders
0
1,000m
0
1,500km
©IISS

Chapter 7

Africa

According to the IMF, some of the fastest-growing economies in the world in 2013 will be in sub-Saharan Africa. At the same time, many Western analysts describe 'an arc of instability' spreading across the Sahel region of West Africa. The juxtaposition of these two judgements encapsulates the continent's current contradictions. While there are varying degrees of hope in two of the most conflict-ridden countries – Somalia and the Democratic Republic of the Congo (DRC) – al-Qaeda-linked militants have found new homes in northern Mali and Nigeria. In the year the African Union (previously called the Organisation of African Unity) turned 50, there was some cause for optimism. Fears of electoral violence in Kenya proved unfounded, and the two Sudans seemed to have resolved their oil dispute. However, the credibility of the African Union itself was damaged by its inability to deal with the recent crisis in Mali, while coups continued in West Africa. The continent's largest and most industrialised economy, South Africa, was haunted by a reminder of its violent apartheid-era past with the deaths of 34 miners in a bitter industrial dispute. Even in some of the most buoyant economies, such as Mozambique, not everyone was sharing in the boom. The mantra of 'African solutions for African problems' still seemed a long way from being realised in the security arena.

West Africa's Troubled Year

Mali: foreign intervention

France sent troops to Mali in January 2013 in response to the upheavals of the preceding year, during which a separatist Tuareg uprising in the remote northern half of the country was hijacked by Salafists linked to al-Qaeda. In March 2012, army officers frustrated by the government's weak response staged a coup in the capital, Bamako.

The Tuareg rebellion in January 2012 was not the first. However the Movement for the National Liberation of the Azawad (MNLA) that led it was bolstered by well-armed fighters returning from the revolution in Libya. President Amadou Toumani Touré's ineffectual government was deposed two months later. In the north, the Salafist group Ansar al-Din briefly joined forces with the MNLA, seizing the opportunity to push its own agenda of installing rigid Islamic law across Mali. The short-lived alliance erupted in fighting in June 2012, at the end of which the Salafists controlled the key northern cities of Gao, Kidal and Timbuktu. They were soon joined by the Movement for Jihad and Oneness in West Africa (MUJAO), a splinter group of al-Qaeda in the Islamic Maghreb (AQIM). Completely sidelined, the MNLA announced in July that it was abandoning aspirations to an independent Tuareg state in favour of 'Quebec-style autonomy'.

Captain Amadou Sanogo and other coup leaders were quickly persuaded by the international community to hand power over to interim President Dioncounda Traoré in April 2012, but the military continued to meddle in politics. Traoré was only accepted as a legitimate leader in July, having survived an assassination attempt, and the military junta went on to force a change of prime minister in November.

With reports that Islamists in the north were destroying historic mausoleums and libraries, flogging locals and enforcing amputations for supposed breaches of sharia law, the 15-member Economic Community of West African States (ECOWAS) and the 54-state African Union (AU) began pushing for a military intervention. In September 2012, ECOWAS agreed with Mali's interim government to deploy a 3,300-strong contingent to the country. Meanwhile, the EU pledged a 250-strong training mission (EUTM Mali) to strengthen the local army (although this did not arrive until March 2013) and up to €270 million in military aid. In December, the United Nations Security Council approved an African-led International Support Mission in Mali (AFISMA) in 2013, but its deployment to Mali was unlikely before September.

On 10 January 2013, more than 1,000 Islamists captured the central Malian town of Konna and threatened to push into southern Mali. With no African force in sight, Mali's interim prime minister asked former colonial power France to intervene. The next day, French President François Hollande confirmed that his country's forces were supporting Malian army operations. Simultaneously, ECOWAS announced the immediate deployment of its mission. France's *Opération Serval*, consisting of 3,500 soldiers in Mali plus 1,100 in Chad and Senegal, was able to go into action so rapidly thanks to the presence of small French contingents in Burkina Faso and elsewhere in Africa. Access to transport and in-flight refuelling aircraft also helped.

In the following three days, the Malian army recaptured Konna with French air support, and French jets pounded Islamist bases in the regions of Gao and Kidal in the north, and the central town of Douentza. Although the Islamists staged a brief comeback in seizing the town of Diabaly, 250 kilometres north of Bamako, they were swiftly driven from there, as well as from Douentza, Gao, Kidal and Timbuktu, by French and Malian soldiers. The first troops from AFISMA began arriving in Mali on 17 January. In April, 18 AFISMA units were deployed across Mali comprising 6,300 soldiers from Chad (2,000), Nigeria (1,200), Niger, Burkina Faso (600), Benin, Ghana, Guinea, Togo and Senegal.

Eventually, the rebels retreated to the Adrar des Ifoghas mountains in the northeast, where French and Chadian forces discovered numerous bases and large amounts of sophisticated weaponry. Many rebels probably also fled into Niger, but several militants – including, in February, AQIM leader Abdelhamid Abou Zeid – were killed in subsequent operations in the Adrar des Ifoghas.

The French intervention was always intended to be brief, with troops scheduled to withdraw by the end of April. However, the Islamists continued to threaten the northern towns through terrorist bombings and guerrilla raids. With questions over AFISMA's ability to hold back the Islamists after the French had departed, the UN suggested beefing up the planned force while the French parliament voted in April to extend *Opération Serval.* AFISMA was to be converted into a UN-mandated peacekeeping force of 11,000 troops, accompanied by 1,440 police, and there was also a proposal for an armed rapid-reaction force to assist the mission. A small French contingent was expected to join the UN peacekeepers due to deploy on 1 July under the banner of United Nations Multidimensional Integrated Stabilization Mission in Mali (MINUSMA), which will take over from AFISMA. China offered 500–600 troops, including at least 155 engineers, to support UN efforts.

French Defence Minister Jean-Yves Le Drian said in May 2013 that Paris would keep 1,000 troops in Mali indefinitely. By mid-year, nearly 4,000 French soldiers remained in the country, awaiting Malian elections in July before half of them would begin to leave.

With campaigning for presidential and parliamentary elections not due to begin until 7 July, and with Tuareg separatists using the rout of the Islamists as an opportunity to resume agitating for northern autonomy, it was possible that elections would not go ahead as planned on 28 July. The humanitarian situation remained dire, with hundreds of thousands thought to have fled the chaos and fighting, and allegations of human-rights abuses by the Malian army, especially towards ethnic Tuaregs, as well as Fulani and Arab citizens. However, tentative plans were under way for the country's reconstruction. Donors meeting in Brussels in May pledged more than €3.25 billion towards rebuilding Mali, but Bamako's two-year plan was queried by development agencies and non-governmental organisations. They said that Mali had limited capacity to absorb such aid rapidly, and money would be wasted if transparency and governance were not improved. The charity Oxfam suggested a 15-year plan to allow the country to address the underlying causes of poverty and implement policy reforms.

The continued volatility of the situation in Mali was exacerbated by the fact that many of the countries contributing forces to the forthcoming African mission faced their own difficulties at home: Nigeria was battling Boko Haram, while in May 2013 there was a failed coup attempt in Chad, where rebels of the Union of Forces of Resistance (UFR) were also threatening to resume violence. The Malian army was plagued by deadly clashes between those who backed Sanogo's coup and those still loyal to ousted President Touré. Even less unity existed among the rebel groups in the north. Tensions existed not only between Tuaregs and their former Islamist allies, but also within Salafist group Ansar al-Din; the new Islamic Movement for Azawad faction broke away from Ansar al-Din in early 2013, vowing to sue for peace. Libyan and Malian extremists formed another group, Ansar al-Sharia, around Gao.

This instability threatened to disturb the wider region. There were knock-on effects in Algeria, where AQIM commander Mokhtar Belmokhtar followed his threat of retaliation for the efforts to dislodge Islamists from northern Mali with a high-profile attack on the In Amenas gas plant. He was also thought to have masterminded two suicide car bombs in Niger in May – one on the Agadez military base and the other on the French-operated Somair uranium mine in Arlit. The coordinated attacks, which killed 26 people and wounded 30, were carried out by MUJAO. After French special forces had to rescue Nigerien cadets taken hostage by the Islamists in Agadez, France and China deployed troops around their uranium mines in Niger.

Indeed, the ramifications of the Malian situation have been felt farther afield. In Senegal, a man was arrested in January for recruiting fighters for Mali. UN Secretary-General Ban Ki-moon warned that Morocco's disputed Western Sahara region might attract militants from Mali, and despite denials from the Sudanese government, Malians were reported to be in North Darfur. French operations pushed many fighters from the Libyan revolution back to Libya. An attack on the French Embassy in Tripoli followed Paris' decision to extend *Opération Serval* in April.

Nigeria: countering militancy

In May 2013, Nigerian President Goodluck Jonathan declared a state of emergency in the country's troubled northeast, before launching the largest military offensive against Islamist insurgents Boko Haram since the group re-emerged in 2010. Jonathan admitted that extremists now controlled towns and villages in the north of Africa's most populous nation, and sent fighter jets and an extra 2,000 troops to quell what he described as a full-blown rebellion that posed 'a very serious threat to national unity and territorial integrity'. Meanwhile, Nigeria faced renewed conflict with militant groups in the southern Niger Delta region. Rumours that Jonathan, a southern Christian, might run for re-election in 2015 – contrary to an unwritten power-sharing agreement – also created rumblings in multi-ethnic Nigeria.

The state of emergency in the states of Borno, Yobe and Adamawa followed an upsurge in violence by Boko Haram, which has been waging a campaign to establish a breakaway Islamist state. Originating on a small scale in 2002, Boko Haram was declared 'defeated' with the killing of its founder Mohamed Yusuf in 2009, but it returned with a vengeance in 2010 under radical and brutal commander Abubakar Shekau. Since then, the group – whose common name 'Boko Haram' means 'Western education is forbidden' in the local Hausa language – has been blamed for more than 3,000 deaths. Using guns, improvised explosive devices, suicide belts and rocket-propelled grenades, it continued in 2012–13 to attack security buildings, government officials, churches, schools, markets, clinics, banks and mobile phone masts across Muslim-dominated northern and central Nigeria.

Major clashes between Boko Haram and the military in the fishing village of Baga, in Borno state, on 16–17 April prompted the president to fly home from southern Africa and declare the emergency. At least 187 people, mostly civilians, were killed and 2,000 homes were destroyed in Baga. However, even before this there were signs of an escalation in Boko Haram activity: security forces said they had uncovered a plot to shoot down Jonathan's plane on his March 2013 visit to Maiduguri, the capital of Borno, in Boko Haram's heartland; and a large weapons cache discovered in April in Lagos was linked to a planned attack on the city's airport. Boko Haram and its Ansaru offshoot also displayed a greater propensity for kidnapping. Ansaru abducted a French national in Katsina in December 2012; seven foreign workers it took hostage in Bauchi in February 2013 were later killed. Boko Haram unusually extended its horizons beyond Nigeria when it kidnapped a French family in Cameroon in February. All five family members were released unharmed in April, following the alleged payment of a $3m ransom. There were increasing fears that the group was receiving help from al-Qaeda-linked groups in other countries, and may have obtained sophisticated weaponry from the 2011 Libyan revolution.

The Nigerian government has long been criticised for not taking the Boko Haram threat seriously enough, but it is now to launch a new strategy for national security, including counter-terrorism, and to set up a counter-terrorism centre.

The first 2,000 extra military personnel deployed under emergency rule were sent to Borno state. Later another 1,000 were reported to be destined for Adamawa, where a curfew was introduced. In all 8,000 troops were expected to be involved in the operation in the northeast to flush out Boko Haram. Early on, each side claimed to be winning. On 16 May, the army raided Boko Haram camps in the Sambisa Game Reserve, claiming within a week to have destroyed the camps, captured up to 200 militants, and rescued women and children held hostage by the sect. Boko Haram was 'in disarray', the military claimed, and fleeing across the border into Niger and Cameroon. However, at the end of May, Shekau said his rebels were fighting back against the military offensive, as Nigerian soldiers dropped their weapons and ran. None of these claims were verifiable, nor were reports that unarmed US spy drones were assisting government operations from a US military base in neighbouring Niger.

The Nigerian military has been accused of human-rights abuses in its long campaign against Boko Haram, which some analysts say hamper its ability to win the support of local populations. In November 2012, Amnesty International accused the military of carrying out extrajudicial killings and torture. US Secretary of State John Kerry later urged the Nigerian military to show restraint.

Moreover, the country's armed forces have been overstretched by overseas operations (for example, in Mali, Somalia and Sudan) and by a decades-old insurgency in the southern region of the Niger Delta. A 2009 amnesty persuaded militants from the Movement for the Emancipation of the Niger Delta (MEND) and similar groups to cease attacks on Nigeria's lucrative oil and gas industry, by giving them monthly payments. These payments – at nearly US$500 a month in a country where the minimum wage is around $130 – remain highly controversial. After payment delays in summer 2012, some former militants threatened to resume attacks. Some actually did: an oil pipeline belonging to Shell Nigeria was bombed in Delta State in June 2012, and one of the company's gas pipelines was set on fire in Delta State in March 2013. In April, MEND threatened to launch attacks against mosques and Muslim clerics in the south unless Boko Haram stopped targeting churches in the north, but was convinced by the federal government and religious organisations not to intervene.

While trying to diversify Africa's second-largest economy away from oil, Finance Minister Ngozi Okonjo-Iweala oversaw annual growth of just under 7% and reduced inflation to single digits, at 9%. She continued steps to tackle endemic corruption, especially in a controversial fuel-subsidy system. A lack of local refinery capacity means most Nigerian crude must be refined abroad and then re-imported to meet local needs. Fuel subsidies to keep gasoline cheap for ordinary Nigerians cost the government billions, but an attempt to remove them in January 2012 had sparked riots. Instead, Okonjo-Iweala tried to tackle fraud in the system, delaying payments to fuel importers to seek better verification of their claims for subsidies. Okonjo-Iweala said that the kidnap of her mother in December 2012 – she was released after five days – was linked to her actions on fuel-subsidy payments.

Meanwhile, Jonathan ran into controversy over hints that he might run for re-election in 2015. Since the return of democracy to Nigeria in 1999 after a long period of military dictatorship, there has been an unwritten agreement to alternate the presidency between the country's Muslim north and the Christian south. The sequence was broken when President Umaru Yar'Adua, a northerner, died in office in May 2010 and was succeeded by his vice-president, the southerner Jonathan. Although Jonathan ran for the top office in 2011 and won, many northerners feel it will be time again for a president from the north. In March 2013, Nigeria's High Court ruled that Jonathan was eligible for re-election provided he won his party's (People's Democratic Party) primary election. A month beforehand, opposition parties had merged to form a grand coalition, the All Progressive Congress, to increase their electoral chances. In May a Northern Elders Forum was established to lobby for the return of power to the north in 2015. Although by mid-2013 Jonathan had insisted he would not run, the conflicting messages coming from his office meant that doubts remained.

Guinea: election delay

Continued failure to hold long-overdue parliamentary elections lay behind a series of violent demonstrations throughout the year in Guinea.

The poll had been due in 2011 to complete the transition to civilian rule after a 2008 military coup. However, at the time of writing it had been pushed back yet again to 30 June 2013. Repeated clashes between opposition protesters, government supporters and police saw hundreds wounded and more than 50 killed. A political stalemate between President Alpha Condé and the opposition fuelled ethnic tensions, raised fears of another military intervention and soured Conakry's international relationships, particularly with former colonial power France, which halted aid.

The president is often accused of favouring his ethnic Malinké people, at the expense of others, in particular the Fulani community, to which about 40% of Guineans belong. Opposition leader Cellou Dalein Diallo is a Fulani. His defeat by Condé in the 2010 presidential election sparked ethnic violence.

Arguments between the president and the opposition over voter registration, the appointment of an electoral commission, and that commission's subjugation to presidential authority continued to delay the parliamentary elections. Even a government reshuffle in October, which included the replacement of three generals with civilian appointees, failed to stem discontent. The military is hostile to Condé, after he implemented army reforms; a former army chief is still awaiting trial for his involvement in a rocket attack on the president's home in 2011 during the reform process.

Guinea's political uncertainty has damaged its economic potential. The country is the world's top exporter of bauxite (the ore used in the production of aluminium) and has the planet's largest iron-ore deposit, at Simandou. However, mining companies BHP Billiton and Rusal have divested some bauxite and iron-ore interests, or suspended operations. Work at the Simandou mine, due to start production in 2015, has all but stalled, with Brazilian mining firm Vale expressing concern about corruption and Rio Tinto reportedly withdrawing 90% of its staff in 2013.

Guinea-Bissau: transition extended

Elections were due before the end of 2013 to complete a transition to civilian rule following an April 2012 coup (see *Strategic Survey 2012*). The vote was initially scheduled for May 2013, but the timetable was put back after another coup attempt in October 2012. At this point, ECOWAS, which first brokered the interim government, accepted that the May deadline for elections looked increasingly unachievable, and in February the transition period was extended until 31 December 2013. Returning in April from a month's medical treatment in Germany, interim president Manuel Serifo Nhamadjo promised to hold elections by the end of the year.

In May 2012, ECOWAS deployed more than 600 troops – from Burkina Faso, Nigeria and Senegal – to support the transition. These were eventually formalised as the ECOWAS Mission in Guinea-Bissau (ECOMIB). However, their presence did not prevent a group of ethnic Felupe soldiers attacking Bissalanca Air Force Base near the capital Bissau in October; seven died in this attempted coup. The subsequent trial of coup leader Captain Pansau N'Tchama heard that the attempt had been ordered by former Chief of Staff of the Armed Forces Lieutenant-General Jose Zamora Induta, with the support of Angola and the Gambia. On 26 April, 12 defendants were jailed for up to five years for their role in the plot.

Guinea-Bissau is plagued by drug trafficking, which the United Nations says increased in the aftermath of the April 2012 coup. Prominent political and military figures have been linked to the business. After years on the United States' wanted list for his involvement in trafficking South American cocaine into Europe via West Africa, former navy chief Rear Admiral Jose Americo Bubo Na Tchuto was arrested in April 2013 and extradited to the United States. Washington has also issued an arrest warrant against Chief of General Staff General Antonio Indjai for weapons and drug-trafficking.

Côte d'Ivoire: rift continues

Ivorian society remained cleft along the same lines as when violence erupted after the 2010 presidential election, after which incumbent Laurent Gbagbo had refused to step down in favour of newly elected Alassane Ouattara. After his arrest in April 2011, Gbagbo was to face trial by the International Criminal Court (ICC) on charges of crimes against humanity and other war crimes. However, in June 2013, the court delayed a decision on whether the case should go forward, and said the prosecution needed to provide more evidence. The former president still enjoys a substantial support network. In February 2013, protests in the commercial capital Abidjan demanding his liberation had to be dispersed by tear gas.

A coup, allegedly planned by exiled senior figures loyal to Gbagbo, was attempted on 13 June 2012. Security forces arrested several people, including Gbagbo's former defence minister, and were reported to have seized documents showing links between the plotters and a group of Liberian mercenaries and pro-Gbagbo militias accused of launching cross-border attacks. The west of the country remained vulnerable to instability, particularly from militias, mercenaries and war criminals who had sought refuge in neighbouring Liberia but regularly clashed with Ivorian forces in villages across the border. Seven peacekeepers belonging to the UN Operation in Côte d'Ivoire (UNOCI) and 15 civilians were killed by militias from Liberia in June 2012, in attacks that prompted more than 13,000 people to flee their homes. Similar attacks, including on police stations, military camps and prisons, continued over the year to mid-2013, further increasing animosity between supporters of Ouattara and those loyal to Gbagbo. Each faction accused the other of being responsible for the violence.

In October 2012, an unreleased report by a UN panel of experts pointed to possible interaction between Gbagbo's allies and Ansar al-Din Islamists from Mali with the purpose of recruiting support for Gbagbo's return to power. The document indicated that Ghana was being used as a base by the former president to destabilise Côte d'Ivoire. Later, Ghana arrested 43 Ivorian ex-combatants believed to be responsible for subversive activities in a refugee camp near the border. In January, it apprehended the former head of the Young Patriots street militia, a close ally of Gbagbo.

Following an initial attempt at political dialogue in July, the government and the opposition Ivorian Popular Front (FPI) finally resumed talks in January 2013. Yet this conciliation was short-lived: when the government announced that it would hold local elections on 21 April, the FPI said it would boycott the vote. In April, 1,500 UN police and 9,500 UN soldiers were mobilised across the country to quell violence following release of the election results.

The Horn, Central and East Africa: Qualified Progress

Somalia: significant advances

Great progress was made in Somalia in the year to mid-2013, after two decades of civil war. The first formal government was established since the overthrow of dictator Siad Barre in 1991; this process began with the swearing in of a new parliament in August 2012, and the legislative election of a new president in September. Meanwhile, government forces and African Union troops – having driven Islamist al-Shabaab fighters from Mogadishu, the capital, in late 2011 – were joined by neighbouring armies in successfully dislodging the Islamists from their strongholds in central and southern Somalia. The government's capture of the southern port city of Kismayo in October 2012 was a major defeat for al-Shabaab.

Piracy off the coast of Somalia fell dramatically as a result of the combined efforts of international naval task forces and shipping companies, and of the improved situation inside the country. By May 2013 there had not been a single successful hijacking in the region for the past year.

Somalia's political and military developments were the culmination of a road map adopted in September 2011, which set out a timetable for writing a new constitution, beginning a process of political reconciliation, reforming parliament and other institutions, and securing the country from extremists. The Transitional Federal Government (TFG), which had been nominally in charge of Somalia for the past eight years, signed the document with representatives of the semi-autonomous Puntland region, the central Galmudug region, and the pro-government militia Ahlu Sunna Wal Jamaa. Representatives of the UN, AU and other regional organisations also signed the deal.

The new constitution was adopted on 1 August by a conclave of 645 Somali clan leaders called the Somali Constituent Assembly. It provided for, among other things, a federal state of Somalia with a bill of rights and Islam as its sole religion. It also made provisions for the establishment of a Truth and Reconciliation Commission and the peaceful settlement of border disputes. Afterwards, the clan elders selected the 275 members of the lower house of Somalia's new parliament – an increase of 50 from the 225 originally agreed upon.

The presidential election was delayed by political wrangling over the final composition of parliament, with the TFG's mandate expiring three weeks before the vote. However, on 10 September, in a run-off poll following an inconclusive first round of voting, MPs elected Hassan Sheikh Mohamud, an academic and civil-rights campaigner, as Somalia's new president. Despite some allegations of corruption and bribery, the election results were accepted by incumbent President Sheikh Sharif Sheikh Ahmed, outgoing Prime Minister Abdiweli Mohamed Ali and most of the international community.

With little political experience, Hassan was an unexpected winner. Some analysts deemed his victory a protest vote, since many Somalis had been keen to elect anyone outside the TFG. Others believed his good reputation and humanitarian work had helped. In a country long plagued by clan rivalries, Hassan had established in 2011 the social democratic Peace and Development Party, which has no clan allegiances. He appointed as prime minister fellow independent Abdi Farah Shirdon Saaid, a businessman with significant experience in Kenya, who was also seen as untainted by clan politics. Shirdon in turn appointed a cabinet in November with few ethnic loyalties. The slimmed down, ten-member cabinet consisted mainly of newcomers and included the first female foreign minister, Yusuf Haji Adan.

Despite the success in forming a government, Somalia's democracy remained fragile. It was unclear whether the new president could maintain control over powerful rivals who had lost out in the election. In May 2013, more than 90 MPs threatened to table a motion of no confidence in the prime minister, over the slow pace of change within the country. Mogadishu continued to face calls for greater autonomy from provincial Jubaland in the south, while the breakaway Somaliland region was rebuffing calls for a unified Somalia.

Although security was much improved, al-Shabaab continued to perpetrate terrorist attacks. In a move that began in late 2011 to capture towns surrounding Mogadishu from the Islamists, government forces and troops from the African Union Mission in Somalia (AMISOM) captured the port of Merca in August 2012 and the outpost of Birta Dheer. They then advanced south towards Kismayo, al-Shabaab's last urban stronghold, where they were joined by Kenyan troops and local militia

Ras Kamboni in launching assaults on the city in August and September. On 29 September, al-Shabaab announced its retreat from the city.

The capture of Kismayo deprived al-Shabaab of access to the sea and of 'taxes' on lucrative shipments abroad of charcoal, the impoverished country's biggest export. However, the loss of territory across Somalia had not destroyed the group, which withdrew tactically from battles with pro-government troops to avoid significant losses. As it pulled back en masse from each city, smaller groups of al-Shabaab fighters switched to guerrilla tactics. For example, despite the group's announced withdrawal from Kismayo after the arrival of Kenyan troops and the Ras Kamboni militia, many al-Shabaab fighters remained to target civilians and soldiers in small-arms and bomb attacks around the city. Clan and other violence in Kismayo, previously suppressed by al-Shabaab, increased in the Islamists' absence.

Al-Shabaab also began to launch terror attacks on Kenyan targets, as well as expanding its operations into Puntland and parts of Somaliland. One of its bolder attacks was the attempted assassination of President Hassan by two suicide bombers on his second day in office. In May 2013, the group claimed to have shot down a US reconnaissance drone that crashed in the southern region of Lower Shabelle.

In light of constant threats to Somalia's stability, the UN Security Council extended AMISOM's mandate until March 2014. However, the 18,000-strong AMISOM force (now comprised of troops from Burundi, Uganda, Sierra Leone, Djibouti and Kenya) was hampered by its small budget and its troops were accused of human-rights abuses.

Despite a turnaround in Somalia's fortunes and a greater sense of optimism than had been felt for many years, the government's writ still did not extend far beyond Mogadishu and other individual towns. The threat of al-Shabaab violence still loomed, Somali forces were still unable to fight alone, and political tensions continued within the new administration. Former Prime Minister Abdiweli Mohamed Ali admitted in a speech to the IISS in London, in March 2013, that the country was 'not out of the woods yet'.

The two Sudans: oil deal agreed

Juba and Khartoum finally agreed in March 2013 to restart the flow of South Sudanese oil through Sudanese pipelines, after a lengthy row and the shutdown of the South's oil sector, on which it relied for 98% of its income. Production resumed in April, but the deal later seemed to be at risk following violence in two Sudanese cities. In addition, two years after South Sudan's secession from Sudan, issues over their border and the oil-rich Abyei region had yet to be resolved.

Sudan has lost billions of dollars in oil revenues since South Sudan became independent in July 2011 under a 2005 peace deal that ended two decades of civil war. The newly created South Sudan took with it about three-quarters of Sudan's oil reserves, but was left dependent on the North's pipeline and port to transport its crude to global markets via Port Sudan on the Red Sea coast. In January 2012, Juba shut down its oil output of 350,000 barrels per day over failures to agree transit fees with Khartoum. The move damaged both economies, which depend upon foreign currency from oil sales and pipeline fees to buy food and other imports.

There were fears of renewed war in April 2012, particularly with skirmishes between the two armies around the border town of Heglig (see *Strategic Survey 2012*, p. 290). This prompted the United Nations Security Council to warn both sides that they would face sanctions if they did not negotiate peacefully. Stop-start peace talks, overseen by AU mediator (and former South African president) Thabo Mbeki, eventually produced the March 2013 agreement.

The breakthrough began in September 2012, when Sudanese President Omar al-Bashir and his southern counterpart Salva Kiir Mayardit met in the Ethiopian capital, Addis Ababa, to adopt a series of agreements intended to pave the way for the resumption of oil exports. This focused on several key areas, including the creation of a demilitarised zone around the border, as well as agreement on economic cooperation and the protection of each other's citizens.

However, it took months for the countries to move towards implementation of the Addis Ababa Accord. Khartoum refused to allow oil exports via its territory until Juba ceased support for Sudan People's Liberation Movement–North (SPLM–N) rebels in the Sudanese states of South Kordofan and Blue Nile. South Sudan blamed the delays on Sudanese concerns over border security in the contested strip of land bordering the Darfur region in Sudan and the Bahr el-Ghazal region in South Sudan.

In January 2013, both capitals were still jockeying for position, with South Sudan announcing plans to sell petroleum to its ally Israel in January 2013, and politicians in Khartoum vowing to block any such move – especially after the bombing of the Yarmouk military complex in Khartoum in October 2012, for which they held Israel responsible. (Israel, while neither confirming nor denying responsibility, accused Sudan of acting as a conduit for the supply of Iranian weapons to Islamic militant groups Hamas and Hizbullah.) However, at an African Union Peace and Security Council meeting in Addis Ababa, Bashir renounced plans to seek $1.8bn compensation from South Sudan for the acquisition by its state oil company, Nilepet, of assets owned by Sudan's state firm, Sudapet. South Sudan had insisted on this renunciation as a condition for supporting Khartoum's bid to have some $40bn of external debt cancelled.

The deal signed in March set out a timetable for the resumption of oil pumping and for the withdrawal of troops from the border area, thus creating a demilitarised buffer zone. However, the return to production was slow, because of damage to infrastructure inflicted during skirmishes in April 2012. Diplomats warned of potential further difficulties. In May, violence in the Sudanese cities of Um Rawaba and Abu Kershola added new strains to relations between the two countries. Bashir ordered oil transfers through Sudan to be halted following claims that South Sudan was supporting rebels in Darfur, South Kordofan and the Blue Nile region. Sudanese officials said the ban would take effect in 60 days.

Meanwhile, there was no timetable for a final determination of the status of Abyei. Both sides claim the oil-rich border region, which is being administered by an interim UN security force. The competing claims rest on a land dispute between farmers from the Dinka people (who are allied to South Sudan) and Misseriya Arab nomads from the North who traditionally herd their cattle through Abyei. Juba and Khartoum also cannot agree on who has the right to vote in a mooted regional referendum. The situation remains volatile, with Dinka chief Kual Deng Majok killed by Arab Misseriya militia when touring the region with a South Sudanese delegation in May 2013. UN peacekeepers were also reported wounded.

In Sudan, there was a wave of protests over a government austerity package. According to IMF estimates, Sudan lost about $6.6bn in revenue in 2012, or 12.9% of GDP, because of its oil dispute with the South. With the country already facing high unemployment, inflation and rising corruption, Bashir announced in June 2012 a devaluation of the Sudanese pound, higher taxes on consumer goods, public-sector cuts and the removal of fuel subsidies. The moves were unpopular, but demonstrations against them were short-lived.

Far more obdurate were the crises in Blue Nile and South Kordofan, where rebels associated with the South Sudanese war of independence continued to battle Khartoum for greater autonomy. Clashes continued between government forces and SPLM–N insurgents. Sudan was repeatedly criticised by human-rights groups for attacking and aerially bombarding civilians, especially in the Nuba Mountains of South Kordofan, which borders South Sudan.

Fighting also flared again in Darfur in early 2013. In January, tens of thousands fled as two rival ethnic communities fought over access to gold mines in the Jebel Amir area of North Darfur state; gold is Sudan's key commodity after oil. Drought wracking the region also provoked several tribal disputes over access to pastures and water. In April, the UN reported that 50,000 people from southwestern Darfur had escaped to neighbouring Chad from clashes between the Misseriya and the Salamat tribes. Battles between the Sudanese army and rebels from the Sudan Liberation Army-Minni Minawi displaced thousands in East Darfur state. Renewed ethnic clashes erupted between the Gemir group and the Beni Halba community in June over land producing gum arabic. In total, the UN calculated, at least 150,000 people had been displaced by renewed violence in the first quarter of 2013.

South Sudan, one of the continent's least-developed countries, introduced its own austerity measures after shutting down oil production. Spending was slashed by 26%, although salaries were unaffected. The measures were not immediately lifted when the flow of oil resumed. Four million South Sudanese, out of a population of ten million, were short of food, according to the World Food Programme, and the country was still plagued by insecurity.

Central African Republic: another coup

President François Bozizé was ousted in a coup in March 2013, the fifth since CAR's independence from France in 1960. The takeover by the Séléka movement, a coalition of five northern militias, followed months of fighting in the country's northeast, where Séléka accused Bozizé of reneging on a 2007 peace deal. Casting aside a brief power-sharing agreement brokered by the Economic Community of Central African States (ECCAS) in January, coup leader Michel Djotodia suspended the 2004 constitution and declared himself president until elections to be held in 2014.

In the run-up to the coup, the armed forces offered little resistance to an advance by 1,000–5,000 Séléka fighters. The rebels were temporarily halted in January by the presence of 2,000 Chadian soldiers requested by Bozizé, and by extra troops from Cameroon, the Republic of Congo, the DRC, Gabon and South Africa sent to reinforce the ECCAS Mission for the Consolidation of Peace in Central African Republic. However, the power-sharing Libreville Accord that resulted from negotiations at this point did not hold. Bozizé, who had seized power in 2013 with the help of the Chadian army and whose personal guards had been provided until last year by Chad's President Idriss Deby, accused Chad of having aided the rebels that toppled him. He said that during the rebels' final advance on Bangui, the capital, Chadian special forces had led a sustained attack on the South African base in the capital, killing 14 of the 200-strong South African contingent.

After African neighbours and Western powers refused to recognise Djotodia, a 105-member interim council was formed, including Nicolas Tiangaye, the prime minister agreed on by both Bozizé and Séléka during the brief government of national unity. In April, the council confirmed the presidency of Djotodia, formerly a low-profile consul in Sudan. He promised not to run in the 2014 elections.

Djotodia declared that he was looking into mining contracts signed by Bozizé with South African and Chinese companies, with the goal of reconsidering any that had been 'badly done'. However, his most pressing concern was to restore law and order. After the coup, humanitarian workers reported chaos in Bangui, with frequent power cuts and reports of looting, rape and killing. Séléka members were accused of involvement in human-rights abuses. The UN reported that tens of thousands of people had fled the country for Cameroon and the DRC. As illegal weapons proliferated across the country, and reports grew of discord among Séléka members about the new government's direction, it was unlikely that Djotodia would achieve his stated wish 'to be the last rebel chief president of Central Africa'.

Democratic Republic of the Congo: beefed-up mission

The eastern provinces of the Democratic Republic of the Congo (DRC) continued to be unstable as fighters from the March 23 (M23) group looted and killed their way across North Kivu Province in particular. Some 800,000 people fled their advance. The latest of some 20 armed groups in the region, the M23 emerged in April 2012 after an army mutiny and seized Goma, capital of North Kivu, in November with little resistance from government or UN troops. Though persuaded to withdraw from the city, they remained a menace, even after notorious rebel leader Bosco 'The Terminator' Ntaganda made a surprise surrender to the International Criminal Court (ICC) in March 2013.

There was a ray of hope for the DRC when, after a regional peace deal reached with its neighbours in February 2012, the World Bank pledged a $1bn regional aid package to assist with energy, infrastructure, agriculture, health, education, trade and jobs. On a visit with World Bank President Jim Yong Kim in May, UN Secretary-General Ban Ki-moon said the DRC had the best chance in years to secure peace. A new 2,500-strong UN 'intervention brigade' – given an offensive as well as defensive mandate – was to be deployed in mid-2013 to neutralise the region's many armed groups. However, after decades of civil war and instability in the DRC, an easy resolution remained unlikely.

Most of the M23 defectors from the Congolese army in April 2012 were ethnic Tutsi former rebels from the National Congress for the Defence of the People (CNDP) who had been integrated into the army under a 23 March 2009 peace deal. The mutineers accused the government of failing to implement several provisions of the 2009 agreement, and defected in two waves. The first several hundred fighters left with Ntaganda, having reportedly got wind of a plan to take him into custody. The second, larger wave exited when President Joseph Kabila attempted to redeploy CNDP army units out of North and South Kivu. The ex-CNDP rebels had been granted significant privileges on their integration into the DRC army in 2009, and operated a parallel command structure in the Kivus, collecting taxes from illegal checkpoints, looting villages and smuggling the DRC's precious minerals into Rwanda. Kabila's move threatened these lucrative arrangements.

The relative ease with which the M23 managed to seize Goma in November was an embarrassment to the army and the UN Stabilisation Mission in the DRC (MONUSCO). Local media reported that soldiers and peacekeepers had abandoned their positions as the M23 entered the city – although the UN later insisted it had fired rockets at the rebels to try to halt their advance. After occupying Goma, M23 leaders threatened to march on the city of Bukavu, in South Kivu, and the national capital, Kinshasa. Only 11 days later, after an agreement brokered by neighbouring countries in the Ugandan capital, Kampala, did the rebels withdraw from Goma.

Negotiations between the DRC government and the rebels then began in Kampala, but were hampered by a split in the rebel movement. One faction, led by Sultani Makenga, was willing to sign a peace deal. Another, led by Ntaganda, wished to continue fighting. The friction led to violent clashes and tit-for-tat killings by each leader's supporters.

Meanwhile, a broad political plan to bring stability to the region was set in motion in February on the sidelines of the AU summit in Addis Ababa in February 2013. Eleven countries signed the Peace, Security and Cooperation Framework Agreement for the DRC: the DRC, Rwanda, Uganda, Angola, Burundi, the CAR, the Republic of Congo, Tanzania, South Africa, South Sudan and Zambia. All pledged to stop interfering in Congolese internal affairs and to support civil-society reform in the country.

Rwanda's signature of the DRC Framework agreement was particularly noteworthy, because of frequent accusations that it was backing the M23. Many Hutu militias implicated in the 1994 Rwandan genocide had taken refuge in the DRC in the years afterwards, and Rwanda has sponsored several Tutsi rebel groups – including the M23's forerunner, the CNDP – in an effort to protect both its own borders and Congolese Tutsi. In late 2012, the UN Group of Experts on the DRC, a six-person panel, reported that 1,000 Rwandan troops had provided direct military support to the M23 during their advance on Goma. This led the United Kingdom to join countries such as the United States and Germany in suspending aid to Rwanda. In February, UN Secretary-General Ban said the rebels must have had 'external support' to capture Goma, but declined to specify from where. The government of Uganda was also believed to have provided logistical support to the M23.

The humiliation of UN peacekeepers in Goma prompted the Security Council to approve its first 'offensive' peacekeeping brigade deployed to 'carry out targeted offensive operations' to neutralise armed groups in the eastern part of the country, including the Hutu Democratic Forces for the Liberation of Rwanda (FDLR). The new intervention brigade was provided for in February's DRC Framework Agreement, and was to initially include troops from South Africa, Tanzania and Malawi, who would join current MONUSCO peacekeepers to make a nearly 20,000-strong force. The government of the DRC said the brigade's main mission should be to secure the DRC's borders with Rwanda and Uganda. Surveillance drones for this task were later authorised by the Security Council.

Ntaganda appeared to have feared for his own safety in the wake of the M23 split, and on 17 March 2013 he walked into the US Embassy in Kigali, Rwanda, asking to be transferred to the ICC in The Hague. Wanted on ten counts of war crimes and crimes against humanity for abuses – including the enlistment of child soldiers, murder, rape and sexual slavery – allegedly committed with an earlier rebel movement, he was transferred to the Netherlands. In May, he made his first court appearance, pleading not guilty.

Although Ntaganda's surrender ended violent infighting between the two M23 factions, no official peace deal was reached between the M23 and the DRC government. Even as Ban Ki-moon arrived in the DRC in May 2013 to promote peace, there was renewed fighting in the country's east, despite an M23 truce. Ban, the World Bank's Kim and UN Special Envoy to the Great Lakes Mary Robinson bolstered mediation efforts and helped to bring M23 back to the negotiating table. In June 2013, M23 announced a temporary cessation of hostilities so as to pursue negotiations.

Kenya: mostly peaceful transition

Kenya's March 2013 presidential election passed off relatively peacefully, despite fears that the violence following the 2007 contest might be repeated. However, the winning candidate, Uhuru Kenyatta, and his deputy, William Ruto, faced charges of crimes against humanity at the ICC, for their alleged roles in the 2007–08 violence. The men promised to cooperate with the ICC, but both denied the charges and asked the court to postpone their trials in The Hague. Ruto's trial was delayed until September 2013 but a decision on Kenyatta, due for trial in July, was still awaited.

Some 1,300–1,500 people were killed and more than 300,000 internally displaced after the 2007 disputed re-election of President Mwai Kibaki; the violence pitted ethnic Kalenjins and Luos, who supported the opposition led by Raila Odinga, against Kibaki's Kikuyu community. A new constitution in 2010 addressed some of the issues that led to the unexpected 2007–08 violence, including an overly powerful presidency and a weak legislature and judiciary; on the other hand, decades-old ethnic rivalries over land, resources and political power were not eradicated. With clashes in Coast Province in August 2012, riots in Mombasa after the assassination of a Muslim cleric that same month, reports of the growth of ethnic militias, and the death of one election worker in riots in January following disputed local primaries, the spectre of violence hung over the election.

On polling day, however, incidents were isolated, with four police reportedly killed in an ambush by a separatist group in Mombasa, and eight government officials and civilians dying in three attacks in the town of Kilifi. Nearly 100,000 soldiers, police officers and other security personnel guarded 33,400 polling stations. More than 22,000 election observers monitored the vote.

The new constitution required presidential candidates to win a majority of votes and at least 25% of the popular vote in more than half of Kenya's 47 counties. Opinion polls predicted neither the Kenyatta/Ruto ticket nor their chief rivals, Prime Minister Raila Odinga and Kalonzo Musyoka, would reach the 50% threshold, so a run-off was expected. However, after several days of delayed results, Kenyatta and Ruto prevailed with 50.07% of the vote. A Supreme

Court challenge by Odinga, who claimed voting irregularities were significant, failed, and Kenyatta was ruled the winner. Riots in the Odinga stronghold of Kisumu were contained, although police shot and killed two rioters.

Wider unrest appeared to have been averted because constitutional reforms gave Kenyans some faith in new institutions, including the Independent Electoral and Boundaries Commission, and the devolution of power to newly created counties reduced the stakes of the presidential contest. Politicians and civil-society leaders urged peace, while a huge police presence worked to enforce it.

The ICC indictments hanging over Kenyatta and Ruto as they campaigned also limited the idea that they could act with impunity. The 51-year-old Kenyatta – son of Kenya's first president, Jomo Kenyatta – became the country's fourth president on 9 April. He is the first person under ICC indictment to be elected to lead a country. Western countries were wary of this happening; Britain's High Commissioner to Kenya suggested that the UK, for example, would only have 'essential contacts' with Kenyatta if he won. After the elections, Western countries appeared to soften their stance, perhaps not wishing to alienate a critical partner in regional counter-terrorism operations and East Africa's largest economy. In May, Kenyatta attended a conference on Somalia in London at Britain's invitation.

Despite a new constitution, peaceful elections and nearly 5% GDP growth in 2012, Kenya still faced major security challenges, especially after its military involvement in neighbouring Somalia. The country sent its armed forces across the border in October 2011, before several thousand of its troops were integrated into AMISOM, the AU mission in Somalia. The Kenya Defence Forces played a major contribution in the fall of Kismayo, an al-Shabaab stronghold. This prompted an increased number of al-Shabaab-linked attacks within Kenya, often involving improvised explosive devices and grenades. While Garissa, in the northeast, bore the brunt of the attacks, an unsettling number occurred in the main cities of Nairobi and Mombasa. The government was planning to revive the Kenyan Police Reserve, an armed civilian police corps, to help counter terrorism in Garissa.

Southern Africa: Quest for Integration

There was further movement in implementing the Free Trade Area (FTA) initiated within the South African Development Community (SADC) in 2000. Most of SADC's 15 member states reduced protective tariffs, and a single tourist visa allowing freedom of travel between neighbouring countries was piloted by Zimbabwe, Zambia, Namibia and Mozambique. However, Botswana continued to resist the mechanism over security fears. Issues of national sovereignty, and the membership of East and Central African regional organisations, also dulled the push towards a 2015 SADC common market and 2018 single currency. Instead, SADC's most visible role was as a regional mediator, pressing for credible polls in Zimbabwe (due mid- to late 2013) and in Madagascar (in July 2013).

Zimbabwe: election nerves

Zimbabwe's often fractious 'unity' government briefly lived up to its name in pushing through a new constitution by popular referendum in March 2013. However, President Robert Mugabe's ZANU–PF party and the Movement for Democratic Change (MDC) of Prime Minister Morgan Tsvangirai continued to wrangle over the timing of fresh national elections. ZANU–PF and the two factions of the former opposition, the main MDC–T and the splinter MDC–M, were brought together in a power-sharing deal mediated by SADC in the wake of Zimbabwe's bloody 2008 election. ZANU–PF wanted new polls to be held before or just after the expiry of the parliamentary term on 29 June 2013. However, the power-sharing mechanism and the constitutional law process stipulated October 2013 as the last month by which elections must be held. The MDC insisted the elections should be delayed until voter registration was completed and other steps had been taken to ensure a fair election. These included the reform of the military and the opening up of Zimbabwe's state-owned broadcasting industry.

Finance Minister Tendai Biti revealed in March that Zimbabwe did not have the estimated US$130m needed for the polls and would have to raise revenue from donors. ZANU–PF, which ruled Zimbabwe as a one-party state for almost three decades after independence from Britain in 1980, was lobbying for funding with as few conditions as possible.

It rejected a UN offer of money for the election in return for admitting international monitors. By contrast, the MDC was keen for observers to be an integral part of any funding package. Bitai, of the MDC–T, warned that ongoing doubt over the election date was damaging Zimbabwe's fragile economy, which had begun to recover after years of decline and hyper-inflation. From 2009 until the middle of 2012, Zimbabwe's economy grew by an average of 7% a year.

For much of 2012, ZANU–PF had threatened to hold elections without a referendum, but the SADC summit in June 2012 in Luanda, Angola, reaffirmed that a referendum must come first. After three years in which the Constitutional Select Committee of parliament had laboured to fashion a draft constitution acceptable to all, the document was put to the people on 16–17 March, and was passed with 95% approval. The vote was largely peaceful, with the three government parties all campaigning for a 'yes' vote. Zimbabwe's electoral commission claimed around 3m voters turned out, but many observers felt the true figure was half that.

The new constitution replaced the one introduced at independence, namely the December 1979 Lancaster House Agreement. Signed into law in May, it limits future presidents to two five-year terms, removes presidential powers to veto legislation and abolishes the position of prime minister. It enshrines certain human rights, allows Zimbabweans to hold dual citizenship, and provides for an independent prosecuting authority, a peace and reconciliation commission, and an anti-corruption commission. The constitution also makes it impossible to legally challenge the controversial land redistributions of 2000 – when 170,000 black farmers occupied 4,500 white-owned commercial farms. However, it commits to compensating foreign nationals whose farms were seized.

Crucially, the document sets out new voting procedures and reforms that must be implemented before new elections can be held. All three government parties faced internal problems going into the election. There were ferocious power struggles within ZANU–PF, especially between Vice-President Joice Mujuru and Defence Minister Emmerson Mnangagwa, who were both positioning themselves to succeed Mugabe. Support for the MDC–T declined significantly after revelations of leader Tsvangirai's numerous romantic liaisons. A survey by the US-based

Freedom House group in August found the MDC–T's popularity had almost halved from 38% to 20%, while support for ZANU–PF increased from 17% to 31% – a trend also recorded by an Afrobarometer poll in October. Meanwhile the smaller MDC–Ncube that replaced the MDC–M lost senior personnel to the MDC–T.

The threat of political violence continued to hang over the elections, after nearly 200 people died in the aftermath of the 2008 poll, thousands were injured and tens of thousands displaced. Human-rights and international lawyers' groups called on ZANU–PF supporters and the state security apparatus to stop harassing and intimidating MDC activists, civil-society groups and NGOs. In one high-profile case, lawyer Beatrice Mtetwa was imprisoned for more than a week in March 2013 after being charged with obstructing justice for intervening in a police raid on MDC headquarters. Four aides to MDC leader Tsvangirai were also arrested in the case. Separately, there was unrest in Manicaland and Mashonaland provinces in 2012–13, with an escalation in assaults on MDC–T activists by ZANU–PF, war veteran, criminal and other groups. There was also intra-party violence within ZANU–PF amidst power struggles over the structure of District Coordinating Committees, which were eventually dissolved by the party because of the mayhem.

The military still wielded great political influence. In May, the Zimbabwe Democracy Institute called for urgent reforms to bring security chiefs under the control of civilian leaders. Mugabe has resisted army reforms such as prohibiting high-ranking officers from holding political allegiances.

South African facilitators mandated by SADC to work with Zimbabwe's leaders were snubbed by ZANU–PF over Pretoria's insistence that reforms must be fully implemented before the elections. In May 2013, a team led by Lindiwe Zulu had to leave Harare empty-handed after ZANU–PF failed to attend a meeting. However many countries relaxed sanctions on Zimbabwe in recognition of its political progress. In March 2013, the EU suspended sanctions on all but ten Zimbabweans, including Mugabe, and later that month Interior Minister Patrick Chinamasa attended a Friends of Zimbabwe meeting in London, making the first official visit by a ZANU–PF minister to the UK since 2002. The United States and Australia also lifted restrictions on varying numbers of

Zimbabwean individuals. Nevertheless, the single most pressing issue was the timing of the elections. South Africa and SADC were under pressure to mediate a date acceptable to all sides.

Malawi: worries about dependence on donors

President Joyce Banda – Africa's most powerful female leader, according to *Time* magazine – hung on to her global popularity, despite resentment at home towards some of her policies. On taking office in April 2012, Banda had moved swiftly to reverse the economic decline of her predecessor Bingu wa Mutharika's twilight years, when donor aid had been reduced to a trickle and farm input subsidies had stalled. This meant that Malawi, which exported grain surpluses from 2005–10, had been forced to rely on imports in 2011 and 2012.

Banda went on a charm offensive with donors. In June 2012, the IMF, which had withheld funds from Mutharika, promised a three-year loan of $157m, after Banda devalued the local currency, the kwacha, lifted currency-trading controls and removed fuel subsidies. Other donors followed suit. However, the currency devaluation and removal of fuel subsidies raised the cost of living, as did a drought later in the year. By January 2013 the UN estimated that more than one million Malawians were at risk from food shortages. Demonstrations erupted in the city of Blantyre against the cost of living; in February, several service sectors went on strike.

Unemployment remained a pressing issue. The government made agreements with South Korea, Kuwait and Dubai under which thousands of Malawians aged 19–40 would be sent as migrant workers to jobs in those countries' agricultural and hospitality sectors. The scheme was controversial: it was praised by some as a practical way of providing employment and international experience for young Malawians, while others said it would lead to exploitation of Malawians as 'slave labour'.

Banda remained firmly in power; in April 2013 Peter Mutharika, brother of the late president, and three other former ministers went on trial for perjury and treason for attempting to block then Vice-President Banda's constitutional accession when the previous president died in office. However, she was accused of being too compliant to the demands of the IMF and other donors, raising questions as to whether she could win the election in 2014. The sometimes-fraught relationship between donor and recipient was illustrated in a complicated row with American pop star Madonna over the building of girls' schools.

Meanwhile, relations with Tanzania soured over sovereignty of Lake Malawi, known in Tanzania as Lake Nyasa: Malawi claims the entire lake, while Tanzania insists it should be partitioned equally. Oil and natural gas are thought to lie beneath it, and Malawi angered Tanzania in 2011 by granting exploration licences in disputed waters. Malawi pulled out of talks in October 2012, claiming Tanzania was harassing Malawian fishermen, but returned to the table in May. Former Mozambican President Joaquim Chissano was mediating the dispute, but Malawi has threatened to take it to the International Court of Justice.

Madagascar: countdown to elections

With presidential and general elections due to be held in 2013, President Jakaya Kikwete of Tanzania and former Mozambican president Joaquim Chissano mediated throughout 2012 on behalf of the SADC between Madagascan President Andy Rajoelina and his ousted predecessor Marc Ravalomanana, in search of a road map to peaceful polls. In late 2012, SADC negotiated an agreement that neither man would contest the polls. The Rajoelina government had already threatened Ravalomanana, who fled Madagascar in March 2009, with arrest if he returned to take part.

On 6 May 2013, Madagascar's Special Electoral Court (CES) published the names of 41 presidential aspirants, including Ravalomanana's wife, Lalao. Citing a conspiracy to contest the presidency 'by other means', Rajoelina announced that he would run after all. SADC mediator Chissano insisted that this was against the spirit of the agreement, but a list of approved candidates published by the CES in April included Rajoelina and Lalao Ravalomanana. Former President Didier Ratsiraka was also on the list.

The decision by Lalao Ravalomanana, Ratsiraka and Rajoelina to contest the polls proved controversial and destabilising. In June, the government announced that elections would be postponed from July to August, after a number of donors withdrew funding for the poll. Crisis talks were due to be held in Addis Ababa.

Mozambique: inequality clouds promise

Mozambique was Africa's fastest-growing economy, with the IMF predicting 8.4% growth for 2013. There was plenty for Mozambique to be optimistic about, with some of the world's largest natural-gas and other energy reserves, and Brazil, Portugal, South Africa and the UK all major investors. Companies such as ExxonMobil and ENI were partnering with the government in exploiting large oil and gas finds in the Rovuma Basin off Mozambique's northern coast. The government was also investing heavily in refurbishing port and railway infrastructure, as Mozambique reasserted itself as a strategic gateway to East and Southern Africa.

However, experts raised concerns about levels of inequality. Mozambique ranked 185th out of 187 on the UN's 2013 Human Development Index and most employees still earned less than $130 a month. After riots in 2010 over rising food and fuel prices, the government implemented a plan to reduce poverty. This involved reintroduction of fuel and bread subsidies, promotion of small and medium-sized enterprises and an increase in agricultural production. In 2012, public-works programmes were stepped up to provide jobs, and more literacy campaigns were rolled out. However, the UN special rapporteur on poverty and human rights, Magdalena Sepúlveda, warned in April 2013 that Mozambique still needed to do more with its resources boom.

The Renamo opposition movement highlighted this inequality during a new political crisis. Renamo, which fought a 15-year civil war against the ruling Frelimo party, threatened to resume the conflict unless Frelimo shared Mozambique's resource wealth with 'the people'. It claimed responsibility for a series of attacks, and violent clashes between Renamo and Mozambican police in Muxungue in central Mozambique followed, after police surrounded the Renamo base in the Gorongosa mountains. With general elections scheduled in 2014, there was pressure on both sides to resolve the dispute.

South Africa: preparing for 2014

Jacob Zuma shrugged off controversy and competition to win a second term as the president of the ruling African National Congress (ANC). The victory put him in pole position to win another term as South African president in general elections in 2014. But continuing economic equality, corruption and the police killing of 34 workers at the Marikana mine caused growing dissatisfaction with the party that had led the struggle against minority white rule. Nobel laureate Desmond Tutu wrote in May 2013 that he could no longer vote for the ANC. He also warned South Africans to prepare themselves for the eventual death of their iconic first black president, Nelson Mandela, who was seriously ill in hospital at mid-year, at the age of 94. Despite the return of wealthy businessman Cyril Ramaphosa to the ANC as deputy leader, fears persisted about the health of Africa's largest economy.

Despite suggestions that Zuma would face a real leadership test at the ANC's elective conference in Mangaung, in Free State Province, in December 2012, the president had lobbied hard enough beforehand to secure his position at the head of the party. Winning 2,986 out of 3,977 votes, he left his challenger, Deputy President Kgalema Motlanthe, a distant second. Ramaphosa, whom Zuma chose as his running mate, received 3,018 votes – more than Zuma himself – to confirm his place as the new ANC deputy leader. A one-time ANC secretary-general, Ramaphosa had been touted as a successor to Mandela, but left politics to pursue a career in business. He was chairman of South African Breweries, and director at mining group Anglo American, before making millions with his own Shanduka investment group; his return to the ANC was welcomed by South Africa's business community.

Zuma's decisive victory was a setback for former ANC Youth League (ANCYL) leader and *enfant terrible* Julius Malema. Malema, an outspoken Zuma critic, had been suspended by the ANC in 2011 for creating internal divisions and bringing the party into disrepute. However, the ANCYL had refused to accept the suspension and Malema continued to agitate from the sidelines, particularly during the Marikana mine dispute. Malema, who had backed Motlanthe in the ANC leadership contest, was further marginalised by Zuma's victory. Several convictions for fraud left Malema with little political legitimacy.

Other South African politicians positioned themselves to do battle in the 2014 election against the ANC. The main opposition Democratic Alliance, which made gains against the ANC in the 2011 elections, joined civil-society groups in forcing amendments to authoritarian ANC legislation, particularly the Protection of Information Bill. This provided for increased state regulation of 'sensitive' national security information, but was seen by many as an attack on media freedom. In February 2013, high-profile anti-apartheid activist and academic Mamphela Ramphele launched a new political party, Agang, to challenge an ANC that she described as riddled with 'corruption, nepotism and patronage'.

Much public discontent with the ANC derived from the country's continued inequality, which seemed further entrenched by a faltering economy. Although South Africa was ranked the 29th richest country in the world by the IMF in 2012, and is a member of the G20 and the BRICS group of developing nations, it remained one of the most unequal countries in the world. Of its nearly 52m people, 15m were living off minuscule state grants, among them the elderly, the disabled and children in poor households. Official unemployment was around 25%, but about 70% among under-35s. Of the 14m or so who made up the country's labour force, fewer than 5m were paying income tax; the low wages of the other 9m left them below the tax threshold.

The miners' strike at the Lonmin platinum mine near Marikana highlighted these deep inequalities. For years, it has been an annual tradition for South Africa's powerful trade unions to stage 'strike seasons' (normally at the start or middle of the year) as an expression of the discontent of poorly paid workers. However, the Marikana strike was of a different magnitude. It began on 10 August 2012 over miners' demands for the British-owned Lonmin to increase wages, with tensions fuelled by a power struggle between rival unions over membership among South Africa's platinum miners. Six days later, in scenes reminiscent of the country's violent apartheid era, it resulted in 34 workers being shot point-blank by police.

The 'Marikana massacre' as it became known, shocked South Africa and the world. It was followed by a wave of wildcat strikes across the country; an estimated 75,000 miners went on strike until the immediate dispute was resolved in September when Lonmin and mine workers agreed an 11–22% wage increase. However, the killings cast a longer shadow over South African society. Although a commission of inquiry was still dragging on in mid-2013 into whether the miners shot had been unarmed or whether police shot in self-defence, Marikana greatly diminished public confidence in the police. It added to the impression of increasing police brutality created in June 2012 when an innocent 15-year old, Kwezi Ndlovu, was killed in Durban by members of the police organised-crime unit in the Cato Manor area of Durban, who burst into his home and indiscriminately opened fire. The image of police impunity was reinforced in February 2013 when a Mozambican taxi driver was tied to a police car and dragged to his death in broad daylight in downtown Johannesburg. The public outcry after this last incident forced parliamentary and public hearings to be held about the police, while the oversight and investigative powers of the Independent Police Investigative Directorate were substantially increased.

Further political ramifications from Marikana also seemed likely, as a significant cause of the crisis was the power struggle between two workers unions. The newer, more militant Association of Mineworkers and Construction Union (AMCU) accused the dominant National Union of Miners (NUM) of being too cosy with company bosses and politicians. The NUM has close links to the ANC through the Congress of South African Trade Unions (COSATU), and Marikana and the strikes following it saw the emergence of an alternative voice to the ANC in the industrial sphere. Although it was too early to determine whether the AMCU would become or join another political party, it was clear that the ANC and its ally, COSATU, would have to pay heed to it.

Despite government commitments to infrastructure development and education, Zuma admitted that labour unrest and slowing economic growth were hurting his development agenda. The rand plunged to a four-year low in May 2013, and figures showed slow economic growth.

On the international stage, South Africa was keen to maintain its profile as first amongst equals in SADC, particularly with regard to Zimbabwe where it was the regional interlocutor. However, it was also keen to recover status lost over its tardy recognition of the new Libyan authorities (see *Strategic Survey 2012*, p. 297), and took a greater role in mediation and peace operations further afield in Africa. It was among the powers that brokered a regional peace deal on the DRC, and the South African National Defence Force (SANDF) lost 14 soldiers during a 13-hour battle against Séléka rebels in Bangui, the CAR capital, in March 2013. This incident raised questions about whether the government had properly planned and resourced the mission in CAR. In May, when preparing to deploy SANDF troops to the new UN intervention brigade in the DRC, army chief Lieutenant-General Vusumuzi Masondo said the army had learned lessons from the Bangui experience.

Having failed to defeat incumbent Jean Ping in the January 2012 elections to head the AU Commission, former South African Foreign Minister Nkosozana Dlamini-Zuma (the former wife of President Zuma) succeeded at her second attempt in July 2012. There were strong hopes that she would build AU capacity while reforming the institution itself.

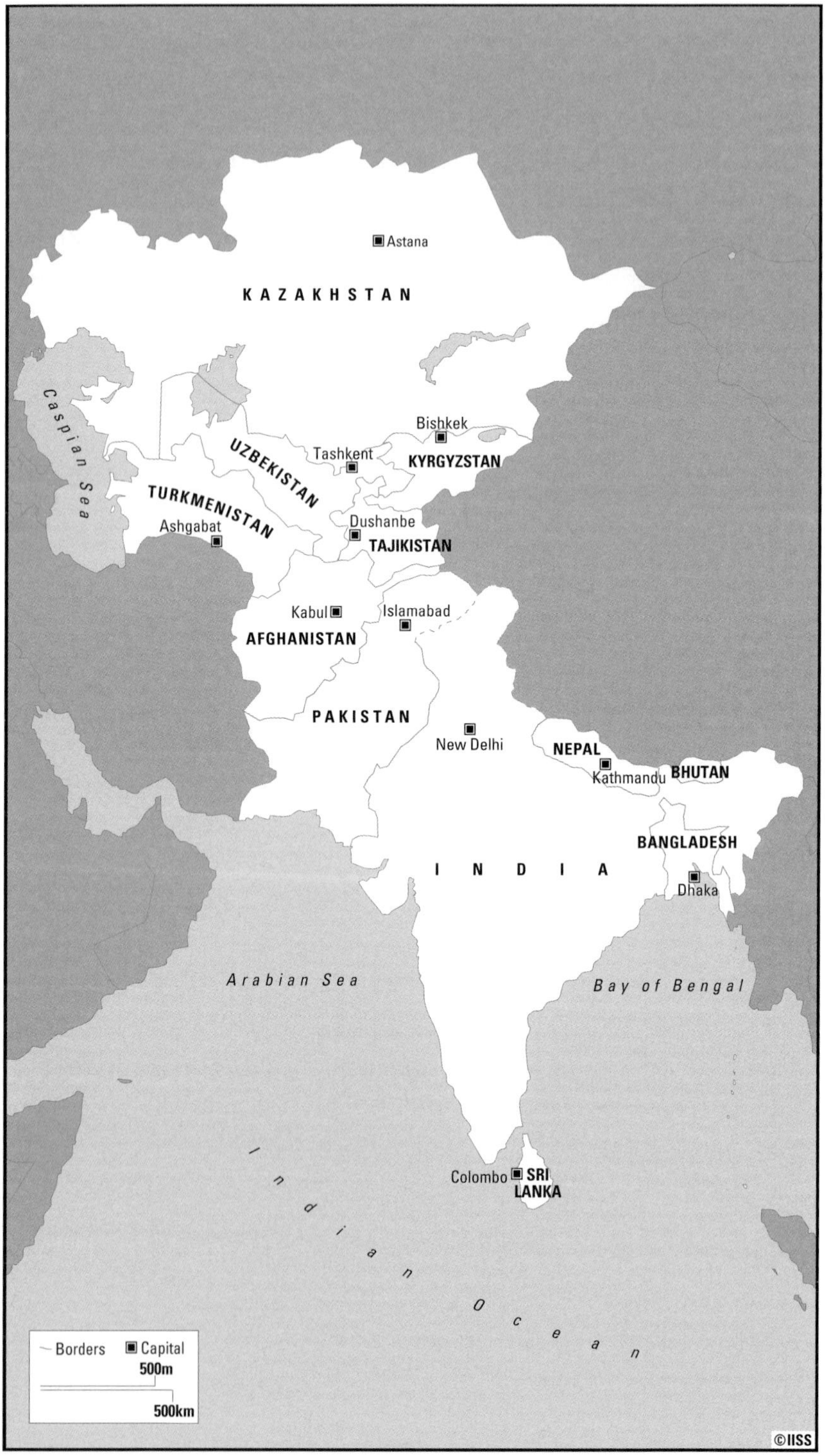

Astana
KAZAKHSTAN
Caspian Sea
Bishkek
Tashkent
UZBEKISTAN
KYRGYZSTAN
TURKMENISTAN
Ashgabat
Dushanbe
TAJIKISTAN
Kabul
Islamabad
AFGHANISTAN
PAKISTAN
New Delhi
NEPAL
Kathmandu
BHUTAN
BANGLADESH
INDIA
Dhaka
Arabian Sea
Bay of Bengal
Colombo
SRI LANKA
Indian Ocean
Borders
Capital
500m
500km
©IISS

Chapter 8

South Asia and Afghanistan

India's weakest economic growth rate in a decade forced the Congress Party-led United Progressive Alliance (UPA) coalition to take bold decisions on economic reforms. But this led to it losing a key coalition partner and becoming a minority government dependent on mercurial regional parties for survival. With the next general elections scheduled in less than a year, the government seemed to be marking time. In Pakistan, the Pakistan People's Party (PPP)-led coalition became the first civilian government to complete its full five-year term, but was ousted in elections in May 2013. Nawaz Sharif's election victory and his appointment as prime minister for the third time showed voters' desire for change, but he faced economic and security challenges. Meanwhile, though Sri Lanka was censured by the UN Human Rights Council in Geneva, it remained on track to host the November 2013 Commonwealth heads of government meeting in Colombo, its highest-profile international meeting since the end of the civil war.

In Afghanistan, a momentous year approached as NATO's preparations for the withdrawal of combat troops by the end of 2014 were fully under way, while a presidential election loomed. The spotlight was on the country's security forces as they took over the battle against Taliban insurgents. The Taliban kept up the pressure with targeted attacks, but efforts at political dialogue with the aim of including them in the country's political process continued.

India: Slow Economy Prompts Contentious Reforms

India's $1.8 trillion economy, the third-largest in Asia after China and Japan, saw growth fall to 5% in 2012 from 9.3% two years previously. Weak infrastructure was most visible when three major electricity grids failed in July 2012, resulting in a power outage that affected 600 million people for several hours. Major risks to the economy were high fiscal and current account deficits, the latter at a high of 6.7% of GDP in the October–December quarter. The Indian rupee weakened, but foreign exchange reserves of nearly $300 billion, as well as inflation at a three-year low of less than 5%, provided strong underpinning.

The economic slowdown was due partly to low growth and debt problems in the Western world and partly to political indecision on economic reforms. Prime Minister Manmohan Singh delayed change largely to keep the ruling coalition together, fearing that some parties would not support liberalisation measures. The Congress Party was weakened by its rout in the Uttar Pradesh state elections in March 2012, as well as in Punjab where it had been expected to unseat the incumbent Akali Dal government. But the worsening economic and financial situation led to fears of a crisis such as had occurred two decades earlier. There was pressure on the government from international credit-rating agencies, which threatened to downgrade India's rating to below investment-grade, as well as from Indian and multinational companies keen to move forward on the reform agenda. Singh and the Congress Party eventually felt that with general elections approaching, the window of opportunity was fast closing. The appointment of P. Chidambaram as finance minister in August 2012 was a positive sign that reform would be pursued.

In September, the government finally carried out several controversial reforms to boost confidence and attract foreign investment, with the aim of reviving economic growth and reducing the fiscal deficit. These were the boldest economic decisions the government had taken in the past nine years, and were dubbed 'big bang' or 'second generation' reforms after those the prime minister had undertaken in the early 1990s as finance minister. The most controversial was an executive order allowing 51% foreign equity in multi-brand retail companies, enacted in spite of fears of job losses among small shop-owners. The government also removed a 51% limit on foreign investment in single-brand retail outlets, while relaxing a stipulation that these must be 30% sourced from small industries. In an attempt to lower the fiscal deficit, the government raised the price of diesel fuel and allowed further small increases, as well as reducing the supply of subsidised LPG cylinders. Even though diesel still remained subsidised by about a fifth, this led to large demonstrations and protests by opposition parties. Separately, the government announced it would sell off stakes in several large state-owned enterprises, increased railway passenger fares (by 20%) for the first time in ten years, and set up a cabinet committee to fast-track large investment projects. Innovative cash-transfer arrangements were introduced to improve the fairness of social benefits and welfare distribution, using a new national biometric identity scheme.

Although the reforms were welcomed by the Indian business community, foreign investors remained wary. Nine months after the multi-brand retail order, there was still no formal application to invest from large international retailers, who preferred to wait for the impending elections. Foreign companies also remained concerned about tax. Even though the implementation of contentious tax-avoidance rules was postponed until 2016, there was little progress on the vexed issue, which stemmed from 2012 budget proposals to introduce a raft of retroactive corporate taxes. This compounded foreign investors' fears, sparked by a separate high-profile tax case involving the telecom giant Vodafone.

The political cost of the reforms was high. The second-largest party in the ruling coalition, the West Bengal-based Trinamool Congress, which opposed the retail and diesel changes, pulled out of the government and its six ministers resigned. This resulted in the coalition becoming a minority government in the Lok Sabha, the lower house of parliament, dependent for survival on the support of two north Indian regional parties, the Samajwadi Party and the Bahujan Samaj Party. These parties enabled the government to win a crucial test of strength in the Lok Sabha in December.

Disturbed politics

Even as the government sought to liberalise the economy and to stimulate growth, opposition parties instigated unprecedented disruptions of parliamentary business. They also organised demonstrations against alleged multi-billion dollar corruption scandals.

This meant that many measures could not be passed, given the government's minority status. For example, liberalisation of the insurance and pensions markets appeared unlikely to get through parliament, and the same fate could befall a land-acquisition bill that would smooth the way for infrastructure and mining projects. A vote-winning $24bn food-security bill, intended to provide subsidised foodgrains to two-thirds of the population, also seemed difficult to pass. In December 2012, public attention focused on the brutal gang-rape of a student by six men on a Delhi bus. She died a week later in a Singapore hospital. This triggered nationwide public protests and led to an anti-rape bill in March prescribing life imprisonment or even the death penalty for repeat offenders.

Even as further controversies emerged in a long-running scandal on the allocation of the 2G telecoms spectrum, the government was accused of corruption in the allocation by auction of coal blocks. In August 2012 the national auditor reported that faulty allotment of blocks had resulted in a loss of $33bn to the exchequer between 2006 and 2009. As Prime Minister Singh had held additional charge of the coal ministry during this period, opposition parties demanded his resignation and continued to disrupt parliament. But in September the Supreme Court provided some relief by stating that it was not necessary to auction all national resources, thereby accepting that the government had the right to decide its policies and that maximisation of revenue could not serve as the sole criterion in all situations. Nonetheless, in a fresh embarrassment, the chief of the agency tasked to investigate the corruption scandal stated in an affidavit that the law minister, Ashwani Kumar, and other officials had suggested four significant changes in the agency's final report two days before it was submitted to the Supreme Court in March 2013. This led to a political outcry, forcing Kumar to resign. Another investigation began into the 2010 purchase of 12 AgustaWestland helicopters for $750m, following the arrest of the chief executive of the manufacturer's Italian parent company Finmeccanica.

In an attempt to boost a tired government, Singh carried out ministerial reshuffles in October 2012 and June 2013. The first brought in 17 new members, including Salman Khurshid as external affairs minister.

In January, Rahul Gandhi, son of Congress Party leader Sonia Gandhi, was appointed the party's vice-president, a step closer towards taking over its leadership.

In March 2013, the departure of another coalition partner, the Tamil Nadu-based Dravida Munnetra Kazhagam, because the government had not censured the Sri Lankan government over its treatment of Tamils, further increased its dependency on other parties. Yet the main opposition Bharatiya Janata Party (BJP) did not appear to want to bring down the government or trigger an early election. It faced corruption allegations against the party president, Nitin Gadkari, who subsequently did not seek another term in office, and was also uncertain about future leadership. The BJP and its coalition partners in the National Democratic Alliance were bitterly divided over whether the dynamic but controversial chief minister of Gujarat, Narendra Modi, who won a third term in December, should become the party's leader for the general election. Modi was alleged to be responsible as chief minister for the killing of Muslims in riots in 2002. His appointment as head of the BJP's campaign committee in June resulted in the withdrawal of a coalition partner, the Janata Dal (United), led by Bihar chief minister Nitish Kumar.

Security: Maoist attacks

Even as India's overall security environment improved, left-wing Maoist/Naxalite violence remained a serious threat, along with communal riots in the northeast and public unrest in Indian-controlled Kashmir.

Although Naxalite attacks decreased for the sixth year running, it was not clear if this was a result of counter-insurgency operations by the state or a tactical reconfiguration by Maoist cadres. The Maoists appeared to have suffered dramatic reverses in Andhra Pradesh and West Bengal, but remained strong in Jharkhand, Chhattisgarh, Bihar, Odisha and Maharashtra. The number of casualties also remained high. According to government figures, there were 1,407 incidents involving Maoists in nine states in 2012, in which 415 people including 300 civilians were killed. Among more notable incidents, small-arms fire caused an air-force helicopter to crash in January 2013, and on 25 May in Chhattisgarh, Maoists attacked a Congress Party convoy of vehicles, killing nearly 30 people including several senior party figures.

In Kashmir, deaths from terror attacks declined to 30 in 2012, the lowest in two decades. However, the execution in February 2013 of Afzal Guru, a Kashmiri convicted of a 2001 terrorist attack on parliament in Delhi, resulted in mass protests and tension. The government imposed a curfew and disrupted Internet and mobile-telephone services. On 13 March 2013, in the first suicide attack in Kashmir in three years, two Pakistan-based militants belonging to Lashkar-e-Taiba (LeT) attacked a paramilitary camp in Srinagar, capital of the Indian state of Jammu and Kashmir, killing five soldiers.

In July–August 2012, more than 85 people died and around 400,000 people were forced to flee their homes after clashes between Bodo tribes and Muslim villagers in the northeastern province of Assam. This resulted in more than 30,000 migrants from the northeast leaving their jobs in cities across India to return home for fear of Muslim reprisals.

Indian Home Minister Sushil Kumar Shinde controversially stated that training camps for terrorism were being organised by the right-wing Rashtriya Swayamsevak Sangh (RSS) organisation, closely allied to the BJP. Subsequently, a senior government official stated that there was evidence against at least ten people allegedly involved in terror attacks linked to the RSS or affiliated organisations. But following a political furore caused by the remarks, Shinde was subsequently forced to express regret for linking terrorism to any religion and for accusing political organisations of organising terror camps.

Chinese incursion

Although India and China had decided to resume bilateral military exercises after three years, relations were seriously affected in April 2013 by China's intrusion 19 kilometres across the Line of Actual Control (LAC), which marks the de facto border between the two countries. New Chinese premier Li Keqiang's visit to India, his first destination on his first foreign tour, calmed the situation but did not dispel a growing perception of Chinese assertiveness towards India.

In September 2012, Chinese defence minister Liang Guanglie visited India, the first such visit in eight years. Confidence-building measures that were agreed included a resumption of joint military exercises stalled in 2010, along with high-level official exchanges and training of armed forces personnel at each other's facilities. The two sides agreed to promote port calls by naval ships, to conduct joint maritime search-and-rescue exercises, and to strengthen cooperation between naval forces in counter-piracy operations in the Gulf of Aden and off the coast of Somalia. In April 2013 bilateral discussions on Afghanistan took place for the first time.

Yet these developments were overshadowed by the intrusion of a People's Liberation Army platoon on 15 April in the Depsang valley in Ladakh, close to the Karakoram Highway connecting China and Pakistan. Unlike similar incidents in the past, the Chinese troops did not quickly return across the LAC but instead established a tented post. Indian troops established a camp just 500 metres from the Chinese tents. Amidst a shrill reaction from Indian media and politicians, three flag meetings between local commanders failed to broker a compromise. Finally, as India considered cancelling a visit by External Affairs Minister Khurshid to Beijing, which would in turn have jeopardised Premier Li's visit to India, the two sides reached an understanding. The three-week stand-off ended as both sides agreed to leave the area, and the Indian army began dismantling bunkers recently built in the Chumar area in Ladakh.

India–Pakistan relations: positive signs

Even as an unprecedented liberalised visa regime was introduced, relations between India and Pakistan suffered a serious setback with the escalation of violence across the Line of Control (LoC) that divides the disputed region of Kashmir. This led to Indian Prime Minister Singh saying that there could not, for the time being at least, be business as usual between the two countries. However, the new Pakistani government of Prime Minister Nawaz Sharif appeared to be interested in taking forward the peace process.

In September 2012, the two countries reactivated, after seven years, a Joint Commission, a high-level body to facilitate exchanges and cooperation on agriculture, education, environment, health, information technology, science and tourism. A liberalised visa regime was agreed, providing citizens aged 65 and above 45-day visas on arrival at the Attari-Wagah border posts and introducing business and group tourist visas. In addition, visa restrictions for business people and pilgrims were relaxed.

However, India remained concerned over the slow pace of the trial in Pakistan of the LeT operational commander Zaki-ur-Rehman Lakhvi and six other conspirators charged with planning, financing and executing the 2008 terror attacks on Mumbai. Islamabad also rejected Delhi's calls for action against LeT founder Hafiz Mohammad Saeed, the alleged mastermind of the attacks, claiming India had not provided any evidence to facilitate his prosecution. Singh pressed President Asif Ali Zardari for a speedy trial, and the issue became the key factor in Singh's reluctance to visit Pakistan. The lone surviving participant in the attacks, Ajmal Kasab, was executed in an Indian jail in November 2012.

Meanwhile, moves towards lifting trade restrictions were having a positive impact on the peace process. In a surprise move, Pakistan had decided in principle in November 2011 to grant most-favoured nation (MFN) trade status to India – a big shift in its position, and one that the army supported. MFN status could result in a three-fold increase in bilateral trade to $6bn within three years. In response, in August 2012 India announced it would allow investment from Pakistan in all sectors with the exception of defence, space and atomic energy. The possibility of allowing banks from both countries to open cross-border branches was discussed. Talks were held on facilitating trade and travel across the LoC in Kashmir. Cricketing ties were resumed, with the Pakistani team touring India and thousands of Pakistani fans obtaining visas to watch the matches. Talks on importing electricity and petroleum products from India were held. Ahead of awarding MFN status, Pakistan switched from a 'positive list' that listed items that could be traded to a 'negative list' that specifically identified products that could not be traded. This had the effect of opening the Pakistani market to about 7,000 types of Indian goods, up from about 2,000 earlier. However, the final move to grant MFN status at the end of 2012 was delayed because of concerns that the interests of Pakistani farmers and manufacturers could be damaged.

The brutal killing and mutilation of two Indian soldiers on 8 January 2013 in the Poonch sector of Indian-controlled Kashmir raised tensions. India believed the operation to have been carried out by the Pakistani army's Special Services Group along with militants from LeT and Jaish-e-Mohammed. This led to a steep rise in firing across the LoC. The Indian army was put on high alert. On 14 January the army chief warned that India's military reserved the right to retaliate at a time and place of its choice, adding that 'we won't remain passive when attacked.' Singh said on 15 January there could not be 'business as usual' with Pakistan. The crisis, during which three Pakistani soldiers were killed, was de-escalated on 16 January after talks between the directors general of military operations of the two sides. Both agreed to adhere to the 2003 ceasefire agreement and to exercise restraint. However, the incident had a lingering impact as some previously agreed steps on visas and sporting events were delayed.

Tensions were raised again in April with an attack on an Indian prisoner in a Pakistani jail. Sarabjit Singh, who died a week later in hospital in Lahore, had been convicted in 1991 for terrorist acts in Lahore and Faisalabad in which 14 people were killed. On the return of his body to India, he was given a state funeral and declared a martyr by the government of Punjab state. In an apparent retaliation, Pakistani prisoner Sanaullah Ranjay, serving a life term after being convicted of terrorism following his arrest in 1999, was assaulted by a fellow prisoner in Jammu prison and died in hospital.

Water issues became important in the bilateral relationship. Pakistan remained concerned over India's construction of a 330 megawatt hydroelectric project on the Kishanganga river in Indian-controlled Kashmir. In a February 2013 report, the International Court of Arbitration in The Hague upheld India's right under the Indus Waters Treaty to divert waters from the river to the project. But the court also held that India would have to maintain a minimum flow of water in the Kishanganga.

A notable feature of Pakistan's election campaign was the lack of anti-India rhetoric, including over the Kashmir dispute, among the mainstream political parties, which favoured a normalisation of relations. Sharif publicly expressed interest in picking up the peace process from when he was last prime minister in 1999, and Singh reciprocated by congratulating him on his victory and conveying his desire to chart 'a new course' in bilateral relations.

Pakistan: Sharif Returns

Landmark elections on 11 May 2013 resulted in Pakistan's first-ever democratic transition from a full-term civilian government to another elected government. Although Nawaz Sharif, leader of the centre-right Pakistan Muslim League-Nawaz (PML-N), had been widely expected to win, the extent of his victory was a surprise. He became prime minister for the third time.

The last year in office of the Pakistan People's Party (PPP)-led coalition government was not without its trials, as the judiciary sought to pressure the government over allegations of corruption. Yousuf Raza Gilani had been forced to step down as prime minister in June 2012, after refusing the Supreme Court's demand to reopen a corruption case against President Asif Ali Zardari, widower of the assassinated former prime minister Benazir Bhutto. New prime minister Raja Pervez Ashraf then formally reopened the case, but there was no tangible progress in it.

In spite of these tensions, Army Chief General Ashfaq Kayani played a key role in the democratic transition, emphasising the need for participation by all political parties. To ensure that general and provincial elections took place and were not disrupted by violence, 91,000 troops were deployed, including at polling stations. During the campaign, 145 people were killed, and the three main 'secular' parties, the PPP, Awami National Party (ANP) and the Muttahidda Qaumi Movement (MQM), were targeted by militants from the Tehrik-e-Taliban Pakistan (TTP). On election day, 38 people were killed and over 130 injured. Yet there was a high turnout of 55%, some 45m people, the highest since the 1980s. The elections were relatively fair, although not without allegations of blatant poll-rigging and violence in some constituencies in Karachi and Lahore, leading to new polls in several constituencies.

Sharif's victory represented a desire for change among the electorate, which was tired of severe power cuts, a fragile economy and corruption. His party won 124 seats, a near-majority of the 272 seats contested. Subsequently, it was allocated 35 of 60 seats reserved for women and six of ten seats reserved for minorities, raising the tally to 165 of a total of 342 seats in the National Assembly. With the support of independents who rushed to join him, Sharif achieved a clear majority and formed a government without the need for a coalition.

Receiving 33% of the vote, Sharif's party sharply increased its tally of seats from 92 held in the previous parliament. But the rise of cricket star-turned-politician Imran Khan's Pakistan Tehreek-e-Insaf (PTI) Party was also significant, as it won 27 seats and a larger vote share than the PPP; it also emerged as the single largest party in Khyber Pakhtunkhwa province, and as the main opposition party in Punjab. The vote share of the religious parties also doubled to over 5% with an increase in seats to 13.

Meanwhile, the PPP was reduced to the level of a regional party. Not only did its seats in the National Assembly dramatically decline from 125 to 31, of which 29 were in Sindh province, the Bhutto family's home base, it was also badly beaten in provincial elections in the most populous province of Punjab, where it won only six seats compared with 107 seats previously. Another major loss was that of the ANP, which won only one seat in the National Assembly and just five seats in the Khyber Pakhtunkhwa assembly.

Though Sharif formed a majority government, his mandate was not uncontested. His party's vote share was well down from the 46% it had won in 1997. The PPP continued to control the Senate, whose support was required for the passage of any significant legislation. Regional and ethnic fault lines were accentuated: while the PML-N continued to govern Punjab, the PPP, with the MQM-controlled Sindh and the PTI, led a coalition government in Khyber Pakhtunkhwa. This divided mandate at the provincial level was a change from the past: the PPP with alliance partners had governed in coalition in three of Pakistan's four provinces. In view of the 18th amendment of the constitution in 2010, which gave greater power to the provinces, Sharif would be forced to engage with opposition parties in the states. In an encouraging move, he awarded the posts of chief minister and governor of the troubled province of Baluchistan to non-PML members.

Sharif's relationship with the army, which has been highly emotive and tense since he was overthrown in a coup by General Pervez Musharraf in 1999, would remain an important factor. It would be tested by the judicial fate awaiting Musharraf, as well as by the appointment of Kayani's successor as army chief, due late in 2013. Musharraf, who ruled Pakistan for nine years until 2008, returned from abroad with the intention of contesting the elections. However, he was soon placed under house arrest over the killing of a Baloch nationalist leader, as well as charges over the assassination of Bhutto, imposition of emergency rule and detention of judges. On 24 June, Sharif said Musharraf would be tried for treason.

Sharif inherited an economy in poor shape. Even though it grew by 3.7% in 2012, it was afflicted by crippling power cuts lasting up to 20 hours a day in some parts. Inflation exceeded 10%, there was a large budget deficit, the rupee was falling, and foreign exchange reserves of $8bn were sufficient to cover only two months' imports. Fewer than 1% of the population filed tax returns. Pakistan, struggling to repay an IMF loan, would be forced to renegotiate its terms. Nonetheless, foreign remittances increased to a high of $14bn and Sharif's victory boosted the stock market.

In an attempt to overcome energy shortages, a $7bn gas pipeline project linking Iran and Pakistan was under way. With Iranian contractors having finished nearly 900km of the pipeline in Iran, work started on the Pakistan section. However, the project was contentious, and its route through insurgency-prone Baluchistan province made the work hazardous and prone to disruption. The United States warned Pakistan that construction may result in sanctions; financing was, as a consequence, a significant problem, though China reportedly offered a $500m loan. However, it was unlikely that Sharif would make the Iran project a priority in view of his close links with Saudi Arabia.

Sectarian attacks

Even though the number of terror attacks within Pakistan declined overall, including a decrease in suicide attacks by a third to 33, the number of victims remained high at over 2,050 dead in 2012. At least 2,284 people died in ethnic, sectarian and politically linked violence in Karachi. There was also an increase in sectarian attacks by Sunni extremist groups such as the Lashkar-e-Jhangvi (LeJ) against the Shia community. In January 2013, 87 people, mostly from the Hazara Shia community, were killed by a car bomb in Quetta, prompting mass protests, the imposition of governor's rule in Baluchistan province, and deployment of the army in the city. A month later, the Hazara Shia community was again targeted in Quetta, with 88 people killed in a bomb attack. In March, two bombs in the Abbas Town area of Karachi killed 45 people, and subsequent mass protests paralysed Pakistan's financial capital. The LeJ was believed to have set up several training camps for militants, with access to large quantities of weapons and explosives.

Meanwhile, the TTP continued to strike at military and government establishments. In August 2012, nine militants stormed the air force's Minhas air base, about 70km from Islamabad, sparking an eight-hour gun battle between the militants and security personnel. In October, TTP militants shot in the head a 14-year-old schoolgirl activist, Malala Yousafzai, who had been campaigning for girls' education. The attack, seen as symbolising the TTP's brutality, was condemned globally, and Yousafzai was transferred to a British hospital, where she recovered. In December 2012, the TTP launched an assault on Bacha Khan airport in Peshawar, in which five Uzbek militants failed to gain entry after firing RPGs and exploding a car bomb. In February 2013, the TTP offered a conditional dialogue with the government, naming Sharif (then in opposition) and leaders of two religious parties as guarantors. But both the army and the civilian government insisted on the laying down of arms and acceptance of the supremacy of the state as prerequisites – not acceptable to the TTP which aims to turn Pakistan into an Islamic state under sharia law. The TTP withdrew the offer in May 2013 after the killing by a drone strike of a senior leader in North Waziristan. At the same time, the army's operations intensified in the Tirah valley in the Khyber agency bordering Afghanistan, seeking to wrest control over key areas from militants, including the TTP.

The intensity and persistence of terror attacks appeared to lead to a shift in Pakistan's security focus. In August 2012, Kayani said in an Independence Day speech that the fight against extremism and terrorism was not only the army's war but that of the whole nation. He indicated that the army's focus would now be on internal security. However, Pakistan appeared to lack an effective counter-terrorism strategy, even though it made progress in strengthening anti-terrorism laws. In September 2012 the cabinet approved the 2012 Anti-Terrorism (Amendment) Bill, creating the offence of financing terrorism. And in one of the last acts of the PPP government, the senate passed the 2013 Anti-Terrorism Amendment Bill, which had been before parliament for more than three years, allowing the preventive detention of suspects for 90 days. It also set up a National Counter-Terrorism Authority to improve coordination between security agencies.

A bitter seven-month impasse between Pakistan and the United States, following the killing of 24 Pakistani soldiers in a US air-strike in November 2011, ended with an apology from Washington. Pakistan reopened NATO supply lines with Afghanistan and agreed not to seek additional commercial fees for transit. A memorandum of understanding was signed, allowing transport of commercial cargo to NATO forces in Afghanistan through Pakistan, but not weapons.

The number of US drone strikes in Pakistan's tribal areas reportedly decreased as the United States focused on high-value targets. Several key al-Qaeda, Afghan Taliban and TTP leaders were killed, including Badruddin Haqqani of the Haqqani network and Waliur Rehman, a leader of the TTP in North Waziristan. But public anger against the attacks persisted because of associated civilian casualties. Although drone strikes were prominent in election campaign rhetoric, the Zardari government's tacit acceptance of them led to an increase in counter-terrorism cooperation with the United States. In May 2013, President Barack Obama announced he would tighten criteria for the use of drones.

Sri Lanka: UN Censure

Sri Lanka was censured by the UN Human Rights Council in Geneva in March 2013 when a tough US-sponsored resolution was passed with 25 countries voting in favour, including India, 13 against and with eight abstentions. The Council encouraged Sri Lanka to conduct an independent and credible investigation into alleged war crimes committed during the country's long civil war. The text contained strong language on concern at reports of enforced disappearances, extra-judicial killings, torture, threats to the rule of law, religious discrimination and intimidation of civil-society activists and journalists.

Nonetheless, Sri Lanka remained on track to host the November 2013 Commonwealth heads of government meeting in Colombo, by far its highest-profile international meeting since the end of the civil war.

Canadian Prime Minister Stephen Harper said he would boycott the summit, and there was concern in Colombo that other leaders may well do so closer to the event.

The government of President Mahinda Rajapaksa claimed that it had implemented many of the recommendations of its Lessons Learnt and Reconciliation Commission (LLRC), set up following the end of Sri Lanka's long civil war. The LLRC, in its report in December 2011, had exonerated the military of large-scale abuses against civilians, but called for specific allegations of serious violations of human rights to be investigated. The government's critics argued that no mechanism had been set up to identify adults who had gone missing during the latter stages of the civil war, nor had there been any prosecutions resulting from investigations of disappearances.

The government focused on rehabilitation and de-radicalisation of former Liberation Tigers of Tamil Eelam (LTTE) combatants and detainees, as well as de-mining. While progress was made in these areas, it said reconciliation would be a long process.

Political tensions were raised in September 2012 when Chief Justice Shirani Bandaranayake ruled that a bill submitted by Basil Rajapaksa, younger brother of the president, proposing a $614m development budget, needed to be approved by nine provincial councils. After weeks of wrangling, a committee of pro-government MPs concluded that Bandaranayake was unfit to hold office on 14 charges of unexplained wealth and misuse of power. Though she was unable to contest the charges in parliament and the Supreme Court judged the impeachment to be illegal, she was removed by the president in January.

Afghanistan: Elections Loom as Foreign Troops Depart

The assumption by Afghan armed forces of greatly increased responsibility for the country's security dominated the year to mid-2013, as NATO-led troops prepared to complete their scheduled withdrawal by the end of 2014.

As the Afghan military took responsibility in June 2013 for the regions that were still under NATO's control, military convoys could be seen leaving the country, heading to ports in Pakistan from where heavy weapons and equipment would be shipped back to the United States. President Barack Obama announced in February 2013 that US troop levels would continue to decline from the previous level of 68,000 throughout the year, halving by the end of the 2013 fighting season. Other countries were also reducing troop levels ahead of the end-2014 deadline, with the remaining forces mainly assisting with training the Afghan National Security Forces (ANSF).

While much of the military focus was on the capability of the ANSF and preparations to maintain security in Afghanistan post-2014, the country was also gearing up for presidential elections scheduled for April 2014, seven months before NATO's scheduled withdrawal. Concerns remained about the country's political system and what form the government would take after the elections. Some high-ranking politicians had been mired in corruption scandals, and Kabul remained dependent on foreign financial support. It was clear that the Afghan government's legitimacy and capability would have a crucial part to play in determining whether a positive momentum could be created after the departure of NATO combat forces.

There was also the question of whether some kind of political agreement with the Taliban would be possible. NATO and the United States began a process of negotiation with the Taliban in mid-2013. A successful transition, leaving Afghanistan with a stable security situation and a legitimate and effective government, was by no means assured.

Future arrangements

An important point was reached on 18 June 2013 with the transfer of responsibility for security in 95 remaining districts across the country from NATO to Afghan control. This followed a joint Afghan–NATO transition board meeting in Kabul to assess the readiness of the Afghan forces to take on the task. President Hamid Karzai labelled the transfer 'a historic moment'. However, NATO Secretary-General Anders Fogh Rasmussen may have more accurately described the situation by stating that the handover proved that 'we have kept to our timetable'.

One focus of the transition process was to reassure the Afghan government that neither the United States nor NATO would abandon the country diplomatically or financially after 2014. As part of this extended exercise, the United States awarded Afghanistan the status of a major non-NATO ally, making Washington's funding, arming and training of the Afghan army more straightforward after 2014. Meanwhile, the international community committed itself to supporting Afghanistan through the transition by pledging $16bn until the end of 2015. However, continued concerns about pervasive corruption were evident in a clause stating that 20% of the funding was conditional on progress in dealing with the problem.

Bilateral negotiations between Kabul and Washington centred on solidifying their relations after 2014. A Strategic Partnership Agreement signed in July 2012 was designed to transform the relationship into one operating between two sovereign states, and was to be followed by a Bilateral Security Agreement that would regulate the number, role and legal immunities of American soldiers in Afghanistan after 2014. Delicate negotiations on this began in November 2012, but the immunity issue was so controversial that discussions about it were set aside for later in the process. This left the number of US troops stationed in the country after 2014 as the main issue to be negotiated.

Obama said the United States wished to conduct 'two long-term tasks, which will be very specific and very narrow: first, training and assisting Afghan forces and, second, targeted counter-terrorism missions against al-Qaeda and its affiliates.' NATO was planning that the current International Security Assistance Force (ISAF) would be replaced by Operation Resolute Support, a non-combat mission focused on training, advising and assisting the Afghans.

Although there was fear within Afghan society about the instability that a quick withdrawal of NATO troops might trigger, there was also resentment directed at a foreign occupying force that had at times been heavy-handed in its use of lethal force. Mindful of this, the United States committed itself to a 'light security footprint' after 2014. In March 2013, the head of US Central Command, General James Mattis, put forward a figure of 13,600 US troops, with other NATO countries potentially bringing the total to 20,000. In June 2013, Secretary of Defense Chuck Hagel told Congress that, although the United States had not confirmed the final number of troops to remain in Afghanistan after 2014, negotiations were now in their final phase.

Uncertainty about the country's future was voiced from many quarters. In November 2012, the Afghan energy and water minister, Ismail Khan, a former mujahadeen commander and regional power-broker in the western province of Herat, called on the Afghan people to 'step forward, take arms and defend the country' in places where the security forces could not guarantee security. In March 2013, Britain's acting ambassador to Kabul, Nic Hailey, admitted it was inevitable that parts of Afghanistan would not be under Afghan government control at the end of 2014. The departing French ambassador, Bernard Bajolet, stated that the whole mission was 'on thin ice'. He pondered how the international community in Afghanistan had created the 'perfect storm' in 2014. How was it that a presidential election was going to take place in the same year that responsibility for security was transferred from NATO to the Afghan government?

Politics and the 2014 elections

Afghanistan's politics were dominated by speculation over, and preparations for, the 2014 presidential election. There was widespread concern that badly run presidential elections or contested results in 2014 could delegitimise the government and destabilise the country just as NATO troops were leaving. A botched or stolen election would also make it more difficult for foreign states to continue to provide aid.

The Afghan state that had been built in the 12 years since regime change remained profoundly weak, its institutions undermined by corruption, and its politicians having lost a great deal of the legitimacy they had gained.

Karzai, sworn in as interim president immediately after the Taliban government was ousted in December 2001, went on to successfully contest elections in 2004 and 2009. The constitution prevents him from seeking a third term, but there had been speculation in 2012 that he would seek to engineer one, by either rewriting the constitution or suspending it. In May 2013, he made it clear that he would do neither. However, by taking himself out of the running he triggered speculation that he would instead seek to anoint a trusted successor who would not pursue anti-corruption investigations against him. Although Karzai himself was not giving public backing to anyone, several names were attracting attention amongst the ruling elite in Kabul. In May 2013, Karzai's younger brother, Mahmoud, added to this speculation by declaring that their older brother, Qayum Karzai, would announce his candidacy. Other potential candidates include Abdul Hadi Arghandiwal, the minister for commerce and industries, and Hanif Atmar, a former minister of interior.

The 2009 presidential elections and the 2010 parliamentary elections had been marred by widespread vote-rigging and electoral fraud. In both years, the Electoral Complaints Commission, supported by the UN, intervened and tried to make the electoral process more legitimate. However, in 2012, Karzai argued that the presence of foreign observers on the Electoral Complaints Commission weakened Afghanistan's sovereignty and he wanted them removed. This raised concerns that Karzai was seeking to weaken electoral oversight so that he could control who would succeed him as president. In spite of this, the Independent High Electoral Commission announced that the presidential election would take place in April 2014, with nominations required by October 2013, so that a full list of contestants could be published by November. Voter registration began in May 2013.

Another significant political development was the Afghan parliament's partial success in attempting to remove the minister of defence, Abdul Rahim Wardak, and the interior minister, Bismillah Khan Mohammadi. In August 2012, parliament passed a vote of no confidence in Wardak and Mohammadi following their failure to stop cross-border shelling from Pakistan. Wardak had been defence minister for nearly eight years and had previously been deputy defence minister. Mohammadi, a former mujahideen commander, was army chief of staff from 2002–2010 and an influential politician in the opposition group, the Northern Alliance.

The vote against two such senior politicians was initially seen as a largely futile attempt by parliament to assert influence over the presidency. Karzai had in the past simply ignored parliament's moves against ministers that he wanted to keep. However, this time, in the wake of the vote, the president issued a statement that neither condemned parliament's actions nor supported the ministers. To the surprise of many, he then agreed to comply with the vote and remove both ministers. At the time this was regarded as a potential risk for Karzai, since Mohammadi had a powerful support base. In the event, Karzai circumvented the problem by appointing Mohammadi as minister of defence. He then used the shake-up of the security portfolios to sack another Northern Alliance politician, Rahmatullah Nabil, who was the head of Afghanistan's intelligence agency, the National Directorate of Security, and replaced Nabil with a close ally, Asadullah Khalid. The effect was that Karzai successfully used a potentially damaging parliamentary vote to increase his control over the security services.

Endemic corruption

Rising levels of corruption have alienated the population from its government, undermined the legitimacy of the state itself and corroded the civil and military institutions built since 2001. A UN report estimated that $3.9bn was spent on bribes in Afghanistan in 2012, 40% more than in 2009.

Among instances of alleged malpractice in the year to mid-2013, Finance Minister Hazrat Omar Zakhilwal attracted unwelcome publicity when, in August 2012, the Afghan television station Tolo reported that he had over $1m deposited in foreign bank accounts. Zakhilwal vehemently denied the accusations, first claiming that the money had come from his own private-sector work before he became a minister and then arguing that it resulted from his financial management of Karzai's re-election campaign in 2009.

The scandal arose just before the main protagonists in the $900m Kabul Bank fraud stood trial. The collapse of Kabul Bank – described as, in effect, a vast Ponzi scheme in which deposits were stolen instead of invested – had been accompanied by allegations of high-level political involvement in its malfeasance. Karzai's brother, Mahmoud, and Vice-President Mohammad Fahim's brother, Haseem, were major shareholders, but neither had faced prosecution. The trial ended in March 2013 with the bank's former chairman, Sherkhan Farnood, and chief executive, Khalilullah Ferozi, convicted on the comparatively minor charge of 'breach of trust', allowing them to serve shorter sentences. As a result the missing money would be harder to recover and wider beneficiaries of the fraud would remain undetected. Its scale, and the opaque manner in which it was investigated and prosecuted, showed that politically sanctioned corruption remained endemic.

A *New York Times* article published in April 2013 reported that the CIA had been sending suitcases of cash – apparently not subject to the conditions placed on US aid – to Karzai's office on a regular basis. This was thought to have helped fuel corruption. Karzai confirmed he had been receiving cash payments from the United States, but said they had been small amounts and had been used legitimately, a claim he had made earlier about cash payments from Iran.

Security: mixed picture

In spring 2012 the Taliban had declared a counter-offensive to push back ISAF and Afghan forces. This failed and the UN reported a 30% decrease in security incidents over the year, with insurgent attacks using improvised explosive devices (IEDs) falling by 20%. The majority of insurgent attacks were on the edges of territory under Afghan government control, some 80% of attacks occurring in 20% of Afghan districts. With the ANSF taking the lead in many areas, deaths of Afghan National Army (ANA) soldiers doubled in 2012 to 1,056. Whilst 42% of the 315 NATO fatalities in 2012 were from IEDs, over 80% of ANA fatalities were caused in this way, stark demonstration of its lower level of counter-IED capability.

However, UN figures showed that civilian deaths rose 24% in the first half of 2013. There were also indications that the Taliban was focusing on more high-profile attacks, targeting major government buildings in Kabul for suicide attacks and specifically seeking to assassinate government and military officials who would be responsible for running the country after NATO troops leave.

The additional 33,000 US 'surge' troops deployed in 2010 withdrew by October 2012, leaving 68,000 US troops alongside 32,000 troops from other nations. The ANA's responsibilities increased, with 21 of 26 Afghan brigades operating independently of ISAF, or with ISAF support limited to advisers. In many areas there was a significant reduction in NATO's footprint: for example British bases in Helmand province fell from 80 in April 2012 to just 12 in April 2013. In June 2013, as military leadership of the campaign moved from NATO's joint headquarters to the new Afghan Ground Forces Command, NATO reduced the number of mentoring teams.

Afghan forces were leading counter-insurgency and policing operations across most of the country. This included holding areas that had been cleared of insurgents during the US surge. In the first half of the 2013 fighting season Taliban attacks as usual increased, as militants overran some ANSF posts and made determined efforts to wrest back control of outlying areas. As the ANSF counter-attacked, there was heavy fighting. There were credible reports that ANSF deaths had at times reached 100 a week and that up to 1,000 members of the ANSF were killed in the first half of the year.

Kabul, the capital, was the location of only 1% of security incidents in 2012. Concerted efforts by the Haqqani network, a Pakistan-based militant group, to launch spectacular attacks on the capital were successfully countered by Afghan forces between April and December 2012. But suicide attacks on government buildings and security bases in Kabul and Jalalabad in 2013 demonstrated the insurgents' continuing ability to launch well-planned attacks.

ANSF challenges

As planned, NATO's training mission shifted efforts from increasing the size of the army to building logistic and support capabilities including medical, counter-IED, fire support and intelligence. Two new ANA brigades were created to form a 'mobile strike force' which would provide much-needed reserves. And NATO evinced greater confidence in army and police special forces as well as the Afghan National Directorate of Security, the country's intelligence service.

However, in spite of earlier optimistic pronouncements by NATO, the ANSF remained over 7,000 personnel short of a planned strength of 350,000. This was partly due to higher attrition within the army, border police and civil-order police. Army desertion rates were estimated to be running at 7–10% per year, and the military was using financial incentives to attempt to reduce it. Soldiers cited Taliban intimidation and low morale as reasons for leaving, as well as poor food and lack of medical care, partly caused by widespread corruption amongst the officer corps.

The ANSF still relied on NATO for artillery and air-strikes, airborne intelligence-gathering, and for help in getting logistic and administrative systems working properly. A report released by the US Department of Defense in December 2012 found that just one of the Afghan army's 23 battalions was able to operate independently of US or NATO support. In addition, the US Special Inspector General for Afghanistan Reconstruction estimated that the Afghan army would not be able to maintain the $12bn-worth of facilities that the US military had built for them. This was partly due to high levels of illiteracy, chronic lack of skilled technicians and corruption.

The Afghan Local Police, a village self-defence force mentored by embedded teams of US special forces, reached a strength of 18,000 operating at 86 sites. However, whilst these forces were aiding stability, concerns remained over human-rights abuses, impunity, vetting and the potential re-emergence of ethnically or politically biased militias. The spectre of a return of warlords' militias was raised by Ismail Khan in November 2012 when he issued his call to arms to address the security threat.

There were ambitious plans to build the Afghan Air Force's airlift and attack capability. The Pentagon assessed that its development lagged behind all the other Afghan forces, due to the shortage of educated and trained personnel, and estimated that 2017 would be the earliest that the air force could achieve full capability.

'Insider' or 'green-on-blue' attacks carried out by Afghan troops and police greatly increased in autumn 2012. Sixty ISAF personnel died in this way in 2012, a 40% increase from 2011. Although attacks were invariably claimed by the Taliban, analysis by the Pentagon suggested that only 11% were the result of Taliban infiltration, with the rest caused by grievances or provocation. Issues ranging from night raids and civilian casualties to insults had been triggers for insider attacks. NATO and the Afghan authorities announced initiatives aimed at improving security against Taliban infiltration, including improved vetting and counter-intelligence. This included NATO troops providing armed guards for trainers and mentors. The level of attacks greatly reduced in 2013. But it was likely that war fatigue and accumulated Afghan resentment of the NATO presence were major motivating factors, so improved security measures may not have a decisive effect: although such attacks would decline as NATO troop levels fell, they would probably continue until NATO troops withdrew completely.

The ANSF seemed strong enough to continue to hold the main cities and key rural areas that had been cleared of insurgents during the surge. And NATO's efforts to build supporting and technical capability could be expected to continue to improve their capabilities over the next year. However, the government in Kabul continued to depend both financially and militarily on Washington, and there remained considerable uncertainty about the military capacity and political intentions of the Taliban.

Talking to the Taliban

An important part of the West's strategy was to engage in negotiations with the Taliban. Exploratory meetings between US officials and the Taliban began in Qatar in January 2011. However, these soon broke down when the Taliban requested the release of five 'high-level' detainees from the US military prison at Guantánamo Bay in Cuba as a sign of goodwill. The US government, constrained by public opinion and congressional opposition, was unable to meet this demand.

Negotiations between the US and Afghan governments and the Taliban were hindered by a lack of clarity over each party's ultimate goal. When the United States first embarked on negotiations, its aim was to split the Taliban, offering 'moderate' members of the leadership incentives to stop fighting whilst demobilising war-weary fighters, making it easier to defeat the 'irreconcilables' and secure victory. However, the Taliban proved to be a cohesive and homogeneous organisation. The senior leadership remained united, and only 5,000 former fighters took advantage of amnesty and demobilisation initiatives.

The Taliban's motivations became clearer in a series of interviews conducted by Michael Semple, former deputy to the EU's Special Representative for Afghanistan, with two former Taliban ministers and a senior commander between July and September 2012. The Taliban were clearly aware that they could not defeat NATO on the battlefield. Instead, they were willing to pursue a dual strategy, maintaining the fight in Afghanistan whilst simultaneously negotiating. By engaging in talks with the United States they hoped to make the point that it was not they who were prolonging the conflict. Those Semple talked with made it clear that they had distanced themselves from al-Qaeda. This point was reinforced when, in a statement issued in August 2012, the head of the Taliban, Mullah Omar, said the organisation 'will not allow anyone to use the soil of Afghanistan against any one', a reference to al-Qaeda's use of the country to plan the 2001 terrorist attacks on the United States.

There was also an awareness among Taliban representatives that their previous approach to women's rights, the enforcement of strict religious rules of behaviour and their approach to international relations had been counter-productive and destructive. They expressed interest in joining a future Afghan government, where their role could focus on the implementation of sharia law and the fight against corruption. To facilitate negotiations, the Qatari government agreed to host a Taliban negotiating team in Doha, and the Taliban formally opened an office in Qatar in June 2013.

However, no sooner had talks begun between Taliban representatives and the US special envoy for Afghanistan and Pakistan, James Dobbins, when they ran into unforeseen difficulties. In June 2013, the main stumbling block was the Afghan government which was worried that Taliban talks with the United States would undermine its own sovereignty. This sensitivity was exacerbated by the Taliban's Doha office adopting the trappings of a legitimate government and raising the Taliban flag. The Taliban had made clear its contempt for the government, arguing that Karzai had no constituency within the country and no control over the forces arrayed against the Taliban.

From the Afghan government's point of view, talks between the Taliban and Washington threatened to sideline it in any potential peace deal. To avoid this outcome, Kabul had since June 2011 been pursuing its own negotiations. In December 2012, a leak from the government's negotiating team, the Afghan High Peace Council, shed light on Kabul's approach to talks: the 'Afghan Peace Process Roadmap to 2015', envisaged that talks between Kabul and the Taliban would start in 2013 in Saudi Arabia, not Qatar. The aim was to negotiate a ceasefire and the integration of Taliban forces into the Afghan army. To facilitate this process, the chairman of the Afghan High Peace Council, Salahuddin Rabbani, travelled to Pakistan in November 2012, seeking the release of 18 Taliban commanders held in prison there. Rabbani succeeded in securing the freedom of 12 Taliban prisoners, an indication that Pakistan was minded to facilitate a peace deal ahead of the withdrawal of NATO troops in 2014.

Talks between the United States and the Taliban looked set to continue in Qatar after US Secretary of State John Kerry reassured the Afghan government that any substantive peace deal would have to be 'Afghan-led'.

Regional relations

While India viewed the drawdown of NATO forces with concern, Karzai sought to improve the bilateral relationship. Visiting India twice in seven months, he solicited Indian investment in Afghanistan as well as additional military training for Afghan security forces. Karzai also sought military equipment from India, reportedly to include artillery pieces, helicopters and mortars, as well as Indian military trainers for a new Sandhurst-style military academy being set up. While these much-publicised requests were an attempt to boost Afghan security force capability, they were also a signal to Pakistan at a time of tension between Kabul and Islamabad. For its part, India – though still unwilling to deploy troops to Afghanistan – appeared keen to strengthen Afghan military capability but was also mindful of not alienating Nawaz Sharif, the new Pakistani prime minister.

Meanwhile, an initial improvement in Pakistan's relations with Afghanistan was soon spoiled by tensions and border clashes. In an encouraging move in November 2012, Pakistan released about a dozen Afghan Taliban detainees in support of the reconciliation process between the Taliban and Karzai's government. It also guaranteed safe passage for those involved in peace talks, and later announced that it would soon free all its Afghan Taliban detainees, expected to include the pro-dialogue Taliban leader Mullah Abdul Ghani Baradar.

In further conciliatory moves, General Ashfaq Parvez Kayani, Pakistan's army chief of staff, took part in a trilateral meeting in Kabul with Afghan and ISAF commanders, and reiterated the need for improved border coordination. He renewed offers of training for ANA officers in Pakistan, probably in an effort to counter Indian training of

Afghan forces. At a trilateral Afghanistan–Pakistan–UK summit hosted by UK Prime Minister David Cameron in February 2013, Islamabad and Kabul agreed to 'structured interaction' and to establish a hotline between their respective militaries and intelligence wings. Pakistan said it would support and facilitate talks with the Taliban via its Doha office. All these developments marked a significant shift from Islamabad's previous obstruction of dialogue between the Taliban and the Afghan government.

However, days later Karzai accused Pakistan's Inter-Services Intelligence agency of derailing the peace process and providing safe havens for the Taliban leadership in Quetta and Karachi. He later accused Pakistan of eliminating pro-peace Afghan Taliban members, an allegation strongly denied by Islamabad. At the same time, Pakistan accused Karzai of supporting cross-border attacks on its troops by allowing Tehrik-e-Taliban Pakistan leader Maulana Fazlullah to operate from Afghanistan's Nuristan and Paktika border provinces. At least ten cross-border clashes took place over several months, prompted by shelling from one or the other side, with both countries accusing the other of starting the clashes. As mutual trust deteriorated, a proposed bilateral Strategic Partnership Agreement was delayed, even though it had been largely agreed upon. Resentment of Pakistan amongst the Afghan people and media was at a peak.

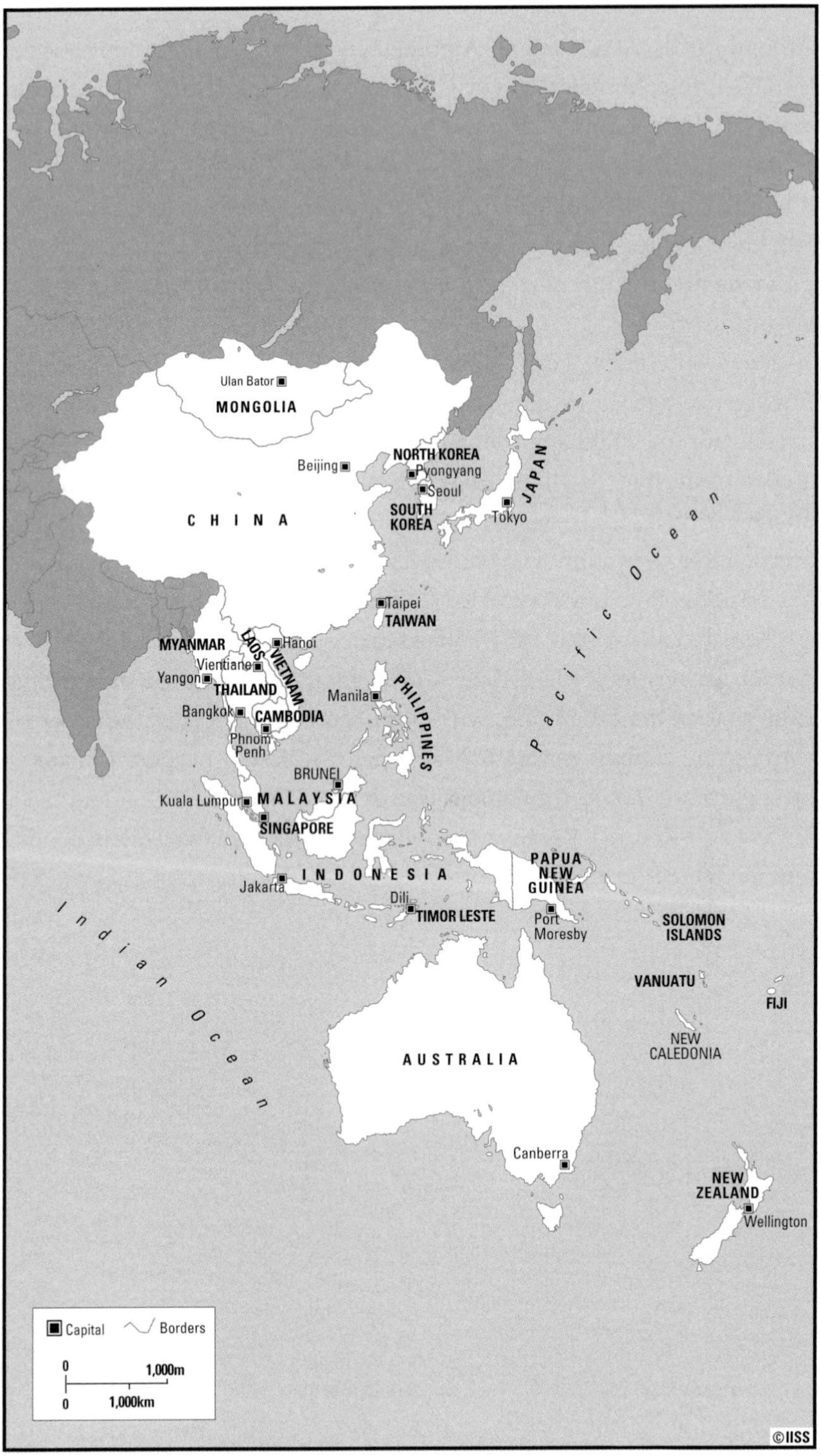

Ulan Bator
MONGOLIA
CHINA
Beijing
NORTH KOREA
Pyongyang
Seoul
SOUTH KOREA
JAPAN
Tokyo
Pacific Ocean
Taipei
TAIWAN
MYANMAR
LAOS
VIETNAM
Hanoi
Vientiane
Yangon
THAILAND
Bangkok
CAMBODIA
Phnom Penh
Manila
PHILIPPINES
BRUNEI
Kuala Lumpur
MALAYSIA
SINGAPORE
INDONESIA
Jakarta
Dili
TIMOR LESTE
PAPUA NEW GUINEA
Port Moresby
SOLOMON ISLANDS
VANUATU
FIJI
NEW CALEDONIA
Indian Ocean
AUSTRALIA
Canberra
NEW ZEALAND
Wellington
Capital
Borders
0
1,000m
0
1,000km
©IISS

Chapter 9

Asia-Pacific

The three main powers of northeast Asia all went through changes of leadership in the year to mid-2013. China's carefully prepared transfer of power to Xi Jinping was accomplished after considerable factional manoeuvring within the Chinese Communist Party. In Japan, the Liberal Democratic Party returned to power after three years, and Prime Minister Shinzo Abe embarked on an ambitious project to revive the economy. A conservative leader was also elected in South Korea, where Park Geun-hye became the country's first female president. Her government was immediately subjected to a wave of bellicose abuse from North Korea, where new leader Kim Jong-un was seeking to make a mark both at home and abroad. Relations between neighbours remained tense, with China and Japan especially at odds over islands in the East China Sea. Long-running disputes over islands in the South China Sea were also no closer to resolution. Myanmar continued its process of reintegration into the international community. In Australia, Kevin Rudd returned as prime minister, ousting his Labor Party rival Julia Gillard three years after she had similarly removed him.

China: New Leadership

The transfer of leadership to Xi Jinping, who was appointed General Secretary of the Chinese Communist Party (CCP) and President of China in succession to Hu Jintao, was the most significant event of the year to mid-2013. Addressing the National People's Congress (NPC) in March 2013, he called for a rejuvenation of the Chinese nation.

Xi inherited a system that was starting to show the strain of 30 years of unrestrained economic growth and development. Evidence of this was visible; much of China was swathed in toxic smog, and thousands of dead pigs contaminated Shanghai's water supply. Before the handover, the Communist Party had been hit by scandal that exposed the inner workings of the political elite. The fall of Chongqing Party Secretary Bo Xilai and his purge from the party, following the murder by his wife of British businessman Neil Heywood in 2011, threw the spotlight on the leadership's factional networks and family interests. It also exposed the systemic corruption that plagues the CCP.

Xi emerged as paramount leader largely unscathed by these events. He lost no time in placing the fight against corruption at the top of the agenda, and reiterated his determination to maintain party discipline. This was a sure indication that party reform would not take place during his tenure, meaning that the CCP would not allow political liberalisation.

The NPC's completion of the change of leadership marked the end of a predominantly introspective period: apart from crisis management in its immediate neighbourhood, most facets of China's global outreach had been put on hold, with attention and energy focused inwards. However, rising tension with Japan in a territorial dispute over the island chain called Diaoyu by China and Senkaku by Japan (see pp. 332–333) created disquiet in relations with the United States.

There was debate within the Chinese establishment over what role the US military, the long-time resident superpower in the Pacific, would play in the decade ahead, especially in light of US President Barack Obama's decision to 'rebalance' forces towards the Pacific. The People's Liberation Army (PLA) continued to showcase new capabilities, exhibiting what was interpreted by many foreigners as a more assertive stance. Milestones included the launch of China's first aircraft carrier. Controversially, reports emerged in 2013 of the PLA directly targeting the US Department of Defense (DoD) through cyber attacks.

The rise of Xi Jinping

In November 2012, China's new leadership emerged from the wings of the Great Hall of the People to meet the press. After many weeks of speculation about rifts within the Politburo, the handover was complete, and was later formalised at the NPC in March. Xi and new premier Li Keqiang were the first top leaders to have been born after the People's Republic was founded in 1949.

Xi had risen swiftly, attaining access to the inner sanctum of the Communist Party at a young age. Born in 1953 in Beijing, his start in life owed much to his pedigree as the son of one of China's veteran leaders of the communist guerrilla movement, Xi Zhongxun, who served as the party's chief of propaganda and at the top of the NPC during the future president's childhood. In 1963, Xi Zhongxun became the victim of one of Mao Zedong's purges and was dispatched to a factory in Luoyang city in Henan Province. Five years later as the Cultural Revolution tore through China, Xi Zhongxun was jailed and Xi Jinping was sent to the Wen'anyi commune in Shaanxi province in 1969, where he was well-received because of the respect his father – despite his reversal of fortunes – still commanded in the area.

By his own carefully cultivated biographical account, Xi's years of labour as part of the commune's Liangjiahe brigade had a transformative effect, shaping his ideological credentials. He joined the Communist Party in 1974 – according to Xi, after he had applied ten previous times – and was named party secretary of the Liangjiahe brigade soon after. Xi returned to Beijing in 1975 to study organic chemistry at Tsingua University, and during this period was taken under the wing of his father's former comrade-in-arms, Vice Premier Geng Biao. He soon caught the eye of the top leadership, and in 1979 was appointed secretary of the General Office of the State Council and the Central Military Commission (CMC), China's most senior military decision-making body.

Xi spent his formative political years in China's coastal provinces. He was sent to Hebei Province in 1982 and became party chief of Zhengding county the year after, then moved to Fujian Province to become deputy mayor of Xiamen city. He remained in Fujian for almost two decades as Deng Xiaoping's reforms brought investment and development opportunities.

He also maintained links to Beijing, studying Marxist theory and ideological and political education at postgraduate level and gaining a law doctorate at his alma mater, Tsinghua University.

Xi was appointed deputy party secretary in Zhejiang Province in 2002 and became acting governor the following year, a post he held until 2007. When Shanghai Party Chief Chen Liangyu was dismissed during a social-security corruption scandal, Xi was tapped to replace him. In 2008 he was appointed vice-president of China and in 2010 he became vice chairman of the CMC. Soon after his appointment as president and general secretary, Xi travelled to the south of China to pay homage to Deng Xiaoping's reforms and to launch his own campaign, the 'Chinese Dream'.

Committee changes

New Chinese premier Li Keqiang, like his predecessor Wen Jiabao, was known to be an economic reformer. His experience as party secretary of Henan Province, an important agricultural producer, and Liaoning Province, an industrial powerhouse, was expected to help him connect with the Chinese populace. In addition, his legal background and a focus on urbanisation were viewed as important credentials in tackling the mounting problems resulting from rapid economic development, such as the economic disparity between the poor rural hinterland and China's fast-growing cities.

In the 2012 leadership handover, appointments to other positions attracted considerable attention, as did the fate of those who failed to advance. One significant change was a reduction from nine to seven members in the Politburo Standing Committee, the elite executive body presiding over the broader Politburo of 25 members. Ten years previously, Jiang Zemin had increased the membership to nine in what was seen as an attempt to constrain the power of his successor, Hu Jintao.

Two significant losers in the reduction of the Standing Committee were Wang Yang, party secretary of Guangdong Province, and Li Yuanchao, chief of the powerful Organisation Department of the Central Committee, both of whom had been contenders for seats. Li was appointed vice-president as a consolation prize. Commentators suggested both men were advocates of reforming the CCP in order to reduce its political control; their exclusion was a signal that neither Xi nor Li would back such reforms.

The 18th Party Congress also saw a transfer of power at the top of the CMC. Jiang had retained the CMC chair for an additional two years after quitting other top leadership posts, but Hu did not follow suit, stepping down from power completely. This paved the way for Xi to become leader of both the CCP and its armed wing, the PLA.

General Fan Changlong, not previously a CMC member, was promoted to first vice chairman, directly from his position as Jinan military region commander. General Zhang Qinsheng, who had allegedly fallen out of favour with both Hu and former Chief of the General Staff Chen Bingde over the role of the PLA as the CCP's military wing, failed to win a place on the commission. Fallout from the Bo Xilai scandal appeared to affect two other contenders, General Liu Yan and General Zhang Haiyang, who were also not elevated to the CMC.

One of the surprises of the leadership transition was the role of Jiang, who was China's president from 1989–2002, and his efforts to balance Hu's influence in the new Politburo. In the new generation of leaders, six of the seven members are believed to be members of Jiang's 'princeling clique' or 'Shanghai clique', a faction whose members share the pedigrees of the founding fathers of the People's Republic, or whose political ascent to power was intricately linked to the financial powerhouse of Shanghai. Hu, a non-princeling, had begun his political career as a stalwart of the Communist Youth League (CYL), many members of which followed his ascent to power and joined him as members of the Politburo. It was widely held that outgoing CCP leaders attempted to secure their legacies by aligning their patronage networks up to a decade in advance, thus creating an orderly cycle of transition and political succession.

A great deal of speculation among China-watchers before the 18th Party Congress had focused on perceived rivalry between the 'princeling' and CYL factions within the CCP. Ultimately, however, factional loyalty may have been overstated by foreign observers; the line-up for the Politburo had more to do with the tight feudal loyalties and personal patronage networks of Jiang and Hu. Another element of the factional rivalry was the rumoured early retirement of the man in charge of state security on the Politburo Standing Committee, Zhou Yongkang. Several sets of events had embarrassed the party: the Bo Xilai scandal, the escape of the blind lawyer dissident Chen Guangcheng and his asylum in the United States, continuing self-immolations of Tibetan protesters and simmering unrest in Xinjiang. Perhaps because of these, there was reportedly a heated debate during the leadership's summer retreat over the powers wielded by Zhou as the head of the Central Political and Law Committee (CPLAC). Zhou, supposedly an ally of Bo Xilai and a supporter of the populist 'Chongqing model', was succeeded at the Party Congress by the former minister of public security, Meng Jianzhu, who was not elevated to the Standing Committee. Standing Committee member Yu Zhengsheng was allegedly now the final arbiter of state security issues.

Ling Jihua, director of the CCP Central Committee General Office and close confidant of Hu Jintao, had been a favourite for elevation to the top of the party, but appeared to be another casualty of the Bo corruption scandal. After Ling's son was killed in a high-speed car crash, a cover-up over the mysterious circumstances of the accident eventually led to Ling's removal from office and a demotion to the relative backwater of the CCP's United Front Work Department.

Addressing the NPC in March, Xi called on party deputies to strive to 'achieve the Chinese dream of great rejuvenation of the Chinese nation'. He stressed interdependence between the Communist Party and the people, united on the 'road of socialism with Chinese characteristics'. Earlier, he had urged party cadres to abide by the 'eight disciplines' designed to encourage frugality, in particular curbing lavish banquets for party officials and their guests.

Postscript: the fall of Bo Xilai

Senior party members, including outgoing premier Wen Jiabao and Xi Jinping, became extremely sensitive to accusations of extravagance and decadence within China's privileged elite, after the *New York Times* and Bloomberg published details of the wealth of the families of senior leaders. Foreign attention on such issues had been stirred by the Bo Xilai scandal.

In 2011, Bo, the 'princeling' son of veteran revolutionary Bo Yibo, seemed on the verge of being promoted to the Politburo Standing Committee. He had powerful patrons within the CCP, including Jiang

Zemin, and had secured a Politburo seat during the 17th Party Congress when he was appointed party secretary of the city of Chongqing. There, he adopted a populist approach that appealed to the 'new left' in China and stirred memories of the fervent activism of the Mao Zedong years. However, his anti-corruption drive made enemies in Chongqing, as the party committee reportedly confiscated tens of millions of yuan from businessmen who fell foul of his campaign.

Bo launched a campaign to gain a seat on the Politburo Standing Committee, tactics that created ripples through the CCP Central Committee, which had thus far favoured a consensus-led approach to promotion and policymaking. Bo's effort to find an alternative way to the top of the party, in the view of his critics, caused a fissure within it, and left it vulnerable to more serious fracture.

Bo's ambitions collapsed after his wife, Gu Kailai, was accused of the murder of British businessman Neil Heywood. Gu had apparently cultivated Heywood as a close confidant of the family after he had facilitated her son's entry into a British private school. Heywood, who had become involved in the family's private business affairs, fell into a dispute with Gu so serious that she orchestrated his murder by luring him to a hotel in Chongqing. With the help of a family servant, she poisoned him with cyanide. The Chongqing police blamed the death on alcohol poisoning and his body was cremated without scrutiny by British consular officials. Wang Lijun, Bo's police chief in Chongqing, apparently discovered the murder, and later sought asylum at the US consulate in Chengdu.

In China, Gu's trial was a hotly anticipated event. In July 2012, Gu and her accomplice, Zhang Xiaojun, were formally charged with murder. During her one-day trial in August, Gu admitted Heywood's murder, gave an account of the killing and stated that she was ready to accept any sentence. She was given a suspended death sentence and sent to prison. Zhang received nine years in prison. Gu's arrest and conviction shook the Chinese leadership to the core. The enemies whom Bo had made within the CCP pounced on the opportunity to bring him down. He was stripped of his party and government positions in Chongqing, his place in the Politburo, the Party Central Committee and the NPC and in early November 2012, he was expelled from the party itself. With Bo out of the way, the Politburo ushered in the next generation of leaders.

Streamlining government

In a move to cut red tape and limit corruption, State Councillor Ma Kai announced an overhaul of Chinese ministry-level bodies and mergers of subordinate agencies and departments. It was the seventh such overhaul in three decades aiming to rid the bureaucracy of duplication of effort and overlapping management. This had created loopholes for corruption to flourish and for some administrative bodies to accumulate far more power than their remits would suggest.

The railways ministry – which had been plagued by corruption allegations and safety scandals including a serious train crash – was incorporated into the ministry of transport, and the business arm of China's rail operations was converted into a company in its own right. Following food contamination and hygiene scares, the Food and Drug Administration was upgraded to ministry status, combining five separate agencies, and was given powers to tackle crime and corruption. In addition, in a move to tighten the CCP's grip on an increasingly diversified Chinese media sector, two regulators were merged to administer the press, films, radio and television.

China's State Oceanic Administration was restructured to enhance maritime law enforcement, and to strengthen the protection and exploitation of China's marine resources. With only one maritime law-enforcement agency under its jurisdiction, it had faced personnel and equipment challenges in patrolling more than 18,000 kilometres of coastline and 875,000 square nautical miles, including those that are the subject of territorial disputes. With calls at the 18th Party Congress for China to become a 'big maritime power', the shake-up merged the coastguard forces that were previously under the ministry of public security, the fisheries law-enforcement command previously under the ministry of agriculture, and maritime anti-smuggling authorities previously under the customs administration. The restructured body would focus on asserting China's maritime claims.

Dip in the economy

China's economy grew at its slowest pace for 13 years in 2012, at 7.8%, down from 9.3% in 2011, due to continued recession in the eurozone, a slow US recovery, and weakened internal demand.

Measures taken in 2011 to cool economic overheating and a property-market bubble, such as tightening monetary policy and new restrictions on the purchase of investment property, had been particularly effective in stabilising prices. House prices settled and the 2.6% inflation rate in 2012 was less than half the 2011 level of 5.4%. However, these measures also resulted in a decline in property investment across the country, which acted as a drag on overall economic activity.

Nonetheless, lower inflation combined with salary and pension increases to boost real income across the country. According to the Asian Development Bank, real income grew on average by 9.5% in urban areas and 10.7% in rural areas. Consequently, consumption exceeded investment expenditure in 2012, supporting the government's continued attempts to reorient the economy away from an export-oriented model towards a more domestic-demand-driven approach.

With inflation in check, China's central bank was able to continue with the expansionary actions it commenced in late 2011, cutting interest rates and the amounts that banks needed to keep as reserves. However, strong growth in credit issuance and non-traditional lending sources resulted in a disproportionate rise in liquidity and indebtedness across the economy, particularly at the local government level. This meant that by early 2013 the People's Bank of China had begun to taper off its injections of liquidity into the money markets.

In 2012 China embarked on a gradual, multi-year policy of liberalisation of capital controls, interest rates and exchange rates, as part of the government's aim to internationalise the renminbi and rebalance the economy towards consumption-led growth. These measures contributed to the renminbi's appreciation in 2012 by an average of 2.4% against the dollar and 10.6% against the euro.

In the first half of 2013, China's economic growth was still losing momentum. In May, exports were at their lowest annual growth rate in almost a year at 1%, after a crackdown by authorities on currency speculation disguised as export trades to circumvent capital controls. Reining in excessive credit also posed challenges, with the central bank's tightening actions triggering a brief cash crunch in short-term money markets in late June 2013, with short-term inter-bank rates briefly rising to 28%, bond repurchase rates jumping temporarily to 10.8%, and the Shanghai stock exchange falling 15% over just three days. Overall, domestic economic activity struggled to pick up, causing analysts to speculate that China would miss its 2013 growth target of 7.5%.

Burst of diplomacy

After China's period of introspection, Xi embarked on a round of international diplomacy, to which the US 'rebalancing' to Asia was an important backdrop. His first visit was to Russia. Many Western commentators interpreted the warmth between Xi and President Vladimir Putin as symbolic of a counterweight to US global strategic influence. The two leaders described Sino-Russian friendship as a guarantor of strategic balance and peace. China agreed a loan of US$2 billion to Russian energy giant Rosneft, which offered to triple energy supplies; Russia's Gazprom agreed plans for a new gas pipeline to China. Xi sealed deals to buy Su-35 fighter jets and submarines.

China and Russia were aligned closely over issues such as the civil war in Syria and the security of the Korean peninsula. In August 2012, Russian Foreign Minister Sergei Lavrov underlined Sino-Russian opposition to Western intervention in Syria, a week after a senior envoy dispatched by Syrian President Bashar al-Assad, Bouthaina Shaaban, had held talks in Beijing with Chinese Foreign Minister Yang Jiechi.

In March 2013 Xi visited Africa, where he completed a tour of South Africa, Tanzania and the Republic of the Congo, cementing agreements to build ports in Tanzania and the Congo. Amid criticism that China was engaged in neo-colonial resource-grabbing, Xi said the arrangements were on a basis of equality between developing countries.

China's international diplomacy continued to gather pace in April, when US Secretary of State John Kerry visited Beijing and the two countries showed unexpected common resolve in the face of belligerent rhetoric from North Korea. China's more assertive stance towards Pyongyang indicated its increasing displeasure with its only military ally (see Koreas, pp. 333–348). As North Korea stepped up threats against South Korea and the United States, Beijing became increasingly alarmed as its appeals for calm seemed to fall on deaf ears in Pyongyang.

China's Defence White Paper

Pre-empting the release of the Pentagon's annual report to Congress on China in May, the State Council Information Office issued China's latest Defence White Paper on 16 April 2013. Entitled 'The Diversified Employment of China's Armed Forces', the document marked a significant departure from its predecessors since 1998, which had been called 'China's National Defence'. It resonated with suggestions of increasing rivalry with the United States and its regional allies.

The paper differed from previous iterations by taking a subject-based rather than doctrinal approach and dispensing with much formulaic jargon. The authors attempted to incorporate into the nation's defence planning the concerns that were driving the strategic debate in China over the US rebalancing to the Asia-Pacific region. Some observers suggested that the change in substance and tone of the paper demonstrated the more assertive hand of the new leadership.

Japan was described as 'making trouble' over the Diaoyu/Senkaku dispute (see pp. 322–323), and the paper observed that the US military pivot was making the regional situation in Asia more tense. Resonant of Hu Jintao's discourse on the historic mission of the PLA a decade before, and reflecting China's drive to become a big maritime power, the paper emphasised the need for blue-water naval capabilities – the capacity to sustain operations across oceans – to protect China's sovereignty, sea lines of communication and maritime resources. The White Paper's message was that China's new military capabilities now presented a challenge to the previously unfettered access to the Asia-Pacific region hitherto enjoyed by the US military and its allies.

The Pentagon described China's approach as an anti-access/area denial (A2/AD) strategy, whereby the PLA would seek to deny US forces entry into theatres of operations of strategic importance to China. Washington asserted that without freedom of access, economic growth in Asia would be impeded and global economic recovery would stall. However, Chinese observers viewed this as an excuse to protect American intelligence-gathering activities in China's littoral, and as part of a strategy intended to contain China. Many observers believed that the PLA, constantly irked by the US ability to mount what it perceived as aggressive surveillance missions at sea and in the air along the entire length of China's coast, had abandoned its policy of strategic restraint and was adopting a more assertive and strident posture in the western Pacific.

The annual US Pentagon report to Congress on China's military repeated the usual refrain of encouraging the transparency of China's military modernisation programme. According to figures released at the NPC in March by China's Ministry of Finance, China's defence budget increased by 10.7% to 720bn yuan ($114.3bn), a slight slowing from the official 2012 defence budget increase of 11.2% to $106.4bn. However, US analysts asserted that this figure was about 50% below the real amount being spent on defence. The Pentagon report suggested that as détente continued in relations with Taiwan, China's *casus belli* with the island had been eclipsed by broader aspirations for power projection. But it said China had been less than candid in spelling out how it would use its rapidly modernising forces to protect or enforce its territorial goals. China repeated its customary retort that China's national defence budget accounted for just 1.7% of GDP, compared with the United States figure of more than 4%. It noted that the 2013 White Paper revealed a considerable amount of information about the PLA for the first time, including details of new military equipment and the scheduling of military exercises.

Chinese space capabilities in particular featured prominently in the first half of 2013. According to media reports, on 13 May, China fired a missile into space from the Xichang Satellite Launch centre. Soon afterwards the US DoD released some limited details, confirming the missile reached an altitude of at least 10,000km. The launch did not send anything into orbit and burned up on re-entry, raising US suspicions that it was part of China's anti-satellite programme. The United States was particularly concerned because the range of this missile, if weaponised, would place it in the geosynchronous orbital range of US communications, intelligence and positioning satellites.

The completion of Hainan's Wenchang Space Launch centre – China's answer to Cape Canaveral – will significantly increase China's heavy payload capability. China is planning to launch 100 satellites by 2015, augmenting its already growing space-based imaging and remote-sensing capabilities. The increased pace of launches and China's growing sophistication in this area have significant implications for the PLA's situational awareness using space assets.

The commissioning of China's first aircraft carrier on 25 September 2012 represented a milestone for the PLA Navy after years of speculation over the fate of a Ukrainian hull that had been towed from the Black Sea to China a decade before. The *Liaoning* will serve as a training platform for China's first carrier battle group and may be deployed to the South Sea Fleet's Sanya naval base, allowing force projection into the South China Sea. Two months after commissioning the carrier, on 26 November the PLA performed its first J-15 fighter take-offs and landings on it.

Meanwhile, the Shenyang J-31 multirole stealth fighter completed its maiden flight at the end of October. This fifth-generation fighter, smaller than the J-20 stealth fighter rolled out two years before, was China's answer to the US F-35 *Lightning*. These new stealth-fighter platforms, when integrated with China's increasingly sophisticated intelligence and surveillance networks in the years ahead, could become an important element of the PLA's anti-access and power-projection capabilities in the Western Pacific, the Pentagon suggested. The PLA hinted that, instead of focusing its efforts against US surveillance close to its littoral within and around the first island chain, it had 'reciprocated' US operations in or near China's Exclusive Economic Zone by deploying PLA Navy assets close to Guam and the Pacific Command's base in Hawaii.

China–US cyber attacks

Perhaps the biggest source of Chinese–US friction in 2013 was the accusation that China had targeted the US defence sector with cyber attacks, in pursuit of intelligence that could aid China's defence industry and economic and foreign policy. US official reports and the media noted numerous intrusions orchestrated by the Chinese government and military against the DoD's computer networks, for the purpose of exfiltrating information in a concerted Computer Network Exploitation (CNE) operation.

The Pentagon said the PLA had integrated CNE into its intelligence-gathering infrastructure, and warned that such capabilities could ultimately be used in a similar fashion in a computer network attack designed to disable and disrupt the DoD's operational capabilities during war,

Deadlock in the East China Sea

China and Japan's relationship dipped to a new low as competing territorial claims over the Senkaku/Diaoyu islands in the East China Sea fuelled a number of incidents in waters near the islands. These skirmishes occurred against the backdrop of heightened tension caused by changes to the regional military balance, including China's military build-up and Washington's rebalance towards the Asia-Pacific.

The group of five uninhabited islands and three rocks, named Senkaku by Japan and Diaoyu by China, are officially administered by Japan, but China asserts that the islands have been part of its territory at least since the Ming dynasty. The islands are close to strategically important shipping lanes and fishing grounds, and may contain oil deposits.

In April 2012, Tokyo's right-wing governor, Shintaro Ishihara, revealed plans to purchase three of the five islands from their private owners. The Japanese government, fearful that Ishihara could use them to agitate against China, bought the islands itself in September 2012, effectively nationalising them. This move was regarded by China as an extreme provocation. In response, anti-Japanese riots broke out, with demonstrations in around 85 Chinese cities. Many Japanese-owned businesses were vandalised. Beijing cancelled celebrations for the 40th anniversary of the normalisation of bilateral ties, and its leaders refused to meet Japan's prime minister, Yoshihiko Noda, at various international gatherings. In the UN General Assembly in New York at the end of September, Chinese Foreign Minister Yang Jiechi accused Tokyo of violating China's sovereignty.

In December, the Japanese Air Self-Defense Force (JASDF) scrambled eight F-15 fighters to intercept a Chinese maritime surveillance aircraft of the State Oceanic Administration that flew over the Senkaku/Diaoyu islands. Japanese fighter aircraft were again scrambled in January 2013 in response to PLA Air Force J-10 fighters which were operating near the islands. Only days later, China's state news agency announced that China's mapping agency intended to conduct a survey of the islands as part of a programme to map China's 'territorial islands and reefs' and 'safeguard its maritime rights and interests'. The announcement was interpreted by some as a signal that China intended to challenge Japan's sovereignty further by setting foot on the islands, although it did not specify when the survey would be conducted.

In Japan, Shinzo Abe's return to power in December 2012 could have provided an opportunity to reduce tensions. During his first tenure as Japan's prime minister in 2006–07, he had managed to improve relations and stressed the importance of the bilateral relationship. During his campaign Abe talked tough on the Senkaku/Diaoyu issue and refused to acknowledge the territorial dispute, but once in office he attempted to engage with China. Beijing showed little interest in dialogue and Abe responded by emphasising Japan's sovereignty over the islands. Abe had also signalled that he intended to bolster Japan's national defence forces and amend its pacifist constitution, moves which could provoke China and indicate that Japan would take a more aggressive stance over the islands in the future.

Perhaps the most fraught incident occurred in January, when the Japanese Ministry of Defense claimed that a PLA Navy vessel had activated its missile-guidance system and 'painted' a Japanese Maritime Self-Defense Force (JMSDF) vessel with its fire-control radar (FCR) system. According to the ministry, the Japanese vessel had been conducting surveil-

lance operations 100–150km north of the islands. This followed a similar incident earlier that month when a PLA Navy frigate had briefly painted a Japanese helicopter with its FCR.

China denied the accusation, claiming that its vessels had only been using surveillance radars at the time the incident was meant to have occurred. Japan's defence minister, Itsunori Onodera, said the radar lock-on amounted to a threat of force and was a violation of the UN Charter. Though Japan had been under pressure to release the technical specifications of the radar signature, it has not done so, and while it insisted that the radar signature had all the hallmarks of an FCR system, experts acknowledged that this type of radar can be employed for positioning and scanning without necessarily indicating an intention to open fire.

The FCR lock-on incident brought the PLA and Japanese Self-Defense Forces (JSDF) closer to a clash than ever before, drawing in both countries' navies: until then, involvement was limited to vessels belonging to the Japanese coast guard and China's various maritime enforcement agencies. The US State Department warned that such incidents escalated tension and increased the risk of miscalculation.

While China and Japan seemed reluctant to allow the dispute to escalate into direct military confrontation, diplomatic sparring on the international stage, as well as incidents in the waters around the islands, continued throughout the first half of 2013.

In April, the PLA missile destroyer *Lanzhou* and missile frigate *Hengshui*, both from the PLA Navy's South Sea Fleet, entered waters near the Senkaku/Diaoyu islands via the Miyako Strait to conduct exercises. China's state news agency pointed out that the naval exercises had taken place on the anniversary of the Treaty of Shimonseki, when China ceded Taiwan and affiliated islands to Japan. The treaty was reversed with Japan's defeat in 1945.

In May, an article in China's state newspaper questioned Japan's sovereignty over the island of Okinawa, where 25,000 US troops are stationed, sparking fears that China intended to broaden the territorial dispute. Towards the end of May and into June, China continued to send maritime vessels into waters around the islands.

By June 2013, the situation was at a stalemate. No summit talks between Japan and China had been held for months, after they had agreed to talks the previous June, and progress on an official agreement to set up a 'maritime liaison mechanism' to avoid an accidental clash had also stalled. Following a summit between US President Barack Obama and President Xi Jinping of China, Japan's Abe agreed during a telephone call with Obama on the importance of dialogue with Beijing. But neither side seemed prepared to back down on their entrenched positions. China continued to call for Japan to acknowledge that there was a territorial dispute, while Japan maintained that no such dispute existed.

or in concert with conventional capabilities. Amid growing US frustration over persistent cyber intrusions from China into commercial and government computer networks, the US–China Economic and Security Review Commission's Report to Congress, released in November 2012, devoted a considerable portion to China's impact on US security interests through malicious cyber attacks. It called for congressional committees to conduct an in-depth assessment of Chinese cyber-espionage practices.

In February 2013 the computer network-security company Mandiant released a report which for the first time identified the PLA as responsible for cyber attacks on the US government and corporations. The report went into more detail than any US government information so far made public. It described a secret Chinese military unit, known as Unit 61398, belonging to the PLA General Staff Department's third department, known in intelligence circles as '3PLA', responsible for communications intelligence (COMINT) and Computer Network Operations (CNO).

The report alleged that since 2007, when Unit 61398's new facility had been built in the Pudong suburb of Shanghai, the PLA had systematically hacked into 141 different companies and had exfiltrated enormous amounts of data from its English-speaking targets, predominantly from the United States. It identified three PLA hackers from among the hundreds suspected at Unit 61398, as well as the techniques they employed to compromise, control and exploit the digital networks of their targets.

The United States and China sparred over the issue. President Obama then referred directly to alleged Chinese cyber attacks in a March 2013 television address, revealing that the United States had been talking sternly with China over attacks targeting US companies and government departments. Billions of dollars and industrial secrets had been lost, according to Obama, although he avoided specifics and bellicose language, stating that some attacks had been state-sponsored and some the result of criminal activity.

The Chinese government dismissed Obama's accusations and said China too had been the target of cyber attacks. China's defence ministry had stated in February that Chinese military websites had been attacked from abroad 144,000 times per month on average in 2012, with around 60% of these attacks originating from the United States. China's Internet-security authority, the National Computer Network Emergency

Response Coordination Centre, said 1.9m mainframes in China had been targets of cyber attacks, and that in the first two months of 2013, 6,747 overseas servers had been discovered using malware to exploit the mainframes. China thus sought to deflect attention from the Mandiant report by focusing on the vulnerability of servers located in China to penetration by malware and viruses from abroad.

When Xi and Obama met for their June summit in California, the subject was such a large concern for the United States that the White House tabled cyber security on the summit agenda at a very late stage, which, according to insiders, irritated Xi considerably. The leaks by the former National Security Agency contractor Edward Snowden that came to light later in June may have created a sense of vindication for China, and the issue remained a serious thorn in the side of the Sino-US relationship as the US–China Strategic and Economic Dialogue got under way in July.

Japan: Abe's Radicalism

After a traumatic period in which Japan's turbulent domestic politics were overshadowed by natural disasters and the Fukushima nuclear accident, the country experienced yet more instability and change in the year to mid-2013. The Democratic Party of Japan (DPJ), elected in a landslide in 2009 with a pledge to install a new political regime after almost 60 years of rule by the Liberal Democratic Party (LDP), was swept aside in December 2012 elections. The LDP returned to power, and Shinzo Abe became Japan's seventh premier in six years, a record turnover even for Japan's eventful post-war period. Abe, who had been prime minister for a year in 2006–07, was the first person to return to the office since the 1950s.

The full implications of the shift back to the LDP were not yet clear. On the one hand, Abe's radical approach to economic policies, briefly glimpsed during his previous tenure, seemed to offer a chance of freeing Japan from the economic stagnation of the last two decades. Abe introduced fiscal and monetary stimulus measures that were quickly dubbed 'Abenomics'. In addition, he sought a more dynamic security role within the US–Japan alliance with a view, among other things, to containing China's expanding power. A more sceptical view, however, was that the LDP's return would offer a familiar mix of pork-barrel policies and collusion with special-interest groups, accompanied by high-risk growth strategies and a nationalist view of Japan's imperial legacy that would incense its neighbours.

DPJ's travails

The DPJ's crushing defeat seemed to shut the door, for the time being at least, on the party's ability to influence the national policy agenda. It had taken power in September 2009 after winning 308 lower house seats out of 480, hoping to end the LDP's era of supremacy, which had been characterised by political-bureaucratic collusion, protection of special interests in agriculture and construction, and failure to escape from economic malaise. The DPJ sought to dilute the power of the bureaucracy and direct public spending away from vested interests. It emphasised a welfare- and consumer-oriented growth model.

In practice, the DPJ government found few opportunities to implement this ambitious agenda, encountering resistance from the electorate and within its own party, which was riven by infighting. It was also criticised for its handling of the aftermath of the March 2011 earthquake and tsunami, which killed some 16,000 people.

Its first prime minister, Yukio Hatoyama, found his premiership destabilised from the start by party funding scandals. He resigned after failing to reach agreement with the United States over proposals to relocate the US Marine Corps (USMC) Futenma air station on the island of Okinawa, to which the prefectural government and local municipalities are strongly opposed. Hatoyama's successor, Naoto Kan, had to deal with the 2011 disasters and the resulting Fukushima nuclear accident, consequent demands for the abolition of nuclear power, and a heated debate over whether to raise consumption tax to boost the government's ailing finances. Yoshihiko Noda inherited these issues, and eventually passed legislation in mid-2012 to raise consumption tax from 5% to 10%, but backtracked on promises to seek the abolition of nuclear power. Meanwhile, the DPJ itself began to disintegrate as power broker Ichiro

Ozawa and some of his allies, highly critical of shifts in party policy, formed a splinter party. By the time Noda called elections, the DPJ was being increasingly harried by a reinvigorated Abe, who became party leader in September.

Just as important, however, was the DPJ's failure to implement its policy manifesto. As it lacked government experience, bureaucrats with interests in industrial policy and a desire to control spending still drove much of the policy agenda. The DPJ failed to redirect budgetary priorities to welfare programmes such as special allowances for child-raising; and the implementation of the consumption-tax hike actually contradicted its attempt to focus on consumer-led growth. Indeed, the DPJ seemed to shift further to the right under each successive prime minister, until it began to adopt policies markedly similar to those of the LDP government that it had replaced.

Therefore, the DPJ was ripe for a resounding electoral loss. The LDP added a net 176 seats in the lower house, winning a total of 294 and an absolute majority. In contrast, the DPJ lost 173 seats and was reduced to a rump of 57 members, the worst performance by a governing party in the post-war period. It only just beat the newly-formed Japan Restoration Party (JRP), created through the merger of parties led by Osaka governor Toru Hashimoto and former Tokyo governor Shintaro Ishihara, both local reformers with a strong right-wing nationalist bent. The JRP, as a conservative party, had been expected to challenge the LDP, but in fact its 54 seats took a larger bite out of the DPJ's constituencies.

The LDP's dominance was tempered by its need to form a coalition with the more moderate New Komeito Party to hold a two-thirds supermajority in the lower house, because its lack of a majority in the upper house would otherwise mean that legislation could be blocked there. (Upper house elections were due in July 2013.) Nevertheless, the electorate had decisively rejected the DPJ, swinging Japanese politics back to the right.

'Abenomics'

Abe's 2007 downfall had been caused, at least in part, by a perceived overemphasis on foreign policy at the expense of domestic priorities. This time around, his government was careful to focus first on economic issues.

Measures to revive the economy included a highly expansionary monetary policy; reversal of the DPJ's tax hike; government fiscal stimulus of more than ¥10 trillion through short-term, large-scale spending on construction; and structural reform through easing regulations on companies. This set of steps was designed decisively to break the deflationary cycle that had impeded Japan's growth for close to two decades. Monetary easing was intended to stimulate economic activity and to depreciate the high-valued yen to make exports more competitive, creating a cycle in which jobs, wages, the stock market, consumer spending, company earnings and investment would all rise. The return of inflation to a targeted level of 2% – consumer prices have fallen for most of the last 20 years – would end the deflationary syndrome in which consumers would perpetually put off purchases in the hope of ever-lower prices. Since many Western governments with high debts were attempting a combination of monetary stimulus and fiscal austerity, the 'Abenomics' combination of both monetary and fiscal stimulus was experimental and risky.

Early results were positive. In May 2013, the sharp weakening of the yen took its rate against the dollar above ¥100 for the first time since April 2009, and the stock market was riding high. Abe's dynamic approach was enjoying approval ratings of around 60%. However, the government had few options for fiscal stimulus, given its very high debt-to-GDP ratio. Moreover, any reversal in the depreciation of the yen, or signs that growth was too sluggish, could undermine the approach. There were also signs that 'Abenomics' was making some Japanese uneasy, because inflationary effects were spilling over into long-depressed consumer prices. Further, in the long term, the weakening of the yen threatened to raise prices of energy and food imports on which Japan depends. Signs of potential problems for Abe emerged in May and June with sudden large falls in the stock market and a weakening of the dollar against the yen.

Abe's approach was undoubtedly high-risk, and its chances of success were hard to assess. But the policy underlined his radical style, which could very well be applied to other policy areas if the LDP were to secure control of the upper house. Abe pledged to restart Japan's nuclear-power reactors, which had been shut down after the Fukushima accident, and indicated that in due course he would follow through with other plans left unfinished in 2006–07. This could include revising Japan's apologies over its colonial past, particularly regarding the forced prostitution of South Korean and Chinese women, known as 'comfort women', to serve Japanese Imperial Army soldiers during the Second World War. In 1993, Prime Minister Yohei Kono issued a statement acknowledging the suffering caused by the practice. As prime minister in 2006, Abe made statements that played down Japan's culpability, and after leaving office he advocated revising the apology. In May 2013, the government claimed there were no plans to revise the 1993 statement, but weeks later Toru Hashimoto, the nationalist governor of Osaka, rekindled tensions by suggesting 'comfort women' had been necessary for troop discipline.

Abe also wanted to rewrite parts of the constitution, particularly Article 9 which limits the use of military force to purposes of national security. However, on this controversial issue too, he was initially cautious, although by the run-up to upper house elections in the summer Abe was beginning to talk of making it a key electoral issue.

Bolstering defence and the US alliance

The DPJ had failed to realise its ambitious plans for foreign and security policy, particularly a shift in the focus of Japan's international engagement. It sought to achieve some degree of autonomy from the US–Japan alliance, believing that it restricted Japan's options in international relations and risked embroiling Japan in US-led wars. Although it did want to maintain the alliance, it also wished to restore ties with China and to develop East Asian regional frameworks. However, the DPJ found little opportunity to pursue these objectives. It was pulled into disputes over territory and history with its neighbours, and also locked horns with Washington over the Futenma issue. Consequently, its prime ministers quickly defaulted to focusing on the US alliance and found it difficult to advance regional ties. Thus, in foreign affairs as in domestic, the DPJ was unable to depart much from previous LDP policies.

The DPJ had, however, taken a more proactive defence stance, introducing the concept of 'dynamic defence' in revised National Defense Programme Guidelines in 2010. This enabled Japan for example to build on military ties with Australia and India, and to approve exceptions to the ban on the export of military technology. Abe's government made clear it would go further, seeking an increase of about 1% in the defence budget, the first hike in 11 years, designed to boost the manpower and surveillance capabilities of the Japanese Self-Defense Forces (JSDF) in southwest Japan, and to support Japan's position in the East China Sea island dispute with China. Abe said he would implement his long-held goal of creating a National Security Council to improve government coordination in responding to security crises and natural disasters.

Abe declared that the US alliance was his top priority and that the pace of bilateral security cooperation would be picked up. He confirmed that Japan would press ahead with agreements to relocate the Okinawa facility to Henoko in Nago City in the north of the prefecture, in spite of local resistance. In March, the government took the first steps towards relocation, applying for prefectural authority to begin landfill activities for the construction, off the coast, of the new facility's runway.

Abe signalled willingness to look beyond the issue of Okinawa to discuss wider military cooperation issues. Japan and the United States thus initiated a review of the bilateral Defence Guidelines, which specify areas for cooperation in regional contingencies and had not been revised since 1997. The revised guidelines were expected to focus on augmenting the intelligence, surveillance and reconnaissance activities of the JSDF, particularly in reaction to the growing strength of China's navy, as well as improved cooperation on cyber terrorism, anti-piracy and UN peacekeeping operations. The LDP's interest in relaxing restrictions on Japan's use of armed force is certain to be welcomed by the United States, as it would increase the scope of Japan's potential participation in future US-led bilateral and coalition operations.

Tokyo and Washington were hoping to forge a broader strategic relationship through Japanese membership of the Trans-Pacific Partnership (TPP), a trade agreement under negotiation between the US and Pacific Rim economies. The DPJ government had shown interest in joining, but was mindful of the political drawbacks of liberalising domestic agricultural markets. Abe, also reluctant to alienate the LDP's agricultural base, promised in March 2012 to seek safeguards for domestic producers. Japanese commitment to the TPP would put Japan in line with a US strategy to establish trade standards across the Asia-Pacific region that others, including China, would be encouraged to follow. While Abe and President Barack Obama held a cordial meeting in Washington in February 2013, the precise course of the relationship was likely to depend on Abe's ability to overcome entrenched resistance in Okinawa to the Futenma plans, and to counter domestic opposition to the TPP.

Relations with China on the rocks

Abe was aware of the importance of a strengthened US–Japan relationship so as to have a stronger foundation for approaching, amongst other issues, challenges from China. Sino-Japanese relations, despite the best intentions of the DPJ, deteriorated under Kan and Noda. In the last months of the Noda administration, Japan's territorial dispute with China over islets in the East China Sea called Senkaku by Japan and Diaoyu by China was as fraught as it had ever been (see pp. 322–323).

Abe's election could have been an opportunity to improve Sino-Japanese relations. Despite his nationalist sentiments, Abe had in the past demonstrated pragmatic recognition of the importance of relations with China. He was responsible during his first premiership for a successful initiative to restore ties after a low point under his predecessor, Junichiro Koizumi; he crafted a so-called 'mutually beneficial strategic partnership' that guided relations for several years afterwards. After taking office again, Abe described China as one of Japan's most important partners and as an 'indispensable country' for its economic prosperity.

By mid-2013, though, Abe had been unable to make progress. Beijing showed little interest in dialogue, and Abe responded by repeatedly stressing Japan's undisputed sovereignty and stating that China was stoking nationalist sentiments to boost the legitimacy of the new government of President Xi Jinping. Abe also revisited a theme from his first premiership: the promotion of liberal democratic 'value-oriented' diplomacy, as distinct from Beijing's support for authoritarian regimes. Abe visited Mongolia in March 2013 seeking to promote these values, and planned to visit Russia, the Middle East and South Korea to explore shared interests in constraining China's rising power.

Japan and the Korean peninsula: no progress

Japan also encountered tension with South Korea over colonial history and disputed territory. In June 2012, South Korea unilaterally postponed the signing of a new agreement meant to promote bilateral information sharing in the event of North Korean missile tests. The delay was apparently caused by domestic opposition to closer military ties with Japan, the former imperial power. Ties cooled further when there was a resurgence in South Korea of commemoration of the plight of 'comfort women'. President Lee Myung-bak's visit, the first by an incumbent president, to the disputed Takeshima/Dokdo islets in the Sea of Japan did nothing to reduce the tension.

During Abe's first tenure as prime minister in 2006, he had improved Japan's relationship with South Korea from a low point, but by mid-2013 he had not been able to repeat the achievement, even though the arrival of new leaders in both countries had sparked hopes for a fresh start. Abe dispatched a special envoy, LDP member Fukushiro Nukuga, to Seoul to meet with President-elect Park Geun-hye to emphasise that South Korea was 'Japan's most important country'. However, Park maintained a hardline stance on Japan's colonial history and the island dispute, and was watchful for any signs that Abe would revise Japan's apologies.

Relations further soured over a visit by four cabinet members and more than 100 MPs to the controversial Yasukuni Shrine in April 2013. The shrine honours Japan's war dead, but because this includes several war criminals, is offensive to South Korea, China, and also Australia, who see it as a denial of Japan's culpability for war-time aggression. After the visit, South Korea cancelled its foreign minister's planned trip to Japan. Abe himself had not so far visited the shrine.

Japan–North Korea relations remained difficult. The two states restarted bilateral dialogue in November 2012 following North Korea's failed rocket test in April, but talks were suspended following North Korea's subsequent successful rocket launch. Abe, long a critic of North Korea for its missile and nuclear programmes, had been vocal in demanding redress from North Korea for the abduction of Japanese citizens in the 1970s and 1980s. Following North Korea's third nuclear test in February 2013, Japan tightened its own bilateral financial sanctions in addition to toughened UN sanctions. Abe openly talked of North Korea's potential collapse if it were to continue its provocations.

Electoral test

The return of Abe and the LDP raised questions over Japan's domestic and international trajectory, but these would only begin to be answered after upper house elections scheduled for July 2013, and as the effects of 'Abenomics' began to be seen in the economy. By mid-year, the prime minister had not yet gone ahead with much of his domestic and foreign policy agenda, mindful of the need to maintain favourable public opinion ahead of the vote. However, his party appeared to enjoy robust support, and capture of the upper house could enable it to press ahead with changes to the country's defence stance and the constitution, as well as to its position on the country's colonial history. All of this would be provocative to Japan's neighbours, and could sharpen tensions over territorial disputes.

The Koreas: New Leaders Face Old Challenges

Soon after succeeding his father as ruler of North Korea in December 2011, Kim Jong-un punctured all hopes that his youthful years at a Swiss boarding school would make for a less antagonistic state. Instead, in the year to mid-2013, continuing his father's 'military first' policies, he defied both friends and foes by launching a rocket and testing a nuclear device in contravention of UN Security Council mandates. Among other provocations, he also broke off all communications and economic relations with South Korea and issued threats of nuclear war. Relations between North Korea and the rest of the world thus reached a nadir.

Internal politics partly accounted for his actions. Manufacturing a defence crisis was a way to quell any questions about his fitness for leadership. The young leader also appeared to solidify his domestic position by replacing a number of key generals and giving the Workers' Party a greater role in managing the economy.

Reasons for his belligerent actions were also to be found in foreign relations. Kim may have wanted to test Park Geun-hye, who won a December election to become South Korea's first female head of state. He also sought leverage to press for negotiations with the United States on a peace treaty finally to replace the Korean War armistice. This was a stretch. The US policy of 'strategic patience' makes any negotiations, such as a resumption of long-stalled Six-Party Talks, conditional upon North Korea first taking steps towards denuclearisation, but the North insisted it would never give up its nuclear deterrent until the United States also disarmed.

North Korea's nuclear brinkmanship

A tense five-month period over the winter and spring followed a familiar pattern. On 12 December, the Democratic People's Republic of Korea (DPRK) conducted a successful space launch, then used the UN Security Council's condemnatory response to justify a third nuclear test. It accompanied these actions with a heavy dose of bellicose rhetoric. The December launch came relatively soon after a failed attempt in April 2012. This time, after four failed long-range missile launches over the past decade, the *Unha*-3 rocket succeeded in putting a small satellite into orbit. It was launched from the Tongchang-ri site on North Korea's west coast on a southern trajectory to avoid flying over the Republic of Korea (ROK) or Japan. Pyongyang had bested Seoul, which put its own first satellite into orbit several weeks later. However, the North Korean satellite failed to stabilise, rendering it useless for its ostensible purpose of weather observation.

Much of the world saw a military purpose behind the space launch, which was in contravention of Security Council resolutions that prohibit any activity related to ballistic-missile technology. After successfully recovering the front section of the North Korean missile, South Korea concluded that it was designed to accommodate a nuclear warhead. The successful three-stage separation of the *Unha*-3 had clear implications for development of an intercontinental ballistic missile (ICBM). The UN Security Council responded with a new sanctions resolution which added more individuals associated with the missile programme to a travel-ban and asset-freeze list, but did not explicitly impose any new sanctions on the regime itself. North Korea nevertheless used the Security Council resolution to justify conducting a third nuclear test.

The 12 February nuclear test had an estimated yield of 4–8 kilotonnes, larger than those of the first two tests in 2006 and 2009 of about 0.5kt and 4kt respectively, but less than the approximately 20kt yield that has been the norm for the first nuclear tests of other states. The DPRK government claimed it had exploded a miniaturised device, suggesting progress towards a weapon capable of being mounted onto a North Korean missile. Pyongyang did not indicate whether the device was based on plutonium or highly enriched uranium, and radioactive isotopes collected in Japan two months after the test had decayed too much to determine a specific signature. Many experts suspected that a uranium-based bomb had been detonated. If so, this would indicate the DPRK has a second path to nuclear weapons that is both easier to hide than plutonium and easier to sell because it can more simply be fashioned into crude weapons, even by non-state actors.

The nuclear test sparked another set of sanctions, this time intended to inflict real penalties. Among other provisions, Resolution 2094 targeted illicit activities of DPRK diplomatic personnel, transfers of bulk cash and the nation's banking relationships, and specified a list of several luxury goods denied to North Korea. To the surprise of most observers, China went beyond these measures by cutting ties with the DPRK's Foreign Trade Bank following moves by the United States and Japan to deny that bank access to their financial systems. Several other North Korean bank outlets in China also reportedly had accounts closed.

The extent of North Korea's strategic capabilities remained open to debate. The US Defense Intelligence Agency expressed 'moderate confidence' in the DPRK's ability to deliver a nuclear weapon via a ballistic missile. This assessment was not shared by other US intelligence agencies, however, and US Director of National Intelligence James Clapper said: 'North Korea has not yet demonstrated the full range of capabilities necessary for a nuclear armed missile.' In May 2013, the US Department of Defense assessed that the missile used in the 12 December space launch 'could reach parts of the United States if configured as an intercontinental ballistic missile capable of carrying a nuclear payload', but noted that the space launch did not test a re-entry vehicle. The DPRK sought to enhance its power-projection capability by releasing photographs of supposed target sites for a missile strike on the US mainland. For the time being, however, the missiles in North Korea's inventory that are known to have been tested threaten only South Korea and Japan. In April, North Korea deployed to its east coast two untested road-mobile *Musudan* missiles, estimated by the United States to have a maximum range of 4,000km – enough to reach Guam – although several private experts believe the range is considerably less.

Notwithstanding the nuclear test, the DPRK's adversaries and neighbours remained reluctant to conclude that it possessed deliverable nuclear weapons. On political grounds, South Korea, Japan, the United States and even China (privately) repeated that they could not accept North Korea as a nuclear-armed state. North Korea is known, however, to have enough plutonium for up to ten bombs. In April 2013 the North announced its intention to restart the 5MW(e) reactor at Yongbyon, which several years ago had produced that plutonium but which had been dormant since 2007. As of June, the reactor appeared one to two months away from start-up. An experimental light-water reactor under construction at Yongbyon and apparently on track for completion in mid-2014 would also be able to produce plutonium. The uranium-enrichment programme that North Korea revealed in 2010 may be capable of producing enough fissile material for one or more weapons a year, but nothing is known about whether it has been put to weapons purposes.

The nuclear and missile tests were merely two episodes in the North's brinkmanship in the year to mid-2013. In response to the Security Council sanctions and an annual US–ROK military exercise, North Korea threatened to conduct a 'pre-emptive nuclear strike' on the United States and released clips on YouTube depicting attacks on the White House. One, copied in part from an American video game, depicted a dream sequence of an attack on New York City. Among other rhetorical flourishes, Kim was quoted telling front-line troops: 'Once an order is issued, you should break the waists of the crazy enemies, totally cut their windpipes and thus clearly show them what a real war is like.' Repeating past threats, the North stated the armistice that ended the Korean War was 'totally nullified', announced that South–North relations had entered a 'state of war' and said Seoul would be reduced to a 'sea of fire' if the

North itself was attacked. The DPRK advised foreigners to leave Seoul and told diplomats in Pyongyang that their safety could not be ensured in the event of a conflict. A military hotline to the South was cut, and so too was a Red Cross hotline. In April, in addition to restoring its plutonium-production capability, North Korea closed the Kaesong Industrial Complex. Cyber attacks on South Korean businesses in March were traced to North Korea. Tensions subsided in early May when North Korea reportedly moved two *Musudan* missiles back from a launch site on the east coast, only to briefly flare again when the North fired six short-range rockets over three days. There was no telling, however, whether the *Musudan* or other missiles might be tested later or when a new atmosphere of crisis could again be triggered.

A combination of domestic politics, North–South rivalry and a desire for negotiations with the United States may best explain the logic behind Kim's mounting provocations. Although his succession following his father's death had proceeded more smoothly than many had expected, the manufacturing of an external crisis may have been intended to solidify internal unity, which might otherwise have been frayed by a series of purges and bureaucratic power shifts. North Korea also has a history of mounting provocations to test new South Korean leaders. Some analysts even suspected the December 2012 missile test was timed to ensure victory by the conservative Park Geun-hye rather than her leftist opponent in order to maintain a convenient arch-enemy.

There was also no doubt that North Korea wanted a peace treaty with the United States that would formally end the Korean War. Pyongyang sought to negotiate on equal terms with the nuclear-powered United States, relegating South Korea to a minor role. The desire for dialogue was evident when former US basketball star Dennis Rodman visited Pyongyang and spent time with Kim Jong-un, the first and only American to meet the young leader. Upon Rodman's return to the United States, he relayed that Kim 'wants Obama to do one thing: call him'. President Barack Obama was in no mood to do so, however. His administration emphasised that the United States would maintain the policy of 'strategic patience', forgoing negotiations, either bilaterally or multilaterally via the Six-Party Talks (which remained moribund), until North Korea took actions to demonstrate a renewed commitment to denuclearisation.

Kim Jong-un's report card

While 'military first' remained North Korea's national credo, underscored by bristling weapons programmes, the political role of the military was taken down a notch. Through a series of high-level purges and moves to elevate the position of the Korean Workers' Party (KWP) relative to that of the military, Kim Jong-un consolidated power and appeared to be in full control. In the most surprising of these moves, Kim convened an unusual Sunday meeting of the Workers' Party Central Committee Politburo on 15 July 2012 to remove the head of the army, Vice Marshal Ri Yong-ho. As one of the four military officers among the seven casket bearers at Kim Jong-il's funeral, Ri was considered to be a key mentor for the young successor. In November, Kim Jong-gak, another pall-bearer and vice marshal, was removed from his position as minister of the People's Armed Forces and later purged from other top positions. The man who replaced him lasted only six months. A third pall-bearer, U Tong-chuk, director of the North's secret police and spy agency under Kim Jong-il, had been quietly purged in March 2012, and another military official among the pall-bearers was also demoted.

These purges were undoubtedly related to a power struggle between the military and the Workers' Party, which had been subordinate for most of Kim Jong-il's tenure. It was reported that Kim had taken away the military's control over foreign currency-earning operations, such as mineral exports and illicit trade, a large source of power and prestige in the DPRK system. The repeated changes of defence ministers and other key military positions may also be an attempt by Kim to protect against any prospect of a military coup.

Meetings of the Workers' Party and Supreme People's Assembly in March and April 2013 further elevated government bureaucrats and party officials at the expense of the military. The Workers' Party Central Committee was downsized from 19 to 17 members, demoting three positions for military members from full membership to alternate while adding a full membership position for another official, meaning that government and party officials now outnumbered the military by seven members instead of only three. This shift was highlighted by the return of reformer Pak Pong-ju, who served as premier from 2003–07 during a time of limited economic experimentation.

The meetings also determined that possession of nuclear weapons should be fixed as a matter of law, never to be traded away, and that nuclear and missile programmes should serve as a means of supporting economic development and foreign trade and investment, defying critics who pointed out the incompatibility of this approach. South Korea estimated that the North's strategic weapons had cost roughly US$3bn over the last 15 years, and that the missile launch cost US$850m, enough to buy 2.5m tonnes of corn. The nuclear and missile tests also led to the loss of foreign trade and investment.

In his style, demeanour and even girth, Kim Jong-un consciously emulated his charismatic grandfather, the country's founding father Kim Il-sung. In contrast to the public reticence of Kim Jong-il, who is recorded as having spoken but a single sentence in public during his 17-year reign, Kim Jong-un kept up a series of public addresses, including one on New Year's Day that replaced the traditional New Year's newspaper editorial that annually laid out the regime's policies. Joined by his stylish wife, Ri Sol-ju (who gave birth to a girl in December), the new leader was featured attending amusement parks and pop concerts featuring Mickey Mouse costumes and music by Frank Sinatra. The Moranbong Band, a new all-female musical group reportedly created personally by Kim Jong-un, shunned traditional Korean clothing for short black dresses. Kim also paid many visits to military units, with whom he was often photographed grinning and pressing the flesh.

The smiling change of style was not accompanied, however, by any clear-cut positive changes in policy. Adopting a conciliatory tone, for example, Kim said in his New Year's address it was time to 'remove confrontation between the North and the South'. Yet two days later, North Korea's highest state body, the National Defence Commission (NDC), reverted to form in a threatening statement that condemned the ROK leadership in vile terms. Kim continued – and even stepped up – the regime's domestic control and political suppression. Tougher border security to crack down on refugees leaving the country probably accounted for the near-halving of North Korean defectors to South Korea: 1,508 in 2012 compared to 2,706 in 2011. As another means of stemming the tide, the government began holding press conferences featuring confessions of re-defectors: people who had fled North Korea for China and then South

Korea, only to return. Although Kim reportedly closed Camp 22, a concentration camp for political prisoners near the Chinese border, satellite imagery suggested the regime had expanded the notorious Camp 14, further inland near Kaechon. UN High Commissioner for Human Rights Navi Pillay said in January 2013 that North Korea's deplorable human-rights situation 'has no parallel anywhere in the world' and in June expressed concern over the role Laos and China played in repatriating nine North Korean orphans who had sought asylum. In March the UN Human Rights Council agreed to establish a Commission of Inquiry to investigate violations, with a view toward possibly finding the DPRK leadership guilty of crimes against humanity.

In one reform, the North Korean government allowed foreigners to bring in their own telephones and to access the Internet inside the country, though foreign phones could not call DPRK citizens and North Koreans were still banned from using the Internet. The North also opened the border city of Sinuiju to Western tourists for the first time. Meanwhile the North's scaremongering rhetoric worked on at least one of the few prominent Western companies willing to invest: Kempinski Hotels pulled out of contract negotiations in April 2013 after previously indicating its intention to finish construction of the long-abandoned Ryugyong Hotel in Pyongyang.

Hints of economic reform

Through the strategic-weapons programmes, Kim sought to fulfil at least one half of his father's pledge to lead the DPRK to become a 'strong and prosperous' nation. He failed to deliver, however, on his pledge to ensure that North Koreans would no longer have to 'tighten their belts again'. In a speech on 28 June 2012, Kim foretold reforms for agricultural policy somewhat similar to China's path under Deng Xiaoping, based on incentivising production through greater private control over harvests and smaller work teams. It took many months, however, for evidence to emerge that this change was being put into practice. On the same day that the reformist premier Pak was rehabilitated, the government announced greater freedom for local managers of farms, factories, and enterprises to set wages and even offer pay rises. The most significant economic change, however, was not planned. Use of the local currency was being supplanted by demand for Chinese yuan and US dollars, a development that undercuts the state's control over the marketplace.

All was not grim in North Korea. Harvests in 2012 were up by roughly 10%, according to the UN World Food Programme. The country still could not produce enough food to feed its population, but the shortfall shrank 30% to 210,000 tonnes. In March 2013, North Korea reportedly reinstated a system of state food distribution that had been largely dormant for two decades. Living conditions visibly improved in Pyongyang, with more electricity, mobile phones, kiosks, restaurants and automobile traffic. Yet rural residents remained impoverished and suffered from malnutrition. Meanwhile, increased access to sources of foreign information – albeit still restricted – made clear to a growing number of North Korean citizens that their cousins in South Korea and neighbours in China were living much better lives. Whether this knowledge was leading to the kind of discontent that sparked grass-roots movements for change in the Arab world was hard to say due to the state's near-absolute control over public speech and assembly.

To earn more hard currency to finance the regime, the government dispatched tens of thousands of labourers to work in China, Russia and other countries. The regime collects upwards of 75% of the workers' salaries directly, although they still make five times more than they would at home.

US–DPRK relations

Washington responded forcefully to North Korea's provocations by strengthening its alliances with South Korea and Japan, as well as increasing its military activity in the region. Augmenting the regularly scheduled large-scale *Foal Eagle* military exercise with South Korea in March–April 2013, the US sent nuclear-capable B-2 and B-52 bombers to fly near the border and simulate bombing runs, along with an F-22 combat aircraft, as much to reassure the South as to deter the North. A nuclear attack submarine and two *Aegis* missile destroyers were deployed off South Korean waters. In direct response to North Korea's missile threats, the United States bolstered missile defences in the region, announcing that the Terminal High Altitude Area Defense system would be sent to Guam and 14 additional ground-based missile interceptors would be deployed to Alaska to join 30 already located there and in California. Secretary of State John Kerry and General Martin Dempsey, Chairman of the Joint Chiefs of Staff, separately visited South Korea and Japan to reassure them of the US commitment to their security and the credibility of extended deterrence. The ROK, however, declined to participate in an integrated US ballistic-missile defence system on the grounds that the high-cost hardware would not add appreciably to South Korea's independent low-tier missile shield and could harm relations with China.

The United States accompanied its military posturing with offers for talks with Pyongyang, even though, in accordance with the policy of 'strategic patience', a resumption of Six-Party Talks on denuclearisation and related issues is conditioned on DPRK progress towards denuclearisation. In return, Pyongyang made future talks conditional on an end to Washington's 'hostile' policies and acceptance of the DPRK as a nuclear state. The United States has conducted secret discussions with the DPRK on numerous occasions since Kim Jong-il's death, but to no avail. Officials from the White House and intelligence community reportedly flew to Pyongyang in April and August 2012 and State Department officials met sporadically with the DPRK's ambassador to the UN. However, these contacts did not produce any significant improvement in relations, as North Korean interlocutors repeatedly expressed the DPRK's rejection of the 19 September 2005 Joint Statement, the last significant agreement to denuclearise the peninsula. Kenneth Bae, a naturalised US citizen arrested in North Korea in November 2011, apparently while leading a tour, was sentenced in May to 15 years of hard labour for allegedly attempting to overthrow the government. Pyongyang announced that it would not follow the pattern of previous cases in which five US citizens who were similarly arrested were released after high-profile visits by US envoys.

DPRK–China relations

In addition to antagonising its adversaries, North Korea angered its main ally by ignoring China's demands to stop its provocations. After a flurry of diplomatic visits throughout the summer of 2012, political relations between the two allies turned cold, then icy.

In August 2012 Chinese Politburo member Wang Jiarui visited Pyongyang as the first foreigner to meet Kim Jong-un after his succession. This appeared to set the stage for Kim's first visit to Beijing. But Kim never made the trip, reportedly rebuffing numerous invitations. In November, Politburo member Li Jianguo led a delegation to Pyongyang carrying a letter from new leader Xi Jinping, but failed to persuade Kim to abandon plans for a missile launch. China criticised the December space launch and February nuclear test and voted in favour of both new UN sanctions resolutions. The Bank of China's halting of all dealings with the DPRK's Foreign Trade Bank reflected a new get-tough attitude, although this may not have been the result of a direct order from the highest levels of the Chinese government. After the nuclear test, Xi said: 'No one should be allowed to throw a region and even the whole world into chaos for selfish gain.' New premier Li Keqiang warned that: 'Provocations on the Korean Peninsula will harm the interests of all sides and it is the same as picking up a rock to drop it on one's feet.' There was also unprecedented public discussion of China's policy towards the DPRK, including prominent academics calling for China to abandon North Korea and government officials revealing debates over whether to 'keep or dump [...] fight or talk' with North Korea. Exacerbating China's increasingly negative public sentiment toward the North, Chinese fishermen were kidnapped in May 2013 by uniformed North Koreans and held for two weeks before being released. The Chinese media implicated the Korean People's Army in more direct coverage than a similar incident in May 2012.

In an attempt to repair ties, Kim sent Vice Marshal Choe Ryong-hoe, who ranks about third in the North Korean hierarchy, to Beijing in late May. It was not clear whether Choe accomplished his objective, other than to be accorded a meeting with President Xi, who told him to stop the nuclear testing. The official Chinese media reported that Choe signalled a willingness to return to Six-Party Talks, but the DPRK media was conspicuously silent on this point. In any case, North Korea showed no hint of returning to the denuclearisation pledge that is a sine qua non for the United States, ROK and Japan to resume the talks.

Under Xi, China appeared more willing to pressure North Korea and to give higher priority to denuclearisation. Unconfirmed reports also emerged that Beijing now understood the need to discuss contingency planning in the event of a systemic breakdown in the DPRK, a once taboo topic. North Korea also figured prominently in discussions between Xi and Obama in June 2013, possibly signalling increased interest in pursuing closer cooperation with the United States. Despite these changes, however, China was still unlikely to abandon Pyongyang, given the longstanding military and party ties between the two.

The economic side of the relationship stagnated as bilateral trade grew just 5.4% in 2012 to $6bn, a dramatic slowdown from the over 60% increase in 2011. North Korea's eagerness to expand trade was emphasised during a visit to Beijing by Kim's uncle Jang Song-taek in August 2012. The visit concluded with a series of agreements reconfirming China's commitment to two joint economic zones along the border, but progress was slower than expected. The withdrawal of China's largest investor, the Xiyang Group, from its $40m investment in an iron-ore mine near the southwest coast, accompanied by public accusations that the DPRK government had forcefully seized property, revived concerns about North Korean capriciousness.

South Korea: presidential election

Park Geun-hye, of the conservative Saenuri (New Frontier) Party, defeated Democratic United Party candidate Moon Jae-in with 51.6% of the vote in South Korea's presidential election on 20 December 2012. However, Korea's first female leader for thirteen centuries did not get a honeymoon period as she faced significant challenges, including the North's aggression.

The presidential campaign was unprecedented for South Korea in that a third-party candidate seemingly stood a chance of winning. But the candidacy of Ahn Cheol-soo, a software tycoon turned independent politician, threatened to split the liberal vote and to hand Park an easy victory. Ahn therefore sacrificed his campaign in favour of Moon, but to no avail. Park won by amassing a large majority of the elderly vote in a country that is rapidly ageing. The main campaign issue for all candidates was 'economic democratisation', which meant lifting social spending and curbing the power of the *chaebol*, family-run conglomerates that dominate the South Korean economy and are often seen to unfairly squeeze smaller rivals. The combined assets of the top five *chaebol* are equal to 57% of the country's GDP, and the companies have had a cosy relationship with successive governments in Seoul. With Moon promising to abolish the circular shareholding system that keeps the founding families in control, the *chaebol* were undoubtedly relieved by Park's victory. She took over a country with diminished growth prospects, meaning any such moves would likely be watered down anyway. The government's growth estimate for 2012, at 2.1%, was the weakest for three years, and exports fell 5.5%, partly due to the won rising strongly against the US dollar in 2012. Exports represent about 50% of South Korea's GDP, making it unlikely that Park would in any case manage to break the dominance of major exporters like Samsung, LG, and Hyundai.

In contrast to poor export figures, the nation's cultural exports rose to new heights, with continued popularity of Korean pop stars and soap operas throughout Asia, including North Korea. One artist in particular, who goes by his initials, PSY, garnered global fame when his 'Gangnam Style' song-and-dance number became the most-watched YouTube video ever.

Inter-Korean stand-off

Park's election meant Kim was no longer the newest leader on the peninsula, nor the only child of a Korean political elite in power. She had been born into Korean political royalty; her father, Park Chung-hee, was South Korea's leader from 1961 until his assassination in 1979. She had filled in as 'first lady' after her mother was killed in 1974 by a North Korean assassin who was aiming for her father.

Park campaigned on a policy of 'trustpolitik' with North Korea, calling for more engagement and a three-step approach to economic assistance, starting with humanitarian aid decoupled from the nuclear issue. Pending denuclearisation, large-scale economic cooperation would be provided. However, North Korea's third nuclear test, which came shortly before her 25 February inauguration, put 'trustpolitik' ambitions out of reach for the time being. After her inauguration, North Korea cited the 'venomous swish of skirt' as the cause of tensions on the peninsula.

By spring 2013, inter-Korean relations had reached their lowest point in years, with no substantial political or economic contact between the two nations at all. The only communication was the onslaught of North Korea's threatening rhetoric. Having heard it all before, most South Koreans went about their daily lives without disturbance. Opinion polls did, nevertheless, show a slight shift in favour of South Korea acquiring its own nuclear-weapons capability – two-thirds of the public voiced support in both 2012 and 2013, but the number voicing 'strong support' went up about 5%.

The closure of the Kaesong Industrial Complex eliminated the last significant form of cooperation between the two Koreas. The hallmark of former president Kim Dae-jung's 'Sunshine Policy', the jointly run economic zone located just north of the demilitarised zone started in 2003, combining South Korean capital, materials and eventually 1,000 managers with 53,000 inexpensive North Korean labourers. On 3 April, North Korea stopped access to the site from South Korea. Most managers stayed put, expecting the shutdown to be temporary, as had happened before. However, to spite those in South Korea who predicted that Pyongyang would not deprive itself of US$90m in annual hard-currency earnings, North Korea removed all workers from the site six days later, dispersing them to work elsewhere, including in China. By May the plant was completely closed.

Difficult regional relations

Like the North in its relations with China, South Korea annoyed a major partner when, in August 2012, Lee Myung-bak became the first ROK president to visit the Dokdo Islands, which Japan also claims under the name of Takeshima. The trip came ahead of the 67th anniversary of Korea's liberation from Japan and followed controversy over a set of low-level military cooperation agreements with Japan that were supposed to be signed in June 2012 but were postponed indefinitely by the ROK National Assembly. Lee used his Dokdo trip to strengthen his party's nationalist credentials before the presidential election. Japan repaid the offence in the spring when four cabinet members of its new government visited the controversial Yasukuni Shrine, which honours war criminals (along with 2.5m other Japanese war dead) and the popular mayor of Osaka said the system of 'comfort women', which forced many Korean women into prostitution, had been necessary R&R for Japanese soldiers.

China and South Korea meanwhile have had a frayed relationship since Beijing's muted reaction to North Korean provocations in 2010. Efforts were made, however, to improve ties through exchanges of envoys and letters between the two new leaders. In March 2013 South Korea held the first round of talks for a trilateral free-trade agreement that would include Japan. In April, China and South Korea opened a hotline for consultations on North Korea policy.

Seoul tests Washington

The US–ROK alliance remained strong in the face of the common DPRK adversary, but it did not go untested. At a 7 May 2013 bilateral summit, the two presidents reaffirmed shared values and the 2011 KORUS bilateral free-trade agreement. They also expressed agreement on North Korea policy, including US support for Park's 'trustpolitik' should her government deem it appropriate to give economic carrots to Pyongyang in case of a moderation in North Korean behaviour.

Seoul, nevertheless, had sought exemption from two kinds of US non-proliferation restraints. One request was granted and the other postponed. In October 2012, Washington accepted Seoul's call to extend the range of its own missiles from 300km to 800km, in order to bring all of North Korea within range. Even though this exceeded the limits of the Missile Technology Control Regime and was potentially destabilising in terms of Pyongyang's reaction, the United States agreed following direct and repeated appeals by Lee to Obama.

The ROK also asked for exemption from a bar on reprocessing US-origin nuclear fuel and on enriching uranium, contained in a bilateral nuclear cooperation agreement that was to expire in March 2014. Such prohibitions are included in most US bilateral nuclear cooperation agreements, but not those with Japan and India. A desire for parity with Japan motivated Seoul's request, although the arguments were couched on economic and technical grounds. Despite the South's insistence that the dual-use technologies would only be used for peaceful purposes, and that the United States should trust its ally, Washington could not ignore the growing murmurs in South Korean political circles that the nation should have its own nuclear-weapons option in response to North Korea. In May it was decided simply to extend the current agreement for two more years, and to postpone the disagreement. As a coincidental compensation, South Korea finally succeeded in an eight-year campaign to win US congressional approval for the purchase of four *Global Hawk* unmanned aerial vehicles to assist with surveillance of the North. However, a price of up to US$1.2bn, nearly three times Seoul's first estimate, could prove prohibitive.

Can US policy be maintained?

So far, 'strategic patience' has not succeeded in bringing about positive change in North Korea. Pyongyang is instead moving further away from the denuclearisation pledge and closer to projecting nuclear power over long ranges. With President Park still intent on engagement based on 'trustpolitik', there is a danger of divergence between the allies. If North Korea refrains from further provocations, it is possible that the Obama administration will look for ways to re-engage – for example, if the North were to put real emphasis on economic development, as potentially signalled by the 'reformist' prime minister.

However, the more likely scenario is that North Korea's impetuous young leader will remain intent on demonstrating his power. If he does so by conducting the kind of cross-border attacks that left 50 South Koreans dead in two incidents in 2010, Seoul will be determined to respond forcefully. Developments from that point on would be anyone's guess. Possessing nuclear weapons could make Kim bolder, and lead to the nightmare of a full-scale war. Preventing such an outcome will be a high priority for Washington and its allies.

Australia: Policy Initiatives Precede Leadership Change

Australia's Labor government produced three important policy documents in the year to mid-2013: an 'Asian Century' White Paper, a National Security Strategy and a Defence White Paper. All were designed to signal new directions, and their delivery within the space of a year was also intended to lend a greater sense of coherence to foreign and defence policy. The last of the trio, the Defence White Paper, noted that 'these three documents should be seen together as a statement of the priority the Government places on Australia's security and prosperity, and on maintaining a strong Australian Defence Force to meet Australia's national security challenges.'

As fiscal conditions tightened, the release of three White Papers was arguably designed to demonstrate the credentials of an increasingly unpopular government. However, the defence policy debate was more than overshadowed by the government's political difficulties, and in June 2013 Kevin Rudd was reappointed prime minister after a party coup that mirrored his removal three years previously, when he had been unceremoniously replaced by Julia Gillard. On both occasions, senior Labor parliamentarians decided that their electoral fortunes would benefit from a leadership change. Since the 2010 election, in which Labor and opposition parties won an equal number of seats, Gillard had headed a government that depended for survival on support from a small number of independent MPs. Throughout this difficult tenure, her leadership was under threat from a vengeful Rudd, who was seen as more popular with the electorate but less so among cabinet colleagues, many of whom resigned when Gillard was ousted. Elections must be held by end-November 2013, and polling in July showed Labor closing on its conservative rivals, with now an even chance of winning.

Trio of papers

The timing and content of the three policy documents were criticised by some commentators for their politicised nature. Despite being ranked by the Organisation for Economic Co-operation and Development (OECD) as the world's 'happiest' industrialised nation for the third year running, economic storm clouds were gathering on the horizon for Australia, a country that in 2008–09 was the envy of most of the Western world as it avoided the worst effects of the global financial crisis. While strong Asian demand for raw materials contributed toward that outcome, flagging demand has since given rise to warnings – particularly from opposition politicians – of an emerging 'budget emergency'.

The first document, on 'Australia in the Asian Century', was the least well-received. Commissioned by Gillard in 2011, its publication was troubled and did not occur until October 2012. A task force led by former Treasury department secretary Ken Henry was initially charged with producing a document of 150–200 pages. When a 500-page draft was delivered, however, the government seconded Allan Gyngell, Director General of the Office of National Assessments, an intelligence agency, to undertake a rewrite. The resultant White Paper sought to provide a 'roadmap' for Australia to 'navigate' its way through the so-called 'Asian century', and included 25 national objectives to be achieved by the year 2025. It was criticised for being overambitious and under-resourced.

The National Security Strategy, released in January 2013, received a kinder reception. Considerably thinner at 48 pages, it 'lays out the pillars of Australia's national security and sets direction for the next five years'. Produced by the Department of the Prime Minister and Cabinet, it was the first such document written by an Australian government, following on from a National Security Statement delivered to parliament by Rudd in December 2008.

The strategy proclaimed an end to the '9/11' decade and emphasised a return of great-power competition – particularly in Asia – coupled with the emergence of a growing cyber-security challenge. An eminent defence academic and former official, Paul Dibb, described it as 'highly focused, disciplined and concentrating on the hard-edged risks'. Former Secretary of the Department of Foreign Affairs and Trade Michael L'Estrange said it signified 'a change of direction that is clear and important'. However, praise was not universal: former army chief Peter Leahy criticised as 'dangerous' the presumption that the 9/11 decade was over. In his terms, 'the global terrorist threat remains strong. We will most likely endure many more decades during which terrorism will feature as a persistent and dangerous threat.'

The final document, the Defence White Paper, received a more mixed response. Released in early May 2013, it was praised in part for its more nuanced approach to rising China. This stood in marked contrast to its 2009 predecessor, which was reportedly influenced heavily by Rudd and implied that Canberra viewed China as an adversary. The 2013 version stated that Australia 'does not approach China as an adversary' and did not need to 'choose between its longstanding Alliance with the United States and its expanding relationship with China'. Yet it was criticised by some commentators for 'kowtowing' to China, Australia's leading trading partner, which had openly expressed its displeasure at the contents of the 2009 version.

A more conciliatory approach to Beijing notwithstanding, the 2013 Defence White Paper restated the Australian government's commitment to purchasing advanced air and naval platforms. Canberra confirmed that Australia remained committed to purchasing the US-made F-35 *Lightning*. As the aircraft is delayed, with first deliveries not expected in Australia until 2020, the government announced plans to purchase an additional 12 US F-18 *Super Hornet* fighter aircraft fitted with the *Growler* electronic warfare system. Canberra remained committed to purchasing 12 submarines with the caveat that these would be manufactured in Australia and based either on an evolution of the existing *Collins* class or on a new design.

Most criticism of the paper centred on the mismatch between promised platforms and lack of detail on how these would be funded. At about 1.5% of gross domestic product (GDP), the defence budget is at its lowest level since 1938. The White Paper announced an aspiration to return defence expenditure to 2% of GDP when fiscal conditions permitted, with no time frame specified. The government sought to justify the spending decline as a 'peace dividend' following the winding down of military operations in Afghanistan and Iraq.

Such logic did not play well in Washington, with strains in the US–Australia alliance reportedly due to Canberra's unwillingness to take on a greater share of the defence burden in an increasingly contested and strategically demanding region. The issue was raised formally at the annual bilateral ministerial meeting held in November 2012. However, such strains were not readily apparent in any of the three documents. The Defence White Paper referred to the US–Australia alliance as 'our most important defence relationship' while the National Security Strategy characterised the alliance as a 'pillar' of Australia's approach to national security. That said, while much of the focus of the previous year had been on the rotation of up to 2,500 marines through Darwin in the north of Australia – announced by US President Barack Obama during his November 2011 visit to Australia – slight signs of cooling were evident on the Australian side. The Defence White Paper, for instance, raised the issue of possible collaboration in Western Australia at the HMAS Stirling base near Perth, but observed that 'decisions on future options for increased US naval cooperation in Australia require further consideration by both governments'.

Particularly following the softer tone towards China evident in the Defence White Paper, there was some speculation that Canberra's reticence towards Washington was also born of deference to Beijing. Such conjecture was fuelled by an April 2013 visit to China by Gillard, who announced the establishment of a new 'strategic partnership' between the two countries. This had apparently been proposed by Beijing during the premiership of John Howard, but was turned down. Revived by Gillard, it will see the Australian prime minister meet annually with the Chinese premier. Separate foreign minister and treasurer dialogues will be held, in addition to 'working level' talks between the Australian Department of Defence and the People's Liberation Army on regional-security issues. Some Australian commentators were sceptical, saying this was simply a repackaging of measures already in place. Others were concerned that it sent the wrong message and lurched back too far in the opposite direction from the tone of the 2009 White Paper.

There was speculation that these foreign- and defence-policy initiatives had been driven predominantly by electoral considerations. During much of Gillard's premiership, she battled flagging public support while Rudd – whom she deposed in June 2010 – remained popular with the public, though less so within the Labor Party. Rudd had contested the party leadership in February 2012 after resigning as foreign minister. When another contest was offered in March 2013, Rudd opted not to take part and issued a statement that: 'There are no circumstances under which I will return to the Labor Party leadership in the future.' Gillard remained unopposed as leader. In January 2013 she made an unusually early announcement that the next general election would be held in September. Then, in June, Rudd finally had his revenge as Gillard was forced by political manoeuvring to call an instant vote within the parliamentary party, and was ousted. After three years of bitter politics, Rudd said: 'Let us try, just try, to be a little kinder and gentler with each other in the deliberations of this parliament.'

New Zealand: US Relations Deepen

As signs of strain emerged in the US–Australia strategic relationship, security ties between Washington and Wellington continued on their upward trajectory. In June 2012, the New Zealand Defence Minister and US Secretary of Defense signed the so-called Washington Declaration, a companion to the 2010 Wellington Declaration that had brought an end to a 25-year freeze in bilateral defence relations.

Though non-binding, the June 2012 agreement established regular high-level dialogues and increased US-New Zealand cooperation in maritime security, counter-terrorism and counter-proliferation in the Asia-Pacific. For the first time in 28 years, New Zealand joined the annual *Rimpac* military exercises in mid-2012 – though New Zealand naval vessels were not permitted to dock at US military ports due to a ban still in place following the ANZUS crisis of the mid-1980s over US nuclear-ship visits to New Zealand. In September 2012 Leon Panetta became the first US Secretary of Defense to visit New Zealand in 30 years, and announced that the ban on New Zealand vessels would be lifted. However, US naval ships remained barred from New Zealand.

The year to mid-2013 period saw the withdrawal from Afghanistan of New Zealand forces which since 2003 had been operating as part of a Provincial Reconstruction Team (PRT), serving primarily in Bamyan province, which had been among the most peaceful. As one of the first provinces to be transitioned to local control, however, it attracted increased Taliban attention. In August 2012 two New Zealand Defence Force (NZDF) soldiers were killed and six wounded in a firefight. Two weeks later, a further three were killed by a roadside bomb. The government had already announced that the NZDF would withdraw from Afghanistan in late 2013, a year earlier than scheduled. The five fatalities – bringing the total of New Zealand troops killed in the campaign to ten – sparked a public debate as to whether the withdrawal should be brought forward even further; it was, as troops began pulling out in April 2013, with the exception of a small number to be stationed in Kabul in non-combat roles.

Southwest Pacific: Steps to Democracy

Following a constitutional crisis that saw Papua New Guinea (PNG) having two prime ministers, two cabinets, two governors-general, two police commissioners and a state of emergency declared in May 2012, the following year saw elections completed that resolved the dilemma and brought some sense of political stability.

While the elections were held from 23 June–6 July, 181 Australian military personnel were deployed to help provide security. Nevertheless, more than 20 people were killed during the campaigning and voting stages, and there were allegations of large numbers of eligible voters being left off the electoral roll, as well as electoral corruption. However, election observers were satisfied that the elections did not fail completely and were an improvement on some previous ballots.

The election was won convincingly by incumbent Prime Minister Peter O'Neill of the People's National Congress, which won 27 seats. Parliament re-elected him by a 94–12 majority, though his former deputy prime minister, Belden Namah, became leader of the opposition. Previous Prime Minister Michael Somare, whose dismissal from parliament had sparked the constitutional crisis, won his own seat, but his National Alliance Party fared poorly, winning only a handful of seats. Amongst the sitting members defeated was Somare's son Arthur. Following this crushing defeat, the elder Somare stepped down as party leader at the age of 76.

One of the first steps taken by the new government was to repeal a controversial law – the so-called Judicial Control Act – which had effectively allowed parliament to suspend judges during the constitutional crisis. Reflecting overwhelming support for O'Neill, in February 2013 parliament also extended from 18 to 30 months the period during which a no confidence vote could be brought against a prime minister following an election.

Meanwhile, another constitutional crisis developed in Fiji, which has had a military government led by Frank Bainimarama since 2007. The atmosphere had seemed more promising when Australia and New Zealand agreed to reinstate High Commissioners (ambassadors), and indicated willingness to relax travel sanctions imposed after the regime failed to hold promised elections in 2009. While these positive moves were ostensibly in return for assurances that elections would be held in Fiji in 2014, some commentators felt they reflected the failure of the hardline diplomatic approaches pursued by Canberra and Wellington. Fiji, though suspended from the Commonwealth and the Pacific Islands Forum (PIF), has been highly effective in attracting aid from alternative sources, particularly China, without political strings attached. In August 2012 PIF leaders agreed to allow Bainimarama to attend a meeting being held parallel to a forum meeting.

This positive trajectory appeared to continue into 2013, when in his New Year address Bainimarama announced that the country would get a new flag and that a new constitution would be completed by March, drafted by constitutional expert, Yash Ghai, a Kenyan law professor. However, in January 2013 the military seized copies of Ghai's draft constitution and burnt them, citing 'security reasons'. The regime said there were concerns about the draft and that its own legal team would rewrite the document. A new constitution was subsequently announced in March 2013, and Bainimarama indicated that he would contest the 2014 elections. As he enjoyed a public approval rating of approximately 66%, and had introduced new electoral regulations forcing the deregistration of at least 14 of Fiji's 17 political parties, his prospects for victory looked promising, should the elections ultimately be held.

Southeast Asia: Back to the 1960s?

During the year to mid-2013, conditions in Southeast Asia sometimes appeared to hark back to those of the 1960s. Though there was no contemporary equivalent to the Vietnam War, the sub-region did seem increasingly to be on its way to becoming a cockpit of major-power rivalry.

China continued to flex its political and naval muscles, particularly in relation to the South China Sea (as well as the wider region), and the United States pursued its strategy of 'rebalance' towards the Asia-Pacific, including increased military deployments in and around Southeast Asia.

There were also signs of Japan asserting its interests more strongly in the sub-region. The Association of Southeast Asian Nations (ASEAN) continued to provide a framework aimed at enhancing collaboration both among Southeast Asian states and between the region and external powers exercising significant roles there.

However, the Association's members sometimes appeared to be as divided and fractious as they had ever been, ASEAN's politico-security role appearing to be particularly severely challenged by the question of how to respond to Chinese pressure on ASEAN member states' territorial claims in the South China Sea. At the same time, in a number of Southeast Asian states there was heightened domestic political unease, and significant new security challenges for Malaysia and Myanmar. In both the Philippines and Thailand, peace negotiations with Muslim insurgents offered only limited promise of restored security.

China keeps up South China Sea pressure

Maintaining a trend in evidence since 2011, Chinese pressure on Southeast Asian states' claims to features in the South China Sea continued. In July 2012, the Central Military Commission in Beijing announced it had authorised establishment of a garrison command in Sansha City (on Yongxing or Woody Island) in the Paracel Islands. China almost simultaneously officially announced for the first time that Sansha would be the capital of a prefecture responsible for administering the Paracels, the Spratly Islands and other features in the South China Sea, even though many of these were occupied by Taiwan, Vietnam, Malaysia and the Philippines. These moves provoked protests from the Philippines and Vietnam. In December, China's National Energy Administration identified the South China Sea as the country's primary offshore site for natural gas production.

China continued to use its maritime paramilitary forces to assert its territorial claims, while the PLA Navy extended its operations in Southeast Asian waters. Some observers noted an escalation in Beijing's pressure after Xi Jinping, who had reputedly taken a special interest in the South China Sea, assumed leadership of the Chinese Communist Party in November 2012. In early December, Hanoi alleged that a Chinese 'fishing boat' had cut a seismic cable attached to a Vietnamese vessel exploring for oil and gas, repeating an incident the previous May which had provoked major anti-China protests in Vietnam. In response, Hanoi said that it would deploy marine-police and border-protection vessels to prevent foreign violations of fishing grounds in waters that it claimed. In January 2013, Philippine President Benigno Aquino III claimed that Chinese vessels had harassed two of his country's fishing vessels near Scarborough Shoal, over which China had effectively asserted control since a bilateral stand-off in mid-2012 when other Chinese ships had prevented the Philippine Navy from arresting allegedly illegal fishing boats from China. During March 2013, China Maritime Surveillance (CMS) vessels confronted a Vietnamese fishing boat in the Paracel Islands. Later that month, a Chinese naval flotilla surprised Southeast Asian governments by conducting exercises as far south as James Shoal, just 50 miles from the coast of the Malaysian state of Sarawak. In early May 2013, Manila protested over the presence of Chinese naval, CMS and fishing vessels near Ayungin Shoal, 105 miles from the Philippine island of Palawan and well inside Manila's Exclusive Economic Zone. For approximately ten days in mid-May 2013, China's navy conducted major exercises in the South China Sea involving ships, submarines, aircraft and marines from all three of its constituent fleets. Speaking at the IISS Shangri-La Dialogue in Singapore in early June 2013, Lieutenant-General Qi Jianguo, PLA Deputy Chief of the General Staff, underlined China's assertiveness and confidence by claiming that Beijing had 'sovereign power over the East China Sea and South China Sea' and that Chinese patrols in the South China Sea were 'totally legitimate and uncontroversial', and 'in our own territory'.

ASEAN's response to growing maritime tensions remained incoherent and unimpressive, particularly in light of the grouping's objective to establish an ASEAN Politico-Security Community by 2015. In relation to the South China Sea, the association remained divided between those claimant states committed to resisting China's creeping encroachment on their interests (the Philippines and Vietnam), claimants prepared to acquiesce in bilateral accommodation with China (Brunei and Malaysia), member states with no direct claims but nevertheless strong interest in preserving a stable regional maritime order (Indonesia and Singapore), and those mainland Southeast Asian states that many observers assessed as having become subject to significant Chinese influence (Cambodia, Laos, Myanmar and Thailand). After the annual ASEAN Ministerial Meeting (AMM) in July 2012 ended in acrimony when the Cambodian chair (allegedly as a result of Chinese pressure and economic inducements) refused to issue a joint statement mentioning the dispute over Scarborough Shoal, Indonesian foreign minister Marty Natalegawa engaged in intensive shuttle diplomacy in order to broker a consensus that might restore some credibility to the association. As a result, ASEAN's foreign ministers approved six principles constituting ASEAN's common position on the South China Sea, most importantly that member states remained committed to the Declaration on the Conduct of Parties in the South China Sea (DOC) agreed in 2002, to 'early implementation' of a more ambitious and constraining regional Code of Conduct (COC), and to the peaceful resolution of disputes in accord with international law and particularly the 1982 United Nations Convention on the Law of the Sea (UNCLOS).

However, beneath the brittle surface of the common position that Natalegawa brokered, individual Southeast Asian states continued to assert distinctly national policies towards the South China Sea. Some ASEAN members displayed much greater willingness to accommodate China's maritime interests. Although the joint statement that Brunei agreed with China when Sultan Hassanal Bolkiah visited Beijing in April 2013 paid due obeisance to the principles agreed by ASEAN foreign ministers with respect to the South China Sea, it also highlighted the agreement by the two countries' leaders 'to carry out joint exploration and exploitation of maritime oil and gas resources'. Though a claimant in the Spratly Islands, Malaysia's government maintained a positive attitude towards China, its most important trading partner. In June 2013, Malaysian Prime Minister Najib Tun Razak called for South China Sea claimant-states to develop resources there jointly in order to prevent conflict and intervention by extra-regional powers to protect freedom of navigation and the safe passage of shipping.

The Philippines, however, continued to resist Chinese pressure. In January 2013, Manila responded to Chinese encroachment on disputed areas that it claimed in the 'West Philippine Sea' by referring the matter to the United Nations for arbitration through a tribunal as provided for under UNCLOS. In May, Philippine Foreign Minister Albert del Rosario made much of the fact that the tribunal had been fully constituted since late April and was expected soon to begin work, though its deliberations might take 'two to three years'. However, in February China had made clear its refusal to cooperate with UN arbitration, and it remained to be seen if the tribunal would even decide that Manila's dispute with Beijing fell under its jurisdiction.

Tensions between Beijing and Manila escalated further in mid-2013, after the Philippines moved additional troops to the Ayungin and Scarborough Shoals, prompting China to warn in late June of a 'counter-strike' if what it claimed were provocations continued. At the annual meeting of the ASEAN Regional Forum in Brunei only days later, Philippine Foreign Minister del Rosario expressed concern over the South China Sea's 'increasing militarisation'. ASEAN members and China agreed to begin consultations on the proposed COC in September (following a special ASEAN ministerial meeting in Bangkok aimed at coordinating members' positions the preceding month), but China warned that progress would depend on countries abiding by the existing DOC, which it accused the Philippines of violating.

America's rebalance and Southeast Asian reservations

China's growing assertiveness and the related phenomenon of rising insecurity in the waters of Southeast Asia and the wider region continued to provide an important context for the United States' rebalance to the Asia-Pacific. That the rebalance was a priority not only for the Pentagon was clear from Secretary of State Hillary Clinton's gruelling schedule of diplomatic visits, which saw her travel to all ten ASEAN member states, as well as Timor Leste, between late 2011 and late 2012. In July 2012, Clinton was in Cambodia to participate in the ASEAN Regional Forum for the fourth consecutive time. In November, President Obama visited Southeast Asia on his first foreign trip after his re-election, joining Clinton for a visit to Myanmar (the first ever by a serving US president) with a view to encouraging further political and economic reforms, to Thailand where they met Prime Minister Yingluck Shinawatra 'to underscore our strong alliance', and to Cambodia.

Obama's visit to Cambodia, which held the ASEAN chair, underscored US willingness to support ASEAN's centrality in Asian regional multilateralism. It came at a time when China's strategy – evident at the AMM in July, and again at the ASEAN Summit in November – had seemed aimed at disrupting ASEAN unity, at least in relation to the South China Sea. Obama participated in the East Asia Summit – the first time the United States had done so – and co-chaired a US–ASEAN Leaders' Meeting, which agreed to institutionalise itself on an annual basis 'as a further step towards raising the US–ASEAN partnership to a strategic level', in the words of the White House.

From the US perspective at least, there was an important economic imperative for this incipient strategic partnership: with a total population of 620m and a combined annual GDP of more than US$2.2 trillion, the ASEAN states were collectively already America's fourth-largest export market and constituted a potentially significant motor for helping to restore US economic momentum. At the same time, expanding economic ties could work in favour of Washington's broader influence in a sub-region that has seemed increasingly in thrall to the rapidly expanding economic power of China. The US–ASEAN Expanded Economic Engagement Initiative, launched in Phnom Penh, provided for 'concrete joint activities' aimed at expanding trade and investment, and preparing ASEAN countries for joining 'high-standard trade agreements', such as the Trans-Pacific Partnership which the United States was negotiating with Brunei, Malaysia, Singapore, Vietnam and six other Pacific Rim states.

The Obama administration consistently denied that rivalry with China had motivated the US rebalance to the Asia-Pacific, and sought both to maintain equable relations with Beijing and to reassure ASEAN member states that the strong military and security element of America's new interest in Southeast Asia did not indicate the beginnings of a new Cold War, which might ultimately force them to take sides. In this vein, Assistant Secretary of State Kurt Campbell went to Beijing in placatory mode immediately before the ASEAN Regional Forum meeting in July 2012. Meanwhile, the commercial dimension so much in evidence in Phnom Penh may have been partly intended to demonstrate that the rebalance was not simply a matter of sharp-edged power politics. Nevertheless, it was widely understood in Southeast Asia that the US rebalance was at core a reaction to China's growing power, confidence and assertiveness in a part of the world that Washington assessed to be strategically important. Indeed, there was a widespread appreciation in most Southeast Asian states of a considerable harmony of interests with the United States in this respect. Rising Southeast Asian concern over the geopolitical implications of China's assertiveness in the South China Sea meant that the rebalance was seen more positively than might have been the case had Beijing's regional behaviour been more obviously in accord with the 'peaceful development' narrative that it used to characterise its international policies.

In his address to the IISS Shangri-La Dialogue in June 2013, US Secretary of Defense Chuck Hagel enumerated recent manifestations in Southeast Asia of the US rebalance's military dimension. He noted the arrival in Singapore in April of the first of an eventual four Littoral Combat Ships that would be forward-deployed in Singapore. He also mentioned discussions with the Philippine government regarding 'an increased rotational presence of US forces', and continuing efforts to enhance the 'maritime capacity' of Manila's armed forces; the November 2012 Joint Vision Statement for the Thai–US Defense Alliance; expanding defence cooperation with Vietnam in maritime security, search-and-rescue, and other areas; growing maritime cooperation with Malaysia, including the first-ever visit in October 2012 by a US aircraft carrier to Sabah; 'new habits of cooperation' with Indonesia; and 'carefully calibrated military-to-military engagement' with Myanmar.

However, the reaction of Southeast Asian states to the new activism in American policy towards them was generally measured. While ASEAN members harboured concerns over China's growing strategic extroversion, economic imperatives meant that developing relations with China was an important aim for most Southeast Asian governments, which often also had domestic political reasons for wishing to avoid overly close identification with US foreign and defence policy. There were also reservations in Southeast Asian capitals regarding the likely durability of the military dimensions of the American rebalance, particularly in light of Washington's financial constraints. In these circumstances, the majority of Southeast Asian governments were determined to keep their strategic options open.

There were reservations even in the case of the Philippines, where the government led by Aquino needed US diplomatic backing and potentially military support in the face of Chinese pressure on its maritime claims. Conscious that approval from the Philippine Senate (which was traditionally protective of Philippine sovereignty and in 1992 had voted to close US bases) would be required for any new agreement allowing US forces access to Philippine military facilities going beyond that allowed by the 1999 Visiting Forces Agreement, Aquino's government had to emphasise that American forces and their equipment would only be in-country temporarily.

Despite US efforts to intensify security relations with Thailand, and notwithstanding Bangkok's concerns over Chinese assertiveness in the South China Sea at the expense of fellow ASEAN members, Thai foreign policy continued to follow its traditional course of 'bending with the wind', which resulted in the elevation of relations with Beijing to a 'strategic partnership' in April 2012. In June 2012, Bangkok's apparent fear of offending China forced NASA to abandon a plan to fly U-2 atmospheric-research aircraft from U-Tapao airfield. In July 2012, a powerful Thai military delegation led by Defence Minister Sukumpol Suwanatat visited Beijing. A major Thai arms-procurement project, revealed in September 2012, will use Chinese technology to develop a guided multiple-rocket launch system.

Unlike the Philippines and Thailand, Singapore is not a US ally, but its defence and security relations with Washington, expanded and codified under a confidential Strategic Framework Agreement signed in 2005, are in some ways closer. But while Singapore is apparently content, for example, to allow the quasi-basing of US Navy ships, and was manifestly discomfited by China's activism in the South China Sea, the preponderance of ethnic-Chinese in its population and its intimate economic relations with China ensured that it remained determinedly neutral with regard to US–China tensions.

Other Southeast Asian states responded even more cautiously to the core security aspects of the US rebalance. Vietnam evidently saw advantages in a revived United States interest in Southeast Asia if this helped to constrain China's behaviour. However, Hanoi had no interest in further undermining its relations with Beijing as a consequence of developing closer military links with the US, and continued to strictly ration US Navy port calls in the face of intense American interest in regaining access to Cam Ranh Bay naval base, which then-Secretary of Defense Leon Panetta visited in June 2012.

Malaysia and Indonesia are both Muslim-majority states where Islamic fundamentalism, anti-Zionism, trenchant nationalism and neutralism are central elements of political discourse. Their governments continued to tread carefully with respect to their relations with the United States for fear of alienating important domestic constituencies. Indeed, Malaysia's first bilateral 'defence and security consultation' with China in September 2012, when the two countries agreed to strengthen bilateral 'mutual exchange and cooperation' in the military sphere, indicated the Malaysian government's wish to maintain a semblance of even-handedness in its security relations with Washington and Beijing. There is no doubt that relations with the United States form an important part of Indonesia's increasingly confident international diplomacy. However, the strategic benefits of this partnership for the United States may be limited. Like Malaysia and Thailand, Indonesia places great emphasis on further developing relations with China, and not only in the economic sphere. In August 2012, Beijing agreed that Indonesian industry could produce Chinese anti-ship missiles under licence. Moreover, in a remarkable assertion of Indonesia's freedom of action, in September Jakarta's defence ministry even spoke of strengthening military links with North Korea.

China and the United States were not the only outside elements in the evolving regional distribution of power. The election of a new Japanese government led by the LDP's Shinzo Abe in December 2012 quickly led to a new confidence and assertiveness in Tokyo's policies towards Southeast Asia, based partly on the assessment that Japan and some ASEAN members faced similar and related challenges from China towards their maritime claims. In January 2013, Abe's first foreign visits were to Thailand, Vietnam and Indonesia, in the wake of an earlier trip by Foreign Minister Fumio Kishida to the Philippines, Singapore and Brunei. Tokyo found a willing partner in the Philippines, where concerns regarding China now overshadowed previous resentment against Japan because of its military's abuses during the

Second World War. In Manila, Kishida and Philippine Foreign Minister del Rosario expressed 'mutual concern' over the maritime disputes, and del Rosario cited his president as thinking that a 'stronger Japan, acting as a counterbalance in the region, would help promote stability'. In concrete terms, Tokyo and Manila agreed to intensify intelligence exchanges and Japan responded positively to a Philippine request for assistance for its coast guard, agreeing to donate ten patrol vessels. However, enthusiasm for Japan's newly assertive role was muted elsewhere in Southeast Asia, one Singapore newspaper columnist remarking that 'ASEAN must not be dragged into an anti-China coalition with Japan'.

India's role in Southeast Asia continued to appear hesitant and under-developed, despite New Delhi's two-decade-old 'Look East' foreign policy doctrine, annual 'operational cruises' by Indian Navy flotillas in Southeast Asian waters (such as one commencing in May 2013 that included an exercise with Singapore's navy and port visits in Malaysia, the Philippines and Vietnam), and Chief of Naval Staff Admiral D.K. Joshi's claim in December 2012 that his service was preparing for the possibility that it might be called upon to protect Indian economic interests in the South China Sea. Distracted by continuing tensions with Pakistan, insurgencies in northeast India as well as Jammu and Kashmir, and concerns over Afghanistan's future, India apparently had little energy for closer engagement with Southeast Asian states. At the same time, notwithstanding New Delhi's concerns over Beijing's strategic assertiveness (not least on the two countries' Himalayan border), India's key economic interest in developing trade with China, and its ambivalence regarding relations with the United States, militated against its adopting a more assertive posture in Southeast Asia that might precipitate more clear-cut strategic rivalry.

Peace in the Philippines; a small war in Malaysia

Though its maritime contest with China exacerbated Manila's external threat perceptions, there were tentative signs that internal security was improving, with decades of lethal domestic conflict in the Philippines potentially coming to an end. President Aquino, who took office in June 2010, revived efforts to bring peace to the southern Philippines and, in October 2012, almost 16 years of stop-start negotiations between the

Philippine government and the Moro Islamic Liberation Front (MILF) culminated in the significant Framework Agreement on Bangsamoro (FAB). The FAB envisaged the creation of an autonomous region in Mindanao to be known as Bangsamoro – effectively covering Muslim-majority areas of the southern Philippines – the government of which would control its own budget, derive a share of revenues from resource extraction in the region, operate its own police force, and have the right to impose sharia law on Muslim residents. In exchange for these important concessions, MILF (which still controlled 12,000 paramilitary personnel) would end its armed rebellion permanently, and acknowledge Manila's continued control of security and foreign policy. Bangsamoro would replace and expand the existing Autonomous Region in Muslim Mindanao, established in 1986 following an earlier political settlement with the Moro National Liberation Front (MNLF). The timescale set out in the FAB anticipated that a self-governing transitional authority would be established by mid-2015, with elections scheduled for the following year.

Though the FAB was a major achievement, its implementation faced serious obstacles because of legal questions over the compatibility of the proposed basic law for Bangsamoro with the Philippine constitution, potential opposition from the Christian and indigenous minorities in the region as well as from the Sulu archipelago, and the potential for MILF to splinter and for elements to resume fighting if implementation of the agreement proved difficult. Though the two sides had established a Transition Commission to draft the basic law, by mid-2013 talks between Manila and MILF had stalled over key issues including power- and wealth-sharing, leading MILF to warn the government of its frustration. During June 2013, text messages circulating in the Philippine south warned that MILF would resume armed operations in the event of any prolonged deadlock in the talks. MILF denied this was true, but several Western governments nevertheless issued adverse travel advisories relating to the region.

One unexpected indirect result of the success of the October 2012 FAB was that in February 2013 Malaysia had faced a severe security challenge when more than 200 Philippine supporters of Jamalul Kiram III, a claimant to the throne of the Sultanate of Sulu, arrived by boat at a village near Lahad Datu on the coast of Sabah State on the island of Borneo. Calling themselves the 'Royal Security Forces of the Sultanate of Sulu and North Borneo' and led by Kiram III's brother, the group included women and children as well as armed guerrillas, some of whom may have previously exercised in the area with Malaysian government acquiescence as members of the MNLF. Kiram III had been slighted by his exclusion from the peace negotiations and the FAB, and announced in November 2012 his intent to assert his claimed entitlement to sovereignty over Sabah, a development that both the Philippine and Malaysian governments apparently overlooked or ignored.

The Malaysian police cordoned off the area that the intruders occupied but no effort was immediately made to dislodge or capture them. Fighting broke out on 1 March, when a group tried to break out of the cordon, leading to the deaths of 12 of the Filipinos. Only after gunmen apparently closely connected with the armed lodgement ambushed a police detachment near Semporna (160km from Lahad Datu) and killed five police officers, including a senior special branch officer, did the government take decisive action. *Operation Daulat* (Sovereignty) began on 5 March with air-strikes on the Lahad Datu intruders, followed by mortar fire and a joint army and police mopping-up operation. In all, 56 intruders, nine Malaysian security-force personnel, and six civilians were killed during this small war, which recalled the most intense phases of Indonesia's 'Confrontation' with Malaysia during the mid-1960s. One important result was the Malaysian government's effort to reinforce security in the region in order to prevent similar incidents in future. In March it quickly established an Eastern Sabah Security Command to control existing and newly deployed military and police units, and in July announced that two new army brigades and a paramilitary police brigade would be set up under the command.

Malaysia: a crucial election

While the focus of many extra-regional observers was on the impact of the South China Sea dispute and the US rebalance on Southeast Asia, most ASEAN member states' governments continued to be concerned as much with domestic politics as with external security. This was certainly true in Malaysia, where the Barisan Nasional (BN) administration led by Prime Minister Najib Tun Razak and dominated by his United Malays

National Organisation (UMNO) had been preparing since early 2012 for a general election, which needed to be called before the end of April 2013. For the first time since the 1960s, it seemed possible (if still less than likely) that the opposition – now in the form of the Pakatan Rakyat (PR) coalition, led by former BN Deputy Prime Minister Anwar Ibrahim – could displace the UMNO-led regime which had been in place since the country's formation 50 years previously. Despite its own internal tensions and what many Malaysians interpreted as government efforts to undermine Anwar through smear campaigns and prosecution, the PR (comprising Anwar's Parti Keadilan Rakyat, the Islamic Party known as PAS, and the liberal Democratic Action Party) had substantially increased its parliamentary representation in the 2008 general election, removing the BN's psychologically important two-thirds majority; the PR also had control of five state administrations.

The BN government waited until early April 2013 – only 26 days short of the deadline – before calling the election. During the preceding months, Prime Minister Najib had travelled intensively throughout Malaysia, impressing many observers with his openness and popular touch, and significantly boosting his personal popularity ratings. Simultaneously, the government implemented a range of popular policy measures including a statutory minimum wage, state-sector salary increases, and cash hand-outs for the poor. The economy remained buoyant, with GDP growth of 5–6% expected in 2013. But while Najib and the BN had waited until conditions were as near-perfect as possible before calling the election, widespread resentment of the BN's alleged abuses of power, corruption and lack of accountability – together with many non-Malay (particularly ethnic Chinese) citizens' indignation over the discriminatory New Economic Policy and the dominance of UMNO within BN – meant the opposition appealed to many voters.

In the event, the general election on 5 May demonstrated that while Malaysia's opposition had continued to gain strength it did not yet have sufficient appeal to eject the incumbent BN from office. On a turnout of 85% of eligible voters, the PR won 89 out of 222 federal seats, and control of three state governments. While it was clear that the BN faced a strengthening opposition, it was likely to be secure in power for a further term of up to five years. Najib, who continued as prime minister, blamed the BN's losses on a 'Chinese tsunami': it was clear that large numbers of ethnic Chinese voters had deserted the BN's Malaysian Chinese Association and Gerakan (the Malaysian People's Movement Party) in favour of the opposition Democratic Action Party. For his part, Anwar made the entirely unsubstantiated claim that the BN victory resulted from the 'worst electoral fraud in history'.

Thailand: stability returns?

During Prime Minister Yingluck Shinawatra's second year in power since the Pheu Thai Party's July 2011 election victory and the subsequent formation of a coalition government including four smaller parties and holding almost two-thirds of the seats in the lower house, Thailand's deep-seated political conflict appeared muted compared with the period of crises and violence between 2005 and 2010. The country's economy recovered quickly from the major floods of 2011, registering 6.4% growth in 2012 and facilitating the expensive policies, such as the rice-mortgage and first-time car buyer schemes, which formed important elements of efforts by the government (which was widely acknowledged to be controlled remotely by Yingluck's elder brother and former prime minister, Thaksin Shinawatra) to maintain and increase its popularity. These schemes, along with the government's plan to borrow two trillion baht (US$64bn) to fund major improvements to the nation's rail system and other infrastructure, provoked considerable criticism from the government's opponents. However, while street protests by conservative groups against the government continued on a smaller scale, the anti-Thaksin Yellow Shirt movement appeared to have lost much of its momentum due to internal conflicts. Moreover, despite the Democrat Party's candidate, Sukhumbhand Paribatra, being re-elected as governor of Bangkok in March 2013, the leading opposition party seemed unlikely to be in any position to challenge Pheu Thai electorally for some years at the national level, particularly as its leader, Abhisit Vejjajiva, faced criminal charges for authorising the army to use lethal force against Red Shirt demonstrators against his government in 2010. In a December 2012 opinion survey by Bangkok University, 52% of respondents identified the prime minister as the country's 'most constructive' politician, compared with only 16% who voted for Abhisit. And, as leading Thai political scientist Thitinan Pongsudhirak wrote in a newspaper op-ed in February 2013, 'anti-Thaksin fatigue seems to have set in'.

Meanwhile, Yingluck's government had been careful not to provoke other key power centres. Yingluck personally demonstrated due deference to the country's king and the institution of the monarchy, and the government made no effort to revise the country's lèse-majesté law, which was invoked in response to even oblique criticism of members of the royal family. Yingluck also cultivated links with the armed forces (which had intervened with a coup to overthrow Thaksin's government in 2006), and in June 2013 removed Deputy Prime Minister Chalerm Yubamrung from his post in a cabinet reshuffle, reportedly because he had disagreed with military leaders over policy towards the insurgency in southern Thailand; at the same time, Yingluck herself assumed the defence portfolio in order to facilitate communication with the armed forces.

Yingluck's government also demonstrably wished to avoid any crisis provoked by disagreement with the courts, but nevertheless still wished to implement reforms aimed at changing parts of the constitution that it saw as contradicting its own interests. In July 2012, after the Constitutional Court ruled that the government's efforts to pass legislation amending the constitution as a whole would be unconstitutional without a referendum, despite its clear mandate and parliamentary majority, the government stepped back from confrontation and effectively sidelined the matter by establishing expert committees to investigate how to proceed. After baulking at the prospect of a referendum in which there would need to be at least 50% support for a complete revision of the constitution from at least 50% of eligible voters, the government decided to revise individual elements of the constitution, and April 2013 saw the first parliamentary reading of bills to establish a fully elected senate and to make it more difficult for the courts to disband political parties.

Despite the apparent return of stability to Thailand's politics, the potential for major upheaval remained. In mid-2013, it seemed almost certain that the next parliamentary session, beginning in August, would see the first readings of an amnesty bill proposed by the government, with the only thinly veiled aim of allowing Thaksin Shinawatra to return to Thailand and resume a more direct leadership role. And while the great majority of Thais might wish for its indefinite deferment, the issue of monarchical succession inevitably became ever more imminent. An unspoken but widespread concern was that the conjunction of these two developments would have unforeseeable but possibly inflammatory consequences.

In Thailand's far south, where more than 5,500 people had been killed in violent incidents since 2004, a familiar pattern of violent attacks by ethnic Malay rebels continued, mainly against 'soft' targets. However, in mid-February 2013, 16 rebels were killed in a raid by an estimated 50 insurgents on a marine base in Narathiwat Province. Though the raid was ineptly executed, it may have indicated increasing confidence on the part of rebels. Soon afterwards, the militants launched a wave of apparent reprisals for their losses in the raid, with near-simultaneous bombings and arson attacks against 29 targets in six districts of Pattani Province. Nevertheless, there was greater evidence of a political response by the government to the violence than previously. In Malaysia at the end of February, Hassan Taib, leader of the Barisan Revolusi Nasional (BRN), a rebel faction, and Lieutenant-General Paradorn Pattanathabutr, Secretary-General of Thailand's National Security Council, signed an agreement to begin talks aimed at ending violence in the south. The agreement, brokered by Malaysia's government and supported by Thaksin Shinawatra, was soon criticised (not least by army commander General Prayuth Chan-ocha) on the grounds that the BRN had little influence over the insurgents, who belonged to a specific militant faction, BRN-Coordinate, which had broken away from the mainstream BRN. In addition, Thailand's army was concerned that the talks might lend legitimacy to the insurgents.

During the following months to mid-2013, the commencement of talks between Bangkok and the BRN did nothing to stem violence in southern Thailand. Indeed, the insurgents targeted higher-ranking officials and in early April killed the deputy governor of Yala Province, Chaovalit Chairuek. The dialogue between the BRN and the Thai government continued, but with little evidence of agreement on anything other than to continue talking. At the third round of talks, in June 2013, the BRN came with a list of demands, including that Malaysia should mediate the talks; the Thai government should release 'political prisoners' unconditionally; the BRN should be recognised as the Pattani region's liberation movement; other ASEAN governments should join the talks; and that the Organisation of the Islamic Conference and NGOs should be observers. None of these demands was acceptable to Bangkok. However, while the dialogue with the BRN was increasingly criticised as a 'dead-end', in early July it was reported that the National Security Council had begun parallel, but secret, talks with other insurgent groups.

Myanmar: unforeseen complications

In Myanmar, President Thein Sein's government continued with its programme of political and economic reforms, but developments raised important questions about the direction in which the country was heading. On the positive side, in July 2012 Aung San Suu Kyi, the internationally respected leader of the opposition National League for Democracy (NLD), entered parliament for the first time as one of 43 NLD members elected in the April by-elections. In August, the government removed more than 2,000 names from a blacklist of people who had previously been forbidden to enter or leave the country. During November, President Obama made a milestone trip to Myanmar, capping a series of important developments in US–Myanmar relations over the preceding months, including the appointment of a US ambassador in June, the lifting of US investment sanctions in July, President Thein Sein's visit to the United States during September, and the suspension of import bans on goods from Myanmar during the same month.

Human-rights groups criticised Obama's visit as premature, particularly given that conflict and violence continued in areas of Myanmar. In the northeast, fighting continued between government forces and the Kachin Independence Organisation (KIO) as a result of the collapse in 2011 of a 17-year-old ceasefire. The KIO's military wing, the Kachin Independence Army, deployed more than 4,000 armed personnel. Fighting escalated in December 2012, with Myanmar's armed forces using heavy artillery, helicopter gunships and fixed-wing air-strikes against the insurgents. More than 90,000 people were displaced, and a statement of concern released by the neighbouring Wa and other ethnic-minority groups in January 2013 suggested that the continued fighting might expand into a wider war as a result of other ceasefires breaking down. In early 2013, the fighting involving ethnic Kachin led China to intervene by sponsoring negotiations between Myanmar's government and the KIO, which reached agreement at the end of May to de-escalate the conflict. However, clashes continued almost daily during the following weeks.

In October 2012, there was a new outbreak of violence in western Myanmar's Rakhine State, where long-term persecution of Muslim Rohingya people (mostly descended from immigrants from Bangladesh, and in many cases stateless) had escalated into a pogrom in June, when at least 80 people were killed and 75,000 displaced. In the new violence, at least 200 people (mainly Muslims) were killed and a further 36,000 displaced in organised attacks led by Rakhine nationalists and incited by Buddhist monks. Some reports alleged that local security forces abetted the violence. While central government forces might have done more to control the violence, they did on occasion fire into Rakhine crowds in an effort to prevent attacks on Rohingya. In December, the UN General Assembly unanimously adopted a resolution welcoming positive changes in Myanmar, but expressing concern over the violence in Rakhine State and calling on the government to protect the human rights of the Rohingya, including 'their right to a nationality'. However, many who had hitherto admired and respected Aung San Suu Kyi were puzzled by her failure to directly condemn the violence. In March 2013, violence against Muslims spread to other parts of Myanmar, often sparked by minor incidents. The main outbreak was in Meiktila in late March, when 40 people were killed and 18,000 displaced after an altercation in a gold shop and the murder of a Buddhist monk. From Meiktila, the violence spread to other parts of central Myanmar, including 14 villages in the Bago Region. In Yangon, Myanmar's largest city, Muslim residents set up barricades to protect their community. There were further anti-Muslim riots in April and May. There is substantial evidence that the '969' movement, led by an extremist Buddhist monk, Ashin Wirathu, instigated at least some of the violence against Muslims.

Thein Sein's government was disappointingly ineffective in preventing communal violence; in November 2012, it also oversaw the repression by its security forces of large protests by Buddhist monks and villagers against the expansion of a Chinese-financed Myanmar Wanbao copper-mine project near Monywa in central Myanmar. The protesters had resisted the mine's expansion on the grounds that it would involve unlawful widespread land confiscation and the destruction of holy sites. It was subsequently revealed that the pre-dawn, paramilitary operation included the use of military-issue white phosphorus grenades against the protesters, more than 70 of whom were injured. The incident was reminiscent of the military's strong-arm tactics against opponents before Thein Sein began his programme of liberalisation, and is believed to have contributed to increasing strains in his relations with Aung San Suu Kyi. However, Aung San Suu Kyi accepted the president's invitation to chair the Latpadaung Inquiry Commission into the copper-mine protests.

In March 2013, the commission's report, while condemning the police tactics against demonstrators and noting the mine project's potential environmental damage and the fact that it would not create local employment, concluded that the project should continue, particularly because its cancellation might affect future foreign investment and damage relations with China. Local residents were enraged and made this clear to Aung San Suu Kyi when she visited Monywa. In her discussions with them, she remarked that 'we have to get along with the neighbouring country [China] whether we like it or not', an assessment that accorded closely with the views of many other Southeast Asian politicians.

Chapter 10

Prospectives

The abiding impression of international affairs in 2013 was of a constant flow of events that political leaders, governments, international organisations, opinion formers and people of all kinds were doing their best to manage. It was the year of living tactically.

Frustration was regularly expressed about the insolubility of conflicts, the iterative management of international tensions and the quick fixes that at best bought time for other unsatisfactory approaches. This amounted to a loud lament that strategy, let alone 'grand strategy', was now impossible. It was not only that the 24-hour news cycle and the dominance of social media commentary bled away the capacity for perspective and long-term planning. The lack of strategy derived also from a failure of leadership and a reluctance to pursue grander designs that might deliver longer-term or more lasting dividends.

This was the year in which the United States confirmed the developing tendency to see foreign policy as a series of procedures to be carried out, rather than as a means either definitively to solve problems or to mark new directions with strategic purpose. That tendency emerged not just out of weariness with the wars of the first decade of the twenty-first century, but from an analytical judgement that most foreign-policy problems fell into the 'too hard' category. Attempts by other countries to fill the gap in decisive leadership only confirmed how slim were the chances of success in any given case.

The next year, too, will be a year of living tactically. However, there are developments on the horizon of potential strategic consequence that will call out for larger, more coordinated, designs. In their absence, the sense that we live in a state of sublimated strategic anarchy will persist.

The international approach to Syria has been, perhaps necessarily, the most tactical of all. With no UN diplomatic umbrella raised over the problem, regional and ad hoc initiatives competed for temporary effect. The humanitarian impulse fell into conflict with complex realpolitik. The uniqueness of the geographical and political terrain appeared to constrain options. On the demand side, the proliferation of potential beneficiaries of support within the opposition, numbered at over a thousand groups, fragmented the chances of decisive shifts in the local balance. On the supply side, the diversity of political preferences for whom to support in the opposition had the same effect. Russian and Iranian tacit or direct support for the regime affected not just the chances of success, but the calculations by outside powers of risk and opportunity cost. Balancing these multiple global, regional and local players defied a diplomatic solution. It will be somehow up to the Syrians to manage the centrifugal forces that are pulling their society apart.

In current circumstances, a strategic approach would need to examine the Levant in its wider context. Containment is rarely an ideal policy, but it is almost always the second-best policy. It can build the conditions for a better outcome, when other factors permit. Has sufficient thought been given to the stability of Lebanon and Jordan and how these countries are affected by Syria's inadvertent suicide? Could there be a containment strategy developed with economic, political and perhaps military elements that would not resolve the tragic humanitarian crisis, but might help to limit the regional collateral damage? These questions are bound to form a larger part of the debate in the coming year, as the regional situation deteriorates, and the Sykes-Picot arrangements of the early twentieth century are fatally compromised by the raft of changes in regional domestic politics.

In Western circles, the word containment is rarely uttered in respect of Iran's nuclear programme and its possible exercise of a weaponisation strategy. In the United States, the abhorrence of the idea of a nuclear Iran is universal. Israel has every reason to fear an existential threat. But under-appreciated in the international debate is the severe intolerance of a prospectively nuclear-armed Iran among most of the other Gulf states. Iran is seen by most of the Gulf monarchies as the principal strategic challenge, and one that would be impossibly greater for them if Tehran took the nuclear route. Saudi Arabia and the United Arab Emirates (UAE) in particular worry that discussion of containment is tantamount to throwing in the towel.

So far, even with a highly unsatisfactory diplomatic process, Iran's hand has been stayed to a sufficient degree that the oft-threatened 'military option' to retard and temporarily disable Iran's capacity has not had to be urgently contemplated. Proof that Washington has a contingency plan has also helped to curtail unilateralist urges in Israel. However, the growing consensus is that 2014 could well be the year of reckoning, assuming that Iran continues to stockpile enriched uranium and make predicted advances in other areas. Admittedly, in the last several years, various thresholds of the nuclear programme's progress have been successively proclaimed, ignored, redefined, recalibrated or in some way finessed. And it is possible that the new Iranian presidency will generate a negotiating attitude that allows for the exploration of a modus vivendi. It is also conceivable that the desire to see some relaxation of sanctions will result in a demonstrable slowing down of the nuclear programme's progress that eases the international pressure. But it is equally possible that the binary choice between a military strike and acceptance of a nuclear Iran will have to be confronted. Putting in place a containment strategy is not just a contingency plan, it strengthens the hand of those dealing with Iran. By itself, it invites consideration by Iran of whether the single-minded pursuit of a nuclear option is in its own strategic interest.

Outsiders engaging in other parts of the Middle East have had trouble defining strategic interest and balancing the advance of principle with the practical need for stability. The disappointments of the 'Arab Spring', manifested in all countries where it initially took root, became legion. The palette from which political outcomes have been painted has been at best varying shades of grey. New governments have not been as inclusive as promised. Many protests have not been peaceful or fuelled uniquely by desires for democracy. The detritus of military intervention in Libya took the form of weapons proliferation and more violence in the Sahel. Tunisia's transition has been better, but has still fallen short of initial hopes. In Bahrain, a ruling family with progressive and modernising forces is coping with more extreme Sunni tendencies, a radicalising Shia population and some new terrorist activity. A meeting of minds among moderates and modernisers remains possible. There is certainly a need for measured outside support for the development of institutions and programmes that can underpin a stronger social contract.

But it is in Egypt that the challenges have been most dramatic. There, democratic principle and democratic action stood in unhappy conjunction. Following the overthrow of Hosni Mubarak and the election of a Muslim Brotherhood government, some hoped that a pluralist and democratic transition would take hold. But violence continued to erupt in various places. President Muhammad Morsi attempted to put himself above a hastily drafted and unsatisfactory constitution. The fear spread, rightly or wrongly, that the Brotherhood was manoeuvring to make itself the permanent party of government. With the economy failing and frustration mounting, the 30 June 2013 protests were, by some measures, the largest in history. The army removed Morsi and installed a technocratic government.

What had happened? Western governments initially wrestled with the vocabulary more than the substance of events. Was it a coup or something else that could withstand legal examination? For some, a democratic process had been aborted and usurped by a military coup that could only result in the forces of political Islam believing that the democratic path could offer no fair results. For others, 22 million people, many more than had voted for Morsi, impeached the president through a self-generated plebiscite in the absence of a constitutional route for doing so, and the army executed that popular will in the interests of stability. Some focused on the fact of democratic election; others on the experience of non-democratic rule. There were also those who chose to adopt the longer historical perspective, perceiving the event as a second stage in a multi-stage revolution. Finally, still others viewed the events as the restoration of the Egyptian 'deep state'.

The more enduring question for global powers will be how to support the slow development of inclusive politics in a wounded society, now awakened to political action. For this, constructive engagement will be the only strategic approach. For the region, the central question will be how to deal with political Islam. Even among the members of the Gulf Cooperation Council, two opposite views had taken shape in the previous year: the UAE would not tolerate any Muslim Brotherhood sympathisers, while Qatar chose initially to bankroll what it saw as the prevailing trend. After the events in Egypt, and with a new emir in office in Qatar, the future of political Islam in the Middle East will be one of the most demanding questions. It remains unclear whether Saudi Arabia and the UAE can sustain politically and financially anti-Brotherhood coalitions, but also support moderate Salafist factions.

In Asia, the balance of tactics and strategy will perhaps be uncomfortably weighted in favour of the latter. Chinese leaders have been hotly debating how China's new-found soft and hard power can be harnessed during what they describe as an important period of 'strategic opportunity'. Xi Jinping has taken very firm command of foreign policy, is resolute in defence of China's 'core interests' and wants China to be seen as a great power, indeed as an equal of the US. His mantra is 'rejuvenation', and his goal the realisation of the 'China Dream.' A bolder foreign-policy approach, that resonates with conservatives and the populist 'new left' together, will find one of its greatest challenges in the attitude to Japan. As relations with Japan continue to sour, Xi will have to demonstrate to his population that China will stand up to perceived provocation, without prompting a regional military escalation.

China's stance towards territorial disputes is likely to harden, with every opportunity taken to interpret the historical record favourably and to assert claims unremittingly. In this effort, the new leadership will be mindful of Sun Tzu's dictum: 'Strategy without tactics is the slowest route to victory. Tactics without strategy is the noise before defeat.' In the recent past, pursuit of tactical success has temporarily backfired. ASEAN members were appalled by Chinese pressure on Cambodia, as the association's rotating chair, to omit a reference to South China Sea disputes from a communiqué. To a degree this stiffened their resolve to insist on a multilateral approach that China resists. But in general, a confident Chinese leadership will iteratively seek to strengthen its position and consolidate its regional sway with determined strategic intent.

This will take place as Japan moves to pass legislation creating a National Security Council infrastructure, including an intelligence bureaucracy. The constitution is likely also to be reinterpreted to allow Japan to participate in collective self-defence activity, most notably with the United States, and that will permit more extensive participation in peacekeeping operations. There is more overt consensus not just among policymakers but within society at large that China, North Korea and Russia are the primary threats to Japanese security. Both of East Asia's large powers are moving to develop external policies more in keeping with their economic weight and global political standing, and are also seeking to defend more plainly their national interests. This imposes on Washington, which has announced its rebalance to Asia, and implicitly its rebalance *within* Asia – diversifying and deepening its engagements – a requirement to act also with careful strategic purpose. It must reassure allies without emboldening them, and it must hedge against Chinese assertiveness while engaging with its resident peer.

That delicate task would, perhaps, be made easier as Asian power became more plural. For with more, rather than fewer, assertive actors, the risks of diplomatic mistakes become sufficiently high to deter brinkmanship. Strong 'middle powers' like South Korea, Indonesia and Australia are key to creating this complex regional balance, but the role of India could also be a vital factor. The last year has seen India internally absorbed. The Indian government has appeared to be marking time and has perhaps lacked the strategic confidence to fulfil the complete promise of its earlier 'Look East' policy. The region certainly welcomes a more extrovert Indian role, but this has not been exerted in part because of the weakness of the present government but also because of the tragic magnetic pull that southwest Asian developments have on the Indian strategic attention span.

For India, 'neighbourhood policy' is likely to become more fully absorbing as the international drawdown from Afghanistan approaches. The air is thick with suggestions that an Indian–Pakistan proxy war could take hold in Afghanistan after 2014, yet both countries seem sensibly aware of the risks of blowback such a conflict could provoke on their own territories. India has made clear it would not put 'boots on the ground' in Afghanistan, and Pakistan is gradually accepting an

Indian role in Afghanistan's regional reconstruction. However, mutual suspicions remain perilously high. A trilateral dialogue between India, Pakistan and Afghanistan would be an important diplomatic institution to establish in order to reduce suspicion but, as always in such situations, it would require some prior confidence-building. India's looming general elections are therefore of strategic consequence. Pakistani Prime Minister Nawaz Sharif seeks greater engagement with the region through economic diplomacy, trade, foreign investment and economic cooperation. The chance of doing so turns greatly on the political choices made by the Indian electorate. Similarly, a self-confident government in Delhi, able to re-animate the Indian economy, might be able to present itself as a stronger pole in the broader Asian political order.

Political transitions in Asia can still easily unsettle the regional dispensation, and each election and change in leadership is looked at with forensic interest, as it can have huge ramifications. Economic accomplishment remains generally high, but wherever that success wavers or shrinks so too does strategic self-confidence. The sensitivity to expressions of 'people power' remains high in Asia, and this can heighten the risk of populist nationalism. Understanding domestic politics in Asia is vital to appreciate the scope for foreign-policy ambition and its shape. The vaunted rise in middle-class capacities and interests in the higher-growth economies will inspire more disrespect for oligarchical styles of government or business. The prospects for sudden political change have constantly to be monitored.

The potential restraint on foreign-policy ambition that can be a consequence of such domestic disquiet is evident in Russia where various forms of domestic insecurity have narrowed the scope of Russia's strategy. North Americans and Europeans, who have struggled to manage collaborative policies with Russia on either European or Middle East questions, would welcome the chance to coordinate approaches to Asia, where a wider set of strategic interests could be shared. Russia's decision-makers have indicated their own interest in a pivot to Asia, and clearly recognise the growing importance of the region, yet it was striking that Moscow's 2013 Foreign Policy Concept had the strengthening of Russia's presence in the Asia-Pacific listed only 33rd in the list of 'regional priorities'. Engagement with the Asia-Pacific remains episodic, and so the prospects for effective collaborative action with others are slimmer than they should be.

The Russian leadership, however keen it is to express a global personality, is drawn ever more inwards and ever more towards the immediate neighbourhood when contemplating foreign-policy questions. Efforts have been focused on the Customs Union between Russia, Belarus and Kazakhstan. A genuine supra-national body has been created, but enlargement poses challenges: Kyrgyzstan's and Tajikistan's prospective membership would make the open-border policy a nightmare to implement. Ukraine's leadership recognises that its own membership would split the country and unsettle the business leadership from which it gathers support. If Ukraine were offered an association agreement with the EU, then membership of the Customs Union would be ruled out and the body's ambitions constrained.

In general, foreign-policy aims are viewed in Moscow through the prism of regime maintenance. While President Vladimir Putin has been able to contain threats to the political system that he leads, has mobilised his core supporters and stabilised his approval rating at around 60%, he remains a weaker figure than before the job swap he engineered with now Prime Minister Dmitry Medvedev. There is therefore more systemic uncertainty in Russian politics than for some time, though the degree of elite splits has not reached the level where dramatic transformation can be considered probable. As ever, the strength of the oil price and the economy will have a bearing on whether real political pressure can be brought for change. In the meantime, grand strategy by the Russian leadership will be centred to a great degree on designs within the internal political chessboard.

The proliferation of 'people power' and organised dissent has cut down (no doubt temporarily, but still significantly) the strategic swagger of a number of rising powers. The large demonstrations in Turkey made it harder for Prime Minister Recep Tayyip Erdogan and his party to argue with the same degree of self-confidence that the Turkish model of politics was the gold standard against which others in the broader region might wish to benchmark themselves. The coincidence that these protests occurred just before the Muslim Brotherhood fell from office in Egypt was significant, in that Turkey then also lost an ideological ally in its efforts to project power in the wider region. The even larger and more widespread demonstrations in Brazil that took place in the same early weeks of June 2013 reduced President Dilma Rousseff's popularity by a sharp 20%, even raising questions about her ability to win the 2014 election.

While the protests in Brazil will not have had a systemic impact, they demonstrate the constant attention that all have to pay to the domestic political imperative. Foreign policy, at least extra-continental foreign policy, becomes a specialist and luxury commodity in these circumstances, and one of the first things that is dispensed with when political times are hard.

Many powers in Latin America, Africa, Asia and the Middle East are now able to take useful and important foreign-policy initiatives. The diversity of strategic actors continues to grow. Yet setting strategic objectives and sticking to them has become nearly impossible. Developing a *sustainable* foreign policy is a challenge for the largest powers. Strategic surprises can derail well-laid plans. The test of an effective strategic approach is its adaptability to change. That adaptability requires governments to connect as much with societies as with government leaders. These tasks are only going to become harder as people come to recognise the change happening in all societies because of the so-called 'Big Data' revolution.

By one estimate, in 2000 about 75% of all data was non-digital. Now, perhaps 98% of all information stored is digital. A great deal that was valuable and difficult to gather has now become more accessible and easier to manage. Private companies, governments and individuals all deal with the reality of 'Big Data' in some way. The evolution of Big Data has fundamentally changed mankind's relationship to information and called into question previous assumptions about privacy. In parallel, the emergence of information and communications technology (ICT) systems with a low barrier to entry has enabled many nations to develop an intelligence reach and a capacity to gather information that they previously could not contemplate. With this has come the risk of the militarisation of cyberspace, and since so many military capabilities are ICT-enabled and cyber-dependent, new sources of conflict arise. At the June 2013 US–China summit in California, the one central issue on which there was little meeting of minds was the question of cyber intrusions.

It is easy to become pessimistic about the ability of states to act strategically and easy to fear that developments are hard to control and manage. The announced resumption in July 2013 of peace talks between Israel and the Palestinian Authority, brokered by US Secretary of State John Kerry, invited much doubt and scepticism. But it was a reminder that political leadership still has a commanding place in human relations. If more leaders were certain of their domestic strength, then genuine strategic action could be a more regular feature of international affairs. And yet, nothing is more dangerous than hubris in international relations. Perhaps another year of living tactically is better than a year of strategic conceits.

Index

A

Abashidze, Zurab 174
Abbas, Mahmoud 218, 219
King Abdullah II (Jordan) 186, 187, 188, 207
King Abdullah bin Abdulaziz Al Saud (Saudia Arabia) 205
Abe, Shinzo 25, 309, 322, 323, 325, 32ff, 363
Abhisit Vejjajiva 368
Abidjan (Côte d'Ivoire) 257
Abkhazia 174
Abu Dhabi (UAE) 208
Abu Kershola (Sudan) 262
Abyan (Yemen) 215
Abyei (Sudan) 261, 262
Acapulco (Mexico) 82
Adamawa (Nigeria) 252, 253
Adan, Yusuf Haji 259
Addis Ababa (Ethiopia) 261, 262, 266, 274
Adrar des Ifoghas mountains (Mali) 249
Afghanistan 17, 23, 28, 29, 48, 77, 135, 137, 141, 142, 163, 166, 168, 212, 281, 287, 293, 294, 295–307, 351, 353, 364, 380, 381
  Afghan National Army 163, 301, 302, 306
  Afghan National Security Forces 296, 301ff
  Air Force 303
  Electoral Complaints Commission 299
  Ground Forces Command 302
  High Peace Council 305
  Independent High Electoral Commission 299
  Local Police 303
  National Directorate of Security 300, 302
Africa 24, 48, 122, 123, 138, 139, 143, 247–280, 318, 383
African-led International Support Mission in Mali 249, 250
African National Congress (South Africa) 275ff
  ANC Youth League 276
African Union 202, 247, 248, 258, 261, 262, 266, 269, 279
  African Union Mission in Somalia 259, 260, 269
  Peace, Security and Cooperation Framework Agreement for the DRC 266
Agadez (Niger) 251
Agang (South Africa) 277
AgustaWestland (UK-Italy) 284
Ahlu Sunna Wal Jamaa (Somalia) 258
Ahmadinejad, Mahmoud 194, 222, 230, 231, 233
Ahmar, Ali Mohsen al- 215
Ahn Cheol-soo 344
Ahrar al-Sham (Syria) 181
Airbus 50, 54
Akali Dal (India) 282
Akcakale (Turkey) 144
Akhromeyev, Sergei 43
al-Aqsa mosque 187
Alasania, Irakli 173
Alaska (US) 342
Alawites 184, 190
Aleppo (Syria) 179, 180
Alevi (Turkey) 148
Algeria 20, 28, 115, 121, 122, 190, 202, 203–204, 251
  Ministry of Religious Affairs and Endowments 204
Algiers (Algeria) 122
Ali, Abdiweli Mohamed 259, 260
al-Islah (UAE) 207, 208
Al Jazeera 195, 197, 239
Almaty (Kazakhstan) 226ff
al-Muthanna (Iraq) 241
al-Nour Party (Egypt) 193, 196
al-Qadisiyah (Iraq) 241
al-Qaeda 20, 27, 28, 146, 175, 181, 190, 208, 215, 247, 248, 252, 294, 297, 305
al-Qaeda in the Arabian Peninsula 214, 215
al-Qaeda in the Islamic Maghreb 120, 121, 199, 204, 248, 249, 251
al-Qaeda in Mesopotamia 242, 243
al-Qassim (Saudi Arabia) 206
al-Qatif (Saudi Arabia) 205
al-Shabaab 258, 259, 260, 269
al-Wataniya (Libya) 198
al-Zaatari (Jordan) 188
Amano, Yukiya 226
Amazon 99
América Móvil (Mexico) 80
Amman (Jordan) 187, 188
Amnesty International 253
Anan, Sami 191
Anbar (Iraq) 237, 241
Andhra Pradesh (India) 285
Anglo American (UK) 276
Angola 256, 266, 271
An-Nahda Party (Tunisia) 200, 201
Annan, Kofi 183, 235
Ansar al-Din (Mali) 248, 251, 257
Ansar al-Sharia (Mali) 199, 200, 215, 251
Ansaru (Nigeria) 252
Antarctic 163
Anti-Ballistic Missile Treaty 166
Anwar Ibrahim 367, 368
Apple (US) 27
Aquino III, Benigno 357, 362, 364
Arabian Sea 208

Arab League 182, 183, 212
Arak (Iran) 225, 226
Aramco (Saudia Arabia) 178, 207, 235
Arbil (Iraq) 145
Arctic 170
Argentina 78, 102, 103–106
National Institute of Statistics and Census 104
Arghandiwal, Abdul Hadi 299
Arizona (US) 71
Arlit (Niger) 251
Ar-Raqqah (Syria) 180
Asadi, Bagher 232
Asa'ib Ahl al-Haq (Iraq) 243
Ashin Wirathu 372
Ashraf, Raja Pervez 290
Ashton, Catherine 140, 226, 227
Asia 23, 41, 46, 54, 55, 102, 122, 141, 178, 230, 282, 319, 350, 380, 381, 383
Asian Development Bank 317
Asia-Pacific 75, 141, 165, 309–374, 381
Asia-Pacific Economic Cooperation 158, 165
al-Assad, Bashar 22, 75, 144, 145, 146, 151, 167, 168, 169, 175, 177ff, 182ff, 188, 190, 195, 206, 207, 208, 213, 220, 234, 245, 318
Assam (India) 286
Assange, Julian 97
Association of Southeast Asian Nations 356ff, 366, 371, 379
Declaration on the Conduct of Parties in the South China Sea 358, 359
Ministerial Meeting 2012 358, 360
Regional Forum 2012 359, 360
Regional Forum 2013 359
Ataturk, Mustafa Kemal 143
The Atlantic 187
Atmar, Hanif 299
Augier, Jean-Jacques 116
Aung San Suu Kyi 371, 372, 373
Aurora (US) 71
Australasia 46
Australia 272, 309, 329, 332, 348–352, 353, 354, 380
'Asian Century' White Paper 348, 349, 350
Australian Defence Force 349
Defence White Paper 348ff
Department of Defence 352
National Security Strategy 348, 350, 351
Autonomous Region in Muslim Mindanao (Philippines) 365
Awami National Party (Pakistan) 290, 291
al-Awlaki, Anwar 215
Ayungin Shoal 357, 359
Azevêdo, Roberto Carvalho de 77, 102

B

Babil (Iraq) 241
Bae, Kenneth 342
BAE Systems (UK) 56
Baga (Nigeria) 252
Baghdadi, Abu Bakr al- 242
Baghdad (Iraq) 241ff
Bago (Myanmar) 372
Bahrain 208–209, 211, 228, 235, 378
Bahrain Center for Human Rights 209
Bahrain Independent Commission of Inquiry 209
Bahr el-Ghazal (South Sudan) 261
Bahujan Samaj Party (India) 283
Bainimarama, Frank 354
Bajolet, Bernard 298
Balad Party (Israel) 217
Balkans 141
Baloch (Pakistan) 292
Baluchistan (Pakistan) 291, 292
Bamako (Mali) 120, 121, 248, 249, 250
Bamyan (Afghanistan) 353
Banda, Joyce 273
Bandaranayake, Shirani 295
Bangkok (Thailand) 359, 368
Bangkok University 368
Bangladesh 31, 372
Bangsamoro (Philippines) 365
Bangui (Central African Republic) 264, 278, 279
Bani Walid (Libya) 198, 199
Ban Ki-moon 202, 251, 265, 267
Bank Mellat (Iran) 228
Bank Saderat (Iran) 228
Baradar, Abdul Ghani 306
Barak, Ehud 223, 224
Barents Sea 170
al-Barghathi, Mohammed 198
Barisan Nasional (Malaysia) 366, 367, 368
Barisan Revolusi Nasional (Thailand) 370, 371
Al-Barrak, Musallam 211
Barre, Siad 258
Barzani, Masoud 240
al-Bashir, Omar 261, 262, 263
Basra (Iraq) 241
Bastrykhin, Aleksandr 155
Bauchi (Nigeria) 252
Bavaria (Germany) 124
Beijing (China) 287, 311, 312, 318, 322, 323, 331, 343, 344, 351, 352, 356, 357, 358, 360, 362, 363, 364
Beirut (Lebanon) 186
Bekaa Valley (Lebanon) 184
Belaid, Chokri 201
Belarus 382
Belize 86
Belmokhtar, Mokhtar 204, 251
Benghazi (Libya) 66, 75, 190, 198, 199
Beni Halba (Sudan) 263
Benin 249
Benkirane, Abdelilah 202
Bennett, Naftali 217
Bergoglio, Jorge Mario 106
Berlin (Germany) 37, 41, 167
Bharatiya Janata Party (India) 285, 286
BHP Billiton (Australia) 255
Bhutto, Benazir 290, 292
Biden, Joe 163, 227
Big Data 75, 383
Bihar (India) 285
Bilateral Security Agreement (US-Afghanistan) 297
bin Fahd, Mohammed 205
bin Laden, Osama 76
bin Nayef, Mohammed 207
bin Sultan, Bandar 207
Birta Dheer (Somalia) 259
Bissalanca Air Force Base (Guinea-Bissau) 256
Bissau (Guinea-Bissau) 256
Biti, Tẹndai 270, 271
Black Sea 321
Blanco, Herminio 102
Blantyre (Malawi) 273
Bloomberg, Michael 72
Bloomberg (US) 314
Blue Nile (Sudan) 261, 262, 263
Boehner, John 68, 69, 72
Bogota (Colombia) 91
Boko Haram (Nigeria) 28, 250ff
Bolivarian Alliance for the Peoples of Our America 77, 108
Bolivarian Revolution 93, 94
Bolivia 78, 102
Bolkiah, Hassanal 358
Bono de Desarrollo Humano 95
Booz Allen Hamilton (US) 76
Borneo 365
Borno (Nigeria) 252, 253
Bosnia 48
Boston (US) 28, 164
Botswana 270
Bouteflika, Abdelaziz 122, 203
Bo Xilai 18, 310, 313, 314, 315
Bozizé, François 264
BP (UK) 170
Brahimi, Lakhdar 183, 184, 235
Brazil 18, 19, 25, 57, 77, 78, 99–103, 108, 255, 275, 383
BRICS 277
British Broadcasting Corporation 136
Brown, Scott 67
Brunei 357, 358, 359, 360, 363
Brussels (Belgium) 128, 147, 250
Bubo Na Tchuto, Jose Americo 256
Buenos Aires (Argentina) 105, 106
Bukavu (Democratic Republic of the Congo) 266
Burkina Faso 120, 249, 256
Burundi 260, 266
Bushehr (Iran) 225
Bush, George H.W. 60
Bush, George W. 29, 59, 60, 62, 63, 68, 69, 77, 162, 165

C

Cabello, Diosdado 93, 95
Cahuzac, Jérome 116
Cairo (Egypt) 189, 194, 204, 220

Calderón, Felipe 79, 81, 82
California (US) 325, 342, 383
Cambodia 358, 359, 360, 379
Cameron, David 113, 114, 129, 131ff, 307
Cameroon 252, 253, 264, 265
Campbell, Kurt 360
Campos, Eduardo 101
Cam Ranh Bay naval base (Vietnam) 363
Canada 135, 230, 295
Cancún (Mexico) 82
Cape Canaveral (US) 320
Capriles Radonski, Henrique 90, 92, 93, 95
Caracas (Venezuela) 94
Caribbean 98
Carney, Mark 135
Cartagena (Colombia) 91
Carter, Jimmy 62
Catholic Church 63, 119
Caucasus Emirate (Russia) 168
Cayman Islands 116
Central African Republic 264–265, 266, 278
Central America 82–87, 98, 108
Central Asia 168
Centre for Strategic Research (Russia) 154
Chad 120, 249, 250, 263, 264
Chalerm Yubamrung 369
Chaovalit Chairuek 370
Chávez, Hugo 87, 91, 92, 93, 94, 95, 96, 97, 98, 107
Chechnya 28
Chen Bingde 313
Chengdu (China) 315
Chen Guangcheng 314
Chen Liangyu 312
Chevron (US) 244
Chhattisgarh (India) 285
Chicago (US) 59
Chidambaram, P. 282
Chile 88, 102
China 18, 20, 22, 25, 26, 28, 31, 36, 42, 46, 47, 78, 99, 164, 213, 222, 230, 235, 250, 251, 264, 282, 286, 287, 292, 309–324, 326, 329, 331, 332, 335, 336, 340ff, 346, 347, 350, 351, 352, 355ff, 367, 368, 372, 373, 379, 380, 383
  17th Party Congress 315
  18th Party Congress 313, 316
  Bank of China 343
  Central Military Commission 311, 312, 313, 356
  Central Political and Law Committee 314
  China Investment Corporation 213
  China Maritime Surveillance 357
  Cultural Revolution 311
  Defence White Paper 319
  Exclusive Economic Zone 321
  Food and Drug Administration 316
  General Office of the State Council 311
  Ministry of Finance 320
  National Computer Network Emergency Response Coordination Centre 324
  National Energy Administration 356
  National People's Congress 310, 311, 314, 315, 320
  People's Bank of China 317
  People's Liberation Army 287, 310, 313, 319ff, 352, 356, 357
    General Staff Department 324
      Unit 61398 324
    Navy 323, 356
      South Sea Fleet 321, 323
  Politburo 311, 312, 313, 315, 343
  Politburo Standing Committee 312, 313, 314, 315
  State Council Information Office 319
  State Oceanic Administration 316, 322
Chinamasa, Patrick 272
Chinese Communist Party 18, 309, 310ff, 356
  Central Committee 312, 315
    Organisation Department 312
  Communist Youth League 313
  General Office 314
  United Front Work Department 314
Chissano, Joaquim 274
Choe Ryong-hoe 343
Chongqing (China) 310, 314, 315
Christian Democratic Union (Germany) 124, 125
Christian Social Union (Germany) 124, 125
Cilvegozu (Turkey) 144
CITIC Capital Holdings (China) 213
Citizens' Revolution (Ecuador) 96, 99
Civil and Political Rights Association (Saudi Arabia) 206
Clapper, James 335
Clarín Group (Argentina) 105
Clegg, Nick 129
Clinton, Bill 63
Clinton, Hillary 359
'Cold Start' doctrine (India) 35, 36
Cold War 31, 32, 37, 39ff, 48, 164, 360
Colombia 87–91, 94, 97, 102
  Law of Public Order 87
Colombia Opina 89
Colombo (Sri Lanka) 281, 294, 295
Colorado (US) 66, 71
Commonwealth 281, 294, 355
Community of Latin American and Caribbean States 77, 108
Computer Network Exploitation 321
Conakry (Guinea) 255
Condé, Alpha 255
Conference on Security and Co-operation in Europe 42
Congress of South African Trade Unions 278
Congress Party (India) 281, 282, 285
Connecticut (US) 70
Conservative Party (UK) 113, 118, 129ff
Consulta Mitofsky–TCS 86
Coordinating Council (Russia) 159
Copé, Jean-François 118, 119
Copts 193, 196, 200
Corn, David 66
Correa, Rafael 95, 96, 97, 99
Côte d'Ivoire 120, 256–257
Council of Europe 164
Croatia 206
Cuba 89, 93, 94, 97, 304
Cuban missile crisis 41
Customs Union 382
Cuyahoga County (US) 59
Cyprus 113, 147, 148

D

Damascus (Syria) 180, 220, 234, 245
Darfur (Sudan) 261, 262, 263
Darwin (Australia) 351
da Silva, Luiz Inácio 'Lula' 77, 78, 99, 100
Deby, Idriss 264
Delhi (India) 19, 284, 286, 381
del Rosario, Albert 359, 364
de Maizière, Thomas 124, 125, 140
Democratic Action Party (Philippines) 367, 368
Democratic Alliance (South Africa) 276
Democratic Forces for the Liberation of Rwanda 267
Democratic Party of Japan 325ff
Democratic Party (US) 24, 59ff, 66, 67, 69, 71, 72, 73
Democratic Republic of the Congo 247, 264, 265–267, 278, 279
Democratic Tribune (Kuwait) 210
Democratic United Party (South Korea) 344
Democrat Party (Thailand) 368
Dempsey, Judy 126
Dempsey, Martin 342
Deng Xiaoping 311, 312, 340
Denmark 52
Denver (US) 66
Deraa Military Council (Syria) 188
Der Spiegel 127
Dheeb al-Ajami, Ibn al- 213
Dhi Qar (Iraq) 241, 242
Diabaly (Mali) 249
Diallo, Cellou Dalein 255
Diaoyu Islands 310, 319, 322, 323, 331
Dibb, Paul 350
Dinka (South Sudan) 262
Diyala (Iraq) 237
Djibouti 138, 260

Djotodia, Michel 264, 265
Dlamini-Zuma, Nkosozana 279
Dmitriev, Mikhail 154
Dobbins, James 305
Doha (Qatar) 212, 218, 305, 307
Dokdo Islands 332, 346
Donilon, Thomas 166
Douentza (Mali) 249
Draghi, Mario 19, 111, 112
Dravida Munnetra Kazhagam Party (India) 285
Dubai 273
Durban (South Africa) 278

E

E3+3 222, 226, 227
EADS 56, 117
East Asia 380
East China Sea 18, 309, 322, 330, 331, 357
East Darfur (Sudan) 263
Eastern Province (Saudi Arabia) 205
Eastern Siberia 170
East Germany 39, 125
East Jerusalem 213, 219
Economic Community of Central African States 264
Economic Community of West African States 248, 249, 256
  ECOWAS Mission in Guinea-Bissau 256
Ecuador 78, 91, 95–99, 102
Egypt 17, 18, 20, 21, 22, 75, 175, 177, 187ff, 190–197, 200, 205, 206, 208, 212, 218, 219, 220, 234, 378, 379, 382
  Constituent Assembly 192
  Egyptian Army 188
  Shura Council 193
  Supreme Constitutional Court 193, 196
  Supreme Council of the Armed Forces 191, 192
Egypt–Israel Peace Treaty 220
Eisenhower, Dwight 41, 64
ElBaradei, Mohamed 195, 196, 197
El Salvador 82ff, 109
  Supreme Court 85
England 129, 131, 135, 137
ENI (Italy) 275
Ensour, Abdullah 186, 187
Erdogan, Recep Tayyip 143, 144, 145, 148ff, 183, 382
Ethiopia 261
Etilaf al-Mu'aratha (Kuwait) 210
Eurasia 153, 164, 173
Europe 19, 23, 24, 25, 37, 38, 44–57, 61, 64, 65, 111–152, 155, 201, 229, 381
European Air Transport Command 50
  Heavy Airlift Wing 50
European Central Bank 19, 111, 112
European Commission 115, 140
European Council 46, 121, 133, 138, 140
European Economic Community 130
European Union 22, 25, 45, 46, 53, 102, 113, 114, 117, 118, 121, 123, 126ff, 136ff, 147, 168, 174, 226, 228, 229, 248, 272, 304, 382
  Common Security and Defence Policy 46, 121, 123, 137ff
  EUAVSEC South Sudan 138
  EUBAM Libya 139
  EUCAP NESTOR mission 138
  EUCAP SAHEL Niger 138
  European Defence Agency 56
  EUTM Mali 139
  operation *Atalanta* 138
  'pooling and sharing' programme 45, 53
  Stability and Growth Pact 118
  Strategy for Security and Development in the Sahel 121
eurozone 112, 113, 117, 118, 126, 127, 130, 131, 133, 316
ExxonMobil (US) 244, 275

F

Fahim, Haseem 300
Fahim, Mohammad 300
Faisalabad (Pakistan) 289
Fakhrawi, Karim 209
Falkland Islands 105, 106
Fallujah (Iraq) 237
Fan Changlong 313
Farage, Nigel 131
Farnood, Sherkhan 300
Fatah 218
Fayyad, Salam 219
Fazlullah, Maulana 307
February 20 movement (Morocco) 202
Fédération Internationale de Football Association 103
Felupe (Guinea-Bissau) 256
Fernández de Kirchner, Cristina 103, 104, 105, 106, 107
Ferozi, Khalilullah 300
Fiji 354, 355
Fillon, François 118, 119
Financial Times 23, 126
Finland 52
Finmeccanica (Italy) 284
First Capital Command (Brazil) 103
Florida (US) 60
Foal Eagle military exercise 341
Forbes 126
Fordow (Iran) 224, 227
Fox News 59
France 22, 23, 24, 44ff, 49ff, 55, 62, 113, 114–123, 139, 141, 171, 178, 199, 204, 208, 222, 248ff, 255, 264, 298
  Fifth Republic 118
  Fourth Republic 119
  Livre Blanc 52
  National Assembly 119
  White Paper 115, 122, 123
Franken, Al 67
Frankfurt am Main (Germany) 39
Free Democratic Party (Germany) 124, 125
Free Democrats Party (Georgia) 173
Freedom and Justice Party (Egypt) 191
Freedom House group (US) 272
Free State (South Africa) 276
Free Syrian Army 181, 234
Frelimo (Mozambique) 275
Friends of Syria 188
Friends of Yemen 216
Fujairah (UAE) 208
Fujian (China) 311
Fukushima (Japan) 125, 325, 326, 328
Fulani (Mali) 250, 255
Fulda Gap (Germany) 39
Fundamedios (Ecuador) 96
Funes, Mauricio 84, 85, 86
Futenma air station (Japan) 326, 329, 331

G

G8 162
G20 166, 277
Gabon 264
Gadhafi, Muammar 120, 189, 197, 198, 199, 200
Gadhafi, Saif al-Islam 199
Gadkari, Nitin 285
Gallois, Louis 117
Galmudug (Somalia) 258
Gamaa Islamiya (Egypt) 191
Gambia 256
Gandhi, Rahul 285
Gandhi, Sonia 285
Gangnam Style 345
Gao (Mali) 120, 248, 249, 251
Garissa (Kenya) 269
Gaskarov, Alexei 160
Gaza 148, 187, 195, 213, 218, 219
Gazprom (Russia) 158, 170, 244, 318
Gbagbo, Laurent 256, 257
Gemir (Sudan) 263
Genel Energy (Turkey) 145
Geneva Discussions (Russia-Georgia) 174
Geng Biao 311
Georgetown (US) 73
Georgia 166, 170–174
Georgian Dream party (Georgia) 171, 172, 173, 174
German/Netherlands Corps 51
Germany 19, 25, 39, 46, 50, 51, 56, 62, 111ff, 117, 118, 124–127, 133, 140, 141, 145, 147, 222, 256, 267
  Bundesbank 111
  Bundestag 124
Gezi Park (Turkey) 143, 149
Ghai, Yash 355
Ghana 249, 257
Giffords, Gabrielle 71
Gilani, Yousuf Raza 290
Gillard, Julia 309, 349, 352
Golan Heights 183
Golos (Russia) 156

Goma (Democratic Republic of the Congo) 265, 266, 267
Google (US) 27
Gorbachev, Mikhail 38
Gordillo, Elba Esther 80
Gordon, Philip 133
Gore, Al 72
Gorongosa mountains (Mozambique) 275
Greece 19, 112, 116, 127, 134
Green Movement (Iran) 232
Green Party (France) 117, 118
Guadalajara (Mexico) 86
Guam 321, 336, 341
Guangdong (China) 312
Guantánamo Bay (Cuba) 304
Guardian 76
Guatemala 82, 83, 84
  Constitutional Court 84
Gudkov, Dmitry 157
Gudkov, Gennady 157
Guinea 249, 254–255
Guinea-Bissau 255–256
Gujarat 285
Gu Kailai 315
Gul, Abdullah 148, 151
Gulf Cooperation Council 209, 210, 211, 213, 235, 379
  Peninsula Shield Force 209
Gulf of Aden 287
Gulf of Mexico 108
Guriev, Sergei 153
Guru, Afzal 286
Gyngell, Allan 350

H

Habayit HaYehudi party (Israel) 217, 218
Habra, Saleh 215
Hadash party (Israel) 217
Hadi, Abd Rabbuh Mansour 214, 215
Hagel, Chuck 74, 297, 361
The Hague (Netherlands) 199, 267, 268, 289
al-Haidari, Faraj 240
Hailey, Nic 298
Hainan (China) 320
King Hamad (Bahrain) 208
Hamad bin Jassim al-Thani 212
Hamad bin Khalifa al-Thani 212
Hamas 177, 195, 213, 218, 219, 234, 262
Hama (Syria) 180
al-Hamid, Abdullah 206
Haqqani, Badruddin 294
Haqqani network 294, 302
Harare (Zimbabwe) 272
Harper, Stephen 295
Harvard 65
al-Hashemi, Tariq 232, 236, 242
Hashimoto, Toru 327, 329
al-Hassan, Wissam 184
Hassan Taib 370
Hatnuah Party (Israel) 217, 218
Hatoyama, Yukio 326
Hausa (Nigeria) 252
Havana (Cuba) 87, 88, 89
Hawaii (US) 321
Heath, Edward 130
Hebei (China) 311
Heglig (Sudan) 261
Helmand (Afghanistan) 301
Helsinki Accords 42
Henan (China) 311, 312
Henoko (Japan) 330
Henry, Ken 350
Herat (Afghanistan) 298
Hernández, Juan Orlando 85
Heywood, Neil 310, 315
Hijab, Riad 188
Hitto, Ghassan 182
Hizbullah 22, 145, 175, 177, 183, 185, 186, 206, 220, 221, 262
Hollande, François 24, 114ff, 120ff, 128, 133, 249
Homs (Syria) 180
Honduras 82, 83, 85, 87, 109
Hong Kong 76
Houthi (Yemen) 214, 215, 235
Howard, John 352
Hu Jintao 310, 312, 313, 314, 319
Human Development Bond 96
Hungarian uprising 41
Hungary 50
Hutu 266, 267
Hyundai (South Korea) 345

I

Iceland 52
Idriss, Salim 181
Ilopango (El Salvador) 84
IMF 247, 263, 273, 275, 277
In Amenas gas plant (Algeria) 204, 251
Independent High Electoral Commission (Iraq) 240, 241
India 18, 19, 25, 27, 31ff, 39, 40, 42, 43, 57, 230, 281, 282–289, 294, 306, 329, 347, 364, 380, 381
  Defence Research and Development Organisation 34, 37
  Lok Sabha 283
  'Look East' policy 380
  National Security Advisory Board 35
  Nuclear Command Authority 43
  Supreme Court 284
Indian Ocean 123
Indjai, Antonio 256
Indonesia 357, 358, 361, 363, 366, 380
Indus Waters Treaty 289
Induta, Jose Zamora 256
Institutional Revolutionary Party (Mexico) 79, 81
International Atomic Energy Agency 32, 225, 226
  Convention on Nuclear Safety 226
International Court of Arbitration 289
International Court of Justice 274
International Criminal Court 199, 256ff
International Energy Agency 243, 244
International Monetary Fund 77, 104, 105, 115, 117, 194, 201, 202, 214, 215, 247, 292
International Security Assistance Force 137, 141, 142, 297, 301, 303, 306
Iran 17, 19, 22, 27, 28, 74, 75, 145, 146, 163, 166, 169, 175, 177, 178, 180, 182, 183, 185, 194, 195, 205, 206, 208, 215, 220, 221–235, 226ff, 232ff, 245, 292, 301, 376, 377
  Air Force 236
  Central Bank of Iran 228
  Guardian Council 232
  Iran Revolutionary Guard Corps 234
    Aerospace Force 234
  Majles 231
  National Security Council 232
Iraq 17, 23, 29, 48, 63, 71, 77, 135, 145, 146, 150, 168, 175, 178, 180, 182, 206, 211, 234, 236–245, 245, 351
  Board of Supreme Audit 238
  Higher Judicial Council 238
Iraq Body Count 242
Iraqi Airways 211
Iraqiyya (Iraq) 236ff
Irbid (Jordan) 187
Ireland 112, 116, 147
Ishihara, Shintaro 322, 327
Islamabad (Pakistan) 36, 39, 40, 293
Islamic Action Front (Jordan) 178, 187, 188
Islamic Dawa Party (Iraq) 240
Islamic Jihad 219
Islamic Movement for Azawad (Mali) 251
Islamic Republic News Agency 231
Islamic Supreme Council of Iraq 241, 242
Ismailia (Egypt) 193
Israel 27, 33, 74, 75, 148, 177, 183, 185, 187, 188, 195, 216–221, 222, 223, 234, 262, 376, 377, 384
  Israel Defense Forces 219, 220
  Israeli Air Force 219
  Knesset 216, 217
  Tal Law 216, 218
al-Issawi, Rafi 236, 237, 238
Istanbul (Turkey) 143, 149
Italy 19, 111, 112, 113, 126, 128, 199
Ivanishvili, Bidzina 170ff
Ivorian Popular Front (Côte d'Ivoire) 257

J

Jabari, Ahmed 219
Jabhat al-Nusra (Syria) 146, 181, 188
Jafari, Mohammad Ali 234
Jaish al-Mahdi (Iraq) 238

Jaish-e-Mohammed 289
Jalalabad (Afghanistan) 302
Jalili, Saeed 226, 228, 232, 233
James Shoal 357
Jammu and Kashmir (India) 286, 364
Jammu prison (India) 289
Janata Dal (United) Party (India) 285
Jang Song-taek 344
Japan 18, 25, 126, 282, 309, 310, 319, 322, 323, 325–333, 326, 328ff, 341, 342, 343, 346, 347, 356, 363, 364, 379, 380
  Bank of Japan 25
  Japanese Air Self-Defense Force 322
  Japanese Imperial Army 329
  Japanese Maritime Self-Defense Force 322
  Japanese Self-Defense Forces 323, 330
  Ministry of Defense 322
  National Defense Programme Guidelines 329
  National Security Council 330, 380
Japan Restoration Party 327
Javanfekr, Ali Akbar 231
Jebali, Hamadi 190, 201
Jebel Amir (Sudan) 263
Jharkhand (India) 285
Jiang Zemin 312, 313, 314
Johannesburg (South Africa) 278
Johnson, Lyndon 61
Joint Commission (India-Pakistan) 287
Jonathan, Goodluck 251, 252, 254
Jordan 22, 177, 178, 182, 186–188, 206, 237, 376
Joshi, D.K. 364
Jubaland (Somalia) 259
Juba (South Sudan) 260, 261, 262
Judis, John B. 62, 63
Justice and Development Party (Morocco) 201, 202
Justice and Development Party (Turkey) 143, 145, 147, 151
Just Russia Party (Russia) 157

K

Kabila, Joseph 265, 266
Kabul (Afghanistan) 296, 298, 299, 301, 302, 304, 305, 306, 353
Kabul Bank (Afghanistan) 300
Kachin Independence Organisation (Myanmar) 371, 372
  Kachin Independence Army 371
Kadima Party (Israel) 217
Kaechon (North Korea) 340
Kaesong Industrial Complex (North Korea) 337, 346
Kaiser Family Foundation (US) 70
Kalenjin (Kenya) 268
Kampala (Uganda) 266
Kandil, Hisham 193
Kan, Naoto 326, 331
Karachi (Pakistan) 290, 292, 307
Karak (Jordan) 187
Karakoram Highway 287
Karasin, Grigory 174
Karbala (Iraq) 241
Karzai, Hamid 29, 296, 298ff, 305ff
Karzai, Mahmoud 299, 300
Karzai, Qayum 299
Kasab, Ajmal 288
Kashmir 35, 40, 42, 285, 286, 288, 289
Katsina (Nigeria) 252
Kayani, Ashfaq Parvez 290, 291, 293, 306
Kazakhstan 226, 382
Kelly, Megan 59
Kempinski Hotels (Switzerland) 340
Kennedy, Edward 67
Kenya 138, 247, 259, 260, 268–269, 355
Kenyatta, Jomo 269
Kenyatta, Uhuru 268, 269
Kerry, John 60, 75, 167, 184, 216, 219, 221, 230, 253, 306, 318, 342, 384
Keynesianism 19, 61, 113, 134
Khalid, Asadullah 300
Khalid Bin Ahmed al-Khalifa 235
Khalid bin Ali al-Khalifa 209
Khamenei, Ali 28, 222, 227, 230ff
Khan, Imran 291
Khan, Ismail 298, 303
Khartoum (Sudan) 260, 261, 262, 263
al-Khatib, Moaz 182, 184, 212
Khrushchev, Nikita 41
Khurshid, Salman 284
Khushab (Pakistan) 33
Khyber Pakhtunkhwa (Pakistan) 291, 293
Kibaki, Mwai 268
Kidal (Mali) 120, 248, 249
Kidwai, Khalid 43
Kigali (Rwanda) 267
Kiir Mayardit, Salva 261
Kikuyu (Kenya) 268
Kikwete, Jakaya 274
Kilifi (Kenya) 268
Kim Dae-jung 346
Kim Il-sung 339
Kim, Jim Yong 265
Kim Jong-gak 338
Kim Jong-il 338, 339, 342
Kim Jong-un 20, 28, 309, 333, 334, 336ff, 343, 345
King, Mervyn 135
Kinshasa (Democratic Republic of the Congo) 266
Kiram III, Jamalul 365, 366
Kirchner, Néstor 104
Kirkuk (Iraq) 241
Kirov (Russia) 159
Kishanganga river (India) 289
Kishida, Fumio 363, 364
Kismayo (Somalia) 258, 259, 260, 269
Kisumu (Kenya) 269
Kobler, Martin 211
Koizumi, Junichiro 331
Konna (Mali) 249
Kono, Yohei 329
Korean War 334, 336, 337
Korean Workers' Party (North Korea) 333, 338
  Central Committee 338
  Central Committee Politburo 338
Kornelius, Stefan 127
Kosovo 48, 168
Koulikoro (Mali) 121
Kufra (Libya) 199
Kumar, Ashwani 284
Kumar, Nitish 285
Kurdish Regional Government 241, 243, 244, 245
  Peshmerga forces 243
Kurdistan 238, 239, 244–245
Kurdistan Democratic Party (Iraq) 238, 239, 240
Kurdistan Regional Government 145, 146
Kurdistan Workers' Party (Turkey) 149, 150
Kuwait 197, 210–211, 214, 273
  Ministry of Interior 211
Kuwait Airways 211
Kuwait City (Kuwait) 210
Kyrgyzstan 382

L

Labor Party (Australia) 309, 348, 349, 352
Labor Party (Israel) 217
Labour Party (UK) 61, 129, 131, 134
Ladakh (India) 287
Lagos (Nigeria) 252
Lahad Datu (Malaysia) 365, 366
Lahore (Pakistan) 289, 290
Lake Malawi 274
Lake Nyasa 274
Lakhvi, Zaki-ur-Rehman 288
Lancaster House Agreement 271
Lancaster House treaties 51
  Combined Joint Expeditionary Force 52
Lanza, Adam 70, 71
Laos 340, 358
Lapid, Yair 217
Larayedh, Ali 201
Larijani, Sadegh 231
Lashkar-e-Jhangvi 292, 293
Lashkar-e-Taiba 286, 288, 289
Lasso, Guillermo 96
Latin America 77–110, 383
Lavrov, Sergei 318
Leahy, Peter 350
Lebanon 22, 145, 175, 178, 180, 182, 184–186, 205, 206, 376
Le Drian, Jean-Yves 120, 122, 250
Lee Myung-bak 332, 346, 347
Left Party (Germany) 124
Le Monde 114
Le Pen, Marine 116, 118
L'Estrange, Michael 350

Levada Center (Russia) 156, 157
Levant 175, 178, 205, 206, 376
LG (South Korea) 345
Liang Guanglie 286
Liaoning (China) 312, 321
Liberal Democratic Party (Japan) 309, 325ff, 332, 333, 363
Liberal Democrat Party (UK) 129, 131
Liberation Tigers of Tamil Eelam (Sri Lanka) 295
Liberia 257
Libya 23, 28, 45, 66, 75, 120, 121, 123, 139, 168, 169, 188, 189, 190, 193, 197–200, 203, 204, 248, 251, 252, 278, 377
  General National Congress 197, 198
  National Transitional Council 197
Lieberman, Avigdor 217
Li Jianguo 343
Li Keqiang 286, 287, 311, 312, 343
Likud Beiteinu (Israel) 217, 218
Likud Party (Israel) 216
Line of Actual Control 286
Line of Control 40, 287, 288, 289
Ling Jihua 314
Liu Yan 313
Livni, Tzipi 216, 217
Li Yuanchao 312
Lobo Sosa, Porfirio 85
London (UK) 28, 97, 129, 131, 136, 206, 260, 269, 272
Lonmin (UK) 277
López Obrador, Andrés Manuel 79
Los Angeles (US) 86
Los Cabos (Mexico) 166
Luanda (Angola) 271
Lugo, Fernando 107
Lukoil (Russia) 244
Luo (Kenya) 268
Luoyang (China) 311
Luxembourg 50, 228
Luxor (Egypt) 191

M

M-18 (El Salvador) 84
M23 (Democratic Republic of the Congo) 265, 266, 267
Maastricht Treaty 130
Madagascar 270, 274
Madonna 274
Maduro, Nicolás 90, 92, 93, 94, 95
Magarief, Mohammed 198
Magnitsky, Sergei 165
Maharashtra (India) 285
Maiduguri (Nigeria) 252
Majok, Kual Deng 262
Major, John 130
Ma Kai 316
Makenga, Sultani 266
Malawi 267, 273, 273–274, 274
Malay rebels (Thailand) 370
Malaysia 356, 357, 358, 360, 361, 363ff, 366–367, 368, 370
  Eastern Sabah Security Command 366
  New Economic Policy 367
Malaysian People's Movement Party 368
Malema, Julius 276
Mali 24, 28, 114, 120–121, 123, 138, 139, 199, 203, 204, 247, 248–251, 253, 257
al-Maliki, Nuri 178, 182, 236ff
Malinké (Guinea) 255
Management & Fit (Argentina) 106
Manama (Bahrain) 209
Manama Dialogue 208
Manchin, Joe 71
Mandela, Nelson 276
Mandiant (US) 324, 325
Mangaung (South Africa) 276
Manicaland (Zimbabwe) 272
Manila (Philippines) 364
Mansour, Adly 196, 197
Mao Zedong 311, 315
Mara Salvatrucha (El Salvador) 84
March of Millions 159
Marikana (South Africa) 276, 277, 278
Marxism 312
Mashaei, Esfandiar Rahim 231, 232
Mashal, Khaled 234
Mashonaland (Zimbabwe) 272
Masondo, Vusumuzi 279
Massachusetts (US) 64, 65, 67
Mattis, James 297
Mauritania 138
Mauritius 138
MBDA (France/UK) 55
Mbeki, Thabo 261
MDC–M (Zimbabwe) 270
MDC–T (Zimbabwe) 270, 271, 272
Medellín (Colombia) 86
Mediterranean 123, 145, 186
Medvedev, Dmitry 154, 156, 160, 161, 162, 168, 382
Meiktila (Myanmar) 372
Memorial (Russia) 156
Meng Jianzhu 314
Merabishvili, Vano 173
Merca (Somalia) 259
Mercosur 102, 107, 108
Meretz Party (Israel) 217
Merkel, Angela 112, 113, 117, 118, 124ff, 133
Mersin (Turkey) 145
Mexico 77, 78, 79–82, 83, 86, 94, 97, 102, 108, 166
  Pact for Mexico 79, 81
Mexico State (Mexico) 79
Mhamadjo, Manuel Serifo 256
Middle East 17, 21, 22, 23, 26, 48, 75, 123, 143, 145ff, 175–246, 331, 377, 379, 381, 383
Mikati, Najib 178, 185, 186
Miliband, Ed 129
Minas Gerais (Brazil) 101
Mindanao (Philippines) 365
Minhas air base (Pakistan) 293
Minnesota (US) 67
Miranda (Venezuela) 92
Misseriya (Sudan) 262, 263
Mitterrand, François 62
Miyako Strait 323
Mnangagwa, Emmerson 271
Modi, Narendra 285
Mogadishu (Somalia) 258ff
Mohammadi, Bismillah Khan 299, 300
King Mohammed VI (Morocco) 201, 202
Mohamud, Hassan Sheikh 259
Mombasa (Kenya) 268, 269
Mongolia 331
Monywa (Myanmar) 373
Moon Jae-in 344, 345
Mopti (Mali) 120
Moranbong Band 339
Morocco 201–202, 204, 251
  Makhzen 202
Moro Islamic Liberation Front (Philippines) 365
Moro National Liberation Front (Philippines) 365, 366
Morsi, Muhammad 20, 21, 75, 175, 177, 188, 190ff, 206, 220, 234, 235, 378
Moscow (Russia) 76, 155, 158, 159, 165, 226
Mother Jones 66
Motlanthe, Kgalema 276
Moussa, Amr 196
Movement for Democratic Change (Zimbabwe) 270, 271, 272
Movement for Jihad and Oneness in West Africa 248, 251
Movement for the Emancipation of the Niger Delta (Nigeria) 253
Movement for the National Liberation of the Azawad (Mali) 248
Mozambique 138, 247, 270, 274, 275, 278
Mtetwa, Beatrice 272
Mubarak, Hosni 20, 21, 177, 191, 194, 196, 378
Mugabe, Robert 270, 271, 272
Mujuru, Joice 271
Mullah Omar 305
Mumbai (India) 288
Munich Security Conference 163, 227
Muqrin bin Abdulaziz 207
Murdoch, Rupert 136
Muscat (Oman) 214
Musharraf, Pervez 291, 292
Muslim Brotherhood (Egypt) 20, 21, 175, 177, 178, 181, 182, 183, 188ff, 200, 205ff, 212, 213, 378, 379, 382
Musyoka, Kalonzo 268
Mutharika, Bingu wa 273
Mutharika, Peter 273
Mutlaq, Saleh al- 237, 241
Muttahidda Qaumi Movement (Pakistan) 290, 291

Muxungue (Mozambique) 275
Myanmar 309, 356, 358, 359, 361, 371–374
  Latpadaung Inquiry Commission 373
Myanmar Wanbao copper-mine 373

N

Nabil, Rahmatullah 300
Nago City (Japan) 330
Nairobi 269
Najaf (Iraq) 242
Najib Tun Razak 358, 366, 367
Namah, Belden 354
Namibia 270
Naqshabandi, Jaish Rijal Tariqah al- 243
Narathiwat (Thailand) 370
Nasrallah, Hassan 185
Nasralla, Salvador 85
Natalegawa, Marty 358
Natanz (Iran) 224, 225
National Action Party (Mexico) 79, 80, 81
National Alliance Party (Papua New Guinea) 354
National Coalition (Qatar) 212
National Coalition (Syria) 181, 184
National Congress for the Defence of the People (Democratic Republic of the Congo) 265ff
National Democratic Alliance (India) 285
National Democratic Coalition (Kuwait) 210
National Dialogue Conference (Yemen) 214
National Forces Alliance (Libya) 197, 198
National Front (France) 116, 118, 119
National Journal 71
National League for Democracy (Myanmar) 371
National Liberation Front (Algeria) 203
National Pact for Growth, Competitiveness and Employment (France) 117
National Rifle Association (US) 71, 72
National Salvation Front (Egypt) 195
NATO 22, 31, 32, 37ff, 45, 47ff, 52, 53, 123, 136, 137, 141, 142, 146, 147, 166, 168, 174, 183, 281, 294ff, 301ff, 306
  Able Archer exercise 41
  Chicago Summit 2012 45, 53, 142
  Connected Forces Initiative 141, 142
  NATO Forces 2020 141
  Operation *Resolute Support* 297
  Response Force 142
  Smart Defence 45, 46, 48, 49, 51, 53, 55, 141, 142
  Strategic Airlift Interim Solution 50
Navalny, Alexei 157, 159, 160
Naxalites 285
Ndlovu, Kwezi 278
Netanyahu, Benjamin 74, 216, 217, 218, 220, 221, 223, 224
Netherlands 50, 51, 147, 267
Neves, Aécio 101
New Deal (US) 61, 65
New Delhi (India) 32, 35, 36, 40
New Economic School (Russia) 153
New Hampshire (US) 64
New Komeito Party (Japan) 327
New START agreement 163, 167
New York Times 43, 60, 301, 314
New York (US) 72, 78, 105, 231, 322, 336
New Zealand 353, 354
  New Zealand Defence Force 353
Nicaragua 97, 109
Niger 138, 249, 251, 253
Niger Delta 251, 253
Nigeria 28, 136, 247, 249, 250, 251, 251–254, 252, 253, 254, 256
Nilepet (South Sudan) 262
Nimr, Nimr al- 205
9/11 62, 76, 162, 166
9/11 350
Nineveh (Iraq) 237, 241
Nixon, Richard 60, 61, 62, 64, 76
Nobel Peace Prize 137
Noda, Yoshihiko 322, 326, 327, 331
Non-Aligned Movement 194, 235
Noonan, Peggy 60
Nordic Defence Cooperation 52
North Africa 178, 188–204, 189, 205
North America 46, 142, 381
North American Free Trade Agreement 82
North Atlantic 123
North Atlantic Treaty 147
North Carolina (US) 60
North Caucasus 168
North Darfur (Sudan) 251, 263
Northern Alliance (Afghanistan) 299, 300
Northern Distribution Network 163
Northern Ireland 129
North Kivu (Democratic Republic of the Congo) 265, 266
North Korea 20, 28, 309, 318, 332, 333, 333–344, 334, 335, 336, 337, 338, 339, 340, 341, 342, 343, 344, 345, 346, 347, 348, 363, 380
  Foreign Trade Bank 335, 343
  Korean People's Army 343
  National Defence Commission 339
  Supreme People's Assembly 338
North Waziristan (Pakistan) 293, 294
Norway 52, 89, 170, 244
Ntaganda, Bosco 265, 266, 267
N'Tchama, Pansau 256
Nuba Mountains (Sudan) 263
Nuclear Non-Proliferation Treaty 222
Nuclear Suppliers Group 32
Nujaifi, Osama al- 237
Nukuga, Fukushiro 332
Nuristan (Afghanistan) 307

O

Obama, Barack 17, 21, 23, 26, 28, 59, 60, 63ff, 114, 133, 165, 166, 167, 169, 187, 220, 221, 222, 224, 227, 228, 236, 294, 296, 297, 310, 323, 324, 325, 331, 337, 344, 347, 348, 351, 359, 360, 371
Oboronservis (Russia) 157, 158
Ocalan, Abdullah 150
Oceania 102
Odah, Salman al- 205
Odinga, Raila 268, 269
Odisha (India) 285
OECD 115, 116
Ohio (US) 59, 66, 76
Okinawa (Japan) 323, 326, 330, 331
Okonjo-Iweala, Ngozi 254
Olympic Games 102, 206
Oman 200, 213, 213–214, 214
  Shura Council 214
O'Neill, Peter 354
Onodera, Itsunori 323
Opération Serval 120, 121, 249, 250, 251
Organisation of Islamic Cooperation 204
Organisation of the Islamic Conference 371
Organisation for Economic Co-operation and Development 349
Organisation for Security and Co-operation in Europe 164
Organization of American States 91, 97, 107, 108
  Inter-American Commission on Human Rights 97
Orlando Hernández, Juan 85
Osaka (Japan) 327, 329, 346
Osborne, George 134
Oslo (Norway) 87
Ottoman Empire 143, 148
Ouattara, Alassane 256, 257
Oxfam 250
Ozawa, Ichiro 326

P

Pacific Alliance 77, 91, 102, 108
Pacific Islands Forum 355
Pacific Rim 330, 360
Pakatan Rakyat (Malaysia) 367
Pakistan 27, 28, 31ff, 42, 43, 281, 286, 287, 288, 289, 290–294, 296, 302, 305, 306, 307, 364, 380, 381
  Anti-Terrorism (Amendment) Bill 2012 293
  Anti-Terrorism Amendment Bill 2013 293

Directorate for Inter-Services Intelligence 36
Inter-Services Intelligence agency 307
National Assembly 290, 291
National Counter-Terrorism Authority 294
Senate 291
Special Services Group 289
Strategic Plans Division 43
Supreme Court 290
Pakistan Muslim League-Nawaz Party 290, 291
Pakistan People's Party 281, 290, 291, 293
Pakistan Tehreek-e-Insaf party 291
Pak Pong-ju 338, 340
Paktika (Afghanistan) 307
Palawan Island (Philippines) 357
Palestinian Authority 213, 218, 384
Palestinian Territories 74, 75, 187, 188, 213, 216, 217, 218–219
Panetta, Leon 235, 353, 363
Panov, Roman 158
Papa Air Base (Hungary) 50
Papua New Guinea 354
Judicial Control Act 354
Paracel Islands 356, 357
Paradorn Pattanathabutr 370
Paraguay 107, 108
Parchin (Iran) 226
Paris (France) 122, 250, 251
Park Chung-hee 345
Park Geun-hye 309, 332, 334, 337, 344, 345, 348
Parti Keadilan Rakyat (Malaysia) 367
Party of the Democratic Revolution (Mexico) 79, 80, 81
Pastrana Arango, Andrés 88
Patriarch Kirill I 155, 159
Patriotic Union of Kurdistan (Iraq) 239
Pattani (Thailand) 370, 371
Peña Nieto, Enrique 79, 80, 81, 82
Pennsylvania (US) 71
People's National Congress (Papua New Guinea) 354
Peres, Shimon 223
Pérez Molina, Otto 83, 84
Perm (Russia) 158
Pernambuco (Brazil) 101
Perot, Ross 63
Perth (Australia) 352
Peru 102
Peshawar (Pakistan) 293
Petrocaribe 98
Pheu Thai Party (Thaland) 368
Philippines 183, 356, 357, 358, 359, 361, 362, 363, 364–366
Exclusive Economic Zone 357
Framework Agreement on Bangsamoro 365, 366
Senate 362
Transition Commission 365
Visiting Forces Agreement 362
Phillips, Kevin 62, 63
Phnom Penh (Cambodia) 360
Pillay, Navi 340
Ping, Jean 279
Pirate Party (Germany) 124
Plutonium Management Disposition Agreement (US-Russia) 163
Poland 133
Polisario Front (Western Sahara) 202
Ponomarev, Ilya 157
Pope Alexander VI 102
Pope Francis 106
Port Said (Egypt) 193
Port Sudan (Sudan) 261
Portugal 102, 112, 116, 275
Prague (Czech Republic) 167
Prayuth Chan-ocha 370
PSY 345
Pudong (China) 324
Punjab (India) 39, 282, 289
Punjab (Pakistan) 33, 291
Puntland (Somalia) 258, 260
Pussy Riot 158, 159
Putin, Vladimir 153ff, 161, 162, 163, 165, 166, 318, 382
Pyongyang (North Korea) 337, 340, 341, 342, 343

Q

al-Qahtani, Mohammed 206
Qalibaf, Mohammad Baqer 232
Qatar 21, 144, 175, 177, 178, 181, 183, 195, 197, 201, 205, 206, 212–213, 219, 234, 304, 305, 306, 379
Qatar Investment Authority 213
Qi Jianguo 357
Quetta (Pakistan) 292, 307
Qusair (Syria) 185

R

Ra'am Ta'al party (Israel) 217
Rabat (Morocco) 202, 203
Rabbani, Salahuddin 305, 306
Rachman, Gideon 23
Radical Party (France) 117
Radonski, Henrique Capriles 92
Rafsanjani, Akbar Hashemi 232
Rajab, Nabeel 209
Rajapaksa, Basil 295
Rajapaksa, Mahinda 295
Rajasthan (India) 39
Rajoelina, Andy 274
Rakhine (Myanmar) 372
Ramadi (Iraq) 237
Ramaphosa, Cyril 276
Ramphele, Mamphela 277
Rand, Ayn 70
RAND Corporation 208
Ranjay, Sanaullah 289
Ras al-Khaimah (UAE) 207
RasGas (Qatar) 178
Rashid, Sarbas Mustafa 240
Rashtriya Swayamsevak Sangh (India) 286
Ras Kamboni (Somalia) 260
Rasmussen, Anders Fogh 45, 46, 137, 141, 296
Ratsiraka, Didier 274
Ravalomanana, Lalao 274
Ravalomanana, Marc 274
Reagan, Ronald 60, 62, 64, 166
Red Command (Brazil) 103
Red Cross 337
Red Sea 261
Red Shirt movement (Thailand) 368
Rehman, Waliur 294
Renamo (Mozambique) 275
Renault (France) 122
Repsol (Spain) 104
Republican Party (Georgia) 173
Republican Party (US) 24, 59ff, 71, 72, 73, 74, 118
Republic of Congo 264, 266, 318
Revolutionary Armed Forces of Colombia 87ff, 97
Reyhanli (Turkey) 144, 183
Rifi, Ashraf 186
Rigby, Lee 135, 136
Rio de Janeiro (Brazil) 103
Ríos Montt, Efraín 83, 84
Rio Tinto (UK) 255
Ri Sol-ju 339
Ri Yong-ho 338
Robinson, Mary 267
Rockefeller, Nelson 64
Rodman, Dennis 337
Romney, George 64
Romney, Mitt 59, 60, 61, 63, 64, 65, 66, 74, 76, 221
Roosevelt, Franklin D. 61, 65
Rosneft (Russia) 170, 318
Ross, Christopher 202
Rouhani, Hassan 20, 27, 75, 222, 232, 233, 235, 236
Rousseff, Dilma 99, 100, 101, 383
Rove, Karl 59, 63
Rovuma Basin (Mozambique) 275
Rudd, Kevin 309, 349, 350, 352
Rusal (Russia) 255
Russia 22, 23, 34, 38, 41, 46, 47, 57, 153–170, 171, 174, 183, 184, 216, 222, 225, 243, 244, 318, 331, 341, 376, 380, 381, 382
Bilateral Presidential Commission 163
Duma 155, 157, 160, 165
Foreign Policy Concept 381
Investigative Committee 155, 157, 160
KGB 157
Skolkovo Innovation Centre 157
Russian Orthodox Church 155, 159
Ruto, William 268, 269
Rwanda 266, 267

S

Saakashvili, Mikheil 170ff
Sabahi, Hamdeen 196
Sabah (Malaysia) 361, 365, 366
Sa'dah (Yemen) 215
Sadr, Moqtada al- 238
Saeed, Hafiz Mohammad 288

Saenuri (New Frontier) Party (South Korea) 344
Safeway (US) 71
Sahel 247, 378
Salamat (Sudan) 263
Salam, Tammam 186
Saleh, Ahmed Ali 215
Saleh, Ali Abdullah 215
Salehi, Ali Akbar 227, 234
Saleh, Mudher 238
Salman al-Khalifa 208, 209
Salman bin Abdulaziz 207
Salmond, Alex 136
Samaha, Michel 184
Samajwadi Party (India) 283
Sambisa Game Reserve (Nigeria) 253
Samsung (South Korea) 345
Sana'a (Yemen) 214, 215
Sandy Hook (US) 70, 71
Sanogo, Amadou 248, 250
San Salvador (El Salvador) 84
Santos, Juan Manuel 87ff, 97
Sanya naval base (China) 321
São Paulo (Brazil) 18, 101, 103
Saran, Shyam 35
Saraswat, Vijay Kumar 34
Sarawak (Malaysia) 357
Sarkozy, Nicolas 115, 116, 118
Saudi Arabia 144, 164, 175, 177, 183, 186, 188, 194, 197, 204, 205–207, 208, 210, 212, 215, 216, 292, 305, 377, 379
  General Intelligence Directorate 207
  National Security Council 207
  Shura Council 206
Scandinavia 44
Scarborough Shoal 357, 358, 359
Schröder, Gerhard 127
Scotland 129, 136
Scottish National Party (UK) 136
Sea of Japan 332
Second World War 329, 364
Ségou (Mali) 120
Séléka (Central African Republic) 264, 265, 278
Sellal, Abdelmalek 203
Semdinli (Turkey) 150
Semple, Michael 304, 305
Senegal 249, 251, 256
Senkaku Islands 310, 319, 322, 323, 331
al-Senussi, Abdullah 199
Seoul (South Korea) 332, 336, 337
Sepúlveda, Magdalena 275
Serdyukov, Anatoly 157, 158
Serdyukov, Yulia 158
Seychelles 138
Shaaban, Bouthaina 318
Shaanxi (China) 311
al-Shabibi, Sinan 238
Shafiq, Ahmed 20, 191
Shamoon virus 207
Shanduka investment group (South Africa) 276
Shanghai (China) 310, 312, 313, 317, 324
Shangri-La Dialogue 357, 361
Sharif, Nawaz 281, 287, 289ff, 306, 381
Sharif Sheikh Ahmad 259
Shas party (Israel) 217
Sheikh al-Azhar 196
Shekau, Abubakar 252, 253
Shell (Netherlands) 253
Sherman, Wendy 228
Shia Party (Lebanon) 175
Shinde, Sushil Kumar 286
Shirdon, Abdi Farah 259
Shtokman gas field (Russia) 170
Shuvalov, Igor 165
Sierra Leone 260
Sikorski, Radek 133
Silva, Marina 101
Silver, Nate 60
Simandou (Guinea) 255
Simla Agreement 42
Sinai (Egypt) 190, 220
Sinai Peninsula 177, 191, 193
Sindh (Pakistan) 291
Singapore 284, 357, 358, 360ff
Singh, Manmohan 282, 284, 287, 288, 289
Singh, Sarabjit 289
Sinuiju (North Korea) 340
Sisi, Fattah al- 191, 194, 196
Six-Party Talks 334, 337, 342, 343
Skrynnik, Elena 158
Slim, Carlos 80
Snowden, Edward 26, 27, 76, 325
Sobyanin, Sergei 159
Sochi 158, 174
Social Democratic Party (Germany) 124, 125, 126
Socialist Party (France) 117, 118
Somair uranium mine (Mali) 251
Somalia 28, 138, 247, 253, 258–260, 269, 287
Somali Constituent Assembly 258
Somaliland (Somalia) 259, 260
Somare, Arthur 354
Somare, Michael 354
South Africa 247, 261, 264, 266, 267, 272, 273, 275–279, 318
  National Defence Force 278, 279
South African Development Community 270, 271, 272, 273, 274, 278
  Free Trade Area 270
South Asia 31, 32, 35, 37, 39, 40, 42, 43
South Caucasus 168
South China Sea 309, 321, 355ff, 364, 366, 379
Southeast Asia 355–374
Southern Cone 103, 108
South Kivu (Democratic Republic of the Congo) 266
South Kordofan (Sudan) 261, 262, 263
South Korea 20, 273, 309, 318, 329, 331ff, 336, 337, 339, 341ff, 344–348, 380
  National Assembly 346
South Ossetia 174
South Shields (UK) 131
South Sudan 138, 260–263, 266
Soviet Union 31, 32, 37, 38, 39, 41, 42, 43, 154, 163, 164, 166, 171, 173
Spain 19, 84, 102, 104, 111, 112, 113, 116, 126, 128
Spratly Islands 356, 358
Sri Lanka 281, 285, 294–295
  Lessons Learnt and Reconciliation Commission 295
  Supreme Court 295
Srinagar (India) 286
State of Law (Iraq) 236, 239, 241, 242
Statoil (Norway) 170, 244
Steinbrück, Peer 124, 125
Stevens, Christopher 23, 75, 190, 199
Strait of Hormuz 208
Strategic Framework Agreement (US-Singapore) 362
Strategic Partnership Agreement (US-Afghanistan) 297
sub-Saharan Africa 202, 247
Sudan 163, 193, 251, 253, 260–263
Sudan Liberation Army-Minni Minawi 263
Sudan People's Liberation Movement North 261, 263
Sudapet (Sudan) 262
Suez (Egypt) 41, 193
Sukhumbhand Paribatra 368
Sultan Qaboos (Oman) 213
Sulu (Phiippines) 365
Summit of the Americas 2012 83, 91, 97
Sun Tzu 379
Supreme Military Council (Syria) 181, 182
Surkov, Vladislav 161, 162
Suwanatat, Sukumpol 362
Sweden 52, 97
Switzerland 333
Sykes-Picot 376
Syria 17, 20, 22, 23, 28, 75, 142, 144ff, 151, 167, 168, 169, 175, 177, 178, 179–184, 185ff, 194, 195, 199, 200, 206, 207, 211, 212, 220, 221, 228, 234, 235, 237, 243, 245, 318, 376
Syrian Islamic Front 181
Syrian Islamic Liberation Front 181
Syrian National Council 181, 182, 200, 206, 212

T

Taiwan 320, 323, 356
Tajikistan 382
Takeshima Islands 332, 346
Takfiri Salafism 204
Taksim Square (Turkey) 143
Talabani, Jalal 238
Taliban 212, 281, 290, 294, 296, 298, 301ff, 353
Tamarod (Egypt) 190, 196

Tamil Nadu 285
Tamils 285
Tamim bin Hamad al-Thani 212
Tantawi, Mohammed Hussein 191
Tanzania 138, 266, 267, 274, 318
Tarhuna (Libya) 198
Tawergha (Libya) 199
Tbilisi (Georgia) 173
Tea Party (US) 63, 67, 70, 76
Tehran (Iran) 178, 194, 221, 222, 225, 226, 227, 229, 231, 232, 235
Tehrik-e-Taliban Pakistan 290, 293, 294, 307
Teixeira, Ruy 62, 63
Tel Aviv (Israel) 219
Televisa (Mexico) 80
Tennessee (US) 72
Thailand 356, 358, 359, 362, 363, 368–370
  Constitutional Court 369
  National Security Council 370, 371
Thai–US Defense Alliance 361
Thaksin Shinawatra 368, 369, 370
Thatcher, Margaret 62, 130, 135
Thein Sein 371, 372, 373
Thitinan Pongsudhirak 369
Tiangaye, Nicolas 264
Tibet 314
Timbuktu (Mali) 120, 248, 249
Timor Leste 359
TNK-BP (Russia-UK) 170
Togo 249
Tokyo (Japan) 322, 327
Tongchang-ri (North Korea) 334
Toomey, Pat 71
Total (France) 244
Toubou (Libya) 199
Touré, Amadou Toumani 248
Transitional Federal Government (Somalia) 258, 259
Trans-Pacific Partnership 91, 102, 330, 331, 360
Traoré, Dioncounda 120, 248
Treaty of Rome 113, 130
Treaty of Shimonseki 323
Treaty on Open Skies 41
Treaty on the Non-Proliferation of Nuclear Weapons 32
Trinamool Congress (India) 283
Trinidad and Tobago 86
Tripoli (Lebanon) 184
Tripoli (Libya) 251
Tsingua University (China) 311, 312
Tsvangirai, Morgan 270, 271, 272
Tuaregs (Mali) 24, 120, 248, 250, 251
Tucson (US) 71
Tunisia 188, 189, 190, 197, 200–201, 203, 204, 378
  Constituent Assembly 200
Tunis (Tunisia) 189, 200
Turkey 18, 19, 22, 26, 142, 143–151, 175, 177, 181, 183, 212, 220, 228, 234, 244, 245, 382
  National Intelligence Organization 150
Turki, Abdel Basset 238
Turkish Republic of Northern Cyprus 147
Tutsi 265, 266
Tutu, Desmond 276
Tymoshenko, Yulia 173

U

Udaltsov, Sergei 160
Uganda 138, 260, 266, 267
Ugulava, Giorgi 173
UK Independence Party (UK) 131
Ukraine 173, 321, 382
Um Rawaba (Sudan) 262
Union of Forces of Resistance (Chad) 250
Union of South American Nations 77, 107, 108
Union pour une Majorité Populaire (France) 118, 119
United Arab Emirates 177, 183, 194, 197, 205, 207, 208, 210, 213, 214, 377, 379
United Kingdom 20, 22, 23, 25, 26, 28, 33, 44ff, 49, 51, 54, 55, 56, 61, 62, 106, 113, 114, 118, 129–136, 141, 170, 178, 199, 208, 222, 228, 269, 270, 272, 275, 277, 293, 298, 301, 307, 310, 315
  Bank of England 25, 134, 135
United Malays National Organisation (Malaysia) 367
United National Movement Party (Georgie) 170ff
United Nations 22, 33, 40, 120, 121, 147, 169, 179, 183, 185, 188, 202, 206, 211, 216, 218ff, 223, 231, 235, 240, 242, 249, 250, 251, 256, 257, 258, 260f, 265, 266, 267, 271, 273, 275, 279, 281, 294, 299, 300, 301, 322, 323, 330, 333, 334, 340ff, 359, 372, 376
  Conference on Disarmament 33
  Convention on the Law of the Sea 358, 359
  General Assembly 223, 231, 322, 372
  Group of Experts on the DRC 266
  Human Development Index 275
  Human Rights Council 281, 294, 340
  Multidimensional Integrated Stabilization Mission in Mali 250
  Operation in Côte d'Ivoire 257
  Security Council 163, 168, 169, 202, 226, 233, 249, 260, 261, 262, 267, 330, 333ff
    DRC Framework Agreement 267
    Resolution 2094 335
    UNSCR 1973 168
  Stabilisation Mission in the DRC 266, 267
  World Food Programme 216, 341
United Progressive Alliance (India) 281
United Russia party (Russia) 160, 161
United States 17, 19ff, 32, 33, 37, 38, 41, 45, 46, 47, 54, 57, 59–76, 77, 82, 85, 87, 96, 97, 102, 105, 107, 108, 114, 118, 120, 121, 123, 133, 141, 146, 147, 156, 158, 162ff, 177, 178, 181, 182, 184, 187, 188, 190, 193, 194, 195, 197, 199, 202, 203, 207, 208, 212, 215, 216, 218ff, 226, 227, 228, 230, 234, 235, 236, 240, 242, 243, 253, 256, 260, 267, 271, 272, 292, 294, 296, 297, 298, 301ff, 310, 314, 315, 316, 318, 319, 320, 321, 323ff, 329, 330, 331, 334, 335, 336, 337, 341, 342ff, 347, 348, 350, 351, 352, 353, 355, 359ff, 366, 371, 375, 376, 379, 380, 383, 384
  Agency for International Development 162
  Air Force 38
  Army 38
  Central Intelligence Agency 26, 215, 301
  Congress 62, 66, 67, 68, 69, 165, 228, 230, 319, 320
  Congressional Budget Office 70
  Court of Appeals 67
  Defense Intelligence Agency 335
  Department of Defense 236, 303, 310, 320, 321
  Department of Energy 170
  Department of State 97
  Environmental Protection Agency 73
  FBI 71
  Federal Reserve 24, 25
  Foreign Agents Registration Act 156
  House of Representatives 67, 69
  Internal Revenue Service 76
  Iran Freedom and Counter-Proliferation Act 228
  Marine Corps 326
  Medicaid 69
  Medicare 69
  Missile Technology Control Regime 347
  NASA 362
  National Security Agency 26, 27, 76, 325
  National Security Council 166
    Principals Committee 166
  Navy 235
  Pacific Command 321
  Pentagon 23, 43, 303, 319, 320, 321, 359
  pivot to Asia 123
  Senate 62, 65, 66, 67, 69, 71, 74
  Sequestration 69
  Sergei Magnitsky Rule of Law Accountability Act 158, 165
  Social Security 68, 69

Special Inspector General for Afghanistan Reconstruction 303
State Department 155, 165, 323, 342
Supreme Court 73
US–China Economic and Security Review Commission's Report to Congress 324
United Torah Judaism (Israel) 217
Urals (Russia) 155
Uribe, Álvaro 88, 89, 91, 97
Uruguay 102
US–ASEAN Expanded Economic Engagement Initiative 360
US–China Strategic and Economic Dialogue 325
U-Tapao airfield (Thailand) 362
U Tong-chuk 338
Uttar Pradesh (India) 282
Uzbekistan 293

V

Van Rompuy, Herman 46, 133, 137
Vasilieva, Yevgeniya 158
Vázquez Mota, Josefina 79
Venezuela 78, 87, 88, 90, 91–95, 96, 97, 98, 102, 107
National Assembly 93, 94
Vietnam 355, 356, 357, 360ff
Vietnam War 61, 355
Vladivostok 165
Vodafone 283
Volodin, Vyacheslav 155

W

Wales 129
Wall Street Journal 60
Wa (Myanmar) 371
Wang Jiarui 343
Wang Lijun 315
Wang Yang 312
Wardak, Abdul Rahim 299
Warren, Elizabeth 65
Warsaw Pact 37, 41, 43
Washington DC (US) 133, 157, 188, 331
Washington Declaration (US-New Zealand) 353
Washington Post 60, 76
Wasit (Iraq) 241
Watergate 62
Wellington Declaration (US-New Zealand) 353
Wenchang Space Launch centre (China) 320
Wen Jiabao 312, 314
West Africa 120, 247, 248–256
West Bank 75, 213, 218, 219, 220
West Bengal (India) 283, 285
Western Pacific 321
Western Sahara 202, 203, 251
Western Siberia (Russia) 170
West Philippine Sea 358
West Virginia (US) 71
WikiLeaks 76, 97
Will, George 60
Wilson, Harold 130
Winter Olympics 2014 158, 174
WMD 122
Woody Island 356
Workers' Party (Brazil) 77, 101
World Bank 77, 109, 265, 267
World Cup 2014 (football) 102
World Economic Forum 157
World Health Organisation 94
World Trade Organisation 77, 102, 163, 165

X

Xiamen (China) 311
Xichang Satellite Launch centre (China) 320
Xi Jinping 18, 309, 310ff, 318, 323, 325, 331, 343, 344, 356, 379
Xinjiang (China) 314
Xiyang Group (China) 344
Xi Zhongxun 311

Y

Yachimovich, Shelly 217
Yala (Thailand) 370
Yang Jiechi 318, 322
Yangon (Myanmar) 372
Yar'Adua, Umaru 254
Yarmouk military complex (Sudan) 262
Yasukuni Shrine (Japan) 332, 346
Yellow Shirt movement (Thailand) 368
Yeltsin, Boris 38
Yemen 28, 138, 214–215, 235
Coast Guard 235
First Armoured Division 215
Ministry of Defence 215
Yesh Atid party (Israel) 217, 218
Yildiz, Taner 145
Yingluck Shinawatra 359, 368, 369
Yisrael Beiteinu party (Israel) 216, 217
Yobe (Nigeria) 252
Yongbyon (North Korea) 336
Yongxing Island 356
Younes, Abdel Fattah 198
Young Patriots (Côte d'Ivoire) 257
Yousafzai, Malala 293
Youssef, Bassem 192
YouTube 65, 336, 345
YPF (Argentina) 104
Yusuf, Mohamed 252
Yu Zhengsheng 314

Z

Zakhilwal, Hazrat Omar 300
Zambia 266, 270
ZANU–PF (Zimbabwe) 270, 271, 272
Zardari, Asif Ali 288, 290, 294
Zaydan, Ali 198
Zeid, Abdelhamid Abou 249
Zelaya, Manuel 85
Zelaya, Xiomara Castro de 85
Zhang Haiyang 313
Zhang Qinsheng 313
Zhang Xiaojun 315
Zhejiang (China) 312
Zhengding (China) 311
Zhou Yongkang 313, 314
Zimbabwe 270–272, 278
Zimbabwe Democracy Institute 272
Zogby Research Services 234
Zubkov, Viktor 158
Zulu, Lindiwe 272
Zuma, Jacob 275, 276, 278, 279
Zwai (Libya) 199